ECONOMIC REPORT OF THE PRESIDENT

TRANSMITTED TO CONGRESS | MARCH 2023

TOGETHER WITH THE ANNUAL REPORT
OF THE COUNCIL OF ECONOMIC ADVISERS

Contents

---

*For a detailed table of contents of the Council's *Report*, see page 11.

Economic Report of the President

Economic Report of the President

To the Congress of the United States:

Our Nation has faced tremendous challenges in recent years. A deadly pandemic and unprovoked war in Ukraine have tested our economy unlike any time since the Great Depression. When I was sworn into office, COVID-19 was raging and our economy was reeling. Millions of workers were out of a job, through no fault of their own. Hundreds of thousands of businesses had closed, our supply chains were snarled, and many schools were still shuttered. Families across the country were feeling real pain.

Today, two years later, 230 million Americans have been vaccinated, and COVID no longer controls our lives. We have created a record 12 million jobs, which constitute the strongest two years of job gains on record. Unemployment is at a more than 50-year low, with near-record lows for Black and Latino workers, and manufacturing jobs have recovered faster than in any business cycle since 1953. Growth is up, wages are up, and inflation is coming down. At the same time, a record 10 million Americans have applied to start small businesses—each of their applications an act of hope. More Americans have health insurance today than ever before in our history, and real household wealth is 10 percent above what it was before COVID. It is safe to say: Our economic plan is working, and American families are starting to have a little more breathing room.

It is important to remember, however, that the economic anxiety so many have felt did not start with the pandemic. For decades, the backbone of America, the middle class, has been hollowed out. Too many American jobs have been shipped overseas. Unions have been weakened. Once-thriving cities and towns have become shadows of what they used to be, robbing people of hard-earned pride and self-worth.

I ran for President to rebuild our economy from the bottom up and middle out, not from the top down—because when the middle class does well, the poor have a ladder up and the wealthy still do well. We all do well. And that is what we have been working for. This past year, we made critical investments to secure America's future. Together, the Bipartisan Infrastructure Law, the CHIPS and Science Act, and the Inflation Reduction Act represent the biggest public investments in our history—expected to draw more than $3.5 trillion in public and private funding for infrastructure, the digital economy, and clean energy over the next decade.

First, the Bipartisan Infrastructure Law is an investment in America and our competitiveness. You cannot be the number one economy in the world unless you have the best infrastructure in the world. That is why this once-in-a-generation law is finally rebuilding our roads, bridges, railroads, ports, airports, and more—to keep our people safe, our goods moving, and our economy growing. Families across the Nation will have safe drinking water and high-speed Internet. A network of electric vehicle charging stations will allow more of us to drive cleaner cars. To date, we have funded over 20,000 construction projects all across the country, creating tens of thousands of well-paying new jobs. Americans everywhere can take pride in seeing shovels in the ground.

Second, the CHIPS and Science Act, which I signed in August, will make sure that America once again leads the world in developing and manufacturing the semiconductors that power everything from cars to refrigerators to smartphones. The United States invented these chips; it is time to again manufacture them at home, and to make sure our economy never again relies so heavily on foreign chipmakers. Private companies have already announced more than $300 billion in new investments in American manufacturing in the last two years, many of them thanks to this law, creating tens of thousands more jobs of the future in every corner of the country.

Third, the Inflation Reduction Act, also enacted last August, takes on powerful special interests to cut costs for working families. It lowers health care and prescription drug costs—for example, capping insulin at $35 a month for seniors on Medicare, and capping drug costs at $2,000 a year for seniors with Medicare Part D starting in 2025. It extends the Affordable Care Act's subsidies, saving families an average of $800 a year. It also makes the Nation's most significant investment ever in combating the existential threat of climate change, investing in everything from climate-smart agriculture to more resilient electric grids. It builds a new clean energy economy, creating thousands of green jobs in communities too often left behind, while also lowering home energy bills for families.

Meanwhile, my Administration has taken wide-ranging executive actions to help level the playing field and promote competition. From easing the burden of crippling student debt, to providing relief to families at the gas pump, to cracking down on unfair junk fees, we are building an economy that gives everyone a fair shot and a little more breathing room.

Throughout, we have shown that we can invest in our future and be fiscally responsible at the same time. We are helping to pay for these historic programs by finally making the wealthy and corporations pay their fair share, without raising taxes on anyone making under $400,000 a year. And we cut the deficit by $1.7 trillion during my first two years in office, the largest reduction in history, with more to come.

I have often said that a job is about more than a paycheck; it is about dignity and respect. This is why we are not only investing in record job growth; we are also providing historic support for workers and unions at a time of big shifts in our workforce. We plan to ban noncompete agreements for 30 million workers who have been unfairly locked in their jobs, giving them the right to be paid what they are worth. We have boosted pay and labor protections for Federal contractors, we have pushed to extend these same protections to all workers, and we have passed laws to ensure safe and fair workplaces, including for pregnant and nursing workers and workers who face sexual assault and harassment on the job. We are investing in job-training programs and registered apprenticeships, which give so many people a ladder up to well-paying jobs on which they can raise a family without a college degree.

Now, it is time to finish the job. We have much more to do to build an economy that benefits everyone—from cracking down on the deadly fentanyl epidemic and investing in mental health care and recovery, to fighting for childcare and paid family leave for millions of working families struggling to care for their loved ones, so no one ever again has to choose between the paycheck they need and the family they love.

Our Nation is at an inflection point that will determine our future for decades to come. But today, because of the choices and investments we have made, jobs are coming back, pride is coming back, and the United States of America is better positioned to lead than any other country on Earth. Our blue-collar blueprint to rebuild America is proving that democracy can deliver, building an economy that is fairer and stronger and leaves no one behind.

The White House
March 2023

The Annual Report of the Council of Economic Advisers

Letter of Transmittal

Council of Economic Advisers
Washington, March 20, 2023

Mr. President:

The Council of Economic Advisers herewith submits its 2023 *Annual Report* in accordance with the Employment Act of 1946, as amended by the Full Employment and Balanced Growth Act of 1978.

Sincerely yours,

Cecilia Elena Rouse
Chair

Jared Bernstein
Member

Heather Boushey
Member

Contents

Appendixes

Figures

Tables

Boxes

Chapter 1

Pursuing Growth-Enhancing Policies in Today's Changing World

Economists often tout the value of economic growth. They argue that as the size of the economic "pie"—the value of all goods and services produced in a year—increases, everyone can get a larger slice of it, making them better off. Of course, growth is not the only economic goal a society may prioritize. Many societies also have notions of fairness and justice such as lower poverty and inequality, so they are attentive to how the slices of the pie are shared. That said, sustained economic growth is an important priority for most societies and, over long swaths of history, is an indispensable driver of improvement in human well-being.

Economic growth is constrained, however, when the size of the economy reaches what economists call "potential gross domestic product (GDP)" or "capacity." An economy's long-run capacity depends on such factors as a growing and skilled labor force, high-quality physical infrastructure, and the efficiency of the production process. Actions that affect any of these factors can either constrain or enhance the capacity of the economy over time. Investing in increased economic capacity enables the economy to accommodate more demand in the medium to long run, which can make it more resilient to economic shocks and minimize the risk of inflationary episodes. The core of the Biden-Harris Administration's economic agenda is building a foundation for steady, sustainable, and shared growth by increasing economic capacity.

Over the last 50 years, the United States' social and economic context has changed, leading to both opportunities and challenges for increasing economic capacity. This has been for a variety of reasons, but three important ones are worth noting. First, women have surpassed men in educational attainment, and they joined the labor force in historic numbers through the late 1990s, though there has been a slowdown in their labor force participation gains in recent years. Women's increased participation—and thus an increase in the size of the labor force generally—helped drive economic growth in the second half of the 20th century. At the same time, a lack of public investment in care has challenged workers, especially working women, with caregiving responsibilities.

Second, soaring carbon emissions in the second half of the 20th century have exacerbated global warming, and the resulting climate change will increasingly become a barrier to economic growth without effective adaptation. Interrelated with the climate crisis, the damage to ecosystems continues to accelerate, creating significant risks for businesses and the wider economy (World Economic Forum 2020).

Third, computers have entered virtually all aspects of life and can now perform tasks that previously were thought not able to be automated. The Internet has changed how people find information, learn, do business, and communicate with one another. These changes have spurred growth and helped some industries weather economic shocks like the COVID-19 pandemic better than they otherwise would have. But they have also raised important issues about how established economic policy can and should adapt to the new digital world.

To expand the potential growth of the U.S. economy, policymakers need to adjust how the Nation invests in response to these kinds of changes. This year's *Report* highlights selected areas where the changing economic and social context calls for a new approach to increasing the capacity for economic growth. The *Report* discusses how the relevant context in these areas has changed, analyzes pressing current challenges to sustained economic growth, and highlights potential strategies to confront these challenges.

Investing in Production Drives Economic Growth

The inputs to sustained economic growth can be understood through the lens of an aggregate production function, which is explained in box 1-1. According to such a function, an economy's output depends on its stock of human and physical capital as well as on a productivity factor that summarizes how efficiently workers, machines, and other types of inputs are put to use. Thus, sustained output growth relies on continuing private and public investments in the economy's workforce, physical capital, and productivity (Mankiw 2010).

In general, well-functioning markets incentivize households and firms to make investments that expand the economy, even when these households and firms do not have the larger economy in mind as they make their individual decisions. For example, a high school graduate who anticipates enhanced career opportunities from attaining a higher degree will likely pursue a college education. A firm that wants to grow but is having trouble hiring may invest in making its workplace more attractive to potential employees or pursue a management strategy to improve the efficiency of its existing workforce. These decisions are made independently throughout the economy without considering their effect on aggregate production, yet they jointly increase total economic capacity and growth.

Unlike the private sector, the public sector is designed to invest in the economy with explicit consideration of the aggregate context. This is reflected in the types of investments it should ideally make, many of which are aimed at markets' overall efficient functioning. The public sector operates the basic institutions that enforce the rule of law and property rights and thus enable households and firms to engage in the complex market system. It is also tasked with promoting competition and preventing socially destructive profit-seeking behavior, ensuring the stability of the financial infrastructure that greases the economy, and representing the interests of the U.S. economy in negotiating terms of trade with the rest of the world.

In addition, when the private sector underinvests, the public sector can step in to invest in human and physical capital. Private underinvestment occurs for various reasons but often entails some combination of coordination failure, externalities, and credit constraints. For example, although virtually all firms benefit directly or indirectly from having functional roads running across the United States, it would be nearly impossible for them to coordinate a plan of action to build them. Compared with what would be best for society, firms tend to underinvest in the use of clean energy because they do not bear the full burden of the cost of pollution (costs are externalized). And information asymmetries in private credit markets can make it difficult for some entrepreneurs to access funding for upfront investments

Box 1-1. What Is an Aggregate Production Function?

An "aggregate production function" summarizes the process whereby an economy transforms inputs into goods and services. Consider a tomato farmer. She needs the input of *labor*—workers—to run and maintain her farm; the input of *human capital*—the education, training, skills, health, and other valuable resources embodied in a person—to know how to plant, raise, and harvest the tomatoes; and the input of *physical capital*—raw materials like seeds, along with harvesting and hydration equipment. The farmer uses these inputs to produce tomatoes as her output. Some of these tomatoes will be sold to consumers at the grocery store or at farmers' markets as final goods; others will themselves become inputs into different products like ketchup and pizza sauce. When all the individual production functions like this farmer's are combined in an economy, the result is an *aggregate* production function, which gives the aggregate output of the entire economy resulting from all its inputs.

Aggregate output increases when there are more workers with in-demand skills, when these workers work more hours, and when they have access to more and better facilities and equipment to help them effectively perform their jobs. Physical capital also captures the broader infrastructure of roads, bridges, and broadband that allows goods, services, and information to move throughout the economy; note that this infrastructure is often public.

An economy also grows when it becomes more efficient at combining labor and capital to produce output—that is, when it can produce more output with the same amount of inputs. Economists call this "total factor productivity." In the tomato farmer example, agricultural innovations such as better farm management techniques, including crop rotation, have enabled farmers to grow tomatoes more easily.

When total factor productivity grows, output increases, even if an economy's inputs—labor, human capital, and physical capital—are kept constant, because the economy becomes more efficient at using these inputs.

Economists tend to discuss total factor productivity in shorthand as "technology"; but in reality, total factor productivity has many different drivers and constraints beyond what one might typically think of as technology. For instance, culture and norms can have a substantial impact on output (Guiso, Sapienza, and Zingales 2006). And corruption holds back economic growth not just by disincentivizing investment in human and physical capital, but also by decreasing the amount of economic growth that an economy sees from a given amount of human and physical capital (Mauro 1995).

Summarizing aggregate production as a function of physical capital, human capital, and total factor productivity is a useful abstraction that provides a framework to understand differences in economic activity across time and countries. For certain questions, it makes sense to extend the basic model. One increasingly relevant extension is explicitly to include natural capital—the stock of water, land, air, and renewable and nonrenewable resources—as a distinct production factor in addition to built or produced physical capital. In the example given above, factors such as soil quality and quantity, climate, irrigation water, and the populations of insect pollinators provide important contributions to the tomato farmer's output production. As natural capital becomes an increasingly important driver of variation in economic activity due to climate change, more questions will benefit from a direct inclusion of natural capital. Indeed, the Biden-Harris Administration recently launched a multiyear effort to put nature on the nation's balance sheet for the first time (White House 2023).

in their businesses, even when those investments promise private and social returns in the future, resulting in credit constraints.

The United States' Economic Growth Over Time

The last two centuries have seen remarkable gains in material well-being around the world, driven by rapid output growth. The United States is an excellent example of a country that has experienced this economic transformation.

Estimates of historical output suggest that in 1800, the United States was not even among the world's 10 largest economies (Groningen Growth and Development Centre, n.d.). But its rapid growth ever since—averaging about 3.5 percent a year between 1800 and 2021—has turned the United States into the world's largest economy in nominal terms. Figure 1-1 decomposes U.S. economic growth since 1800. Total output can be mechanically separated into (1) labor supply (how many workers there are)—which in turn depends both on population size and labor force participation—and (2) how much average output these workers produce. Output per worker reflects the growth drivers other than labor supply mentioned above: human capital, physical capital, and total factor productivity.

This decomposition of economic growth highlights how the relative importance of the American workforce's size versus its productivity in driving growth has changed over time. Productivity-driven economic growth is ultimately what spurs sustained growth in output per capita, which better reflects how growth translates into improved living standards for individuals. In the first half of the 19th century, aggregate growth was driven mainly by the country's increasing population and by its larger workforce. This

Figure 1-1. Average Annual U.S. Real GDP Growth since 1790, by Decade and Contributor

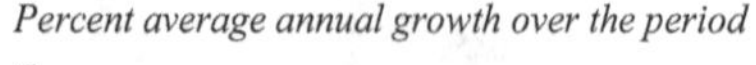

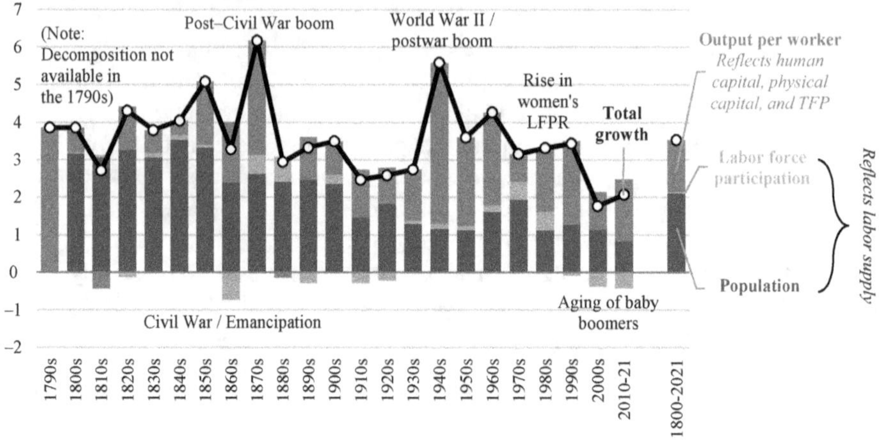

Sources: Weiss 1999; Lebergott 1966; Bureau of Economic Analysis; Bureau of Labor Statistics; Census Bureau; CEA calculations.
Note: LFPR = labor force participation rate; TFP = total factor productivity.

implied comparatively more limited gains in material well-being for the average person. In contrast, aggregate growth in the 20th century was driven mostly by an increasingly productive workforce and thus translated more directly into higher individual output and incomes.

Productivity-driven output growth in the United States has been the result of private and targeted public investment in the skills of its workforce, its equipment and infrastructure, and the technologies that enable its workers to most efficiently use their skills.

Two decades in particular—the 1870s and 1940s—stand out for having the highest average growth in American history. These decades serve as case studies for some of the factors that drive economic expansion.

Economic historians sometimes mark the 1870s as the start of a period of advancement called the "Second Industrial Revolution" (e.g., DeLong 2022). Some of the investments during this decade were made to repair the infrastructure that had been damaged or destroyed during the Civil War. But investment in the 1870s went well beyond replacement. In 1860—on the eve of the Civil War—there were about 31,000 miles of railroads in operation in the United States. By 1870, this had increased to 53,000 miles; and by 1880, to 98,000 miles (see figure 1-2). In 1869, Western Union operated about 105,000 miles of telegraph wires and handled just under 8 million messages annually. Ten years later, it had doubled the mileage of its wires and was handling more than three times the number of telegraph messages (Carter et al. 2006, series Dg 9 and Dg11). And this surge in investment in the 1870s was not limited to physical infrastructure but also extended

Figure 1-2. Miles of U.S. Railroads, 1830–90

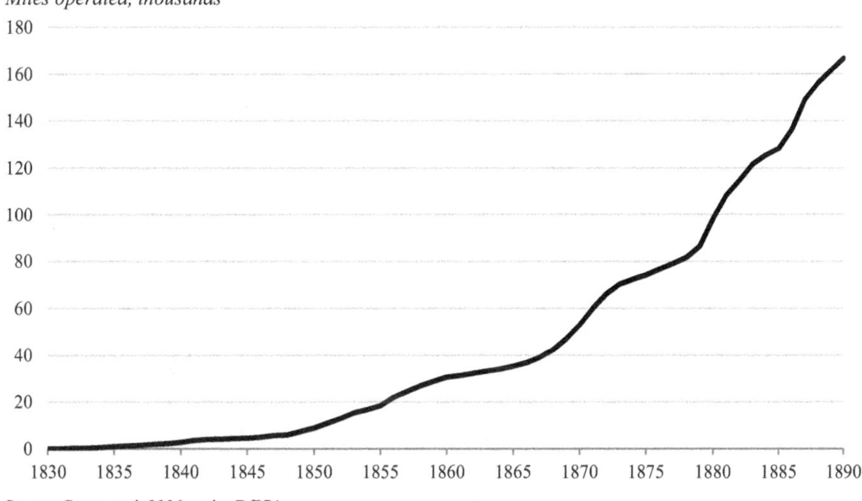

Source: Carter et al. 2006, series Df874.

to ideas. The United States issued roughly 72,000 patents for inventions between 1860 and 1869; the next decade, it issued about 125,000 (see figure 1-3). Moreover, the Nation's labor supply grew strongly during the 1870s: the U.S. labor force was about 35 percent larger in 1880 than it was in 1870, thanks both to natural population growth and immigration (Migration Policy Institute, n.d.). In comparison, the labor force grew by a total of 5 percent between 2011 and 2021.

The expansion of physical capital and ideas, combined with the increasing labor force, corresponded with strong growth in the 1870s and beyond.

Like the 1870s, the 1940s came on the heels of a catastrophe—in this case, the Great Depression. However, growth in the 1940s was less about an increase in the labor supply, given that the labor force grew at about half the rate it did in the 1870s. Instead, growth in the 1940s was driven by a combination of public investment and greater utilization of a labor force with a high unemployment rate at the start of the decade: although unemployment had fallen substantially from its 1932 peak of 22.9 percent, in 1940 it was still at an elevated rate of 9.5 percent (Carter et al. 2006, series Ba475).[1]

The United States' entry into World War II accelerated this growth. The number of active-duty military personnel grew from just over 300,000 in 1939 to 12 million by the war's end in 1945 (National World War II

[1] This series treats workers participating in Federal emergency New Deal programs like the Works Progress Administration and Civilian Conservation Corps as "employed"; official labor market statistics, which were still in their infancy at the time, classified these workers as "unemployed."

Figure 1-3. U.S. Patents Issued, 1790–2000

Patents issued for inventions, thousands

Source: Carter et al. 2006, series Cg30.

Museum, n.d.). This mobilization, in combination with increased private hiring (driven itself in large part by wartime government orders) pushed the unemployment rate down to 1.2 percent by 1944 and expanded women's labor force participation (Acemoglu, Autor, and Lyle 2004; Carter et al. 2006, series Ba475; National Archives, n.d.).

Public investment in physical capital also skyrocketed. The Federal Government's gross investment rose from $12 billion in 1940 to $270 billion in 1944 (inflation-adjusted).[2] Growth in government consumption and investment was responsible for adding 10 percentage points to real GDP growth in 1941 and an astounding 28 percentage points in 1942 (see figure 1-4).

The end of the war did not mean a return to the prewar economy of the 1930s that was characterized by high unemployment and depressed output. Demobilization led to a mild recession in 1945, as the United States began shifting away from the wartime economy, and the unemployment rate crept back up in the years after the war. But it did not return to its prewar levels of 9.5 percent and above (Carter et al. 2006, series Ba475).

Even as Federal investment retreated in the years following World War II, private investment picked up. Between 1944 and 1950, real Federal defense investment fell by $257 billion (in 2021 dollars). But real private fixed investment rose by $224 billion over that same period, and real personal consumption was $444 billion higher. Indeed, increased private

[2] This is measured in inflation-adjusted 2021 dollars.

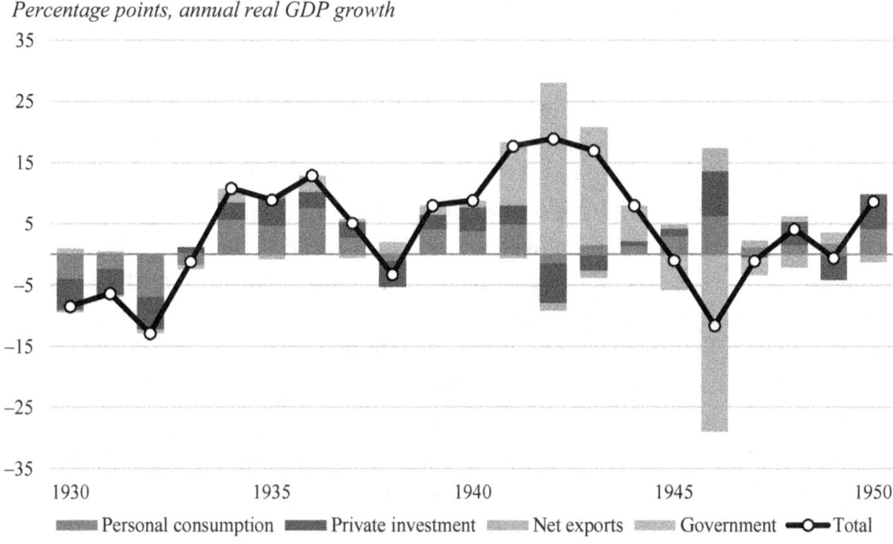

investment and consumption were even able to substantially offset the massive 29-percentage-point deduction to GDP growth from the postwar demobilization in 1946 (see figure 1-4). Government investments during World War II helped pave the way for private investments that sustained renewed economic growth throughout the latter half of the 20th century (Goodwin 2001).

The Inputs to U.S. Economic Growth Over Time

The economic growth of the United States over the last two centuries would not have happened without investments in the labor force, the physical capital stock, and total factor productivity. The previous pages of this section discussed what some of these investments looked like during two key rapid-growth decades: after the Civil War, and around World War II. This subsection steps back and considers each of these factors over a wider span of American history, highlighting key public and private investments for each one and discussing selected available measures of how they have evolved over time.

The labor force. Over the past 200 years, both public and private actors have invested in the skills and size of the labor force. Consider the key input of education. For centuries, the United States has been a world leader in public education. Beginning in the 1700s, American communities began to establish publicly funded or free schools, along with land grants to support the creation and maintenance of schools (Kober and Rentner 2020). Over time, an array of private and nonprofit institutions—including private schools, universities, and vocational training programs—have also become integral to the U.S. educational landscape. Investments in education transformed the skills of American workers. In the first several decades of the 20th century, the United States underwent what is now termed the "high school movement" (see figure 1-5); between 1910 and 1940, the share of those age 18 years with a high school diploma (from a private or public institution) rose by over 40 percentage points (Goldin and Katz 2009). However, progress has at times been uneven; segregation and other forms of race and gender discrimination in the education system have presented barriers to educational attainment for women and people of color.

The U.S. labor force has also grown—from roughly 1.5 million workers in 1800 to over 160 million today—with particularly rapid growth in the second half of the 20th century, although there has been a gradual decline in the growth rate since the 1980s (see figure 1-6).

The physical capital stock. Investment has also focused on physical capital and productivity. This has included investments by the public sector, such as under the Rural Electrification Act of 1936, which provided loans to farmers and investors to expand electricity to rural communities, with remarkable results, as depicted in figure 1-7 (Sablik 2020). Later in the 20th century, the United States built out the Interstate Highway System, which is often described as one of the greatest public works projects in history

Figure 1-5. U.S. Secondary School Enrollment and Graduation Rates, 1890–1991

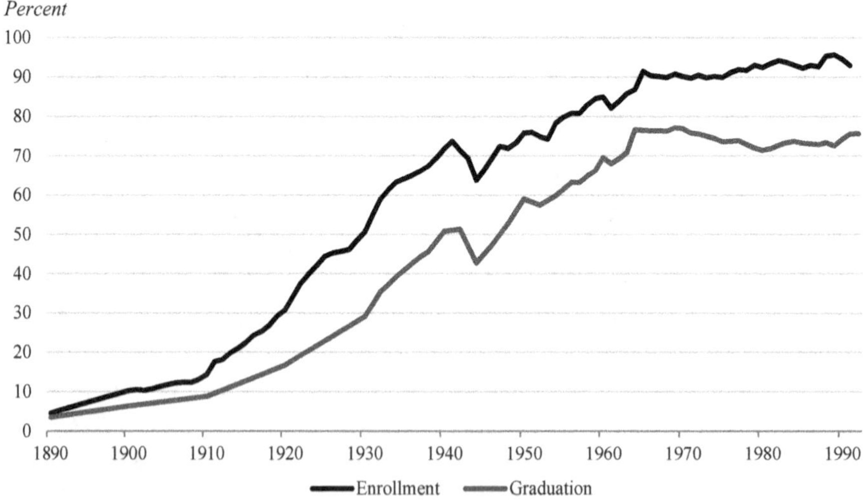

Sources: U.S. Department of Education; Goldin and Katz 2009; CEA calculations.
Note: Graduation data were reported every 10 years before 1930; some years are missing after 1930.

(Capka 2006; Pfeiffer 2006). In parallel with the public sector's investments, the private sector has invested in physical capital, such as by constructing

Figure 1-6. The U.S. Labor Force, 1800–2021

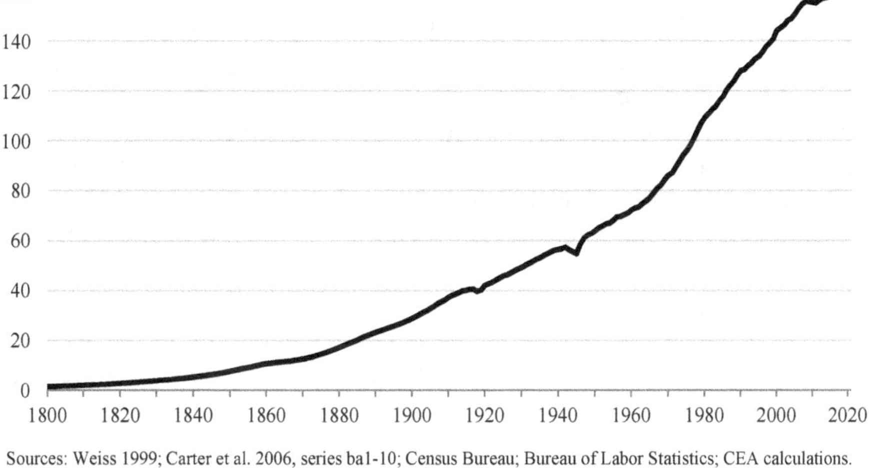

Sources: Weiss 1999; Carter et al. 2006, series ba1-10; Census Bureau; Bureau of Labor Statistics; CEA calculations.

Figure 1-7. U.S. Residences with Electricity, 1920–56

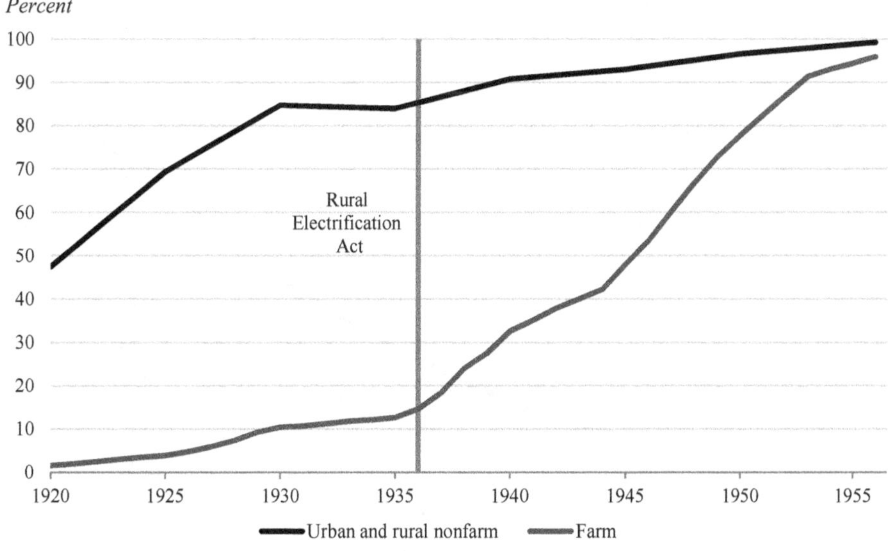

Sources: U.S. Census Bureau 1975, table S 108-119; Sablik 2020.
Note: Data on the percentage of dwelling units with electric service in urban and rural nonfarm settings are only available every five years.

factories, farms, and office buildings—in 2021, gross private domestic investment exceeded $4 trillion (FRED 2022).

Public and private investments have combined to facilitate the continued growth of the Nation's capital stock over the past century, as highlighted in figure 1-8. (The capital stock includes physical capital, ranging from trucks to houses to software to roads.)

Total factor productivity. As discussed above, total factor productivity is the most amorphous input into economic growth. It captures many aspects, from technological innovation to the quality of institutions that promote competition and the efficient allocation of scarce resources.

Consequently, historical public and private investment in total factor productivity is multifaceted and not always straightforward to measure. For example, one paper estimates that between 20 and 40 percent of growth in aggregate output per person in the United States between 1960 and 2010 can be explained by improved talent allocation brought on by reduced discrimination and changing preferences among Black and white women and Black men (Hsieh et al. 2019). The Civil Rights Act of 1964 likely contributed to this reduced discrimination and thus, in addition to rectifying long-standing injustices, it functioned as an investment in the economy. But this type of investment is difficult to quantify, given that it is concurrent with broader social change.

Figure 1-8. U.S. Capital Stock, 1925–2021

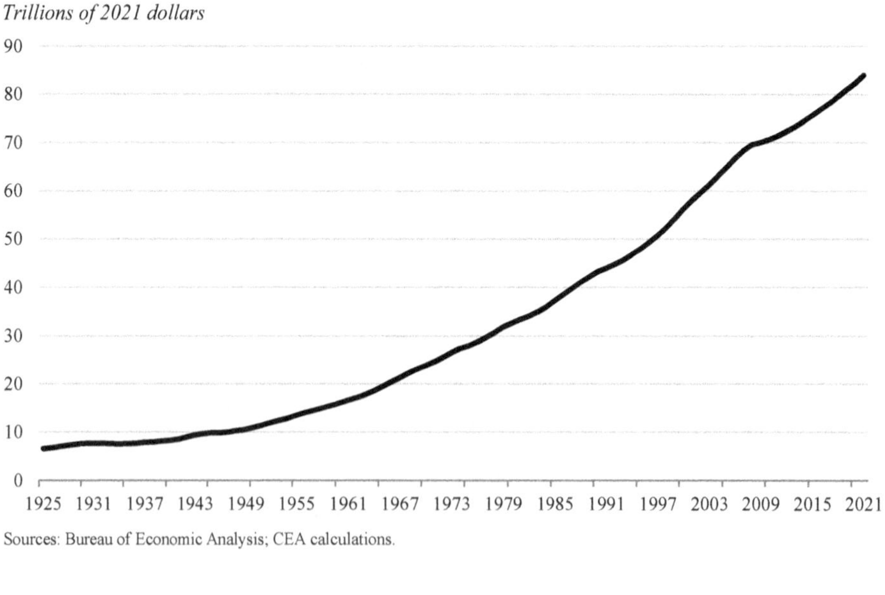

Trillions of 2021 dollars

Sources: Bureau of Economic Analysis; CEA calculations.

Other forms of investment are more tangible, such as investments in research and development. The United States is consistently one of the top spenders on research and development (OECD 2022a). The majority of this spending comes from the private sector, but the public sector also plays an important role, especially in funding basic research (Burke, Okrent, and Hale 2022).

The information technology revolution exemplifies the complementary roles of public and private investment in the economy. The government played an essential role in developing groundbreaking technologies, such as the Internet and the Global Positioning System. These early-stage investments were arguably too risky for any private firm to undertake (Mazzucato 2013). But it was the private sector that transformed these base technologies into the market-oriented ones that have shaped the way people work and live. Unlike the number of workers or the stock of physical capital, the return on these investments cannot be measured directly. However, economists can infer that total factor productivity is changing when total output changes more or less than would be expected based on observed changes in the labor force and the physical capital stock. That is, a greater-than-expected increase in total output suggests that total factor productivity has increased, whereas a smaller-than-expected increase suggests that it has decreased.

Figure 1-9 shows total factor productivity growth in the United States since 1953. In the short term, productivity growth fluctuates considerably,

Figure 1-9. Total Factor Productivity Growth, 1953–2021

Percent annual growth, five-year moving average

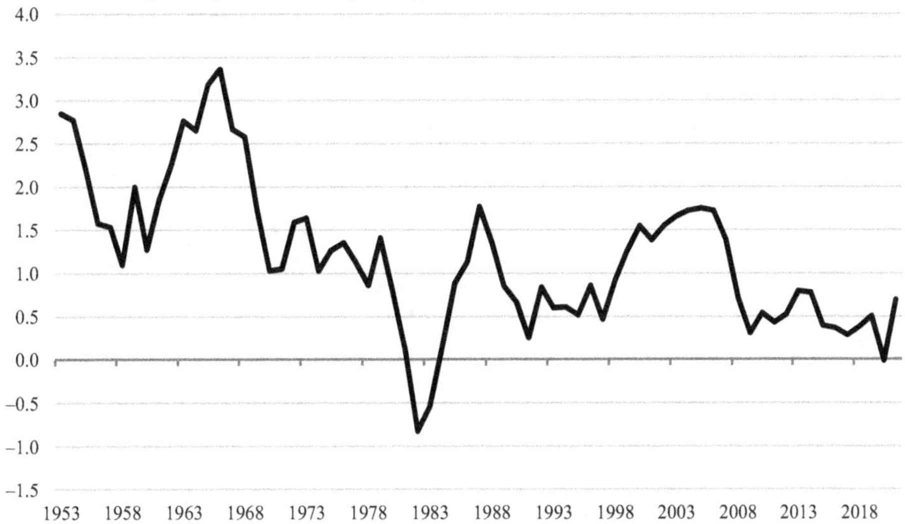

Source: Bureau of Labor Statistics.

partly because it can only be inferred from other measurements. Still, there are some notable trends over time. The postwar decades were marked by relatively high productivity growth, before a notable slowdown in the 1970s and through the mid-1990s. Productivity growth picked up again into the 2000s, but it fell during the Great Recession. The decade of slow productivity growth in the 2010s was common to most advanced economies, and it is still not fully understood (Dieppe 2020).

U.S. Economic Growth in Context

Although economic growth in the United States over the past 200 years has led to enormous gains in material well-being and life expectancy, and has given the United States an economic and political leadership role on the global stage, it cannot be taken for granted. For example, in the 1800s, the United States' GDP per capita was about 70 percent larger than that of Argentina. But faster average U.S. GDP growth starting in the second half of the 20th century caused the two countries to diverge further, and today U.S. GDP per capita is about three times as large as Argentina's (figure 1-10). Singapore, conversely, experienced slower growth for much of the 20th century before growing rapidly—more quickly than the United States—beginning in the 1960s; the country's GDP per capita is now above that of the United States.

Figure 1-10. GDP per Capita for the United States, Argentina, and Singapore, 1800–2018

Log scale, real GDP per capita, 2011 dollars

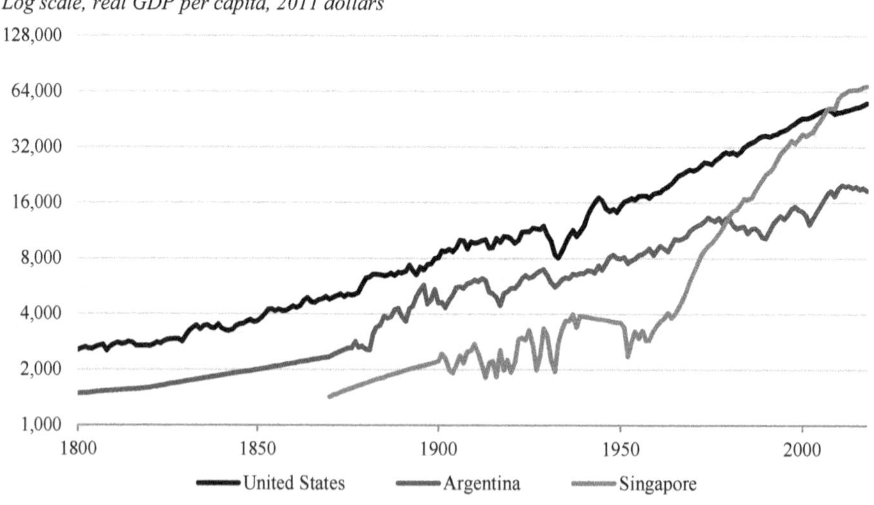

Source: Groningen Growth and Development Centre, n.d.
Note: Missing values are interpolated.

Economies have diverged widely in modern history, and though there have been various factors in this divergence, both public and private institutions—and economic policies—are a central part of the story. Indeed, Argentina and Singapore are telling case studies in this regard. The Argentine economy accelerated in the late 1800s thanks to immigration, exports, and foreign investment. However, productivity and economic growth in the country stagnated in the 20th century in the context of the Great Depression and political instability, beginning with the military coup in 1930 (Spruk 2019). Singapore's economic growth, conversely, is generally considered an example of successful economic policy. The rapid rise of Singapore and the other "East Asian Tigers" has been attributed to a set of common, market-friendly economic policies that targeted macroeconomic stability, public infrastructure and education, and export orientation (World Bank 1993; Lee 2019).

Sustaining Economic Growth in Today's Changing World

The preceding discussion highlighted the importance of past and continued private and public investments in the U.S. economy. Many of these historical investments remain relevant today. The Nation must continue to make investments to ensure access to high-quality education, from childhood through adulthood; to maintain its physical infrastructure; and to ensure that markets remain fair and competitive.

However, these investments are not being made in a vacuum. They are influenced by changes in society and the economy that have an impact on the need for, and value of, different kinds of investments—in human and physical capital, as well as in total factor productivity. Sometimes the private sector adapts quickly and well to these changes; other times, the public sector needs to spur private investment and provide the necessary guardrails to protect individuals and the U.S. economic system.

Investing in Human Capital and the Labor Supply: Implications of More Women Participating in the Labor Force

Millions of American women entered the labor force in the latter half of the 20th century—with substantial implications for society, economic growth, and public policy. Between 1970 and 2000, U.S. women's labor force participation rose from roughly 43 percent to 60 percent (figure 1-11). Although this overall trend masks important differences in levels of participation by dimensions such as race, age, income, and family status, virtually all groups of women saw large participation gains over these decades.

This period has been termed the "Quiet Revolution" by the economist Claudia Goldin, who has identified turning points in the late 1960s and early

Figure 1-11. Women's Labor Force Participation Rate, 1970–2022

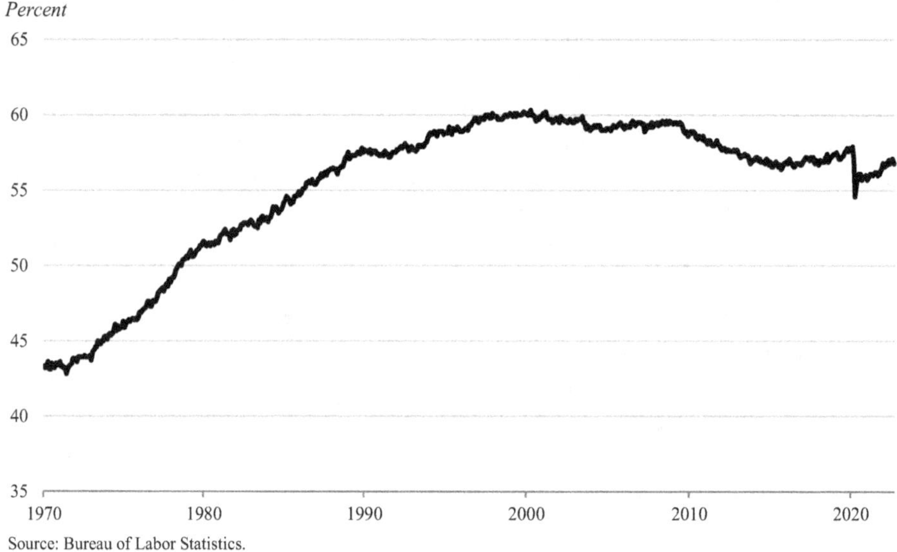

Source: Bureau of Labor Statistics.

1970s in the marriage age, college graduation rate, and extent of professional school enrollment for women—along with the gradual lifting of some discriminatory barriers for women, shifts in social norms for women's family and career decisions, and factors accounting for women's life satisfaction (Goldin 2006). Thus, Goldin attributes the increase in women's labor force participation to many factors, such as reduced labor market discrimination against women and women's increased choice in making reproductive decisions through the invention, dissemination, and legalization of the birth control pill.

In addition to women's labor force participation, women's educational attainment increased drastically relative to men's. Today, women earn the majority of bachelor's, master's, and doctoral degrees (figure 1-12).

The economic consequences of these trends are significant. Using a methodology similar to the one used in the 2015 *Economic Report of the President*, updated CEA calculations indicate that the U.S. economy was almost 10 percent larger in 2019 than it would have been without the increase in women's employment and hours worked from 1970 to 2019 (Council of Economic Advisers 2015).

However, starting in about 2000, women's labor force participation plateaued and began to decline. Men for their part have also seen a multidecade decline in participation, although they continue to participate at a higher rate than women. Removing barriers to women's and men's participation and educational attainment would ease labor constraints on firms

Figure 1-12. Percentage of Postsecondary Degrees Received by Women, 1980–2020

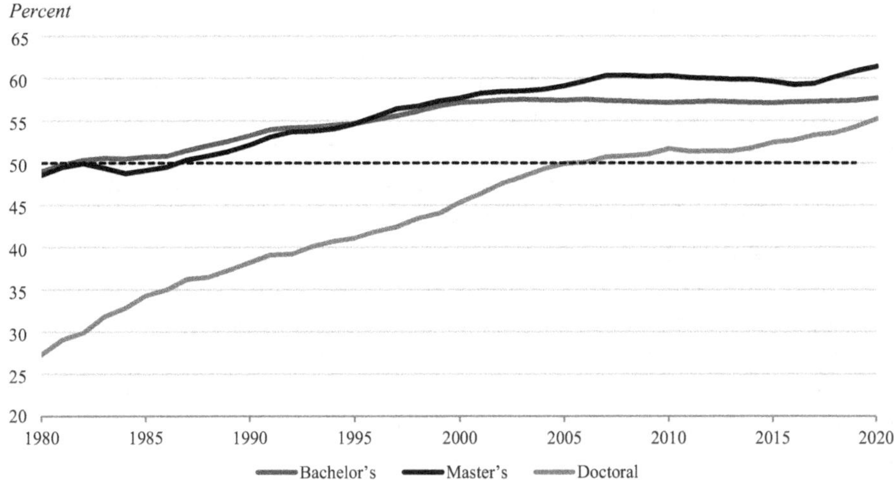

Source: U.S. Department of Education, National Center for Education Statistics.
Note: The dashed line indicates 50 percent. Doctoral degrees include all doctoral degrees, including M.D., J.D., and Ph.D.

that want to open or expand, boost long-run economic growth, and increase prosperity.

One factor affecting labor force participation, particularly for women, is household, community, and care responsibilities. Before entering the labor force in large numbers, women had long provided a large share of unpaid work in their homes and communities, including household maintenance tasks, raising children, caring for elder family members, and volunteering for community projects—work typically not captured in economic measures like GDP. Today, women working outside the home continue to disproportionately undertake these tasks; one recent study found that in heterosexual marriages, even when women's wages are more than double those of their spouses, women do 44 percent more household work (Siminski and Yetsenga 2022).

At the same time, in recent decades, the aging of the so-called baby boom generation (people born roughly between 1946 and 1964) and reduced fertility rates have increased the demand for senior care while constraining the supply of younger workers. The ratio of people age 65 and above to the number of people age 16 to 64, sometimes called the old-age dependency ratio, has more than doubled during the past seven decades. This has contributed to increased demand for care from adult children, creating the so-called sandwich generation of people who have care responsibilities for both older and younger family members (figure 1-13). In 2017 and 2018, more than 8 million parents of children under 18 also provided senior care, including nearly 5 million mothers (BLS 2019).

Women's shift into the labor force and demographic changes were associated with an increased demand for paid workers to provide what was previously unpaid labor, particularly caring for young children and older or disabled adults (figure 1-14). These care workers are often paid very low wages and are disproportionately women, particularly women of color.

To meet care needs, in recent years, multiple States and cities have passed legislation to provide paid family and medical leave for workers (National Partnership 2022). Additionally, private firms have increasingly provided paid family and medical leave, remote work adjustments, and other benefits to help workers balance their care and work responsibilities (figure 1-15). However, the lack of a national paid family and medical leave program, of adequate affordable child care, and of Federal labor laws to guarantee flexibilities for workers with care responsibilities has limited the ability for caregivers, especially women, to remain in the labor force.

The actions of the private sector have not been enough to meet the scale of the problem. Inequality in who has access to these benefits means that workers in the top 10 percent of the wage distribution are nearly eight times as likely as the lowest-paid workers to have access to paid family leave and more than four times as likely to have access to childcare through their work (BLS 2022a). Low-wage and hourly workers can particularly struggle to

Figure 1-13. Percentage of Households with a Child under 18 That Have an Adult over Age 65 Years, 1989–2021

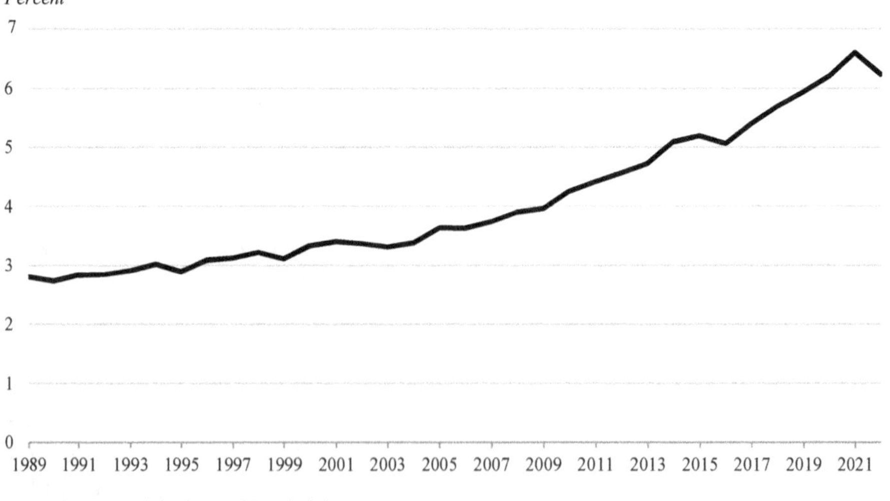

Sources: Current Population Survey; CEA calculations.

Figure 1-14. Consumption of Nursing Home and Childcare Services and Women's Labor Force Participation, 1960–2022

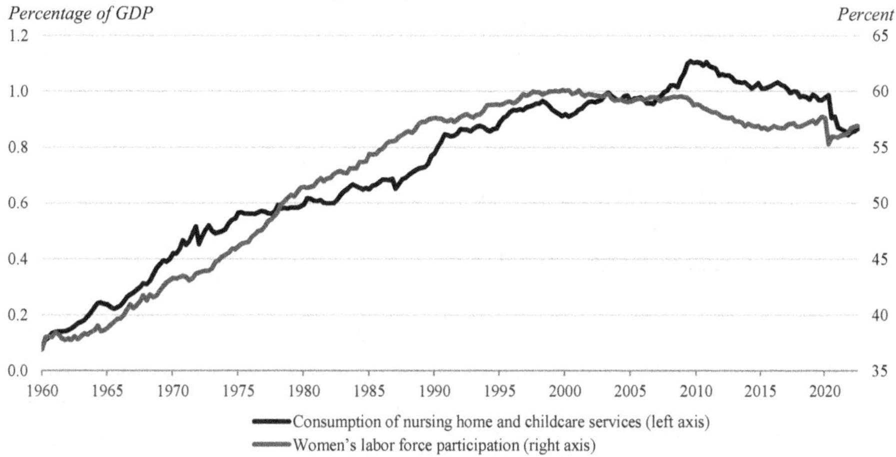

Sources: Bureau of Economic Analysis; Bureau of Labor Statistics; CEA calculations.

Figure 1-15. Share of Private Industry Workers with Access to Benefits

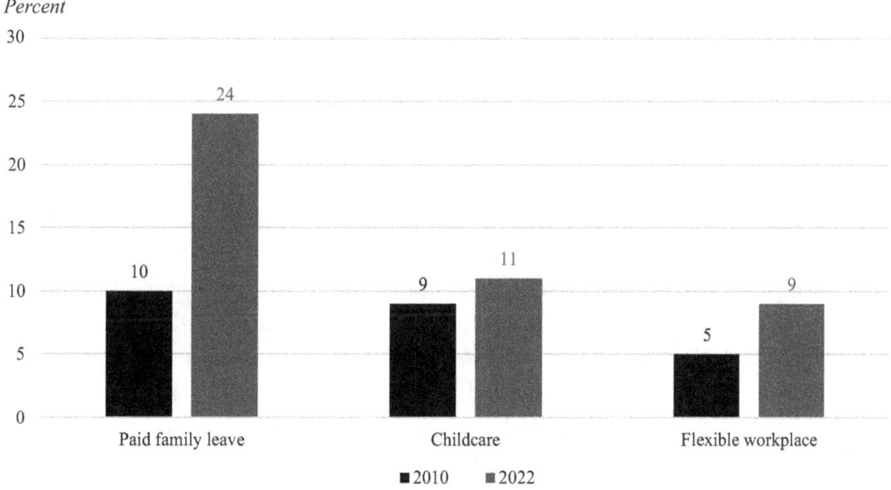

Source: Bureau of Labor Statistics.

manage work and care responsibilities due to limited workplace flexibilities, such as fair and predictable scheduling. Although data are limited, evidence suggests that the market and public sector underprovide both childcare and senior care. For example, the CEA's analysis of the 2019 National Survey of Early Care and Education indicates that nearly three-quarters of childcare centers are experiencing excess demand (i.e., have a waiting list or reject children due to limited capacity).

There are many reasons that the care industry has not been able to evolve to meet current needs. Among other issues, even as other service-providing industries have benefited from productivity-enhancing technological advances, the care industry has not; it still takes roughly as many people to watch 10 children today as it did 50 years ago, and the cost of childcare has risen in part due to increases in provider wages (although they are still quite low).[3] Between 1990 and 2021, the price of childcare rose by 225 percent while the median household income rose by roughly 150 percent. In addition, because families face liquidity constraints, like the inability to borrow against future income, they are often unable to afford the childcare that best meets their needs.

These challenges have a negative impact on labor force participation, particularly for women. In 2022, 14.6 percent of women between the age of 25 and 54 said that they were not in the labor force because they were caring for their home or family, representing roughly 60 percent of all the prime-age women not working. While some women may prefer providing family care to participating in the labor force, research suggests that for others, the cost of care limits their choices. Studies indicate that government policies that reduce the costs of care can strengthen participation, particularly for women (Morrissey 2017; Shen 2021). But relative to its peers, the United States provides few policies that could help families meet these care needs, such as paid family and medical leave and childcare investments—an observation researchers often make when discussing trends in U.S. female labor force participation (Blau and Kahn 2013). Whereas in 1985, the participation rate among women age 25 to 54 in the United States exceeded the rate in Canada, the United Kingdom, Japan, Australia, and the European Union, in recent years, the United States has experienced *lower* women's participation than Canada, the United Kingdom, Japan, Australia, and the European Union (OECD 2022b).

Further, care responsibilities affect men's participation in the economy along with women's, particularly as gender norms evolve (figure 1-16). In 2022, 2 percent of men between the age of 25 and 54 said they did not work due to home or family responsibilities, up from 0.9 percent in 1995. Subsidizing care for families while simultaneously investing in the supply of childcare would likely increase the overall number of workers who are able to enter the workforce, and thus facilitate economic growth.

[3] The Baumol-Bowen cost disease is what economists call this tendency for wages and costs to rise in industries that see smaller productivity gains in response to increases in wages and costs from industries that have seen larger productivity gains (Maiello 2017).

Figure 1-16. Nonparticipation in the Labor Force, by Reason

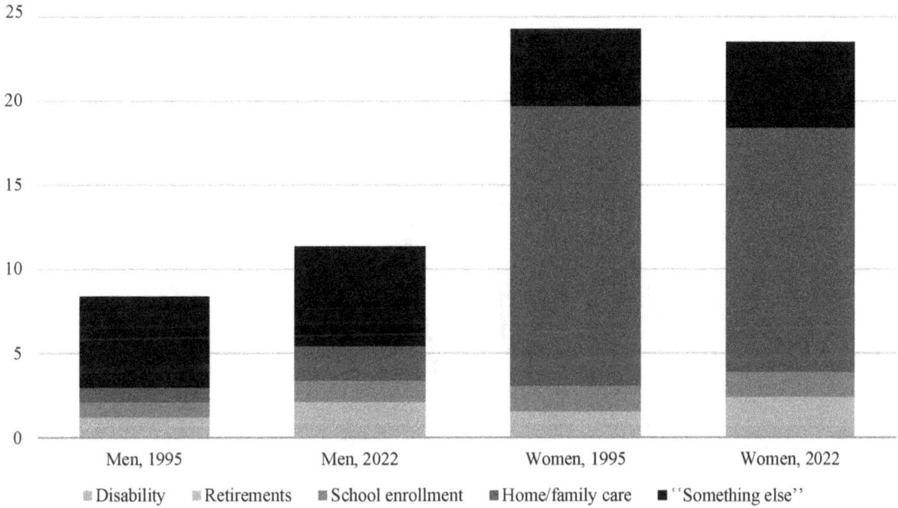

Sources: Current Population Survey; CEA calculations.

Investing in Physical Capital: Adapting to the Increasing Effects of Climate Change

Physical capital is the next important input for economic growth. The kinds and quantities of physical capital needed are in a constant state of flux. For much of human history, infrastructure was designed around animal power, such as horses. In the 19th century, infrastructure began shifting to railroads, while the 20th century saw rapid shifts toward infrastructure for automobiles and airplanes. Although much of the transportation infrastructure built in the 20th century remains useful today, the 21st century has seen massive investments in network infrastructure to allow for faster and more reliable communications and Internet access.

At the same time, the large and growing effects of climate change pose a significant, broad-based risk for physical capital. Over the past century, the level of carbon dioxide (CO2) in the air has risen drastically (figure 1-17). In 2013, atmospheric CO2 concentration surpassed 400 parts per million for the first time in recorded history (Blunden 2014). In 2021, it averaged nearly 415 parts per million (Lan, Tans, and Thoning 2022). Climate models find that the increased level of greenhouse gases in the atmosphere is in turn responsible for rising sea levels, hotter weather, and more common and severe extreme weather events—trends that are predicted to continue even with an ambitious reduction of greenhouse gas emissions.

Figure 1-17. Carbon Dioxide Levels Over Time

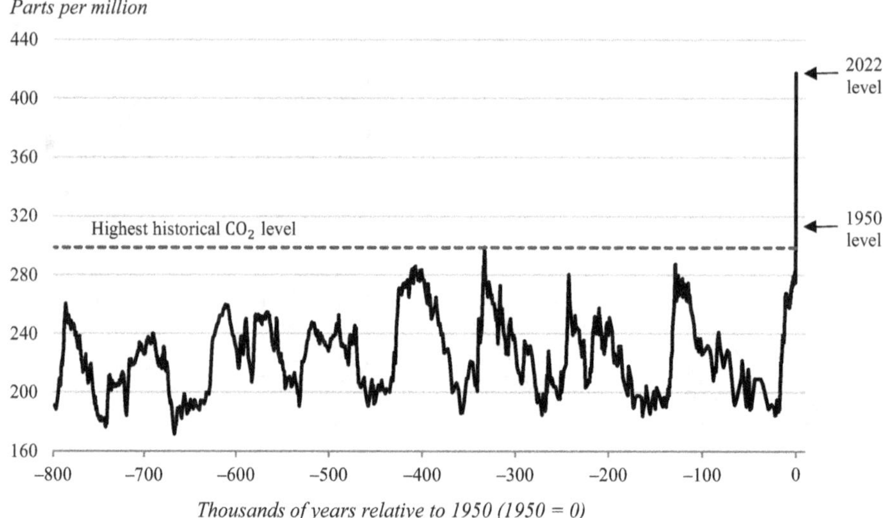

Source: Lüthi et al. 2008.
Note: Data come from reconstructions from ice cores.

The economic damage from climate change has already begun to accrue and have an impact on communities around the globe. Some of these types of damage emerge in human capital: beyond the effects on human health (e.g., Carleton et al. 2022), researchers have documented the effects of climate change on migration flows (Missirian and Schlenker 2017; Jessoe, Manning, and Taylor 2018), violent crime (Ranson 2014), labor productivity (Graff Zivin and Neidell 2012), and learning (Park et al. 2020; Park, Behrer, and Goodman 2021). However, this damage has also been observed in physical capital. In the United States, the damage from billion-dollar disasters (see figure 1-18) now averages roughly $120 billion a year (Smith 2023). Costs from rising extreme weather are being driven both by the changing climate and by rapid development in risky areas (Climate Central and Zillow 2018; Iglesias et al. 2021). Climate change has been found to affect crop yields and agricultural productivity, and increasingly frequent heat waves will likely exacerbate increasing strain on electrical grids (Woetzel et al. 2020; Auffhammer, Baylis, and Hausman 2017). Instability due to climate change is expected to cause new systemic risks for financial markets (Financial Stability Oversight Council 2021; Brunetti et al. 2021). In insurance markets, extreme weather events are driving higher payouts, which can raise premiums and reduce insurance availability (Lara 2019; Botzen, van den Bergh, and Bouwer 2010). Large disasters could cause insurance companies to fail altogether—as seen after Hurricane Andrew's $15.5 billion in property damage in 1992, and along the Gulf

Figure 1-18. Number of Billion-Dollar Natural Disasters in the United States, 1980–2022

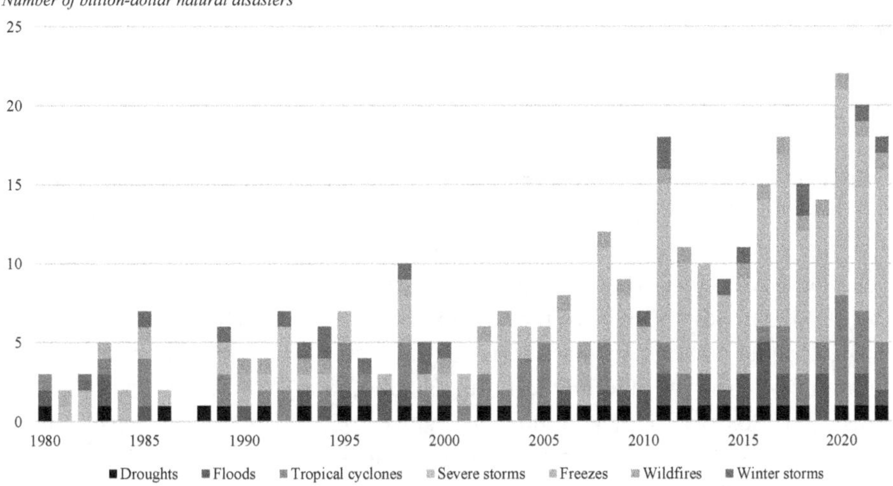

Source: NCEI 2022.
Note: Disaster costs are adjusted for inflation using the Consumer Price Index for All Urban Consumers.

Coast after more recent hurricane strikes (Gelzinis and Steele 2019; Elliott 2022). Even if markets continue to adapt to past experiences, rising climate uncertainty may increase the risks of future failures as unanticipated costs rise for insurance companies.

These effects of climate change have important consequences for physical capital and will likely require adaptation by institutions—from insurance and financial markets to construction firms, energy producers, and the government. To lessen the economic damage of climate change, these institutions, and many other actors throughout the global economy, will need to quickly transition away from fossil fuels and emit fewer greenhouse gases (known as "mitigation"). They will also need to protect physical capital from damage ("adaptation"), such as by building resilient infrastructure, employing nature-based solutions to improve resilience in the face of more frequent extreme weather events, and shifting new investments away from high-risk areas. The scale and timing of climate change have led many researchers to conclude that both mitigation and adaptation are necessary (IPCC 2014). Adaptation measures may range from actions on the individual level, like raising the foundations of houses to accommodate rising sea levels and changing agricultural cropping practices, to community-level actions, like building seawalls and expanding reservoirs' capacities to deal with more variable rainfall.

Climate change is also expected to alter the productivity and value of different forms of capital in complex ways. The existing infrastructure, which was designed for older climate conditions, may underperform in these new conditions. For instance, major hydropower dams in the Southwest may soon cease being able to produce electricity because of the decades-long drought (Ramirez 2022; Partlow 2022; Kao et al. 2022). In contrast, other forms of capital may become more valuable. Existing sea-walls and riverine flood defenses provide greater value in the face of the changing climate that is increasing coastal and inland flooding risks. Additionally, with the rise of clean energy technologies, some resources like the Sun and wind have acquired new value and have become important kinds of capital. For example, though societies have used windmills for centuries, wind has only become a widely used source of electric power in the last few decades as technological advances have met the energy needs in a changing climate.

Climate change is already reducing—and will very likely continue to reduce—growth in GDP (Burke, Hsiang, and Miguel 2015; Newell, Prest, and Sexton 2021; Kalkuhl and Wenz 2020); this type of harm could be reduced with greater investment in adaptation. A recent summary of the literature from the Council of Economic Advisers and the Office of Management and Budget (2022) shows substantial variation in the estimates of the impact of global warming on U.S. GDP. For example, the Congressional Budget Office estimates that climate change will reduce the average annual GDP growth rate by 0.03 percentage point from 2020 to 2050 (Herrnstadt and Dinan 2020), which implies that the level of U.S. GDP would be just under 1 percent lower by 2050, whereas a study by the Bank of England (2021) finds that climate damage could reduce U.S. GDP by over 11 percent by 2050 in a worse-than-expected scenario. These estimates only capture a fraction of climate change costs, however, since many effects, such as increasing mortality risk and ecosystem disruption, are not fully reflected in market transactions or GDP estimates (Rennert et al. 2022; Bastien-Olvera and Moore 2021). By one estimate, more than half of global GDP is moderately or highly dependent on nature, which is being lost or dramatically altered by human activity (World Economic Forum 2020).

Investing in the Economy's Productivity: The New World of Digital Markets

Rapid advances in information technology in recent decades have had a substantial impact on how Americans work and live. Computer and information technology occupations now account for 3 percent of all employment in the United States, and the Bureau of Labor Statistics (BLS) projects that the number of these jobs will increase by 15 percent over the next decade (BLS 2021, 2022b). Moreover, other occupations that are not explicitly computer-related increasingly also rely on strong digital skills (Muro et al. 2017).

The spread of computer use is not limited to the workplace. In 1984, 8.2 percent of households had a computer at home; by 2021, this share had climbed to 95 percent (File 2013; U.S. Census Bureau 2021). More recently, information technology has been applied to traditionally analog devices—telephones, cars, watches, and the like—in what is sometimes referred to as the "Internet of Things" (Armstrong 2022). Figure 1-19 shows how rapidly Internet use has expanded in recent decades, with almost all adults using the Internet in 2021 compared with just over half in 2000.

New technology is changing the way people interact with each other, both in markets and socially. Online sales now account for 14.8 percent of total retail sales, more than doubling their share over the last decade (U.S. Census Bureau 2023). Most job seekers now look for jobs online (Hernandez 2017). And people increasingly connect with each other on digital social media platforms to exchange ideas and information. The largest such platform, Facebook, counted 2.96 billion monthly active users as of December 2022 (U.S. Securities and Exchange Commission 2023).

Through the lens of the aggregate production function, the contribution of recent technological advances to economic growth has been twofold. First, it has increased the physical capital stock of the American economy. The fall in the cost of computing power and the more recent rise of machine learning and artificial intelligence have led to a proliferation of computers in workspaces and robots in factories, which are helping workers specialize

Figure 1-19. Percentage of Adults Who Report Using the Internet Over Time

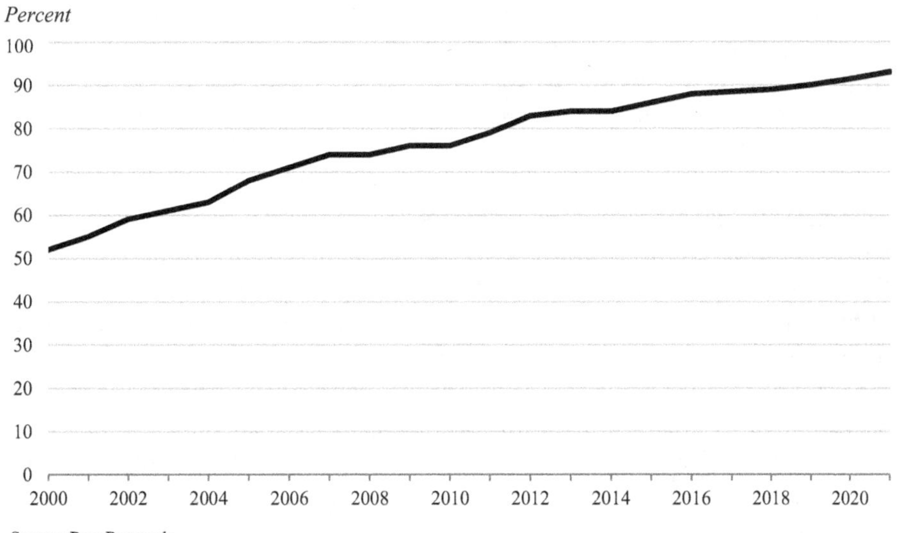

Source: Pew Research.

in tasks for which they have the greatest comparative advantage, like big-picture strategizing, designing products, and interacting with consumers.

Second, at least in theory, recent technological advances have increased total factor productivity by enabling new production processes and making the allocation of resources more efficient. Indeed, increased investments in computers and software arguably played a substantial role in the fast productivity growth of the late 1990s and early 2000s (Weller 2002). The economic benefits of broadband Internet access, for example, have been widely accepted. One study comparing countries that belonged to the Organization for Economic Cooperation and Development between 1996 and 2007 found that a 10-percentage-point increase in broadband penetration increased per capita economic growth by 0.9 to 1.5 percentage points (Czernich et al. 2011). In the United States specifically, one study of the expansion of broadband access between 1999 and 2007 estimates that ubiquitous broadband access within a county would increase that county's employment rate by 1.8 percentage points compared with no broadband access (Atasoy 2013). And when the COVID-19 pandemic prevented many Americans from participating in in-person work and school, new online technologies enabled people to continue learning and working.

The practical importance of the productivity effect of more recent developments in machine learning and artificial intelligence remains a topic of debate, however, especially because the last decade saw the slowest productivity growth in the post–World War II era (according to CEA calculations using BLS data). One viewpoint is that recent innovations in technology have been more incremental and not as groundbreaking as previous technological changes (Gordon 2016). Other scholars, in contrast, have argued that traditional output measures fail to capture the full value of these new innovations and that their productivity gains will materialize in time (Brynjolfsson and Petropoulos 2021).

In addition to the direct effects of those technological advances on output growth, policymakers are paying increased attention to the more indirect ways that these advances are affecting the structure of the U.S. economy. For example, blockchain technology has fueled the rise of financially innovative digital assets that have proven to be highly volatile and subject to fraud (White House 2022). The Internet and other new technologies have allowed for the provision of digital services, increasing the ability of people to perform and access services remotely, which affects trade, given that technological advances make it easier for countries to import and export services than in the past. Additionally, technological advances have raised distributional concerns, both in terms of access and their usage. Black, Hispanic, and lower-income Americans are less likely to have home access to a computer and broadband and the opportunities that those technologies provide (Pew Research Center 2021b, 2021c). And artificial intelligence has been argued to deepen racial and economic inequities by perpetuating discrimination in areas such as housing, the criminal justice system, or mortgage lending (ACLU 2021).

Addressing these areas of concern often draws on the traditional tools of policymakers in new contexts. For example, policymakers have focused on the high level of market concentration in the digital economy. Economic theory has long seen market power and monopolization as threats to productivity and output growth. The digital economy—broadly capturing the platforms that facilitate the online exchange of goods and information—is characterized by high levels of concentration, where markets are often dominated by a small set of firms (Digital Competition Expert Panel 2019). This concentration can be the result of the economic fundamentals of these platforms, whose scale can produce value for participants. Inherently, many of these markets exhibit some form of network externality. For example, buyers and sellers on an e-commerce platform are generally better off when more sellers and buyers are on the same platform.

The economics underlying the susceptibility of digital markets to concentration is not new. But the scale of digital markets is amplified by the fact that they typically allow for a virtually unlimited number of participants without congestion. This implies that the "winners" in digital markets—the small set of firms that dominate the market—end up being larger and are of significantly greater importance for the overall economy. Because it is notoriously hard to define markets and there are many ways to measure concentration, it is difficult to precisely quantify the degree of concentration in digital markets. Nevertheless, big tech firms such as Amazon, Alphabet, and Meta have provided some of the most widely used services in recent years and generally have few direct competitors that come close to their size.

From a policy perspective, these advances pose new challenges. The degree of concentration in digital markets raises long-standing concerns about whether dominant players in these markets leverage their market power to stifle competition and innovation. But unlike in some traditional markets, much of the value of digital companies comes from network effects—so antitrust actions may face greater challenges in preserving value for consumers while addressing problems associated with concentration. A world where digital technologies make services increasingly easy to trade requires adjustments to international trade policy. And digital assets require updating at least some regulations.

In the future, the Internet and digital markets—and further innovation—will have the potential to drive continued increases in productivity. However, careful policymaking to address both the new and old challenges presented by these technologies will be necessary to ensure that productivity and output gains remain strong.

Conclusion

This year's *Report* sheds light on these and other changes in the United States' economic and social systems and how they challenge established economic thinking and policymaking.

Chapter 2 summarizes the Nation's economy during the past year, characterizing how the continuing recovery from the COVID-19 pandemic and the impact of Russia's invasion of Ukraine have shaped the economy, and how sustained demand imbalances, supply chain delays, and pandemic policies have affected growth, inflation, and unemployment. It also presents the macroeconomic forecast underpinning the Biden-Harris Administration's Fiscal Year 2024 Budget.

Chapter 3 describes trends in international trade and investment in 2022 and characterizes how shifts over past decades in global interconnectedness have led to new challenges and opportunities for the United States. There is a need to balance the considerable benefits of globalization through economic linkages with the risks for economic and national security that international economic interconnectedness can entail. Working in concert with U.S. allies and partners can enable the Nation to effectively address shared challenges and take advantage of new opportunities in the changing global environment.

Chapters 4, 5, and 6 point to shortcomings in, respectively, the supply of care, the supply of higher education, and the supply of labor—and highlight their significance for economic prosperity. Chapter 4 illustrates the significance of early childhood care and education for economic well-being and prosperity, focusing on the effects of childcare on children and families as well as the broader societal benefits. The chapter characterizes gaps in access and availability, and it details how challenges in the childcare industry, including the high cost of providing care, prevent the market from delivering childcare of an optimal quantity or quality. The chapter explains how policies that address these challenges by supporting families accessing care and providers supplying care can have substantial, long-run economic benefits.

Chapter 5 highlights the importance of higher education in this context, with a particular focus on the role that postsecondary institutions play in creating the skilled workforce. The chapter notes that various features of the higher education market suggest that promising institution-focused policies and programs could meaningfully improve student outcomes and ensure that all students have access to a college degree of value.

The recovery from the COVID-19 global pandemic has highlighted the importance of the labor supply for the economy. Chapter 6 shows that current labor supply shortfalls in the United States are not merely a lingering effect of the pandemic but are also due to population aging and long-run declines in labor force participation. Policies to draw more adults into the labor force will be needed, without which the labor supply is likely to be constrained for the foreseeable future.

Chapter 7 describes the significance of digital markets in the modern U.S. economy and the tension for this market environment's regulators between promoting competition and enabling economies of scale. Digital markets have grown rapidly, and high levels of consolidation suggest that the government has a role in protecting consumers and promoting innovation through antitrust action. The importance of network effects means that regulatory interventions in the digital economy have nuanced effects.

Chapter 8 explores recent developments in digital assets, along with their opportunities and risks. Although advocates often claim that digital assets, particularly crypto assets, are a revolutionary innovation, the design of these assets frequently reflects an ignorance of basic economic principles that have been learned in economics and finance over centuries, and this inadequate design is often detrimental to consumers and investors.

Finally, chapter 9 describes the physical risks that the changing climate poses for U.S. economic production, the well-being of U.S. communities, and the fiscal position of the Federal Government, as well as opportunities to manage and reduce these risks. International and domestic climate policy has historically focused on policies to reduce greenhouse gas emissions, which are critical for mitigating the worst effects of climate change. However, the effects of climate change are already being felt across the United States and, even with ambitious emission reductions, will continue to increase until net global emissions fall to zero. Policies that enable households, businesses, and communities to plan for the changing climate and to manage evolving weather risks are an important complement to emission reductions in reducing the costs of climate change. Chapter 9 thus describes the economic foundations of these adaptation policies and outlines four pillars that could inform the Federal adaptation strategy.

Chapter 2

The Year in Review and the Years Ahead

The U.S. economy in 2022 continued to navigate an unprecedented global pandemic, and weathered an additional price shock to energy and food caused by Russia's unprovoked invasion of Ukraine. Despite these and other challenges, the economy remained resilient with moderate output growth, strong employment growth, and inflation that peaked and then started to moderate late in the year (figure 2-1). In the face of supply constraints and changes in the composition of demand, the primary goal of fiscal and monetary policy in 2022 was to restore balance to supply and demand, fight inflation, and return the economy to a path of stable, steady growth.

Russia's invasion of Ukraine in February created acute supply constraints to energy, food, and other commodities that raised inflation globally. In

Figure 2-1. The U.S. Economy, 2018–22

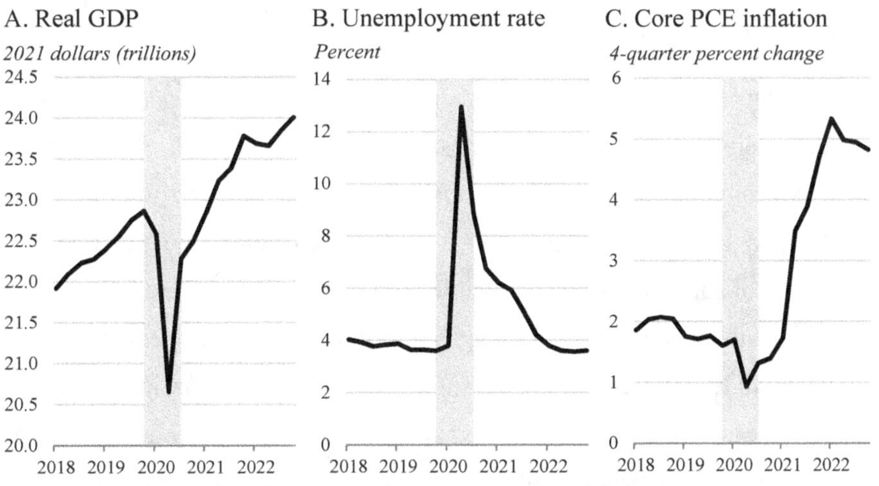

Sources: Bureau of Economic Analysis; Bureau of Labor Statistics; CEA calculations.
Note: Nominal GDP was converted to 2021 dollars using the GDP Price Index. PCE = Personal Consumption Expenditures Price Index. Core PCE inflation excludes volatile food and energy inflation. All values are seasonally adjusted.

addition, in the first half of the year, the COVID-19 virus continued to weigh on economies across the world—in the same ways, if to a different extent, as it had in 2021 (Chetty et al. 2022)—especially when its Omicron variant caused cases and fatalities to surge in the United States and abroad. Due to pandemic-related disruptions, global supply chains were stressed. To support the U.S. economy, the Federal Reserve kept the target range for the Federal Funds Rate near zero until March. Although the majority of direct household relief funds from the CARES Act, the American Rescue Plan, and related legislation had been dispersed by the end of 2021, many of these funds had not been spent by households, and Americans entered 2022 with historically elevated savings.

Recessions can leave lasting scars, but thanks to the fiscal and monetary support provided in 2020 and 2021, the United States' real gross domestic product (GDP) in 2022 was close to what it had been forecasted before the pandemic (CBO 2019) to be in 2022. After muted growth for much of the previous two years, growth in real consumer spending on services was particularly strong during the four quarters of 2022, as spending patterns started to return to normal. By most measures, the labor market was extraordinarily tight in 2022, creating some of the most favorable conditions for job seekers in decades.

As this chapter shows, the government's comprehensive response to the pandemic helped achieve the solid positive outcomes of 2022. At the same time, the combination and interaction of numerous factors exacerbated the elevated inflation. Although it is difficult to determine the relative importance of each factor, the pandemic, and responses to it, had substantial effects on both the supply and demand sides of the economy. Specific factors of note include pandemic-induced supply disruptions, shifts in consumer demand, the accumulation of excess savings, and stimulative fiscal and monetary support throughout 2020 and 2021.

In 2022, monetary policy turned to fighting inflation and fiscal policy focused on strategies to complement that fight, while also working to guide the economy to stable and steady growth, in 2022 and in the future. Even before the year began, government spending and deficits fell closer to prepandemic trends. In March, the Federal Reserve began to reverse its asset purchase program and started what became a swift series of interest rate hikes; stock markets and residential investment declined quickly. President Biden authorized a drawdown of the Strategic Petroleum Reserve to lower gasoline prices after Russia's invasion of Ukraine. In July and August, major pieces of legislation were passed to boost the economy's long-term supply side. Some measures of labor market tightness and inflation began to moderate, with inflation showing an easing at the end of the year. The fight against inflation is expected to continue into 2023, resulting in a near-term outlook of below-trend GDP growth, a modestly rising unemployment rate, and falling inflation.

This chapter begins with a review of the economy in 2022, first examining the recovery of GDP and its subcomponents, and then summarizing the conditions of labor markets and financial markets. Next, the chapter describes inflation in 2022, discussing possible causes along with the government's response. Finally, the chapter presents the forecast underpinning the President's Fiscal Year 2024 Budget and summaries of the near-term and long-term outlooks.

The Year in Review: The Continuing Recovery

This section summarizes the U.S. economy in 2022. By many measures, the economy had recovered from the recession induced by the COVID-19-pandemic by the end of 2022; by a few measures, the economy had not. For example, real GDP was near the level it would have been if it had continued to grow at its average 2010–19 pace from its prepandemic peak in 2019:Q4. The unemployment rate was near its prepandemic low for most of the year, and other labor market indicators showed more tightness than they had in 2019:Q4. On average, wages adjusted for inflation declined over the year, though they saw growth in the second half. The stock market started the year at a record high, but fell over the year, partly due to rising inflation and tighter monetary policy. By most measures, and especially compared with recoveries from previous recessions, the economy in 2022 was healthy.

Output in 2022: A Return to Near Its Trend

Real GDP grew by 0.9 percent during the four quarters of 2022, a deceleration from its 5.7 percent pace during 2021. After a rapid decline in 2020 and a large bounce-back in 2021, the level of GDP in 2022 was roughly at its prepandemic trend. But GDP growth in 2022 was uneven, negative in the first half and positive in the second half. Some components increased and others contracted, reflecting the ongoing adjustment back to "normal" and away from the atypical spending and investment patterns seen over the past three years.

As shown in figure 2-2, real GDP in 2022 had rebounded to a level that was at or above a log-linear trend extrapolated from preceding years of GDP growth, an important achievement. In some previous economic cycles, including the recovery from the Great Recession of 2007–9, the economy took much longer to return to its extrapolated trend, meaning that workers and consumers suffered negative consequences for a longer period. (See figure 2-3, panel H, for a comparison of this recovery with other recoveries.) The longer-run trend level of GDP is a simple estimate of what is sometimes called potential GDP, which is a measure of what the economy can produce at full capacity at a particular point in time. Recessions can cause output to

Figure 2-2. GDP and Trend GDP, 2012–22

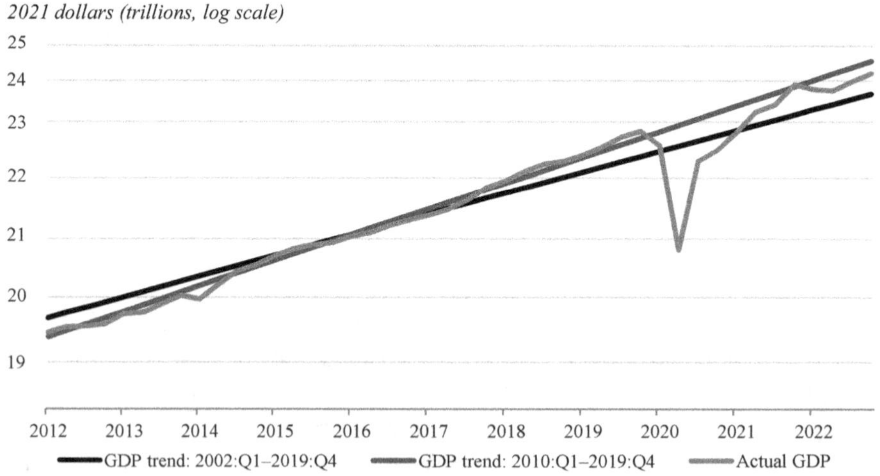

2021 dollars (trillions, log scale)

25
24
23
22
21
20
19

2012 2013 2014 2015 2016 2017 2018 2019 2020 2021 2022

GDP trend: 2002:Q1–2019:Q4
GDP trend: 2010:Q1–2019:Q4
Actual GDP

Sources: Bureau of Economic Analysis; CEA calculations.
Note: GDP trend lines were calculated by regressing the log of real GDP on time for the specified intervals, and plotting predicted values from that regression. Nominal GDP was converted to 2021 dollars using the GDP Price Index. All values are seasonally adjusted.

Figure 2-3. The 2019–22 Period Compared with Previous Business Cycles

Index = 100 at business-cycle peak; 2019–22 cycle peak is 2019:Q4

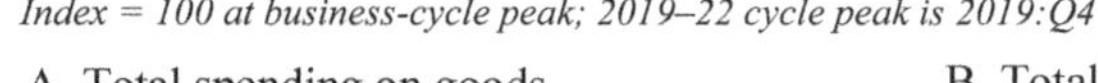

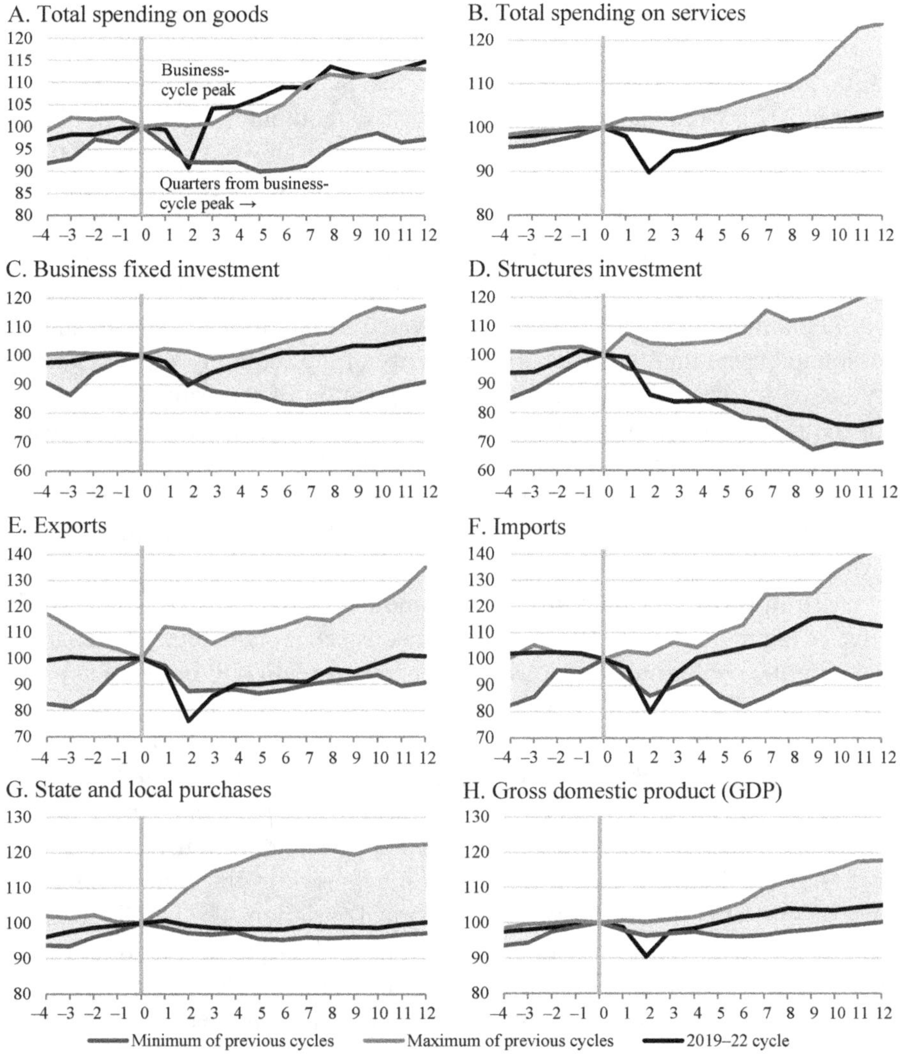

Sources: Bureau of Economic Analayis; CEA calculations.
Note: Panels A and B include spending on goods and services by consumers, businesses, government, and as part of international trade, as defined in table 1.2.6 in the "National Income and Product Accounts." Panel D includes business, residential, and government structures investment, also from table 1.2.6. All values are seasonally adjusted.

run below its trend, which may be followed by faster growth that returns the level of output toward its trend. Growth can also be so fast that the level of output rises above its trend, a situation that may lead to high inflation as aggregate demand outstrips the capacity of the economy to produce the desired level of goods and services; this is often referred to as an overheated economy. Usually, high inflation provokes a policy response—for example, an interest rate hike by the Federal Reserve—that cools the economy and returns output to its trend.[1]

Estimating the trend of GDP is not straightforward. Figure 2-2 plots two log-linear trend lines estimated over different intervals. The longer estimation interval suggests that the United States' output was above its trend in 2022, while the shorter one suggests that output was below it. Many other measures suggest the economy was running above its trend in 2022, including signals of tight labor markets, the elevated inflation rate and the growth of consumption without corresponding growth in investment or imports. Further, given the turmoil associated with the pandemic—lower labor force participation, demand shifts for specific skilled labor categories, and population movement—and the elevated inflation rate, there is ample reason to expect that the productive capacity of the economy was temporarily below its usual position in 2022. The position of the economy matters for the interpretation of growth in 2022, and has implications for the near-term economic outlook. If GDP was above trend, the slowdown of growth in 2022, influenced by the Federal Reserve's rate hikes, would mean the economy was returning to its trend, and may also presage continued slow growth in the near term.

To illustrate the strength of the economic recovery in 2021 and 2022 relative to previous recoveries, figure 2-3 consists of eight "butterfly charts" that plot the evolution of various components of real GDP before and after the 12 post–World War II business-cycle peaks in the United States, as determined by the National Bureau of Economic Research. To construct these charts, each highlighted component of GDP was normalized to equal 100 in the quarter at the peak of each business cycle. The orange lines in the figure show the maximum paths of each component during the 11 business cycles before the current cycle; the light blue lines show the minimum paths; and the gray areas show the range of historical variation. The dark blue lines plot the postpandemic recession recovery. If, to the right of the green vertical line, a dark blue line is closer to an orange line than to a light blue line, this means that, relative to previous recessions, the recovery was stronger for that component.

As can be seen in panel A of figure 2-3, the cumulative growth of real spending on all goods since the previous business cycle peak in 2019:Q4 through 2022 was at the top of historical experience. Conversely, in panel B of figure 2-3, real spending on all services was far below the range of historical experience at the end 2021, and growth through 2022 was only enough for it to recover to the lower historical bound by the end of 2022. As shown in panels C and D of figure 2-3, though real business fixed investment remained at the middle of its historical range, real investment in residential

[1] While higher GDP is generally beneficial, high inflation poses costs to the economy. It is these costs that the policy responses seek to avoid.

Table 2-1. Real GDP Growth and Its Components, 2022

Component	Q4/Q4 Growth (percent) (1)	Contribution to Q4/Q4 GDP Growth (percentage points) (2)	Contribution to the Deviation of 2022:Q4 GDP from Its Trend (percentage points) (3)
Total	0.9	0.9	−1.1
Consumer spending	1.8	1.2	0.5
Goods	−0.9	−0.2	0.9
Durables	0.5	0.0	0.3
Motor vehicles and parts	−1.5	0.0	−0.3
Nondurables	−1.7	−0.3	0.5
Services	3.2	1.4	−0.4
Investment	−4.0	−0.7	−2.3
Business fixed investment	4.3	0.6	−1.4
Nonresidential equipment	4.0	0.2	−0.8
Nonresidential structures	−3.3	−0.1	−0.9
Intellectual property	8.5	0.4	0.4
Housing investment	−19.0	−0.9	−1.1
Change in private inventories	–	−0.4	–
Net exports	–	0.3	–
Exports	5.2	0.6	−1.1
Imports	1.8	−0.3	−0.3
Government	0.8	0.1	1.3
Federal	0.1	0.0	1.2
Defense	−0.2	0.0	0.6
Nondefense	0.5	0.0	0.5
State and local	1.3	0.1	0.2

Sources: Bureau of Economic Analysis; CEA calculations.

Note: Column 2 lists the contribution of each component to the annual rate of growth of real GDP. These may not precisely sum to totals because of approximations to the formulas used in the National Income and Product Accounts. Column 3 shows that that GDP was 1.1 percent below prepandemic trend in 2022:Q4 and how much each component of GDP contributed, negatively or positively, to this deviation from trend. It was calculated by regressing the log of each real GDP component on time from 2010 to 2019, calculating the percent difference of the 2022:Q4 level predicted by that regression from the actual 2022:Q4 level of each component, and multiplying by the importance of that component to overall GDP (the average of the 2019:Q4 and 2022:Q4 ratios of that nominal component of GDP to total nominal GDP).

and other structures fell in 2022, and its recovery has remained near the bottom of its historical range.

Table 2-1 breaks down real GDP growth into its subcomponents. The first column lists the four-quarter growth rate for each component over 2022. The second column lists the contributions of each category to overall real GDP growth over those quarters. Contributions can be negative or positive. For example, because real exports grew 5.2 percent during the four quarters of the year and constituted about 11.7 percent of GDP, its contribution to real GDP growth was 0.6 percentage point. The first row of the third column compares the 2022:Q4 level of real GDP with what it would have been if it had followed its 2010–19 log-linear trend (the light blue line in figure 2-2); all other rows show the approximate contribution of that real GDP component to this deviation. The major sectors that grew noticeably faster than overall GDP in 2022 include consumer spending on services, equipment investment, intellectual property investment, and exports. Imports also experienced relatively fast growth, but these reduce GDP. Expenditure categories that grew slower than overall GDP include consumer spending on goods, nonresidential and residential investment, Federal Government purchases, and inventory investment. State and local expenditures grew, but only slowly.

Consumer spending. The nominal goods-to-services consumer spending ratio—which had been in a long-term decline—increased during 2020 and 2021, reaching its highest level since 2006. Real consumer spending on services fell sharply when the pandemic hit, as in-person activities such as dining out and traveling became more difficult. In contrast, real goods spending, after initially falling during the first two pandemic quarters, rebounded and spiked above its prepandemic level, as people stuck at home spent a larger share of their total real consumption on goods like furniture, appliances, and sporting equipment and a smaller share on services.

During 2022, the goods-to-services spending ratio started to normalize; real goods spending fell 0.9 percent during the four quarters of 2022, while real consumer services spending grew 3.2 percent. Even so, this ratio remained well above prepandemic norms. Overall, real consumer spending grew modestly during the four quarters of 2022, at a 1.8 percent annual rate, with all of that growth accounted for by services.

Investment. Real business fixed investment increased 4.3 percent during the four quarters of 2022, continuing its steady recovery from its pandemic-induced low. Investment growth was particularly strong in intellectual property, as it has been for the last decade. But investment by businesses in structures fell 3.3 percent during the four quarters of the year, with declines in investment in commercial and health care structures and power and communication structures. Investment increased in manufacturing and petroleum and natural gas mining structures.

Increases in business fixed investment were offset by declines in fixed investment in residential and other structures, as the housing market cooled due to the rise in mortgage rates associated with the Federal Reserve's tightening cycle. Both business fixed investment and fixed investment in residential and other structures were below their prepandemic trends. Overall, spending on structures was near the lower end of the business-cycle range, as shown in panel D of figure 2-3.

Some of the slowing GDP growth in 2022—which followed strong growth in 2021—was accounted for by inventory investment. The overall real inventory-to-sales ratio shrank to the lowest on record in 2021:Q2, as firms fought supply chain bottlenecks and then began to rapidly recover, with inventory investment at high levels in 2021:Q4 and 2022:Q1. The stock of real inventories continued to grow strongly in 2022, but because inventory investment was lower in 2022:Q2 and 2022:Q3 than in 2022:Q1, inventory investment subtracted from real GDP growth in those quarters and over the four quarters of the year.

Government spending. The Federal Government's real purchases (expenditures and gross investment) edged up slightly, by 0.1 percent, during the four quarters of 2022. Most of the surge in Federal spending that had supported households, businesses, and State and local governments in 2020 and 2021 consisted of transfers and subsidies that are not directly part of GDP; while these transfers and subsidies fell, purchases were little changed. Defense expenditures and gross investment barely changed during the four quarters of the year, while nondefense purchases edged up. State and local government purchases increased slowly, by 1.3 percent, during the four quarters of the year. Relative to the average cyclical response, State and local purchases were near the lower end of the business-cycle range, as shown in panel G of figure 2-3.

Imports and exports. Finally, real exports grew faster than overall GDP during the four quarters of 2022, growing by 5.2 percent at an annual rate, reflecting the continued reopening of the world economy. Although real imports grew more slowly than real exports during the four quarters of the year, at 1.8 percent, that import pace exceeded the growth of real GDP by 0.9 percentage point. Due to the stronger growth in real exports relative to imports, real net exports partially recovered from their pandemic-induced decline in 2022, contributing 0.3 percentage point to overall real GDP growth. (See chapter 3 of this *Report* for an in-depth discussion of international trade and investment in 2022.)

The Historic Strength of Labor Markets in 2022

Labor markets were very tight in 2022, as the strong economy led firms to continue to hire workers after pandemic-induced layoffs and hiring pauses. At the end of the year, the unemployment rate was 3.5 percent, matching the lowest rate—tied with September 2019 and prepandemic 2020—since 1969. Other labor market measures also showed a historically high degree of tightness, including the ratio of job openings per unemployed person, shown in figure 2-4, and the quit rate, considered by some to be the best measure of labor market tightness (Furman and Powell 2021), which reached at least a 20-year high at the end of 2021 and remained elevated through 2022.

Figure 2-4 shows the ratio of total job openings divided by the total number of unemployed people. During recessions, this measure tends to fall, as firms slow hiring, reduce job openings, and lay off workers, and it plummeted in 2020. By April 2022, however, the measure had climbed to the highest level on record, indicating that the labor market was unusually

Figure 2-4. Job Openings per Unemployed Person, 2000–2022

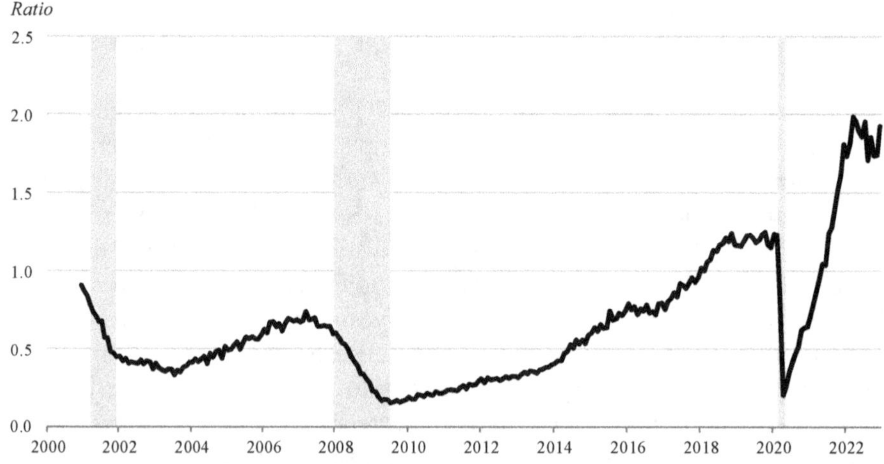

Sources: Bureau of Labor Stastistics; CEA calculations.
Note: All values are seasaonally adjusted.

Figure 2-5. The Beveridge Curve at Two Intervals

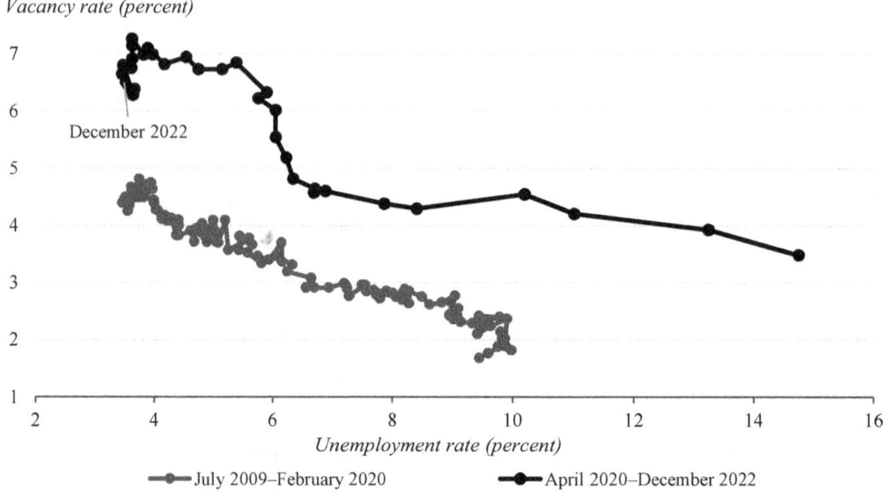

Sources: Bureau of Labor Statistics, CEA calculations.
Note: All values are seasonally adjusted.

tight. In the second half of the year, job openings decreased and the number of unemployed persons increased slightly.

Figure 2-5 shows another view of the labor market: the Beveridge curve, the relationship between the unemployment rate and the percentage of job openings relative to labor demand, known as the "vacancy rate."[2] The

[2] Labor demand equals job openings plus employment.

Beveridge curve during the pandemic-recession recovery, represented by the dark blue dots, shifted up and out, possibly due to increased pandemic-related difficulties in hiring and retaining workers. All the months of 2022 are located in the upper-left-hand corner of the figure, where vacancy rates are high and unemployment rates are low, indicating that labor markets were tight and that labor demand was high relative to labor supply.

Economists disagree about how much of this labor market tightness was due to a shortage in the supply of workers versus an excess demand for workers. On the demand side, the high aggregate demand described later in this chapter led to an increased demand for workers by businesses. There are a range of potential supply-side factors, which are discussed in chapter 6 of this *Report*.

The Cooling of Financial Markets in 2022

The stock market recovered quickly from large declines during the COVID-19 pandemic, reaching a new peak at the end of 2021. In early 2022, as inflation rose and the Federal Reserve began hiking the Federal Funds Rate to cool off the economy, stock prices declined. The losses in 2022 reversed only part of the gains made during the previous two years (figure 2-6).

Along with stock prices, bond prices also fell.[3] The price of 10-Year Treasury Notes, which moves inversely to the yield, began the year near historical highs but ended the year quite a bit lower, likely due in part to upward revisions in market expectations for the future path of inflation and associated revisions in market participants' expectations for the path of the Federal Funds Rate.[4]

From near the beginning of the COVID-19 pandemic to the end of 2022, the correlation between changes in stock prices and long-term bond prices was reversed from its previous sign. From 2000 until the beginning of the COVID-19 pandemic in 2020, the correlation between changes in stock prices and bond prices was generally negative (Rankin and Idil 2014). During this 20-year period, the Federal Reserve lowered the Federal Funds Rate, increasing bond prices. These increases were primarily in response to negative aggregate demand shocks, which drove down stock prices, as during a typical recession.

As shown in figure 2-6, the pandemic-induced recession fit this pattern in early 2020: stock prices fell and bond prices rose. In contrast, in 2022 inflation led the Federal Reserve to raise the Federal Funds Rate, causing both stock and bond prices to decline. This relationship can be seen in

[3] Bond prices, rather than bond yields, are discussed here in order to simplify the comparison with stock prices. The spot price of the 10-Year Treasury Note is calculated from the market yield, assuming no coupons.

[4] A complete description of the drivers of changes in the interest rate on 10-Year Treasury Notes is beyond the scope of this chapter; see Stigum and Crescenzi (2007).

Figure 2-6. Stock Market and Bond Prices, 2019–22

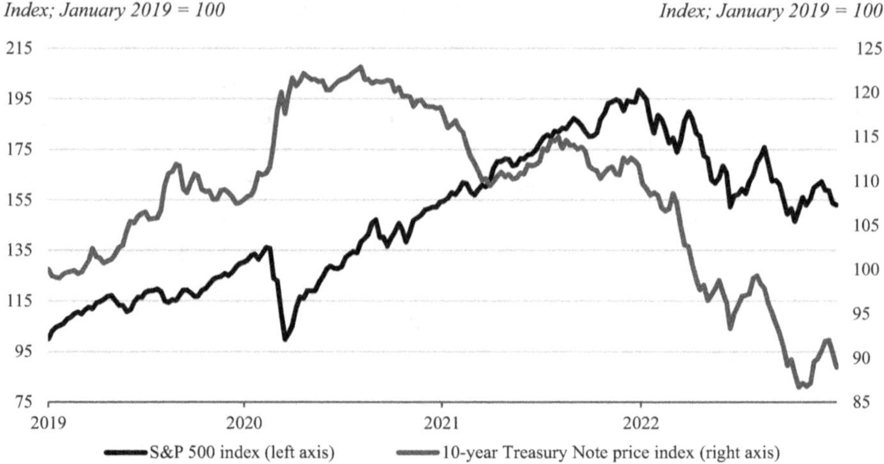

Sources: Federal Reserve System; Standard & Poor's (S&P).
Note: The prices of 0 coupon 10-Year Treasury Notes are shown relative to January 2019.

figure 2-6, starting slightly before the tightening cycle began, possibly due to markets anticipating monetary actions. The change in the sign of this correlation after the start of the pandemic suggests that negative supply shocks were important for U.S. financial markets in 2022; these shocks moved the price level higher and output lower—thus hurting stock prices—and led to increasing interest rates, thus hurting bond prices.

Inflation in 2022

Beyond the developments summarized above in discussing output growth, the historically strong U.S. labor market, and financial markets, the rise of inflation in 2021 and its continued elevation through 2022, exacerbated by Russia's invasion of Ukraine, were important aspects of 2022's overall economic picture. For most of the 2010–19 period, the rate of inflation was below the Federal Reserve's long-term 2 percent target. Then the COVID-19 pandemic hit the United States in early 2020. Prices fell briefly in the spring of 2020, when the pandemic initially struck, interrupting many forms of economic activity; but prices, and the economy, quickly recovered.

Inflation began to climb in 2021. Although, at the end of 2021, many forecasters predicted that inflation would quickly fall, inflation instead persisted in 2022.[5] The year 2022 was one of historically elevated inflation, but it was also a year that saw many actions taken to bring that elevated inflation

[5] E.g., the 2022:Q1 annualized CPI inflation rate predicted by the December 2021 Blue Chip consensus was 3.3 percent, close to the Federal Reserve's target and much lower than the actual quarterly inflation rate of 9.2 percent.

Box 2-1. Measures of Consumer Price Inflation

Inflation can be challenging to precisely define and measure. This box describes what inflation is not and what it is, how the government measures inflation, and what information key inflation measures provide.

Defining inflation. Inflation can be tricky to talk about. First, inflation is the rate of change of the price level, not the level of prices. High inflation means that prices are rising rapidly, not that prices are high. Second, increases in the prices of specific goods and services do not always reflect inflation. Due to changes in *relative* demand and supply, prices for specific goods and services rise and fall *relative* to each other all the time. For example, during the COVID-19 pandemic, demand for television sets rose, and their prices increased. Concurrently, demand for airline tickets fell, along with their prices. Price indices—such as the Consumer Price Index (CPI) and the Personal Consumption Expenditures (PCE) Price Index, which are discussed below—aggregate prices in the economy in an attempt to measure the price level. Inflation is a positive rate of change in the price level.

Measuring inflation. Measuring the price level, and therefore inflation, is a difficult task. This chapter frequently references two measures that approximate the level of prices faced by consumers: the CPI, produced by the Bureau of Labor Statistics (BLS); and the PCE Price Index, produced by the Bureau of Economic Analysis (BEA).

(The main text refers exclusively to the CPI-U, which follows the market basket of urban consumers. The description "urban" refers to anyone not living in extremely rural areas, and covers about 90 percent of the U.S. population. The BLS also supports several other versions of the CPI. The CPI-W follows the market basket of wage earners; the CPI-E follows the market basket of the elderly; and the chain CPI follows the same consumers as the CPI-U, but it aggregates with a formula that allows for more substitution.)

The CPI measures the prices of a fixed basket of consumer goods and services (BLS 2020). The basket, which was updated every two years from 2002 to 2022 and will be updated every year in the future, approximates the average consumption of a household as surveyed in the annual Consumer Expenditure Survey. The assumption of a fixed consumption basket makes comparing the prices of the same goods and services across time relatively easy, but it can misrepresent the rate of price changes households actually face (or experience) if households change what they consume when prices change. For instance, if the price of oranges falls relative to the price of apples, consumers will usually buy more oranges and fewer apples. The PCE Price Index, in contrast to the CPI, uses a formula that allows for such substitution. Further, while the CPI focuses on out-of-pocket expenditures, the PCE Price Index captures a wider range of consumer costs—including, for example, employer-provided health insurance. Largely because the PCE Price Index allows for more substitution (but also due to other differences), the 12-month change in the PCE Price Index has averaged 35 basis points less than the corresponding change in the CPI for the last 20 years.

Headline inflation versus core inflation. Economists and policymakers focus on price indices that exclude goods and services with volatile prices, such as food and energy, in order to get a better sense of persistent movements in inflation (Gordon 1975). Food and energy prices are erratic largely because they are influenced by weather and international commodity markets, and therefore can move independently from the other goods and services whose prices are determined domestically to a greater extent. The *core* CPI and the *core* PCE Price Index exclude food and energy, whereas the corresponding *headline* CPI and *headline* PCE Price Index include food and energy. Of course, because consumers buy food and energy, headline inflation measures better reflect the costs consumers actually face.

Monthly versus yearly inflation. Each month, the BLS and BEA update the CPI and the PCE Price Index, respectively, and the month-over-month percent change in each price level. They also report 12-month percent changes, which are substantially less volatile because they accumulate month-over-month percent changes over 12 months. Measures of annualized 3-month or 6-month inflation—the 3-month or 6-month percent change mathematically adjusted to be comparable to 12-month, or yearly, rates—can also be calculated from the raw price indices. These measures are less volatile than monthly inflation but are more timely than yearly inflation. Figure 2-i plots annualized 6-month inflation for four price indices: the headline CPI, the core CPI, the headline PCE Price Index, and the core PCE Price Index. All four inflation indices began to increase in 2021 but turned downward in the second half of 2022.

Figure 2-i. Types of Consumer Price Inflation, 2011–22

Percentage change, 6-month annualized

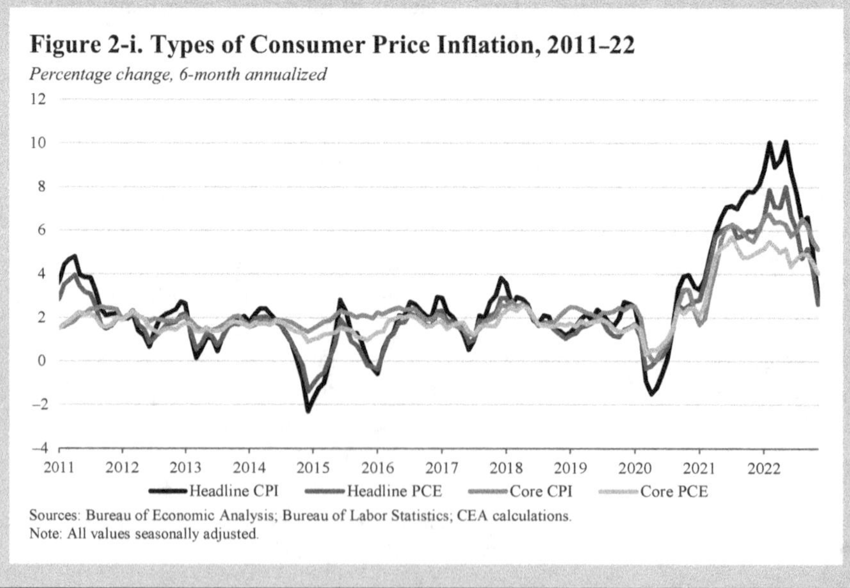

Sources: Bureau of Economic Analysis; Bureau of Labor Statistics; CEA calculations.
Note: All values seasonally adjusted.

Figure 2-7. The Expectations-Augmented Phillips Curve at Two Intervals

3-month annualized core CPI inflation (percent), controlling for expected inflation (see note)

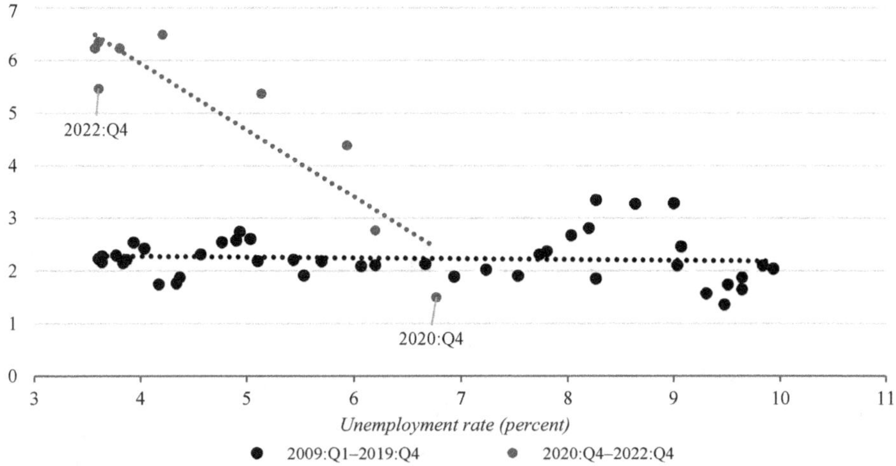

Sources: Bureau of Labor Statistics; Federal Reserve Bank of Philidelphia.

Note: CPI = Consumer Price Index. The y axis shows a measure of the actual rate of inflation minus the difference betwen the expected rate of inflation and the long-term rate of inflation, or π - (E[π] - π^*), where π = core CPI inflation, E[π] = 1-year lagged median 1-year ahead core CPI inflation expectations from the Federal Reserve Bank of Philidelphia's Survey of Professional Forecasters, and π^* = the long-term (post-2000) average of core CPI inflation, 2.3 percent. Actual CPI inflation values are seasonally adjusted.

down. As discussed in box 2-1, there are many ways to measure inflation. One of the most common, the 12-month rate of change in the headline Consumer Price Index (CPI), peaked at 9.1 percent in June 2022—a pace not seen since 1981. The fight against inflation has not been an easy one, but progress has been made as of December 2022, when the 12-month rate of change in the headline CPI inflation was 2.6 percentage points lower than in June.

The unexpected nature of the inflation in 2021 and 2022 is exemplified by figure 2-7. The figure shows an estimate of the Phillips curve, the relationship between inflation, unemployment, and inflation expectations from 2009 until the last prepandemic quarter in 2019:Q4 (dark blue dots), and during the economic recovery from 2020:Q4 through 2022:Q4 (light blue dots). The light blue dots are substantially above the dark blue dots, indicating that inflation moved more strongly with unemployment during the economic recovery than in the previous economic expansion. Investigating why inflation responded so strongly, and the fiscal and monetary responses to it, occupies much of the rest of this chapter. (Also see box 2-2.)

Measures of inflation can be approximately decomposed into contributions from subcategories of goods and services. Figure 2-8 plots the decomposition of annualized three-month headline CPI inflation into five categories: food; energy; core goods, which exclude food and energy goods; shelter, which includes rent and "owners' equivalent rent," and core services

Figure 2-8. Decompostion of Inflation, 2019–22

Contributions to quarterly headline CPI inflation, percentage points, quarterly annualized rate

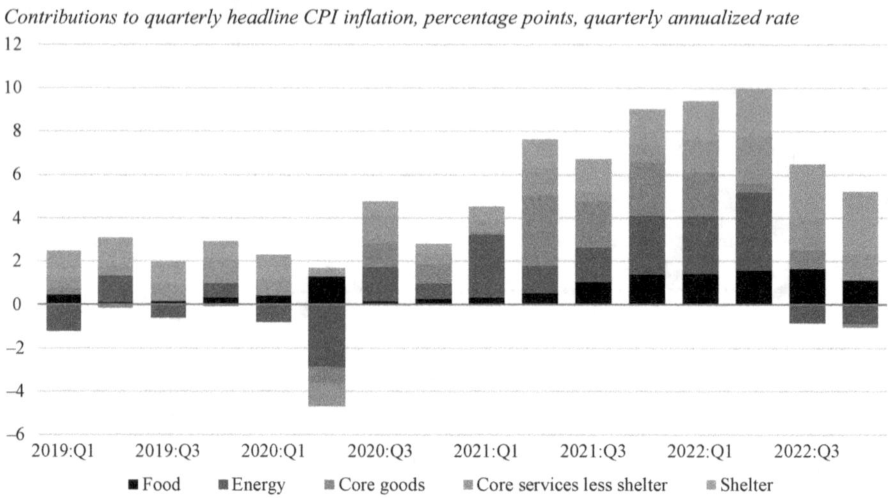

Source: Bureau of Labor Statistics.
Note: All values seasonally adjusted.

less shelter, which also excludes food and energy services. The figure shows that inflation during 2022 in the United States was broad-based, with each of the subcategories contributing substantially to overall inflation.

The timing of these contributions differs and tells an interesting story. In early 2021, the contribution of core goods inflation to overall inflation rose as consumer purchases rotated from services to goods during the pandemic, when supply chains snarled and productive capacity could not rise fast enough to match the rise in demand. As consumer behavior and supply chains both normalized in 2022, monthly core goods inflation declined and actually turned negative in late 2022. The contribution of food and energy inflation rose in 2021, and continued in 2022. Russia's invasion of Ukraine in February 2022 increased pressure on global oil and agricultural commodity markets. Partly as a consequence, the contribution of food and energy to inflation rose both domestically and globally. Inflation in core services, which was the primary contributor to overall inflation in the decade before the pandemic, was only slightly above its prepandemic pace in 2021 but increased sharply in 2022.

The decomposition shown in figure 2-8 is informative, but it is only an accounting exercise: it does not explain the underlying economic factors that led one category to move relative to another. If one category "contributed" more than another in a certain quarter, it means that prices in that category were increasing *relative* to prices in the other category, not necessarily that price increases in that category were the underlying *cause* of inflation. For example, it is possible for headline CPI inflation to be 0.0 percent, with core

Figure 2-9. Global Measures of Consumer Price Inflation

12-month percent change in national consumer price indices

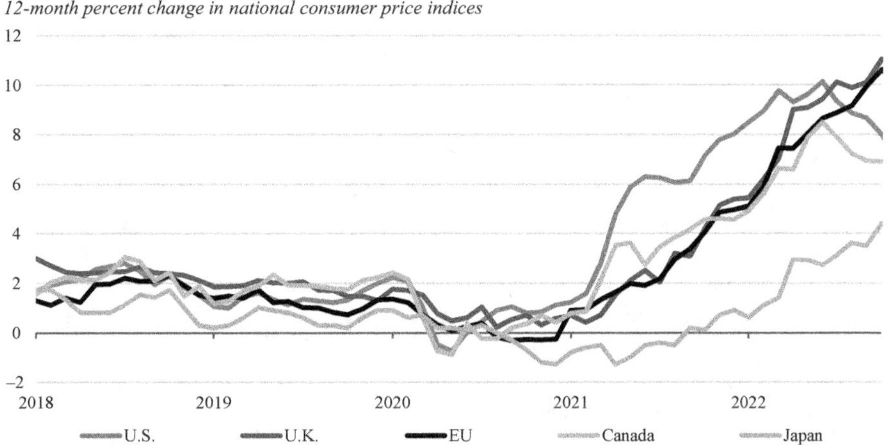

Sources: U.S. Bureau of Labor Statistics; U.K. Office for National Statistics; Eurostat; Japanese Ministry of Internal Affairs and Communications; Ministry of Statistics and Programme Implementation of India; Statistics Canada, CEA calculations.
Note: Measures are of headline consumer price inflation less owner-occupied housing (sometimes called the Harmonized Index of Consumer Prices).

goods inflation contributing negative 2.0 percent and core services inflation contributing positive 2.0 percent. The difference in goods and services inflation would mean that services prices were increasing relative to goods prices, not that either was causing inflation. In the next subsection, possible causes of U.S. inflation in 2022 are examined in detail.

High inflation in 2022 was not just a U.S. phenomenon, as shown in figure 2-9. In 2021, after years of relative stability, inflation began to climb across a number of countries. In the second half of 2022, inflation in the EU and the United Kingdom was higher than in the United States, partially reflecting the EU countries' and the United Kingdom's greater exposure to the war in Ukraine, and specifically the war's effect on energy prices. Inflation in some other countries, such as Japan, remained relatively low, though well above its prepandemic norm.

Factors That Had an Impact on Inflation in 2021–22

As discussed in box 2-2, the root causes of inflation are imperfectly understood, and economists use many theoretical frameworks to model and study it. Because the most common framework used to analyze inflation is aggregate supply and demand, this subsection first discusses what are generally thought of as "supply" factors and then examines what are generally thought of as "demand" factors. The role of expectations, a common theme in many inflation frameworks, is also discussed. Fiscal and monetary actions are both

Box 2-2. The Phillips Curve and Other Models of Inflation

Economists have spent much time and effort trying to explain and predict inflation, using a variety of methods and approaches. This box explains one common model, the Phillips curve; describes its recent history; and discusses each of its components—inflation; economic tightness, or "slack"; inflation expectations; and other factors—before briefly discussing theories of inflation that do not depend on a Phillips curve–type relationship.

The term "Phillips curve" is used to refer both to the empirical relationship between forms of inflation and measures of economic tightness or slack, used in the macroeconomic model developed by Klein and Goldberger (1955) and noted by Phillips (1958) (with regard to wage inflation and unemployment), and to the theoretical relationship between the two. Today, policymakers and forecasters often refer to the "expectations-augmented Phillips curve," which recognizes that inflation expectations can influence inflation independently from measures of economic tightness or slack.

As shown in figure 2-7 in the main text, the empirical relationship between the unemployment rate, one measure of tightness, and Core CPI inflation can change drastically, even when controlling for inflation expectations. The Phillips curve appeared to have become "flat" in about 2000, as discussed in the 2016 edition of the *Economic Report of the President* (CEA 2016). More precisely, the coefficient on the unemployment rate was near zero (hence, the adjective flat). This flatness during the 2009–19 business-cycle expansion is shown by the dark blue dots in figure 2-7 and the accompanying flat dark blue dashed line. Elevated unemployment rates failed to lower inflation during the first half of this cycle, while the low unemployment rates during the second half of that cycle failed to increase inflation.

Viewed from the end of 2022, the Phillips curve has substantially changed, as the decline in the unemployment rate to near historic lows in 2022 coincided with the first major increase in U.S. inflation since the 1980s, as shown by the light blue dots in figure 2-7 and accompanying steeply sloped light blue dashed line. The increase in inflation during 2021 and 2022 was much larger than the consensus economic forecast, perhaps because most forecasters had come to believe in a flat Phillips curve anchored by stable inflation expectations (Federal Reserve Bank of Philadelphia 2020).

One of the important questions facing the economy in 2023 is whether the Phillips curve will remain steeply sloped as inflation continues to cool. If the Phillips curve remains steep, this implies that inflation may fall without much of an increase in the unemployment rate. A Phillips curve that returns to near its prepandemic slope would imply that inflation may fall, but with a larger increase in the unemployment rate than in the second half of 2022.

Measures of inflation in the Phillips curve. As described in box 2-1, measures of inflation that include food and energy prices are volatile for reasons that have little to do with the domestic economy. Thus, core inflation measures, which exclude food and energy, fit better and are preferred for forecasting applications. Some practitioners use estimates of a deeper, more persistent, underlying inflation rate—as described or suggested by Ascari and Sbordone (2014), Yellen (2015), and Rudd (2020)—in order to enhance the fit and predictive power of the Phillips curve. Figure 2-7 uses annualized 3-month core CPI inflation.

(Simple estimates of this underlying inflation rate involve a menagerie of methods and measures, as discussed by Detmeister 2011. These measures include averaging across months of inflation data, using the inflation rate on specific categories of spending, such as the median CPI, from the Federal Reserve Bank of Cleveland 2023; and trimming categories that see the most and least inflation when calculating the inflation rate, such as the Trimmed-Mean PCE from the Federal Reserve Bank of Dallas, n.d., among others.)

Measures of economic tightness or slack in the Phillips curve. Choosing an appropriate measure of economic tightness or slack is a difficult conceptual issue. "Slack" refers to the intensity of resource utilization in the economy (Yellen 2015). Figure 2-2 shows one possible measure of slack: the difference between real GDP and a longer-run trend of real GDP. The situation at the end of 2022, when real GDP was higher than its trend, indicates that resource utilization was higher than normal, which may have fed through to inflationary pressures via increased costs to firms to produce a unit of output (Boehm and Pandalai-Nayar 2022).

Another commonly used measure of slack is the deviation of the unemployment rate from the natural rate of unemployment, the rate of unemployment that would exist when the economy is stable in the long-term and not disrupted by shocks. Estimating the natural rate of unemployment, which is by nature unobservable, is a difficult task. (Many practitioners estimate the natural rate of unemployment together with the Phillips curve. But to have separate measurement power, that natural rate estimate would need to come from a method external to estimation of the Phillips curve itself, as was done by Michaillat and Saez 2022.) For simplicity, figure 2-7 uses the unemployment rate alone, without an external estimate of the natural rate.

Inflation expectations in the Phillips curve. The expectations-augmented Phillips Curve includes inflation expectations because many theories of inflation suggest that expectations may in some cases be self-fulfilling—in other words, if people believe that inflation will rise, inflation will rise; and if people believe that inflation will fall, it will fall. Empirically, expectations are important to explaining the decline in inflation since the 1970s, and its stability in the 2010s (Blanchard et al. 2015). The exact link between inflation expectations and actual inflation is still debated (Rudd 2021; Bernanke 2007, 2022; Werning 2022). Figure 2-7 uses projections of core CPI inflation from the Survey of Professional Forecasters.

Given the importance of inflation expectations, managing expectations is an important aspect of managing inflation. Inflation expectations are said to be "anchored" when they do not change much, even when the economic environment changes. Though many believe that the Federal Reserve had an implicit inflation target at which it wanted to anchor inflation starting in the 1990s or earlier, it was only in 2012 that the Federal Reserve announced an explicit longer-run target of 2 percent annual PCE Price Index inflation (Federal Reserve 2012). In 2020, the Federal Reserve revised its "Statement of Longer-Run Goals and Monetary Policy Strategy" to indicate that it would conduct policy in a way that seeks to anchor inflation expectations at 2 percent and results in inflation that averages 2 percent over time (Federal Reserve 2020). As can be seen below in the text, even though inflation in 2021 and 2022 rose well above 2 percent, measures of long-run inflation expectations remained relatively stable, lending support to the idea that the Federal Reserve had successfully anchored inflation expectations.

Other factors. While Phillips curves are often parsimonious models of inflation, factors other than expectations and slack may be used to help empirically estimate the curve and control for other influences. Yellen (2015) highlights the importance of changes in imported goods prices, which are an input to many production processes and can proxy for exchange rate dynamics. In a similar vein, below the text highlights a measure of supply chain pressures and its relation to a producer-side measure of inflation. The price of energy may also be included, although pass-through from energy prices to measures of core or underlying inflation has diminished in recent years (Clark and Terry 2010).

Alternative models of inflation. The Phillips curve is one of most common frameworks that economists use to understand inflation, but it is far from the only one. For example, when economists talk about how supply and demand affect inflation, they are usually referring to the Keynesian Aggregate Demand and Aggregate Supply (AD-AS) model, which evolved from attempts by John Hicks to formalize the ideas of John Maynard Keynes in the 1930s (Hicks 1937; Keynes 1936). The Phillips curve is often considered to be part of Keynesian theory because, due to the link between employment and real output, something similar can be implied from the AD-AS model. Keynesian theory can be understood as one explanation for the connection between inflation and slack observed in the empirical Phillips curve. New Keynesian theory, which is a modern, mathematically formal development of Keynesian theory, offers a related explanation (Galí 2015). The standard New Keynesian Phillips curve relates inflation to the theory's measure of slack and features a larger role for expectations than most Keynesian models.

Monetarism is both a theory that describes a group of formal mathematical models and also a set of less formal ideas. As a theory, it is most associated with Milton Friedman, who famously said, "Inflation is always and everywhere a monetary phenomenon, in the sense that it is and can be produced only by a more rapid increase in the quantity of money than in output" (Friedman 1970). Monetarist models emphasize inflation as a consequence of the growth of the quantity of money compared with the level and growth of output, rather than a connection between inflation and slack.

Finally, a number of models of inflation emphasize the importance of government debt. One of the best-known of these models, the Fiscal Theory of the Price Level (FTPL), argues that increases in government debt that are not backed by credible promises of repayment via increases in future tax revenue or reductions in future spending lead to inflation (Cochrane 2023). Proponents and critics of the FTPL disagree over the direction of causality in this relationship, and the implicit assumptions that such causality implies (Bassetto 2008).

usually considered to be demand factors in the near term; because they are both especially important, they are discussed separately.[6]

Over the last two years, many hypotheses about the causes of the current inflation situation have been proposed by academics, journalists, and politicians. The goal of this subsection includes reviewing prevalent propositions, not to argue for a single hypothesis or set of hypotheses. The possible causes discussed here likely played some role in the level and elevated nature of inflation in 2022—and the pandemic was a large exacerbating cause to each. Interactions between causes likely worsened inflationary pressures. Frequently cited hypotheses include the shock to energy, food, and other commodity prices associated with Russia's invasion of Ukraine; pandemic-related supply chain issues; the extension of zero interest rate monetary policy and accompanying quantitative easing; household transfers

[6] In the medium to long terms, both monetary and fiscal actions can influence supply. For example, low interest rates can spur long-term investment. Government spending can build infrastructure—e.g., Donaldson and Hornbeck (2016)—and support research and development—e.g., Gross and Sampat (2020), as discussed in the paragraphs about legislative and executive actions in the text below. In general, these supply-side factors take longer to impact the economy than do demand-side effects of monetary and fiscal actions.

Figure 2-10. Supply Chain Pressures and Producer Inflation, 1990–2022

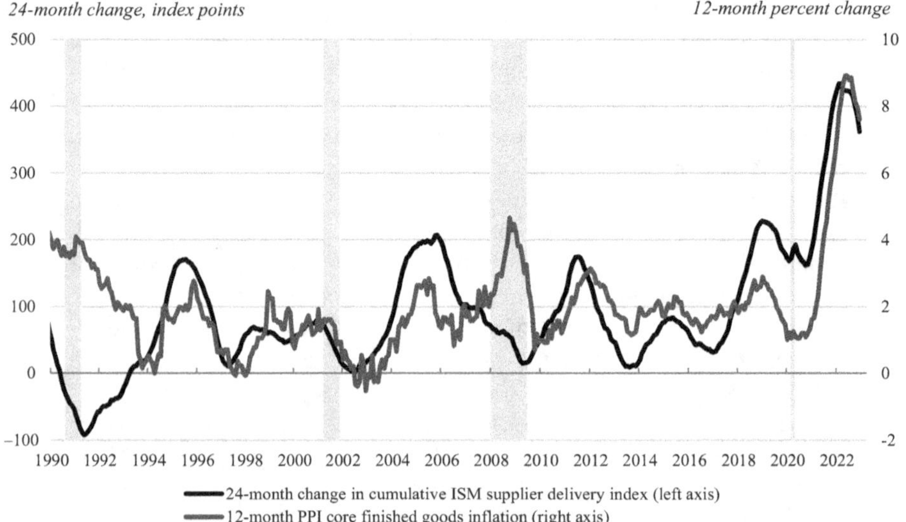

Sources: Bureau of Labor Statistics; Institute of Supply Management (ISM).
Note: PPI = Producer Price Index. The dark line is equal to $\Sigma(S_i - 50)$ with $i = 0{,}23$, where S_i = the ISM supplier deliveries index, which is equal to 50 if the number of manufacturers that report lengthening delivery times is equal to the number of manufacturers that report shortening delivery times. Longer lags include more information, and the 24-month changes fit with recent data on the change in PPI inflation.

legislated as part of the CARES Act, the American Rescue Plan, and related legislation; and households' accumulation of "excess savings."

The impact of supply factors on inflation. As described in the 2022 edition of the *Economic Report of the President*, the COVID-19 pandemic introduced challenges to the labor force and constraints on the supply of goods and services (CEA 2022). In mid-2022, these disruptions finally began to ease.

As shown in figure 2-10, increases in supply chain pressures were strongly correlated with rises in goods inflation in 2022. The measure of supply chain pressures in the figure is derived from an Institute for Supply Management (ISM) survey, in which supply managers are asked whether delivery times for their raw materials are shorter, the same, or longer than the preceding month. Because the resulting ISM measure captures monthly *changes* in delivery times, these responses must be cumulated over time to make an index of the *level* of delivery times.[7] In figure 2-10, the change

[7] The ISM supplier deliveries index is calculated by subtracting the percentage of supply managers saying that delivery times are longer from the percentage of supply managers saying that delivery times are shorter, dividing by 2, and adding 50. To construct this index of delivery time levels, 50 is subtracted from the ISM and the index is cumulated over 24 months. The ISM delivery index indicates only the one-month change in delivery lags, so cumulating more months includes more information. Cumulating over the preceding 24-month period fits the recent data on the change in PPI inflation.

Figure 2-11. Commodity Pressures and PCE Inflation, 2006–22

Sources: Bureau of Economic Analysis; U.S. Energy Information Administration; Bloomberg Agriculture Spot Index.
Note: FAO = Food Agriculture Organization of the United Nations. Data are displayed on two axes because commodity and gasoline prices are much more volatile than inflation. The PCE Price Index is seasonally adjusted.

in this measure of delivery times, over an appropriate interval, is plotted against the change in the core Producer Price Index (PPI) for finished goods. The PPI measure reflects prices charged by manufacturers. The relatively high correlation between the change in delivery times and core PPI finished goods inflation since 1990 suggests that supply chain issues have a significant impact on finished goods inflation.

According to the ISM survey, suppliers' delivery times started lengthening substantially shortly after the start of the COVID-19 pandemic, and most supply managers were reporting lengthening delivery times until September 2022. Delivery times shortened during the final three months of the year, but were still elevated at the end of 2022. Another measure of supply chain stress, the Global Supply Chain Pressure Index, produced by the Federal Reserve Bank of New York, also increased notably in 2020–21, but fell for most of 2022. Collectively, these measures indicate that supply chain delays stopped getting worse and even began to unsnarl toward the end of the year. Still, overall inflation remained high, indicating that the drivers of inflation had broadened, including to the service economy (Powell 2022a).

Figure 2-11 shows that commodity prices, as represented by gas and food price inflation, started rising in 2021. These commodities are traded on international markets, and their prices influence inflation globally. Then, in February 2022, Russia invaded Ukraine. The resulting chaos, both directly and indirectly, led food prices to quickly jump higher, and gasoline and natural gas prices soon followed. As commodity suppliers adapted to the

Figure 2-12. Employment Cost Index and Inflation, 2013–22

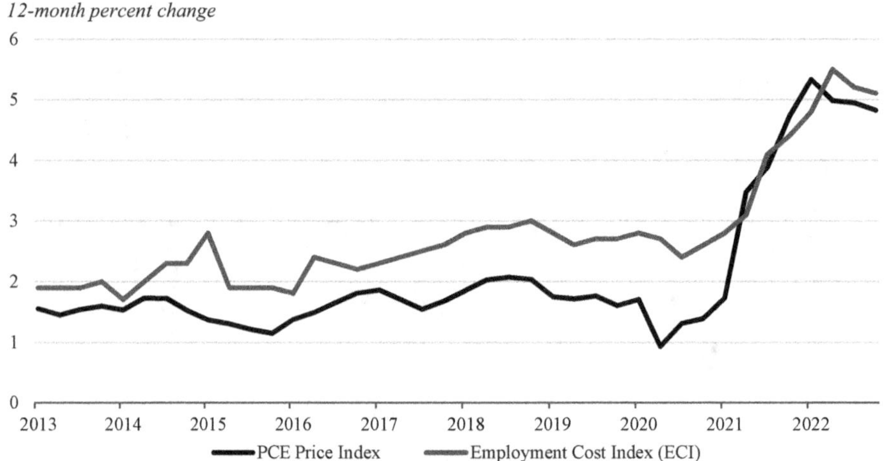

Sources: Bureau of Labor Statistics; Bureau of Economic Analysis; CEA calculations.
Note: The PCE Price Index is seasonally adjusted, but the ECI is not.

disruption caused by the war, commodity prices fell. Since commodities are a basic input to most production processes—and consumers directly purchase some commodities such as food, gasoline, and natural gas directly—higher commodity prices can quickly feed into overall inflation. Russia's status as a major oil exporter led to a spike in many energy prices, and the price of regular gasoline in the United States peaked at $5.02 a gallon in June. But by the end of the year, the price of regular gasoline had fallen to $3.20 a gallon, partly due to the Biden-Harris Administration's decision to draw down the Strategic Petroleum Reserve, which is further discussed below.

As the economy continued to recover from the recession in 2020 and consumer demand for goods and services increased, demand for workers to produce these goods and services also increased. Illustrated by the ratio of vacancies to unemployment shown in figure 2-4, the demand for workers relative to their supply has been high during much of the recovery from the pandemic-related recession. If firms are having difficulty hiring workers, then the relative price of workers—that is, hourly compensation—should increase. Figure 2-12 displays the Employment Cost Index, a measure of hourly compensation that adjusts for changes in the composition of the workforce, showing that inflation in 2022 was accompanied by rising wages. But rising wages can be both a cause and a consequence of inflation (Jordà et al. 2022). The BLS's measure of real average wages, or wages relative to the overall price level, declined overall in 2022, falling in the first half of 2022 before rising in the second half. Some parts of the labor income distribution saw better real wage outcomes than others, with outcomes positive in the lowest quartile (Federal Reserve Bank of Atlanta, n.d.).

Although there were fears during 2022 of a "wage-price spiral"—where workers expecting increased inflation would demand higher wages, which would lead to higher realized inflation, and then workers would demand even higher wages, and so on—those fears lessened toward the end of 2022, as inflation and wage growth showed broad slowdowns. Notably, as shown below with the University of Michigan's survey results (see figure 2-19), consumers' short-term inflation expectations remained well below actual inflation throughout the year, and longer-term expectations remained anchored.

Some have pointed to another factor that may have influenced the reaction of prices and thus inflation to the COVID-19 shock: increased market concentration in U.S. industries. More U.S. industries have become dominated by a few, large firms over the last 20 years. There is some evidence that these firms increase prices in response to cost increases more than firms without market power would have done in the past (Bräuning, Fillat, and Joaquim 2022). However, the link between market power and pricing when subject to shocks like the pandemic is not clear (Syverson 2019). Measuring market power is a difficult task, and measuring the prices firms charge above the cost of their inputs, their "markup," isolated from the effects of the increased demand and constrained supply of 2022, is even more fraught.

The impact of monetary factors on inflation. By controlling short-term interest rates, and through them, longer-term interest rates, the Federal Reserve is able to influence when consumers and businesses spend money versus save money, thereby affecting aggregate demand. In both traditional Keynesian and New Keynesian aggregate supply-and-demand frameworks (see box 2-2), higher interest rates lead to decreases in real output and inflation, all else being equal (Miranda-Agrippino and Ricco 2021). Figure 2-13 shows that the Federal Reserve kept the Federal Funds Rate close to zero from April 2020 until it began to raise the Federal Funds Rate in response to rising inflation in March 2022. By the end of 2022, the Federal Reserve had increased the Federal Funds Rate to a range between 4.25 and 4.50 percent. The rapid increase in the Federal Funds Rate was an attempt to bring demand into better alignment with supply and cool inflation. It is important to note that the Federal Funds Rate alone is not enough to judge the stance of monetary policy. The Federal Funds Rate is a nominal rate, so its effect on the real economy depends on inflation. The real Federal Funds Rate is approximated in figure 2-13 by subtracting short-term expectations of consumer inflation.[8]

Another perspective on the stance of monetary policy is the real rate relative to r^*, the long-term real rate consistent with the economy growing at its long-term trend. Though it is hard to estimate, there is evidence that

[8] Exactly which measure of inflation is appropriate to use to deflate the nominal Federal Funds Rate is outside the scope of this chapter.

Figure 2-13. Nominal and Real Measures of the Policy Rate, 2016–22

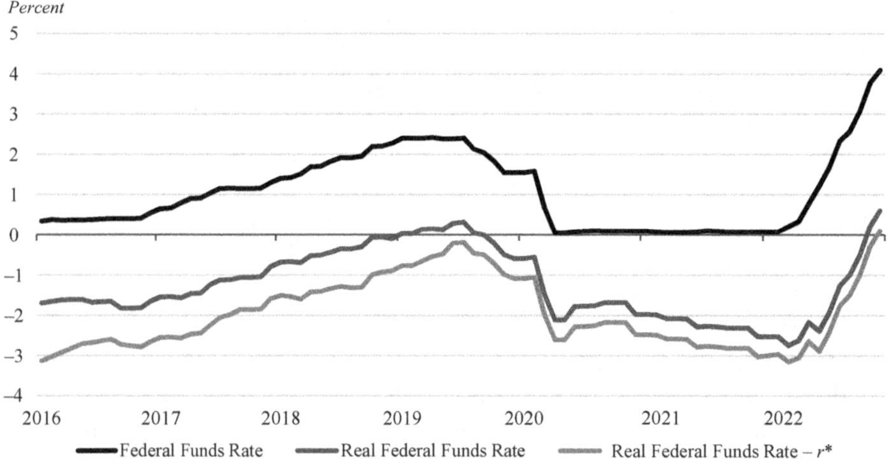

Sources: Survey of Professional Forecasters (SPF); Federal Reserve System; CEA calculations.
Note: The bright blue line subtracts 1-year-ahead expected inflation from the SPF from the dark blue line. The orange line subtracts the median estimate of the appropriate long-term Federal Funds Rate from the Federal Reserve quarterly Summary of Economic Projections (SEP) from the bright blue line.

r^* declined during recent decades (Powell 2018). Because of this decline in r^*, and depending on inflation expectations, low Federal Funds Rates may not be as stimulative as they were in the past (Jordà and Taylor 2019). The Federal Open Market Committee (FOMC), in its December 2022 "Summary of Economic Projections" (Federal Reserve 2022a), suggested that long-run r^*, calculated by subtracting the longer-run inflation rate (2.0 percent) from the longer-run Federal Funds Rate (2.5 percent), was 0.5 percent. The difference between the real Federal Funds Rate and r^*, shown by the orange line in figure 2-13, is a plausible measure of the stance of monetary policy. At the end of 2022, the stance of monetary policy, as measured by both the real Federal Funds Rate and the real Federal Funds Rate minus r^*, was above 0 percent, indicating a restrictive monetary policy.

An additional factor in judging the stance of monetary policy is the Federal Reserve's balance sheet. In 2020, following the playbook used during the 2007–8 financial crisis, the Federal Reserve announced additional measures to support the economy, including emergency lending and asset purchase programs, sometimes known as "quantitative easing." Figure 2-14 shows that assets held by the Federal Reserve—the sum of Treasuries, mortgage-backed securities, and all others—grew to $8.2 trillion by the end of 2021—more than double their size before the COVID-19 pandemic.

The increase in the size of the Federal Reserve's balance sheet contributed to a substantial increase in measures of the money supply. As discussed in box 2-2, in 2020, a monetarist would have predicted that the substantial

Figure 2-14. The Composition of the Federal Reserve's Balance Sheet, 2007–22

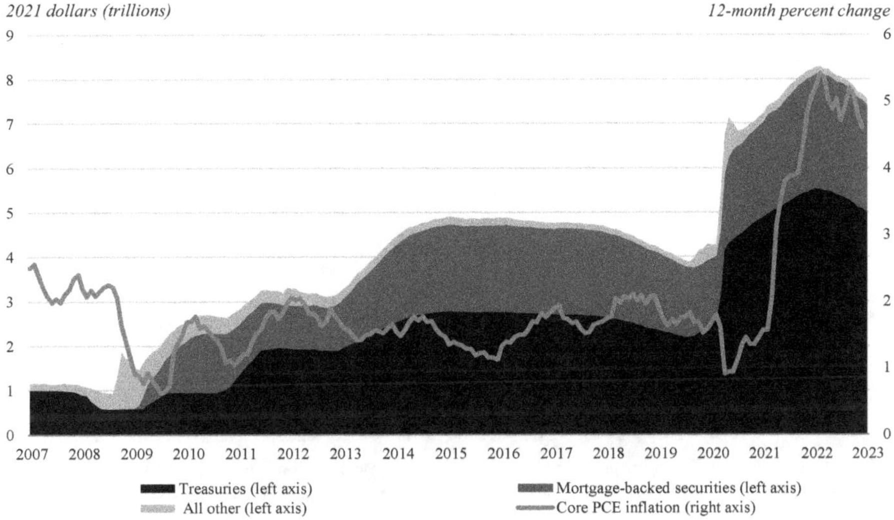

2021 dollars (trillions)
12-month percent change
9
8
7
6
5
4
3
2
1
0
6
5
4
3
2
1
0
2007
2008
2009
2010
2011
2012
2013
2014
2015
2016
2017
2018
2019
2020
2021
2022
2023
Treasuries (left axis)
All other (left axis)
Mortgage-backed securities (left axis)
Core PCE inflation (right axis)

Sources: Bureau of Economic Analysis; Federal Reserve Bank of St. Louis; CEA calculations.
Note: Excludes unamortized premiums and discounts on securities held outright. Nominal dollars were converted to 2021 dollars using the PCE Price Index. The PCE Price Index is seasonally adjusted.

increase in "money" at a time when real output was shrinking would lead to inflation. In 2021 and 2022, with some lag, they would have been right.

But 10 years ago, they would have been wrong. When the Federal Reserve more than quadrupled its balance sheet in the five years after the 2007–9 financial crisis, inflation did not rise by much, and it quickly returned to a stable rate below 2 percent. There are important differences: the 2007–9 recession was longer and deeper; households and firms had worse balance sheets; the unique, pandemic-related supply-side challenges were not present; and the fiscal response to the crisis was smaller (Guerrieri et al. 2021). Nevertheless, the drastically different result in 2007–8 makes it hard to draw a straight line between the Federal Reserve's balance sheet actions in 2020–22 and inflation (Crawley and Gagnon 2022).

The impact of fiscal factors on inflation. Extraordinary monetary policy in 2020 and 2021 was accompanied by expansive fiscal policy. In 2020, the pandemic prompted an increase of slightly more than 10 percentage points in the Federal Government's outlays relative to GDP, the largest such increase since the increase of nearly 20 percentage points when the United States entered World War II. Much of this increased spending was distributed in economic impact payments made directly to households. Support was also provided via large temporary expansions of unemployment benefits and funds offered to small businesses to maintain payrolls and extend operations.

Figure 2-15. The Fiscal Impulse and Inflation, 2012–24

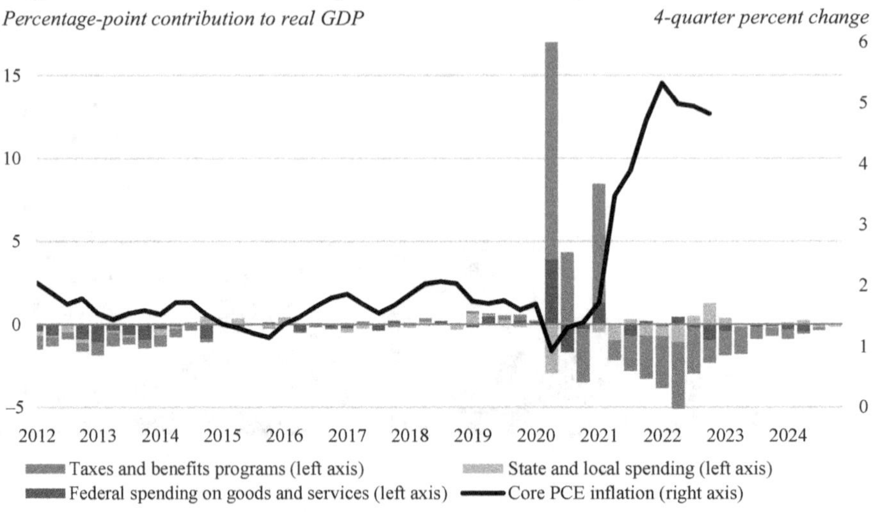

Sources: Hutchins Center at Brookings Institution; Bureau of Economic Analysis.
Note: All values are seasonally adjusted.

Aggregate supply-and-demand frameworks predict that, all else being equal, increases in government outlays will increase output and inflation. Estimates of the "fiscal multiplier," or the ratio of the change in total real output to an expansionary fiscal policy action, vary considerably, with different estimates suggesting that government spending increases total output by more, or by less, than the government spending itself (Ramey 2019). Empirical estimates of the impact of government spending on inflation are mixed; a recent meta-analysis found that increases in government spending, offset by tighter monetary policy, often tend to be *deflationary* rather than inflationary (Jørgensen and Ravn 2022).

Figure 2-15 plots the Hutchins Center's Fiscal Impact Measure (FIM), which uses information on the Federal Government's spending on goods and services, State and local government spending on goods and services, and taxes and benefit programs to approximate the contribution of fiscal policy to total real GDP growth each quarter (Belz, Sheiner, and Campbell 2022). A positive fiscal impulse means that the contribution of fiscal policy to real GDP is larger than it was the quarter before. Figure 2-15 shows that the FIM spiked in 2020:Q2, mainly due to an expansion of transfer programs, and was positive for two of the next three quarters, but was a significant drag throughout 2022 and is projected to remain negative in 2023 and 2024, using projections for fiscal policy by the Congressional Budget Office in its current services baseline.

Table 2-2 highlights legislative and executive actions that cannot be easily characterized as "fiscal policy"—and hence are outside the scope of

Table 2-2. Selected Legislative and Executive Actions in 2022

Date	Action	Goal
April to October	Release of 180 million barrels of crude oil from the Strategic Petroleum Reserve	Increase the supply of gasoline to lower its price, and the prices of other goods
May	Additional funding for domestic fertilizer production and technical assistance in agriculture, and expansion of eligibility for double-cropping insurance	Encourage farmers to expand production, lowering and stabilizing food prices
May	Housing Supply Action Plan	Increase the supply of available homes to lower housing costs
June	Ocean Shipping Reform Act	Lower shipping costs and improve supply chains by fostering compeition
July	President Biden announces a series of actions that incentivize solar adoption and energy efficiency upgrades	Lower demand for fossil fuels and lower energy prices
August	IRA promotes clean energy adoption, authorizes Medicare to negotiate drug prices, and caps annual out-of-pocket prescription costs at $2,000	Increase the supply of clean energy to lower the price; reduce prices and lower markups in the pharmecutical industry
October	Executive Order on Promoting Competition in the American Economy	Lower fees and hidden costs and increase consumer and small business bargaining power

Note: IRA = Inflation Reduction Act. This table only captures some of the many actions taken in 2022.

the FIM—which by most economic definitions is primarily concerned with the levels of government revenue and spending and the path of deficits. The actions can be roughly divided into two categories. First, there are measures to promote competition in 2022 and in the future, such as the Ocean Shipping Reform Act, President Biden's Executive Order on Promoting Competition in the American Economy, and the Inflation Reduction Act (IRA).[9] Second, there are measures meant to either directly or indirectly expand the supply of particular goods or services, such as the President's decision to tap into the Strategic Petroleum Reserve to reduce gasoline prices, and executive actions in May intended to help increase agricultural production and add to the stock of affordable housing. The actions listed in table 2-2 have likely lowered costs for specific goods or services, many of which are key inputs to other industries, and increased the future supply of many products. The long-term impact of these plans should be disinflationary.

Figure 2-16 shows the Federal Government's historic primary deficits, or total revenues minus total spending not including interest payments on outstanding debt, and those deficits projected for the next 10 years by the Office of Management and Budget (OMB), which uses the economic

[9] Procompetitive IRA measures include provisions that granted Medicare greater bargaining power in prescription drug cost negotiations with pharmaceutical companies. The IRA's clean energy provisions will boost supply in targeted industries in the long term.

Figure 2-16. OMB's Primary Deficit Forecast, 2017–33

Percentage of annual fiscal year GDP

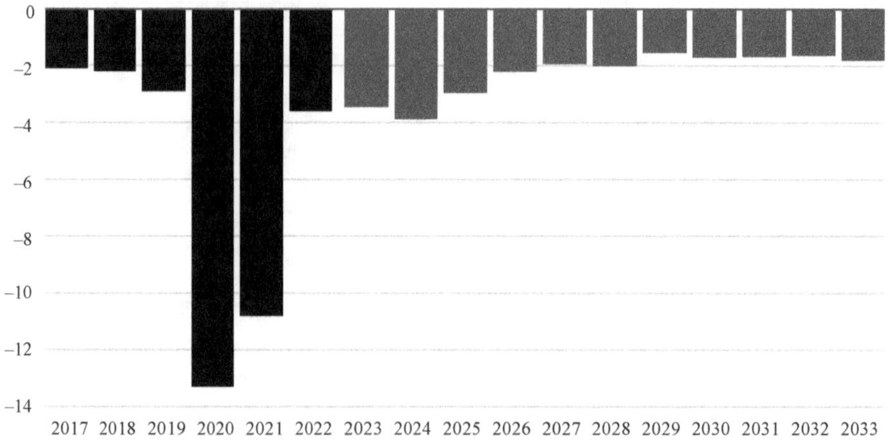

Sources: Office of Management and Budget (OMB); CEA calculations.

assumptions from the Administration forecast presented in the next section. The winding down of spending under the CARES Act, the American Rescue Plan, and related legislation, combined with higher tax revenue due to the recovery in GDP, led to a smaller deficit in 2022 as a share of GDP than in 2020 and 2021, or the 3 years after the 2007–8 financial crisis; but the deficit was higher than the post–World War II prepandemic average. One of the intentions of the reforms to the tax code made during the Biden-Harris Administration—including an increase in the corporate minimum tax, an increase in the Internal Revenue Service's funding to help it bring in uncollected taxes and close loopholes, and a new excise tax on stock buybacks—is to reduce future deficits (Gleckman and Holtzblatt 2022; Congressional Research Service 2022).

In an op-ed on May 30, 2022, President Biden said that he expected the reduction in the Federal deficit in 2022 to help ease price pressures (Biden 2022). Some theories suggest that lower deficits (or higher surpluses) over time can ease inflationary pressures (see box 2-2). Empirical estimates of the impact of government deficits on inflation do not provide consistent answers (Catão and Terrones 2005; Banerjee et al. 2022). Nevertheless, the global coincidence of unprecedented, deficit-funded fiscal actions begun in 2020, and the highest rate of inflation in 40 years has convinced some economists that the two are related (Bordo and Levy 2021).

In 2020 and 2021, partially due to pandemic-era fiscal measures, and pandemic-related constraints on in-person spending, consumer income exceeded consumer spending by substantially more than it usually does,

Figure 2-17. Excess Savings and Inflation, 2016–22

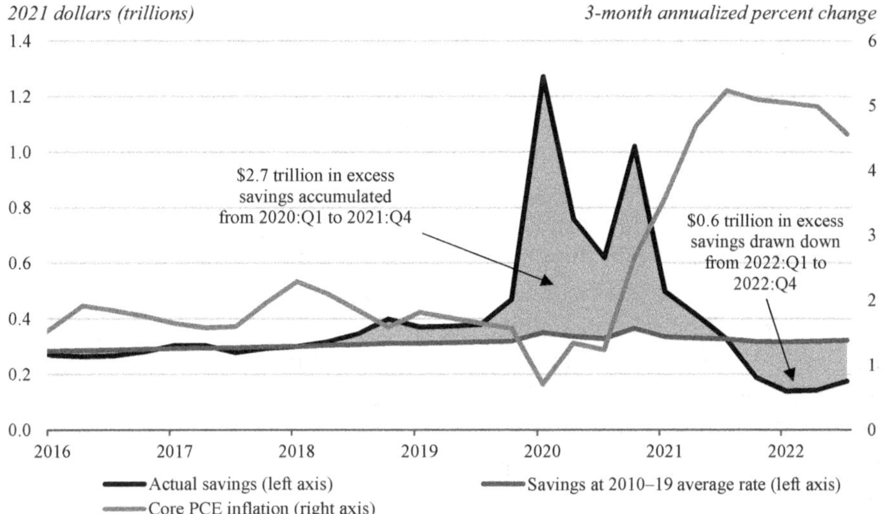

Sources: Bureau of Economic Analysis; CEA calculations.
Note: The average saving rate from 2010 to 2019 was 7.3 percent. Nominal dollars were converted to 2021 dollars using the PCE Price Index. All values are seasonally adjusted.

leading to a surplus of savings beyond what would have occurred if the saving rate (i.e., saving as a share of disposable income) had remained at prepandemic levels. The buildup of excess savings was due to the increased precautionary savings and pandemic-related constraints on spending that led consumers to spend less and save more than usual (Bilbiie et al. 2021) paired with the direct payments and income support program expansions included in the CARES Act, the American Rescue Plan, and related legislation. Figure 2-17 plots one measure of excess savings; the dark blue line represents the deviation of actual saving from what it would have been under the average quarterly saving rate from 2010 to 2019 (7.3 percent); and the green shaded area between the dark blue line and the light blue line is the excess savings in the quarter. By the end of 2021, the amount of cumulative excess savings peaked at about $2.7 trillion, or more than two months of usual prepandemic consumer spending.

Given the excess savings, households had the potential to spend more than they normally would without incurring debt, even after the withdrawal of some fiscal recovery programs. In an aggregate supply-and-demand framework, if households spend their excess savings, the spending will increase aggregate demand, exacerbating inflation when supply is constrained (Aladangady et al. 2022). Excess savings, as shown in figure 2-17, were drawn down by about $0.6 trillion in 2022, and consumer spending rose, counteracting the aggregate demand effect of the negative fiscal impulse shown in figure 2-15. If the drawdown of excess savings, together with current income, boosted aggregate demand, it could have contributed to high inflation in 2021 and 2022.

Additional demand factors affecting inflation. The pandemic and recovery, supported by funds provided by the CARES Act, the American Rescue Plan, and related legislation, also generated large and unusual shifts in consumer demand—most importantly, away from in-person services and toward distancing-friendly goods, and then back again, as shown in panels B and C of figure 2-18. In April 2021, possibly driven by this unusual spending on goods, inflation in the price of goods over the preceding 12 months, as measured by the PCE Price Index, was higher than inflation in the price of services for the first time in nearly a decade, as shown in panels D through F of figure 2-18. In the second half of 2022, goods inflation settled some, but the consumer demand rotation back to services caused services inflation to increase. Correspondingly, the ratio of the consumption of real goods to that of real services also rose, and then fell back somewhat toward prepandemic levels, but remained elevated.

Because consumer spending makes up nearly 70 percent of GDP, it is informative to look at consumer spending on its own, as a measure of where the economy in 2022 was relative to its trend, as shown in figure 2-2 above. Figure 2-18, panel B, shows that goods consumption remained above its

Figure 2-18. Consumer Goods-Services Rotation, 2018–22

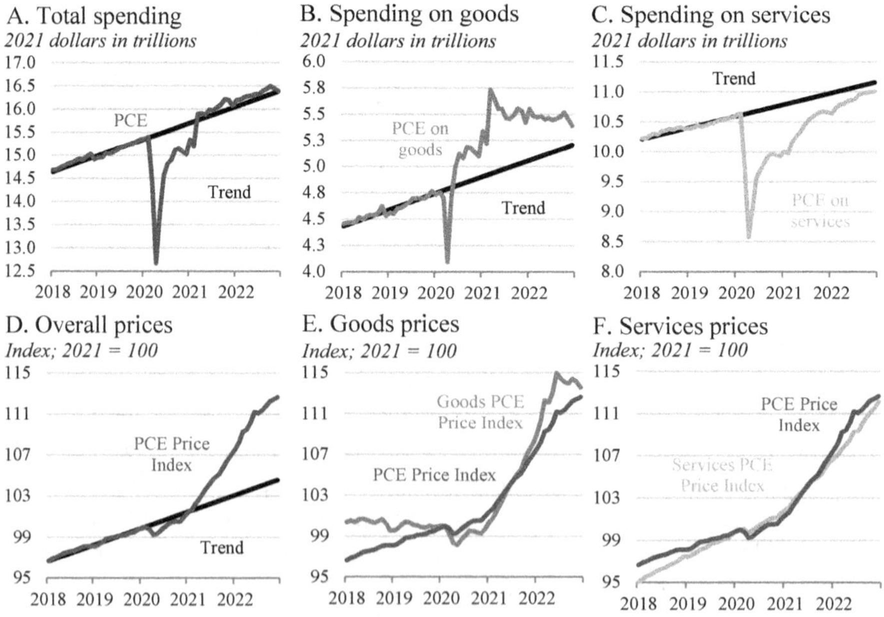

Sources: Bureau of Economic Analysis; CEA calculations.
Note: PCE = Personal Consumption Expenditures. Trend lines were calculated by regressing each respective series on time from 2015 to 2019. All values are seasonally adjusted.

trend through 2022. Services consumption—as shown in figure 2-18, panel C—recovering from the obstacles to in-person services during the pandemic and seeing a rapid rise in prices, remained below its trend. Overall, as shown in panel A of figure 2-18, consumer spending was near its trend. Business fixed investment, as broken out in figure 2-3—which is necessary to add to domestic productive capacity—did not see the same rapid increase as consumption. This disconnect between above trend goods consumption and the lack of increased production, whether due to supply constraints on production or slow investment, means that domestic supply was not able to provide the level of goods and services demanded. As supply chain disruptions made it challenging to address this imbalance through increased imports, inflation rose as goods prices increased (Guerrieri et al. 2021).

The impact of inflation expectations. Expectations play an important role in the major frameworks that economists use to analyze inflation, as described in box 2-2. Some economists think that higher expectations of future inflation can be self-fulfilling, making efforts to fight inflation more difficult or painful. If businesses, consumers, and financial market participants expect inflation to be high, they will behave in ways consistent with this expectation and that may bring about actual higher inflation. For example, workers with high inflation expectations may demand higher wages, and businesses with high inflation expectations may price goods higher. The back and forth between these effects can lead to further increases in inflation. In 2022, long-term inflation expectations stayed near their historical levels, and short-term expectations moved with actual inflation, pointing

Figure 2-19. Actual and Expected Inflation, 2012–22

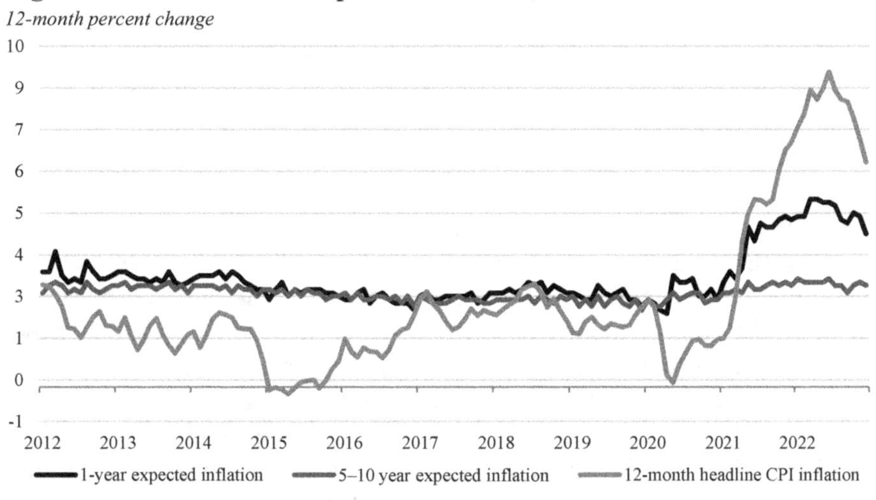

Sources: University of Michigan; Bureau of Economic Analysis; CEA calculations.

to inflation expectations that were dependent on actual inflation rather than being driven independently in a way that could lead to further inflation.

When inflation began to rise in 2021, long-term inflation expectations had been steady for decades, and even as inflation started to climb, these expectations remained low. Figure 2-19 plots two of the most commonly tracked measures of inflation expectations: the median expected annual price change over the next 12 months, from the University of Michigan's monthly survey of households; and the median expected average annual price change over the next five to 10 years, from the same survey. Although both measures increased during 2022, they did not increase by nearly as much as realized inflation. Long-term inflation expectations (5–10 year expected inflation, the light blue line) in particular were reassuringly stable, indicating that although elevated inflation was expected in the short run, it was not expected to last. As discussed in box 2-2, this stability was taken as evidence that inflation expectations were anchored. Still, toward the end of 2022, some economists worried that the modest increases in long-run inflation expectations, and the possibility of sustained increases in expectations, would make it harder to bring inflation down (Powell 2022b).

The Forecast for the Years Ahead

The Biden-Harris Administration finalized the latest version of its official economic forecast on November 28, 2022. This forecast provides the Administration's estimated projections of key economic variables over the next 11 years, from 2023 to 2033, and also includes its forecast for 2022. During the interval between when this forecast was finalized and the publication of this *Report*, more 2022 data have become available, so that the official forecast discussed in this chapter differs from those published more recently.

This overall forecast is a critical input to the President's Fiscal Year 2024 Budget, because it is an input into the budget projections of many Federal agencies, and to projections of tax revenues. The forecast development also provides insight into what challenges lie ahead and where the economy might need additional investment and support.

COVID-19 continues to generate forecasting uncertainty. Although U.S. COVID-19 fatalities surged to 1,700 a day in 2022:Q1 due to the new Omicron variant, they declined to 500 per day in April and then the four-week moving average fluctuated in the range of 300 to 500 per day for the rest of the year—held down by vaccinations, increasing immunity, and new treatments. Further COVID-19 declines or future surges pose upside and downside risks for the forecast. The potential for future supply chain disruptions due to COVID-19 surges abroad or wartime disruptions provide further risks; the Russian invasion of Ukraine is another source of uncertainty.

Table 2-3. Economic Projections, 2021–33

Year	Percent Change (Q4 to Q4)			Level (percent)			
		Inflation Measures		Unemployment Rate		Interest Rates	
	Real GDP	GDP Price Index	CPI	Annual	Q4	3-Month T-Bills	10-Year T-Notes
Actual							
2021	5.7	6.1	6.7	5.4	4.2	0.0	1.4
2022	0.9	6.4	7.1	3.6	3.6	2.0	3.0
Forecast							
2022	0.2	6.6	7.6	3.7	3.8	2.0	3.0
2023	0.4	2.8	3.0	4.3	4.6	4.9	3.8
2024	2.1	2.1	2.3	4.6	4.5	3.8	3.6
2025	2.4	2.1	2.3	4.4	4.4	3.0	3.5
2026	2.0	2.1	2.3	4.3	4.3	2.5	3.4
2027	2.0	2.1	2.3	4.2	4.2	2.3	3.4
2028	2.0	2.1	2.3	4.1	4.1	2.2	3.4
2029	2.1	2.1	2.3	4.0	4.0	2.3	3.4
2030	2.2	2.1	2.3	3.9	3.8	2.4	3.4
2031	2.2	2.1	2.3	3.8	3.8	2.4	3.4
2032	2.2	2.1	2.3	3.8	3.8	2.5	3.4
2033	2.2	2.1	2.3	3.8	3.8	2.5	3.4

Sources: Bureau of Economic Analysis; Bureau of Labor Statistics; Department of the Treasury; Office of Management and Budget; CEA calculations.

Note: These forecasts are based on data available as of November 28, 2022; actual data for 2022 arrived later. The interest rate on 3-month (91-day) Treasury Bills is measured on a secondary-market discount basis.

Averaging these risks, the Administration presents a central forecast; table 2-3 summarizes its kcy aspects.

The Near Term

For this *Report*'s near-term forecast, two questions were paramount. First, does real GDP currently exceed its short- or long-run potential level? And second, how soon will inflation return to the Federal Reserve's 2 percent target, and how will this return influence output and employment?

The Administration forecast largely followed the consensus of Blue Chip forecasters by revising its GDP forecast downward. Over the six months between March and October 2022, the Blue Chip consensus economic forecast was revised to show substantially lower real GDP growth and higher inflation during the two years 2022 and 2023 (see table 2-4). This combination of revisions suggests that the consensus—implicitly—recognized that demand had exceeded available supply during 2022; the consensus panel did not make any offsetting upward revisions during the subsequent two years. The lack of a bounce-back in the consensus forecast for real GDP growth in

Table 2-4. Evolution of the Blue Chip Consensus Real GDP Forecast

	Percent Growth, Annual Average to Annual Average				
	2022	2023	2024	2025	2026
Real GDP					
March 2022	3.5	2.5	2.1	2.0	2.0
October 2022	1.6	0.2	1.5	2.1	2.1
Revision	–1.9	–2.3	–0.6	0.1	0.1
CPI					
March 2022	6.2	2.6	2.3	2.2	2.2
October 2022	8.0	3.9	2.4	2.2	2.2
Revision	1.8	1.3	0.1	0.0	0.0

Source: Blue Chip Economic Indicators.
Note: The Blue Chip panel revises its long-term forecast in March and October, with growth rates that are annual average to annual average.

2024 and 2025 may reflect that the constraints on supply during 2022 partly reflected long-term factors. Between October and December 2022, inflation in 2022 came in lower and real GDP growth during 2022 came in stronger than the Administration had predicted as of November. In light of the new data available since the forecast was finalized, a forecast assembled today would differ from that finalized in November.

The forecast given in table 2-3 predicted slow (0.4 percent) real GDP growth for the four quarters of 2023 because GDP growth may need to be less than trend growth to alleviate the current tight labor market. The Blue Chip consensus panel also predicted that 2023 real GDP growth would be slow over the four quarters of the year.[10]

The second question, how soon will inflation return to levels consistent with the Federal Reserve's target, depends on the success of monetary and fiscal policy, and the legislative and executive actions discussed above. As a consequence of the FOMC's decision to raise the target Federal Funds Rate from close to 0 percent in February 2022 to between 4.25 and 4.50 percent in December, other short-term rates also increased, including the yield on 91-day Treasury Bills, which rose 4.2 percentage points during the 12 months of the year to 4.3 percent by the end of the year. Though nominal interest rates on long-term securities also rose, they did not increase by as much as short-term rates, perhaps reflecting market confidence that inflation will recede over the next 10 years. As of November 2022, the Administration predicted that interest rates would continue to increase during 2023, but would then begin to decline in 2024. The Administration further predicted that inflation would fall quickly in 2023 from its 2022 pace as supply chains unsnarled, and would return to rates consistent with the Federal Reserve's

[10] In October, the Blue Chip panel predicted that Q4-to-Q4 real GDP growth would be 0.4 percent, which was lowered to –0.1 percent in the December survey.

long-term targets by 2024 (see, e.g., the FOMC's December 14, 2022, statement: Federal Reserve 2022b).

Consistent with slow GDP growth, in November 2022 the Administration expected the unemployment rate would edge up in 2023, averaging 4.3 percent but peaking at 4.6 percent in 2023:Q4. The combination of this rising unemployment, slow GDP growth, a falling vacancy rate, the effects of expected fiscal policies and executive actions, and continued confidence in the Federal Reserve's commitment to its 2 percent target rate was expected to lower the rate of CPI inflation to 3.0 percent during 2023, and to 2.3 percent during 2024. As mentioned in box 2-1 above, CPI inflation tends to outpace the PCE Price Index; hence, a 2.3 percent CPI inflation rate is consistent with the Federal Reserve's target of a 2 percent PCE Price Index inflation rate. Another measure of inflation, the price index for GDP, was expected to fall from a forecasted 6.6 percent rate during 2022 to 2.1 percent during 2024.

Post–World War II history suggests that bringing down inflation, via monetary policy or otherwise, will likely lower employment growth and output growth. Recognizing this relationship, in November the Administration expected that unemployment would increase during the four quarters of 2023, before starting to decline in 2024. From its expected 4.6 percent peak in 2023:Q4, the unemployment rate was expected to edge lower to 4.5 percent by the end of 2024, eventually falling—in 2030—to the long-term rate of 3.8 percent that the Administration considers to be consistent with stable inflation.

The Administration's near-term forecasts for real GDP growth in 2023–24, near-term inflation, the unemployment rate, and interest rates were roughly consistent with the forecast of the Blue Chip Economic Indicators (the consensus), and that of the FOMC as of November 2022.[11]

The Long Term

In contrast to the near-term outlook, the Administration's long-term forecast for real GDP growth exceeded the October 2022 Blue Chip consensus long-term forecast by an average of 0.2 percentage point a year during the nine years 2025–33. The Administration believed that potential real GDP growth in the long run would be modestly higher because of the expected effect of the President's proposed economic policies, assuming that they are enacted, including a range of programs to enhance human capital formation, provide childcare, and reform immigration policy. In addition, the Administration recognized that the downward pressure on labor force participation from the

[11] The Congressional Budget Office's forecast is absent from this list because its latest 2022 forecast (during the interval that the Administration forecast was in play) was finalized on March 2, 2022, before the release of much data on GDP and inflation, and was therefore out of date.

Table 2-5. Supply-Side Components of Forecasted Real Output Growth

		Percentage-Point Contribution to Annual Real Output Growth				
		1953:Q2–2019:Q4	1990:Q3–2001:Q1	2001:Q1–2007:Q4	2007:Q4–2019:Q4	2019:Q4–2033:Q4
	Component	(1)	(2)	(3)	(4)	(5)
1	Population	1.4	1.2	1.1	1.0	0.7
2	Labor force participation rate	0.1	0.1	–0.3	–0.4	–0.2
3	Employed share of labor force	0.0	0.1	0.1	0.1	0.0
4	Average weekly hours	–0.2	–0.1	–0.2	–0.1	0.0
5	Output per hour	2.0	2.4	2.4	1.4	1.6
6	Output per worker differential	–0.3	–0.3	–0.6	–0.4	–0.2
7	Sum: Real GDO	3.0	3.5	2.4	1.7	1.9

Sources: Bureau of Economic Analysis; Bureau of Labor Statistics; Department of the Treasury; Office of Management and Budget; CEA calculations.
Note: These forecasts are based on data available as of November 28, 2022. Total may not add up due to rounding. 1953:Q2, 1990:Q3, 2001:Q1, 2007:Q4, and 2019:Q4 are all quarterly business-cycle peaks. Population, labor force, and household employment have been adjusted for discontinuities in the population series. Detailed row defintions: (1) civilian noninstutional population, 16 + (4) nonfarm business average weekly hours (5) nonfarm business output per hour; output is measured as the average of income- and product-side measures (6) difference between output-per-worker growth in the economy as a whole and in the nonfarm business sector (7) gross domestic output (GDO) is the average of GDP and gross domestic income (GDI).

retirement of baby boom cohorts is likely to wane during the last five years of the budget window (2028–33), as discussed in box 2-3.

Although the circumstances surrounding this year's near-term forecast were unique to 2022, the key issues affecting the long-term forecast are less tied to recent events. These issues can be described most clearly in terms of the supply-side components of GDP, which, although erratic in the short run, have more understandable long-term movements.

The first set of key issues has to do with the long-term labor supply. As discussed in chapter 6 of this *Report*, the U.S. population is aging. The first row of table 2-5 shows that the Administration's forecast expected that the civilian, noninstitutional population age 16 years and above would grow by an average of 0.7 percent at an annual rate from 2019 to 2033, below the average 1.0 percent annual growth rate from 2007 to 2019.[12] Much of this expected growth will likely come from immigration.[13] The labor force participation rate was projected to continue its decline, reflecting the aging of the baby boom cohorts into retirement. This downward pressure on the

[12] The civilian, noninstitutional population excludes individuals who are incarcerated or are living in mental health facilities or homes for seniors, or who are on active duty in the Armed Forces. Projected growth rates come from demographers at the Social Security Administration. Table 2-5 shows projected growth rates for the 15 years since the business cycle peak in 2019:Q4. The choice of this long period to discuss these supply-side components is because many of these components move sharply for business-cycle reasons (workweek and productivity), and others have large erratic components in the short run (labor force participation rate and the productivity differential).
[13] Also see Social Security Administration (2022a).

Box 2-3. Aging and Growth

The United States, like most advanced countries, is going through a demographic transition, and this will have a large impact on a variety of economic variables for years to come. In figure 2-ii, the blue line plots the age distribution of the United States in 2011, the bars show the current age distribution, and the orange line plots the expected age distribution in 2033. Although the U.S. population is still growing, the center of mass of the age distribution is shifting to the right—that is, to older ages.

Of particular note is the baby boom cohort, whose members were between 58 and 76 years of age in 2022. Most baby boomers are now

Figure 2-ii. The Evolution of the U.S. Population's Age Composition

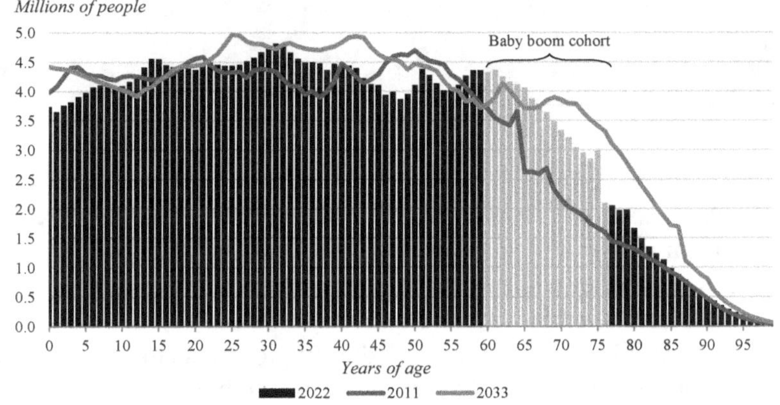

Source: Social Security Administration (2022b).
Note: The U.S. Social Security population differs slightly from the U.S. civilian noninstitutional population.

Figure 2-iii. Age–Labor Force Participation Rate Profiles in 2019

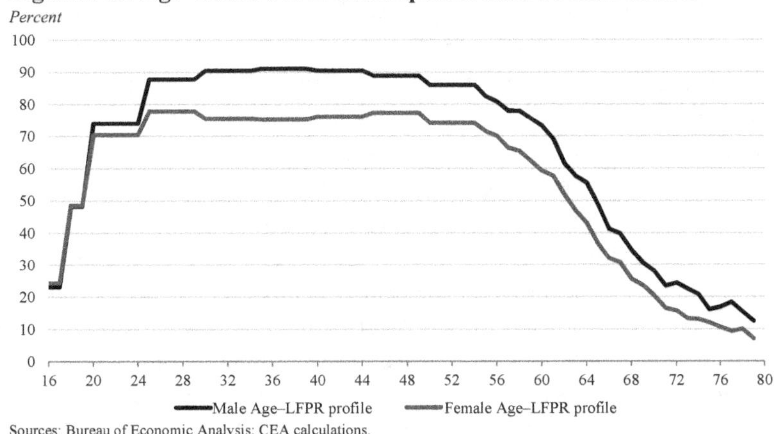

Sources: Bureau of Economic Analysis; CEA calculations.
Note: LFPR = labor force participation rate.

at or above the age of retirement. As they age, the baby boomers will continue to push out the right tail of the distribution.

Most people retire when they are between the ages of 62, the earliest age of eligibility under Social Security, and 70, as can be seen from the sharp decline in participation for those ages shown in the age–participation rate profiles given in figure 2-iii. Using the Social Security Administration's projections for the age distribution through 2033, together with these age–participation profiles, overall participation is projected to drop about 0.4 percent (or about 0.2 percentage point) a year for the next five years. But during the last five years of the forecasted interval, this downward pressure on the overall labor force participation rate will be reduced to about 0.2 percent a year, because most of the baby boom cohort will have already retired. Using the identity shown in table 2-5, the less negative growth in the participation growth rate is expected to have a positive impact on GDP growth.

participation rate was projected to wane after 2028, however, as discussed in box 2-3. The workweek (row 4 of table 2-5) was projected to stabilize after a long historical period of decline attributable to the entry of women, who, on average, have shorter workweeks than men, and to the declining share of manufacturing in total employment.

In the Administration's forecast, the employed share of the labor force was projected to remain close to its level at the 2019 business-cycle peak, and therefore made no net contribution over the forecast interval. Productivity growth (measured as output per hour) was projected to grow 1.6 percent a year over the 15-year interval, somewhat more slowly than its 2.0 percent long-term average but faster than the 1.4 percent growth rate during the 2007–19 business cycle. Finally, the output per worker differential, which is the difference between the output per person for the economy as a whole and the output per person in the nonfarm business sector, was expected to be negative, because of the national income accounting convention that productivity does not grow in the government or household sectors. Because productivity growth is assumed to be zero for these sectors of the economy, while productivity growth was forecasted to be positive in the nonfarm business sector, the differential was necessarily negative. That said, this differential was projected to be less negative than the historical average because of the projected declining share of government in total output.

The long-term forecast of the inflation rate was based on the assumption that the Federal Reserve will succeed in hitting its target of 2 percent for inflation, as measured by the PCE Price Index. Forecasts for future interest rates were informed by the FOMC's near-term forecast of the Federal Funds

Rate. Projections for the yield on 10-year Treasury Notes lie between the Blue Chip consensus forecast and the implicit forecast provided by forward rates derived from the market prices of U.S. Treasury securities.

Conclusion

The forces that have buffeted the U.S. economy since the beginning of the COVID-19 pandemic only began to calm in 2022. The United States found itself in an enviable position among advanced economies, with substantial growth during 2021 and positive growth in 2022, a low unemployment rate, and lower inflation than some other countries. Moreover, inflation pressures abated from their mid-year highs by the end of 2022, both in terms of headline and, more importantly for the future, core inflation. The U.S. economy has, by some economic measures, such as the record low unemployment rate and the return of output to—or even above—the trend, fully recovered from the COVID-19-induced recession.

As discussed in this chapter, the rise in inflation during this period appears to have been driven partly by the intersection of constrained supply and strong demand. These dynamics reflected the effects of the pandemic on consumer demand and supply chains, along with the strong fiscal and monetary support that was necessary to offset the unique and powerful negative shock caused by COVID-19. Though these fiscal and monetary interventions contributed to the strong demand that played a role in the ensuing inflationary pressures, they also set the stage for the historically strong 2021–22 labor market and supported smoothly functioning financial markets. At the same time, these interventions helped avoid the deep and lasting hardships that otherwise would likely have beset millions of American households. In this uncertain environment, as President Biden said at the time, the risk of doing too little exceeded the risk of doing too much (White House 2021).

Overall, the recovery from the pandemic-induced recession progressed far enough in 2022 that the U.S. economy is well situated to weather the anticipated below-trend growth over the near term. The speed and strength of the pandemic recovery testifies to the power of fiscal and monetary policy to fight even the largest negative shocks. The government is united in working toward sustainable growth, low inflation, and inclusive prosperity.

Chapter 3

Confronting New Global Challenges with Strong International Economic Partnerships

In 2022, the global economy continued to face challenges as the economic shocks associated with the COVID-19 pandemic persisted into their third year. In addition, Russia's unprovoked invasion of Ukraine disrupted global commodity markets and caused businesses and governments to reevaluate key trade and investment linkages. Nevertheless, in the United States, persistently strong global economic ties contributed to the continuing recovery of manufacturing output, strong consumption, deepening business investment (BEA 2023a), and resilience to shocks. They also provided strategic room to counter geopolitical aggression.

The global economic shocks of the past three years have highlighted the need for policies that balance the benefits of these economic ties with the risks to economic and national security that they can entail. The policy response to external challenges, along with the pursuit of greener and more inclusive economic growth at home, will transform the international economic linkages that manifest through global markets for goods, services, and data. Strong partnerships between governments are essential to effectively address these challenges.

This chapter begins by describing how the global economic events of 2022 were reflected in the United States' robust international trade and investment flows. It then examines how ongoing COVID-19 disruptions, more recent geopolitical tensions, and the expansion of the digital economy have affected global economic policymaking priorities. It closes by underscoring the critical role of international partnerships between the United States and its allies and partners in ensuring the effectiveness of their collective response to these shared challenges.

The United States' International Trade and Investment in 2022

As the headline-grabbing supply chain challenges associated with the persistence of COVID-19 retreated, and despite Russia's invasion of Ukraine, U.S. international trade and investment reached record highs in 2022. Trade in goods and services (exports plus imports) increased by 8 percent compared with 2021 in real, inflation-adjusted terms, surpassing the record set in 2019 (figure 3-1) and reflecting robust imports and exports of goods, despite headwinds from slowing global growth and the strong U.S. dollar (BEA 2023a).

Record imports were driven by a surge in the first quarter of 2022, which retreated in the second half of the year. Although they declined from their first-quarter high, they remained strong in historical terms. In contrast, exports increased relatively steadily to the third quarter, with a shallow fourth-quarter decline. These distinct paths are reflected in the sharp increase and subsequent narrowing of the trade deficit (exports minus imports) in 2022 (figure 3-2). The trade deficit shot to 4.5 percent of gross domestic product (GDP) in the first quarter of 2022—the largest since the

Figure 3-1. Real U.S. Trade in Goods and Services, 2012–22

Trillions of chained 2021 dollars, quarterly, seasonally adjusted at annual rates

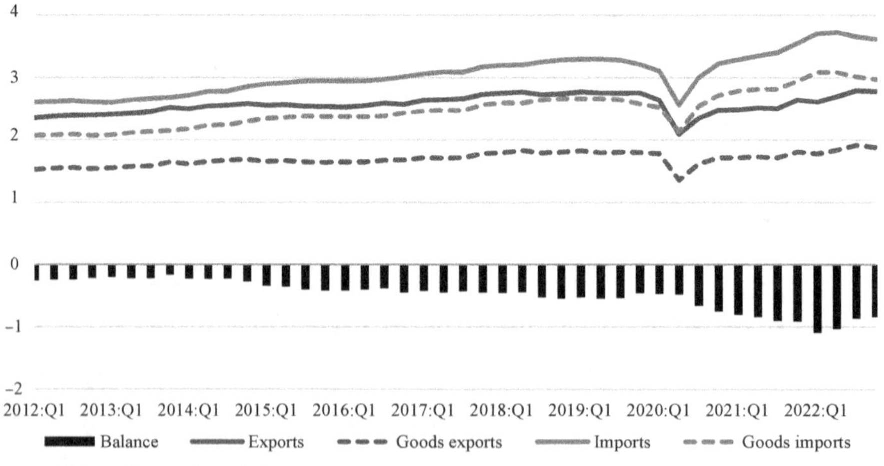

Sources: Bureau of Economic Analysis; CEA calculations.

Figure 3-2. U.S. Trade Balance, 2018–22

Percentage of GDP, quarterly

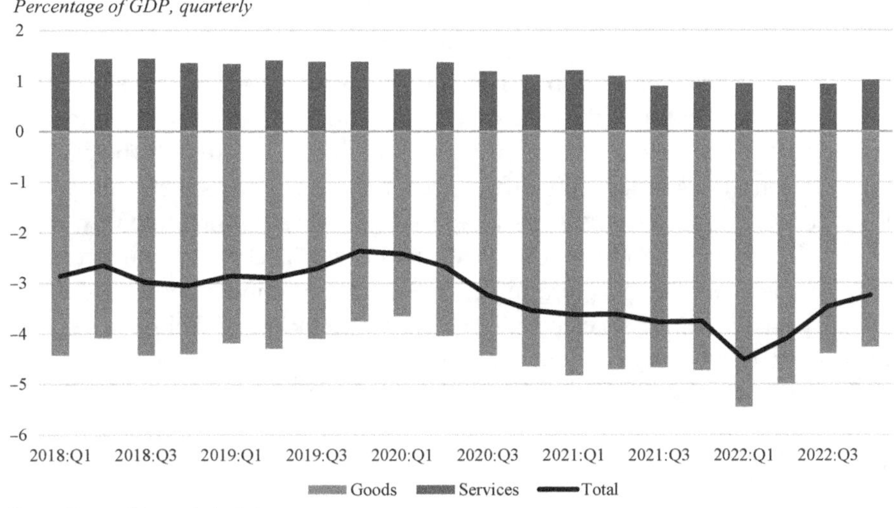

Source: Bureau of Economic Analysis.

Figure 3-3. Real U.S. Services Trade, 2012–22

Billions of chained 2021 dollars, quarterly, seasonally adjusted at annual rates

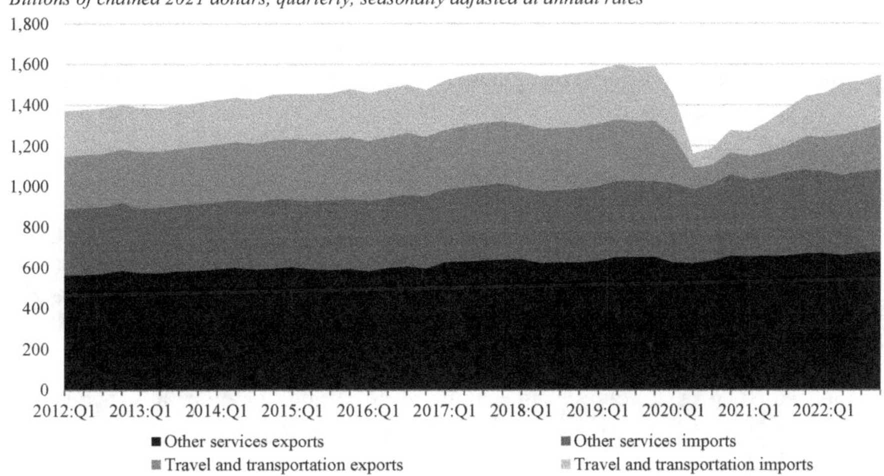

Sources: Bureau of Economic Analysis; CEA calculations.

third quarter of 2008. The deficit then declined as imports fell from their peak, reaching 3.2 percent of GDP in the fourth quarter.

Over the past 20 years, the U.S. goods trade deficit has been partially offset by a surplus in services trade. That is, U.S. exports of services have consistently exceeded imports of services. However, services surpluses have been depressed since the abrupt halt in international movements at the onset of the COVID-19 pandemic as exports of travel and transportation services have recovered more slowly than imports.[1] In 2022, real travel and transportation services exports had only reached 67 percent of their 2019 level, whereas imports were at 89 percent (figure 3-3).

In 2022, stronger growth in travel services imports (spending by U.S. travelers abroad) compared with exports (spending by foreign visitors to the United States) was likely driven in part by the dollar's strength (box 3-1). For transportation services, the differences in recovery paths were compositional: U.S. transportation services exports are typically dominated by passenger air services, so fewer foreign visitors due to COVID-19 suppressed these exports. While the plurality of U.S. transportation imports are also typically passenger air services, a large share are maritime freight services. Since most shipping companies are foreign-owned, record goods imports pushed these services imports higher (BEA 2023b).

[1] In official U.S. data on services trade, this category is named "transport" rather than "transportation."

Box 3-1. Effects of the Strengthening U.S. Dollar on the U.S. Economy

In 2022, the U.S. dollar strengthened against the currencies of its main trading partners, particularly other advanced economies. The Federal Reserve's broad, real exchange rate index increased by 10.7 percent between January 2022 and its peak in October 2022, falling back at the end of 2022 to realize a 5.4 percent year-over-year increase in December 2022 (figure 3-i). The dollar's rise was driven by strong U.S. growth and rising interest rate differentials, as well as by the appeal of U.S. assets as safe haven investments as Russia's invasion of Ukraine stoked global uncertainty. The weakening of the dollar at the end of the year reflects the Federal Reserve's signal that the pace of rate hikes would slow and signs of relatively strong economic conditions in other advanced economies.

Dollar exchange rates have an important influence on trade patterns because they determine the price of U.S. goods and services in the national currencies of the Nation's trading partners. When the dollar is strong, it takes more foreign currency to purchase dollar-denominated goods and services. At the same time, it reduces the dollar cost that U.S. buyers pay for imported goods and services denominated in foreign currency, effectively making them cheaper. All else being equal, these changes in relative prices encourage U.S. buyers to substitute away from goods and services produced in the United States and toward foreign-produced goods and services (i.e., imports), deepening the U.S. trade deficit.

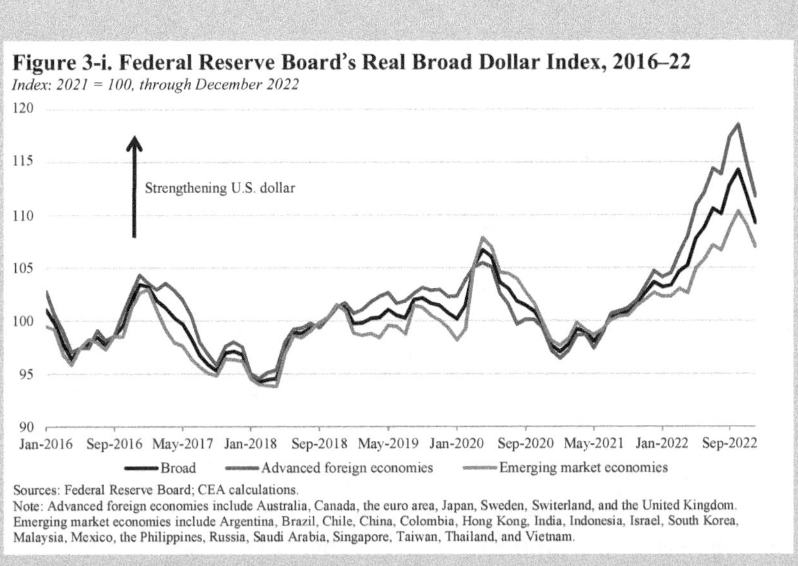

Figure 3-i. Federal Reserve Board's Real Broad Dollar Index, 2016–22

Sources: Federal Reserve Board; CEA calculations.
Note: Advanced foreign economies include Australia, Canada, the euro area, Japan, Sweden, Switerland, and the United Kingdom. Emerging market economies include Argentina, Brazil, Chile, China, Colombia, Hong Kong, India, Indonesia, Israel, South Korea, Malaysia, Mexico, the Philippines, Russia, Saudi Arabia, Singapore, Taiwan, Thailand, and Vietnam.

In 2022, the dollar's strength was only one of many strong currents shaping trade patterns. As such, it is difficult to distinguish its effects from other forces. However, as an example, it is likely that the strength of the dollar contributed to the comparatively stronger rebound in imports relative to exports of travel services, as depicted in figure 3-3. This is because when the dollar is strong, as explained above, it has more value in foreign currency terms, making travel budgets go further and thus incentivizing increased spending on hotels, restaurants, and other goods and services by Americans abroad. The opposite effect makes travel in the United States more expensive for foreign visitors.

The strong dollar also likely dampened U.S. exports of agricultural commodities like soybeans, cotton, and corn in 2022 (Jiang et al. 2022). Indeed, exports in the Bureau of Economic Analysis' (BEA's) broad end-use category of food, feed, and beverages, which includes these agricultural products, fell to its lowest level in real terms since 2015, another period of the dollar's strengthening. (The BEA classifies traded goods in six broad end-use categories: consumer goods; foods, feed, and beverages; industrial supplies and materials; capital goods; automotive vehicles, etc.; and other goods.)

Because agricultural commodities tend to have relatively few intrinsic differences across countries of origin, it is particularly attractive for buyers to substitute away from U.S. varieties when a strong dollar increases their relative prices. Indeed, research suggests that exchange rates are a particularly relevant factor for buyers of less-differentiated commodities, and U.S. agricultural exports tend to decline in periods of real dollar strength (Cooke et al. 2016; Mattoo et al. 2017).

The strong real exports of manufactured goods in 2022 seemingly conflict with the deterioration of U.S. currency competitiveness. (These exports are defined as goods exports under the North American Industry Classification System, chapters 31–33; U.S. Census Bureau 2023b; BLS 2023.) However, this may be explained in part by two offsetting forces. First, the dollar's strength lowers the dollar costs of imported inputs and capital equipment priced in foreign currencies, thus increasing the cost-competitiveness of U.S. manufacturers that rely on these imports (Goldberg and Crockett 1998). Second, in 2022 U.S. manufacturers' loss of currency competitiveness was likely offset by a deterioration of cost-competitiveness in other countries that were more exposed to rising input costs from energy price hikes.

A strong dollar can also lower the dollar price of imported consumer goods, dampening inflationary pressures. In practice, however, the dollar's impact on movements in U.S. consumer price inflation has historically been limited, due to the relatively low pass-through of exchange rate movements to U.S. import prices (Gopinath and Itskhoki 2021; Gopinath, Itskhoki, and Rigobon 2010). Moreover, imported goods constitute a relatively small share of the basket of goods used to calculate common measures of inflation—representing only 12.6 percent of the Consumer Price Index by one estimate (Borusyak and Jaravel 2021)—so declines in prices of imported goods are unlikely to have a substantial impact on measured inflation in a given period.

Pandemic-Related and Macroeconomic Trends Have Shaped Record Goods Imports

Strong demand growth and the unwinding of the pandemic-era supply chain pressures that mounted throughout 2021 underpinned the dramatic increase in goods imports in the first quarter of 2022 (for the top U.S. import partners, see box 3-2). Along with the strengthening dollar, these forces sustained elevated imports through the rest of the year. To illustrate how this pattern unfolded in record imports in the broad end-use category of consumer goods, figure 3-4 splits this category in two. The household goods series depicts trends in real imports of goods most closely associated with household consumption, such as apparel and footwear, cellphones, furniture and household appliances. The other consumption goods series reflects trends in real imports of goods like pharmaceuticals, artwork, and gem diamonds that are less associated with everyday household expenditures.[2]

[2] The CEA is grateful to the International Trade Programs team in the Economic Indicators Division of the U.S. Census Bureau for suggesting this division.

Box 3-2. The United States' Top Goods Trading Partners

Although research suggests that the product composition of goods trade has shifted in recent years, the United States' top trading partners have largely remained the same (Bown 2022a). The top U.S. export destinations and import sources are still China and the European Union—the two largest economies outside the United States—as well as the United States' North American neighbors, Mexico and Canada. Together, these four economies are responsible for over half of U.S. trade (figures 3-ii and 3-iii).

Figure 3-ii. Top Sources of U.S. Goods Imports, 2022

Share of nominal imports

European Union, 17.0%
China, 16.7%
Mexico, 14.0%
Canada, 13.5%
Rest of the world, 38.8%

Source: U.S. Census Bureau.

Figure 3-iii. Top U.S. Goods Export Destinations, 2022

Share of nominal exports

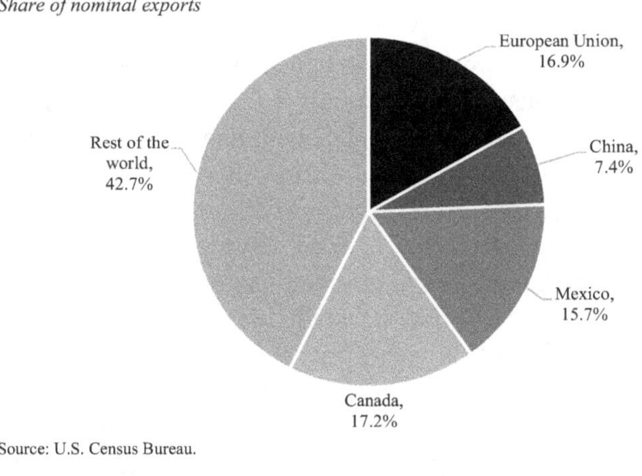

Source: U.S. Census Bureau.

Figure 3-4. Real Imports of Consumer Goods, 2018-22

Billions of 2021 dollars

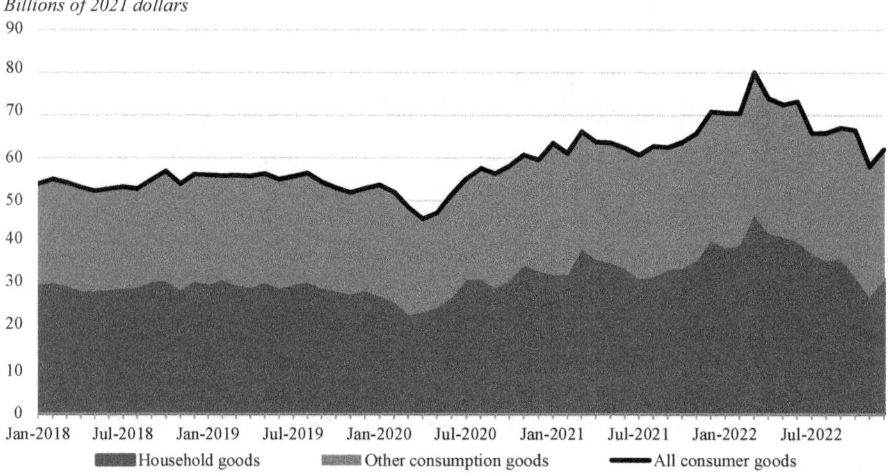

Sources: Bureau of Economic Analysis; Bureau of Labor Statistics; CEA calculations.
Note: Consumer goods exclude automobiles and parts. Household goods include apparel, footwear, and other household goods; furniture and other household goods; household appliances; cell phones and other household goods; and toys, games, and sporting goods. Real series have been adjusted with the Bureau of Labor Statistics' import price indices.

Figure 3-4 reveals that the first-quarter import surge was largely driven by household goods, reflecting the pandemic-induced shift in consumption expenditures to goods and away from services (see chapter 2 of this *Report*). This shift disproportionately increased import demand throughout this period, in part simply because goods are more import-intensive than services. Compounding this, the persistence of remote work and diminished leisure spending outside the home increased demand for goods like computers and home improvement products that are particularly import-intensive in the United States (Chetty et al. 2022; Higgins and Klitgaard 2021; IMF 2022a).

In the first quarter, easing of port congestion—in addition to high inventory investment by businesses responding to global market uncertainty after months of COVID-19-related supply chain snarls and the impending threat of Russia's invasion of Ukraine—further boosted imports. Imports of household goods decreased from their first-quarter peak as consumption expenditures began to shift back to services, supply chain backlogs were cleared, and inventory rebuilding continued (see chapter 2). However, they remained well-above prepandemic levels throughout the first half of the year. In the second half of the year, household goods imports declined even more significantly as rising interest rates began to dampen consumer demand.

Real imports of capital goods also set a record in 2022, exceeding the previous record set in 2021 by 10 percent. Together with robust imports of industrial supplies and materials—fuels, metals, and other key industrial

Figure 3-5. Real Imports of Capital Goods (Excluding Automobiles), 2018-22
Billions of chained 2021 dollars

Sources: Census Bureau; CEA calculations.

inputs—these imports supported a strong rebound in domestic output in 2022 (see chapter 2). Like household goods, capital goods imports surged in the first quarter with relief from pandemic-era port congestion (figure 3-5). Unlike household goods, capital goods imports remained substantially above prepandemic levels as imports of various types of electrical equipment, industrial machinery, transportation equipment, and information and communications technology equipment—including semiconductors—benefited from a combination of easing supply constraints and strong business demand.

Geopolitical Shocks and Global Demand Have Shaped Record Goods Exports

Real exports of goods surpassed their prepandemic heights of 2019 by 2.6 percent in 2022 (see box 3-2 for the top U.S. export partners). Increased demand for U.S. energy exports was a key driver, as many countries—particularly in Europe—looked to replace Russia as a source of crude oil and natural gas supplies. U.S. exports in the broad end-use category of industrial supplies and materials—which includes energy goods—hit a record high in 2022, as did exports of consumer goods. In contrast to consumer goods imports depicted in figure 3-4, the increase in real consumer goods exports was driven by pharmaceutical goods (figure 3-6).

Shocks from Russia's invasion of Ukraine had a significant impact on global commodity markets in 2022 that echoed in U.S. exports. In contrast to other traded goods, commodities like oil—as well as many metals, minerals, and agricultural products are relatively standardized across source countries,

Figure 3-6. Real Exports of Consumer Goods, 2018–22

Billions of 2021 dollars

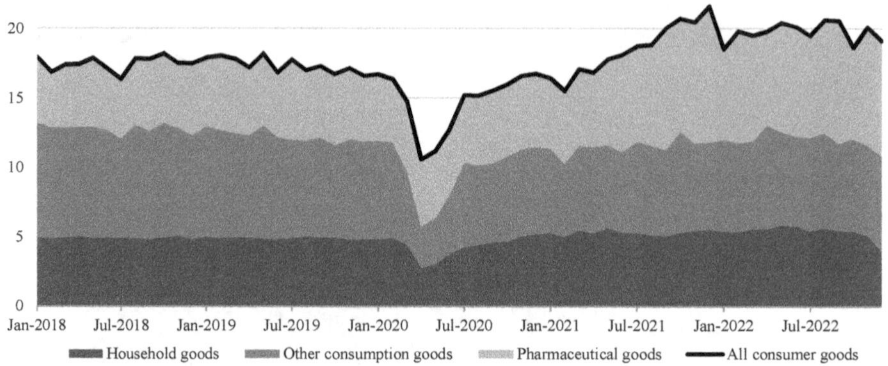

Sources: Bureau of Economic Analysis; Bureau of Labor Statistics; CEA calculations.
Note: Consumer goods exclude automobiles and parts. Household goods include apparel, footwear, and household goods; furniture and household goods; household appliances; cell phones and other household goods; and toys, games, and sporting goods. Real series adjusted with BLS import price indices.

allowing buyers to substitute across source countries fairly easily. Because of this, their price in any given country is largely determined by global market movements. As such, although Russia and Ukraine are relatively small trading partners for the United States—representing only 0.5 percent of U.S. exports and 1.1 percent of U.S. imports in 2021—because they are major producers and exporters of key commodities, disruptions of their exports influence the prices U.S. consumers must pay for food and fuel, and also overall inflation (see chapter 2). In addition, since the United States is an exporter of some commodities also exported by Russia and Ukraine, notably energy and agricultural products, disruptions to supplies or changes in the pattern of exports from these countries can affect U.S. exports as well (IEA 2022a).

Initially, Russia's invasion largely cut off Ukraine—a major exporter of food commodities, especially wheat, corn, and vegetable oil—from global markets, threatening global food security. The loss of Ukraine's export supply, along with the reluctance of global buyers to engage with Russian exporters on the exports of grains and oil seeds and Russia's own export restrictions on fertilizer and other agricultural products, resulted in contractions along key supply lines for food staples and agricultural inputs like fuel and fertilizer, sending prices soaring in the immediate aftermath of the invasion (Glauber and Laborde 2022). Prices retreated as allied nations successfully collaborated to mitigate disruptions. Nevertheless, the uncertainty associated with Russia's domestic actions and aggression toward Ukraine—including the destruction of infrastructure used to store and export food commodities, and the naval blockade of Ukraine's Black Sea

Figure 3-7. U.S. Exports of Liquefied Natural Gas, 2021 and 2022
Millions of cubic meters

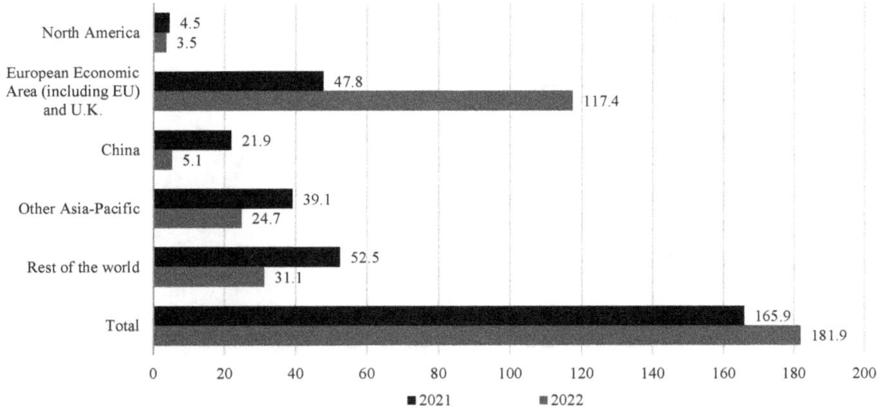

	2021	2022
North America	4.5	3.5
European Economic Area (including EU) and U.K.	47.8	117.4
China	21.9	5.1
Other Asia-Pacific	39.1	24.7
Rest of the world	52.5	31.1
Total	165.9	181.9

Sources: U.S. Census Bureau, accessed with Trade Data Monitor; CEA calculations.
Note: Liquefied natural gas is covered by HS271111. Other Asia-Pacific includes Australia, Japan, South Korea, New Zealand, and all 10 nations that belong to the Association of Southeast Asian Nations: Brunei, Cambodia, Indonesia, Laos, Malaysia, Myanmar, the Philippines, Singapore, Thailand, and Vietnam.

trade route—continued to exacerbate elevated prices. This led U.S. exports of food, feed, and beverages to exceed their 2021 record by 10 percent in nominal terms, even as they fell to their lowest level since 2015 in real terms (Foggo and Mainardi 2022; U.S. Census Bureau 2023b; Yale School of Public Health 2022). Real exports of these products were ultimately depressed by the strong dollar, weakening global demand and other product-specific factors, including adverse weather conditions.

Disruptions from Russia's invasion of Ukraine had a more significant real impact on U.S. exports of energy goods, notably liquefied natural gas (LNG) and crude oil. The quantity of U.S. exports of LNG and crude oil rose substantially over 2021's already-high levels. For LNG, U.S. exports also shifted dramatically to European countries as Russia restricted its once-dominant supply of natural gas via pipeline (figure 3-7). Crude oil exports expanded more broadly across destinations, with the notable exception of a decrease in exports to China (figure 3-8). Although this figure only captures a single year rather than a trend, research suggests that reductions in China's energy imports from the United States in 2022 likely represented a shift to imports from other sources, including Russia, along with a drop in demand due to slower Chinese economic growth (Bown 2022b).

International Trade in Services and Digital Trade Have Been Resilient

Through the end of 2022, U.S. trade in services other than travel and transportation was remarkably stable and resilient amid the continued disruption of the COVID-19 pandemic and rising geopolitical tensions (see figure 3-3). In part, this is because digital technology enables adaptations that allow

Figure 3-8. U.S. Exports of Crude Oil, 2021 and 2022
Millions of barrels

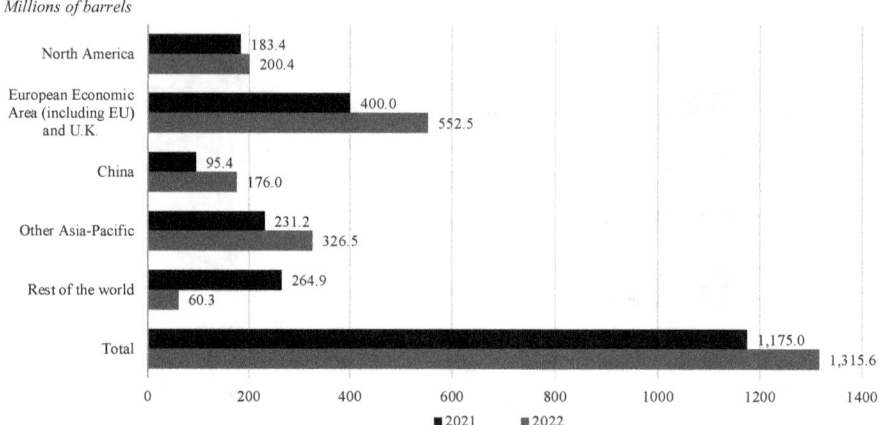

Sources: U.S. Census Bureau, accessed with Trade Data Monitor; CEA calculations.
Note: Liquefied natural gas is covered by HS271111. Other Asia-Pacific includes Australia, Japan, South Korea, New Zealand, and all 10 nations that belong to the Association of Southeast Asian Nations: Brunei, Cambodia, Indonesia, Laos, Malaysia, Myanmar, the Philippines, Singapore, Thailand, and Vietnam.

many traded services to be remotely provided. Further, many countries have made efforts to reduce obstacles to digital trade, including by promoting access to and efficiency of electronic payments (Klapper and Miller 2021). Just as remote work minimized pandemic-related disruptions in many domestic industries that specialize in information, digital technologies allowed movements of service providers to be converted into movements of data and thus minimized interruptions of international trade in these industries (Brynjolfsson et al. 2020; Dingel and Neiman 2020; Espitia et al. 2021; Pei, de Vries, and Zhang 2021). Furthermore, limitations on mobility increased demand for other traded digital services as more household consumption as well as work moved online.

In fact, the pandemic likely accelerated the trend of rising digital trade flows. Though there is no standardized definition of digital trade, it can be conceptualized as including three general types of transactions. The first is traditional e-commerce, whereby the Internet facilitates a purchase that is delivered offline. The second is digitally provided services, which are provided and consumed online. This category includes a wide array of services that are increasingly part of everyday life, including digital media like streaming music and videos; digital platforms that connect individuals to make transactions; the services embedded in the Internet of Things, like "smart" household appliances and connected medical devices; and the cloud computing services relied on for business operations. The third category includes data, which are a basic element of many cross-border transactions but can also be deployed by companies as part of their operations or sold to other businesses to target advertisements, improve manufacturing

Figure 3-9. U.S. Trade in Potentially ICT-Enabled Services, 1999–2021

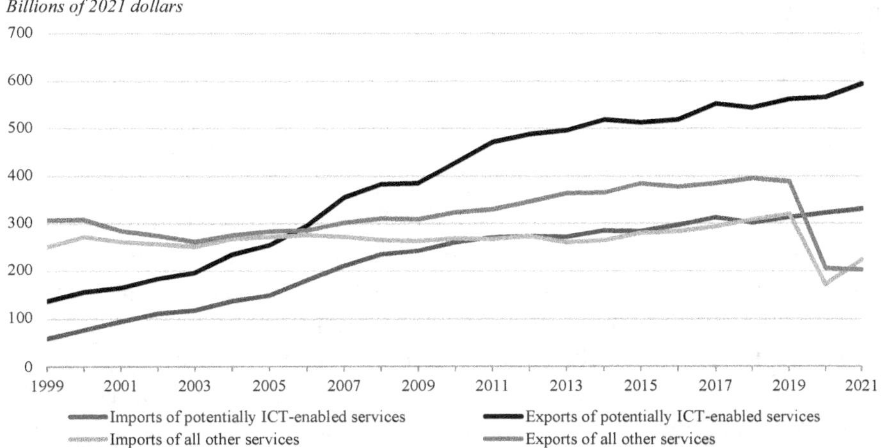

Sources: Bureau of Economic Analysis; CEA calculations.
Note: ICT = information and communications technology. Price indices for exports and imports of potentially ICT-enabled services are calculated as the average of price indices for their components (insurance services; financial services; charges for the use of intellectual property; telecommunications, computer, and information services; other business services; and personal, cultural, and recreational services), weighted by the category's nominal share. The nominal series is then converted with this price index.

operations, and power machine learning for artificial intelligence (AI) tools, among many other uses (Meltzer 2019; OECD 2023a; Staiger 2021a; Wharton 2019).

Although digital trade cannot be precisely measured using current data sources, the evidence suggests that there have been dramatic increases during the last two decades. Cross-border data flows that underpin digital trade transactions are estimated to have increased by a compound annual growth rate of 45 percent between 2010 and 2019 and by about 40 percent between 2019 and 2021 (Birshan et al. 2022). In comparison, flows of goods and services grew at a compound annual growth rate of about 3 and 4 percent, respectively, between 2010 and 2019 (BEA 2023c). Estimates suggest that e-commerce transactions grew at an average annual rate of 14.5 percent between 2010 and 2019 and by 30.3 percent between 2019 and 2021. E-commerce transactions made up an average of 14.5 percent of retail sales by value in 2022, up from 4.5 percent in 2010 and 10.5 percent in 2019 (U.S. Census Bureau 2022).

Likewise, the subset of traded services that the BEA defines as "potentially ICT-enabled" (i.e., information and communications technology–enabled) has grown dramatically over time (figure 3-9).[3] Real exports

[3] Potentially ICT-enabled services trade includes the categories of services trade for which digital technologies are thought to play the most prominent role. These include ICT services themselves, as well as insurance services, financial services, and charges for the use of intellectual property, including royalties and licenses.

and imports of potentially ICT-enabled services grew at an average annual rate of 7.0 and 8.5 percent, respectively, between 1999 and 2021. This was much faster than real exports and imports of all other services, which grew at average annual rates of 0.5 and –1.1 percent, respectively, during the same period.

Unlike traditional trade in goods and services, for many digital trade transactions, there is no physical movement of a good or a person across a border. Rather, the transaction is fully realized by data flows. In great contrast to physical exchanges, the direct, marginal cost to move data across borders is nearly zero. Moreover, the cost difference in procuring an identical digitally delivered service from nearby versus from far away is also close to zero (Goldfarb and Tucker 2019). Absent a sharp increase in regulatory hurdles, digital trade is thus poised for further dramatic increases as digital technology continues to improve, as the Internet of Things continues to spread, and as robotics and artificial information technologies are further developed (Baldwin 2022).

At present, U.S. trade in potentially ICT-enabled services is concentrated among advanced economies (BEA 2022). However, as digital technology develops, and as the infrastructure that enables Internet use improves, there will be more opportunities to draw on workers and consumers from around the world to provide and demand a wide range of digital services. This is likely to propel substantial increases in digital trade with emerging markets (Baldwin 2022) and provide benefits to U.S. consumers, workers, and businesses. However, increased competition from service providers abroad will also likely have negative effects on some American businesses and workers (box 3-3).

Continued Growth for Foreign Direct Investment Despite Elevated Uncertainty

Global foreign direct investment (FDI) flows exhibited strong growth during the first three quarters of 2022; total real global FDI flows grew by 9 percent during the first three quarters of 2022 compared with the same period in 2021; global FDI flows in the first quarter of 2022 reached their second highest level in the past five years, increasing by more than 15 percent year-over-year and by over 40 percent compared with the prior quarter (BEA 2023d; OECD 2023b).[4] Global FDI as a share of world GDP reached about 2 percent of GDP in the first half of 2022, a continued recovery from the sharp contraction in international investment during the onset of the COVID-19 pandemic. Though FDI can sometimes pose risks (e.g., to national security in limited cases), research has found that inward and outward FDI can be

[4] Real FDI flows are calculated as the average of global FDI inflows and outflows in dollars, deflated by the U.S. Personal Consumption Expenditures Price Index (chain type).

Box 3-3. Rising Digital Trade and U.S. Labor Markets

Advances in digital technology that facilitate the remote production and provision of goods and services will create significant opportunities and challenges for U.S. workers (Amiti and Wei 2006; Eppinger 2019; Grossman and Rossi-Hansberg 2008). U.S. workers have a comparative advantage in many tradable services and some sophisticated goods industries due to skill level and education. Access to a larger global market will allow these industries to expand, increasing demand for these skills, which may lift wages and provide opportunities for employment for a portion of the workforce. However, other workers in services industries that compete directly with digitally enabled imports (e.g., a worker for a traditional big box retailer competing with a foreign e-commerce company) may face lower wages and job loss. Importantly, research suggests that these losses may disproportionately affect individuals who are more economically vulnerable, exacerbating economic inequality within the United States (Oldenski 2011). In particular, Baldwin (2022) argues that an expansion of digital services trade may have particularly negative effects on U.S. workers providing intermediate services (e.g., administrative assistants, graphic designers, travel agents, and information technology help staff), who will face rising competition from low-wage counterparts in developing countries.

Labor provisions are a core feature of the Biden-Harris Administration's work with U.S. partners on digital trade and featured in the United States' discussions with the EU in the U.S.-EU Trade and Labor Dialogue under the U.S.-EU Trade and Technology Council (DOL 2022), as well as in Pillar 1 of the Indo-Pacific Economic Framework for Prosperity (USTR 2022b). These provisions aim to ensure that trade policy supports fair competition for U.S. workers in the digital economy, raising the standard for workers abroad rather than facilitating competition on the basis of low labor standards.

Research on previous labor market shocks—notably the so-called China Shock, whereby increased import competition in certain manufacturing sectors led to concentrated and persistent job losses in some communities—has revealed that the costs for many workers to adjust after a change in the demand for their labor can be very high (Autor, Dorn, and Hanson 2013, 2016, 2021; Eriksson et al. 2021). This suggests that there is an essential role for complementary domestic policies to equip U.S. workers who are exposed to increased competition through digital trade with the resources to adapt (CEA 2022, chap. 3; Clausing 2019).

Figure 3-10. Real U.S. Outward Foreign Direct Investment, by Destination, 2012–22

Billions of 2021 dollars, quarterly

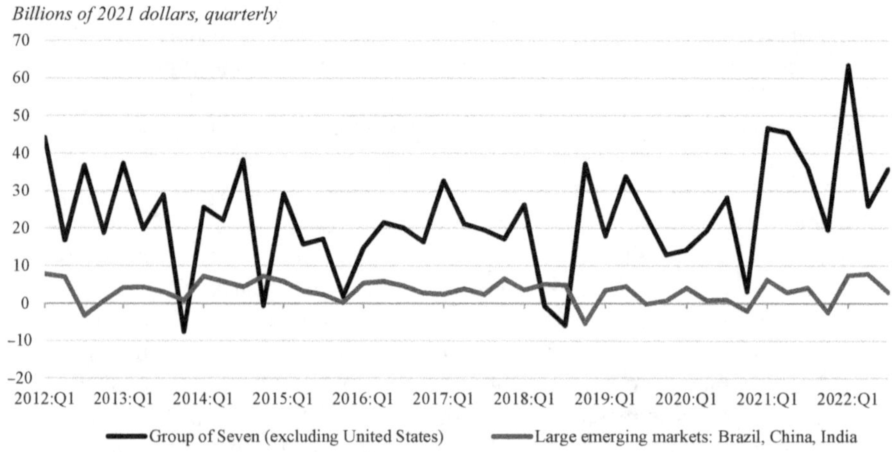

Sources: Bureau of Economic Analysis; CEA calculations.
Note: Data are net financial transactions (without current cost adjustment) on a directional basis, in this case those that relate to outward investment (U.S. direct investment abroad). Nominal series converted to 2021 dollars using U.S. Personal Consumption Expenditures Price Index. Data through 2022:Q3.

the source of significant contributions to economic growth and increased resilience to shocks (Alfaro 2016; OECD 2020a).

Although FDI flows are not directly subject to the same types of physical disruptions as international trade (i.e., the ability to carry out financial transactions is not affected by issues like port closures or physical distance), they are similarly responsive to changes in global economic conditions. Elevated uncertainty about global economic conditions and changes in the economic policy environment can reduce or reverse investment flows (Choi, Furceri, and Yoon 2020; Gulen and Ion 2016; Julio and Yook 2016). Businesses may decide to delay or suspend investment decisions when uncertainty is high and when investors find it difficult to determine when conditions are likely to normalize. Following the strong flows in the first quarter of 2022, elevated global inflation and tightening global financial conditions, as well as the compounding effects of Russia's invasion of Ukraine, resulted in individuals, companies, and governments moderating global FDI flows in the second and third quarters of 2022 (although they still grew 5 percent compared with the second- and third-quarter flows in 2021) (OECD 2023b).

Focusing on the United States, in the first half of 2022, the country was both the largest recipient and largest source of FDI globally (OECD 2022a). FDI flows into and out of the United States are largely flowing from or to advanced economies (e.g., the Group of Seven), especially in comparison

Figure 3-11. Real U.S. Inward Foreign Direct Investment, by Source, 2012–22

Billions of 2021 dollars, quarterly

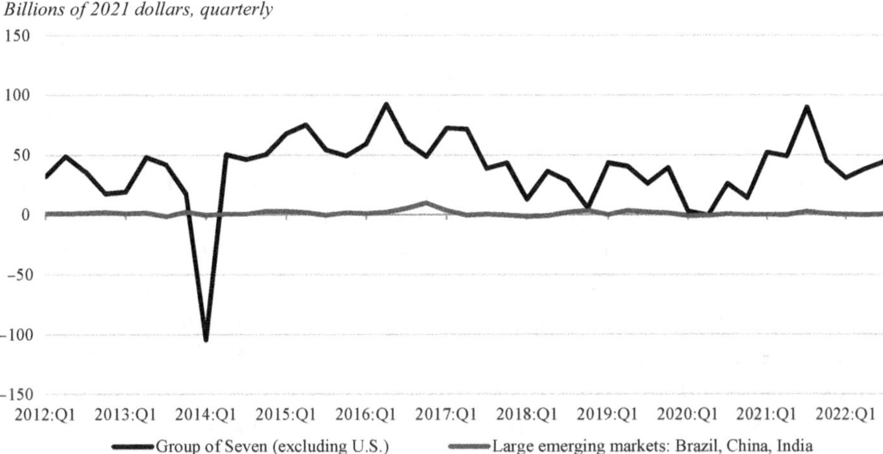

Sources: Bureau of Economic Analysis; CEA calculations.
Note: Data are net financial transactions (without current cost adjustment) on a directional basis, in this case those that relate to inward investment (foreign direct investment in the U.S.). Nominal series converted to 2021 dollars using U.S. Personal Consumption Expenditures Price Index. Data through 2022:Q3.

with FDI to and from large emerging market countries (figures 3-10 and 3-11).

Along these lines, the United States, its allies, and its partners are taking measures to deepen investments in the critical industries in one another's economies as a way of reducing dependencies on other countries that have had an outsized role in these industries, notably China. For instance, the United States, its allies, and its partners are coordinating to increase their collective capacity to produce semiconductors (Shivakumar, Wessner, and Howell 2022). As part of the United States' CHIPS and Science Act, the State Department will manage the International Technology Security and Innovation Fund, which will promote the development of complementary, secure supply chain investments in key partners to strengthen and support the U.S. semiconductor industry (U.S. Department of State 2022a). Similarly, coordinated efforts to catalyze infrastructure investment in emerging and developing countries through the Partnership for Global Infrastructure and Investment—particularly to support the digital economy and the green energy transition—will help reduce uncertainty, strengthen secure supply chains, create new opportunities for businesses and workers, and boost overall economic growth (White House 2022a). The increased policy clarity resulting from these types of commitments and the shared experience of supply constraints during the pandemic may further catalyze mutual investment, thereby deepening the United States' investment relationship with its key allies and partners.

Global Economic Relations Are at a Turning Point

Since World War II, a central focus of the international economic policies of the United States, its allies, and its partners has been reducing barriers to trade and investment in pursuit of greater economic prosperity (Irwin 2022a; CRS 2023). These policies have led to an expanded and strengthened web of integrated economic relationships in the form of global supply chains, and they have supported flows of goods and services across borders that have substantially increased national incomes around the world (CEA 2022, chap. 6; Irwin 2022b; World Bank 2020). However, disruptions of these flows during the global COVID-19 pandemic hit critical nodes of supply chains and hindered production worldwide, amplifying constraints on the supply of certain essential goods to businesses and households (Espitia, Rocha, and Ruta 2022). In addition, Russia's invasion of Ukraine made it imperative for the United States, its allies, and its partners to sever economic relations with Russia that could facilitate its military aggression. The resulting economic sanctions, the reluctance of some international businesses to maintain even permitted economic relationships with Russia, and Russia's retaliatory export restrictions made the risk of undiversified supply chains even more apparent. They also underscored the power of economic integration as a tool of foreign policy (Yellen 2022a; Lagarde 2022).

Alongside these shocks, increased competition from imports over time has also hurt the employment and earnings outcomes for some groups of workers (box 3-3). Long-standing concerns about the associated role of international trade in rising income inequality within the United States (Autor et al. 2014; Chetverikov, Larsen, and Palmer 2016)—along with concerns about the climate crisis, through the greenhouse gas emissions embedded in the consumption of tradable goods and services within the United States—have led to calls to reassess and update the approach to trade policy in the United States and elsewhere (CEA 2022, chap. 3; Tai 2021a, 2021b; WTO 2022).

Although market incentives and current trade rules do not always align production and trade flows with broader social, political, environmental, or national security objectives, international trade and investment can be powerful sources of economic gains. Empirical research has demonstrated that in addition to supporting lower costs for businesses and consumers (de Loecker et al. 2016; Jaravel and Sager 2019), and jobs and higher wages for workers in export industries (Feenstra et al. 2019; National Security Council 2022; Riker 2015; U.S. Department of Commerce 2021), trade and investment facilitate the flow of knowledge across borders, spurring productivity gains and innovation (Goldberg et al. 2010; Keller and Yeaple 2009). Beyond the United States' borders, trade and investment with the United States provides opportunities for many developing countries to fight potentially destabilizing poverty (Irwin 2022b) and can be a foundation for closer relationships with the United States in other domains (Chivvis and Kapstein 2022).

Moreover, as leaders have emphasized, global economic integration is also part of a strategy to promote economic resilience and security (Georgieva, Gopinath, and Pazarbasioglu 2022; Lagarde 2022; Yellen 2022a). Extensive research has found that under a broad set of conditions, businesses are more resilient during supply disruptions when they are able to draw on a geographically diverse set of sources rather than a concentrated source of supply for inputs. Put simply, geographically distributed supplies can act as a "pressure valve" for supply challenges during periods of idiosyncratic supply disruptions (Bonadio et al. 2021; Eppinger et al. 2021; Caselli et al. 2020; D'Aguanno et al. 2021; Espitia, Rocha, and Ruta 2022; Grossman et al. 2021). Although the opportunity to trade does not automatically deliver geographic diversity in sourcing, it does enable it. Similarly, global markets can serve as a backstop for demand, providing alternative markets for businesses when domestic demand is low (Caselli et al. 2020; Lagarde 2022). As such, it is in the interest of the United States to pursue approaches to lower trade costs within greener, fairer, and more secure trade and investment partnerships.

The United States, its allies, and its partners have thus reached a turning point in international economic policy, whereby it is necessary to reckon with a broad mandate: On one hand, it is desirable to maintain the benefits associated with international trade and investment and to facilitate the growth of these benefits in the digital sphere. On the other hand, the focus of trade policy needs to expand beyond reducing barriers. Decisionmakers need to ensure that policy supports increased resilience to global supply shocks; limits the ability of adversarial powers to weaponize economic integration to the United States' detriment; preserves fair competition in the presence of large, nonmarket economies; and minimizes exposure to cybersecurity and regulatory risks, while facilitating digital trade flows. Trade policy can also advance other objectives that interact with international markets, such as fighting climate change, promoting workers' rights and labor standards both at home and abroad, and expanding the benefits of trade to underserved communities (Meltzer and Kerry 2019; USTR 2022e). The mandate to balance these priorities exists both at the level of individual policy measures and for aggregate U.S. policy, making coordination across agencies within the U.S. government and between U.S. partners increasingly important. The approach the United States takes to international economic policy in this challenging environment sends a signal to businesses, consumers, and governments around the world about U.S. priorities. As such, it forms a key element of U.S. foreign policy.

Imperatives of Economic Partnerships in the Changing Global Environment

Confronting systemic vulnerabilities that have become more prominent over the past two years while preserving the benefits of international economic integration to the maximum extent will require close collaboration between the United States, its allies, and its partners. This subsection explores three critical policy objectives where cross-border trade and investment play an essential role in promoting economic well-being and for which there is a need to calibrate trade policy to meet current challenges: (1) building more resilient supply chains, (2) responding to adversarial or unfavorable political and economic policies abroad, and (3) safely advancing digital trade. Although the scope of this chapter is limited to these three areas, the United States and its allies and partners also face a broader mandate to update and strengthen the rules, norms, and institutions that underpin international business and economic relations in the twenty-first century environment. This includes facing sociopolitical challenges and combating climate change (CEA 2022, chap. 3). Existing institutions and frameworks for global dialogue and collaboration remain important as incubators for solutions to complex and evolving challenges (Staiger 2021b). Today's challenges also provide a critical opportunity for the United States to play a global leadership role, working with its allies and partners to chart a modern course for a greener, more inclusive, more resilient, and more secure global economy (box 3-4).

Box 3-4. The United States' New Approach to Economic Partnerships

The Biden-Harris Administration is pursuing deeper commercial ties through economic partnerships that address vulnerabilities to external shocks while making international trade and investment greener and fairer. The Indo-Pacific Economic Framework for Prosperity, a flagship effort, consists of four pillars. The trade pillar seeks to craft high-standard, inclusive, free, fair, and open trade commitments. The supply chain pillar seeks to establish commitments for supply chain transparency, diversity, and coordination. The clean economy pillar seeks cooperation on clean energy, decarbonization, and infrastructure. And the fair economy pillar seeks economic frameworks to enforce tax, antibribery, and anticorruption systems. Commitments within each of the four pillars will be designed to enhance the benefits for workers in the United States and around the world (White House 2022b).

Resilience during Global Supply Shocks

In the early days of the COVID-19 pandemic, disruptions in the supply of manufacturing inputs like semiconductors, consumer products like bicycles, and medical supplies and equipment made Americans acutely aware of the importance of "supply chain resilience"—that is, the ability of businesses and public services to continue to provide goods and services when a source of supply or distribution is suddenly unavailable. The past three years have demonstrated how shortfalls of inputs or equipment in one industry can disrupt production and distribution in linked industries, slowing overall economic output (Cerdeiro and Komaromi 2020). Furthermore, Americans have witnessed how supply disruptions can even put public health and safety at risk. This experience has motivated both firms and governments to take steps to build resilience.

Falling barriers to trade—induced by both policy and technological change—have enabled businesses to reach around the world to source the inputs and equipment that ultimately come together to produce the goods purchased by consumers and public service providers at lower cost, greater variety, and higher quality (Baldwin and Freeman 2022; de Loecker et al. 2016; Fan, Li, and Yeaple 2015; Krugman 1980). However, the inputs and equipment themselves are often also an amalgam of raw materials extracted in one country, processed in another, and combined with more materials in a third country. As a consequence of this global production process, firms and governments often have only a limited visibility of the critical nodes of supply chains, which limits their ability to evaluate or reduce their exposure to rising geopolitical tensions, climate-related disasters, and other risks. As such, researchers have emphasized that government support for initiatives to increase the visibility of supply chains, or to enhance supply chain transparency, can reduce the information costs of broader steps to increase resilience (CEA 2022, chap. 6; National Academies 2022).

Because stages of production take place globally, engaging with partner governments to collect and share information can make efforts to map and monitor supply chains more complete. Such collaboration can alert governments to potentially fruitful avenues to mitigate destabilizing supply dependencies and, because sharing information highlights cross-country interlinkages, it can catalyze coordinated responses during crises. Indeed, experts have argued that a sustained commitment by countries to share information and coordinate policies affecting the supply of critical health-related goods and services will be essential in preparing for future public health crises (Bown 2022c; National Academies 2022). Partnerships to increase supply chain transparency can also reduce the costs of gathering information to satisfy climate and other policies, such as those that aim to eliminate trade in products made with forced labor, like the Uyghur Forced Labor

Prevention Act in the United States (Baldwin and Freeman 2022). More generally, greater supply chain transparency gives both firms and consumers the information they need to "vote with their wallets" by choosing to buy from producers and vendors whose practices are consistent with their own values (Mollenkopf, Peinkofer, and Chu 2022). In this way, transparency can leverage market forces to reward and advance greener, more inclusive, and more secure business practices.

The Biden-Harris Administration has initiated several ongoing dialogues on supply chains that focus on sharing information, designing early warning systems for supply chain disruptions, developing technical standards, and facilitating private investment. These discussions have been held through the U.S.-EU Trade and Technology Council, the Quad Critical and Emerging Technologies Working Group, the Minerals Security Partnership, and the Indo-Pacific Economic Framework for Prosperity. The United States also conducts regular bilateral dialogues on supply chains with a number of countries, including Canada, Mexico, the United Kingdom, Japan, and South Korea.

These and other partnerships can further contribute to maximizing the benefits of government incentives to increase productive capacity for critical goods and materials—that is, traded goods that are essential building blocks for economically and intrinsically important goods and services, such as medical and energy supplies and core technologies (Baldwin and Freeman 2022; Miroudot 2021; IMF 2022a; OECD 2020b; White House 2021a). Cross-country coordination can reduce the risk that competing government subsidies lead to unproductive excess capacity or an oversupply that blunts incentives for further innovation. Likewise, since support from foreign governments can impose economic distortions on domestic competitors, frameworks for allies and partners to resolve differences can help to limit those distortions and avoid costly retaliatory measures (Bown and Hillman 2019; Staiger 2021b; Sykes 2015).

Finally, partnerships to encourage cooperation and communication about industry standards for traded goods and services can enhance the ability for trade to contribute to supply chain resilience. Though there are legitimate reasons for countries to have differing approaches to regulations and standards affecting product design and distribution, fragmentation of entire supply chains because of regulatory differences can decrease resilience. For example, divergent industry standards may make digital systems less interoperable or standard manufacturing inputs less substitutable across production systems, making it more costly to find alternative sources in the event of a supply disruption. As such, forums to develop internationally recognized product standards as well as those that facilitate information sharing on domestic regulatory measures play a critical role in facilitating the ability of trade and investment to promote resilience.

Box 3-5. Coordination Has Been Critical for the Success of the Sanctions Policy toward Russia

Russia's invasion of Ukraine on February 24, 2022 started the largest land conflict in Europe since at least the conflicts in the Balkans in the 1990s. The scale and brutality of this conflict marked an abrupt departure from the post–World War II—and in particular the post–Cold War—rules-based global political and economic order (National Security Council 2022). The coordinated response by the coalition of the United States and more than 30 allied and partner nations to impose costs on Russia and address the associated threats to the global economy highlights how pooling resources and acting in coordination to achieve a policy goal is often more effective than a unilateral approach (Aslund and Snegovaya 2021; Berner, Cecchetti, and Schoenholtz 2022).

To date, the coalition's sanctions against Russia have targeted key aspects of the Russian economy. Extensive financial sanctions have restricted capital flows into Russia, depriving it of revenues necessary to continue funding its war. For example, the United States has prohibited U.S. persons from making new investments in Russia, and the United States and its allies and partners have sanctioned major Russian financial institutions and taken action to remove major Russian banks from the SWIFT financial messaging system (CRS 2022a). Beginning in early 2022 and continuing through the year, foreign direct investment into Russia fell sharply (figure 3-iv), highlighting the scope and strength of coordinated financial sanctions and the private sector's responses to Russian aggression (OECD 2022b).

The coalition's member countries have also imposed extensive export controls and have revoked Russia's normal trade relations status,

Figure 3-iv. Real Russian Foreign Direct Investment Net Inflows, 2017–22

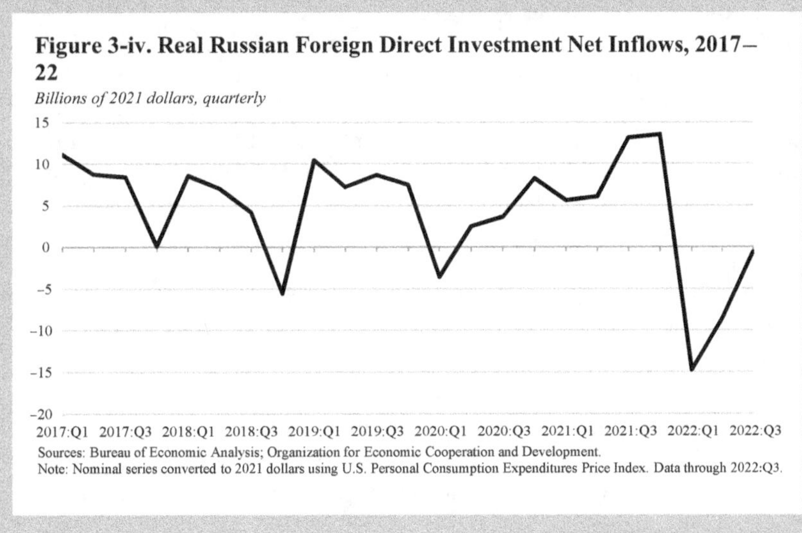

Sources: Bureau of Economic Analysis; Organization for Economic Cooperation and Development.
Note: Nominal series converted to 2021 dollars using U.S. Personal Consumption Expenditures Price Index. Data through 2022:Q3.

thereby increasing tariffs on imports from Russia and thus the cost of doing business with Russia (U.S. Department of Commerce 2022; Tai 2022). The United States' coordination with its allies and partners on export controls has hampered Russia's ability to backfill its imports of military or dual-use items (U.S. Department of State 2022b). Sanctions and export controls contributed to a sharp overall drop in Russia's imports and a shift in Russia's energy exports away from Europe, both of which researchers have characterized as key factors harming the Russian economy (Demertzis et al. 2022).

The International Monetary Fund estimates that the Russian economy contracted by 3.4 percent in 2022 (IMF 2022b). In addition, some analysts estimate that Russia's economy will continue to suffer significantly in the medium to long runs. For example, some predictions suggest that the Russian economy will not return to its prewar level of real GDP for five years or more (Economist Intelligence Unit 2022).

Importantly, recognizing the potential for negative spillovers to the global economy from financial and trade sanctions, the United States and its allies and partners have coordinated to relieve global market stress, including by ensuring trade channels remained open in selected commodities exported by Russia and Ukraine (IMF 2022b; OECD 2022c). This meant going after Russian energy in a measured way, by coordinating with partners and allies to allow energy transactions to continue while also designing price caps on seaborne Russian oil and petroleum products to limit Russia's revenue and ensure a stable global supply of energy (U.S. Department of the Treasury 2022a, 2022b). (The price cap on seaborne oil entered into force in December 2022. The price cap on petroleum products entered into force in February 2023.)

In addition, the United States has carved out agricultural commodities, fertilizer, and medical supplies from sanctions and issued extensive public guidance to ensure these authorizations are well understood (U.S. Department of the Treasury 2022c). The United States has also worked with the United Nations to find a pathway for Ukrainian wheat to reenter global markets: through the Black Sea Grain Initiative, more than 11.1 million metric tons of grains and other foodstuffs left Ukrainian ports between July 22, 2022, when the program took effect, and November 17, 2022 (United Nations 2022).

The global market's spillovers from Russia's war against Ukraine illustrate the broader themes of this chapter: the past year has been marked by profound new and lingering disruptions of global commerce. Nevertheless, global markets remain relatively robust, and economic coordination—a key element of the post–World War II era—between the United States and its allies and its partner countries has been critical. Without coordination in 2022, there was a nontrivial risk that divergent sanctions policies could have increased confusion and uncertainty in markets to the detriment of the global economy, notably global price stability. A lack of coordination also could have lessened the impact on the Russian economy of these sanctions. In coming years, continued coordination between the United States and its allies and partners will remain important for crafting effective policies to respond to these kinds of disruptions and to mitigate the economic and political uncertainty that may arise as a result of rising geopolitical tensions (Georgieva, Gopinath, and Pazarbasioglu 2022).

Responding to Geopolitical Challenges

In today's environment of rising geopolitical tensions and geostrategic competition, the United States' economic strength is one of its most profound sources of global power and influence. This strength is greatly enhanced by the collective economic strength that it can wield, along with its allies and partners that share its support for a free, open, prosperous, and secure world (National Security Council 2022). Coordination between the United States and its allies and partners can enhance the ability of aligned countries to provide shared security against and resilience in facing adversarial actions by, for example, enabling a network of alternative sourcing and market opportunities.

In a recent example, the United States and its allies and partners have been able to impose significant economic costs on Russia in response to its invasion of Ukraine in February 2022 (box 3-5). By coordinating their actions, U.S. allies and partners have been able to limit Russia's access to goods and services necessary to pursue its illegal war. Indeed, research has shown more broadly how coordinated economic actions more effectively limit a targeted country's ability to evade economic consequences than do unilateral measures (Bapat and Morgan 2009; Drury 1998; Peksen 2019).

Equally, economic partnerships can mitigate the economic consequences of adversarial actions targeted at the United States, its allies, and its partners. Just as concentrated dependencies on foreign adversaries can create vulnerabilities, diversified linkages with allies and partners can lessen them. Strong, diverse, and reliable economic linkages between trusted partners give businesses alternative markets to which they can shift their sourcing and sales if necessary, mitigating the impact of adversarial actions (Harrell, Rosenberg, and Saravalle 2018). For example, Russia has sought to weaponize Europe's dependence on its supply of natural gas in an attempt to weaken Europe's resolve to support Ukraine and to continue imposing costs on Russia in retaliation for its aggression. However, trade partnerships with the United States and other allies and partners have ensured that Europe has

Box 3-6. The U.S.-EU Energy Partnership Diminishes Russia's Leverage

One of Russia's biggest sources of economic leverage has been its dominance as a supplier of energy via its natural gas pipelines to Europe. Historically, Russia supplied Europe with roughly one-third of its gas (Corbeau 2022). Since the start of its invasion of Ukraine, Russia has cut pipeline deliveries of natural gas to Europe by more than half, and it may stop flows entirely in 2023 (IEA 2022b).

However, the EU was able to replace some Russian gas with imported liquefied natural gas, including from the United States, thus weakening Russia's ability to impose economic damage by restricting supplies of this critical source of energy for European households and industry. Economists estimate that natural gas shortages in Europe could have caused a contraction in some European economies of up to 6 percent if the global LNG market had been unable to respond (Flanagan et al. 2022). The ability of the United States to contribute to easing natural gas shortfalls has thus been critical.

Since Russia's invasion of Ukraine, the United States and the European Union have strengthened their cooperation on energy security. Through the Joint Task Force on Energy Security, the United States has made commitments to supply LNG to Europe through 2023 (White House 2022c). Through this partnership, the United States and the EU have agreed to address short-term energy supply issues with LNG while minimizing greenhouse gas emissions from LNG through measures to increase energy efficiency, reduce demand for gas, and regulate methane emissions. The task force has also led to additional commitments to advance renewable energy by expediting renewable energy projects and accelerating the deployment of clean energy technologies (White House 2022d).

The United States is also strengthening its bilateral partnerships with European countries to increase energy security, empower global decarbonization efforts, and achieve net-zero economies in hard-to-abate energy sectors through clean nuclear energy technology. In 2022, the United States announced its support for the Front-End Engineering Design study to provide the basis for the deployment of a small modular reactor power plant in Romania (U.S. Department of State 2022c); support for a pilot of commercial-scale production of clean fuels from small modular reactors in Ukraine (U.S. Department of State 2022d); and technical assistance for the inaugural civil nuclear project in Poland (U.S. Department of Energy 2022). These investments will help reduce dependence on Russian energy in Eastern Europe in both the medium and long term.

had the ability to shift to alternative energy sources, limiting the damage of Russia's coercive behavior on households, businesses, and workers (box 3-6).

Promoting Opportunity and Managing Risks in Digital Trade

As discussed earlier in this chapter, digital trade is poised to expand dramatically as work and consumption increasingly take place online; as the Internet of Things digitally connects more everyday objects; and as frontier technologies, for which masses of data are a fundamental input, such as AI, continue to develop. Digital trade may also provide solutions for some of the core challenges to global trade and investment discussed above. For example, with technologies like 3-D printing or other forms of so-called additive manufacturing, digital information flows can potentially facilitate the substitution of entire stages of manufacturing supply chains that currently involve the physical movement of goods, improving resilience in the presence of supply disruptions (Freund, Mulabdic, and Ruta 2022). Likewise, products in the growing "TradeTech" industry use advanced technologies, including AI, to enable supply chain transparency and traceability. These products could reduce the cost of ensuring that supply chains meet security, social, and environmental criteria that make trade safer, greener, and more equitable (Capri and Lehmacher 2021). However, digital trade also creates vulnerabilities that must be managed, especially given rising geopolitical tensions.

Digital trade has two fundamental requirements. The first is the infrastructure and equipment that transmit, store, and process data flows, including the network of underwater fiber-optic cables that carry more than 95 percent of international data (Comini, Foster, and Srinivasan 2021; Morcos and Wall 2021; World Economic Forum 2020). The second is a regulatory environment that permits the flow of data across borders with appropriate safeguards. Absent guardrails, digital trade can introduce potentially critical risks to economic well-being and national security through both of these gateways (Meltzer 2020).

The risks involved are manifest and nontrivial. Among the most salient are cybersecurity risks: The constant flow of large volumes of digital information creates an appealing target for the theft of data. This can allow competitors to capture intellectual property, including trade secrets, that threaten American businesses. It can result in unauthorized access to Americans' sensitive personal information, violating their privacy and potentially enabling financial or other crimes. Digital technology can allow goods and services traders to falsify information, potentially facilitating the evasion of national laws, regulations, and standards. Digital systems can also be manipulated or disabled remotely, potentially compromising national defense and critical infrastructure (Meltzer 2020). Estimates suggest that the economic cost of security breaches of information and technology assets during 2020 were as high as 6 percent of global GDP (or about $6 trillion). Other studies suggest that the costs are disproportionately high for critical industries like health care, transportation, energy, and financial services (IBM 2022; UNCDF 2022).

The expansion of the digital economy modifies existing markets and creates new ones, bringing new challenges to protecting consumers and workers and promoting competition. For example, the difficulties of verifying identity and quality online can compromise consumer protection laws and labor market protections (Goldfarb and Tucker 2019). Likewise, the importance of large userbases and quantities of data, and the ability of digitally enabled companies to attract suppliers of products and consumers from all over the world creates new market concentration dynamics and poses new challenges to regulators focused on competition policy (see chapter 8).

Governments employ a variety of measures to address these challenges by regulating the movement, storage, and processing of data. Regulations affecting digital trade generally fall into a few categories. First, data flow restrictions—for example, limits on access to digital media—may be used to protect intellectual property rights or enhance security, among other objectives. Second, so-called data localization policies—government regulations that determine where and how data related to their citizens, government, and businesses are stored—may be used to enhance consumer privacy and facilitate regulation (Casalini and González 2019; CFR 2022). Such policies may also reflect domestic economic priorities to try to protect industry from international competition.

These regulatory measures can mitigate some risks associated with digital trade, but they can also blunt the very benefits they are put in place to protect (Meltzer 2020). For example, data flow restrictions can hamper innovation, which benefits from sharing information and knowledge across borders (Valero 2016; White House 2022e). These restrictions can be particularly detrimental for the development and use of AI technologies, which rely on the availability of large data sets and are increasingly prominent in business and important for national security. The ability to aggregate, store, process, and transmit data across borders is similarly critical for the financial services sector and its development (Carr, French, and Lowery 2020). Similarly, data localization requirements can increase vulnerability to cyberthreats by concentrating data, thus making systems easier to target (Bauer et al. 2014). These requirements can also make integrated risk management, including monitoring and detecting fraud and cybersecurity risks, more difficult for global firms and institutions to conduct—particularly those in the financial services sector. Mismatches in equipment standards and regulations can limit system interoperability and thus the resilience of digital systems.

International cooperation to define the vulnerabilities associated with data flows and digital supply chains and the regulatory measures that diminish them can reduce the risks and enhance the economic benefits of digital trade (Ahmed 2019; Casalini et al. 2019; Huang, Madnick, and Johnson 2019; OECD 2015, 2022d). Efforts to enhance workers' rights and increase consumer protections from cybercrime and fraud that crosses borders are integral to these efforts. Indeed, scholars, policymakers, and business leaders have all emphasized the importance of creating an international digital architecture that promotes trust in data flows (CFR 2022). To do so, governments must grapple with how to provide a regulatory system that is safe and secure without unnecessarily restricting the benefits of trade. Best practices in international trade suggest that regulations should be transparent, should be nondiscriminatory for like products and services, and should not be more

Box 3-7. U.S. Digital Trade Initiatives

Digital trade is an increasingly prominent element of various international working groups and agreements, reflecting its importance for inclusive economic growth and security and the challenges policymakers around the world face in developing appropriate and consistent regulatory approaches. Attesting to the focus that the Biden-Harris Administration has placed on ensuring that digital trade benefits people as workers and consumers, the United States has led efforts to foster trust in the digital economy, support innovation and competition, promote a resilient and secure digital infrastructure, ensure consumer protection and privacy, and address discrimination. It is pursing these efforts by cooperating in regional partnerships that include the Indo-Pacific Economic Framework for Prosperity, the World Trade Organization's (WTO's) Joint Statement Initiative on Electronic Commerce, the Americas Partnership for Economic Prosperity, and the U.S.-Central Asia Trade and Investment Framework Agreement, as well as bilateral engagements with the United Kingdom, Kenya, Taiwan, and other countries (CRS 2022b; USTR 2021, 2022a, 2022b, 2022c, 2022d, 2022e; White House 2022f). The United States has also actively participated in multilateral forums to exchange information on best practices and promote standards and frameworks for tackling the risks associated with digital trade. These include the WTO, the Asia-Pacific Economic Cooperation forum, the Organization for Economic Cooperation and Development, and the Group of Twenty and Group of Seven, which together cover a broad set of countries around the world (USTR 2022e).

burdensome or restrictive than is necessary to achieve their goals, including enhanced security and economic resilience (Casalini and González 2019).

In this regard, the Biden-Harris Administration is engaging with various forums to build this trusted system (box 3-7). These include working with partners and allies to promote an environment that fosters development of the global economy and facilitates robust cross-border data flows that are consistent with both privacy and security needs. However, given the rapid pace at which the digital economy is evolving and the variety of domestic regulatory objectives, negotiating every aspect of the digital regulation may not always be desirable or possible. In this context, frameworks to establish common principles and provide for regulatory transparency have tremendous value (Staiger 2021a).

Conclusion

The record-setting flows of trade and investment in 2022 demonstrate that the United States remains deeply connected with the global economy. However, disruptions such as those experienced during the COVID-19 pandemic and rising geopolitical tensions pose fundamental challenges to globally connected production systems. Though the shock from Russia's invasion of Ukraine reverberated primarily in global commodity markets, it also increased the level of geopolitical uncertainty, which was already elevated after two years of pandemic-induced stress. The unprovoked invasion of Ukraine has exposed and intensified geopolitical rifts that, along with the experience of the pandemic-induced supply shock, have increased the perceived risk and uncertainty associated with global goods trade and some types of cross-border investments. These uncertainty effects may have longer-term effects on trade as governments adjust their international economic policies and businesses change their global sourcing patterns. Certainly, the economic links between Russia and the rest of the world, and global markets for the commodities in which Russia is a key player, will be transformed. Preserving the benefits from international trade and investment, while protecting national security, addressing the effects of climate change (Tai 2021a; USTR 2022e; White House 2021b), and promoting resilience and equity in a revitalized domestic economy demands new policy approaches to respond to both existing and emerging risks.

Given the global nature of the challenges discussed in this chapter, the policy decisions that the United States, it allies, and its partners make now will reverberate in international trade and investment for some time. The importance of partnerships in the modern global economy cannot be overstated. Enhanced partnerships that feature commitments to share information and coordinate actions are essential to sustaining the economic dynamism and productivity delivered through global economic integration in uncertain times (Yellen 2022b). Institutional arrangements must evolve to ease tensions between openness on one hand, and security and domestic imperatives on the other hand (Staiger 2021b). Effective coordination both across and within governments can help to ensure that the individual policies that sum to the aggregate of international economic policy reflect a deliberate, coordinated policy direction that responds to today's challenges.

Chapter 4

Investing in Young Children's Care and Education

Investments in the earliest years of a child's life can generate substantial benefits, with returns over the child's lifetime that often considerably exceed costs. In particular, a large body of evidence demonstrates that early care and education (ECE) programs can improve children's short-term development and long-term well-being, producing benefits not only for them but for society as well.

ECE programs also support parents' employment, which has become increasingly important with the decline in households where a parent stays home to provide full-time childcare. Women's labor market options have grown considerably over the past 50 years, increasing the opportunity costs of staying out of or reducing time in the workforce (Yellen 2020). Both men and women point to caregiving and family responsibilities as a major obstacle for their career advancement, with mothers particularly likely to report career interruptions and reduced engagement in the labor force (Parker 2015; Pew Research Center 2022). The challenge of balancing work and family looms largest for the parents of young children not yet enrolled in K-12 schooling, and has ramifications across parents' careers.

As a result of these trends, a market for nonparental ECE services has developed. Care for young children is wide-ranging—from informal care (paid or unpaid) by relatives, neighbors, or in-home caregivers to formal care in home-based, center-based, or school settings.[1] This decentralized patchwork of providers caring for children in homes, centers, and schools stands in contrast to, for example, the more structured system of public K-12 education in the United States. Though the ECE market is one upon which many families rely (NCES 2018), and despite ample evidence that ECE programs can both effectively facilitate children's healthy development and support parents' employment, the ECE market often does not function well.

This chapter first presents evidence on the effects of ECE investments for children, their parents, and society. It then discusses ECE market challenges, including workforce turnover and low pay, the high costs of providing high-quality care, price sensitivity among ECE customers, the fragility of the childcare business model, and the resulting underprovision of high-quality ECE relative to what would be socially optimal. The chapter closes with a discussion of the role of public subsidies in supporting a better-functioning ECE market.

The Effectiveness of Early Childhood Investments

Ample research documents the benefits that ECE investments can generate—both directly, for children who participate and working parents who rely on the care, and indirectly, through spillovers to their families and communities. This section summarizes and highlights the relevant evidence on ECE investments' benefits for children and society, the role of ECE quality in improving outcomes, and the benefits of ECE for working parents.

Benefits for Children and Society

ECE investments support children's healthy development and early learning starting at birth, which cascades into longer-term and broader benefits for them, their communities, and the economy. A large body of research points

[1] This chapter employs the term "ECE" to encompass childcare, preschool, and prekindergarten (pre-K) programming, because there is often a significant overlap in how programs are structured, funded, and delivered. Childcare typically refers to programs serving children from infancy through school age, while preschool and pre-K commonly refer to programs aimed at the year or two before formal school entry. As such, preschool programs typically serve children ages three and four years old and often operate on a school-day and school-year schedule. The terms "childcare," "preschool," and "pre-K" are used in the chapter when the policy, research, or data in question pertain to a specific segment of the broader ECE landscape.

to ECE experiences as influential for children's short-term outcomes, such as school readiness and early social-emotional and cognitive skill development, as well as long-term outcomes like educational attainment, executive function, employment, and earnings (Deming 2009; Duncan and Magnuson 2013; Heckman and Kautz 2014; Weiland and Yoshikawa 2013). These long-term, positive effects have been demonstrated in studies of childcare, Head Start, and other model preschool programs (Bailey, Sun, and Timpe 2021; Campbell et al. 2014; Gray-Lobe, Pathak, and Walters 2023; Heckman et al. 2010; Herbst 2017).[2]

Some studies of short- and medium-term program effects find that improvements in test scores fade out over time. However, when these studies also track long-term outcomes, they find substantial improvements in life chances, despite the short-run evaporation of test score gains (Chetty et al. 2011; Deming 2009). Moreover, there are documented complementarities between ECE investments and subsequent school investments (Johnson and Jackson 2019). Recent evidence captures the intra- and intergenerational spillovers of ECE exposure to siblings and the children of those exposed to the ECE program (Barr and Gibbs 2022; García et al. 2021; García, Heckman, and Ronda 2021).

When deployed well, ECE investments can advance both economic efficiency and equity. The return on these investments manifests not only as improved individual life chances but also as societal benefits, in the form of greater productivity and economic growth; less individual reliance on government transfers; and fewer bad outcomes that are costly for society, such as poor health, high school dropout, and crime (Heckman and Masterov 2007). Figure 4-1 presents a stylized depiction of the return on investments at various stages of life, with examples of programs in each period. The figure shows how the Heckman curve, as it is known, maps the economic argument that \$1 invested earlier in life can yield a greater return than \$1 invested later (Heckman 2008). In other words, the efficacy of human capital investments likely declines with age, a conclusion that aligns with the science on a child's developing brain and its malleability during the infant and toddler years (Knudsen et al. 2006; Shonkoff and Phillips 2000). According to this argument, policies and programs targeted at the earliest years of life have the greatest potential to generate large individual and societal returns, followed by investments in the preschool years, when children are three to five years of age.

Research that estimates returns on human capital investments over a wide range of ages is generally consistent with the Heckman curve. In comprehensive assessments of the long-run benefits of specific early childhood programs, researchers estimate a \$7 to \$12 return on every \$1 invested in

[2] Head Start is the federally funded preschool program for children from low-income families; it began in 1965 as part of the War on Poverty (ECLKC 2022).

Figure 4-1. Return on Investment in Human Capital, by Age

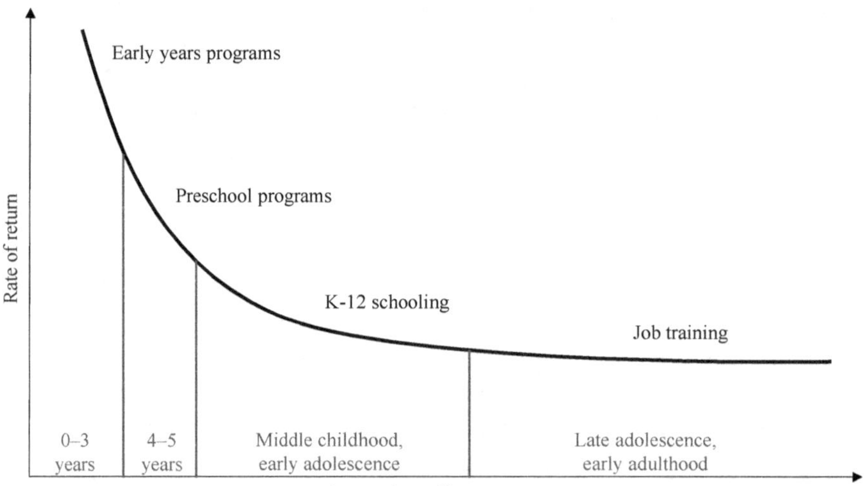

Source: Adapted from Heckman (2008).

Perry Preschool (Heckman et al. 2010), and even higher rates of return for the Carolina Abecedarian Project and the Carolina Approach to Responsive Education programs (García et al. 2020).

Defining Quality in ECE

Although there is solid evidence that ECE investments can be effective in the long run, less empirical evidence speaks directly to the *features* of ECE that matter for improving children's outcomes. This research gap is due in part to limited data on inputs to, and outputs from, ECE programming, and in part to ECE's multifaceted aims. In addition, the quality of the ECE experience is measured relative to the possible alternative settings where children could spend their time, and these settings vary widely. That said, there are some aspects that research suggests are important dimensions of high-quality ECE.

While parents' definitions of "good" ECE settings are likely subjective and include family-specific preferences for location, linguistic and cultural match, hours of operation, and program type, there have been efforts—across the United States' mixed delivery system—to define and measure program quality objectively.[3] Beyond the core safety and security requirements, systematic efforts to boost ECE quality include the Head Start Program Performance Standards and States' quality rating and improvement systems

[3] A mixed delivery system provides care through home-based, community-based, and school-based settings, and can involve funding and accountability from Federal, State, and local sources in addition to families paying directly for ECE services.

(Office of Child Care 2011). These systems rely on various components, depending on the State—including licensure, lead teachers' educational attainment, child–caregiver ratios, and other measures—and most States directly incentivize providers achieving higher levels of quality, as defined in the State's system. States make information on program quality publicly available. Though research has not definitively established links between quality rating and improvement systems and measurable child outcomes (Cannon et al. 2017), the evidence suggests that assignment to a low rating does lead programs to improve on the measured dimensions and influences parents' choices (Bassok, Dee, and Latham 2019).

An important, measurable dimension of ECE quality is the nature of relationships and interactions between ECE staff and children in the care setting. Evidence suggests that stable, attached child–caregiver relationships in children's earliest years provide a critical foundation for their subsequent healthy development (Hatfield et al. 2016; Pianta 1997; Sabol and Pianta 2012). Indeed, research points to the importance of the caregiver's focused attention, which means that having more early childhood educators, or educators who have been trained in how to productively engage with children, could generate economy-wide, long-term productivity gains (Blau and Currie 2006). Relatedly, research suggests that ECE staff turnover is associated with children's weaker language and social skill development (Caven et al. 2021). Childcare workers experiencing economic stress have a more difficult time fully engaging with children and offering a high-quality learning experience (Schlieber and Mclean 2020). Evidence also indicates that improvements in compensation and working conditions can significantly reduce turnover and are associated with better care and improved child outcomes (Bassok et al. 2021b; Grunewald, Nunn, and Palmer 2022; King et al. 2016).

Some comprehensive, model programs have generated large returns, but they are made up of a package of components—including home visits, parenting programs, and health and nutrition offerings—which makes it difficult to isolate the impact of specific features of these programs in that evidence base. Notably, ECE settings provide early academic skill building and educational inputs alongside other types of support for children's healthy development, including play-based and social activities, and physical and mental health and nutrition services. Box 4-1 explains the role of nutrition support in young children's development.

Benefits for Working Parents

In addition to benefits for children, ECE programming can be important for families because it allows parents to participate in the labor market while raising their children. In 2021, 62 percent of families with children under six

Box 4-1. Nutrition Support in Early Childhood

ECE settings often provide services and support beyond the classroom, including programs for parents, health services, and access to food. For example, from its inception in 1965, the Head Start program was designed to be a comprehensive early childhood development program, with an emphasis on health and nutrition components (Vinovskis 2005). Among young children, the Child and Adult Care Food Program (CACFP) provides funding for healthy meals and snacks for children in Head Start and other ECE programs. Research suggests that funding and standard-setting programs like the CACFP are associated with improvements in child nutrition offerings and reductions in households' food insecurity (Heflin, Arteaga, and Gable 2015; Korenman et al. 2013; Ritchie et al. 2012, 2015).

Researchers have established that increased access to healthier food—provided to children through nutrition assistance for their families or through meals while in childcare or at school—lead to improved health, cognitive functioning, and long-term well-being. Evidence from the introduction of both the Food Stamp Program—now the Supplemental Nutrition Assistance Program (SNAP)—and the Special Supplemental Nutrition Program for Women, Infants, and Children (WIC) across the United States suggests that both programs have improved children's early life health outcomes (Almond, Hoynes, and Schanzenbach 2011; Hoynes, Page, and Stevens 2011) and—if provided before age five—long-term economic outcomes (Bailey et al. 2020; Hoynes, Schanzenbach, and Almond 2016).

Young children can also interact with the National School Lunch Program, School Breakfast Program, and Special Milk Program offered in participating childcare, preschool, and pre-K settings. Several studies indicate that school meals can improve nutrition and health outcomes (Gundersen et al. 2012; Bhattacharya, Currie, and Haider 2006). Although there are a few exceptions (e.g., Schanzenbach and Zaki 2014), many studies conclude that higher participation in these meal programs leads to increases in academic achievement and educational attainment (Imberman and Kugler 2014; Frisvold 2015; Hinrichs 2010). These findings are consistent with clinical evidence that nutrition is important for cognitive performance (Alaimo, Olson, and Frongillo 2001; Wesnes et al. 2003).

Food assistance programs are an important tool to reduce food hardship for many Americans, particularly in times of economic distress. Though food insecurity had been trending down in the decade preceding the COVID-19 pandemic, most dramatically for Hispanic and Latino households (figure 4-i), nonwhite children experienced setbacks in food security in 2020 and 2021. Additionally, gaps that predate the COVID-19 pandemic remain between Black and Hispanic or Latino children and

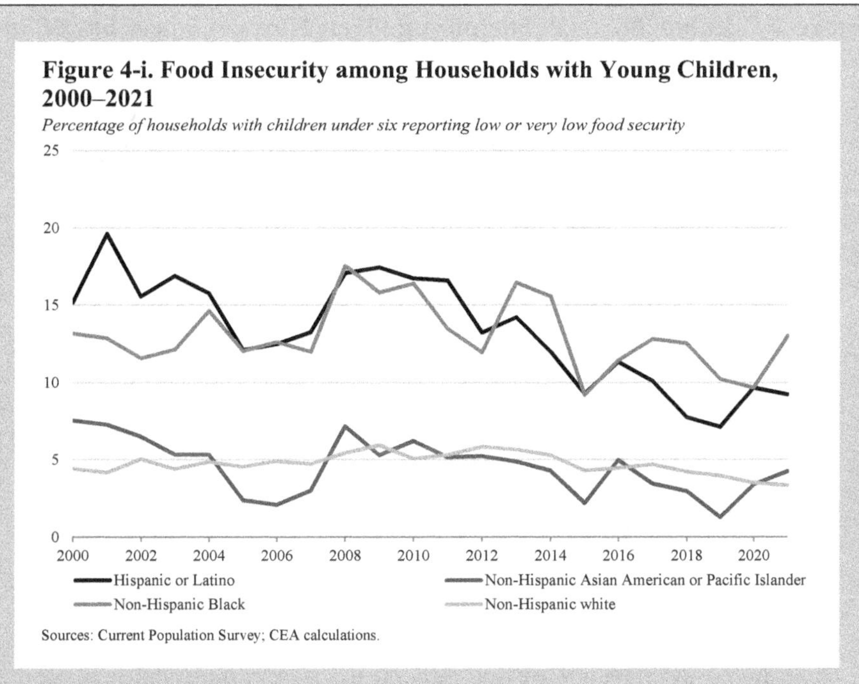

Figure 4-i. Food Insecurity among Households with Young Children, 2000–2021

Percentage of households with children under six reporting low or very low food security

Sources: Current Population Survey; CEA calculations.

white and Asian American or Pacific Islander children (U.S. Census Bureau 2021a). As of 2021, the rate of food insecurity was higher for households with children, for households with children under age six, and particularly for single-woman-headed households than it was for households overall (USDA 2022a).

As households with children face food insecurity, ECE settings and schools will continue to serve as an important source of nutritional assistance for children. Beginning in 2024, as part of ongoing efforts to advance families' food security, children who receive free or reduced-price school meals will have access to a permanent food assistance program to address the summer gap in access to nutrition support (USDA 2022b).

years had all parents in the household working (BLS 2022). In large part, this stems from a rise, over the past half century, in maternal labor force participation. From the mid-1970s to the mid-1990s, participation rates for both prime-age women and prime-age mothers grew by about 20 percentage points. Since then, both rates have plateaued and have even experienced periods of decline, although they remain higher today than in the mid-1970s (figure 4-2).

Figure 4-2. Labor Force Participation Over Time, by Maternal Status

Percentage of prime-age women in the labor force

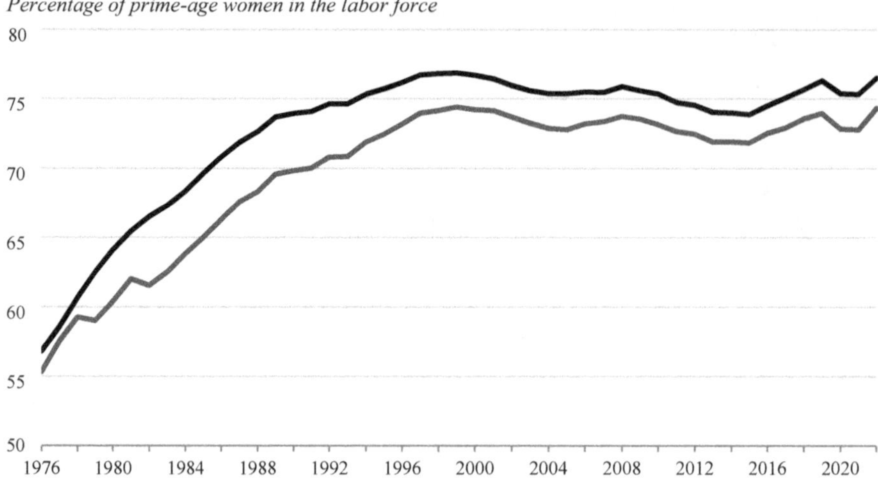

Sources: Current Population Survey; CEA calculations.

As noted in chapter 1 of this *Report*, the rise in maternal labor force participation occurred in tandem with a rise in paid ECE and senior care. Time use data suggest that, among mothers of young children, more highly educated mothers in particular have reduced time spent on care of their children concurrent with the rise in maternal employment (Flood et al. 2022). While increased formal ECE was likely partially the *result* of maternal participation, research indicates that ECE also *enables* it (Herbst 2022; Morrissey 2017). Specifically, research examining ECE availability, expansion, and subsidization finds that ECE has large, positive effects on maternal employment (Blau and Tekin 2007; Gelbach 2002; Herbst 2017). Several studies of programs in other countries—specifically Canada, Germany, and Norway—also confirm the responsiveness of mothers' employment to ECE expansions (Baker, Gruber, and Milligan 2008; Bauernschuster and Schlotter 2015; Finseraas, Hardoy, and Schøne 2016; Lefebrve and Merrigan 2008).

Evidence from across ECE contexts, including childcare subsidy receipt and the introduction of public preschool and kindergarten programs, suggests that certain mothers' employment is most affected. Those mothers who respond to program introduction and availability by working more are those whose youngest child is eligible for the program, and those who are relatively disadvantaged (i.e., single mothers and those with lower levels of education) (Cascio 2009; Cascio and Schanzenbach 2013; Fitzpatrick 2010, 2012; Gelbach 2002; Tekin 2005, 2007). Research on the Head Start program similarly documents that program access improved employment and earnings outcomes for single mothers (Wikle and Wilson 2022).

In addition to increasing parents' likelihood of working at all, policies that expand access to ECE can boost their productivity in the workplace by allowing them to get additional education or job training and increasing the likelihood they will work *full time* (Davis et al. 2018; Herbst and Tekin 2011). These effects may have been especially important in the context of the COVID-19 pandemic, which, according to survey evidence, made parents, and mothers in particular, likely to reduce their work hours or productivity even while remaining in their jobs (Pew Research Center 2022). Increased access to ECE, such as through policies to expand availability and reduce costs, would likely enable more parents to work, which could bolster long-run economic growth and expand the economy's productive capacity. However, as the next section describes, the market for ECE faces fundamental challenges, hampering families' ability to secure ECE that meets their needs.

Challenges in the Market for Early Care and Education

Although, as noted above, investments in children can make a difference not only for the children themselves but also for their families and communities in ways that spill over to society, it is not at all clear the ECE market works for both providers and families. Important questions include: can families that need care access a well-functioning market to meet their needs? And, is the supply of ECE inefficiently low from society's perspective? The evidence indicates that the care economy faces fundamental challenges in terms of both supply and demand, and thus there is an important opportunity for effective policies to improve the functioning of this market.

On the supply side, a core concern is whether care businesses that invest in higher quality—such as through better staff compensation, professional development and coaching for early educators, and lower child–caregiver ratios—can recoup the increased costs while also charging rates that families can afford.

On the demand side, families face liquidity constraints, given that they are more likely to be financially strapped when their children are young and the parents are in the early, and relatively unstable, years of their earnings trajectories (Davis and Sojourner 2021). That is, many families simply lack the resources to invest in high-quality care when it is needed and cannot borrow against future earnings to do so at competitive interest rates. High-quality care can consume a large fraction of families' budgets, especially for low-income families (Landivar, Graf, and Rayo 2023; U.S. Department of the Treasury 2021). As such, many families are sensitive to the price of childcare and may respond by forgoing market-based care and instead relying on parental care or informal arrangements (Morrissey 2017).

Workforce Challenges

Early care and education is a labor-intensive industry, and, as discussed above, a stable, qualified workforce is an essential ingredient in the provision of high-quality ECE services. According to the 2019 National Survey of Early Care and Education (NSECE), a nationally representative survey of childcare providers conducted before the pandemic, the average departure rate of caregivers in center-based care—the share of staff members who work directly with young children who left the focal program in the last 12 months—was 17 percent. Though this rate of turnover is comparable to the public teaching profession (16 percent), half of teaching departures are to another teaching position, whereas evidence suggests that many childcare providers leave the industry entirely (NCES 2016). Research in Louisiana suggests even higher turnover overall—finding that more than one-third of ECE educators depart annually, and that most turnover is a departure from the ECE profession (Bassok et al. 2021a). Evidence also demonstrates that turnover varies considerably across centers, with nearly 10 percent losing more than half their workforce in each year of the three-year study period (Doromal et al. 2022), a and higher turnover in centers paying low wages and those serving infants and toddlers (Caven et al. 2021).

The 2019 NSECE also documents that the average longevity for a home-based ECE provider was relatively short, with about 46 percent of home-based providers having operated five or fewer years (NSECE 2019). Though these survey data predate the pandemic, the evidence suggests that periods of low unemployment in the broader economy are related to higher turnover in childcare employment (Brown and Herbst 2022). Thus, the tight labor market during the pandemic recovery period could exacerbate high workforce turnover and slow the recovery from pandemic-induced job losses in childcare (see box 4-2). Churn in the workforce prevents workers from gaining experience in the field and impedes staff continuity in ECE settings, potentially reducing the quality of care.

The workforce challenges for ECE largely stem from workers' low pay. As described below, this low pay results, in part, from the price sensitivity of consumers and the thin profit margins of care businesses. Childcare workers, who are described in more detail in box 4-3, make low wages relative to typical nonsupervisory workers. In the United States in December 2022, the typical production or nonsupervisory worker made, on average, $28.19 an hour, yet production or nonsupervisory childcare workers earned considerably less, $17.95 an hour (BLS 2023). According to one analysis, childcare workers earn 23 percent less on average than workers in other occupations with similar composition by age, education, and other demographic characteristics (Gould 2015). In particular, comparing the earnings of childcare, pre-K, kindergarten, and elementary school teachers illustrates

Box 4-2. The American Rescue Plan and Support for Childcare

At the beginning of the COVID-19 pandemic, the childcare industry was severely affected. Between February 2020 and April 2020, childcare employment fell more than 35 percent. Recognizing the disruptions of the care infrastructure wrought by the pandemic, the American Rescue Plan (ARP) Act allocated funds to stabilize childcare, including $24 billion in funding for the new Child Care Stabilization Program. Data from the U.S. Department of Health and Human Services (2022; also see White House 2022) indicate that more than 200,000 childcare programs in the United States, with total capacity to serve as many as 9.5 million children, have received funding through these grants, intended to help the industry recover by providing grants to childcare programs to help cover operational costs such as wages and benefits, rent and utilities, and program materials and supplies. As of the fall of 2022, the most common uses of funds were personnel costs at centers, and rent and utilities at family childcare homes.

These grants likely have had economic consequences that extend beyond their effects on childcare workers and providers. As described earlier in this chapter, access to childcare is an important input for parental employment, particularly for women (e.g., Morrissey 2017). This relationship between employment and access to childcare likely helps to

Figure 4-ii. Percent Change in Maternal Employment

Percent change in the 12-month rolling average of the employment–population ratio relative to January 2020

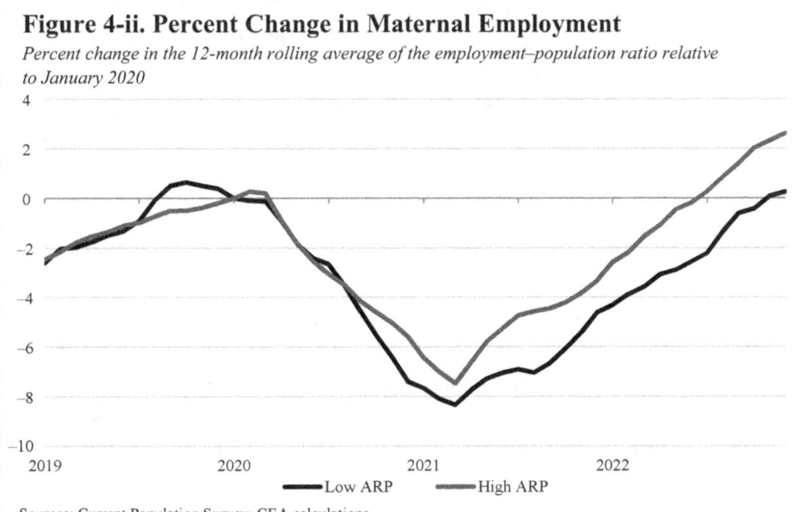

Sources: Current Population Survey; CEA calculations.

Note: Data are restricted to mothers who have at least one child under six. "Low ARP" refers to employment among those living in the half of core-based statistical areas (CBSAs) with the lowest provider capacity covered by American Rescue Plan (ARP) funding per population. "High ARP" refers to employment among those living in the half of CBSAs with the highest provider capacity covered by ARP funding per population.

explain the significant, disproportionate drop that women experienced in their attachment to the labor force at the beginning of the COVID-19 pandemic. Whereas the overall employment–population ratio (i.e., the employment rate) fell by 16 percent between February 2020 and April 2020, the employment rate for women fell by 18 percent. Several studies indicate that during these months, employment for mothers of young children was particularly hard hit (Boesch et al. 2021; Collins et al. 2021; Heggeness 2020; Tüzemen 2021).

The CEA's analysis comparing maternal employment among those living in areas with relatively more provider capacity (as a share of population) supported by ARP funding to employment among those living in areas with less provider capacity supported by funding suggests that maternal employment has recovered more quickly in areas with greater capacity supported by stabilization grants (figure 4-ii). This analysis does not rule out other potential explanations of the differences in maternal employment across low- and high-ARP places, including underlying differences in community characteristics, but it points to an area for further research to better understand the effects of ARP childcare stabilization funds on the childcare industry and the parents who rely on it.

the extent of low compensation among care workers. On average, childcare workers earn less than half, and preschool workers earn just over half, the average annual earnings of kindergarten and elementary school teachers (BLS 2021a). Childcare workers also rarely receive nonwage employee benefits; only 15 percent of these workers belong to an employer- or union-sponsored health insurance plan, compared with 58 percent of all workers (Gould 2015; BLS 2021b).

In their labor-intensive industry, which typically has families' payments as the sole source of revenue, childcare providers have limited options to cuts costs or raise revenue in order to pay higher wages. Low pay means that ECE workers are more likely to have an income below the Federal poverty line; 1 in 7 childcare workers lives in a family with an income below this threshold, compared with about 1 in 16 families overall (Gould 2015). In addition, 53 percent of childcare workers rely on a public assistance program, such as Medicaid or SNAP, compared with 21 percent of the United States' workforce as a whole (Whitebook et al. 2018).

The High Costs of High-Quality Care

Given the importance of ensuring safe, secure, and high-quality ECE for infants and young children, and to make quality more visible to families,

Box 4-3. Who Works in ECE?

Most childcare workers are women, and they are disproportionately women of color (Banerjee, Gould, and Sawo 2021). Figure 4-iii shows the breakdown of childcare employment by gender and race/ethnicity compared with the overall workforce. About 14 percent of childcare workers are Black and about 24 percent are Hispanic, higher than the share of Black and Hispanic workers in the overall workforce (6 and 8 percent, respectively).

Additionally, historical norms that have devalued care work, typically performed by women, and labor market discrimination affecting women and people of color may exacerbate low pay. The current composition of the care workforce has legacies in slavery, when Black women acted as caregivers through coercion and force (Glenn 2012). Since the end of the Civil War, care workers have been shut out from workforce protections, such as those enacted under the New Deal (Burnham and Theodore 2012). Lawmakers continue to exclude many care workers from labor protections and benefits, including minimum wage laws, paid leave, retirement benefits, and overtime pay. The historical roots of the devaluation of care work, and the ongoing barriers to equal treatment that women and people of color face in the labor market, likely continue to affect the pay and working conditions for ECE workers today.

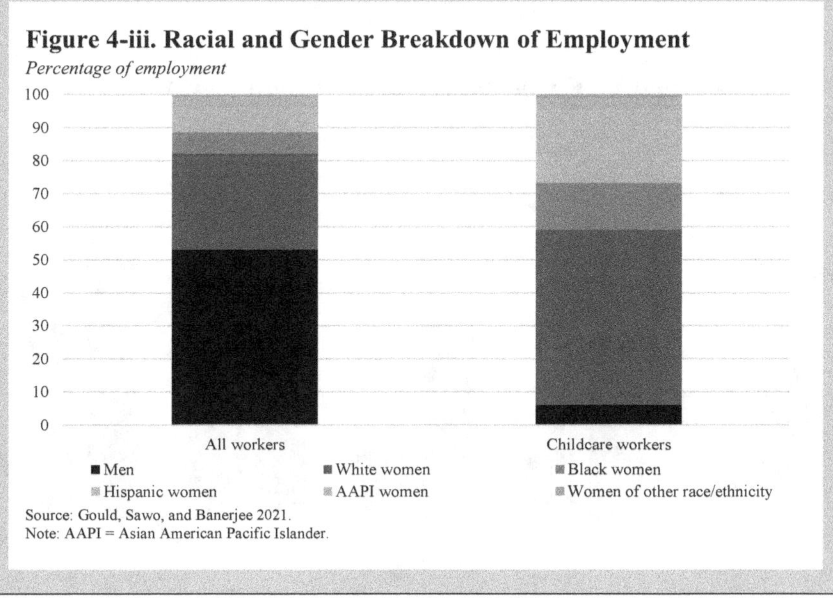

Source: Gould, Sawo, and Banerjee 2021.
Note: AAPI = Asian American Pacific Islander.

there are rules and standards for formal (i.e., licensed and regulated) childcare providers. Some regulations vary by State, and others are Federal. For example, the Child and Adult Care Food Program's Child Care Standards, which some childcare centers must meet to receive certain Federal reimbursements, require childcare centers to have at least one early childhood educator for every four children under age three (but at least six weeks of age), and one educator for every six children between age three and six. These quality regulations are critical for ensuring children's safety and well-being, and insofar as they require higher staffing levels and childcare workers with in-demand skills, they necessarily increase providers' costs of doing business.

Additionally, though industries such as manufacturing have seen large technological advances leading to improvements in quality and labor productivity, these advances are less applicable to labor-intensive, service-based industries such as ECE. Like those for many services, 60 to 80 percent of childcare business expenses are for labor (Workman 2018). Increasing wages in other industries that have higher labor productivity gains means that wages for care workers must also increase for care businesses to compete for workers, thus raising overall prices. As noted above, stable child–caregiver relationships are a key component of high-quality ECE, and one documented way to improve continuity in the ECE workforce is through competitive pay (Bassok et al. 2021b; Grunewald, Nunn, and Palmer 2022).

Figure 4-3. Formal ECE Consumption, by Income Level

Percent

Income quintile	Share of households receiving care	Share of households paying for care
1	29	11
2	34	13
3	37	17
4	37	21
5	60	49

Sources: 2019 National Survey of Early Care and Education; CEA calculations.
Note: Early care and education (ECE) measures are limited to children under age 6 and to "formal" ECE, which includes paid individuals (with no prior relationship), center-based care, preschool, community-based care, and other organizational ECE on a regular and irregular basis.

High-quality ECE is fundamentally an expensive service, so it is not surprising that its use and costs vary considerably across the income distribution. Figure 4-3 shows formal ECE consumption by family income level, giving the proportions of both households receiving care and those paying for care. Both measures increase with income, and families across the income distribution are participating in some subsidized care, though much more pronouncedly, in the lowest income quintiles. Only about 15 percent of households with young children in the lowest quintile pay for ECE, while 53 percent of those in the highest quintile pay for ECE (NSECE 2020).

Although low-income families more often qualify for subsidized services, those that pay for ECE devote a larger fraction of their income to ECE expenses than middle- and high-income families. Recently released data from the Department of Labor's National Database of Childcare Prices document that prepandemic median childcare prices for one child account for between 8 and 19 percent of median family income in communities across the country, with even higher prices for infant care (Landivar, Graf, and Rayo 2023). For low-income families, that burden is even more pronounced. Figure 4-4 shows average annual ECE expenses as a share of income for all households with young children receiving formal ECE and for households that pay for ECE. For those paying for ECE, the share of income spent on ECE declines sharply by income level. The lowest-income families that pay for formal ECE spend one-third of their annual income on ECE,

Figure 4-4. Average Annual Expenses for Formal ECE as a Proportion of Income, by Income Level

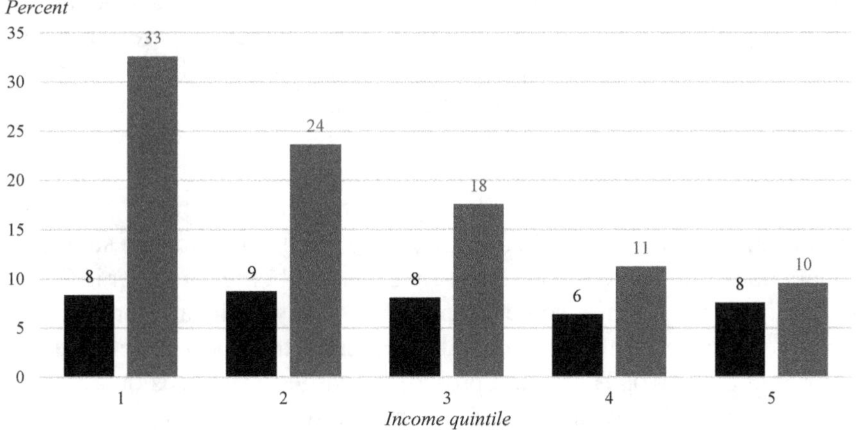

Sources: 2019 National Survey of Early Care and Education; CEA calculations.
Note: Early care and education (ECE) measures are limited to children under age 6 and to "formal" ECE, which includes paid individuals (with no prior relationship), center-based care, preschool, community-based care, and other organizational ECE on a regular and irregular basis.

compared with the highest-income families, which spend about 10 percent of their annual income on ECE.

ECE Pricing and Price-Sensitive Consumers

As noted above, businesses supplying care services face a pool of consumers with financial constraints that may limit their ability to afford the cost of high-quality care. In particular, low- and moderate-income families tend to be more likely than higher-income ones to curtail their purchases of these services if the price rises—by forgoing nonparental care altogether or by relying on informal, unpaid, or lower-quality ECE services.

The budget constraints that families face in turn affect the supply of high-quality care. ECE providers serving families that are more sensitive to prices may be unable to afford costly quality improvements. In supplying care, providers choose their investment in quality at the point where their marginal revenues equal their marginal costs—that is, where an additional $1 invested is equal to an additional $1 earned. Providers serving low-income families have little economic ability to improve quality from a relatively low level; their clients may not be able to pay more for higher-quality care due to their budget constraints. In theory, with full information and accessible credit markets, parents may be willing to borrow against future earnings to access high-quality ECE that meets their and their young children's needs. However, such credit is not generally available. As such, families must pay for childcare out of their current income, which may be particularly constrained when children are young and parents are in the low-earning stages of their careers (Davis and Sojourner 2021).

Providers serving high-income families, conversely, can more easily charge higher prices to recoup the costs of their investments in quality. When these providers invest in better-quality care, their clients are generally able to pay higher prices, in large part because their family budget/income can accommodate it. This aspect of the ECE market gives rise to a stronger relationship between quality and total revenues among providers serving high-income families.

ECE pricing is also complicated by parents who stay home full time and informal care providers. The most recently available evidence suggests that about one in five parents was a full-time, stay-at-home caregiver in 2016 (Livingston 2018). Further, some people who supply childcare services do so while also caring for their own children, altering their cost-benefit calculus (Porter et al. 2010). These care providers charge lower rates on average than larger, licensed providers, exerting downward pressure on prices in the broader ECE market and attracting families that cannot afford center-based care (National Women's Law Center 2018). Parents may also shift to relatives, neighbors, or in-home providers on an ad hoc or more permanent basis when market-based options fail to meet their needs. Evidence suggests that these informal ECE settings are often of lower quality than parental care and center-based care (Bassok et al. 2016; Flood et al. 2022).

In 2018, 88 percent of childcare businesses were sole proprietors (i.e., with no employees other than themselves), and the average receipts per establishment were about $16,000 (U.S. Census Bureau 2018). Even under the unreasonable assumption that providers had no expenses, these receipts put the average sole proprietor at about the 20th percentile of the earnings distribution. Indeed, absent other resources, at these revenue levels, it would be difficult to sustain a family by running a childcare business. These data suggest that some providers may supply care at below-market rates, perhaps as supplementary income while providing care for their own children or family members, with altruistic motives, or because of limited employment options.

Business Model Fragility

As noted throughout this chapter, the ECE market is fundamentally challenged because it cannot provide high quality at prices families can afford. The ECE market has other fundamental characteristics that are factors in its business model, which are vulnerable to economic headwinds. Researchers have confirmed that childcare responds more strongly to negative economic shocks than other low-wage industries and takes longer to recover from recessions than the rest of economy (Brown and Herbst 2022). In sum, ECE is a highly fragmented industry, populated by small firms, often sole proprietorships, that pay low wages, have high labor turnover, and face low profit margins of less than 1 percent for most childcare providers (Carson and Mattingly 2020; Grunewald and Davies 2011; U.S. Department of the Treasury 2021).

Liquidity challenges for childcare business owners explain why even a few weeks without revenue is often untenable for ECE providers, as became evident during the COVID-19 pandemic. According to the CEA's analysis of November 2021 Small Business Pulse data, 82 percent of social assistance small businesses (which include childcare businesses) reported large or moderate negative effects of the pandemic on the business, compared with 66 percent of small businesses in general. In the same data, almost double the number of social assistance businesses (nearly 4 percent) reported temporarily or permanently closing, compared with all small businesses (2 percent). In 2021, social assistance businesses were also more likely to report that they anticipated needing financial support or additional capital in the next six months.

The demographic composition of childcare providers may exacerbate the issue of limited access to capital. The owners of private childcare

Figure 4-5. Ratio of Young Children to Childcare Capacity in 2018

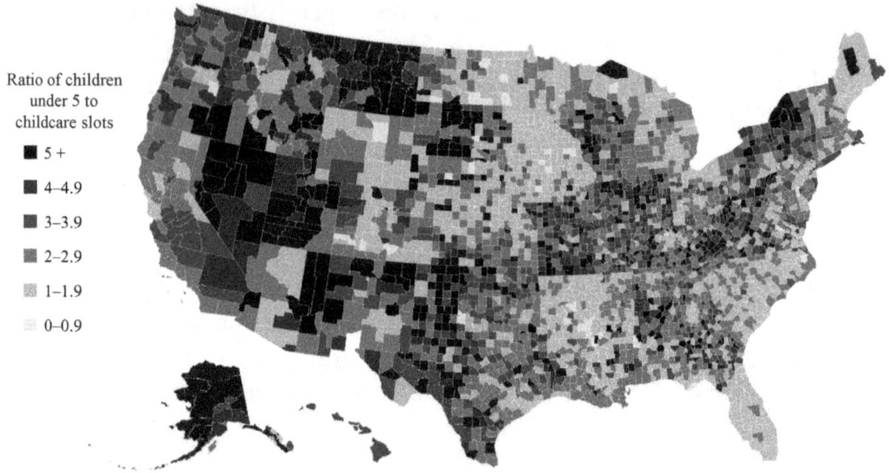

Sources: Center for American Progress (2020); CEA calculations.

businesses are disproportionately women and people of color, aligning with the composition of the ECE workforce (as shown in box 4-2), and these providers may face more pronounced barriers in capital markets. Almost all childcare businesses—nearly 97 percent—are owned by women, while half are minority-owned (National Women's Business Council 2020; Mueller 2020). Yet women and minorities tend to have fewer assets to get them through tough times. One study indicates that even after controlling for other differences, small business owners who are women or people of color have lower loan approval rates and pay higher interest on loans for their businesses (Asiedu, Freeman, and Nti-Addae 2012).

Participation in and Availability of ECE

Data on ECE participation represent the intersection of the supply of and the demand for ECE slots; participation requires both the availability of a slot, referring to its provision, along with take-up of the slot, which incorporates a family's care preferences and needs. That is, for a family to access ECE in the United States, there must be an available slot that also meets the family's needs in terms of cost, location, operating hours, and quality, among other factors. According to data on childcare capacity and population by county, more than half of Americans live in neighborhoods where the number of young children outpaces the availability of licensed childcare slots by three to one or more (Malik et al. 2018). Figure 4-5 maps the ratio of children under age five to licensed childcare slots across U.S. counties.

The ratios of young children to childcare slots are larger when looking at infant and toddler care, as shown in figure 4-6 for counties in States with

Figure 4-6. Ratio of Infants and Toddlers to Childcare Capacity in 2018

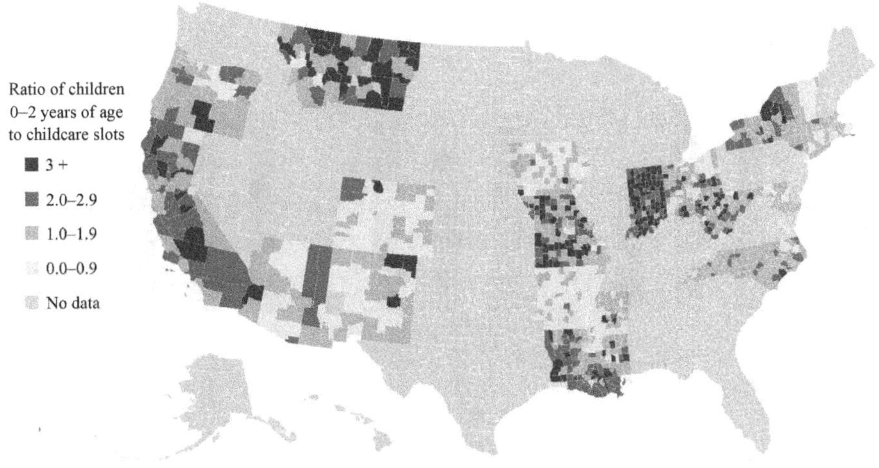

Sources: Malik et al. (2018); CEA calculations.

available data for 2018. In one analysis, researchers found that 80 percent of the counties for which they had data had at least three infants and toddlers for every childcare slot for children under three (Jessen-Howard, Malik, and Falgout 2020). Rural and low-income communities were more likely to have high child-to-capacity ratios—which could reflect lower demand for nonparental ECE in those areas—and Hispanic families were more likely to live in areas with high ratios (Malik et al. 2018).

An undersupply of ECE slots may exacerbate a lack of participation in formal ECE. In 2019, 53 percent of children age three to six years who were not yet enrolled in elementary school were in a formal preschool setting outside the home (U.S. Census Bureau 2021b).[4] Prepandemic data point to existing gaps by race, ethnicity, and family socioeconomic status. Hispanic children, in particular, have historically participated in formal care at lower rates, and Black children more likely to be in the care of relatives than other children (de Brey et al. 2019). Lower-income and disadvantaged families have used nonparental care at lower rates, though participation among families at the lowest end of the socioeconomic distribution resembles that of more advantaged families (de Brey et al. 2019; NCES 2022).

Many argue that the differences by socioeconomic status and region of the country in child participation in ECE is due to a lack of availability of suitable slots. However, is it possible that what appears to be a lack of availability—more young children than capacity—could in fact be the result of lower demand due to parents' preferences? Data sources, including surveys,

[4] In the October School Enrollment Supplement of the Current Population Survey, respondents are asked if the focal child attends "preschool" or "nursery school."

Figure 4-7. Excess Demand by Provider Type

Percentage of providers experiencing excess demand

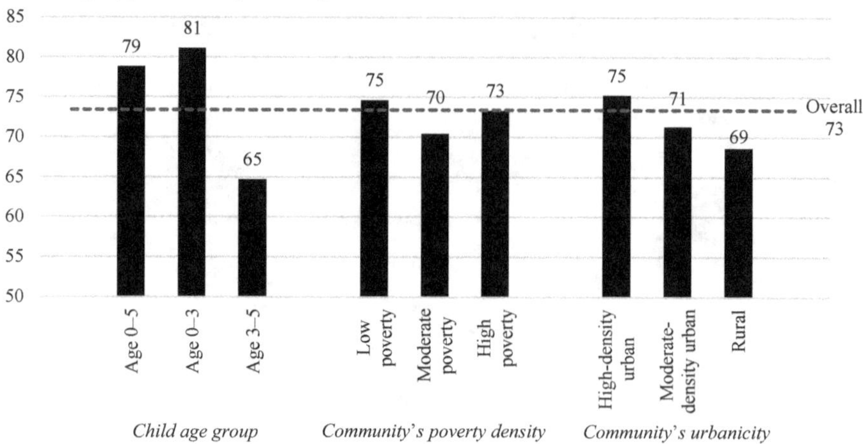

Sources: 2019 National Survey of Early Care and Education; CEA calculations.
Note: Excess demand is defined by whether providers have turned families away due to lack of capacity or had a waiting list in the past year. Line denotes the overall percentage of providers experiencing excess demand (73.4 percent).

can help to identify whether observed participation rates fall short of families' demand for ECE slots for their children. For example, to conduct the National Head Start Impact Study, researchers constructed a nationally representative sample of Head Start grantees. Because excess demand was a critical feature of the study design, grantees could only participate if they expected to be oversubscribed in the fall of 2002; 89 percent of Head Start grantees in the nationally representative sample were not serving all eligible children in the community who wanted Head Start (U.S. Department of Health and Human Services 2005). Analysis of prepandemic data found that there were 63 Head Start slots for every 100 income-eligible, preschool-age children who lived within 5 miles of a Head Start center (Ghertner and Schreier 2022).

In addition to the Head Start program, other data sources similarly document excess demand for ECE providers' limited slots. National Survey of Early Care and Education data for 2019 suggest that 73 percent of center-based care providers experienced excess demand for childcare slots, in that they either rejected families because they were too full or maintained waiting lists. As presented in figure 4-7, excess demand varied by provider type. Providers serving only infants and toddlers and those serving all young children were more likely to report excess demand for their services (81 percent and 79 percent, respectively) than those serving only preschool-age children (65 percent). Though excess demand did not vary linearly with community poverty, the level of urbanicity was important, with providers in rural areas less likely to report excess demand. There is also a limited supply

Figure 4-8. Reasons Households Face Difficulty Finding Care

Percentage of all households that face difficulty finding care reporting primary reason for difficulty

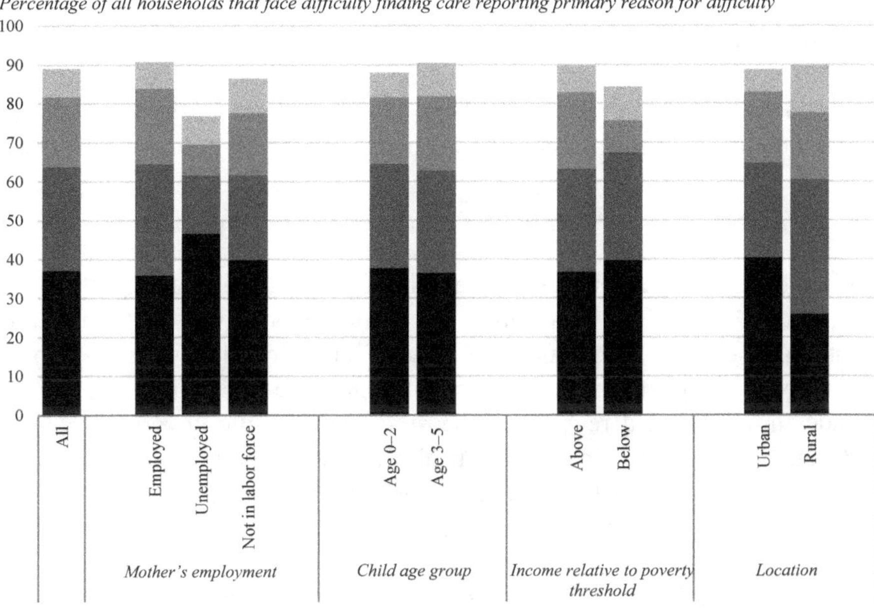

Sources: National Center for Education Statistics (2019); CEA calculations.
Note: Households included are those that reported some or much difficulty finding the type of childcare or early childhood program they wanted for their child, or reported that they did not find the childcare program they wanted. Households are grouped by their response to the question "What was the main reason for the difficulty finding childcare or early childhood programs?" The four most common reasons are displayed, so the bars do not sum to 100.

of childcare subsidies funded by the Federal Government and States; only 16 percent of the children who were eligible for oversubscribed subsidies in 2019 received them (Chien 2022).

On the consumer side, households also report difficulty accessing care that meets their needs. In 2019, 76 percent of households that searched for care for their young children had difficulty finding care that met their needs (National Household Education Surveys Program 2019). Among this group, when respondents were asked the main reason for difficulty, the most common barrier was cost, followed by a lack of open slots (figure 4-8). Other significant barriers in the search for care included locational challenges and insufficient quality. Cost was a particularly pronounced concern among urban households and households with an income below the poverty threshold. A lack of available slots at the ECE providers they contacted was a more salient difficulty for households with working mothers, those above the poverty threshold, and those in rural areas. The disconnect between families' reports of difficulty finding ECE and providers' reports of a lower incidence of excess demand in rural areas perhaps suggests that the types of available care, ages served, or other program features offered in rural areas do not meet families' needs. Previous research also documents more pronounced search difficulty for Black and Hispanic households (NCES 2018). The undersupply of ECE warrants attention because of the documented effectiveness of investments in facilitating parents' labor force attachment as well as in improving children's short- and long-term outcomes, both of which are important for individual well-being and strong economic growth.

The Role of Subsidies in the Market for Care

The sizable social benefits of high-quality ECE and the challenges in the ECE market create an opportunity for policy innovation. Hendren and Sprung-Keyser (2020) document the returns on various investments across the life cycle using a metric called the marginal value of public funds, which includes any increased revenue and cost savings for the government, and find that investments in childhood health and education yield the largest returns. Though other public and private entities also spend money on ECE in the United States, increased Federal funding could help move the quality of care for young children closer to the socially optimal level (Davis and Sojourner 2021). Research indicates that improving ECE—and reaping the social and economic benefits of investing in children—requires (1) broadening access, and in particular, addressing disparities by race, ethnicity, and family socioeconomic status; (2) incentivizing supply building, including workforce support; and (3) ensuring quality.

International Comparisons

Many countries around the world subsidize ECE (Olivetti and Petrongolo 2017). Whereas among all countries that belong to the Organization for Economic Cooperation and Development (OECD), national governments spend an average of 0.74 percent of their gross domestic product on ECE, the United States spends only 0.33 percent (OECD 2021). As discussed in chapter 6 of this *Report*, women's labor force participation in the United States has stagnated and fallen behind participation rates in many other comparable countries. Researchers have advanced the relative lack of family-friendly policies in the United States as one potential explanation for why U.S. women's labor force participation has failed to increase at the same rates as its peer countries (Blau and Kahn 2013).

Among OECD countries, the United States has one of the lowest ECE participation rates among children age three to five years, at 66 percent (OECD, n.d.). This rate was essentially unchanged between 2015 and 2020, measured before the COVID-19 pandemic. Notably, several OECD countries have universal or near-universal ECE participation rates among children age three to five. This group includes Ireland, which experienced a large increase, from 79 percent in 2015 to universal participation in 2020 (OECD, n.d.), concurrent with major reforms of and national investment in ECE, including improved compensation for early educators (Moloney 2021).

Though the United States stands out among advanced economies for its relatively low amount of spending on preschool-age children (age three to five), as measured by spending per child served or as a proportion of gross domestic product, public spending on ECE for the youngest children from infancy to age two is particularly low (OECD 2021). Many other countries, particularly the Nordic ones, spend the most on ECE for infants and toddlers and continue to invest heavily in the years before school entry.

The United States' ECE landscape is different from those of many other OECD countries, and it is also importantly embedded in a different policy context that has implications for the functioning of ECE programs. Of the OECD countries with available data, more than 70 percent have a centralized authority for ECE, with oversight for the system that serves children from birth or age one through primary school entry, unlike the United States; many also have established a right to at least one year of ECE enrollment before age five (OECD 2019). In addition, parental leave policies in many other countries alleviate pressure on the ECE infrastructure for providing infant care, which is the costliest to provide and the least agile in accommodating fluctuations in enrollment, due in part to smaller group sizes and child-to-adult ratios (Landivar, Graf, and Rayo 2023; OECD 2011; Office of Child Care, n.d.). All OECD countries, with the exception of the United States, offer nationwide paid maternity leave (OECD 2016). Many also offer paid paternity leave after the birth of a child, and 23 OECD countries provide paid parental leave that allows parents to share caregiving responsibilities in that time period (OECD 2016).

Subsidies in the United States' ECE Market

Subsidizing the United States' ECE infrastructure more robustly could make it possible for care providers to invest in high-quality services, including adequately compensating workers, at a price that families can afford. Box 4-4 outlines the major Federal investments in ECE.

Two recent working papers find that a combination of subsidies targeting low-income families *coupled with* provider-side investments is the most effective means to expand enrollment in high-quality ECE (Bodéré 2023; Borowsky et al. 2022). Subsidies tied to the cost of providing high-quality care allow providers to invest in costly quality improvements, and adjusting the price childcare consumers pay based on their income makes it easier for families to fit high-quality care into their budgets.

Box 4-4. Federal ECE Investments

Currently, the Federal Government invests in ECE through several channels, some of which direct funding toward private and public organizations to provide free or subsidized services, while others provide financial resources directly to families for spending on ECE services.

Head Start is the federally funded program, operated by public agencies, private nonprofit and for-profit organizations, Tribal governments, and school systems, providing free ECE for preschool-aged children from low-income families (ECLKC 2022). The Early Head Start program serves pregnant women and infants and toddlers from low-income households through home visitation and center-based services (ECLKC 2019).

The Preschool Development Grant–Birth through Five also invests in ECE, with the goal of supporting systemic enhancements in strategic planning, family engagement, workforce development, and quality improvement across all ECE programs, including but not limited to States' preschool programs (OESE 2023; Office of Early Childhood Development 2022).

The Child Care and Development Fund (CCDF), authorized by the Child Care and Development Block Grant (CCDBG) Act, provides funding to States, territories, and Tribal governments to invest in ECE programs as well as directly to low-income families pursing work, education, or training opportunities to spend on childcare (Office of Child Care 2022).

Some ECE benefits operate through the tax code: the now fully refundable Child and Dependent Care Credit, a tax credit that supports working families with childcare expenses (IRS 2022), and the Employer-Provided Child Care Credit, which provides tax credits to employers with qualified childcare expenditures, including operating on-site childcare facilities or contracting with childcare providers to offer services to their employees (Smith, McHenry, and Mullaly 2021).

Recent childcare policy proposals would encourage States to build the supply of high-quality ECE and expand access to it through, in part, incentives for providers to increase investments in quality. In addition, these proposals include subsidies targeting low- and middle-income households. Both these features would allow providers to recoup the cost of additional quality investments, counteracting market frictions that lead to underinvesting in quality, as discussed above.

Investing in quality will require both process improvements and better job quality for care workers to attract and retain people with the appropriate

Box 4-5. New Data and New Methods to Inform Investments in Children

Understanding the current lay of the land in ECE and how to effectively invest in children requires continued innovation in data infrastructure and research methods. There are no systematically collected measures of ECE programming, inputs, and outcomes across the mixed delivery system, and information on ECE enrollment from household surveys lags real time considerably. Misalignment in the timing and incidence of costs and benefits creates challenges for public investments in children; the time horizon over which such investments realize their returns is long, and most budget scoring calculations fail to account for long-term benefits.

Timely, responsive data collection. Issues with the limited data on ECE provision and participation, and the timeliness of its availability existed before the COVID-19 pandemic, but real-time data collection became increasingly important during the pandemic for assessing which programs or elements of programs were achieving their intended goals (Cajner et al. 2022). Two surveys that emerged in response have been widely used in analysis: the Household Pulse Survey and the School Pulse Panel. In theory, these ongoing surveys have much potential to both inform policy and support research, but the Household Pulse Survey has issues with representativeness and low response rates (Bradley et al. 2021). Redesign and incentives could address these problems, and gathering data on households and schools over time holds promise for use in future research and policymaking.

Unlocking and expanding the potential of existing data sources is likely to be more cost-effective than collecting new data. Administrative data, for example, often contain rich information on children's and families' interactions with services. The ability to link administrative data over time and across sources could facilitate many fruitful research pursuits to inform policy and practice (Bigelow et al. 2021).

Measuring long-run effects. Several new methods capitalize on the documented relationships between short-term metrics and longer-term outcomes of interest to project or estimate the long-run and broader impact of interventions. One recent paper documents this evolution in economic research on the effects of the U.S. social safety net on children, as causal methods have evolved, sufficient time has elapsed, and data availability has improved (Aizer, Hoynes, and Lleras-Muney 2022). New and reinvigorated approaches to capturing long-term effects include *life-cycle benefit forecasts* (García et al. 2020), *surrogate indices* (Athey et al. 2019), and the framework of the marginal value of public funds (Hendren and Sprung-Keyser 2020). Ongoing innovation in this space demonstrates that there is interest in, and urgency to, more quickly measuring the broad and full impact of programs. This need is particularly pressing when assessing programs and policies that affect children.

skills. Evidence indicates that labor supply in ECE settings responds to higher wages, which suggests that as ECE jobs become higher quality, more qualified people will remain in care jobs and seek to be hired by care businesses (Blau 1993; Borowsky et al. 2022; Mocan 2007). Therefore, the supply and quality of ECE would increase, helping to counteract the long-standing undersupply of high-quality care.

As discussed in box 4-4, the Federal Government currently invests in ECE programming through multiple avenues, and many States have proceeded with efforts to increase availability and lower costs, often using Federal funding from the ARP. A number of States—including Connecticut, Delaware, Georgia, Maine, Maryland, Oregon, Pennsylvania, and Vermont—are offering one-time bonuses for care workers or are permanently subsidizing pay increases (Child Care Aware 2022). In Texas, for example, lawmakers increased reimbursements to providers serving infants and toddlers from low-income households, and have required childcare programs receiving public subsidies to participate in the Texas Rising Star quality rating and improvement system (Goldstein 2022).

The Federal Government could also play a significant role in improving data infrastructure that supports effective policymaking for ECE through better real-time information on availability and participation, and by building evidence. Box 4-5 discusses some of the new developments on this front, and avenues for improvement.

Conclusion

Early care and education programs play an important dual role for families: (1) contributing to young children's development of cognitive and social-emotional skills; and (2) supporting parents' engagement with the labor market. Both these channels also generate substantial benefits for society. Ensuring that all children have access to high-quality ECE requires investing *both* in families' ability to access programs and in the provision of these programs—including supporting workforce improvements and smart capacity expansion. Such investments in ECE can yield significant long-run benefits not only for the affected children themselves but also for society at large.

Although the COVID-19 pandemic exacerbated many gaps in the Nation's ECE infrastructure, many of these challenges—and particularly disparities by race/ethnicity and family income—existed before the pandemic. There are critical issues in the market for ECE programs and services, and the Nation's economy often fails to support care businesses, care workers, and the families in need of their services. These challenges ultimately lead to low pay for workers and exacerbate the undersupply of high-quality, affordable, and accessible care for families. However, these problems could be mitigated with policy improvements.

Carefully designed government policies would address frictions in the ECE market—including workforce challenges and low pay, the high costs of high-quality care provision, families' price sensitivity, and the fragility of the ECE business model—thereby making childcare more affordable while improving pay for workers and ensuring investments in quality. The government could thus foster a better-functioning ECE market by funding subsidies for childcare providers, including incentives to improve the quality of care and higher caregiver pay, alongside subsidies and publicly provided ECE programming for families. Together, these policies would address both the supply and demand sides of the ECE market, ensuring that providers are willing and able to provide the high-quality, affordable care needed by families and society.

Chapter 5

Building Stronger Postsecondary Institutions

The United States' postsecondary education system is, in many ways, the envy of the world. Relative to most other international systems, U.S. postsecondary institutions are more numerous, diverse, and decentralized, as well as more likely to offer opportunities for exploration, transfer, and reentry. Students are likely to benefit from having flexibility to find the program that fits them best. The high number of institutions relative to those of peer countries may help spur innovation among competing institutions to be responsive to the needs of students. These features help explain why the United States is the top destination for international college students: over 1 million international students were enrolled in U.S. colleges in 2020—more than triple the number in 1980—and now account for one-fifth of all cross-country student migration in postsecondary education (Bound et al. 2021; Institute of International Education 2020).

Nonetheless, as the demand for highly educated workers has increased over the past half century, earning a valuable postsecondary credential has remained a challenge for many Americans. The United States no longer leads the world in postsecondary attainment, and large gaps by income and race have widened over the past several decades. This has consequences both for individuals, who miss out on the personal benefits of postsecondary education, and for society, which forgoes the increased civic participation, lower reliance on public benefits, increased tax revenues, higher economic growth, and other benefits that such education brings. Though college continues to be a good investment on average, increased student debt burdens relative to a generation ago mean this investment includes risks that some students can be left worse off if their education does not yield the labor market benefits they expect.

Federal and State support for postsecondary education has long included direct funding for institutions, but in recent decades the primary form of support has shifted to financial aid for students. These efforts have been essential to help offset rising tuition and fees, which before accounting for financial aid, have roughly tripled in real terms since 1980 and have increased even more at public four-year institutions (Ma and Pender 2022a). Yet policies aimed at institutions and the programs they offer—to build capacity, to support colleges in serving students well, and to hold them accountable when they do not—are a critical complement to policies lowering financial barriers to attendance. Federal policy can influence the quality of postsecondary options with both carrots, such as Federal support to help institutions improve student outcomes, and sticks, such as policies to hold institutions accountable for the economic value they provide. Where there are geographic barriers to access, institution-oriented policies can help facilitate the equitable expansion of high-value programs and deter the expansion of lower-value ones.

Before considering institution-oriented policies, this chapter first describes the landscape of U.S. postsecondary education, documenting the extraordinary variation across such institutions, and summarizing evidence that institutions and their programs are themselves a critical determinant of student success. The chapter next explains the rationale for Federal investment in postsecondary education, and places the U.S. model of postsecondary education finance in historical and international contexts. The decentralized "high tuition, high aid" model currently used in the United States has some advantages but also generates economic risks for students who fail to graduate or whose education does not pay off in the labor market. Imperfections in the market for postsecondary education limit the potential of the market alone to drive improvements. Such imperfections include geographic constraints, informational and behavioral constraints, and production constraints that limit institutions' ability to react quickly to fluctuating demand. The chapter documents one source of production constraints: State appropriations for public postsecondary institutions tend to fall during economic recessions, precisely when demand for enrollment in such institutions tends to rise.

The rest of the chapter considers how Federal policy can help support postsecondary institutions, reviewing a range of options to improve or maintain the quality of such institutions, to hold institutions accountable for student outcomes, and to reduce geographic barriers to access. The institution-oriented policy efforts described in this chapter have the potential to improve the landscape of postsecondary options. Throughout the discussion, the chapter highlights actions that the Biden-Harris Administration has already undertaken to improve the postsecondary institutional landscape, with the ultimate goal of ensuring that all students have access to a college education of value.

The U.S. Postsecondary Institutional Landscape

The degree of heterogeneity in the institutional landscape is a distinctive feature of the U.S. postsecondary system. Colleges in the public, private nonprofit, and for-profit sectors offer a different mix of programs, enroll a different composition of students, and are financed in different ways. Four-year institutions offer bachelor's degrees in fields that can vary substantially in their connection to specific occupations. Community colleges offer a range of credentials, including academic associate degrees (e.g., for students who intend to transfer to a four-year program); occupational associate degrees; short-term certificates intended to help students access the labor market quickly; and, increasingly, bachelor's degrees. Historically Black Colleges and Universities and Tribal Colleges and Universities have an additional mission: to serve communities that have historically been excluded from postsecondary education. In addition, institutions vary in the extent to which their students graduate and succeed in the labor market. This institutional landscape is both a driver and consequence of how the United States supports higher education and has implications for how its quality can be improved.

Figure 5-1. Distribution of Enrollment Across Institution Types, by Student Characteristics
Percentage enrolled in each institution

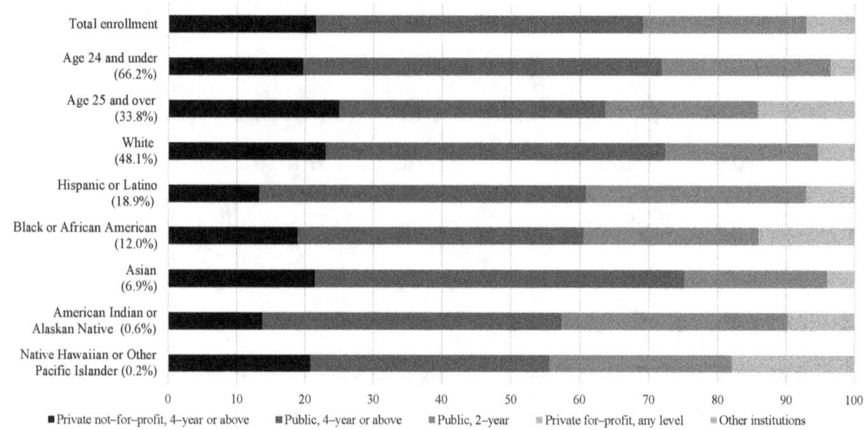

Source: National Center for Education Statistics, Integrated Postsecondary Education Data System Fall Enrollment component, 2021 provisional data.
Note: The category "other institutions" encompasses public institutions and private not-for-profits of less than 2 years, as well as private not-for-profits of 2 years. Reported in parentheses under each category is the percentage of total fall enrollment in all institutions captured by the given population. Percentages do not add up to 100 due to rounding and the omission of students with two or more races, students of unknown race/ethnicity, and students who are nonresident aliens.

Institutions Serve a Diverse Student Population

U.S. college students vary in age and residential status. Only about 13 percent of undergraduates both started college before age 20 and live on the campus of a residential four-year college (NCES 2022a, 2022b, 2022c). Nearly 30 percent of enrolled students started their programs at age 20 or above (NCES 2022a). Among enrolled students younger than 20, about 40 percent attend two-year (or less) institutions, and only about half the remaining students attending four-year institutions live on campus (NCES 2022d, 2022e). Over one-third of enrolled undergraduates are 25 or older, a proportion that rises to nearly 44 percent for community colleges and to nearly 62 percent for the for-profit sector (NCES 2022f).

Undergraduates are, on average, fairly diverse with respect to income and race, and institutions vary substantially in the extent to which they enroll different types of students. In any given year, nearly one-third of undergraduates receive Pell Grants, a proxy for a low family income (NCES 2020a). Institutions vary substantially in the extent to which they serve low-income students, with about 16 percent of campuses having fewer than one-fourth of students receiving Pell Grants and about 22 percent having more than three-fourths receiving them.[1] Overall, low-income students are relatively similarly represented across the two- and four-year sectors and are over-represented in the for-profit sector, where about 53 percent of undergraduate students receive Pell Grants (NCES 2020b, 2020c).

[1] CEA calculations, using data from the College Scorecard. These College Scorecard data were the most recent available publicly, as of September 2022, which for most measures reflect the 2020–21 academic year.

Figure 5-2. Variation in Per-Student Expenditures

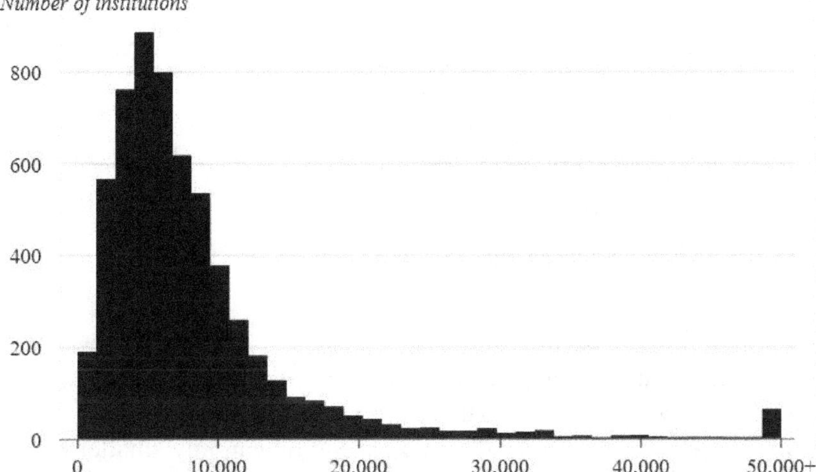

Sources: College Scorecard; CEA calculations.
Note: FTE = full-time equivalent.

Nearly two-fifths of undergraduates self-identify as Black, Hispanic, Asian, American Indian or Alaskan Native, or Native Hawaiian or Pacific Islander. Most such student groups are more heavily represented in community colleges and the for-profit sector. As figure 5-1 shows, students who self-identify as Black, Hispanic, American Indian or Alaskan Native, or Native Hawaiian or Pacific Islander are substantially more likely than white students to attend for-profit institutions. For-profit institutions also disproportionately attract those age 25 or above.

Institutions Vary in Their Prices and Spending on Students

Postsecondary institutions vary not only in the students they serve but also in the prices they charge and the amount they spend on student instruction. As table 5-1 shows, the average institution has an undergraduate sticker price of roughly $13,000 in tuition and fees per year; has a total cost of attendance of roughly $25,000 after housing, food, books, and other expenses are included; and has a net cost of nearly $15,000 after grant aid has been accounted for. Such prices vary tremendously by sector. Private nonprofit and for-profit colleges have undergraduate net costs of over $20,000 a year, while public four- and two-year institutions cost roughly $14,000 and $7,000 for undergraduates, respectively, after accounting for grants.

Institutions also vary widely in the amount of resources they have available and spend on student instruction—the clearest measure available

Table 5-1. College Prices and Expenditures by Sector

Measure	All Institutions	Private Not-for-Profit, 4-Year	Public, 4-Year	Public, 2-Year	Private For-Profit, Any Level
Tuition and fees	$12,602	$34,235	$9,149	$3,338	$14,913
Total cost of attendance	$25,235	$49,401	$22,529	$13,170	$26,204
Net cost of attendance	$14,762	$26,045	$13,812	$7,101	$20,400
Instructional expenditures per FTE student	$9,633	$14,071	$10,617	$6,292	$3,691

Sources: College Scorecard; CEA calculations.
Note: FTE = full-time equivalent. College prices and expenditures are per academic year, for full-time enrollment.

of an institution's financial investment in learning.[2] Figure 5-2 shows that this resource distribution is highly skewed, with 70 percent of institutions spending less than $10,000 per full-time-equivalent student each year and 9 percent spending more than $50,000. Such spending can buy smaller class sizes, higher-quality instructors, better academic support services, and other resources that may contribute to student success. As table 5-1 shows, there is clear variation across sectors in these spending patterns. Across most sectors, higher prices tend to translate into higher spending on students. Private, nonprofit, four-year colleges spend about $14,100 a year on instruction; public four-year colleges spend about $10,600; and public two-year colleges spend about $6,300. The exception to the pattern are for-profit colleges, where students pay relatively high net prices but receive the lowest instructional spending of any sector (about $3,700).

Institutions Vary in Their Student Outcomes

Student outcomes, such as degree completion rates, also vary substantially by postsecondary institution. A relatively high fraction of U.S. undergraduate students who start college do not complete their degrees (Bound, Lovenheim, and Turner 2010; Bowen, Chingos, and McPherson 2009). Though recent research suggests that graduation rates have increased somewhat since 1990, fewer than 60 percent of undergraduates seeking a bachelor's degree complete such a degree within six years of entry (Denning et al. 2022). As panel A of figure 5-3 shows, the average college student attends an institution where about 55 percent of undergraduate students complete their degree within 150 percent of the time expected (i.e., three years for two-year colleges and six years for four-year colleges). This average masks substantial variation, as nearly one-tenth of colleges have undergraduate completion rates under 25 percent and over one-third have completion rates above 75 percent.

[2] The instructional spending measure, available in the Integrated Postsecondary Data System (https://nces.ed.gov/ipeds/), measures total spending across both undergraduates and graduate students, so care should be taken when comparing such figures with undergraduate costs of attendance.

Figure 5-3. Variation in Undergraduate Student Outcomes

A. Variation in Completion Rate

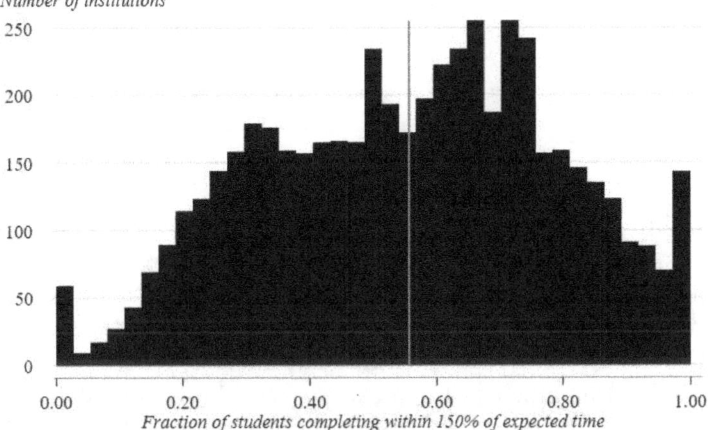

B. Variation in Students' Earnings

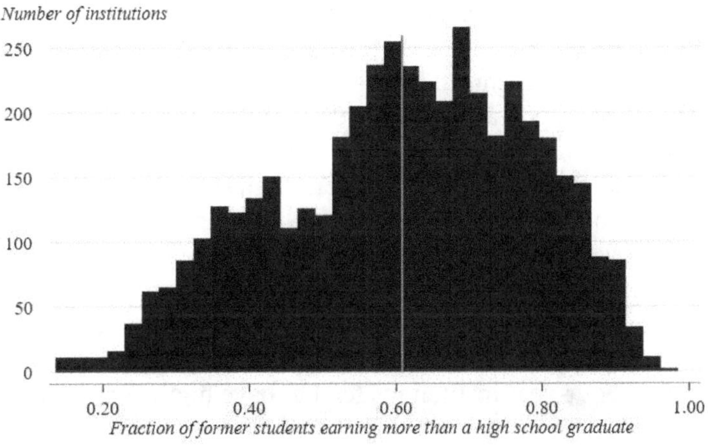

Sources: College Scorecard; CEA calculations.
Note: The orange line in Panel A denotes the average fraction of students completing their undergraduate education within 150% of the expected time. The orange line in Panel B denotes the average fraction of former students earning more than a high school graduate.

Not all noncompletion is problematic. The U.S. postsecondary system allows many students to explore college, even when they are uncertain about the experience. A recent pre-COVID-19-pandemic, large-scale survey of Americans who had attended college but had not completed their degree reveals a range of self-reported reasons for this noncompletion (Gallup 2019). Some students' reasons for leaving suggest that better institutional practices or financial aid policies might have helped them complete their degrees, while other reported reasons indicate that some students leave after learning that college was not a good fit for them. Such exploration can be

Table 5-2. Student Outcomes by Sector (percent)

Measure	All Institutions	Private Not-for-Profit, 4-Year	Public, 4-Year	Public, 2-Year	Private For-Profit, Any Level
Degree completion rate	50	63	56	29	47
Proportion of students out-earning typical high school graduate	70	77	75	59	59

Sources: College Scorecard; CEA calculations.

costly for students attending high-priced institutions. This suggests a policy role for balancing the benefits of exploration with the need to protect students from making poor investments of time and money.

Variation in postcollege earnings by institution is also striking. One such measure, available in the College Scorecard, is the percentage of a given college's Federal-aid-receiving undergraduate students who, 10 years after entry, earn at least as much as a typical worker whose highest level of education completed is high school.[3] Comparing earnings with those of workers who are high school graduates provides a rough proxy for whether a college's enrollees have better economic outcomes than if they had not enrolled in college at all.

The average college student attends an institution where about 60 percent of undergraduate Federal aid recipients out-earn a typical high school graduate. Yet, as shown in panel B of figure 5-3, at 19 percent of colleges, fewer than half of such students out-earn high school graduates 10 years later. Relatedly, colleges also vary widely in the extent to which their students experience upward economic mobility, measured by the fraction of students entering from the bottom quintile of the income distribution who later reach the top quintile (Chetty et al. 2017). Degree completion rates and postcollege earnings indicate striking variation across college sectors, as shown in table 5-2. Four-year institutions tend to have higher completion rates and earnings than two-year institutions. Students at community colleges have similar earnings outcomes to students at for-profit colleges, even though community colleges are substantially less expensive for students to attend.[4]

Institutions Matter for Student Outcomes

The extent to which variation in student outcomes is driven by institutions themselves is challenging to measure. Some outcome differences are due

[3] The College Scorecard (https://collegescorecard.ed.gov/) is a website created by the U.S. Department of Education that gives students, families, and other interested parties information about the cost and value of nearly all higher education institutions. The earnings measure discussed here comes from a national average of the earnings of all those age 25 to 34 who indicated that high school completion was their highest level of education, were working, and were not enrolled in school during the measurement year. This threshold is about $31,000 in 2020 dollars.

[4] The for-profit figures cited here cover all for-profit institutions.

to differences in students across institutions. A large and growing body of literature documents that some portion of undergraduate student outcome differences across institutions is causally attributable to the institutions themselves: colleges appear to vary widely in their effects on students. A given institution's effects do not appear to be inherent, but depend in part upon available resources and how those resources are spent; better-resourced institutions and those that spend more per student on instruction generally produce better outcomes, including higher graduation rates and labor market earnings (Lovenheim and Smith 2022). As the evidence suggests, students of all kinds appear to benefit from attending the college with the best track record available to them, with the worst colleges leaving the typical student worse off than they would have been if they had not attended college at all.

Within the four-year college sector, researchers have found that students are more likely to graduate and have higher earnings when they attend colleges with more resources, academically stronger peers, and better historical student outcomes such as graduation rates and earnings. Such patterns hold even when comparing otherwise similar students who enroll in different colleges (Long 2008; Smith 2013; Mountjoy and Hickman 2021; Cohodes and Goodman 2014). Evidence from States including Texas and California suggests that gaining access to well-resourced flagship institutions increases graduation rates and earnings, including for those whose access comes as a result of "Top Percent" guaranteed admissions policies (Hoekstra 2009; Andrews, Li, and Lovenheim 2016; Bleemer 2021; Black, Denning, and Rothstein 2020).

Public four-year colleges have been documented to have substantially positive effects on students. For example, research in a variety of States shows that students whose academic background gives them access to less selective public four-year institutions are more likely to graduate and have higher earnings than those lacking such access (Zimmerman 2014; Goodman, Hurwitz, and Smith 2017; Smith, Goodman, and Hurwitz 2020; Kozakowski 2023). Consistent with observable resource differences across sectors, enrollment in four-year colleges generally improves student outcomes even more for those choosing between two- and four-year options. Comparing otherwise similar students who differ only in their proximity to two- and four-year options suggests that four-year college enrollment increases the rate of degree completion and may increase earnings (Rouse 1995; Mountjoy 2022).

On average, community colleges have been shown to generate positive effects on students and substantially better outcomes than the for-profit colleges that enroll similar student populations (Cellini and Turner 2019; Armona and Cao 2022). Researchers have found that enrolling and completing an associate degree at a two-year college generally improves outcomes relative to not enrolling or completing one at all (Belfield and Bailey 2017;

Mountjoy 2022). Further, they document that, relative to those who start but do not complete their two-year degrees, graduates of community colleges see substantial increases in their annual income five to nine years after college entry (Jepsen, Troske, and Coomes 2014; Bahr et al. 2015; Liu, Belfield, and Trimble 2015; Bahr 2016; Bettinger and Soliz 2016; Xu, Jaggars, and Fletcher 2016; Dadgar and Trimble 2015; Belfield 2015). The return from a two-year degree is even higher in subsequent years after entry and during economic recessions (Minaya and Scott-Clayton 2022). Some high-demand community college programs, such as nursing, raise students' earnings so much that expanding the number of available slots in such programs would more than pay for itself via increased tax revenues returned to State and local governments (Grosz 2020).

For-profit colleges have been found to generate particularly poor outcomes for their enrollees. Advocates of for-profit colleges have argued that such poor outcomes are due to the disadvantages with which their students start (Cellini and Koedel 2017). Differences in student composition have not, however, been enough to explain the large differences in outcomes between for-profits and other institution types (Deming, Goldin, and Katz 2012; Scott-Clayton 2018a). Community colleges appear to improve earnings more than for-profit colleges, even when accounting for variations in student characteristics (Cellini and Turner 2019; Armona and Cao 2022). Numerous studies comparing the earnings of the same for-profit students before and after enrollment find that such students see little or no earnings increase relative to those who do not attend college or to those enrolled in public colleges (Cellini and Turner 2019; Cellini and Koedel 2017). Résumé audit studies similarly suggest that for-profit degree holders receive employer callbacks less often than otherwise-identical degree holders from public colleges and no more often than those with no college education at all (Darolia et al. 2015; Deming et al. 2016). Enrollment in for-profit colleges increases debt and worsens labor market outcomes relative to other two- and four-year options (Armona, Chakrabarti, and Lovenheim 2022). Nearly two-fifths of for-profit college chains have negative returns for Federal aid recipients compared with returns from simply gaining experience in the labor market (Armona and Cao 2022).

The Rationale for and Delivery of Public Postsecondary Investment

To assess strategies to promote access and improve quality in the postsecondary sector, it is useful to understand the economic rationale for public sector involvement, and to consider the possible forms such involvement can take.

The Economic Rationale for Public Sector Investment

A key motivation for promoting college is its value as an economic investment for both students and society. For example, though students express many reasons for pursuing postsecondary education, including personal exploration and growth, getting a better job tops the list (Fishman 2015; Stolzenberg et al. 2020). From a societal perspective, expanding educational access has been associated with economic growth, much like when the United States in the 20th century led the world in the transition to mass secondary—high school—education. This expansion also helped to dampen inequality (Goldin and Katz 2008).

However, in recent decades, as the demand for highly educated workers has continued to increase, the United States has faced significant challenges in the transition to broad-based postsecondary education and training (Goldin and Katz 2008; Neelakantan and Romero 2017). Although postsecondary enrollment has increased substantially since 1980, the pace has slowed since 2000 (Ma, Pender, and Welch 2019). The United States is no longer a global leader in college degree attainment for adults age 25 to 34 years, and the 43 percent completion rate among those entering associate degree programs in the United States is among the lowest of all countries belonging to the Organization for Economic Cooperation and Development (OECD) that reported their equivalent of this statistic (NCES 2021; OECD 2022). Failing to navigate the transition to broader postsecondary education would represent a missed opportunity, given the substantial private and societal benefits of college (described in box 5-1). Of particular concern is the large and growing gap in bachelor's degree attainment between high- and low-income families, which is wider for cohorts born in the 1980s than for those born in the 1960s (Chetty et al. 2020; Bailey and Dynarski 2011). Racial disparities in college attainment have also grown over a similar time span, particularly among women (Emmons and Ricketts 2017; Ma, Pender, and Welch 2019).

Finally, despite the substantial private and public benefits, many students cannot afford to attend a postsecondary institution without financial assistance. The problem is that the benefits of college accrue over the course of a lifetime, while the bill must be paid in advance. Typically, individuals solve this problem by borrowing to pay for an investment up front, such as when purchasing a car or home. However, private lenders typically do not provide loans unsecured by collateral (e.g., those for a car or a house that can be repossessed) because a college education cannot be returned or resold if the individual fails to make interest payments and defaults on the loan (Barr 2004). The existence of such "credit constraints" provides an important rationale for the public sector providing loans to students at subsidized interest rates.

Box 5-1. The Private and Public Benefits of College

The earnings premium for those with a college education is well documented (Barrow and Malamud 2015). Less well known is that the benefits of college accrue to a broad range of students at a broad range of schools. Students with relatively low grades and test scores who enroll in four-year institutions derive significant earnings benefits from college attendance (Zimmerman 2014; Ost, Pan, and Webber 2018; Smith, Goodman, and Hurwitz 2020), as do the 35 percent of students who enroll in open-access community colleges rather than not enrolling at all (Kane and Rouse 1995; Mountjoy 2022; NCES 2022g). Associate degrees—and even some shorter-course credentials in high-demand occupational fields—yield substantial returns in many fields, including for older students and displaced workers (Grosz 2020; Jacobson, LaLonde, and Sullivan 2005; Jepsen, Troske, and Coomes 2014).

Postsecondary education also serves the public good. College attainment leads to increased civic participation, lower rates of involvement in the criminal justice system and reliance on public benefits, increased tax revenues, higher economic growth, and improved health in the next generation (Dee 2003; Lochner and Moretti 2004; Lochner 2011; Oreopoulos and Salvanes 2011; Hout 2012; Ma, Pender, and Welch 2019; Aghion et al. 2009; Currie and Moretti 2003). Reducing racial disparities in college attainment is particularly urgent, given that underrepresentation in highly credentialed professions can adversely affect the treatment and outcomes of historically excluded groups. For example, recent evidence indicates that students benefit from exposure to instructors of the same race (Fairlie, Hoffman, and Oreopoulos 2014; Gershenson, Hansen, and Lindsay 2021; Gershenson et al. 2022; Lusher, Campbell, and Carrell 2018), and that Black patients benefit from access to Black physicians (Alsan, Garrick, and Graziani 2019; Greenwood et al. 2020). Finally, postsecondary education and training serve as a form of social insurance, increasing workers' resilience during economic shifts and mitigating the negative consequences of recessions (Hyman 2018; Barr and Turner 2015; Minaya and Scott-Clayton 2022; Barnes et al. 2021).

How Public Funds Are Delivered: Student Aid and Institutional Support

Public funding to promote college access and completion can be delivered directly to institutions, to support programming and keep prices below cost, or directly to students, who then use financial aid to help pay tuition and other costs at the institution of their choice. In primary and secondary education, government support is delivered primarily through institutions, in the public provision of free schools, and with supplemental supports such as free meals delivered through those schools. Many countries follow this model, not only for primary and secondary education but also for postsecondary education, with direct institutional support for predominantly public institutions helping to keep tuition prices low (Marcucci 2013). Along these lines, at least 20 States currently offer statewide free community college programs (Mishory 2018; Education Commission of the States 2022), and the Biden-Harris Administration has developed a framework for a nationwide free community college program (White House 2021).

The Federal Government's earliest investments in postsecondary education also focused primarily on expanding capacity and keeping prices low at public institutions, which even today enroll over three-quarters of U.S. undergraduates (IPEDS 2020). The foundations of many of today's State colleges and universities can be traced to direct institutional support—such as the Federal Morrill Land Grant Act of 1862, which granted each State 30,000 acres of public land to establish public postsecondary institutions; the Second Morrill Act of 1890, which directed Federal funds to newly designated Historically Black Colleges and Universities; and the subsequent significant push by States to establish and expand two-year colleges in the 1960s (Cohen, Brawer, and Kisker 2013). State and local direct appropriations for public institutions, which help keep tuition prices below the full cost of provision, remained the largest source of government support for postsecondary education in the United States through the end of the 20th century (Dynarski, Page, and Scott-Clayton 2022).

The Higher Education Act of 1965, which established the foundations of today's Federal student aid programs (including the precursor to Pell Grants), marked a significant shift from institution-focused to student-focused assistance (Fountain 2017; Leslie and Johnson 1974). Delivering support via student aid may conserve public resources by targeting subsidies to those students who are most in need, support institutional quality by bringing in additional resources from those who can afford to pay, and promote competition and choice by enabling students to use their aid at the institutions they judge as highest value (Barr 2004). State and local direct appropriations for institutions have fallen from nearly two-thirds of support for undergraduates in 1990–91 to just under one-third in the academic year 2018–19 (Dynarski, Page, and Scott-Clayton 2022). Student aid is now the primary mode of support in the United States, providing $174 billion in grants, loans, and other direct support for undergraduates in 2021–22, with Federal sources accounting for about half this total, and loans accounting for about half of Federal student aid (Dynarski, Page, and Scott-Clayton 2022; Ma and Pender 2022b). The result, as shown in figure 5-4, is that only England exceeds the United States in the level of both tuition and student

Figure 5-4. Average Public Tuition and Fees and Percentage of Students Receiving Public Financial Aid–Bachelor's Degree Programs, 2019–20

Average public tuition and fees (listed prices in U.S. dollars converted using purchasing power parity)

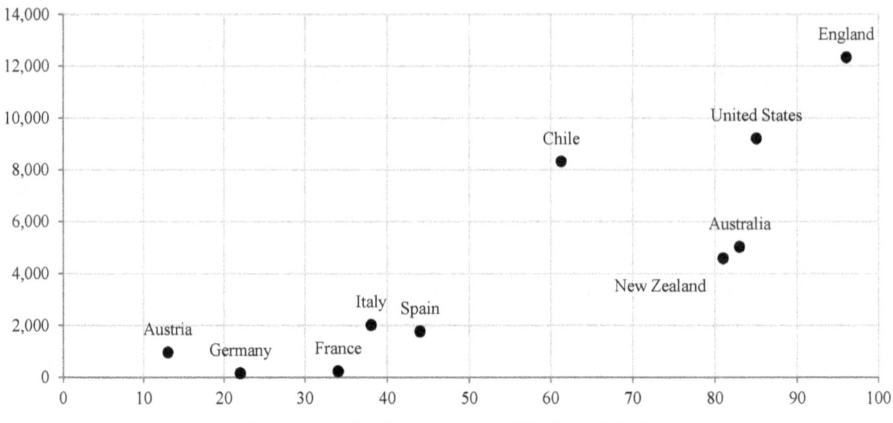

Source: Organization for Economic Cooperation and Development (2021, tables C5.1 and C5.2).
Note: Data refer to the academic year 2019-20 and are based on a special survey administered by the OECD in 2021.

aid (OECD 2021). The contemporary "high-tuition, high-aid" model of U.S. postsecondary finance is thus distinctive in both international and historical contexts.

In line with this high-tuition, high-aid model, inflation-adjusted published tuition and fees before accounting for financial aid ("sticker prices") have since 1980 nearly tripled in the public two-year sector, more than tripled in the private not-for-profit four-year sector, and nearly quadrupled in the public four-year sector, though such prices have stabilized over the past decade (Ma and Pender 2022a, 2022b). At the same time, *net* prices in the United States—tuition and fees minus grants and scholarships—have increased much more slowly than published prices, and have actually remained flat or declined over the past decade (Ma and Pender 2022b). The Biden-Harris Administration has taken a number of steps to continue to improve college affordability and help student loan borrowers, including providing a $900 increase to grant aid for low-income students through the Pell Grant program over the last two years, streamlining and improving student loan repayment, and pursuing debt relief through the HEROES Act.

The model of financing students rather than institutions has helped fuel a system of postsecondary education that is diverse and decentralized, with more opportunities for exploration, transfer, and reentry (Labaree 2017; Goldin and Katz 2008), because students decide where their subsidized dollars will be spent. In contrast, many other countries deliver funding primarily to public institutions that students can attend free (Marcucci 2013) but that often offer fewer spots in a more constrained set of programs. The diversity and flexibility of the U.S. system may help explain why the United States is the top destination for international students (Institute of International Education 2020). In recent decades, some countries that formerly provided fully free public institutions have shifted to the U.S. model as a way to maintain affordability while expanding postsecondary capacity and improving quality (Marcucci 2013; Murphy, Scott-Clayton, and Wyness 2019).

Still, the U.S. model of postsecondary education finance is not without challenges. Over the longer term, the dramatic increases in sticker prices have made it more difficult for today's students and families to pay for college relative to a generation ago. In 2022–23, the maximum Pell Grant, the largest source of grant aid in the United States, only covered 30 percent of published tuition, fees, room, and board at the typical public, four-year institution, down from 50 percent in 1988–89 and nearly 80 percent in 1975 (Ma and Pender 2022b; Baum, Payea, and Steele 2009; Protopsaltis and Parrott 2017).

Despite the availability of aid, research shows that tuition prices still influence students' persistence and degree completion, even after initial enrollment (Acton 2021). Prospective students—particularly those who would be first in their families to attend college—may not even know that financial aid exists and thus may be dissuaded by the sticker price alone (Levine, Ma, and Russell 2022). Research has shown that the process of applying for financial aid is itself a barrier to access (Bettinger et al. 2012), and that students are more likely to apply when aid is guaranteed in advance (Dynarski et al. 2021). Further, research indicates many students are reluctant to borrow (Boatman, Evans, and Soliz 2017). This may reduce the effectiveness of loans relative to grants of the same size.

Further, the decision to invest in college entails risks—in particular, the risk that the earnings students gain will be less than the cost they pay for their education. The breadth, flexibility, and multiple entry and exit points in the U.S. system also mean more risks of making mistakes and falling off track (Labaree 2017; Goldin and Katz 2008; Scott-Clayton 2012). Fewer than two-thirds of students who enroll in college finish any degree within six years (National Student Clearinghouse Research Center 2022a). Even among those who graduate with at least a four-year degree, roughly one in five male college graduates and about one in seven female college graduates has earnings no higher than the typical worker with only a high school diploma (Ma, Pender, and Welch 2019).

Because many students rely on debt to finance a portion of their education, some students who attend college may end up worse off, even though the expected return is high on average. Nearly one-third of students who take on debt do not receive a degree (Miller 2017). More than one in four borrowers experience a student loan default within 12 years of college

Box 5-2. International Comparison of Income-Driven Student Loan Repayment

Like the United States, postsecondary education systems in Australia and England also combine high tuition with high financial support for students. In contrast to the United States, students in England and Australia can fully defer tuition payments until after college and then repay via income-driven repayment (IDR). Under IDR, student loan repayments are capped at a fixed percentage of income, mitigating the risk that college enrollment leads to incomes too low to repay such debts. Research from the United States finds that IDR enrollment reduces borrowers' risk of delinquency and default (Mueller and Yannelis 2019; Herbst 2023).

IDR plans vary substantially across these countries in two important ways. First, U.S. undergraduate loans, though capped below most students' cost of attendance, are available for a wider variety of programs, including short-term credentials and those at thousands of for-profit institutions (U.S. Department of Education 2023a; Ma and Pender 2022a). Both England and Australia allow undergraduates to borrow the full amount of public tuition but restrict the institutions eligible for IDR. England directs IDR primarily to public university students, and Australia originally restricted IDR to four-year colleges, only in 2009 expanding eligibility to vocational programs (Barr et al. 2019; Student Loans Company 2022). Second, IDR is the only loan repayment option in England and Australia, with automated enrollment and payments income-adjusted and collected automatically through the tax authority. In contrast, borrowers in the United States need to opt into IDR and annually update their own income (Barr et al. 2019). Only about one-third of U.S. student borrowers in 2022 were enrolled in such a plan (CEA calculations, based on Federal student loan portfolio data by repayment plan, from the U.S. Department of Education 2022a). The Biden-Harris Administration has proposed reforms of IDR to reduce monthly and lifetime payments, especially for low- and middle-income borrowers, and to eliminate barriers that prevent borrowers from accessing IDR.

entry, including nearly half of Black student loan borrowers (Scott-Clayton 2018b). One tool for mitigating repayment risk in a high-tuition, high-aid model are income-driven repayment plans—but as box 5-2 discusses, the implementation and use of these plans differ substantially by country.

Finally, the global experience suggests that countries expanding student aid to for-profit institutions face challenges in regulating quality to address poor student outcomes in this sector (Usher 2019; Salto 2019).

Although for-profit higher education is not unique to the United States, it is unusual in terms of both its size in the United States and its integration into the student aid system, including access not only to student loan dollars but also to nonrepayable grant aid (Kinser 2016; Levy 2019). For-profit colleges in the United States account for 12 percent of Federal student aid dollars and 30 percent of student loan defaults, even though they enroll only 8 percent of students (Century Foundation 2021).

The Imperfect Market for Postsecondary Institutions

In an idealized market, the United States' approach of providing portable financial aid to support consumer choice might be sufficient to ensure that high-quality choices actually exist. At least in theory, this approach should promote institutional quality by weeding out low-quality institutions or prompting them to improve and encouraging better ones to expand (Barr 2004; Fountain 2017). The postsecondary education market, however, is too imperfect for institutional improvements to emerge simply from students voting with their feet (Leslie and Johnson 1974). Institutions may, for example, be able to attract students regardless of their program quality. Three main types of constraints—geographic constraints, informational and behavioral constraints, and constraints on colleges' ability to expand quickly—diminish the power of market forces to promote productive innovation, improve quality, and drive down prices through student choice and

Figure 5-5. Distance Between Home and College, 2004–16

Percentage of undergraduates

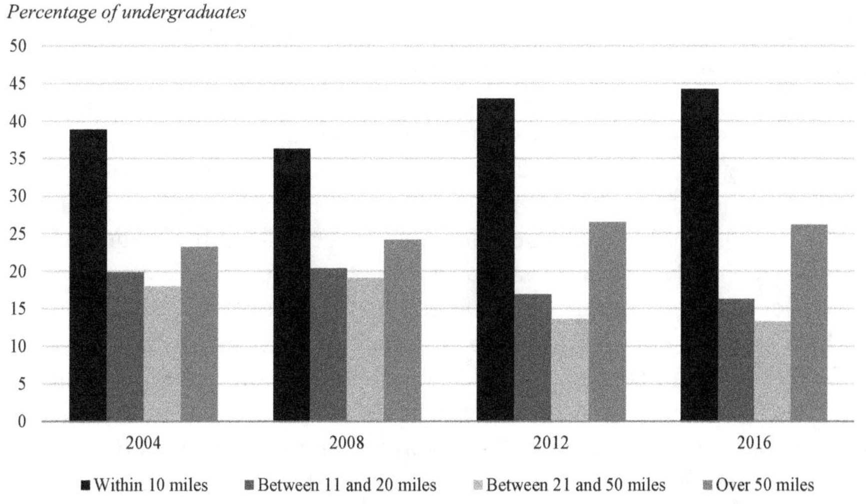

Source: National Center for Education Statistics (National Postsecondary Student Aid Study, 2016 undergraduates).

competition alone. The resulting institutional landscape offers variety, but it is not always clear which aspects of this variety benefit students.

Geographic Constraints

The first main types of constraints, again, are geographic. First, as figure 5-5 shows, most students attend college close to home, limiting the scope for choice and competition. About 60 percent of U.S. undergraduates attend a college within 20 miles of their home, and the fraction attending within just 10 miles of home grew from nearly 39 percent in 2004 to 44 percent in 2016 (NCES 2022h). These proportions are substantially higher for students of color and low-income students (NCES 2022i, 2022j).

These geographic constraints make college markets "thin," as many students do not have a substantial number of options to choose from if they want or need to stay close to home (Hillman 2016; Blagg and Chingos 2016). The median commuting zone has just two colleges of any type or level. About 23 percent of those age 18 to 44 years live in a commuting zone with at most one public four-year college; about 27 percent live in a commuting zone with at most one public two-year college. Students with no options nearby must incur the high cost of relocating or lengthy commuting if they wish to attend college. Those with limited choices nearby may enroll in a program that is a poor fit for their goals (Klasik, Blagg, and Pekor 2018). Online programs provide an alternative but many generate poor student outcomes, as further discussed below.

Informational and Behavioral Constraints

Even for students with options close to home, informational and behavioral constraints can complicate decisionmaking. The United States' college landscape is particularly complex, with 63 percent more bachelor's-degree-focused institutions per capita than Canada, 71 percent more than the United Kingdom, and 67 percent more than Australia (World Higher Education Database, n.d.). The American community college, serving multiple missions including both transfer and terminal associate degrees, is a distinctive type of institution that only recently has begun to develop in other countries (Redden 2010). The United States also has a large for-profit college sector, adding to an already large and varied set of options students face.

College is not a simple consumer good, but an "experience good" for which students may not have well-formed preferences in advance. The decision to enroll in college is made infrequently in one's lifetime, limiting the opportunity to learn from previous decisions. Colleges differ along numerous dimensions, including both content and quality, which may be difficult to observe in advance. Benefits are uncertain and accrue over long time horizons, making it difficult for students to compare options. Even the best-prepared students may oversimplify or avoid decisions when choices are complex, information is limited, and preferences are not well established (Hoxby and Avery 2013; Beshears et al. 2008; Lavecchia, Liu, and Oreopoulos 2016; Ross et al. 2013).

Comparing financial aid offers can be particularly opaque. A recent report from the Government Accountability Office (GAO) found that 41 percent of colleges in a nationally representative survey did not provide information on net prices in their financial aid offers, and an additional 50 percent understated net prices by omitting some costs or including loans that must be repaid (GAO 2022). This complexity also affects students after college as they attempt to navigate student loan repayments (Turner 2021).

Finally, many prospective college students are relatively young and inexperienced financial decisionmakers, which increases both their susceptibility to marketing campaigns and the likelihood of decision mistakes (Beshears et al. 2008; Agarwal et al. 2009). Indeed, reports have found that some for-profit colleges take advantage of this by outspending their public counterparts 20-to-1 on advertising (Cellini and Chaudhary 2020) and using dubious claims about future employment prospects to recruit students (McMillan-Cottom 2017; GAO 2010).

College Expansion Constraints

In a simpler market, increased demand for the best products can induce successful producers to expand and new producers to enter the market. The substantial fixed costs and labor-intensive model of traditional postsecondary

Figure 5-6. Per-Student State and Local Funding for Public Higher Education, 1989–2019

2019 dollars

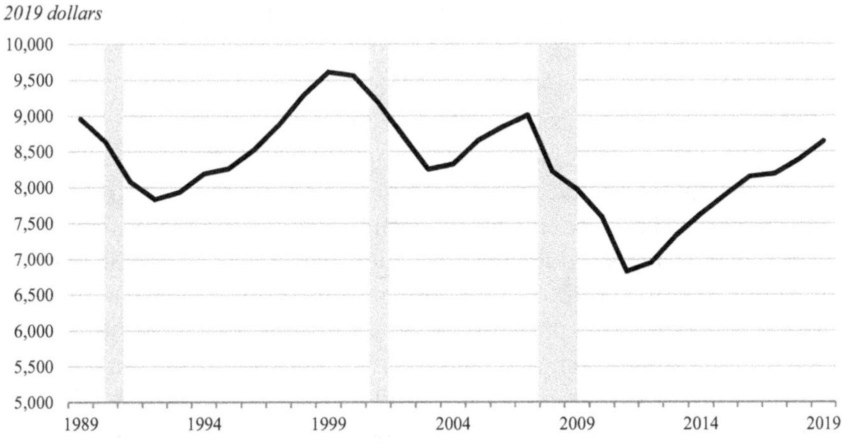

Source: College Board Trends in College Pricing 2021b, as compiled by Ma and Pender (2021).
Note: Shaded areas indicate recessions.

education, however, constrain institutions' ability to quickly respond to increased demand without diluting students' experience, as discussed below.

As figure 5-6 shows, per-student State and local funding is procyclical, falling during times of economic contraction. Demand for postsecondary education is, however, countercyclical, as students tend to seek skill training when employment opportunities are worse since the opportunity cost of enrollment is lower when jobs are scarce (Barr and Turner 2015). The combination of public funding's procyclicality and demand's countercyclicality means that per-student funding shrinks precisely when enrolling in a postsecondary program makes the most economic sense (Ma and Pender 2022b; Kane et al. 2005). This pattern leads to both higher tuition and lower resources provided per student during recessions, which has been documented to harm students' outcomes (Chakrabarti, Gorton, and Lovenheim 2020; Bound, Lovenheim, and Turner 2010; Bound and Turner 2007; Deming and Walters 2017).

Community college enrollments are particularly sensitive to economic conditions, partly because they are open-access institutions to which unemployed or underemployed adults often turn for midcareer training. Community college enrollments rise by about 1 to 3 percent overall for every increase of 1 percentage point in the local unemployment rate, with greater responsiveness among those age 25 and above (Hillman and Orians 2013; Betts and McFarland 1995). The only exception to this pattern has been the weak labor market early in the COVID-19 pandemic, when community college enrollment declined in part because instruction, particularly in fields requiring hands-on training, was disrupted by pandemic conditions (Schanzenbach and Turner 2022).

At the same time, students are more likely to enroll in for-profit institutions when funding for local public institutions decreases (Cellini 2009; Goodman and Henriques Volz 2020). Although causal research does not establish the mechanisms underlying this result, when resources per student fall, four-year colleges may not be able to expand enrollment to meet demand. Community colleges do not typically have enrollment caps, but when public institutions have fewer resources per student, students may have more difficulty registering for the courses they want at the times they want, or they may be discouraged by staffing constraints that affect their ability to navigate registration, financial aid, and other aspects of enrollment. In contrast, for-profit institutions can cut costs and expand more quickly than traditional institutions by offering more highly standardized curricula, a more limited range of programs, fewer in-person courses, and lower-paid instructors (Deming, Goldin, and Katz 2012). A large portion of for-profit programs are fully online, making them particularly attractive to students lacking alternatives close to home (NCES 2019). The heavy concentration of online programs in the for-profit sector may partly explain why for-profit enrollment declined much less than community college enrollment in the first year of the pandemic, when demand for remote learning increased substantially (National Student Clearinghouse 2022b).

Institution-Focused Policies That Promote Access to Postsecondary Value

Research has shown that the quality of institutions matters for student outcomes. Thus, policies aimed at institutions—to build capacity, to support colleges in serving students well, and to hold them accountable when they do not—are critical to ensuring that all students have access to an education of value. Federal policy can influence the quality of postsecondary options by supporting evidence-informed strategies to expand supply and improve outcomes at public institutions, while holding all institutions accountable for the value they provide and protecting students from the worst options.

Supporting the Quality of Existing Colleges and Programs

As more attention has been given to increasing college completion—not just enrollment—the base of evidence has grown for promising programs and policies (e.g., see the recent review by Dynarski et al. 2022). This subsection considers the potential benefits of expanding specific institutional programs with a track record of success, as well as the potential benefits of more flexible institutional support.

Enhanced guidance and advising. Personalized guidance, coaching, and/or mentoring have been shown to help college students overcome both academic and nonacademic challenges. Several randomized-control studies find that such services can help students persist and complete their degrees at higher rates (Dynarski et al. 2022). Bettinger and Baker (2014) find that four-year college students randomly assigned to receive access to individualized student coaching from outside professionals were more likely to persist and graduate. Oreopoulos and Petronijevic (2018) find that one-to-one coaching by upper-year undergraduate mentors improved students' academic performance, while less intense text and email "nudge" interventions did not. Randomized studies have found positive effects of related interventions for community college students as well (Linkow et al. 2017, 2019; Evans et al. 2020).

Comprehensive programs. Comprehensive programs that provide multifaceted financial, academic, and nonacademic supports have shown particularly dramatic effects. Of these, the best known is the City University of New York's (CUNY's) Accelerated Study in Associate Program (ASAP). In addition to waiving tuition and fees, ASAP provides textbook vouchers, free transportation, a dedicated one-to-one adviser, and enhanced tutoring and career counseling. Students are required to enroll full time. A randomized evaluation found that the program nearly doubled associate degree completion rates three years after entry (40 vs. 22 percent), with large effects on completion persisting after six years (Scrivener et al. 2015; Weiss et al. 2019). ASAP has since been successfully replicated in Ohio (Sommo et al. 2018; Miller et al. 2020), and CUNY is piloting a version of the program at several of its four-year campuses (CUNY, n.d.). The version implemented in Ohio, though less expensive per student than the original CUNY model, cost 42 percent more per student than business as usual—but because the program dramatically increased completion rates, it lowered the average cost per graduate (Miller et al. 2020). CUNY's ASAP was estimated to raise degree completion rates enough to more than cover its costs, so that enrolling 1,000 more students was estimated to provide taxpayers with fiscal benefits of $46 million in 2010 dollars (Levin and Garcia 2013).

Direct institutional support. All the programs described above require resources. Research indicates that per-student institutional resources are an important driver of college persistence and completion (Bound and Turner 2007; Bound, Lovenheim, and Turner 2012; Webber and Ehrenberg 2010; Cohodes and Goodman 2014; Deming and Walters 2017). This echoes findings that resources matter for student outcomes in the K-12 context, particularly for low-income students (Jackson, Johnson, and Persico 2015; Hyman 2017). How resources are spent matters but, because the optimal use of funds may vary from context to context, general funding support—with appropriate guardrails—may give institutions the flexibility they need to optimize. Box 5-3 describes some of the Biden-Harris Administration's efforts on this front.

Various scholars have offered proposals for what a more regular program of Federal institutional support for postsecondary education could look like. Existing Federal support for K-12 schools provides one model: Federal grants have long been provided to districts, schools, and States through Title I of the Elementary and Secondary Education Act (Skinner and Cooper 2020). Hiler and Whistle (2018), for example, propose a version of Title I funding for postsecondary education that could be based on the number and proportion of Pell Grant recipients enrolled. Federal grants that match State spending—which have proven effective in increasing State spending on other programs, such as Medicaid (Kane et al. 2005)—could reduce the risk that Federal dollars simply crowd out State investment in public colleges (Deming 2017). Some scholars have suggested that aid be targeted to community colleges, the sector with the greatest need and potential (Goolsbee, Hubbard, and Ganz 2019).

Box 5-3. Policies Focused on Direct Institutional Support

The Biden-Harris Administration has made direct institutional support a priority. The College Completion Fund for Postsecondary Student Success (funded by the Consolidated Appropriations Act of 2022, and following similar proposals in the American Families Plan and the President's Budget Request) in 2022 provided $5 million in competitive grants to postsecondary institutions to support "data-driven and evidence-based reforms that encourage postsecondary retention, transfer, and completion" (U.S. Department of Education 2022b). These funds were targeted to institutions that disproportionately serve students of color and low-income students, with priority given to community colleges. Congress provided an additional $45 million for the program for Fiscal Year 2023 (U.S. Department of Education 2023b).

During the COVID-19 pandemic, direct support for institutions was a key aspect of Federal support for postsecondary education. The American Rescue Plan Act of 2021 provided nearly $40 billion in institutional support via the Higher Education Emergency Relief Fund (HEERF). HEERF, initially established by the Coronavirus Aid, Relief, and Economic Security (CARES) Act of 2020, required institutions to spend half the funds on emergency student aid and the other half on "any costs associated with significant changes to the delivery of instruction due to the coronavirus" (U.S. Department of Education 2020, 2022c). About 90 percent of HEERF-participating institutions reported the program helped them keep students enrolled who might have otherwise dropped out (U.S. Department of Education 2023c). Evidence on similar programs during the Great Recession suggests that they help public research institutions maintain or increase their expenditures on both research and instruction (Dinerstein et al. 2014). Many states have used funding from the American Rescue Plan to expand or strengthen colleges and job training programs, seeing these as core strategies to build back from the pandemic (U.S. Department of the Treasury 2022).

Institutional Accountability

Accountability policies are wide-ranging, and they include (1) strict accountability policies that cut off institutions from Federal or State aid completely if they fail to meet certain minimum standards; (2) performance-based funding, whereby financial assistance is at least partly conditioned on institutional performance; and (3) policies that increase transparency and rely on the market to self-regulate. Evidence regarding each option is discussed in turn.

Strict accountability. A variety of past and current Federal regulations suggest potentially promising results from holding postsecondary institutions accountable for program-level student outcomes as a condition of eligibility for Federal financial aid for students. For-profit colleges are most affected by such regulations, in part because of the legal authority granted to regulators under Federal law and partly because of their poor observed student outcomes (Cellini and Koedel 2017). Cutting off aid from programs that leave students unable to repay their loan debt is at least partly effective in discouraging enrollment in such programs (Darolia 2013). Cellini, Darolia, and Turner (2020) further show that when for-profit colleges experience large drops in annual enrollment due to policy sanctions, most such students shift to community colleges, whose loan default outcomes are substantially better. Kelchen and Liu (2022) demonstrate that having debt-to-earnings ratios in excess of prescribed limits made poor-performing colleges and programs more likely to close, even though the regulations were rescinded by the Trump Administration before any sanctions were actually applied. Box 5-4 describes these regulations further.

Performance-based funding. Currently, roughly 30 States have implemented policies that partly tie higher education appropriations to outcomes such as graduation rates. Known as "performance-based funding," this strategy is an attempt to improve institutional accountability. A review of the evidence shows, however, little sign of such measures inducing institutional improvements in student outcomes such as degree completion (Ortagus et al. 2020). Researchers have also found that performance-based funding can incentivize behavior counterproductive to increasing the available quality of college opportunities, with some public, four-year institutions boosting their outcomes by decreasing admission rates and reducing enrollment of underrepresented students of color (Ortagus et al. 2020; Birdsall 2018). Some States have modified their plans to include additional incentives for improving measures related to equity, with potentially promising evidence that such equity-focused modifications can improve enrollments of low-income students and students of color (Gándara and Rutherford 2018).

Increasing the transparency of student outcomes. Increasing the transparency of student outcomes can potentially make college quality more salient, both to prospective students and to institutions themselves, increasing the competitive pressure to improve. Research indicates, for example, that improving students' information on labor market outcomes can influence their major choice (Baker et al. 2018; Wiswall and Zafar 2015). In addition to the College Scorecard, several States have their own databases of earnings data, organized by institution or industry. For example, the Salary Surfer (salarysurfer.cccco.edu), a collection of earnings data from the California Community College System, provides average salary information two years before, two years after, and five years after graduation, by industry

Box 5-4. Gainful Employment and Other Accountability Regulations

Since its 1965 enactment, the Higher Education Act (HEA) has defined the types of institutions and programs that are eligible to participate in Federal financial aid programs. Under current law, educational programs must lead to a degree at a nonprofit or public institution or must prepare students for "gainful employment in a recognized occupation" in order to be eligible for financial aid under Title IV of the HEA (U.S. Department of Education 2022d). The "gainful employment" requirement was not, however, defined in regulations for the first few decades of the HEA. In 2014, the Obama-Biden Administration finalized regulations defining gainful employment as requiring aid-eligible certificate and degree programs to meet a specific debt-to-earnings ratio for graduates. The Department of Education estimated that 840,000 students' programs would not meet this standard, nearly all at for-profit institutions (U.S. Department of Education 2014). The gainful employment regulation was rescinded under the Trump Administration. The Biden-Harris Administration is in the process of reinstating a new such rule to ensure that Federal funds are not directed to programs that do not lead to gainful employment (U.S. Department of Education 2022e).

The Administration has already taken other actions designed to increase the accountability of postsecondary institutions and programs to students and taxpayers. The Department of Education has solicited public comment on the development of an annual watch list identifying programs with the lowest financial value and announced plans to request improvement plans from the institutions that offer such programs. The Department of Education also reestablished the enforcement unit in the Office of Federal Student Aid to hold institutions accountable, and withdrew authorization from the accreditor ACICS, which oversaw for-profit institutions involved in some of the worst outcomes for students. The Administration also closed a long-standing loophole that encouraged for-profit institutions to aggressively target and recruit veterans and their families. Research indicates that such institutions lower veterans' earnings (Barr et al. 2021) and use this additional revenue stream to raise tuition rather than improve quality (Baird et al. 2022). Recent regulations enacted by the Biden-Harris Administration will ensure that private for-profit colleges derive at least 10 percent of their revenue from non-Federal sources, including veterans' benefits, as required under changes made by Congress to the 90/10 rule in the American Rescue Plan Act.

and subfield. The U.S. Census Bureau has released the Post-Secondary Employment Outcomes data product since 2017, providing earnings data by institution and degree program up to 10 years after graduation, and showing the flows of graduates from various degree programs into employment in various industries.

Evidence from the release of the College Scorecard and earlier efforts at transparency suggests, however, that transparency on its own may have a limited short-term impact on student application and behavior. Publishing annual lists of institutions with the highest levels or changes in costs for students did not appear to affect those institutions' prices or enrollments, at least in the short run (Baker 2020). For the first time, in 2015, the Scorecard made widely available average graduation rates and earnings of students enrolling at thousands of colleges nationwide. Research indicates that this release had limited effects on college search and application behavior, with effects concentrated among more advantaged students (Huntington-Klein 2016; Hurwitz and Smith 2017; Meyer and Rosinger 2019). The longer-term effects of the College Scorecard and other transparency efforts may, however, be more meaningful than the short-term effects, as information takes time to reach students, families, school counselors, and other decision-makers. More research is needed to isolate such longer-term effects of data transparency on college quality.

Addressing Geographic Barriers to Access

Additional policy efforts may be needed to more directly address geographic constraints on access. Though the COVID-19 pandemic has led to increased awareness of the feasibility of remote learning at scale, it has also shown its limitations. This subsection discusses the evidence on the effectiveness of online education as well as other, more promising alternatives to provide more students with access to high-quality college experiences on the campus of their local high school. For older returning students, box 5-5 provides additional information on local workforce training interventions that have demonstrated promise in improving outcomes.

Online programs. Some have suggested expanding online options to reduce geographic barriers to access, but research findings suggest caution about this approach. In some settings, such as four-year colleges, there are examples of students doing equally well across both online and in-person formats (Figlio, Rush, and Yin 2013; Bowen et al. 2014), as well as in blended learning approaches combining online and in-person components (Bowen et al. 2014; Alpert, Couch, and Harmon 2016). Other research finds, however, that courses taught through online formats often lead to worse learning outcomes than their in-person counterparts (Joyce et al. 2015; Alpert, Couch, and Harmon 2016; Krieg and Henson 2016). Research

Box 5-5. Supporting Workforce Training Quality

Community colleges are the primary providers of education and training targeted at labor market needs, with Pell Grants now the largest source of funding for workforce training for low-income Americans (Ma and Pender 2022b; Holzer 2008). Postsecondary institutions that provide such training may, however, be slow to respond to sectoral shifts and changes in employers' specific skill needs (Katz et al. 2022). The traditional academic schedule and program offerings may not always fit the needs of nontraditional students, such as workers displaced midcareer. Though displaced workers are eligible for Federal student aid, they may not be aware of their eligibility or how to use it (Barr and Turner 2018). Federal training resources specifically developed to serve such workers are funded at much lower levels—through the Workforce Investment and Opportunity Act—and with generally positive but somewhat mixed evidence of effectiveness (Rothstein et al. 2022; Holzer 2021).

In this context, sectoral employment and training programs have shown promise. These programs typically involve partnerships between employers or industry associations, training providers (often community colleges), workforce boards, and intermediary organizations such as unions and local nonprofits (Holzer 2015). These programs may improve alignment between training programs and workforce needs, and the wraparound services they often provide may increase students' likelihood of completion. Research on sectoral employment programs, many located at community colleges, concluded that such programs lead to substantial earnings gains for participants (Katz et al. 2022). Additional positive evidence comes from the Trade Adjustment Act Community College and Career Training (TAACCCT) Initiative, which provided $1.9 billion in grants to postsecondary institutions to enhance their workforce training capacity in the wake of the Great Recession (U.S. Department of Labor 2022a). A meta-analysis of quasi-experimental studies of TAACCCT programs concluded that the investments had overall positive effects on program completion as well as labor market outcomes (Blume et al. 2019).

Registered Apprenticeships provide another promising pathway to well-paying jobs. Registered Apprenticeships are formally approved by the U.S. Department of Labor or a State Apprenticeship Agency and are vetted to ensure that they align with industry needs in high-demand fields (U.S. Department of Labor 2022b). In this "earn and learn" model, workers get paid while training under the supervision of a mentor, typically for two to four years, and simultaneously receive supplementary classroom instruction. One study found that, for every $1.00 invested, employers receive $1.44 in direct and indirect benefits in the years during and after training an apprentice (Kuehn et al. 2022). Research on the causal impact of such programs is limited, though descriptive research indicates workers experience strong wage growth in the year after finishing the program (Walton, Gardiner, and Barnow 2022). The Biden-Harris Administration has expanded Registered Apprenticeships through additional funding and efforts like the launch of the Apprenticeship Ambassador Initiative (White House 2022).

during the COVID-19 pandemic found that college students performed worse in courses that shifted or later remained online (Bird, Castleman, and Lohner 2022; Kofoed et al. 2021). Online coursework appears to work least well for less academically prepared students, in both the for-profit sector (Bettinger et al. 2017; Bird, Castleman, and Lohner 2022) and the community college sector (Xu and Jaggars 2013). Many existing postsecondary options that are fully online do not appear to improve students' employment opportunities or earnings relative to no postsecondary education (Deming et al. 2016; Hoxby 2018). Online delivery of coursework may not even be less costly than in-person education (Hemelt and Stange 2020). This evidence suggests that online education is unlikely to fully address geographic barriers to high-quality programs.

Leveraging local institutions. New, high-value college opportunities could also be created closer to home and earlier in students' lives. Local community colleges are increasingly offering bachelor's degrees, which may reduce the distance some students need to travel for such programs. As of 2022, about 15 percent of community colleges offered at least one bachelor's degree program (Love 2022). Evidence is not yet available regarding the impact of such programs. "Dual enrollment" similarly brings college coursework closer by allowing high school students to take college-level courses, often delivered at the high school itself to minimize travel (Marken, Gray, and Lewis 2013). Enrollment in such coursework has grown rapidly in the last two decades (An and Taylor 2019). The limited evidence suggests that dual enrollment improves postsecondary trajectories. For instance, early exposure to dual-credit advanced algebra coursework increases the rigor of high school mathematics coursework taken and raises four-year college enrollment rates (Hemelt, Schwartz, and Dynarski 2020).

Early college high schools are a more intensive version of dual enrollment, in which high schools form partnerships with local colleges to offer students the opportunity to earn an associate degree or equivalent amounts of college credit at little cost to their families (Webb 2014). Students admitted into early college high schools are more likely to earn college degrees and earn them faster than similar students denied admission (Edmunds et al. 2020; Song et al. 2021). Expansion of dual enrollment and early college opportunities should be done with equity considerations featured prominently. Dual enrollment students are more likely to be white, high income, and high achieving than the typical student, likely because higher-income schools are more likely to offer dual enrollment and higher-income students at a given high school are more likely to enroll in such coursework (An and Taylor 2019). Promoting equitable access will require proactive planning and outreach by policymakers and educators.

Conclusion

The diversity and flexibility of the United States' system of postsecondary education are among its greatest assets, and part of what makes it unique globally. These features also introduce complexity and risks for prospective students. In a simpler marketplace, choice and competition might be sufficient to promote quality improvements and to drive bad options out of business. But investing in postsecondary education is not like buying groceries or even a car. Most students are limited geographically, leaving them with a narrow set of options, and the choices they do have may be hard to fully evaluate and compare in advance. Further, public institutions are often constrained in their ability to meet demand, while less-constrained private, for-profit institutions have poor track records with respect to student outcomes. Students today rely more heavily on student loans to pay for college than did their counterparts a generation ago, increasing the risk of financial hardship for those who attend college but leave without gaining valuable skills.

An examination of institution-oriented policy options reveals three major themes. First, a variety of institutional programs—many of them pioneered by community colleges—have demonstrated great potential for improving student outcomes. Many of these promising programs require additional resources to expand, and the Federal Government can both invest directly in postsecondary institutions and encourage States to increase their own investments. Second, discouraging the proliferation of low-quality postsecondary options is important in limiting the potential for students to make enrollment choices with low or negative returns. Finally, policymakers should continue exploring ways to address geographic barriers to college access through programs such as dual enrollment, early college, and community college baccalaureate degrees.

Robust Federal and State efforts to improve the affordability of college have made progress in recent decades in expanding access to college. Yet, as this chapter has documented, making a good educational investment requires attention to both price and quality. Institution-oriented policies can help the U.S. postsecondary system build on its strengths, and ensure that all students who aspire to college have access to options that are both affordable and of high quality.

Chapter 6

Supply Challenges in U.S. Labor Markets

Despite the enormous disruption of the COVID-19 pandemic, U.S. labor markets remained tight throughout 2022. For much of the last year, there were two job openings for every unemployed person—an unprecedented gap between labor demand and supply that has shifted the balance of power between workers and businesses. The resulting surge in hiring empowered many workers to change jobs and careers, with many job switchers experiencing substantial wage gains. Workplace organizing increased, with union representation petitions rising sharply in 2022, as workers sought to use their increased leverage to negotiate better working conditions.

It is tempting to assume that today's hiring challenges are primarily due to the lingering effects of the pandemic. However, tight labor markets predated the pandemic, and demographic trends indicate that labor supply challenges are likely to remain, even as the pandemic recedes. The baby boom generation is aging out of the labor force, and there are not enough younger workers to replace them. This tightening of the supply of labor due to population aging is a principal cause of current hiring challenges, constraining the economy's capacity for growth by slowing the rate at which businesses can expand hiring. Unless efforts are undertaken to mitigate the impact of demographic change—by drawing more adults into the labor market and/or increasing immigration flows—the labor supply is likely to be constrained for the foreseeable future.

This chapter examines both short- and long-run challenges for the U.S. labor supply. In the short run, some lingering effects of the pandemic remain, principally in the form of heightened labor market exits of older workers.

Immigration inflows, which were falling before the pandemic began, fell steeply when the U.S. borders closed and are just starting to recover. Chief among the long-run challenges are demographic trends, particularly population aging, but also falling labor force participation among prime-age adults. The chapter concludes with a description of several options to boost the U.S. labor supply; it also takes a closer look at labor markets experiencing especially acute labor shortfalls to see how macroeconomic forces are affecting specific industries.

Labor Supply Fundamentals

What determines the supply of labor? Simply put, individuals who are able to work decide whether to join the labor force, and if they do, how many hours they will work. Individuals can also decide to leave the labor force—to retire, to seek further schooling, or to care for small children. The aggregate labor supply of a nation is the sum of these individual choices. The aggregate labor supply is also a function of the size of the working-age population, which depends on fertility choices of earlier generations as well as immigration flows.

In the simple framework used in economics textbooks to model the labor supply decision, employment is a choice between earning a wage and the alternative uses of that time (e.g., household tasks, childcare, leisure). Households also require a steady source of income to pay for necessary goods and services. This very simple model ignores many important variables that go into the labor supply decision, such as the psychological and social rewards of work and the nonmonetary aspects of particular jobs. Yet this simple model does allow economists to make useful predictions of how individual decisions are affected by more easily observed factors, such as changing wages and the availability of other household income.

Chief among these inferences is that individuals who cannot meet essential consumption needs without working are highly likely to participate in the labor market. This suggests that individuals without a source of preexisting wealth or nonwage income are more likely to seek formal employment. A second implication is that individuals are more likely to enter the labor market when wages are high, when nonparticipation becomes more costly in lost earnings. This model also predicts that participation will fall when wages decline, for example, due to negative labor demand shocks. As discussed later in the chapter, many economists believe that declining relative wages for non-college-educated workers are chiefly responsible for men's declining participation in recent decades.

Trends in U.S. Labor Market Participation

The labor force participation rate (LFPR) is defined as the share of the population age 16 years and above who are working or who are actively seeking employment (BLS 2022). The labor force participation rate is an important measure of labor market potential and health (box 6-1). Nonparticipation in paid activity is not necessarily a source of concern—many nonparticipants are retirees, students, or parents with young children, many of whom do not desire formal employment. However, low participation rates can indicate an untapped potential labor supply, which includes individuals on the sidelines who would enter the labor market if attractive opportunities were available or obstacles to formal employment were removed.

As shown in figure 6-1, labor force participation rose markedly in the second half of the last century, from 59.6 to 67.1 percent between 1968 and 2000. This growth in participation was due to the increased labor market activity of women—facilitated by changing societal norms, access to birth

Box 6-1. Labor Supply Terminology

Discussions about the labor supply can be confusing, given that the term "labor supply" is sometimes used to indicate the aggregate labor supply and at other times refers to labor force participation. In this chapter, we distinguish which term we are using as follows:

- *Labor supply* typically refers to the aggregate labor supply, which is a function of the adult population (age 16 years and above), as well as the share of the adult population that participates in the labor market. However, analyses of the labor supply often take population trends as given and focus on the labor supply decisions of individuals, which are reflected in the labor force participation rate and the employment rate, as defined next here.
- *The labor force participation rate (LFPR)* is the share of the noninstitutionalized adult population participating in the labor market; this includes people who are currently working or who are seeking employment.
- *The employment-to-population ratio*, or *the employment rate*, is the share of the noninstitutionalized adult population that is employed. It is a participation measure similar to the LFPR but does not include unemployed people in the numerator.

Figure 6-1. U.S. Labor Force Participation Rate, 1948–2022

Participation rate, in percent, age 16 years and above

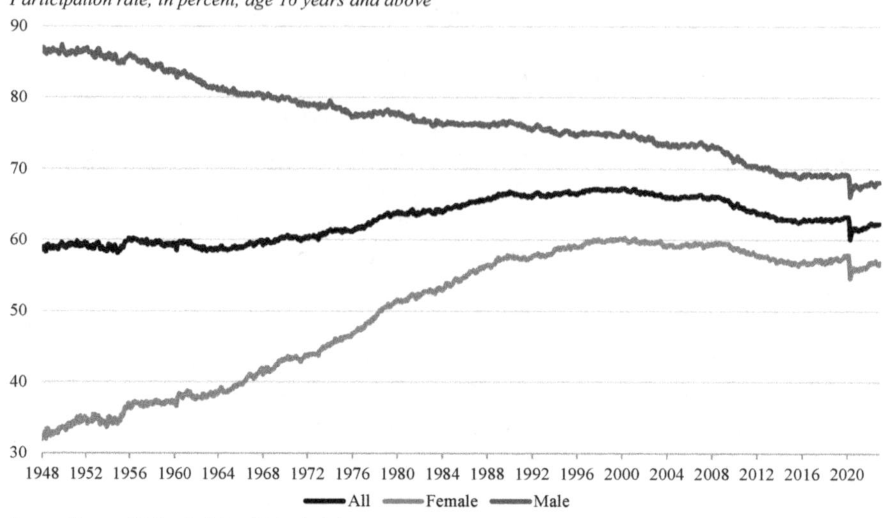

Sources: Bureau of Labor Statistics; CEA calculations.
Note: Data are seasonally adjusted. Rate is for age 16 years and above.

control, and improved education and labor market opportunities—with large gains especially among married women (e.g., Blau and Kahn 2007; Goldin and Katz 2002; Black and Juhn 2000). The increase in women's participation was more than enough to offset the decline in participation among men since the 1950s. As a result of more women entering the labor market and favorable demographic trends (the baby boom generation swelled the ranks of the workforce during this period), the U.S. labor supply grew steadily until 2000.

Labor force participation in the United States began to decline after 2000 due to both supply and demand factors. The U.S. economy experienced two demand shocks during this period: the dot-com crash, which ended the economic expansion of the 1990s; and the global financial crisis, which began in 2007. Women's participation growth also leveled off and began to decline after 2000. But the most significant factor pushing down participation in recent years has been the aging of the workforce, with the oldest baby boomers entering their retirement years at the beginning of the global financial crisis.

Why Worry About Slower Labor Supply Growth?

Declining labor force participation and slowing U.S. population growth mean that there is a dwindling supply of workers. A principal reason to be concerned about slower labor supply growth is that it implies slower economic growth (for further discussion, see chapter 1 of this *Report*). The growth of economic output is determined by labor supply growth, capital investments, and productivity growth—all else being equal, if the labor supply's growth slows, so too does economic growth. As labor market participation declines with age, an aging population also reduces the fraction of active workers in the population, thereby putting downward pressure on output per capita if not accompanied by capital investments or increases in productivity. Strong per capita economic growth was a primary driver of rising living standards over the last century; the aging population could have a negative impact on improvements in U.S. living standards in the future.

Although demographic change is relatively easy to forecast, it is more difficult to account for changes in technology and productivity that may dampen the impact of the aging population on future economic growth. Cutler and others (1990) posit that labor scarcity could spur labor-saving technological innovation that would offset the impact of demographic change on output growth. Most studies have concluded that the relationship between

Box 6-2. Work and Leisure in the United States and Europe

John Maynard Keynes famously predicted that within two generations workers would work only 15 hours a week. For today's Americans, that is simply not the case, despite living in a vastly richer country than Keynes experienced in the early 1900s. After decades of decline, the length of the typical American workweek began increasing in the 1970s, despite widespread expectations that productivity growth would lead to more leisure time for workers. Schor (1993) highlighted the plight of the "overworked American" in an influential book on work and leisure in the United States. She determined that a weakened labor movement and the erosion of workers' power were largely responsible for setbacks in converting productivity gains into a shorter workweek for workers.

Americans in the labor market now work longer hours, have less sick leave, and take fewer vacations than those in other wealthy nations. In 1960, hours of work and labor market participation rates were similar in the United States and Europe. But by 2000, there was a large gap in the work effort of the typical person in the United States compared with their counterparts in Europe. While the typical American works as many hours a year as they did in the 1970s, Europeans generally work much less, working fewer hours and weeks throughout the year. As suggested by Schor, differences in labor regulation and unionization appear to be the dominant factors explaining differences in annual hours worked per year between the United States and Europe (Alesina, Glaeser, and Sacerdote 2005).

Box 6-3. Deaths of Despair in the United States

For white Americans between age 45 and 54, average life expectancy is no longer increasing; in fact, it even declined for several years, a pattern not previously seen outside pandemics or wars. This occurred during a period when Black Americans saw gains in life expectancy, narrowing the enduring gap in outcomes between these two groups. Increases in mortality rates among whites are largely accounted for by higher rates of suicide, opioid overdoses, and alcohol abuse (Case and Deaton 2015). The term "deaths of despair" was coined by Case and Deaton (2020) in their influential book, which documents the impact of declining economic opportunity on the health and well-being of working-class society in the United States. They explain that these deaths of despair primarily affect white Americans without a four-year college degree, living in areas of the country that have a very low share of the working-age population employed.

While economists usually frame employment as a choice between paid work and alternative uses of time, Case and Deaton's (2020) work highlights the importance of good jobs in providing meaning, structure, and purpose to a community. They write: "Destroy work and, in the end, working-class life cannot survive. It is the loss of meaning, of dignity, of pride, and of self-respect that comes with the loss of marriage and of community that brings on despair, not just or even primarily the loss of money." Their research shows how the diminished economic prospects of white working-class Americans constitute not only an economic crisis but also a public health crisis.

Recent papers have challenged the notion that growing deaths of despair are a phenomenon unique to economically disadvantaged whites; deaths from suicide, drug use, and alcohol use have risen even more among Indigenous persons living in the United States (Friedman et al. 2023). Among Indigenous persons, local economic conditions have a heterogenous effect on deaths by suicide and drug use, suggesting that improvements in economic conditions alone may not be enough to reduce deaths of despair (Akee et al. 2022).

an aging population and output is negative (e.g., Gagnon, Johannsen, and Lopez-Salido 2021; Maestas, Mullen, and Powell 2022; and Sheiner 2014). However, Acemoglu and Restrepo (2020) find that the impact on technological change dominates, and that an older workforce increases economic growth. Eggertsson, Lancastre, and Summers (2019) similarly find that population aging can increase growth due to increased national savings that accrue as populations age, driving down interest rates. However, as interest rates approach zero and cannot fall further, this mechanism is disrupted, and they find that the impact of aging on growth becomes negative. Overall, the evidence suggests that aging populations slow per capita economic growth, but the economy's potential to adapt to the tightening of labor supply in ways that spur productivity cannot be discounted.

From an individual perspective, the fact that fewer people are engaged in paid labor market activity is not necessarily negative and could simply reflect personal choices. By way of example, John Maynard Keynes famously predicted in 1930 that technological progress would increase living standards so much that his grandchildren would work just 15 hours a week, devoting the rest of their time to leisure (Keynes 2010; orig. pub. 1930). As noted in box 6-2, this prediction did not come to pass for workers in the United States. But evidence suggests that many nonparticipants, if not otherwise engaged in schooling or caring for young children, are not happier than those who work. Prime-age men who are out of the labor force report low levels of emotional well-being, and derive little meaning from how they spend their time (Krueger 2017). They are also less likely to be married and much more likely to be living in poverty. Localities where employment rates have fallen the most have also seen a sharper rise in opioid deaths and suicides (see box 6-3), suggesting significant community stress in these areas.

Causes of U.S. Labor Supply Challenges

Slowing population growth and declining labor force participation are significant headwinds for U.S. labor supply. If these trends persist, and offsetting increases in productivity or capital intensity fail to materialize, there will not be enough workers to meet long-run demand. Because understanding the causes of current labor supply challenges is necessary to craft effective policy solutions, this section provides an overview of the dominant factors driving slower growth of U.S. labor supply since 2000.

Demographic Trends

Demographic trends are the principal cause of near-term U.S. labor supply challenges. Over the next decade, the share of the population in their prime working years (between age 25 and 54) will decline in the United States and in many other countries, as shown in figure 6-2. These demographic trends are the result of a sharp decline in fertility rates between 1960 and the late 1970s, with fertility remaining at or below replacement rates for the last several decades. Additionally, life expectancy in the United States has also not kept pace with that of other wealthy nations, and was decreasing for some groups even before the COVID-19 pandemic (see box 6-3). Due to low fertility rates, the vast majority of near-term working-age population

Figure 6-2. Percentage of Total Projected Population That Is Prime Age, 2026–50

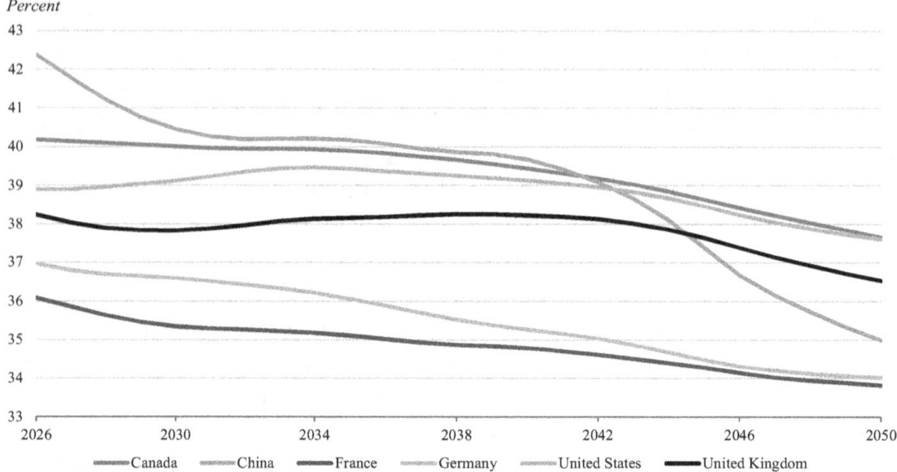

Sources: World Bank; United Nations Population Projections.
Note: "Prime age" is 25–54 years.

Figure 6-3. Prime-Age versus Overall Labor Force Participation, 1990–2022

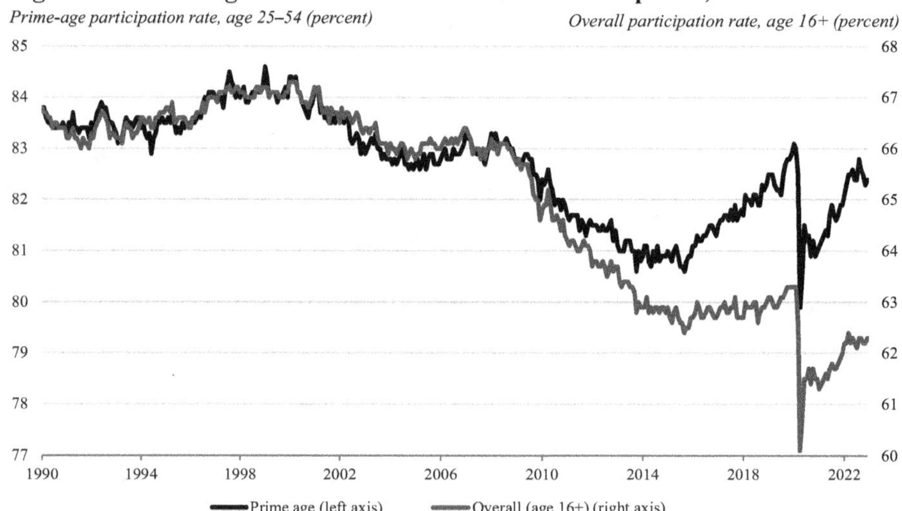

Source: Current Population Survey data.
Note: "Prime age" is 25–54 years.

growth will be accounted for by immigrants and their descendants born in the United States (Blau and Mackie 2017).

The tightening of labor supply conditions due to these demographic trends was well under way before the pandemic, as can been seen in figure 6-3. Between 1990 and 2008, prime-age and overall labor force participation moved more or less in tandem. Starting in 2009, however, the two categories began to diverge, as baby boomers began to enter their early retirement years. Increases in the participation rate among older workers and slack labor demand conditions in the years after the financial crisis dampened but did not completely offset the initial effect of retirements on the labor supply (Aaronson et al. 2014; Abraham and Kearney 2020). As labor demand recovered and labor markets tightened in the years preceding the COVID-19 pandemic, many workers left the sidelines and entered the labor market in response, easing concerns about the labor supply. Then the pandemic arrived, and COVID-19—a virus that is particularly dangerous for older members of the workforce—sped up many of the forces reshaping the labor market. In December 2022, the prime-age LFPR was just shy of its prepandemic peak, but overall participation had fallen by a full percentage point, due primarily to population aging and the increase in the propensity of older workers to retire during the pandemic.

Declining Labor Market Participation Among Men

In addition to population aging, another cause of slowing labor supply growth is the decline in participation among men, particularly those without a college degree. The participation rate for U.S. men in their prime-age working years peaked in the 1950s and has been falling in earnest since the mid-1960s. This decline is sharper than in other advanced economies. Prime-age men in the United States and the United Kingdom had similar rates of participation in the 1980s and 1990s, but the participation of men in the United States continued to fall after 2000, while the United Kingdom's participation rates remained relatively flat. This trend has particularly significant implications for economic growth, because individuals are at their most productive in their prime-age working years.

The underlying causes of declining male participation have been the subject of much scholarly interest but still remain an open debate. This very large body of research is summarized here to explain the potential causes of declining male participation and to illuminate potential policies to counteract the ongoing decline.

Spousal income for heterosexual men. Increases in married women's labor supply could reduce male labor force participation by reducing the cost of nonparticipation and increasing responsibilities at home, such as childrearing and senior care. However, the evidence suggests that this is *not* a significant factor driving down male participation. Men with working wives and men with children have had the smallest declines in participation among all men (Juhn and Potter 2006; CEA 2016). As discussed in more detail in box 6-4, nonparticipating men are more likely than other groups to rely on income from other family members, usually parents. It is plausible that changing trends in household formation, such as more adults living with their parents, will reduce male participation. However, the causality may go

Box 6-4. On What Income Do Jobless Men Live?

How do men between the age of 25 and 54 who do not work fund food, shelter, and other necessities? Figure 6-i documents sources of income for prime-age men who were not in the labor force in 2022. For comparison purposes, we also provide the composition of household income for men in the labor force and for women. A primary source of income for nonparticipating men is other household members, principally parents. In contrast, income provided by other household members accounts for only a small share of income for other groups. Spousal income available to nonparticipants is smaller than it is for men in the labor force, in part reflecting lower marriage rates. Government transfer income, particularly disability insurance, is a key source of income for some nonparticipating men, although, as can be seen in figure 6-i, it accounts for a relatively small share of income for nonparticipants as a group.

Figure 6-i. Sources of Annual Income for Prime-Age Workers by Sex and Labor Force Status, 2022

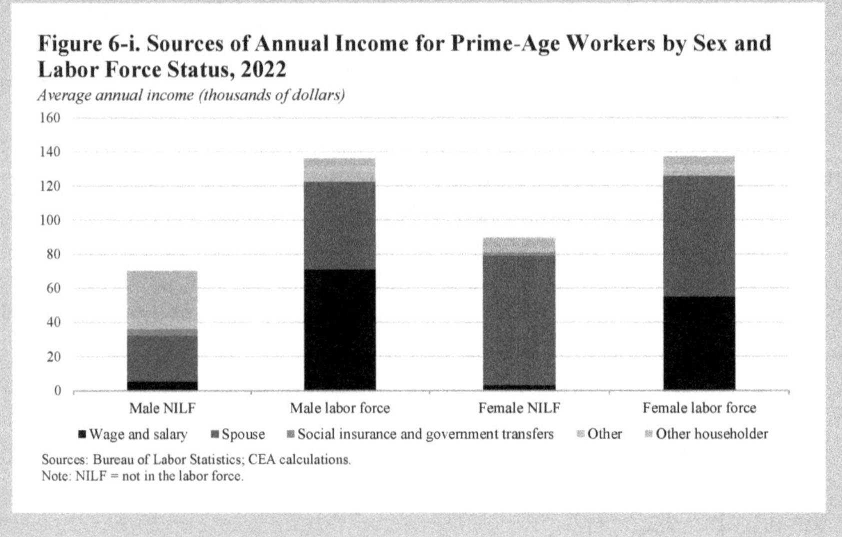

Sources: Bureau of Labor Statistics; CEA calculations.
Note: NILF = not in the labor force.

in the other direction: these trends themselves may be an outcome of higher housing costs and fewer labor market opportunities for young workers (Fry, Passel, and Cohn 2020; Matsudaira 2015).

Disability insurance. Social Security Disability Insurance (SSDI) is another candidate for a supply-side explanation of declines in male labor force participation rates. SSDI receipts increased for several decades before peaking in 2010, after which their incidence fell (CBPP 2021). A substantial body of research indicates that the availability of SSDI benefits lowers participation for workers who are on the margin of eligibility (e.g., Bound 1989; Autor and Duggan 2003; Maestas, Mullen, and Strand 2013; and

Gelber, Moore, and Strand 2017). However, SSDI receipts do not appear to be an important determinant of declining male participation rates. From 1967 until 2014, prime-age male participation fell 7.5 percentage points, while the share of prime-age men who received SSDI benefits increased by 2 percentage points (CEA 2016). Moreover, this 2-percentage-point rise in the SSDI take-up rate among prime-age men should not be interpreted as having caused lower participation, given that many of the men receiving SSDI benefits would likely not have participated due to their disabilities. An analysis conducted by the CEA finds that, under reasonable assumptions, holding SSDI receipts constant for prime-age men during the 1967–2014 period would only have eliminated between 0.3 and 0.5 percentage point of the observed reduction in prime-age men's participation (CEA 2016).

Rising incarceration rates. As shown in figure 6-4, Black men have a lower labor force participation rate in the United States than Hispanic or white men, and participation among Black men has been falling more steeply than that of other groups. A steep rise in incarceration rates beginning in the 1980s is a potential culprit in the declining employment prospects of Black men, who face a much higher risk of incarceration than white men. Because standard labor market statistics exclude institutionalized populations, they understate the impact of rising incarceration rates on employment among Black men. Doleac (2016) shows that accounting for the incarcerated population lowered the employment rate (i.e., the percentage of the population

Figure 6-4. Prime-Age Male Labor Force Participation, by Race, 1976–2022

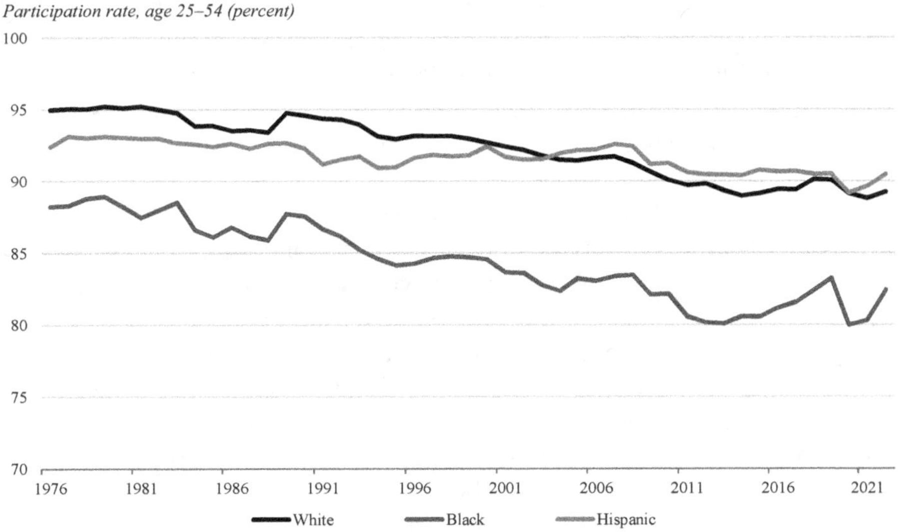

Sources: Bureau of Labor Statistics; CEA calculations.
Note: "Prime age" is 25–54 years. Data are annual averages.

that is employed) of Black men in 2014 by about 4 percentage points, with only a minimal impact on white men's employment.

Incarceration is also likely to have a negative impact on employment after release—an effect that would be reflected in official statistics. Formerly incarcerated people face a number of barriers to formal employment: limited labor market experiences while incarcerated, laws preventing them from being employed in certain jobs, and employer practices that discourage hiring those with criminal records. Résumé-audit studies have found that an applicant's criminal record is a significant barrier to finding employment (Pager 2003). Mueller-Smith (2015) finds that for individuals with a previous formal labor market attachment, incarceration decreases the probability of subsequent employment, especially for those serving longer terms. Some recent papers using administrative data have not found strong evidence of significant scarring effects on postincarceration earnings and employment (Garin et al. 2022; Looney and Turner 2018). However, this empirical result is a consequence of poor labor market opportunities preceding incarceration; formerly incarcerated persons are disproportionately drawn from neighborhoods in extreme economic distress. A reasonable interpretation of these findings is that while incarceration likely does have an impact on future employment and earnings, many of the challenges that formerly incarcerated persons face in the labor market start long before their incarceration begins.

Abraham and Kearney (2020) use estimates of the formerly incarcerated population and Mueller-Smith's (2015) estimates of scarring effects to roughly calculate the impact of rising incarceration rates on declines in the overall employment rate. They estimate that rising incarceration accounted for a decline of 0.12 percentage point in the employment-to-population ratio between 1999 and 2018, a period when the ratio declined 3.8 percentage points. Though admittedly a rough estimate, their calculations suggest that rising incarceration accounts for a small part of observed declines in overall employment. However, rising incarceration disproportionally affects Black communities, so incarceration's role in driving down participation among Black men is likely much larger.

Geographic mismatches. Labor force participation varies dramatically across the United States, with striking gaps even among prime-age adults (Nunn, Parsons, and Shambaugh 2019). Migration flows within the United States were quite high in the mid-20th century. Those picking up stakes generally moved to where they could find work, and migration flows redirected population on net from low-income to high-income regions (Blanchard and Katz 1992). However, since 1980, internal migration has declined, and moves have become less likely to reallocate population to more prosperous parts of the country (Ganong and Shoag 2017). Reduced internal migration may be a result of increased housing costs and/or increased licensing costs for certain occupations and industries (Hsieh and Moretti 2019; Johnson and Kleiner 2020).

Declines in labor migration may have exacerbated declining labor force participation, with workers increasingly exiting the labor market instead of migrating in response to regional shocks (Dao, Furceri, and Loungani 2017). This change has been evident in manufacturing employment declines since 2000; unlike previous downturns, those who lost jobs have been less likely to migrate to other regions and more likely to exit the labor force (Autor, Dorn, and Hanson 2021; Charles, Hurst, and Schwartz 2018). However, some economists have argued that declining mobility is an appropriate response to improved information about distant labor markets reflecting rational expectations about potential employment success in those locations (Kaplan and Schulhofer-Wohl 2017) and to declines in urban premiums for non-college-educated workers (Autor 2019).

The extent to which declining geographic mobility has exacerbated declining labor force participation remains an open question. The fact that out-migration responses to regional downturns have declined suggests that it does play a role, but the importance of this role cannot be fully ascertained with the evidence. However, the reduction in domestic migration to areas with better economic opportunities is well established in the literature. This indicates that policies designed to pull workers into the labor market will have limited success unless they can also improve job opportunities in regions where participation is currently low.

Demand factors: import competition and technological change. The labor supply model outlined earlier in the chapter posits another theory for declining participation: wages. In the model, adverse demand shocks can have a negative impact on an individual's decision to participate through wages alone. The steepest declines in participation since the 1970s have been among men without a four-year degree; these men have also experienced declines in wages throughout much of this period. It is reasonable to wonder, therefore, if declines in labor demand can account for declines in participation, particularly among men without a four-year degree.

Why would demand for labor have fallen disproportionately for men without a college degree? Possible causes include globalization and technological change. These dual forces are thought to be key drivers of "job polarization"—a term used to describe the relative growth of high- and low-skill jobs and the disappearance of middle-skill opportunities (Acemoglu and Autor 2010; Autor and Dorn 2013). Middle-skill jobs generally include tasks that are most vulnerable to automation and offshoring—making it difficult to distinguish the relative impact of each factor on employment. Job losses during the two recessions preceding the COVID-19 pandemic were concentrated among middle-skill jobs, and workers who lost those jobs tended to exit the labor market rather than take lower-paying work (Foote and Ryan 2015).

A number of papers have linked declines in U.S. manufacturing employment to increased import competition from China (e.g., Autor, Dorn, and Hanson 2013; Autor et al. 2014; Pierce and Schott 2016; and Acemoglu et al. 2015). Increased imports from China reduced demand for domestically produced manufacturing goods, which reduced demand for U.S. manufacturing workers, who are disproportionately less-educated men. More recent research by Bloom and others (2019) suggests that the negative impact of the "China shock" on U.S. manufacturing employment was sizable between 2000 and 2007 but has not exacerbated manufacturing declines in more recent years. However, increased import competition is not the only cause of manufacturing employment declines; automation has also increased. Looking specifically at the role of robots in employment declines, Acemoglu and Restrepo (2020) estimate that each robot displaces about 5.6 workers. Using this estimate, Abraham and Kearney (2020) tentatively conclude that increases in the stock of robots between 1999 and 2018 resulted in the loss of 1.1 million jobs during this period.

Many economists believe that demand factors are the principal cause of declining male labor force participation. In their comprehensive review and meta-analysis of recent research on declining overall employment rates, Abraham and Kearney (2020, 636) state that "our review of the evidence leads us to conclude that, among the factors whose effects we are able to quantify, labor demand factors are the most important drivers of the secular decline in employment over the 1999 to 2018 period." However, their estimates indicate that almost half the fall in employment rates during this period is unexplained after accounting for changes in demand. The CEA (2016) also concluded that low wages were the primary driver of male participation declines, with smaller roles for supply factors.

A seeming puzzle with regard to the view that declining wages are driving participation declines is that real wages for lower-skilled men rebounded in the 1990s and the 2010s, periods when the participation of men continued to fall. One possibility, suggested by Wu (2022), is that it is not absolute but relative declines in wages that reduce participation. Widening inequality means that relative wages for men without a four-year degree have declined steadily for many decades, reducing their status, marriage prospects, and job satisfaction. Wu finds that changes in relative wages account for almost half the growth in labor force exits among noncollege men between 1980 and 2019. In a related paper, Binder and Bound (2019) argue that supply and demand factors are likely not additive but interactive, with negative demand shocks for noncollege men leading to less stable employment and lowering marriage rates, in turn leading to changes in household formation that reduce the male labor supply. Together, these papers suggest that demand factors and rising inequality may together have a negative impact on participation by lowering the relative gain in status attainable through work.

Summary of the evidence on the declining male LFPR. Despite significant scholarly interest in the decline of male labor force participation, questions remain. The evidence suggests that demand factors have played an important role, with globalization and automation reducing employment and wages, particularly for men without college degrees. However, a sizable participation gap remains unexplained by changes in labor demand. Supply factors, such as increasing incarceration and disability insurance, have also exacerbated the decline, although the impact of these factors has been small. An open question for research is how changes in gender roles and household formation—particularly declining marriage rates and more adults living with their parents—interact with demand factors and have exacerbated declines in participation.

Despite the incomplete nature of the evidence on participation declines, the extensive research literature does point to policy measures that could boost participation among men. In particular—given the importance of demand factors and rising inequality in driving down participation—efforts to improve wages and working conditions for men without a four-year degree would likely draw more of them into the labor market. Several policy options to boost participation by addressing these factors are discussed in greater detail later in the chapter.

Female Labor Force Participation: The United States Falls Behind

Despite declining labor force participation among men, the U.S. labor supply grew for much of the last century, largely due to the growing participation of women. The many social and economic factors driving the growth of female participation in the last century are the subject of a large body of literature, a review of which is beyond the scope of this chapter. What is more relevant for current labor supply challenges is that the growth in women's participation in the United States leveled off in the 1990s and began to decline. This stagnation did not occur in other advanced economies, where female participation continued to grow. As shown in figure 6-5, female participation levels and trends in the United States were similar to those in Canada and the United Kingdom until about 1995. Female participation continued to grow in these two countries after 1995, unlike in the United States. By 2015, U.S. female participation rates were below those for women in Japan, who were far less likely to work than women in the United States as recently as 2005.

Most of literature on declining female participation since 2000 has focused on factors affecting the *maternal* labor supply. When discussing why U.S. female participation has fallen behind that of other countries, a frequent observation is that the United States lacks publicly provided childcare

Figure 6-5. Prime-Age Female Labor Force Participation, 1984–2021

Participation rate, age 25–54, selected OECD countries (percent)

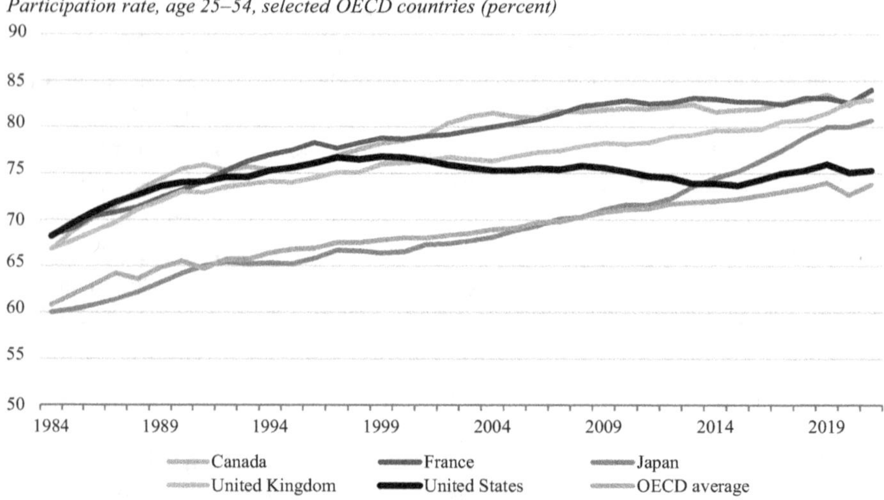

Source: Organization for Economic Cooperation and Development.
Note: "Prime age" is 25 to 54 years.

and paid family and medical leave policies, which are common in most advanced economies. The United States spent only $2,600 on care and early education per child under 6 years of age in 2017, compared with the EU average of $5,500 (OECD 2019). In consequence, childcare in the United States consumes a significant portion of family budgets, with care costing up to one-third of the average earnings of a single mother (Ziliak 2014). Most of the empirical evidence indicates that publicly provided care options for young children boost the maternal labor supply (e.g., Gelbach 2002; Baker, Gruber, and Milligan 2008; and Haeck, Lefebvre, and Merrigan 2015), as discussed in the next section on policy options. Chapter 4 of this *Report* also discusses more broadly the social and economic benefits of greater public support for early care and education.

However, there is no strong evidence tying childcare costs facing families to declines in female participation since 2000. Declines in participation among women are broad-based and are actually steepest among single women without children, whose participation declined by 7 percentage points between 1989 and 2016 (see figure 6-6). In many ways, female participation trends after 2000 resemble those of men in the United States, who also had declining participation relative to other advanced economies during this period. While the factors driving declining participation among men have been the subject of much research, much less attention has focused on declines in women's participation—with a few notable exceptions, such as Black, Schanzenbach, and Breitwieser (2017) and Abraham and Kearney (2020). Although research has been understandably focused on the role of

Figure 6-6. Prime-Age Female Labor Force Participation Rate, 1976–2022

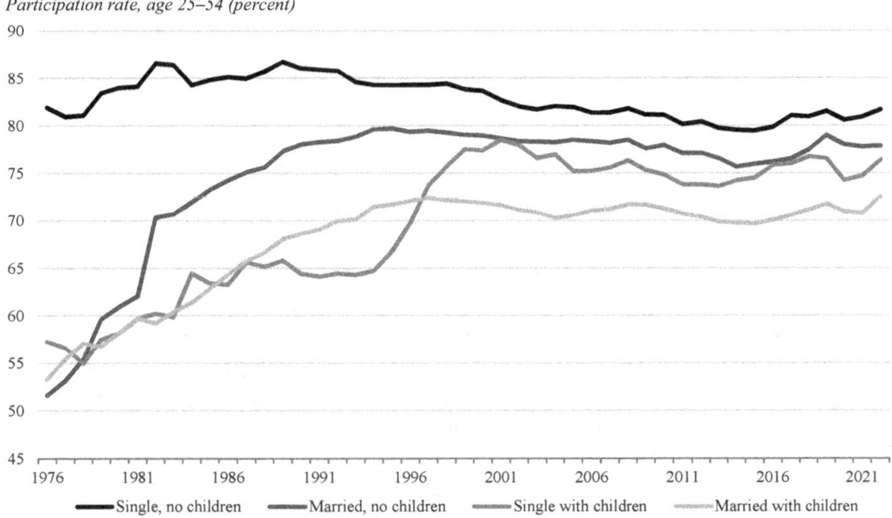

Sources: Bureau of Labor Statistics; CEA calculations.
Note: "Prime age" is 25–54 years. Data are annual averages.

care in boosting the maternal labor supply, the factors driving declining participation among women without children are also worthy of further investigation.

The COVID-19 Pandemic's Lingering Effects on the Labor Supply

The forces constraining the supply of workers at the onset of the COVID-19 pandemic were amplified as countries attempted to mitigate the spread of the virus. Retirements among baby boomers, already fueling hiring challenges in many industries, spiked as older workers faced new and potentially severe health risks at work. Some employers encouraged workers to take early retirement in order to slash workforces in the face of reduced demand. Immigration bans and closed borders halted the flow of foreign-born workers who were critical for many industries, particularly food services and agriculture. The pandemic also disrupted the availability of childcare and in-person school, making it difficult for many parents to return to work.

Prime-age participation has mostly rebounded from the pandemic (see box 6-5), and recent efforts to clear the backlog of applicants have returned immigration flows to prepandemic levels. But the lingering effects on the labor supply remain, principally lower participation rates among older workers. While retirements have increased in previous downturns (Gorodnichenko, Song, and Stolyarov 2013; Coile and Levine 2011), the pandemic-induced recession had a particularly severe impact. Quarterly retirement rates increased by 5 percentage points at the start of the pandemic,

Box 6-5. The Missing Prime-Age Workers

Early during the COVID-19 pandemic, declines in prime-age labor market participation were primarily due to pandemic-related disruptions. Layoffs, illness, and care responsibilities pushed many participants out of the labor market (Garcia and Cowan 2022; Goda and Soltas 2022; Cajner and others 2020). As businesses and schools reopened, and vaccines were rolled out, prime-age participation rebounded quickly (Forsythe, Kahn, Lange, and Wiczer 2022; Hansen, Sabia, and Schaller 2022). Individuals with disabilities actually increased their participation relative to prepandemic levels, likely due to increased telework and remote work practices adopted during the pandemic (Ne'eman and Maestas 2022). Yet despite tight labor markets and steadily rising wages, growth in prime-age participation slowed markedly in the latter half of 2022; at the end of the year, it remained 0.6 percentage point below the level in February 2020. As policymakers had hoped that continued prime-age participation growth would ease ongoing inflationary pressures, concern about these missing workers grew. But why prime-age participation remained below prepandemic levels three years after the start of the pandemic cannot be easily ascertained.

One possibility is that the level of participation at the end of the last expansion was an exception and not the rule. The last expansion pulled many workers into the labor market, and the continued growth in participation between 2016 and 2019 surprised many economists. It may be that participation rates were well above the trend at the end of the long expansion that preceded the pandemic (Barkin 2022).

Another possibility is that participation will keep growing as long as the current expansion continues. That participation decisions can respond to favorable economic conditions with a lag is suggested by Cajner, Coglianese, and Montes (2021), who find that participation declines after a negative shock can last up to four years, with nonparticipants who return to school or shift to care responsibilities during the downturn accounting for much of the lagged response. If households adapted to the pandemic in ways that can take a while to unwind, it may be that more prime-age workers will return to the labor market over time.

a much larger spike in the retirement rate than occurred during the financial crisis (McEntarfer 2022). Unlike previous downturns, the pandemic-induced growth in retirements appears largely unrelated to local economic conditions, suggesting that the retirement surge may have been primarily driven by COVID-19 health concerns (Coile and Zhang 2022). A recent paper suggests that the increase in housing wealth during the pandemic may have also played an important role, with more retirements among older workers in housing markets with stronger price growth (Favilukis and Li 2023).

As of the end of 2022, the growth in the retired share of the U.S. population accounted for nearly all the shortfall in labor force participation relative to prepandemic levels. In a recent paper looking at the surge in retirements during the pandemic, Montes, Smith, and Dajon (2022) estimate that almost half the retirements since the start of the pandemic have been "excess" retirements that would likely have not occurred in absence of the pandemic. They find particularly sharp increases in retirements among workers over 65, among whites, and among those with a four-year degree. Given the advanced age of most excess retirees, it seems unlikely that a large proportion will return to the labor force. The authors also find that flows into retirement remained elevated almost three years after the start of the pandemic. They conclude that it may take some time for retirement behavior to return to prepandemic norms.

Options to Boost the U.S. Labor Supply

As detailed in this chapter, the United States faces long-run headwinds for its labor supply that may have an impact on future economic growth. This section discusses policy options for boosting the U.S. labor supply. Although the focus here is on broad-based measures, labor supply challenges are often unique to specific markets, and policy solutions to increase the labor supply in general may be insufficient to remedy supply issues in specific occupations and industries. To highlight this fact, this section also discusses the supply challenges facing two particular labor markets, medical care (box 6-6) and local public education (box 6-7) in greater detail.

Increasing Immigration

Increasing immigration to the United States is frequently cited as a way to mitigate the consequences of the aging population. Immigration increases potential output by increasing the size of the labor force; because new immigrants are typically working age, it also lessens the effect of the aging population on per capita economic growth. Immigrants also make other important contributions to the U.S. economy. For example, given that they often have fewer long-standing family and social ties, they are more mobile than workers born in the country and are more responsive to local economic conditions (Basso and Peri 2020). Skilled immigrants have been found to boost innovation and technological change, which is an added contribution to overall economic growth (Bernstein et al. 2022; Hunt and Gauthier-Loiselle 2010). Overall, research also suggests that the effects of newly arrived immigrants on the wages and employment of the

Box 6-6. A Critical Shortfall of Nurses and Physicians

Demographic shifts that began before the COVID-19 pandemic had already started to manifest in a noticeable reduction in the supply of health care providers. Researchers have documented the effect of the aging of the U.S. population on the supply of nurses and physicians in certain specialties such as primary care and psychiatry, along with geographic misallocation affecting rural areas (Buerhous, Auerbach, and Staiger 2017; Petterson et al. 2012; Satiani et al. 2018; Ricketts 2005). Given that the youngest members of the baby boom generation are just reaching retirement age, the aging of the population will continue to affect the availability of health care providers for the foreseeable future by simultaneously reducing the supply of providers and increasing demand for health care.

Compounding these predictable shifts, the pandemic exerted a historic shock on the health care workforce, exacerbating existing challenges. Unprecedented rises in the demand for health care overwhelmed providers. Many left their jobs to protect themselves and their families from catching the virus, to care for their young children and elderly parents, and to focus on their physical and emotional health and lessen burnout (Galvin 2021). These actions increased the burden for providers who remained in the system.

Swift, short-term solutions were implemented to stabilize the supply of critical health care workers. Hospitals utilized travel nurses to fill short-term increases in demand (Gottlieb and Zenilman 2020). The wages of these traveling nurse positions were set significantly higher than those of other nurses, which resulted in many nurses being willing to move to areas of the country with the greatest short-term need. Through provider payment incentive modifications, access to telehealth services was expanded for many Americans. Many States also relaxed their scope-of-practice restrictions, allowing for greater utilization of nurse practitioners and physicians' assistants (Volk et al. 2021).

Although these short-term solutions helped during the crisis, improvements in the education and training of health care providers will be required to maintain an adequate supply and distribution of providers in the long run. There are currently too few nurse educators to meet the demand. There are also too few nursing clinical placement spots to provide clinical experience for nursing students. Poor working conditions in many hospitals led to high turnover in the nursing profession well before the pandemic; improvements in patient-to-nurse staffing ratios and management practices would reduce turnover and improve patient outcomes (Vahey et al. 2004; Aiken et al. 2022). For physicians, there is an insufficient number of residency slots. Increasing funding for medical residency programs will also likely be needed to boost the supply of physicians (GAO 2021).

Box 6-7. Staffing Challenges in K-12 Education

Between February 2020 and October 2022, employment in local education fell by almost 300,000 workers, about 3.5 percent of this workforce. According to survey results from a nationally representative sample of public schools, 53 percent indicated that they were entering the 2022–23 academic year understaffed. Among those schools, respondents reported that their highest need areas were special education teachers (65 percent) and transportation staff (59 percent) (U.S. Department of Education 2022). Declines in education employment since the COVID-19 pandemic have not been broad-based but in fact have been concentrated in lower-income communities, as shown in figure 6-ii.

Understanding the cause of these shortfalls is complicated, as there is no single education labor market (Goldhaber et al. 2015). Additionally, the lack of adequate data makes it difficult to identify areas experiencing difficulties in hiring (Nguyen, Lam, and Bruno 2022). Staffing challenges have long plagued schools that serve high proportions of students living in poverty and who belong to minority groups, and hiring challenges are more pronounced in specialty teaching areas such as special education, English language learning, and high school science, technology, engineering, and mathematics (Boyd et al. 2005; Cowan et al. 2016; Murnane and Steele 2007). Qualified teachers are not evenly distributed across schools and students, with poor, Black, and Hispanic students being much more likely to experience novice teachers (James and Wyckoff 2022).

Figure 6-ii. Percent Change in Teacher Employment, 2019–22

Change in the 12-month rolling average of employment relative to January 2020

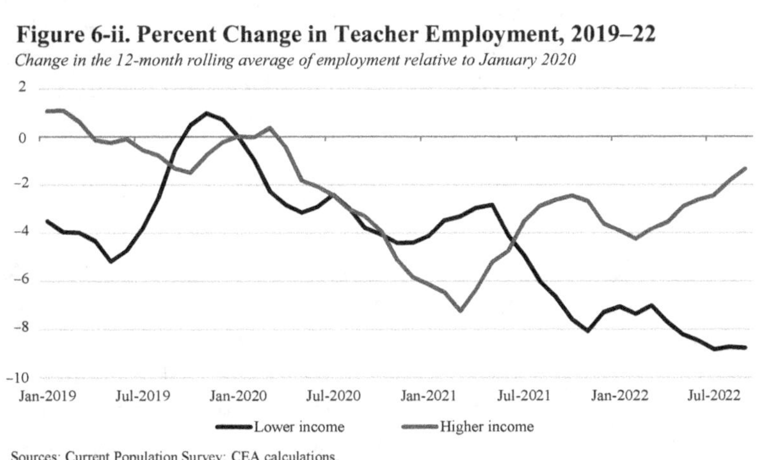

Sources: Current Population Survey; CEA calculations.
Note: Teacher employment is limited to government employees and includes preschool and kindergarten teachers, elementary and middle school teachers, secondary school teachers, special education teachers, tutors, and other teachers and instructors. "Lower income" refers to employment among those living in the half of core-based statistical areas (CBSAs) with the highest share of households with total household income under $50,000. "Higher income" refers to employment among those living in the half of CBSAs with the lowest share of households with total income under $50,000.

When properly diagnosed, policy remedies emerge for areas with particular teacher and school staffing needs. Addressing these localized challenges requires targeted efforts, such as incentives to serve in hard-to-staff schools and high-need areas, and innovation and flexibility about alternative pathways into the profession and licensure reciprocity (Dee and Goldhaber 2017). The keys to addressing teacher and staffing challenges are facilitating mobility into these local labor markets and encouraging retention in high-need positions once they are filled. Some of these measures, such as relaxing licensing requirements, have also contributed to meeting long-term goals such as creating a more diverse teacher workforce (Bacher-Hicks, Chi, and Orellana 2021).

domestic population are quantitatively very small, and that the fiscal effects of immigration are generally positive. For example, as new immigrants tend to be working age, they pay taxes without incurring the fiscal costs of youth and early education (for a comprehensive review of the fiscal and economic impact of immigration, see Blau and Mackie 2017).

There is also a potential pool of laborers already residing in the United States without legal authorization to work and/or a path to citizenship. Legal permanent residence would expand the employment opportunities for a significant portion of this population. As such, immigration reform that provides a path to citizenship for the estimated 11 million undocumented individuals would help to increase the labor supply (Migration Policy Institute 2022). Additional immigration reforms could include removing per-country caps on employment, expanding diversity lottery visas, and expanding the J-1 exchange visa program, which would bring additional faculty, scientists, and students to the United States for training and sharing knowledge and methods.

Drawing More Adults into the Labor Market

Labor force participation among working-age adults in the United States is falling, and it is now lower than that in other developed nations. A likely culprit is the lack of public sector support for workers and families in the United States relative to other wealthy countries. Policies directed at improving the labor market prospects of nonparticipants and removing obstacles to their employment could increase participation among prime-age adults. This subsection outlines several policy options for drawing more adults into the labor market.

Improving care options. Public spending on childcare and senior care in the United States is very low relative to that in other advanced economies.

The United States is also one of the few countries that has no guaranteed paid family and medical leave. In the absence of public support, the economic burden of caring for family members falls chiefly on women, whose labor market participation and lifetime earnings fall in consequence. Given women's low participation rates relative to men, policies that reduce their care burden are a promising avenue for increasing participation and reducing gender disparities.

The preponderance of empirical evidence suggests that childcare and preschool programs have a positive impact on maternal labor force participation (e.g., Bauernschuster and Schlotter 2015; Morrissey 2016; and Wikle and Wilson 2022). Some of the evidence arises from research on a policy change in Quebec, which introduced highly subsidized universal childcare in the late 1990s. These subsidies led to a very large increase in the use of care and a sizable and long-lasting impact on mothers' participation (Baker, Gruber, and Milligan 2008; Haeck, Lefebvre, and Merrigan 2015). Morrissey (2017) evaluates a range of studies and concludes that a 10 percent reduction in the cost of childcare would likely increase maternal participation in the range of 0.5 to 2.5 percent. Paid family and medical leave can also help workers stay connected to their jobs while addressing family-related needs, maintaining good job matches, and boosting long-term attachment to the labor market (Baum and Ruhm 2016; Anand, Dague, and Wagner 2021). Blau and Kahn (2013) estimate that nearly one-third of the gap in U.S. women's participation relative to that in other developed countries can be explained by the relative lack of such family-friendly policies.

Criminal justice reform and removing barriers to reentry. The United States incarcerates people at a higher rate than any other country in the world (World Prison Brief 2021). Reducing the punitiveness of the criminal justice system in the United States would reduce the large fiscal burden of its current system and the collateral damage of incarceration on affected communities. It would also increase the labor supply by reducing both the incarcerated population and the scarring effects of incarceration on employment. In recent decades, several States have experimented with criminal justice reforms aimed at reducing incarceration rates, with noteworthy success. For example, California introduced changes to sentencing for less serious offenses and lessened punitive measures for technical parole violations, changes that caused a sharp decline in incarceration (Lofstrom and Raphael 2013). A series of reforms in New York to divert drug offenders to treatment facilities and to relax mandatory minimum sentencing practices have also sharply reduced incarceration rates in that State (Greene and Mauer 2010). In both States, these periods of reduction in incarceration generally coincided with declining crime rates.

High incarceration rates have also created a large population of formerly incarcerated individuals who face significant barriers to reentry.

Removing barriers to employment for the formerly incarcerated would likely improve their employment prospects after release. One such reform, undertaken by several States in recent years, is to remove occupational licensing barriers for people with arrest and conviction records. In many States, a prior arrest or conviction, no matter how long ago, can prevent one from becoming a licensed barber or cosmetologist, a drug counselor, or a firefighter (Rodriguez and Avery 2016). Noting that information about prior arrests or incarceration decades after the event in question is of limited information value to employers, Piehl (2016) advocates reforms that would set a time limit on information about past convictions for employment background checks.

Expanding the Earned Income Tax Credit. The Earned Income Tax Credit (EITC) is a large government program that raises the after-tax return to work for low- and moderate-income households, particularly those with dependent children. As one factor depressing labor market participation is stagnating wages for non–college educated workers, the EITC can create additional incentives for participation by increasing the returns to work. A large body of research has shown that the EITC increased the labor supply of low-income mothers, a group it principally targeted (e.g., Bastian 2020; Eissa and Liebman 1996; and Meyer and Rosenbaum 2001). However, the maximum credit for families with two or fewer children has remained flat in real terms for many decades (Hoynes, Rothstein, and Ruffini 2017). Increasing the generosity of the current credits and/or expanding the EITC to provide more incentives to low-wage workers without dependent children would likely boost participation.

Regional economic development. Efforts to improve the economic performance of a particular region usually (but not always) target areas that have experienced downturns, with the intent of helping its residents. While not explicitly intended to increase participation, improving economic opportunities in declining areas would likely improve participation in areas with low employment rates by boosting local labor demand.

Regional economic development strategies can take many forms. A common form is that of enterprise zones, which provide tax incentives and sometimes exemptions from regulations, with the intent of spurring business investment and growth. Evidence on the effectiveness of enterprise zones in improving employment opportunities is mixed, and uncertainty remains about which policies work, how they work, and for whom they work (e.g., Neumark and Kolko 2010; Neumark and Simpson 2015; and Ham et al. 2011). However, evidence on the effectiveness of regional economic development programs involving infrastructure expenditures and investments in higher education and research is more promising. Kline and Moretti (2014) find positive long-run effects of the Tennessee Valley Authority, which administers an ambitious regional development plan, on manufacturing employment and income in the targeted region.

The Economic Development Administration (EDA) also encourages economic development in regional clusters, with notable successes, including Milwaukee's water cluster and St. Louis's agricultural technology initiatives (Feldman 2022). An expansion of these efforts was included in the 2021 American Rescue Plan, which funded EDA's Build Back Better Regional Challenge, ultimately awarding 21 coalitions the resources to develop emerging regional industry clusters. The recent CHIPS and Science Act also has an explicitly place-based approach to boosting innovation and commercial activity, and it authorizes the establishment of the new Regional Technology and Innovation Hub Program at EDA to reduce geographic disparities and promote the growth of technology clusters in underrepresented and promising regions.

Other regional economic development strategies include workforce development programs that aim to train people in new and emerging industries and occupations. These programs provide skill upgrading and certification programs for displaced workers and others who would otherwise be unable to access (at reasonable costs) the training required for employment in these industries or occupations.

Nonmonetary incentives and job quality. As noted previously in this chapter, the classic labor supply model frames work as an exchange of effort for monetary compensation. Implicit in this framing is the notion that money alone motivates participation in the labor market. But the evidence suggests that workers care about nonpecuniary aspects of work—such as the meaningfulness of the employer mission, social interaction, greater scheduling flexibilities, and self-direction (Cassar and Meier 2018; Nikolova and Cnossen 2020; Clark 2015). Preferences for nonpecuniary amenities vary across workers, with women and nonwhites tending to value job quality attributes more than white men (Katz, Congdon, and Shakesprere 2022). These preferences can shape lifetime earnings in significant ways. For example, Wiswall and Zafar (2017) find that a quarter of the early career wage gaps for women can be explained by a higher preference among women for jobs with greater flexibility and stability.

Job attributes vary widely across the working population. A national survey of working conditions in the American workplace found that men without a college degree, women, and younger workers generally experience substantially worse working conditions. Specifically, they tend to have less control over their work schedule, experience more verbal abuse and harassment, and have greater exposure to safety hazards (Maestas et al. 2017). Data on preferences indicate that, unsurprisingly, workers prefer work to have more "good job" aspects and fewer "worse job" aspects. This evidence has led many to speculate that improvements in job quality that would improve worker welfare could also potentially increase labor market participation. Some aspects of job quality can be improved through policies such as mandated sick leave or changes to scheduling practices. But many job quality attributes will remain the outcome of business decisions made by employers.

Improving workers' bargaining power. As indicated previously in this chapter, stagnating wages and rising inequality are key drivers of declines in labor force participation. Though many of the factors responsible for demand declines are global, inequality has risen more in the United States than in other advanced economies. This is at least partially due to declining worker power, particularly declines in unionization (Grossman and Oberfield 2022; Stansbury and Summers 2020). Worker power enables workers to negotiate with employers for better pay, safe conditions, predictable working hours, and other aspects of the work environment. Unions have historically been an important force in increasing workers' leverage.

Despite the recent upswing in petitions for union elections, union density in the United States continues to decline, from about one-third of the private sector workforce in 1950 to just over 6 percent today. The consequences of unions' decline for workers include lower wages (e.g., Card 1996), including for nonunionized workers in the same sector (Farber 2005). Union density may also be tied to trends in income inequality, with U.S. inequality rising as union density has fallen (Farber et al. 2021). In short, as unionization has fallen, workers' incomes have stagnated relative to output growth.

Globalization, technological change, and employer concentration are commonly cited as key factors driving declining unionization. However, many economists have pointed out that these factors do not fully explain why unionization in nontradable goods sectors has fallen at a similar rate, or why unionization is lower in the United States than in other Western countries (Levy and Temin 2007; Schmitt and Mitukiewicz 2012). More likely reasons for declining worker power are institutional changes within the United States—particularly the expansion of right-to-work States, greater employer opposition to organizing efforts, and decreased enforcement of labor laws.

The Biden-Harris Administration supports the Protecting the Right to Organize Act, or PRO Act, which would help restore that stated policy of the National Labor Relations Act, to "encourag[e] the practice and procedure of collective bargaining and [protect] the exercise by workers of full freedom of association, self-organization, and designation of representatives of their own choosing, for the purpose of negotiating the terms and conditions of their employment or other mutual aid or protection" by making it easier for workers to unionize by preventing companies from holding mandatory antiunion meetings and by imposing penalties on employers that retaliate against organizers (White House 2021). The Administration has also taken significant steps to improve workers' leverage, appointing former union officials to the National Labor Relations Board, increasing funding to allow the Board to pursue its statutory remit, establishing a task force to promote labor organizing, and adding prevailing wage and apprenticeship requirements to the recent CHIPS and Science Act and Inflation Reduction Act.

Conclusion

The United States faces a large shortfall in its labor supply as it continues to recover from the COVID-19 pandemic. This shortfall is not merely a lingering effect of the pandemic but is also due to long-run demographic trends and declines in labor market participation by adults. Without increased immigration and/or efforts to draw more adults into the labor market, the labor supply is likely to be constrained for the foreseeable future. The shrinking share of adults in the workforce and the Nation's aging population may have a negative impact on its living standards through slower economic growth. More proactive policies to increase the labor supply—such as higher public spending on childcare, increasing immigration, and improving workers' bargaining power—are needed to counteract these demographic trends.

Chapter 7

Competition in the Digital Economy: New Technologies, Old Economics

Digital markets have become an integral part of Americans' daily lives. Over 14 percent of retail shopping now happens digitally (U.S. Census Bureau 2022), and digital markets now account for more than $2 trillion in value (over 10 percent of gross domestic product) and employ 8 million workers in the American economy (Highfill and Surfield 2022). The economic forces operating in digital markets are not particularly new; however, when combined with the scale afforded by digital settings, the low costs of connecting with others, and the large amounts of data being collected, the economics of these markets lead to new implications for how these markets look, how they operate, how they make an impact on the economy and society, and how they should be regulated.

Nearly all digital markets feature positive "network effects"—meaning that the value of a product or service increases as the number of users grows (i.e., as the "network" gets bigger)—so having fewer, larger service providers can benefit users. A social media website, for example, is of little value to its users if it has very few users; it is, in fact, more convenient to have all your friends accessible via the same website. In addition to network effects, digital settings enable a global scale and the unprecedented collection of data, which can all favor the rise of dominant firms. These forces can also act as barriers to entry, preventing new firms from challenging dominant ones.

Healthy competition among many firms pushes companies to produce goods at their lowest possible cost, offer products and services at the best prices, provide better wages and working conditions, create new technologies, and develop and sell new products that people want to buy. This, in turn, ensures that economic agents make the best use of society's resources. In contrast, dominant firms with significant market power may use this power to increase prices, reduce quality, and lower output, making consumers and other market participants worse off. This is why regulations are necessary to ensure that the competitive process is protected and to maintain a level playing field for all market participants.

This chapter reviews some of the potential economic benefits delivered by digital markets, such as lower search costs and increased variety. The chapter also explores other characteristics of digital markets that differentiate them from their offline counterparts, including the ability of firms to gather a huge variety and volume of data on users, potentially without their knowledge, either by running experiments or simply monitoring users' behavior, and rapidly process these data to derive significant value. These data can be used to improve firms' product offerings, which can benefit users, or for other purposes, such as personalized pricing, which may benefit firms but harm users.

The chapter closes with a discussion of the regulation of digital markets. Regulators' challenge is to deliver all the benefits of competition—such as innovation, privacy, and low prices—in a setting where economic factors may drive markets toward fewer competitors. As a result, regulators should seek to lower barriers to entry and also prevent a dominant firm from exploiting its power either in the same or a related market, or to engage in practices that harm consumers or other market participants in other ways. For regulators overseeing digital markets relative to offline ones, new areas of concern include the misuse of consumer data and collusion by pricing algorithms. Overall, digital markets present significant opportunities to benefit society if regulators, enforcers, and courts can adapt to the new digital landscape.

The Benefits of Digital Markets

In this chapter, the term "digital markets" encompasses the interfaces that electronically bring together various agents for economic or social purposes. Although there is no unanimously accepted definition of digital markets or what goods and services they include, the chapter refers to these diverse interfaces—including app stores, operating systems, search engines, social media platforms, web browsers, and online marketplaces. Unlike many offline settings, where buyers and sellers typically transact directly with one another, most digital markets involve an intermediary that brings together different agents and facilitates their interactions. In addition, "marketplaces" include not only traditional marketplaces—where buyers sell tangible items to consumers, as would occur in offline markets—but also markets where different economic agents are being matched. For example, an online job search website would be classified as a "market," as would a ride-sharing application on a mobile phone that connects drivers with riders.

In many cases, users may value the additional convenience of having interactions facilitated digitally (Goldfarb and Tucker 2019). Digital markets have also provided other benefits to consumers by creating new forms of price competition and saving time from travel or searches for goods and services, among others. For example, one early study (Brynjolfsson and Smith 2000) found that Internet retailers' prices were 9 to 16 percent lower and that they changed their prices by increments up to 100 times smaller as compared with traditional retailers, suggesting that they have lower costs for instituting price changes and that these savings are partially passed on to customers. However, other studies have produced more nuanced results, such as a more recent study (Cavallo 2017), which finds that online and offline prices are often identical among the largest firms. In e-commerce, digital markets allow for greatly increased product variety because there is much less of a physical inventory constraint when products are shipped directly to consumers. Digital markets also have benefits for businesses. They can potentially compete in markets that would otherwise be too costly to enter. The next sections further explore the value of these aspects of digital markets.

Reducing Search Costs

The seminal work of Stigler (1961) explores the value of lowering search costs. Digital markets theoretically enable perfect price comparisons across the universe of retailers of the same good at low cost, and also lower the acquisition costs of information. For example, digital marketplaces like eBay and Etsy are able to reduce search costs—such as the costs incurred to find a particular product or service, including the cost of the time spent looking—by bringing together and matching large numbers of buyers and sellers that would otherwise spend a great deal of time searching for one another to transact a unique item. An early study in the digital era (Brown and Goolsbee 2002) found that the Internet led to lower prices for term life insurance. Other studies from the same period found that digital markets reduced prices for consumers, such as estimates of an average of 2 percent saved by customers of online car-buying referral services (Scott Morton, Zettelmeyer, and Silva-Risso 2001) and an average of 16 percent saved by consumers shopping for electronic products using an online price comparison tool (Baye, Morgan, and Scholten 2003). More recently, researchers have investigated the potential trade-offs between reducing search costs and increasing the potential for collusion; issues related to collusion are addressed later in the chapter.

In theory, digital markets should be inherently more competitive, thanks to the low search costs and increased price transparency, all else being equal. However, one natural response by firms to combat this is to introduce obfuscation. Ellison and Ellison (2009) document that firms face a very high price sensitivity of consumers in online marketplaces that make price comparisons easy. As a result, sellers undertake price obfuscation behaviors, such as making product descriptions complicated so that comparisons are difficult, creating multiple versions of the same product, and attempting to "upsell" consumers who were drawn to an initial low price. Such behaviors have been documented in multiple government sources and findings, or engage in so-called drip pricing strategies (Blake et al. 2021; FTC 2017; CFPB 2022; White House 2016).

Increased Variety

Consumers have also benefited from increased access to variety in both products and services that has been enabled by digital markets. Brynjolfsson, Hu, and Smith (2003) estimate that the benefits to consumers attributable to increased product variety among online booksellers may be 7 and 10 times larger than those from increased competition and lower prices. Quan and Williams (2018) estimate that the value of the online footwear market is 5.8 percent greater than the traditional local retail market due to the increased variety available, and Gentzkow (2007) finds that a free online version of a newspaper in Washington was worth $0.35 per reader per day, or a total gain of about $52 million per year in 2021 dollars. One study also found the availability of online services meant that consumers in smaller, less densely populated places could be better connected to national markets, increasing their access to a larger variety of goods and services (Sinai and Waldfogel 2004). It is worth noting, however, that if a particular firm achieves dominance in a market, the variety offered becomes something that this firm can control.

Network Effects Create a Competitive Moat

If network effects at the firm level are sufficiently strong, having larger firms may be better for customers. For example, as noted above, messaging services may be more useful when they have more users. Competition among many small, incompatible messaging services is unlikely to benefit consumers, given the fixed costs and returns to scale. And yet, left to its own devices, a dominant messaging service would likely raise prices above a competitive level, provide lower quality, potentially innovate less, or do all of the above. This would be seen as a market failure, which should be addressed via regulation, nationalization, or antitrust enforcement (Joskow and Rose 1989; Joskow 2007; Smiley and Greene 1983).

Further, network effects have long been recognized as potentially becoming an "economic moat"—a protective barrier that guards a profitable business (the "castle")—in that they lead to customers being locked in to certain products, making mass migration to a new product unlikely unless accompanied by a simultaneous technological advance somewhere else in the ecosystem (Bresnahan 2002). New entrants are less likely to be successful when facing an entrenched firm with network effects or the benefits of scale, eliminating some benefits of competition.

The messaging service example is illustrative, in that a potential solution to bringing back the benefits of competition in the presence of network effects may be interoperability, although interoperability alone may not suffice to fully restore competition. Interoperability expands the benefits of network effects from the firm level to the market level. Requiring that competing services interoperate is one remedy that can dissolve some of the anticompetitive outcomes of network effects because all competitors would share the same network effect. Thus, interoperability would mean that both old and new services would need to compete on other dimensions like quality to keep users on their services.

Another related tool is data portability, the idea that consumers can take, or "port," their data to a different service. This reduces the switching cost created by network effects. For example, imagine that a user wants to switch from one music streaming service to another. One barrier for the consumer would be having to give up their playlists and liked songs. Data portability would allow the user to download and port these playlists to another streaming service, thereby reducing the barrier to switching. Both data portability and interoperability can make it more appealing for a potential entrant to introduce a competing service and increase the likelihood of new innovations being able to succeed.

The Challenge of Preserving Competition in Digital Markets

Traditional competition policy analysis often focuses on estimating changes in prices to assess effects on consumers. However, this approach faces new challenges in digital markets arising from several sources—notably, the provision of free goods and services, and the cross-subsidization in markets with indirect network effects. For "free" goods with no monetary price, in a more competitive market, the true price could be negative (e.g., consumers could be paid to watch ads or fill out surveys with their personal data), or service could be better. As a result, demonstrating anticompetitive harm may require alternative measures rather than prices.

Research into the effects of mergers in digital markets demonstrates heightened complexity in the expression of competitive effects. Chandra and Collard-Wexler (2009) empirically show that mergers of firms in two-sided markets may not lead to higher prices on either side of the market in an application to the Canadian newspaper industry; and Song (2021) shows that mergers between firms in two-sided markets can lead to either higher or lower prices after the merger, but that even agents that experience higher prices may be better off due to increased network effects. Another study, of the merger of two platforms for pet-sitting services (Farronato, Fong, and Fradkin, forthcoming), found that on average consumers were not substantially better off with one platform than two competing ones because the network effects were not large enough to balance the losses due to higher prices and reduced variety after the acquired platform was shut down. In markets with indirect network effects, policies intended to increase competition may need to account for how an intervention on one side will affect the well-being and behavior on both sides of the market because pricing is linked to the costs and price sensitivity of users on both sides (Evans 2003; Wright 2004).

These challenges are exacerbated by the scale of the task of protecting competition in digital markets. For example, large tech companies are highly acquisitive. Figure 7-3 shows that the volume and value of mergers and acquisitions among tech firms is large, a trend that has drawn the attention of antitrust authorities. Reviewing these acquisitions for anticompetitive harm requires significant resources due to the complexity of the markets, the sophistication of the firms, and the need to look beyond the impact on retail prices alone.

Finally, digital markets can be highly dynamic, appearing and evolving rapidly. This can limit the ability of regulators to use current and historical data to analyze market behavior. In addition, it can be quite difficult for regulators to identify nascent competitors and potential entrants in assessing proposed mergers. Further, when antitrust authorities do identify such anticompetitive mergers (DOJ 2020), the lack of prices for the potential entrant

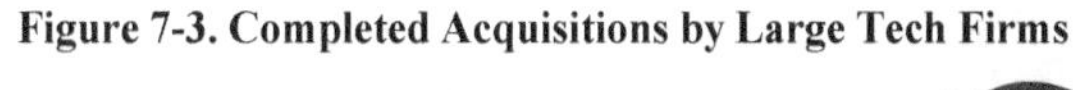

Figure 7-3. Completed Acquisitions by Large Tech Firms

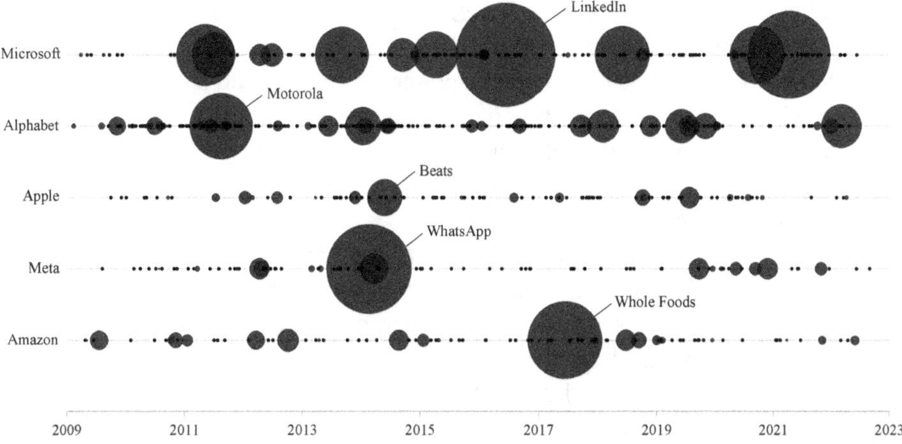

Sources: Bloomberg; Crunchbase; Mergr; Alphabet; Meta; Amazon; Google; Microsoft; TechCrunch.
Note: The dark blue circle radius is proportional to the deal size, and the small black dots indicate acquisitions with no publicly available price. Deals include completed mergers-and-acquisitions deals by the specified firm as of the fall of 2022.

or lack of significant market share for the nascent competitor are again problematic for traditional competition analysis, since anticompetitive harm has often been demonstrated using economic models showing that mergers would lead to higher prices. These challenges underscore the need for further research and approaches to evaluating competitive effects in complex digital environments. This is work the antitrust agencies are well positioned to do, in concert with academics and other stakeholders.

Preventing the Extension of Dominance into Adjacent Markets

Digital markets with network effects, big data, and a global scale have tended to coalesce on a small number of dominant firms. An obvious concern is that firms could exploit their dominance in one market to gain market power in or dominate adjacent markets. This type of conduct could be illegal under Section 2 of the Sherman Antitrust Act.

Today, there are many examples of digital markets where a dominant firm also competes in an adjacent market: Google and Apple operate app stores, in which their own apps compete with other apps; Amazon operates an e-commerce marketplace, where its Amazon Basics brand competes directly with those from other firms; and Microsoft operates a video game marketplace, where they also compete as a video game developer. In these situations, one concern is that the dominant firm could have an unfair advantage for its competitive products, known as "self-preferencing." For example, Apple was alleged to give its own apps higher priority when a person searched its app store (Mickle 2019).

If dominant firms exploit their dominance to give their own offerings an advantage, consumers may not get the full benefits of competition. One approach a regulator or legislature might take to improving the functioning of certain markets is to prohibit self-preferencing and similar practices. However, such a ban could be challenging to enforce, as a regulator would need to show that self-preferencing is intentionally built into a service instead of just occurring organically because, for example, the owner's products have received better reviews.

A related concern about marketplace operators that compete on their own marketplaces is the issue of how competitors' data are used. Marketplace operators are able to gather extensive data on competitors' products and customers, and they may have an incentive to use those data strategically, either in the design of their own competing products or in their pricing or promotional strategies. They could also intentionally limit what data from the site are available to competitors. Any of these actions would further put competing firms at a competitive disadvantage. A regulator may want to prohibit the use of competitors' data or insist on the fair treatment of marketplace data for all firms in order to reset the competitive landscape, although enforcement of such a regulation could be a challenge requiring significant monitoring and oversight.

The ability of a dominant firm to extend its dominance into adjacent markets is a threat to competition. Society may miss out on certain innovative products if entrepreneurs realize that their product may just get copied by a dominant marketplace operator and, therefore, decide against investing in developing it. In addition, the better product may not "win" on an uneven playing field. Regulators can address this market failure by clarifying who owns what rights to the data collected and leveling the playing field for all firms in online markets. An overview of some of the approaches that regulators are taking, both internationally and in the U.S., is presented in box 7-4.

Preventing the Misuse of Consumer Data

Assessing the competitive effects of data usage and policies can be difficult. Research suggests that when data can be used to reduce a firm's exposure to risk, it can lead to increased innovation or efficiencies, potentially driving down prices (Eeckhout and Veldkamp 2022; Kirpalani and Philippon 2020; Competition Bureau Canada 2017). However, data can also become a barrier to entry that insulates firms from competition. Prüfer and Schottmüller (2022) show that under certain conditions, a data advantage can lead to market tipping. In addition, the ability of firms to collect massive amounts of data about individuals raises clear concerns about privacy and also about data protection, as leaks of massive data sets could expose individuals to

Box 7-4. International and Subnational Efforts at Regulatory Reform

Numerous antitrust and consumer protection efforts are occurring both internationally and in the United States at the State level. For instance, the European Commission has proposed a pair of new laws focused on regulating digital markets—the Digital Markets Act (DMA) and the Digital Services Act (DSA) (Council of the European Union 2022).

The DMA aims to promote competition by establishing rules about the types of conduct in which large "gatekeeper" firms can engage (European Parliament and European Commission 2022). In order to be designated a "gatekeeper," in each of the last three financial years, a firm must have had at least 10,000 annual business users established in the European Union, 45 million monthly users established or located in the European Union, and €7.5 billion (about $7.4 billion in 2021 dollars) in annual revenue across the EU or a €75 billion market capitalization (about $74.4 billion in 2021 dollars). It must also provide the same "core platform" services—for example, web browsing, messaging, and social media—in at least three EU member states. To foster competition between firms and reduce barriers to entry, the DMA lays out requirements by which gatekeepers must abide. For example, gatekeepers must allow for data portability and must make messaging services interoperable. They must also be more transparent about their mergers and acquisitions and must allow users to uninstall predownloaded software on the gatekeeper's operating system. At the same time, the DMA also restricts gatekeepers from engaging in certain business practices, like preferencing their own products over those of competitors on their platform ("self-preferencing") or combining users' personal data across the gatekeeper's different core platform services. The DMA also prohibits gatekeeper firms from engaging in certain price-setting practices and creating operating terms that discriminate against certain businesses and app developers. For instance, the DMA makes it illegal for gatekeepers to make business users sign agreements to not offer better terms on other platforms (known as most-favored-nation clauses). These agreements have the potential to dampen competition, raise prices and fees, and reduce entry by competitors offering lower-priced alternatives (Boik and Corts 2016; Baker and Chevalier 2013; Wang and Wright, forthcoming).

While the DMA primarily focuses on regulating the conduct of a few very large firms in an effort to promote competition, the DSA addresses the wider societal implications associated with digital markets and establishes regulations focused on filtering illegal content and protecting the fundamental rights of consumers online (European Parliament and Council of the European Union 2022). For example, the DSA requires that firms inform users about how and why advertisements are being targeted to them. It also bans firms from using personal data to target advertisements if the firm is reasonably aware that the user is a minor. In addition, the DSA includes numerous other provisions, such as requiring online intermediaries to moderate illegal content (including hate speech), while giving regulators wide-ranging powers to request access to very large online platforms' business practices and algorithms.

In addition to new laws being passed abroad, certain States of the United States are also passing new regulations targeting digital markets, with a specific focus on consumers' data rights. As of late 2022, five States—California, Colorado, Connecticut, Utah, and Virginia—had passed comprehensive State-level regulations on consumer data and privacy rights in digital markets (NCSL 2022; Connecticut 2022). For example, Connecticut passed a law in 2022 that gave consumers more control over how their data could be collected, used, or accessed (Connecticut 2022). Once the law takes effect, in July 2023, consumers will have the right to access, correct, and delete records of their personal data. Connecticut residents will also be able to opt out of having their personal data sold or used for targeted advertising.

identity theft or other financial harm (Ichihashi 2020; Chapman and Bodoni 2022; O'Sullivan 2021).

For all these concerns about the misuse of data and protection of privacy, a practical intervention is to regulate how data can be collected, used, shared, and stored. The authors of one study explore mediated data sharing to reduce the correlation between users' data and thus to mitigate externalities that create excessive data sharing (Acemoglu et al. 2022). They propose sharing data with a third party that would transform their data to remove correlation with other users before sharing it with services requested by the user. Other policies that might impose fewer costs include "right-to-be-forgotten" provisions, which create time limits on data retention (Chiou and Tucker 2017).

Monitoring Pricing Algorithms and Collusion

Concerns have been raised that pricing algorithms could facilitate explicit price collusion by reducing uncertainty about consumer demand. O'Connor and Wilson (2021) suggest that this improved forecasting could either lead to lower prices and increased consumer benefits or enhance the ability of firms to support collusive arrangements. Other studies of retail gasoline markets have raised concerns about online price disclosure and experimentation facilitating the coordination of prices across firms (Luco 2019; Byrne and de Roos 2019). A simple example would be the use of posted prices

Box 7-5. Artificial Intelligence and Digital Markets

A fundamental aspect of the operation of digital markets is using artificial intelligence (AI) to translate the data available to firms into actionable predictions, recommendations, and decisions (OECD 2019). Many of the features that make digital markets so appealing to users are powered by machine learning and other algorithmic tools (Brown 2021). Indeed, many of the key features of digital markets—efficient matching, low search costs, an unmatched variety of products, and personalization of prices—are made possible by a combination of data availability and the application of AI techniques like neural networks, natural language processing, or other forms of machine learning. Though the use of these algorithms can improve the experience of users and increase firms' profitability, there are ongoing concerns that they will displace workers; introduce racial or other sorts of bias into these systems; make digital marketplaces even harder to regulate; and meaningfully impact individuals' or communities' rights, opportunities, or access to critical resources or services.

For ride-sharing companies like Uber and Lyft, machine learning is the key to their ability to set prices to assure that there are enough drivers on the road to meet customer demand (Liu et al. 2022). AI also allows social media platforms to optimize their content. TikTok relies on its algorithm's ability to use its wealth of data to select content that will keep users engaged longer (Smith 2021; Wall Street Journal 2021). Further, the ability of firms like Amazon to have the products that a customer is looking for in stock without having to maintain a surplus inventory is driven by AI-based predictions about demand at any given point in the future (Amazon 2021). All these features of digital markets are made possible because of the combination of data and algorithms.

However, the reach of AI in digital markets raises concerns that there could be a wave of automation of jobs (Sisson 2022). Even in cases where AI augments existing labor, as with Uber's algorithmic management of its drivers or Amazon's of its warehouse workers, some workers report deep levels of frustration and resentment due to such concerns as the degree of surveillance and the lack of transparency about AI decisionmaking (Möhlmann and Henfridsson 2019).

AI also has been shown to perpetuate and potentially exacerbate biases already present in society. There is a robust literature on this relationship, with findings of discrimination based on race alone found in algorithmic risk assessments in the health care space, facial recognition systems, and natural language processing (Obermeyer et al. 2019; Furl, Phillips, and O'Toole 2002; Caliskan 2021). Major players in the digital market have long struggled with these issues; for example, Amazon's attempt to build an AI-based hiring program resulted in a system that taught itself to prioritize male candidates and penalize résumés that mentioned women's colleges and made other references to women (Dastin 2018). These biases can be both intentional, as when Facebook's AI-based advertising made it possible for advertisers to exclude specific users based on their race, and unintentional, as when women were shown fewer career ads because the cost to advertise to women was higher online (Zang 2021; Lambrecht and Tucker 2019). Even when an algorithm itself does not increase bias, differential rates of utilization of the algorithm can deepen racial and gender disparities, as in the case of Airbnb's Smart Pricing tool (Zhang et al. 2021).

As governments around the world consider how best to regulate digital markets, they are confronting the fact that AI's role in this market introduces levels of opacity and complexity that can hinder reasonable efforts at oversight (European Parliament 2022; Kroll 2021). Further, complexities emerge in assessing the intent of firms, which can be an important part of many regulatory systems (Chin 2019). Processes like algorithmic audits have been proposed as tools to overcome the "black box" features of AI that can create substantial information asymmetries between firms and regulators (Guszcza et al. 2018). These audits have received attention in areas related to hiring, and they are being actively considered both internationally and within the United States (Lee and Lai 2021; Engler 2021; Digital Regulation Cooperation Forum 2022). In 2022, the Biden-Harris Administration released the "Blueprint for an AI Bill of Rights" (White House 2022), which outlines five principles to guide AI system design that will protect the American public.

online to institute price matching, enabling firms to potentially achieve a higher price than they could achieve if their rivals' price was uncertain, as price-matching policies remove the incentive for competitors to lower prices. There is evidence that artificial-intelligence-based algorithms can potentially adapt to raise prices in a coordinated fashion, even if they have not been explicitly programmed to do so (Harrington 2018). This form of tacit collusion may be difficult to detect. In addition to the possibility of collusion through the use of algorithmic pricing, the use of automated software can support prices above competitive levels. This can intensify merger price effects in ways that are not accounted for in a traditional merger analysis and also generate greater price dispersion in the market (Brown and MacKay, forthcoming). In order to guard against the threats of tacit collusion and explicit price fixing enabled by pricing algorithms, antitrust authorities may require additional resources (i.e., computing, personnel, and financial resources). Box 7-5 explores other ways in which artificial intelligence affects the functioning of digital markets.

Conclusion

Although the basic economics of digital markets are well understood, when combined with the effects of scale and the data collection potential of the digital world, they raise new concerns. Many digital markets have become dominated by a few firms or even one firm, and these dominant firms have incentives to protect their existing position, to extend their market power into other markets, and to exploit the huge amounts of data being gathered on their users.

Governments must ensure that the benefits of competition—such as innovation, privacy, choice, and low prices—are realized while protecting market participants and promoting a fair and contestable playing field. Competition regulation and enforcement must adapt to the changes brought on by the digital revolution, given that harm to competition, market participants, workers, and consumers is now being manifested in novel ways. Creating digital markets that work for everyone would allow their full potential to be shared by all Americans.

Chapter 8

Digital Assets: Relearning Economic Principles

Multiple financial crises have struck the United States during the last two centuries. Many of these crises have been caused by institutions that function like banks but are not registered or regulated as banks, so-called shadow banks. For example, the 1907 crisis—then called a "panic"—was mainly caused by trust companies, which were State-chartered entities that competed with banks for deposits. Because these trusts were not part of the central payments system, and thus processed only a small amount of payments, they did not hold a large amount of cash relative to deposits. To earn profits, they made as many loans as possible. After a series of events in October 1907 set off a rush for withdrawals, several trusts faced a run and were forced to suspend credit and liquidate assets, acting as a catalyst for a larger fire sale in financial markets. To save the financial system, J. P. Morgan, owner of the eponymous bank, and a small number of other financial leaders individually chose which banks to bail out (Moen and Tallman 2015). This helped government policymakers realize that when faced with a crisis, the financial system, as then constituted, would rely on a privileged group of individuals seeking to maximize their own profits rather than on institutions that had an obligation to protect the public's interest. This realization helped lead to the creation of the Federal Reserve—the centralized entity that first aimed to serve as the lender of last resort and, over time, also obtained the exclusive power to issue U.S. dollar notes and manage the Nation's monetary policy.

Fast forward 100 years, and digital asset proponents are now aspiring to create a decentralized financial system without relying on governments and their regulatory frameworks, which were shaped by important lessons learned from multiple previous crises, including the 1907 panic. Digital assets are electronic representations of value and operate as part of a complex and interconnected digital ecosystem. Crypto assets are a subset of digital assets that use cryptographic techniques and distributed ledger technology (DLT) but exclude central bank digital currencies (U.S. Department of the Treasury 2022a). DLTs rely on networks to store and process transactions.

This chapter primarily examines crypto assets, whose proponents have been relearning the lessons from previous financial crises the hard way. In addition to the decentralized custody and control of money, it has been argued that crypto assets may provide other benefits, such as improving payment systems, increasing financial inclusion, and creating mechanisms for the distribution of intellectual property and financial value that bypass intermediaries that extract value from both the provider and recipient. Looking under the hood at these arguments, however, shows a more complicated picture. So far, crypto assets have brought none of these benefits. Meanwhile, the costs generated by several of their aspects—such as those for consumers, the physical environment, and the financial system—are not only substantial but are also being accrued in the present. Indeed, crypto assets to date do not appear to offer investments with any fundamental value, nor do they act as an effective alternative to fiat money, improve financial inclusion, or make payments more efficient; instead, their innovation has been mostly about creating artificial scarcity in order to support crypto assets' prices—and many of them have no fundamental value. This raises the question of the role of regulation in protecting consumers, investors, and the rest of the financial system from panics, crashes, and fraud related to crypto assets. Even so, as companies and governments experiment with DLT, it is conceivable that some of their potential benefits may be realized in the future.

The Perceived Appeal of Crypto Assets

This section reviews the potential benefits that crypto assets may offer, as often touted by their proponents, while the next section evaluates what they have actually achieved. To introduce the digital asset landscape, figure 8-1 illustrates certain types of digital assets. The label "cryptocurrency" is used in the industry to connote a crypto asset that is promoted to be an alternative payment instrument. "Stablecoin" is also an industry label for a form of crypto asset that is purportedly backed by a portfolio of underlying assets and claimed to have a stable exchange value with these assets. While some stablecoins mainly aim to become payment instruments, other stablecoins mainly aim to provide returns from investments. Regardless of the label used, a crypto asset may be, among other things, a security, a commodity, a derivative, or another type of financial product, depending on the facts and circumstances. Nonfungible tokens are the other primary type of crypto asset; they use DLT to track ownership of digital goods but are not a main focus of this chapter.

The term "crypto asset" excludes digital currencies that may be issued by a central bank. Though central bank digital currencies might be designed to operate using DLT, there is no requirement for them to be on DLT, and a central bank digital currency does not necessarily involve using DLT (White House 2022a).

Figure 8-1. A Taxonomy of Digital Assets and Central Bank Money

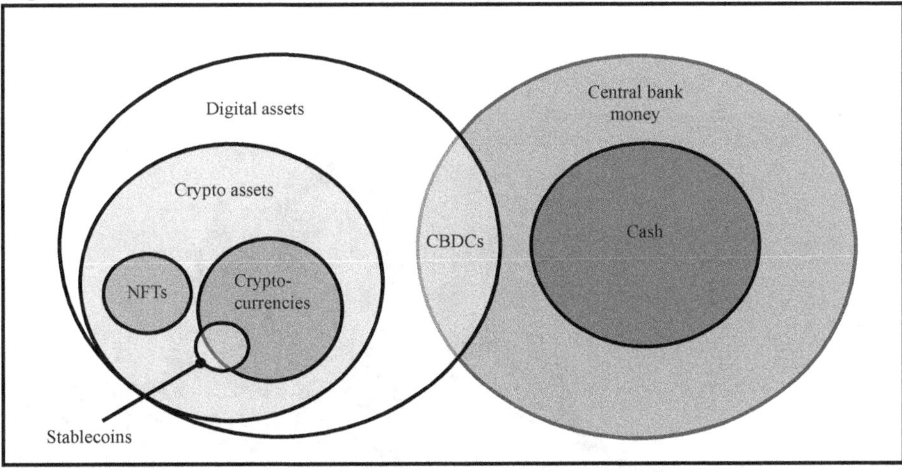

Sources: CEA analysis; Hoffman (2022).
Note: NFTs = nonfungible tokens. Not drawn to scale. Cash represents currency as well as reserves. Regardless of the label used, a crypto asset may be, among other things, a security, a commodity, a derivative, or other financial product, depending on the facts and circumstances.

Crypto assets have gained substantial popularity in recent years—particularly since the beginning of the COVID-19 pandemic in 2020. As shown in figure 8-2, the estimated market values of selected crypto assets have increased significantly in recent years and reached a collective peak of nearly $3 trillion in November 2021. As of the end of December 2022, crypto assets collectively had a reported market value of a little under $1 trillion, due to a large downturn in prices over the year, and largely reflecting the failures of certain prominent crypto asset projects and firms.

The development of crypto assets and their underlying distributed ledger technology have the potential to transform industries and business models. Recognizing both the potential opportunities and actual risks of crypto assets, in March 2022, President Biden signed Executive Order 14067, "Ensuring Responsible Development of Digital Assets" (White House 2022b), which tasked the Administration to study the effects of these novel assets. As a result, departments and agencies of the Federal Government have produced nine reports examining the implications of crypto assets for consumers, businesses, financial stability, national security, and the physical environment (White House 2022c).

The first crypto asset, Bitcoin, was launched in 2009, shortly after the global financial crisis, as something of a repudiation of the existing financial intermediaries that caused the crisis (Nakamoto 2008). Bitcoin was

Figure 8-2. Market Capitalization of Selected Crypto Assets, 2020–22

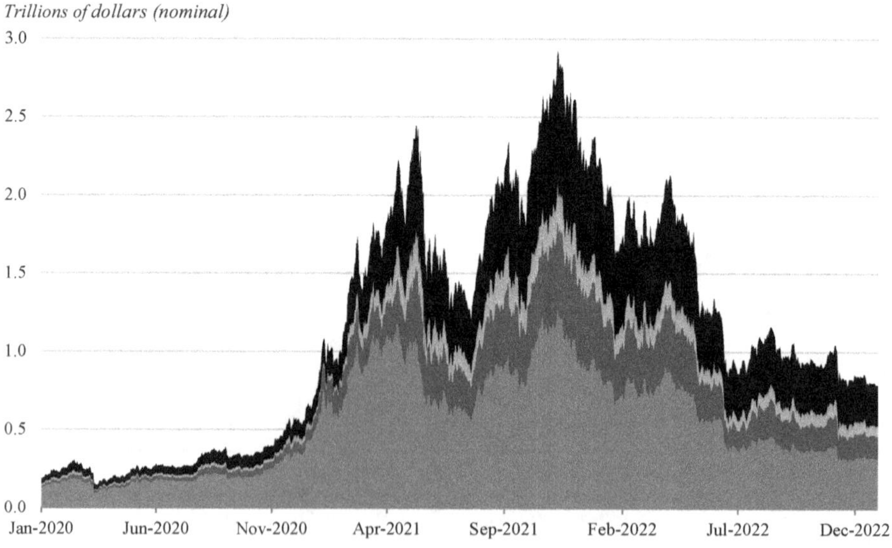

Source: Coin Metrics, Inc; Federal Reserve Board of Governors Financial Stability Report.
Note: Total market cap figures are subject to revision from Coin Metrics.

Box 8-1. What Are the Functions of Money?

In early history, bartering was a common way for people to exchange goods and services. Bartering, however, takes time, because individuals need to find another person who is willing to trade one physical good or service for another. A workaround for this was the invention of money; some of the earliest forms of money appeared in about 1200 BCE (Tikkanen, n.d.). Money's key innovation was to facilitate trade between individuals by using an item that had a common representation of value that was widely agreed upon by members of society. That is, instead of having to take a goat everywhere and hoping to find someone who wanted the goat, money enabled individuals to carry something that everyone valued, such as polished beads, which could be exchanged for a wide variety of goods and services (Jordan 1997).

The first money was in the form of things like seashells, beaver pelts, and even large stones (Tikkanen, n.d.; Hudson's Bay Company History Foundation 2016; Goldstein and Kestenbaum 2010). Eventually, money took the form of "specie," or coins such as gold and silver, which could be produced to a specific standard of weight (Velde 2012). While money like specie money was decidedly more convenient than carrying around a goat, it was still cumbersome to transport. To get around this, paper money was created, which was substantially easier to transport. To ensure that paper money still had financial value, it was "backed" by specie (Tikkanen, n.d.). That is, the paper money essentially served as a promissory note for specie sitting in a bank, and it could be freely redeemed.

This system worked well, but it had a key vulnerability that became a common theme of many crises: banks could earn higher profits by issuing more paper currency than the amount of specie they held in their vault. For example, a bank could hold 50 gold coins, but could issue 100 units of a paper currency, each giving the holder the right to 1 gold coin. Then, if all holders of the currency demanded their money back at the same time, the bank would not have enough gold coins to meet the holders' redemptions (Diamond and Dybvig 1983). This dynamic—referred to as a bank run—also has a long history, dating back to as early as the fourth century BCE (Flood 2012).

Eventually, institutions and faith in currencies—particularly the U.S. dollar—became strong enough that specie was not needed to assuage investors' concerns about what was "backing" the currency. This led to the creation and adoption of "fiat" currency, or currency issued by the government that is not redeemable for specie. Fiat currency's value is largely a function of (1) the currency being the only instrument with which individuals can pay taxes; (2) the strength of the government's institutions, such as the legal system and military; and (3) a shared social trust in the value of the money itself (Bank of England 2020).

Money, as defined in the Uniform Commercial Code and certain other specialized sources, is a medium of exchange currently authorized or adopted by a domestic or foreign government (U.S. Commercial Code, n.d.). In contrast, here the economic functions and common understanding of money are considered. For a type of money to actually be useful in the economic sense, there must be *wide agreement about its value*—either derived from assets backing it (e.g., the gold standard) or from things like institutions and social trust. Money serves three core functions: as a medium of exchange, as a unit of account, and as a store of value (U.S. Department of the Treasury 2022b).

First, money can serve as a medium of exchange if it can be used *widely* to trade for goods and services. For example, the U.S. dollar can be used for purchasing anywhere in the country, and even in many places abroad. In contrast, for example, while cigarettes are often used inside prisons to trade for goods and services, they cannot be used to purchase groceries or buy plane tickets (Lankenau 2007).

Second, money can be considered a unit of account if it acts as a benchmark upon which the values of different goods and services can be compared. For example, instead of estimating how many chickens it would take to trade for one cow, a person can instead simply express the value of chickens relative to cows through their respective monetary values—so if 1 chicken costs $10 and 1 cow costs $2,000, then a person can simply use their relative dollar values to conclude that 200 chickens are worth the same as 1 cow.

Finally, money can be a store of value if its purchasing power does not fluctuate dramatically over short intervals of time. For example, the number of apples a $10 bill can buy does not vary much from one day to the next. This is one reason why very high levels of inflation—so-called hyperinflation—can create uncertainty in the purchasing power of money.

"Sovereign money" is money issued by the governing authority of an independent country. Sovereign money can easily satisfy money's functions to serve as a medium of exchange and as a store of value over time. This is because sovereign money is an information-insensitive asset; it is unlikely that one side of a transaction is acting based on private information about the value of sovereign money (Gorton and Zhang 2022). The more information-sensitive an asset is, the less likely it is to be a medium of exchange. For example, if there is a high possibility that someone is buying gold to protect themselves against losses from holding another asset, the gold seller may decide that it is better not to exchange gold for that asset. Sovereign money is also a liability of the central bank, meaning that its value is backed by the bank. The U.S. dollar is widely accepted as a medium of exchange, and it is also a store of value. Indeed, roughly half of all international trade is invoiced in dollars (CRS 2022). This does not mean that all sovereign currencies have the features of money. For example, Zimbabwe's currency lost its role as a store of value in 2007, when its annual inflation rate rose to over 66,000 percent (Siegel 2008). In Zimbabwe's case, consumers and firms shifted toward the widespread use of other sovereign currencies, which effectively replaced Zimbabwe's currency (Noko 2011).

Bank deposits can also act as money. Banks offer deposit accounts to their customers, and these deposits are pegged one-for-one against sovereign currencies. The value of this private form of money is generally supported by a nexus of regulatory and supervisory requirements, such as capital and liquidity requirements, designed to protect the customer against a possible bank run. This account-based private money is linked to an individual person or entity. In contrast to sovereign currencies, there are limits on account-based money to circulate. For example, if Jeff writes a check to Greta to pay rent, Greta's check from Jeff represents money that belongs to Jeff (i.e., the money is linked to his deposit account), and she can redeem it in exchange for circulating currency (cash). Although Greta is legally allowed to exchange Jeff's check for gasoline, third-party checks are not widely accepted as a payment method. Hence, in reality, Greta first needs to cash the check and then purchase gasoline.

designed as a purported peer-to-peer payment system that does not rely on intermediation by a "trusted authority" to keep track of transactions. Instead, Bitcoin uses cryptography to record transactions across an open ("permissionless") network of computers.[1] These transactions are recorded digitally on a "blockchain," which uses cryptographic techniques to link transactions to each other in a manner that makes it challenging to edit or tamper with previous transactions. Because the Bitcoin blockchain is a public ledger, network participants can view and validate transactions as they happen in real time.[2] The supply of bitcoins is capped to ensure that each unit retains value, since digital assets otherwise could be reproduced perfectly forever, and they would have no value if there were an unlimited supply. This "artificial scarcity" was one important feature of Bitcoin, and has been replicated by many new crypto assets introduced since Bitcoin.

[1] There are also "permissioned" DLTs, where all nodes have to be given permission to participate in the network. However, if the trust in the network is established by authentication, that runs counter to the purpose of the trustless system.

[2] Formally, the network tracks the "unspent transaction output" from transactions for each account, which represents the transfer of specific units (e.g., like coins being transferred between individuals), or by how much available funds exceed withdrawals.

Both the number of crypto assets and their combined market value have risen over time, reflecting their increasing popularity around the world. There are several possible benefits that proponents claim for this popularity of crypto assets. These claims are reviewed in the next subsections.

Claim: Crypto Assets Could Be Investment Vehicles

People invest in assets with the hope of making returns on their investments by accepting a certain level of risk of loss. For example, traditional investments such as equities and bonds offer a certain level of expected returns for their risk exposure. Similar to these traditional types of assets, it has been argued that crypto assets are also investment vehicles that offer an expected return for a given risk exposure. Hence, depending on the risk appetite of investors, one might invest in crypto assets with the hope of quickly making a large profit. Moreover, some have argued that crypto assets can serve as a hedge against inflation, hoping their value will keep pace with or rise more than the rate of inflation.

Claim: Cryptocurrencies Could Offer Money-like Functions without Relying on a Single Authority

One stated goal of cryptocurrencies has been to create a financial system that is "censorship resistant" and unable to be controlled by a government, instead distributing control among pseudonymous global actors that do not rely upon any trust in existing financial institutions. In particular, some cryptocurrencies aim to replace central authorities that issue money by instead relying on a distributed network, with benefits spread across the network that issues representation of value that can be minted and transacted without central authorities. For example, when implementing monetary policy, governments can profit from issuing money because the value of money is generally higher than the cost of issuing it (this is called "seigniorage"). In contrast, many cryptocurrencies aim to distribute the profit from issuing a cryptocurrency by rewarding participants that can verify a transaction through a consensus mechanism (Acemoglu 2021). In this process, participants can be rewarded with the new issuance of a cryptocurrency as well as transaction fees, earning them a profit for supporting the distributed network that maintains the cryptocurrency. This could be seen as a novel way to distribute the profits from issuing new assets. Box 8-1 discusses the functions of money.

Claim: Crypto Assets Could Enable Fast Digital Payments

In recent years, the usage of cash has declined dramatically as the usage of digital payments has increased substantially. Figure 8-3 demonstrates the trends in cash and check transactions against those in debit/credit payments,

Figure 8-3. Payment Types Used in the United States Over Time

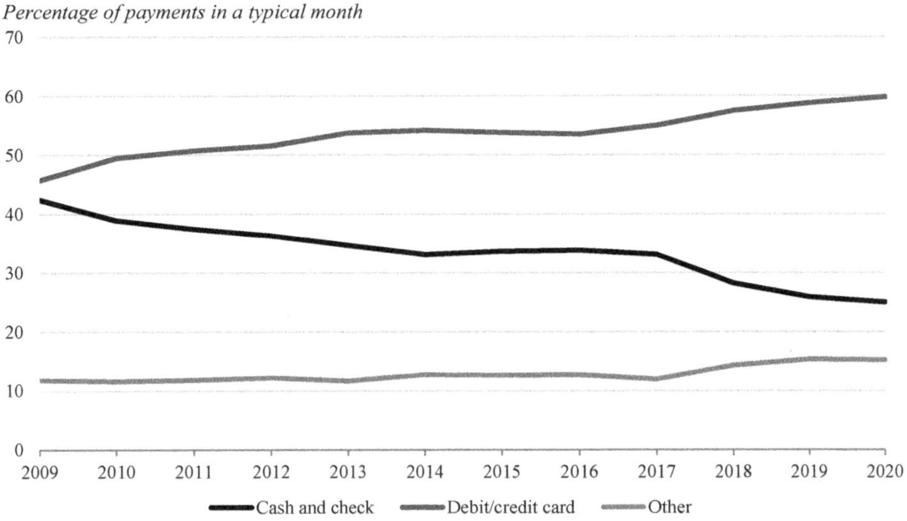

Percentage of payments in a typical month

Cash and check Debit/credit card Other

Sources: Federal Reserve Bank of Atlanta; CEA calculations.

which are forms of digital transactions. In the last decade, payments in cash and checks have declined dramatically, while digital payments have notably increased.

As the demand for digital payments increases, it has been argued that stablecoins could be used as near-instant 24/7 payment instruments (Liao and Caramichael 2022). As of December 22, 2022, there were about 200 stablecoins, with an estimated market size of roughly $140 billion. The two crypto assets Tether and USD Coin alone accounted for roughly 80 percent of the total market of stablecoins.[3] Since stablecoins try to be pegged to a reference asset such as the U.S. dollar (or another currency, or a basket of currencies), proponents argue that stablecoins could eliminate exchange risk when used as a settlement method. That is, if one stablecoin is always worth $1, then an individual using a stablecoin to buy or sell goods has the expectation that its nominal purchasing power will not change dramatically after their transaction. Stablecoins have been suggested as a possible way to simplify cross-border transactions and remittances.

Claim: Crypto Assets Could Increase Financial Inclusion

Some segments of the U.S. population are unbanked, meaning they do not own a bank account. Others are underbanked—that is, they own bank accounts but often use expensive nonbank financial services. Black households have disproportionately higher rates of being unbanked and underbanked (FDIC 2022). Crypto assets often are promoted as a tool for

[3] Market capitalizations exhibit volatility. See, e.g., CoinMarketCap (2023).

reaching these populations to improve their access to financial services and build wealth to achieve upward mobility. For example, many crypto assets do not impose minimum account requirements or charge overdraft fees, in contrast to some traditional banking institutions. Unbanked individuals cite such attributes as primary reasons they do not have bank accounts (FDIC 2022). A recent report found that minority households are more likely to have invested in crypto assets than other households (Faverio and Massarat 2022).

Claim: Crypto Assets Could Improve the United States' Current Financial Technology Infrastructure

The distributed ledger technology that underlies many crypto assets is based on a number of technological advances. It addresses the problem in certain circumstances of establishing trust and a consensus on the true history of transactions among a group of "mutually suspicious" parties. It is effectively a shared database whose contents can generally be trusted, even though it is operated by entities that generally do not have a reason to trust one another. For crypto assets, the database stores the set of transactions that have occurred among network participants. In addition, more recent developments in DLT have enabled new features and improved efficiency, such as "smart contracts," which automatically trigger particular actions without the need for ongoing oversight. Box 8-2 further describes how Bitcoin and distributed ledgers work.

The Reality of Crypto Assets

This section investigates the claimed benefits reviewed earlier in the chapter and presents the risks and costs of crypto assets.

Crypto Assets Are Mostly Speculative Investment Vehicles

As shown in figure 8-4, compared with many other asset types, crypto assets are very volatile, and, hence, highly risky. Because they are very volatile, crypto assets can be used for speculation, an investment strategy that seeks to make a profit from short-run trading. One reason many crypto assets are highly volatile is that many of them do not have a fundamental value. For example, stocks are claims on the future profits of firms and debt is a claim on interest and principal payments. Even commodities such as gold and silver have fundamental values, because they can be used in jewelry and for special manufacturing purposes (Nogrady 2016). Conversely, unbacked crypto assets are traded without fundamental anchors, suggesting that their market prices only reflect speculative demand, or market sentiment, not claims on cash flow. Relatedly, the U.S. Department of Labor (2022) issued

Box 8-2. How Does Bitcoin Work?

This box explains how Bitcoin functions, as it was the first crypto asset. Subsequent crypto assets have often incorporated key features from this design. Bitcoin relies on several innovations, including the novel use of a hash function, a well-established cryptographic technique.

What is a hash function? A hash function, which is sometimes called a "one-way" algorithm or "trap-door" algorithm, uses a mathematical algorithm to take an input (e.g., a number, a string of letters) and produce an output that satisfies three requirements: (1) reproducibility—or running the algorithm on the same input always produces the same output; (2) irreversibility—or even knowing the algorithm, it is not possible to easily invert the output to recover what the input was; and (3) collision avoidance—or any unique input string must produce exactly one unique output. This is a "one-way" function, in that there is no efficient way to recover the input from just the output; the only way would be to hash every possible input to see if it matches the output. Figure 8-i gives examples of hashed output.

The hash function is usually quick and has many applications. For example, most websites do not store a person's actual password on their servers; instead, they store a hash of the password. That way, if there were ever a hack of their systems, the hackers would only have the hashed versions, which would not work as passwords and could not easily be used to determine passwords. When you log onto a website, its server hashes the password you enter and compares that with what is stored in its database and only lets you in if they match. Note that a change of the input as seemingly small as from "hello" to "Hello" usually creates a drastically different hash, and that a vastly different phrase produces a hash that is equally random. Two key participants in the Bitcoin space are users and miners.

Users. Crypto assets generally require a user to have a "wallet." A digital wallet is a software application, piece of hardware, or other device or service that stores a user's public and private cryptographic

Figure 8-i. Examples of Hashed Output

Input Text	Hashed Output (in hexadecimal using the SHA-256 algorithm)
hello	2cf24dba5fb0a30e26e83b2ac5b9e29e1b161e5c1fa7425e73043362938b9824
Hello	185f8db32271fe25f561a6fc938b2e264306ec304eda518007d1764826381969
The quick brown fox jumps over the lazy dog	d7a8fbb307d7809469ca9abcb0082e4f8d5651e46d3cdb762d02d0bf37c9e592

Source: CEA analysis.

keys, which allow users to interact with one or more blockchains and send and receive crypto assets. Users can have custodial wallets, which are provided and maintained by an intermediary or third-party provider, or non-custodial wallets, also known as unhosted wallets, for which users are responsible for their own wallets and private keys. For Bitcoin, wallets have an associated "private key," typically a randomly generated string of digits, which can be hashed to derive a "public key." The public key similarly can be used to generate the wallet's address using a different, known hash function. Anyone can initiate a transfer to a wallet if they know its address. This is used as either the source or destination of transfers on the Bitcoin blockchain. However, to send crypto assets, one needs to know the private key for the wallet that is sending (Outten 2021). In particular, someone wanting to send crypto assets can construct the transaction, create a hash of it, and combine that with a private key to create a digital signature of the transaction. A useful analogy is that the public key is akin to your home address, while the private key is the physical key to your home. It is the difference between letting someone know where you live versus giving them access to your house. Any node of the network can then compare the hash of the digital signature with the public key, and with the hash of the transaction data, and determine if the transaction is valid. Nodes will reject any invalid transactions, so private keys are required to transfer crypto assets.

From the perspective of the user, who typically uses a wallet app to manage this process, all that is needed is the knowledge of the addresses of the sending and receiving accounts, the private key if sending, the amount, and a fee. The fee incentivizes miners to include the user's transaction in an upcoming block. A transaction with a high fee is more likely to be included in upcoming blocks than one with a low (or zero) fee. This means that transactions with low fees may takes days to be processed or may not be processed at all.

Miners. The key part of the Bitcoin ecosystem that is different from physical currency is that there are no central, trusted arbiters of truth. Instead, the system operates by consensus among nodes of the network about what the truth is (i.e., the distribution of bitcoins across all wallets). This means, in theory, that governance of the cryptocurrency is arbitrated by network participants, not a central authority, although control in some blockchains is more centralized as there may be a significant concentration among network participants that effectively consolidates governance between a few parties.

The Bitcoin blockchain uses what is called the SHA-256 algorithm (developed by the National Security Agency and the National Institute of Standards and Technology), which, for any text input, always produces a 64-digit (256-bit) hexadecimal output string (Brown 2002). The Bitcoin blockchain and many other cryptocurrencies use a "proof-of-work" method to achieve a consensus among all the nodes of the network.

Miners monitor the network and maintain a pool of transactions that are yet to be validated. In a proof-of-work network, the network's miners are competing to be the ones to successfully mine the next block of transactions in the chain. The actual way this is accomplished is that the miner puts together a candidate block of transactions to include as well as a "block header," or some metadata for the block (Rybarczyk 2020). These metadata include the hash of the last successfully mined block of the chain, the version of software used, and some technical parameters that are explained just below: the target difficulty, a digital signature unique to the block of transactions they are including (the "Merkle root"), and the "nonce." They then take all the information in the block header, combine it into one string, and push it through the SHA-256 algorithm to get the hash of that information.

Here is the competition aspect: the nonce field is a number that miners can choose arbitrarily. Their goal is to pick a nonce such that the resulting hash—a hexadecimal number—is less than the target—also a hexadecimal number—currently set by the blockchain. Given how the hashing process works, there is no way to do this efficiently; a miner must continue trying different numbers until they are successful. Since the nonce must be an 8-digit hexadecimal number, a little over 4 billion nonces can be tried. If no possibility is successful, the miner needs to get creative in how to try new hashes against the target, such as changing the set of transactions that are included in the block, which changes the Merkle root in the header, thus changing the proposed block's hash. While finding a valid nonce and set of transactions requires a large amount of brute-force computing power, verifying that a proposed block is valid is trivial—nodes just need to compute the hash of the proposed block and compare it with the target—and this means that once a block is found to be valid and is broadcast across the network, a consensus can be quickly reached that it is a valid block. At that point, it is added to the chain, and competition commences on adding the next block of transactions, the next element of truth in the system.

Miners receive two types of compensation for the work that they do: the fees that are included in the transactions they choose to put in a block; and the "miner reward," defined by the blockchain's protocol. For Bitcoin, the mining reward was initially 50 bitcoin for every mined block, but this has diminished due to a "halving rule." This rule limits the total supply of bitcoins to 21 million over the lifetime of the coin and means that every four years, the payout for mining a new block falls in half. The reward was 6.25 bitcoin, as of December 31 2022; but, given prevailing prices, this was worth over $100,000 (Coindesk 2022). The "target" difficulty parameter is adjusted every two weeks to ensure that a new coin is mined roughly every 10 minutes. As the number of resources dedicated to mining has increased, higher levels of difficulty have been required to keep pace. In the five years before October 2022, the number of attempts to mine a typical block of the Bitcoin chain increased by a factor of 19 (BTC 2022). Once the maximum supply of 21 million bitcoins is reached (which is projected to occur in about 2140), miners will only benefit from transaction fees (Timón 2016).

Why does the blockchain mechanism "work"? Once the blockchain is running, suppose a bad actor wanted to modify the history of the blockchain by, for example, inserting a fraudulent transaction in an earlier block. In theory, this would not work, since any other node of the network could immediately verify that this block did not previously belong in the chain because no subsequent block would point to its (changed) hash as being its predecessor. So, a bad actor would need to recompute the entire chain, from the fraudulent block to the current one, with new hashes, which would require an inordinate amount of computing power. This highlights the origins of blockchain technology in ensuring trust among mutually suspicious groups (Chaum 1982). Figure 8-ii demonstrates how a blockchain is formed.

Many other blockchains have a design similar to that of Bitcoin, although with different parameters and features, such as smart contracts. Ethereum, for example, allows more daily transactions than Bitcoin, is calibrated to have blocks added every 12 seconds, and recently switched its consensus protocol to be less energy-intensive (Etherscan 2022). An important criticism of crypto assets is their energy intensity. A more complete discussion of the technological options of blockchain design is beyond the scope of this chapter.

Figure 8-ii. Blockchain Blocks Linked by Hashed Values of Their Contents

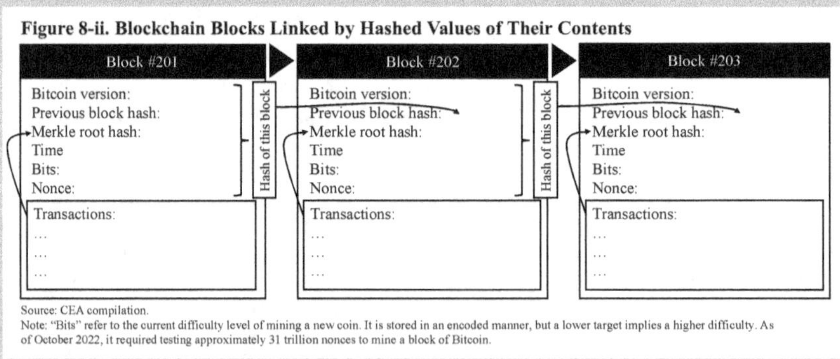

Source: CEA compilation.
Note: "Bits" refer to the current difficulty level of mining a new coin. It is stored in an encoded manner, but a lower target implies a higher difficulty. As of October 2022, it required testing approximately 31 trillion nonces to mine a block of Bitcoin.

Figure 8-4. Volatility of Crypto Assets versus Certain Traditional Assets, 2017–22

Thirty-day rolling standard deviation of daily returns

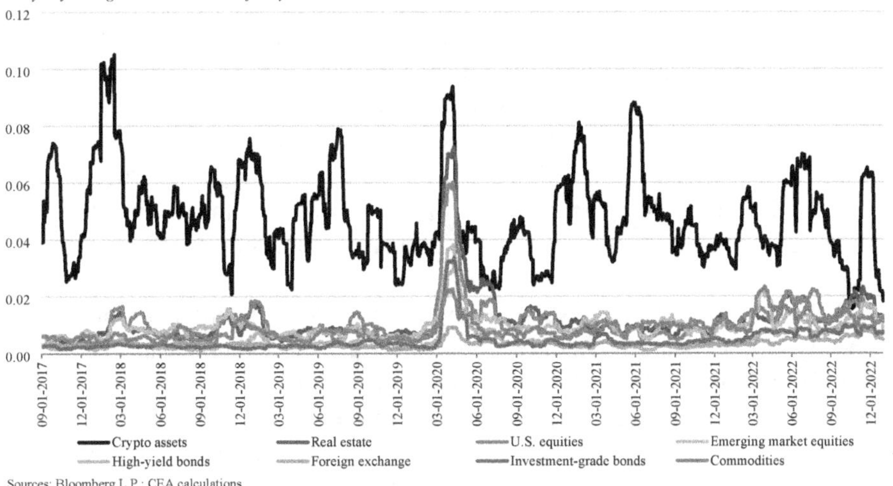

Sources: Bloomberg L.P.; CEA calculations.

guidance to protect investors' retirement plans with respect to this asset type. Recall that one of the purported benefits of crypto assets like Bitcoin was to hedge against inflation, meaning that their value does not erode as inflation increases. But as inflation increased globally in the second half of 2021 and in 2022, the prices of crypto assets collapsed, proving them to be, at best, an ineffective inflation hedge.

Cryptocurrencies Generally Do Not Perform All the Functions of Money as Effectively as Sovereign Money, such as the U.S. Dollar

As discussed in box 8-1, money serves three functions: as a unit of account, which means that it acts as a benchmark upon which the values of different goods and services can be compared; as a medium of exchange, which means that it can be used to trade goods and services; and as a store of value, which means that the amount of goods and services that a unit of the money can buy does not fluctuate dramatically over short intervals of time. Although cryptocurrencies currently serve each of these functions, they only do so in limited ways in the United States, so they do not serve, from an economic perspective, as an effective alternative to the U.S. dollar.

For the first monetary function question, cryptocurrencies can serve as a unit of account, given that the relative values of goods and services can be expressed in cryptocurrency (e.g., a single chicken in commerce is worth roughly 0.0001 bitcoin). However, individuals would likely need to first convert bitcoins or other cryptocurrencies to dollars to understand relative values as cryptocurrencies are not as effective as the U.S. dollar as a medium of exchange (discussed below). Thus, cryptocurrencies currently do not fully serve as units of account.

The second question is whether cryptocurrencies can serve as a medium of exchange. The answer is that in the United States, they are not as effective a medium of exchange as the U.S. dollar. This is because they can be used to purchase other cryptocurrencies and to buy goods and services at a smaller number of firms relative to the U.S. dollar (Modderman 2022). The strength of the U.S. dollar is derived from several important factors, such as faith in government institutions and the legal system, but cryptocurrencies lack these factors.

Third, cryptocurrencies currently experience substantial amounts of volatility, and thus are not stable stores of value. For example, the value of a bitcoin (relative to the U.S. dollar) increased by over 1,000 percent from March 2019 to March 2021, and then decreased by over 70 percent from November 2021 to October 2022. This volatility means that anyone who is using bitcoins to store their savings is subject to high-volatility risk in their purchasing power. As figure 8-4 shows, the volatility of cryptocurrencies outpaces those of many other financial asset types. Cryptocurrencies regularly exhibit a similar amount of volatility as U.S. equities experienced at the onset of the COVID-19 pandemic.

There is also tension in an asset being promoted as both money and an investment vehicle. As money, the instrument should have a stable value, suggesting limited price volatility. But as a risky asset, it should experience price volatility, for which an investor would be compensated with a high expected return. Holding everything else constant, the riskier an asset is, the less likely it can effectively serve as money.

In sum, in addition to generally being speculative assets, cryptocurrencies currently are not effective alternatives to sovereign money such as the U.S. dollar. As mentioned above, most cryptocurrencies do not have fundamental value, but that is not a requirement for them to function as money. In fact, sovereign money does not have a fundamental or intrinsic value (Berentsen and Schär 2018). Even so, sovereign money can easily satisfy money's requirements, as discussed in box 8-2. The main reason for this is that the value of sovereign money is backed by a trusted institution—the central bank. One important feature of many cryptocurrencies is validating transactions through consensus mechanisms, which are a way to distribute profits from new issuance among participants such as cryptocurrency miners that verify the cryptocurrency transactions. (See box 8-3 for the impact of cryptocurrency mining on the physical environment.) Hence, the supply of cryptocurrency generally increases with the number of verified cryptocurrency transactions. In the case of a new issuance of sovereign money, monetary policy reasons play a major role, and the resulting profits from the new issuance of sovereign money accrue to governments. In advanced

Box 8-3. Crypto Asset Mining as a Risk to the Environment

The growth of trading in crypto assets has necessitated a corresponding increase in the mining of crypto assets. As discussed in box 8-2, crypto asset "mining" (cryptomining for short) is a process by which high-powered computers perform calculations to verify transactions using distributed ledger technology for some kinds of crypto assets (White House 2022d).

Cryptomining can be lucrative for successful miners, which are compensated with the crypto assets they are mining but which also consume large amounts of energy. According to recent estimates by Goldman Sachs, cryptomining accounted for more than 2 percent of U.S. power consumption as of early 2022. The amount of electricity used to mine bitcoins in the United States is similar to what is used to power all the country's home computers or residential lighting (White House 2022d). A recent inquiry by Congress into the electricity consumption of cryptominers found that just seven of the largest cryptomining operations in the United States had a combined capacity of 1,045.3 megawatts as of February 2022, with plans to expand capacity significantly in the coming months and years. For comparison, these miners alone could use roughly as much power as all residential units in Houston, the Nation's fourth-largest city (Tabuchi 2022).

While comparing usage across different types of activities is difficult because not all activity is recorded on-chain, some have estimated that in 2021 mining a single bitcoin used roughly the same amount of electricity as nine years' worth of the average American household's consumption (Huang, O'Neill, and Tabuchi 2021). Bitcoin additionally uses more energy than several entire *countries*, such as Finland, Belgium, and Chile (University of Cambridge 2022). Globally, Bitcoin accounts for 0.42 percent of all electricity usage. This effectively means that Bitcoin is using the same amount of electricity as a medium-sized advanced economy.

Not all cryptomining operations consume the same amounts of power. Energy-intensive consensus mechanisms, such as a proof-of-work, use substantial amounts of power by encouraging machines in a network to race against each other to solve a mathematical puzzle. Bitcoin, which accounted for over of a third of all crypto assets' value as of December 2022, is the most notable crypto asset that is mined using proof-of-work. Ethereum, conversely, switched in September 2022 from a proof-of-work consensus mechanism to a proof-of-stake consensus mechanism that selects specific miners to validate a transaction at a given point in time, thereby reducing electricity usage in exchange for reducing the security of the network and increasing the power of individual actors vis-à-vis the network's intensity. There are benefits and drawbacks from different consensus mechanisms, and they have different energy, transparency, and security attributes. Despite Ethereum's switch to proof-of-stake, Bitcoin has not announced plans to make a similar change.

Evidence suggests that cryptomining has substantial costs for local communities and has few, if any, attendant benefits. Cryptomining facilities produce substantial noise pollution, which has been compared to a "jet-like roar" (Williams 2022). Cryptomining facilities can also lead to increases in local air and water pollution (White House 2022d).

Local cryptomining operations also push up community electricity prices, as increased electricity consumption forces generators to rely on more expensive energy sources and, in the case of communities with hydropower where cryptomining operations are often located, reduces electricity surpluses. For example, in the Mid-Columbia Basin of Washington State, an energy surplus produced by hydroelectric dams originally pushed down electricity prices for both residents and businesses. But after cryptomining facilities began placing additional demand on the energy grid, exports of energy surpluses decreased, substantially raising residential electricity prices (Samford and Domingo 2019).

Continuously running an electricity grid at maximum capacity can cause grid equipment that was not designed for such high-intensity usage to degrade over time, increasing the risk of fire in vulnerable communities. In places like Texas, which expects to add 27 gigawatts of additional cryptomining demand in the next four years—equal to roughly 30 percent of the generation capacity of the entire Texas grid—cryptomining could increase the likelihood of power crises, where demand overwhelms the grid's ability to provide sufficient generation (Calma 2022).

Furthermore, the intensive nature of mining bitcoins requires frequently replacing machines, and as the old equipment becomes nonfunctional, it can become "e-waste," which often contains toxic chemicals and heavy metals that can leach into soils if not properly disposed of (de Vries and Stoll 2021). Just as mining energy-usage comparisons are difficult, comparing e-waste across activities is imprecise, especially because old machines used to mine bitcoins may be temporarily retired but then used again if the price increases enough (White House 2022d). With that being said, some have estimated that it would take as much as 114,000 Visa transactions to generate the same amount of e-waste as a single bitcoin transaction. Alternatively, a single bitcoin transaction may generate more e-waste than 2.7 iPhones (Digiconomist 2022).

economies such as the United States, the profits from the issuance of sovereign currency benefit taxpayers by lowering tax needs, as central banks effectively return these profits as government revenue.

Stablecoins Can Be Subject to Run Risk

Some cryptocurrencies, specifically stablecoins, are promoted to have the potential to be fast digital payment instruments. A fundamental problem with stablecoins is one that has been known in the traditional banking sector for centuries: *run risk* (Humphrey 1975). If stablecoin holders wish to redeem their stablecoins for $1 each, this will require the stablecoin issuer to liquidate some of its reserves (Adams and Ibert 2022). Depending on how liquid these reserves are, and the state of broader financial conditions, this liquidation may lead to disruptions in the markets for the reserve assets and reduce the market value of the issuer's remaining reserves because the sales of the reserve assets put further downward pressure on the prices of remaining reserves. If reserves are falling in value at the same time holders are seeking redemptions, then the issuer may receive less than $1 for each $1 placed in stablecoins, thereby causing the stablecoin issuer to become insolvent. In fact, money market funds, which have balance sheet characteristics that a number of stablecoins purport to have, faced runs during the 2008 financial crisis and at the onset of the COVID-19 pandemic in 2020 (Schmidt, Timmermann, and Wermers 2016; Anadu et al. 2021).

Deposits in bank accounts can be used to make payments, and banks aim to maintain parity between deposits and dollars; that is, $1 deposited in a bank account can be withdrawn for $1 at a later point in time. One important distinction between stablecoins and bank deposits is that in the United States, bank deposits are subject to a comprehensive set of regulatory and supervisory requirements. In contrast, stablecoins are not subject to requirements designed to maintain this exchange rate.

A different approach to maintaining a stablecoin that does not fully rely on holding reserves is the so-called algorithmic stablecoin of TerraUSD (and the closely linked Luna token), which had the stated objective to maintain its exchange rate peg with the U.S. dollar using an algorithm (Baughman et al 2022). The idea behind the Terra/Luna coins was that Terra (known as UST) was a stablecoin pegged to $1 and was maintained through arbitrage (Wong 2022). Theoretically, 1 UST could always be traded for $1 worth of Luna. If the value of Terra ever fell below $1, arbitrageurs could exchange 1 Terra for $1 worth of Luna, a different coin. In theory, this would allow the arbitrageur to make a gain, decrease the supply of Terra (the exchanged token was "burned"), and raise the value of Terra. If the value of Terra rose above $1, arbitrageurs could buy ("mint") 1 UST in exchange for $1 of Luna, making a small gain but increasing the supply of Terra and pushing down its value. This was meant to be the mechanism to keep the value of Terra at $1, although there was also a reserve of other cryptocurrencies kept to support the peg, but not enough to fully cover the market value of Terra. At one point, Terra was the world's fourth-largest stablecoin, in part due to the fact that people who were willing to deposit UST on Anchor, a smart contract-lending protocol, which promised investors an annual interest rate of 19.5 percent on their investments (Briola et al. 2023). Eventually, a run occurred as a few major withdrawals in May 2022 knocked UST off its $1 peg, leading to a stampede out of Terra into Luna, depressing Luna's value, and ultimately causing the total crash of the two cryptocurrencies.

Another key risk of stablecoins for U.S. retail users is that redemption may be a secondary concern for liquidity on crypto asset trading platforms. As noted in the Financial Stability Oversight Council's "Digital Asset Financial Stability Risks and Regulation Report," U.S. retail customers cannot directly redeem the two largest stablecoins (Tether and USD Coin) for dollars (U.S. Department of the Treasury 2022a). Stablecoin holders that lack redemption rights may be unable to find willing counterparties to exit their stablecoin positions.

Gorton and Zhang (2021) evaluate a number of solutions to the run risk of stablecoins. For example, they assert that if stablecoins are required to be fully backed by safe assets, they would risk attracting funds that would ordinarily go to banks, which make loans. This would have the potential to hurt credit availability for individuals and firms. In subsequent research, Gorton and Zhang (2022) argue that stablecoins could challenge the government's monetary authority to have an exclusive monopoly on currency issuance and disrupt financial stability.

Stablecoins currently have a few major impediments against becoming fast payment instruments. For one, stablecoins are too risky to satisfy this need at present. Additionally, as discussed below, general concerns about consumer and investor protections in the crypto asset space also apply to stablecoins (U.S. Department of the Treasury 2022a). Nevertheless, there is continuing experimentation in using distributed ledger technology for digital payment systems. While crypto assets are currently not payment or settlement technologies for the rest of the financial system, it is still possible that in the future, their underlying DLT could be adapted into a payment or settlement system for the broader financial system.

Crypto Assets Can Be Harmful to Consumers and Investors

For consumers and investors to use crypto assets to access financial services, the crypto asset industry must have sound consumer, investor, and market protections. However, many participants in the crypto asset industry are not acting in compliance with existing laws and regulations, and some of the most common unlawful activities in the crypto asset industry are scams especially aimed at retail investors (U.S. Department of the Treasury 2022a). One of the principal areas where there is mass noncompliance is disclosure surrounding crypto assets that are securities. This lack of disclosure prevents investors from recognizing that most crypto assets have no fundamental value. For example, many fraudsters develop intricate and professional-looking websites that purport to offer investors an exciting, high-return investment opportunity. When a victim gives crypto assets to the criminal to invest, the criminal can simply abscond with the funds. Examples of this includes a matter in September 2021, when the U.S. Securities and Exchange Commission (SEC) filed an action against the platform BitConnect for allegedly committing $2 billion worth of fraud (SEC 2021a). In its action, the SEC alleged that BitConnect purported to offer investors a "lending" program using a "proprietary volatility software trading bot," but instead simply took investors' crypto assets and transferred them into digital wallets controlled by the criminals. To date, the SEC has filed charges alleging a number of fraudulent offerings and other types of misconduct involving crypto assets (SEC 2022).

In May 2021, the Federal Trade Commission (FTC) released a post detailing the increase in scams involving crypto assets since October 2020 (Fletcher 2021). Between October 2020 and May 2021, more than 7,000 people reported losses from these scams, which totaled more than $80 million, with a median loss of $1,900. One particular type of scam identified by the FTC is "giveaway scams," where promoters claim to instantly multiply a given number of crypto assets but instead appropriate the crypto assets upon receipt. According to the FTC, young people were most susceptible to this type of fraud; those between 20 and 39 years of age lose far more money to investment fraud than any other type, more than half of which was attributable to crypto assets.

In November 2022, the Consumer Financial Protection Bureau (CFPB) released a bulletin summarizing the consumer complaints it had received about crypto assets (CFPB 2022). In a period of less than four years, from October 2018 to September 2022, the CFPB received more than 8,300 complaints related to crypto assets, with the majority received since 2020. In this period, roughly 40 percent of crypto asset complaints handled were primarily frauds and scams. Transactional issues with crypto assets and issues with assets not being available when promised made up about another 40 percent of complaints. Other risks identified in the CFPB's bulletin included romance scams and "pig butchering," difficulty obtaining restitution, and fraudulent transactions.[4]

[4] Pig butchering refers to a practice where scammers develop close personal relationships with a victim in order to convince them to set up crypto asset accounts from which the scammers can steal.

Furthermore, there can be conflicts of interest at crypto asset platforms. For example, some crypto asset platforms combine exchange, brokerage, market making, and clearing agency functions. This vertical integration of products and services has long been prohibited in traditional markets and leads to risks to customers. For instance, a platform that combines exchange and market making functions would have an incentive to trade ahead of its own customers, and would have less incentive to seek out best executions for its customers. FTX, one of the largest crypto asset platforms until 2022, reportedly transferred billions of dollars in customer accounts to its affiliated trading firm, Alameda Research (Goldstein et al. 2022). By borrowing against FTT, the native token of FTX, Alameda Research reportedly made risky bets and lost a large fraction of FTX customers' funds (Tortorelli and Rooney 2022). In November 2022, FTX and its affiliates declared bankruptcy and the price of FTT posted massive losses; at this time it is unclear whether FTX customers and creditors will get their funds back (Ge Huang, Osipovich, and Kowsmann 2022).

There Have Been Limited Economic Benefits from DLT Technology

The ability of DLT to solve the difficult problem of ensuring that two parties that do not have a reason to trust each other can nonetheless transact securely is a notable achievement of computer science. This solution has led to excitement about DLT, with even some enthusiasm that this technology will change the way business is done (Iansiti and Lakhani 2017). DLT and blockchain technology are not necessarily suitable for all applications; some considerations have been proposed for successful blockchain technology applications (Yaga et al. 2018). See box 8-4 for the proposed DLT use cases. However, at its core, DLT is simply a database, and many proposed DLT-based projects do not actually employ decentralization (as discussed below). Some have sought to profit from the hyperbole of blockchain—it has become a common tactic for non-crypto-related businesses to announce a "pivot to blockchain" to generate interest in a product or enterprise (Griffith 2018). For example, in December 2017, a beverage maker named "Long Island Iced Tea" added "Blockchain" to its name—though changing nothing substantive about its business—and its stock shares tripled in value (Cheng 2017). Ultimately, three persons involved with the firm were charged with insider trading by the SEC, which alleged that these insiders used the "pivot to blockchain" tactic to increase the firm's share prices before they sold their stakes in the firm (SEC 2021b).

In addition, many prominent technologists have noted that distributed ledgers are either not particularly novel or useful or they are being used in applications where existing alternatives are far superior. For example, Bruce Schneier (2019), a cybersecurity expert, has called crypto assets "useless"

Box 8-4. Proposed Uses of Distributed Ledger Technology

The excitement generated about DLT has drawn substantial investment capital and has prompted governments and firms outside the crypto asset industry to experiment with its underlying technological processes. In some cases, this excitement has led to large writedowns or failed projects. Here, we review three current cases and give examples of experimentation.

Walmart Canada and supply chains. A commonly touted use for distributed ledger technology is supply chains, where a single, distributed ledger could improve traceability throughout a supply chain and reconcile records between a firm and its multiple suppliers (Laaper, n.d.). In 2021, Walmart Canada launched a blockchain that attempted to handle payment disputes between 70 third-party freight carriers. An article in the *Harvard Business Review* dubbed the experiment "a tremendous success," noting that before the blockchain system, 70 percent of invoices were disputed, but after the rollout, that share dropped to less than 1 percent (Vitasek et al. 2022). Though seemingly impressive, the firm that partnered with Walmart Canada to develop the blockchain platform stated in a report describing the project that the platform ran on "more than 600 virtual machines (VMs) to securely store and manage data points from thousands of transactions per day" (Hyperledger Foundation, n.d.). This implies that each VM is, at a maximum, handling 17 transactions per day. For reference, a minimally configured AWS (Amazon Web Services) RDS (relational data store) database with two VMs configured with best practices could process thousands, if not tens of thousands, of transactions per second (Amazon 2017). Furthermore, a prominent technologist stated that it was not even obvious what functional role blockchain was playing in the system, and that the program was more akin to using an existing technology in an inefficient way (Orosz 2022).

Helium and the decentralized Internet. Helium is a company that is attempting to build a peer-to-peer wireless network by allowing users to buy "hotspots"—small devices that can send data over long distances—that can, together, create a Wi-Fi network. When the company was founded, it did not intend to have crypto assets as a central part of its business model (Roose 2022). Instead, it attempted to use traditional economic incentives for those helping build the network by simply sharing some of the fees from network users to hotspot owners. In 2019, however, the company pivoted and attempted to make crypto assets central to its business model by creating an incentive system where users that purchased hotspots that cost roughly $500 (and thus contributed to the network) were rewarded with Helium crypto asset tokens. If the prices of tokens rose, then so, too, would the reward for owning a hotspot, thus encouraging more users to build out the necessary network infrastructure.

After this pivot, large venture capital firms like Andreessen Horowitz (also known as a16z) helped Helium raise hundreds of millions of dollars in equity (Seward 2021). Alameda Research (the failed hedge fund affiliated with FTX) was also a large investor in Helium. Despite the sizable funding and widespread interest, Helium came under scrutiny in July 2022, when its cofounder tweeted that the company had generated $2 million a month in fees from new users joining (buying hotspots), but only $6,500 (0.3 percent) of that was from users actually using the Internet service (Levine 2022). Furthermore, a Forbes investigation in September 2022 found that the executives of the firm gave themselves and their families a windfall in Helium tokens early in the company's history that was not publicly disclosed (Emerson, Jeans, and Liu 2022). Also, in September 2022, Helium ended the use of its own blockchain, which purportedly incentivized broader provision of Internet access as a core feature ("proof of coverage") and shifted its operations and coins to the Solana blockchain, the same technology on which many other speculative crypto assets are traded, calling into question whether this use could be distinguished from any other type of crypto asset (Yaffe-Bellany 2022). Although these pieces of news may present a significant headwind for Helium's future, the Helium token nonetheless has a market value (as of December 22, 2022) of over $253 million (CoinMarketCap 2022).

Nonfungible tokens and virtual real estate. Nonfungible tokens (NFTs) are digital assets that are not interchangeable. Each NFT is unique, with its ownership recorded on a distributed ledger. Ownership of an NFT can pass between two users by recording the transaction and transferring it on a blockchain. NFTs often contain a pointer to a digital object, such as an image file. As a famous example, in March 2021 Jack Dorsey, the cofounder and former CEO of Twitter, auctioned off an NFT of an image of his first tweet on Twitter from 2006, with the winning bid coming in at more than $2.9 million (Locke 2021). While anyone could create ("mint") a new NFT of the same digital image (and the digital image can be easily reproduced), the original transaction is maintained on a blockchain, so it would not truly be the same (OpenSea 2022). This highlights the "artificial scarcity" view of crypto assets.

Borri, Liu, and Tsyvnski (2022) studied the market for NFTs from 2018 to 2021 and created an index of NFT value based on the repeat sales method. They found the average NFT market return was 2.5 percent a week in this period, although with a weekly standard deviation of 19 percent. This highlights the volatility and variability of NFT returns. The market for NFTs cooled in 2022; the owner of Dorsey's tweet listed it for sale in April 2022 for $48 million, but the highest bid as of January 4, 2023, was about $82,000 (OpenSea 2022).

NFTs can be a natural way to track ownership of virtual real estate. Several different "metaverses" have begun offering "land" in virtual worlds. Ownership of land translates into the title of a virtual property being recorded on a distributed ledger. What one does with their land depends on the platform—on Decentraland, a large metaverse platform, owners are free to develop their land as they see fit: they could open a store selling virtual goods, create a game app for visitors, build a gallery for their virtual art collection, or build a virtual "house" (Kamin 2021). Dowling (2022) studied the value of land in Decentraland and found that the daily values of the virtual land tokens between 2019 and 2021 changed with extreme volatility. As in the physical world, location matters—while the average transaction value for a property in the data set is $1,311, a firm paid $2.5 million for land in Decentraland's Fashion District (Putzier 2021).

Experimentation. The current uses discussed above have demonstrated only limited, if any, economic benefits so far. Even so, proponents still claim that this technology could find productive uses in the future as companies and governments continue experimenting with potential uses; however, they often use "permissioned" networks of machines that have been authenticated as a trusted member of the network (Oracle 2022). For example, it is possible that distributed ledger technologies can be used to improve the settlement and clearing processes of banks (Bech et al. 2020). In fact, as mentioned above, banks are experimenting with distributed ledger technology to improve the efficiency of trading, clearing, settlement, and custody (Yang 2022). In addition, the New York Innovation Center of the Federal Reserve Bank of New York (2022) is participating in an experiment with the notion of a regulated liability network, a conceptual financial market infrastructure that could enable transactions between regulated financial institutions potentially using DLT.

and has noted that despite claims of being decentralized and trustless, blockchain-based applications are in practice neither; often, users access their crypto assets by going to a limited set of crypto asset platforms, and a small group of miners perform the majority of mining in most crypto assets, an activity that has costly implications for the physical environment, as discussed in box 8-3. When it comes to the "trustlessness" of blockchains, Schneier notes that a blockchain does not eliminate the need for trust but simply shifts trust away from individuals and institutions to a technology—along with all its features and bugs.

James Mickens, a leading computer scientist who studies distributed systems, has stated that in addition to not actually being decentralized and trustless, blockchains are often a very poor fit for their purported uses (Mickens 2018). This is primarily because the instant that the identity of a person or firm is needed (as is the case for supply chains, medical records, and land deeds), existing technologies can solve the same problem in a much more efficient way. For example, many of the cybersecurity benefits of an immutable, distributed blockchain can be replicated through existing features like tamper resistance (the ability to not change digital signatures at a later point in time) and nonrepudiation (a receipt of a sender of information's identity that is delivered to both the sender and receiver of information, thus guaranteeing that both parties have processed the information) (World Bank, n.d.; NIST, n.d.).

Proponents of blockchain technology claim that it will not only improve firms' performance but also be the backbone of an entirely new Internet. Web3—the so-called new Internet—purports to retain all the privacy/networking benefits of the earliest versions of the Internet that existed roughly before 2000 (often called "web1," which featured decentralized, community-governed open protocols), while keeping the high functionality of various features of web2 (the current version of the Internet) without the existing dependencies on large centralized firms like Google and Apple (Dixon 2021). However, Moxie Marlinspike (2022), the cryptographer and founder of the messaging app Signal, argues that the reason the current Internet features so much centralization is because it makes things easier, for two specific reasons. First, he argues that a decentralized Internet would require individuals and firms to host their own servers. However, centralized hosting of servers can be done much more cheaply and reliably by large entities and therefore benefits from economies of scale. Second, he notes that protocols—or the rules that Internet systems run on—are much more difficult to change than platforms. That is, centralized, non-open-source protocols can be managed by a single entity (as opposed to many), facilitating a wider variety of features that can change with much greater speed than if they were decentralized. Marlinspike also notes that web3 is already trending toward a centralized structure because of the ease and convenience that centralization brings, but in a much clunkier way than if traditional technology were being used. He specifically notes that "once a distributed ecosystem centralizes around a platform for convenience, it becomes the worst of both worlds: centralized control, but still distributed enough to become mired in time."

Table 8-1. Top Ten Crypto Derivative Platforms by Open Interest

Rank (1)	Exchange (2)	24-Hour Open Interest (Nominal $) (3)	24-Hour Volume (Nominal $) (4)
1	BTCEX	$8,314,364,513	$7,180,531,116
2	Binance	$7,714,660,817	$32,741,616,672
3	BTCC Futures	$5,103,831,418	$7,968,963,153
4	Deepcoin	$4,781,751,226	$9,854,658,307
5	BingX	$4,334,560,170	$5,165,147,675
6	Bitget Futures	$4,331,916,947	$5,414,169,494
7	OKX	$3,586,501,924	$8,449,781,644
8	Bybit	$3,397,272,483	$8,090,497,597
9	MEXC Global	$3,228,041,626	$2,263,323,835
10	Bitmart Futures	$2,707,627,218	$4,283,383,129

Source: CoinGecko. Data were collected on January 19, 2023.

The Risks of Financial Innovation

While the crypto assets ecosystem and its underlying technology introduce the potential for newfound efficiencies, efforts to challenge basic economic principles have frequently resulted in financial calamities. The economist Hyman Minsky hypothesized that financial crises often follow a similar cycle, whereby initially strong investments turn increasingly more speculative until a bubble bursts (Minsky 1992). Further, Minsky stated that this repeatedly happens because regulators are initially vigilant in the immediate aftermath of a crisis; but as time goes on, and the instrument of speculation changes, regulators take a less proscriptive approach to not harm "innovation" (Minsky 2008). According to Minsky, this relaxed regulatory environment invariably leads to another crisis. Indeed, other economists have argued that the most effective financial regulation has been introduced only *after* a crisis has occurred (Gorton 2012). Minsky's theories became popular in the aftermath of the global financial crisis, when complicated financial products involving mortgages that exacerbated the crisis were initially hailed as innovative, and individuals discussing their risks were labeled "Luddites" by prominent commentators (Cassidy 2008; Wheatley 2013).

Minsky's writings, as they apply to past financial crises, may prove instructive for policymakers today. Fortunately, there has not yet been a systemic crisis caused by crypto assets, in part because they are not yet fully integrated with the rest of the financial system, giving policymakers time to act appropriately. The risks presented by crypto assets stem from excessive speculation, high leverage, run risk, environmental harm from crypto asset mining, and fraudulent activities that harm retail investors and corporations. Because crypto assets appear to be here to stay, policymakers should consider these risks to avoid a "Minsky moment" caused by crypto assets.

Other Risks from Crypto Assets

Some risks that apply to crypto assets require further examination. Many of these risks are not unique to crypto assets; combined with innovative technology, they pose challenges for policymakers and regulators trying to minimize risks while encouraging responsible innovation.

Leverage risks. Crypto asset derivative platforms—where investors can buy and sell financial derivatives linked to crypto assets—have seen substantial growth in the past two years (Damalas et al. 2022). Table 8-1 shows that the top 10 platforms for crypto asset derivatives, which account for roughly 76 percent of all volume in these derivatives, have over $47 billion in open interest and roughly $91 billion in daily trading as of January 18, 2023. According to one international regulator, one of the largest platforms, Binance, refuses to provide adequate and reliable information in response to regulatory requests (FCA 2021).

Exchanges frequently tout the high amount of leverage they offer clients, stating that investors can take up to 100-to-1 leverage (debt-to-equity ratios) (Pechman 2021). These derivative platforms can create financial instability because positions with high leverage (debt-to-equity ratios) can amplify a shock to prices of crypto assets and lead to large losses and even defaults (U.S. Department of the Treasury 2022c). In particular, leverage leaves little room for prices to fall in a short amount of time, as steep price declines could induce brokers to issue large margin calls, thus forcing broader liquidation (Carapella et al. 2022).

A relatively new application of DLT in financial markets where there is a relatively unknown amount of leverage is so-called decentralized finance (DeFi). DeFi attempts to offer financial products, such as loans, on the blockchain through the use of "smart contracts" (Carapella et al. 2022). The basic promise behind DeFi is to replace financial intermediaries, instead linking savers directly with borrowers (or buyers with sellers), allowing them to save on the spread that traditional intermediaries charge for creating the match with software. Though DeFi applications claim to help broaden access to credit by decreasing intermediation fees, they create serious risks to investors and cause at least two risks for the broader financial system: the use of significant leverage, and the performance of regulated functions without compliance with appropriate regulations. DeFi platforms acting as unregulated banks, broker-dealers, exchanges and other entities subject to regulation should be operating in compliance with existing regulations and rules. DeFi lending platforms effectively receive funds from investors and use them to generate loans, promising interest to investors. This dynamic inherently causes run risks, where more investors try to redeem more of their funds than the platform can accommodate at a given time, thus causing the platform to either suspend convertibility or fail outright (Carapella et al. 2022). Furthermore, DeFi presents the opportunity for "synthetic leverage," whereby investors can mask the true amount of leverage they are undertaking from the party from which they are borrowing (Tian 2021). If DeFi were limited to small, retail investors, the failure of a DeFi platform could still hurt these investors, but the shock could be relatively contained. Banking agencies issued a statement that expressed concerns with business models that are concentrated in crypto-asset-related activities or have concentrated exposures to the crypto asset sector (Federal Reserve Board 2023).

Price volatility. Most crypto assets experience substantial price volatility. Holding such volatile assets could present challenges for large financial institutions if they were permitted to hold crypto assets, as the volatility would lead to constant changes on the asset side of their balance sheets. This volatility, in turn, could increase funding costs for banks and other financial institutions, thereby requiring banks—which fundamentally borrow so as to be able to lend—to increase the funding costs (interest rates) that they charge, leading to tighter credit conditions.

Currently, this contagion risk is relatively muted, given that banks are limited in their ability to conduct crypto-related activities, such as acting as custodians of crypto assets (i.e., holding crypto assets for clients, not on their own balance sheets) (OCC 2020). Indeed, banking regulators such as the Federal Reserve have issued guidance requiring regulated financial institutions to inform their regulator before engaging in crypto-asset-related activity (Gibson and Belsky 2022). But other, less-regulated financial institutions, such as hedge funds, are increasingly investing in crypto assets. Such activity of lightly regulated or nonregulated entities can lead to "liquidity spirals," as described by Brunnermeier and Pederson (2007). These spirals occur when a dramatic crash in the price of an asset—such as a crypto asset—leads a hedge fund to be margin-called, requiring the fund to sell off other positions to meet the margin call. If enough funds are exposed to the asset or assets with declining prices, then sell-offs could be broad enough to cause a deterioration in market liquidity.

Illicit finance risks. Crypto assets are the standard form of payment extorted from victims of "ransomware," whereby a malicious actor hacks an organization and demands payment to release control of the victim's network and often to purportedly forgo leaking the victim's stolen data. Crypto assets remove a critical friction in performing a ransomware hack. Because the attacker can demand that crypto assets be sent to a pseudonymous wallet

Figure 8-5. Nominal Cyber Insurance Prices Over Time

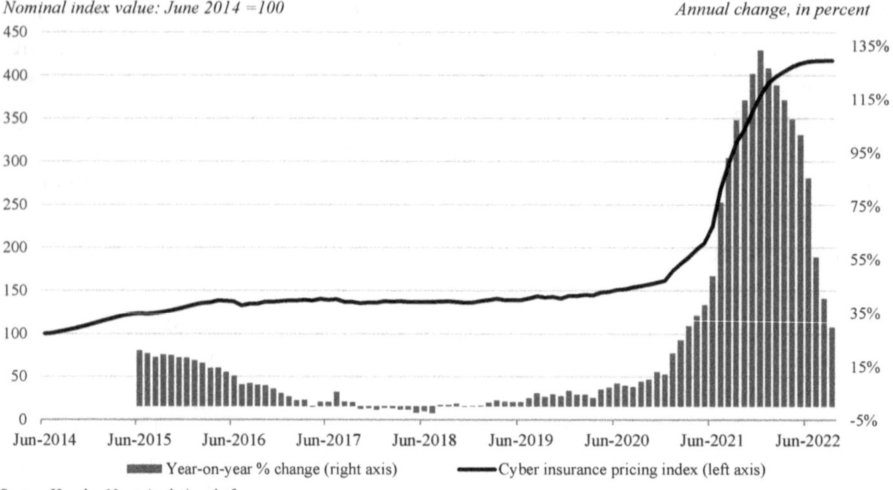

Source: Howden Nova Analytics platform.

instead of a bank account linked to a specific person, attackers can more easily launder or obfuscate payments made to them, in comparison with fiat currency (U.S. Department of Justice 2022). Importantly, like other financial assets, crypto assets can be misused for a range of illicit activities, including ransomware payments. Crypto assets have also been misused by human traffickers, by individuals exploiting children for sexual abuse, and by drug traffickers and scammers; to fund the activities of rogue regimes, such as the recent thefts by the Lazarus Group, which is affiliated with North Korea; and to finance terrorist activities (GAO 2021; U.S. Department of the Treasury 2022d). The other key illicit financing risks associated with crypto assets come from gaps in implementation of the international Anti-Money-Laundering/Combating-the-Financing-of-Terrorism (AML/CFT) standards abroad; the use of anonymity-enhancing technologies; in some cases the lack of covered financial institutions as intermediaries—and thus the absence of AML/CFT controls—in some crypto asset transactions; and service providers that are noncompliant with AML/CFT and other regulatory obligations, including compliance with sanctions obligations. With regard to the last, when crypto asset firms fail to register with the appropriate regulator, fail to establish sufficient AML/CFT controls, or do not comply with sanctions obligations, criminals are more likely to exploit their services successfully, including to circumvent U.S. and United Nations sanctions.

Ransomware uses. As hacking to receive crypto assets becomes more widespread, more firms will attempt to insure themselves against these attacks by purchasing cyber insurance. However, the existence of such insurance may not eliminate the underlying problem, and instead may even

Table 8-2. Ransomware and Downtime Costs by Country, 2020

Country (1)	Total Submissions (2)	Minimum Cost ($, Nominal) (3)	Estimated Costs ($, Nominal) (4)
United States	15,672	5,123,606,318	20,494,425,272
France	4,476	1,452,222,393	5,808,889,571
Spain	4,088	1,332,008,900	5,328,035,599
Italy	3,835	1,255,260,122	5,021,040,489
Germany	3,747	1,214,481,832	4,857,927,329
Canada	3,236	1,058,505,964	4,234,023,855
United Kingdom	2,718	878,155,444	3,512,621,775
Australia	2,072	678,541,158	2,714,164,633
Austria	819	268,888,310	1,075,553,242
New Zealand	265	86,448,688	345,794,755
Total	40,928	13,348,119,130	53,392,476,519

Source: Emsisoft Malware Lab.

create an incentive for hackers to attack insured firms and get paid by insurance. In fact, in an interview with *The Record*, a member of the Russian hacking group REvil was explicitly asked if they targeted organizations that have cyber insurance. The member responded: "Yes, this is one of the tastiest morsels. Especially to hack the insurers first—to get their customer base and work in a targeted way from there. And after you go through the list, then hit the insurer themselves" (Smilyanets 2021).

One can observe evidence consistent with this vicious cycle from cyber insurance prices. The insurance brokerage Howden compiles a "Global Cyber Insurance Pricing Index," which broadly measures premiums for cyber insurance (Howden 2023). As shown in figure 8-5, the cost of cyber insurance has increased more than 300 percent since July 2014.

In addition to paying for ransom costs, companies affected by ransomware attacks typically are unable to maintain their business activity until they have made the payment. In its annual "State of Ransomware" report, the cybersecurity firm Emsisoft estimated the combined cost of ransom payments and business downtime to be $19.6 billion in the United States in 2020, and roughly $51 billion in total across the United States, France, Spain, Italy, Germany, Canada, the United Kingdom, Australia, Austria, and New Zealand (as shown in table 8-2) (Emsisoft Malware Lab 2021).

It is crucial to note that the costs described here are direct costs. The indirect costs are likely higher. Instead of engaging in productive activities where firms have comparative advantages, they must divert resources to activities and products that help fend off attackers, such as buying cyber insurance and adding more personnel for information technology security. Thus, both welfare and economy-wide production decrease by a multiple of the direct dollar costs of resources that firms are using to stop ransomware attacks.

Investing in the Nation's Digital Financial Infrastructure

The growth of crypto assets has revealed a demand for a faster and more inclusive financial system with a real-time payment system and circulating digital money. Some have hoped that crypto assets could act as a form of decentralized money, making the U.S. payment systems faster, cheaper, safe, and more inclusive. This vision has not been realized. That said, there are still other ways near-term progress can be made on at least some of these goals. As a regulator of and participant in the Nation's payment systems, the Federal Reserve has a historical role in maintaining these systems' integrity (Federal Reserve Board, n.d.). For example, in the past decentralized payment systems were costly, in part, because some banks did not pay the full amount of a check from other banks—so-called nonpar collection or nonpar banking (Federal Reserve Board 1988). In some cases, this was done by levying a fee on checks deposited from other banks. Shortly after the establishment of the Federal Reserve System, it started providing payment services to banks, and over time it helped eliminate nonpar banking (Federal Reserve Bank of Minneapolis 1988).

This section first discusses an upcoming improvement to U.S. payments, which will help many consumers and businesses make cheap, instant payments. It then discusses the possibility of introducing a central bank digital currency (CBDC), which is a digital form of money. While operating under the supervision of a trusted authority, both these mechanisms have the potential to realize many of the benefits that crypto asset developers have promised.

The FedNow Instant Payment System

In terms of overall value as of 2020, the largest retail payment system in the United States was the Automated Clearinghouse (ACH) (Federal Reserve Board 2022a). ACH provides an electronic means to exchange funds between banks and other depository institutions (Federal Reserve Bank of San Francisco, n.d.). Typical ACH payments include salaries, consumer and corporate bills, interest payments, dividends, and Social Security payments. Peer-to-peer payment platforms such as Venmo complete transfers that are in and out of their platforms by accessing ACH network services through a participant bank (Venmo, n.d.). The regional Federal Reserve banks and the Electronic Payment Network are the country's two national ACH operators (Federal Reserve Board 2020). The prevalence of ACH offers many benefits; but a larger, more fast-paced economy is starting to arise. ACH payments can be processed in same-day batches between banks, throughout the day, but a standard ACH transfer can take up to three business days for funds to be settled and available to end users. In addition, ACH settlements occur only on business days (Nacha 2021). Businesses and individuals alike are increasingly in need of faster payment systems.

Advances in technology have created an opportunity for significant improvements in the way individuals and businesses make payments in today's economy. In recent years, members of Congress, staff members of the Department of the Treasury, and other experts have called for the Federal Reserve to offer a faster payment system for both businesses and retail users (Warren 2019; Mnuchin and Phillips 2018; Klein 2019). As a result of the COVID-19 pandemic and increased consumer demand for e-commerce options, many businesses have also increased their efforts to offer quicker payment options (Rathjen 2022).

In response, the Federal Reserve has prioritized designing and developing a faster payment system (Federal Register 2019).[5] The Federal Reserve plans to launch this new system, which is called the FedNow Service, later in 2023 (Federal Reserve Board 2022b). Through financial institutions participating in FedNow, businesses and individuals will be able to send and receive payments conveniently, and recipients will have nearly instant access to funds, giving them greater flexibility to manage their money and make time-sensitive payments. This service will be operational 24 hours a day and 7 days a week. This uninterrupted processing of fund transfers is an important improvement over existing payment systems (Federal Reserve Board 2022b, 2022c, 2022d). This service is different from peer-to-peer services such as Venmo in many ways. For example, funds transferred via FedNow will be available more quickly than those that must first exit a peer-to-peer payment service and then enter the ACH bank transfer process, which can take time to settle.

Beyond speed and convenience, near instant payments can yield real economic benefits for both individuals and businesses by allowing them to make time-sensitive payments whenever needed and providing them with more flexibility in managing their money. In particular, near instant payments under FedNow could bring significant benefits to vulnerable segments of the population. Slow payment systems can cost Americans billions of dollars. In addition to incurring bank overdraft fees, consumers can be forced to use high-cost alternatives like check cashers and payday lenders (Klein 2019). In 2019, it was estimated that a fast payment system such as FedNow could reduce these kinds of fees, generating savings of more than $7 billion a year for American households (Klein 2019). Because lower-income individuals are more likely to be hurt by slow payment systems,

[5] Note that there is a private faster payment system, RTP, whose adoption has been low (Clearing House 2022).

they could especially gain from these savings if FedNow is adopted widely. Using innovation productively and responsibly in this way could make banking services more inclusive.

FedNow requires commitment and active engagement by the private sector to make it interoperable, which means connecting and communicating with other payment services (Federal Reserve Board 2022c). According to the Federal Reserve, interoperability is crucial for "payment messages [to be] routed or exchanged and settled such that the sender may initiate a payment that will seamlessly reach the receiver. With interoperability, an individual or business with a bank account would be able to send a payment to another individual or business without having to choose, understand, or even be aware of the path taken by the payment." While noting that interoperability can take different forms, the Federal Reserve has maintained that it alone cannot fully establish the interoperability of FedNow; achieving this will require active partnership and collaboration with the financial industry (Federal Reserve Board 2022c).

Some have suggested that near instant digital payment systems like FedNow may reduce the need for circulating digital money (NAFCU 2022). In this case, the benefits of circulating digital money after FedNow is launched may be minimal. In fact, Federal Reserve governor Michelle Bowman commented in August 2022 that "my expectation is that FedNow addresses the issues that some have raised about the need for a CBDC" (Bowman 2022). Conversely, FedNow is intended to mainly focus on domestic payments and may bring limited improvements to the cross-border payment system, at least initially. In addition, FedNow is not a digital asset, which can be used in settlements or provide transaction programmability, roles that circulating digital money could play in the globally integrated financial system.

Central Bank Digital Currencies

It is important to note that money can come both in a physical format (e.g., cash) and in a digital format (e.g., electronic bank accounts). Thus, a central bank's digital currency is a liability of a central bank similar to cash, but it exists on a digital platform, where it can be exchanged and settled in real time. A CBDC system is made up of the CBDC itself, the public and private sector components that work alongside the CBDC, and the laws and regulations that apply to these digital assets (White House 2022a). A CBDC system can be set up in numerous different ways, such as a wholesale CBDC, which allows for access only by financial institutions (e.g., banks); and a retail CBDC, which allows for access by individuals. "That said, certain design features and questions related to the underlying infrastructure of CBDC may blur these distinctions to some degree" (U.S. Department of the Treasury 2022e).

As of January 5, 2023, 11 countries have launched CBDCs (Atlantic Council 2022). In addition, a number of foreign central banks, including the European Central Bank and the Bank of Japan, are exploring CBDCs; and some central banks, such as the People's Bank of China, are piloting a retail CBDC (Gorton and Zhang 2022). While some countries have considered using DLT for their CBDC, it is worth noting that many of the pilot programs for CBDC systems are not built on DLT; instead, they rely on a trusted central authority—a country's central bank—to operate key aspects of the CBDC system. This seems likely to be the case if a U.S. CBDC is introduced. A White House assessment of a potential U.S. CBDC system recently noted that "while a U.S. CBDC system could, in theory, be mostly 'permissionless' from a governance standpoint, this design choice introduces a large number of technical complexities and practical limitations that strongly suggest a permissionless approach does not make sense for a system that has at least one trusted entity (i.e., the central bank)" (White House 2022a). This is somewhat ironic, given that this is different from an oft-cited founding principle of crypto assets like Bitcoin, whose purported aim was to create decentralized money without any trusted central authority.

A U.S. CBDC—a digital form of the U.S. dollar—would have the potential to offer significant benefits. It could enable a payment system that is more efficient, provide a foundation for further technological innovation, facilitate faster cross-border transactions, and be environmentally sustainable (White House 2022a). It could also promote financial inclusion and equity by enabling access for a broad range of consumers (Maniff 2020). A potential U.S. CBDC could also help support other policy goals. For example, a potential U.S. CBDC could help ensure that such payment systems are aligned with the principles of human rights, democratic values, and privacy (U.S. Department of the Treasury 2022e).

There are also some risks from having a CBDC in the financial system. Similar to one-to-one backed stablecoins, CBDCs may also pose credit availability risks (U.S. Department of the Treasury 2022b). That is, a widely available CBDC could serve as a substitute for commercial bank deposits. Just as in the case of stablecoins that are fully backed by safe assets, this substitution effect could reduce the aggregate amount of deposits in the banking system, which could in turn increase bank funding expenses, and thus could reduce credit availability or raise credit costs for households and businesses. In addition, because central bank money is the safest form of money, a widely accessible CBDC would be particularly attractive to risk-averse users (and likely more so than a stablecoin), especially during times of stress in the financial system. The ability to quickly convert bank deposits into a CBDC could make systemic bank runs more likely or more severe

(Bank of Canada et al. 2021). In addition, CBDCs could cause operational risks. If the CBDC platform could not function due to a system failure or a cyberattack, it could erode investors' confidence.

Recognizing the potential benefits and risks from a U.S. CBDC, the Biden-Harris Administration has developed "Policy Objectives for a U.S. CBDC System," which reflect the Federal Government's priorities for a potential U.S. CBDC (White House 2022e). These objectives flesh out the goals outlined for a CBDC in the Executive Order. According to these objectives, the "U.S. CBDC system, if implemented, should protect consumers, promote economic growth, improve payment systems, provide interoperability with other platforms, advance financial inclusion, protect national security, respect human rights, and align with democratic values."

Conclusion

Innovation in financial services brings both risks and opportunities for the broader economy. It can challenge business models and existing industries, but it cannot challenge basic economic principles, such as what makes an asset effective as money and the incentives that give rise to run risk. Although the underlying technologies are a clever solution for the problem of how to execute transactions without a trusted authority, crypto assets currently do not offer widespread economic benefits. They are largely speculative investment vehicles and are not an effective alternative to fiat currency. Also, they are too risky at present to function as payment instruments or to expand financial inclusion. Even so, it is possible that their underlying technology may still find productive uses in the future as companies and governments continue to experiment with DLT. In the meantime, some crypto assets appear to be here to stay, and they continue to cause risks for financial markets, investors, and consumers. Much of the activity in the crypto asset space is covered by existing regulations and regulators are expanding their capabilities to bring a large number of new entities under compliance (SEC 2022). Other parts of the crypto asset space require coordination by various agencies and deliberations about how to address the risks they pose (U.S. Department of the Treasury 2022a).

Certain innovations, such as FedNow and a potential U.S. CBDC, could help bring the U.S. financial infrastructure into the digital era in a clear and simple way, without the risks or irrational exuberance brought by crypto assets. Hence, continued investments in the Nation's financial infrastructure have the potential to offer significant benefits to consumers and businesses, but regulators must apply the lessons that civilization has learned, and thus rely on economic principles, in regulating crypto assets.

Chapter 9

Opportunities for Better Managing Weather Risk in the Changing Climate

Global temperatures as high as those in recent years are unprecedented in the time span of human civilization and have likely not been seen in at least the last 125,000 years of Earth's history (Gulev et al. 2021). Many nations, including the United States, are working ambitiously to limit the impact of climate change by reining in greenhouse gas emissions and harnessing the opportunities of the clean energy transition. However, given the time it takes to transform the global energy system and for the climate to respond, the climate will continue changing at least until global greenhouse gas emissions fall to zero. In the coming decades, more intense and frequent weather extremes and the uncertainty of the changing climate will present a range of economic and financial risks to the U.S. economy and will confront the Federal Government with related fiscal challenges. Physical climate risks can be managed by anticipating and planning for coming changes in climate, a process known as adaptation. Adaptation presents opportunities to lower climate change costs over the long-term while also building resilience to natural hazards and weather risks today.

The design of climate adaptation policies must recognize that actors across the United States, including individuals and businesses and all levels of government, already face incentives to adapt to climate change. But they also face informational, financial, and legal constraints that may limit their ability to adapt. Targeting adaptation policies to alleviate these constraints and address related market failures should be most effective in supporting private action.

The Federal role in climate change adaptation is complicated by the complex, nested governance structure of relevant policy areas. Many important areas that are relevant to adaptation, from land use planning and zoning to the regulation of insurance markets, are governed at the State or local level. The Federal Government, however, has a strong interest in advancing reforms in these areas to address climate change because of its role in managing risks across the United States, from credit and insurance provision to disaster response and recovery to social safety net programs.

The risks that climate change poses are multidimensional, regionally specific, and vary based on underlying socioeconomic vulnerabilities. Adaptation policies need to be targeted to particular settings and therefore will need to be both varied and complex. This chapter proposes four overarching objectives for structuring further Federal adaptation efforts:

- Producing and disseminating knowledge about climate risk
- Long-term planning for the climate transition
- Ensuring accurate pricing of climate risks
- Protecting the vulnerable.

The United States has joined nations around the world in acting to reduce greenhouse gas emissions. If fully implemented, national pledges may limit global warming to 3.6°F (2°C; Meinshausen et al. 2022), achieving a primary goal of the Paris Agreement (United Nations Climate Change, n.d.). The steeply falling costs of low-carbon technologies and the increasingly ambitious climate policies of many countries are bending the global emissions curve, rendering worst-case outcomes of 8–10°F of warming by the end of the century increasingly unlikely (Hausfather and Moore 2022). The United States has implemented major domestic legislation to achieve its own goals to reduce emissions to 50–52 percent below 2005 levels by 2030 and to reach net-zero emissions by 2050. In particular, the August 2022 Inflation Reduction Act and the November 2021 Bipartisan Infrastructure Law together make $430 billion in investments in American infrastructure, with a focus on the climate challenges facing our Nation (U.S. Department of Energy 2022).

However, even given the ambitious action to rein in emissions that will be required to meet these national commitments, the climate will continue changing for the foreseeable future, for two main reasons. First, it will take decades to completely transform the global energy system, which currently relies heavily on greenhouse-gas-generating fossil fuels. Second, the climate system will take years to respond to changes in emissions. At present, temperatures across the lower 48 States are about 1.8°F above their level in 1900 (Vose et al. 2017, 185); even if all nations meet their emission reduction goals, global warming will at least double by 2100. (Meinshausen et al. 2022).

The effects of global warming are already apparent across the United States, in the form of more extreme heat and longer heat waves (National Oceanic and Atmospheric Administration, n.d.; Lipton et al. 2018; Gutiérrez et al. 2021, p. 2004); more extreme rainfall events and associated flooding (U.S. Environmental Protection Agency 2021; Davenport, Burke, and Diffenbaugh 2021); more frequent and intense droughts driving huge wildfires (Williams, Cook, and Smerdon 2022; Borunda 2021; Burke et al. 2021); and higher sea levels driving coastal flooding and worse storm surges (Hino et al. 2019; Marder 2020). Among the events that have been formally linked to climate change in recent years are the ongoing drought in California (Diffenbaugh, Swain, and Touma 2015); exceptionally dry conditions in the Southwest (Park Williams, Cook, and Smerdon 2022); extreme heat in the Pacific Northwest (Bercos-Hickey et al. 2022); flooding in the mid-Atlantic (Winter et al. 2020); major western wildfires (Yu et al. 2021); the damage caused by Hurricane Harvey, which inundated Houston in 2017 (Frame et al. 2020; World Weather Attribution 2017); and severe, rain-induced flooding in Louisiana in 2016 (van der Wiel et al. 2017).

Fluctuating weather conditions have always presented challenges. The inherent variability of the atmospheric system means that specific weather conditions cannot be predicted—even in principle—beyond a 7- to 10-day predictability horizon. In a stable climate, however, the *probability* of different weather conditions can be accurately estimated. A stable climate allows actors to understand the risks of weather-dependent outcomes and to plan accordingly, in designing infrastructure, allocating investments, and adjusting daily routines and habits. For example, statistical methods currently used to design infrastructure assume a stable and unchanging climate, where the probability of extreme weather over the lifetime of the infrastructure remains constant at historical values (Milly et al. 2018).

With the human-induced climate change of today, however, it is no longer possible to assume that the future will be like the past and to use unadjusted past experience as a guide for the future. Decisions made using only historical weather records will become increasingly inaccurate and costly as weather patterns change (Milly et al. 2018; Electric Power Research Institute 2022). Weather variability occurring in the context of the changing climate will result in repeated experiences of historically unprecedented weather conditions (Fisher, Sippel, and Knutti 2021).

Even small changes in average climate conditions can produce large changes in the probability of previously rare weather events. Social, financial, and infrastructural systems that manage these risks typically have certain tolerances, with steeply increasing costs when these thresholds are exceeded. For instance, construction is often designed to standards based on historical weather conditions, such as a 1-in-100-years rain event, and conditions exceeding these design thresholds can produce dangerous conditions that have high economic and social costs (American Society of Civil Engineers 2018, 239). A shifting climate can quickly render these standards obsolete. In the example shown in figure 9-1 using an illustrative climate distribution, the mean changes by just under 20 percent, but the probability of an extreme event (the area of the distribution to the right of the green line) increases by about 80 percent.

Modern societies have been and continue to be ordered for a climate that no longer exists; therefore, the projected rapid changes in the climate system will pose major, evolving risks for economic, social, infrastructural, and governance systems in coming decades. Recognizing and planning for these risks—a process that is often called adaptation—can reduce costs, improve stability, and protect the most vulnerable people and communities. Because climate change touches many aspects of economic production and societal well-being, adaptation policies need to be equally broad, ranging

Figure 9-1. Small Changes in Climate Can Greatly Increase the Probability of Extreme Weather Events

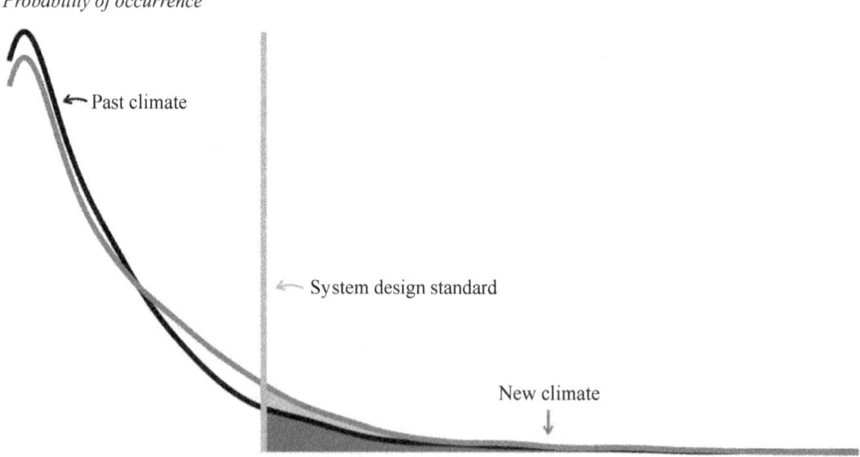

Source: CEA calculations.

from the provision of decision-relevant climate information to the regulation of insurance markets to improved building codes and zoning. Box 9-1 describes some of the ongoing investments being made by the Biden-Harris Administration to build resilience while reducing and managing the costs of a changing climate.

Economic Principles of Adaptation Policy and Planning

The economic principles that support adaptation planning for climate change are both different from, and more varied than, those underpinning the reduction of greenhouse gas emissions, typically referred to as mitigation. Mitigation is a classic example of a public good. The costs of emissions accrue to people all around the world and will last far into the future. Because the market prices of fossil fuels do not incorporate these large social costs, climate change can be understood as a global externality—what Nicholas Stern has termed "the greatest market failure the world has ever seen" (Stern 2006). Private markets have little incentive to provide emissions reduction in the absence of government action. Moreover, because the benefits of reducing emissions accrue globally and are not captured within the borders of a single country, nations must cooperate to address the climate challenge (Nordhaus 2019). Aligning the incentives of private actors and nations throughout the world to account for the climatic effects of fossil fuels requires coordinated action.

In contrast, many adaptation decisions are private goods, in that both the costs and benefits are largely internalized by the decisionmaker (Mendelsohn 2000; Kahn 2021; Kolstad and Moore 2020). For adaptation, communities, households, and businesses all have their own motivations for responding to and planning for climate risks. Examples include a homeowner investing in reinforced windows to defend against stronger storms, a farmer choosing what crops to grow in response to changing drought conditions, and a business adjusting suppliers to reduce weather-related disruptions that are shifting due to climate change. Though there are public goods problems and other market failures related to adaptation (discussed in detail later in the chapter), they are varied, specific, localized, and very different from the global externality problem that characterizes mitigation.

Indeed, there is already evidence that private actors are starting to consider emerging climate risks in their decisions. For example, recent research suggests that both the risks of sea-level rise and the productivity effects of extreme heat are reflected in property and agricultural land prices (Keys and Mulder 2020; Bernstein, Gustafson, and Lewis 2019; Baldauf, Garlappi, and Yannelis 2020; Severen, Costello, and Deschênes 2018). Climate risk premiums are also showing up in longer-term corporate and municipal bonds (Painter 2020; Acharya et al. 2022; Goldsmith-Pinkham, Gustafson,

Box 9-1. Adaptation and Resilience Investments of the Biden-Harris Administration

The 2021 Bipartisan Infrastructure Law (BIL) and the 2022 Inflation Reduction Act (IRA) both contain a number of provisions to build resilience to natural disasters and adapt social and economic systems to reduce the costs of climate change. The Biden-Harris Administration is in the process of implementing these laws, making historic investments in climate change resilience. The BIL in particular provides $50 billion for adaptive investments such as support for energy-efficiency improvements in low-income households, grants to states and territories for resiliency projects and flood mitigation, dedicated funding to improve resiliency of transportation systems, and funding for wildfire defense and coastal adaptation (White House 2022g, 2022h; U.S. Department of Transportation 2022; U.S. Department of Commerce 2022). Resiliency provisions within the IRA include tax credits and rebates for improving home energy efficiency and funding for addressing droughts and improving water infrastructure (White House 2022i).

Beyond the investments provided by the BIL and IRA, the United States is pursuing a multipronged adaptation strategy that includes: inter-agency coordination on climate extremes, building codes and climate-related financial risks; the provision of climate data tools such as the Climate Mapping for Resilience and Adaptation portal; and building resilience into Federal procurement (UN Framework Convention on Climate Change 2021; Climate Mapping for Resilience and Adaptation, n.d.). Principal agencies are now required to develop and implement Climate Adaptation and Resilience plans and report annually on implementation and progress under the plans (White House 2022j). Several programs target assistance to groups that may be particularly vulnerable such as low-income and Tribal communities (White House 2022g, 2022h).

These historic investments are laying the foundation that will be required for building adaption and resilience in the United States. This chapter describes both the broad economic principles that underlie adaptation policy generally and that could support future work building on this foundation. For instance, spending on adaptation and resilience projects will be most effective when coupled with reforms to zoning, building codes and infrastructure standards (mostly governed at the State and local level; see figure 9-3), as well as clear communication of strategic priorities for the management of climate risks at all levels of government.

and Lewis 2021). There is also evidence that property market adjustments are concentrated in regions where more people report believing in climate change, which suggests continuing pricing frictions in areas where there is greater skepticism about climate change (Barrage and Furst 2019; Bernstein, Gustafson, and Lewis 2019; Baldauf, Garlappi, and Yannelis 2020; Severen, Costello, and Deschênes 2018).

The importance of private incentives in shaping climate action has implications for the design of adaptation policy. First, effective adaptation policy will recognize that individuals, households, businesses, and communities will act in response to the shifting climate. But these actions will be defined by legal, informational, and financial constraints, along with the sometimes-distorted or perverse incentives that these actors face. Government action that targets constraints and market failures that impede adaptation should be most effective in supporting and enabling private action rather than crowding out actions that would have occurred anyway. Examples of these constraints and market failures, as well as policies that can address them, are discussed in detail later in the chapter.

Second, government policies and programs already play a role in determining how the costs of weather-related hazards are distributed through society, a role that will likely grow in importance as climate change effects worsen. Individuals with more wealth and a higher income are better able to avoid, prepare for, and recover from weather-related shocks. This means that, in the absence of counteracting policies, climate change costs will likely be disproportionately borne by the poor and marginalized. Programs of public lending, insurance, grants, and welfare can be designed to reallocate some of these risks and thus reduce the regressive nature of climate change costs. However, the existing disaster response and social support system is composed of legacy programs that were designed in a pre–climate change era and thus may not be adequate for addressing climate change. Programs are distributed across multiple agencies and levels of government, often with burdensome applications or complex requirements, making their net distributive effect difficult to determine (Mach et al. 2019; Howell and Elliott 2019). In fact, there is evidence that postdisaster aid can exacerbate rather than mitigate preexisting inequalities (Billings, Gallagher, and Ricketts 2022). Comprehensive reevaluation and reform of the system composed of these interacting support programs, building on the ongoing adaptation work within the Biden-Harris Administration (box 9-1), will be required to ensure that the system is able to protect the vulnerable as climate change damage grows.

The next sections first review new evidence on the economic costs and financial risks that climate change poses to the United States and to Federal finances and then outline the role that a Federal adaptation strategy could play in managing and reducing physical climate risk.

The Economic Costs and Financial Risks of Climate Change in the United States

Shifting climate patterns are producing a wide array of risks affecting the well-being of American communities. Earlier research on climate change economics assumed that higher-income countries like the United States would be able to manage the effects of changing weather conditions relatively easily because of the small share of clearly exposed sectors of the economy, such as agriculture and forestry, and the assumption that adjusting to climate change would be straightforward (Mendelsohn, Nordhaus, and Shaw 1994; Nordhaus 1991, 930). However, this assessment needs to be reconsidered in light of new economic evidence and the increasing intensity and frequency of extreme weather events across the United States that can be formally attributed to climate change (Seneviratne et al. 2021).

The Costs of Climate Change for the United States' Well-Being and Prosperity

Weather variability has a range of effects within the United States. For example, studies have shown that very hot temperatures have adverse effects—including increasing premature mortality and worsening of the health of newborn babies (Deschênes and Greenstone 2011; Deschênes, Greenstone, and Guryan 2009; Barreca and Schaller 2020); decreasing crop yields (Schlenker and Roberts 2009); adversely affecting mental health (Burke et al. 2018); lowering the labor supply in exposed industries (Graff Zivin and Neidell 2014); increasing violence (Mukherjee and Sanders 2021); and reducing students' ability to learn (Park et al. 2020). These effects are not borne equally across geographic regions or economic sectors within the United States, and they are felt most acutely among disadvantaged groups with a high vulnerability to natural hazards (box 9-2).

Climate models predict that extreme heat will become more frequent and intense as climate change continues (IPCC 2021). Today, in many parts of the United States, the heat wave season is nearly three times longer than in the 1960s; in the summer of 2022 alone, 400 U.S. locations broke their monthly temperature records (Lipton et al. 2018; Stevens and Samenow 2022; U.S. Global Change Research Program 2018, figure 1.2b). There is some evidence that people, businesses, and communities can adjust to hotter temperatures over time—for instance, by changing the timing of outdoor activities (Graff Zivin and Neidell 2014; Dundas and von Haefen 2020) or by using more energy for cooling (Auffhammer 2022; Deschênes and Greenstone 2011). But these adaptations are costly, do not eliminate climate change costs, and may reduce the quality of life (Deschênes 2022).

Box 9-2. Climate Change Will Most Likely Interact with and Exacerbate Existing Inequalities

The effects of climate change are not evenly distributed across the U.S. population by income, race, or ethnicity. Lower-income communities have fewer resources to prepare for or respond to extreme weather events, leaving them more vulnerable to their effects. For instance, residents of lower-income communities are less likely to evacuate away from the path of hurricanes and tend to live in more vulnerable structures, leaving them at a higher risk of mortality or injury (Deng et al. 2021; Fothergill and Peek 2022). Low-income Americans are less able to adjust their activities to avoid exposure to wildfire-induced air pollution or to adjust air-conditioning in response to extreme heat (Burke et al. 2022; Cong et al. 2022). They are more likely to work in industries such as agriculture and construction that are highly exposed to dangerously high temperatures (U.S. Environmental Protection Agency 2021). Major natural disasters are more likely to lead to financial hardships, such as debt defaults and bankruptcies in low-income and minority communities (Billings, Gallagher, and Ricketts 2022; Jerch, Kahn, and Lin 2022).

Injustices throughout U.S. history mean that these effects are also strongly differentiated by race. For instance, because of forced relocation away from their tribal homelands, many Native American people live on marginal lands that are highly susceptible to wildfires, extreme heat, and droughts (Farrell et al. 2021). Minority and low-income areas within cities, including formerly redlined neighborhoods, are substantially hotter than wealthier, whiter, and nonredlined areas (Hoffman, Shandas, and Pendleton 2020; Benz and Burney 2021); Black and Hispanic students are more likely to attend schools without air-conditioning (Park et al. 2020); and minority communities are more likely to be affected by expected increases in extreme heat and coastal flooding due to climate change (U.S. Environmental Protection Agency 2021; Wing et al. 2022).

Wealth and assets allow households to avoid, prepare for, respond to, and recover from weather-related shocks, leaving minority populations that lack these assets more exposed to intensifying weather extremes. Minority populations, particularly African Americans, were barred from accessing avenues for wealth accumulation for centuries—for instance, through discriminatory home-lending practices that persisted through much of the 20th century—leading to stark disparities today in wealth and assets by race and ethnic group; the median wealth of white households is almost eight times that of Black households (Rothstein 2017; Derenoncourt et al. 2022; Cook 2014; Bhutta et al. 2020).

Moreover, disadvantaged and racial minority communities have generally received less financial assistance after disasters than affluent white communities (National Advisory Council 2020), partly because some of this aid is tied to property ownership, from which minorities have been historically excluded. The Biden-Harris Administration is working to address these inequities. The Federal Emergency Management Agency (FEMA) has committed to establishing an equitable and fair distribution of Federal aid and assistance and to increase access for underserved populations (U.S. Department of Homeland Security 2022). In response to past inequities, the U.S. Environmental Protection Agency recently created the Office of Environmental Justice and External Civil Rights, which seeks to coordinate and prioritize environmental justice within the agency and in its partnerships with other Federal agencies (U.S. Environmental Protection Agency, n.d.). More generally, the Biden-Harris Administration is working to direct 40 percent of the benefits of climate and clean energy investments to disadvantaged communities. Several programs in the IRA and BIL, most notably the $27 billion Greenhouse Gas Reduction Fund, also target those communities (U.S. Environmental Protection Agency 2022; White House, n.d.).

Beyond extreme heat, climate change is associated with a host of other costly events. About one-third of the cost of major flood events since 1988, totaling $79 billion, has been attributed to climate change (Davenport, Burke, and Diffenbaugh 2021). The western United States is currently having the worst drought in at least 1,200 years, requiring costly cutbacks in water use and endangering the functioning of the Lake Meade and Lake Powell reservoirs (Wheeler et al. 2022; Park Williams, Cook, and Smerdon 2022; Borunda 2021). California and the Pacific Northwest have suffered devastating wildfires that blanketed cities under thick smoke, undermining decades of air quality gains driven by the Clean Air Act and forcing preemptive blackouts to avoid igniting wildfires, temporarily cutting off power to millions of customers (Burke et al. 2022; Childs et al. 2022; Goss et al. 2020; Chediak 2019). Hurricane Ian struck Florida in September 2022, causing a coastal storm surge of up to 18 feet and widespread inland flooding; it will end up being one of the costliest storms on record, with losses to residential and commercial property estimated at between $36 billion and $62 billion (CoreLogic 2022; Paquette and Kornfield 2022).

Unprecedented extreme events are exposing the weaknesses of aging U.S. infrastructure, which was designed to operate in different climate conditions. Multiple infrastructural systems gradually built over many decades—including electricity grids, dams and irrigation systems, coastal and riverine defenses, roads and railways, and ports—will need to be quickly redesigned, retrofitted, or rebuilt to maintain their functionality in the changing climate. And this investment in climate resilience will need to be made while also addressing the estimated $2.6 trillion in deferred infrastructure investments required over the next 10 years just to restore existing infrastructure to working order. These costs will likely be borne by cities, States, and the Federal government, along with specific infrastructure user groups such as electric utility customers or irrigation district members (American Society of Civil Engineers 2021).

The complexity of global supply chains means that extreme weather events around the world can ripple through international trade networks, to affect American producers and consumers (Woetzel et al. 2020a). Pankratz and Schiller (2022) show how disruption from extreme heat and flooding in supplier locations is transmitted through supply chains to affect the revenues of customer firms. As climate change intensifies, the chances of major disruptive weather events occurring simultaneously in multiple regions will increase, causing larger and more systemic threats to supply chains. The summer of 2022 saw major heat and drought events in the United States, Europe, and China disrupt global production, which prevented the transporting of agricultural products along rivers and shut down electricity generation for car and electronics factories, and thus exacerbated supply chain challenges (Ahmedzade et al. 2022; Bradsher and Dong 2022; Plume 2022).

Crop failures and other effects of climate change could also exacerbate volatile conditions in fragile nation-states, leading to instability and conflict—with spillover effects to the United States via migration and escalation of local conflicts into national security concerns (Missirian and Schlenker 2017; Benveniste, Oppenheimer, and Fleurbaey 2020; Mach et al. 2019; White House 2015a). Studies have suggested that both the conflict in Syria and the flows of migrants from Central America have been exacerbated by climate-related stressors (Ash and Obradovich 2019; Kelley et al. 2015; Lustgarten 2020). Recent massive flooding in Pakistan led to the inundation of one-third of the country by floodwaters, internal displacement of 33 million people, massive disruption of the agricultural sector, and a sovereign debt downgrade (Lu 2022; Fitch Ratings 2022). By shifting where nonhuman species live and how they interact with humans, climate change could even increase the risks of zoonotic disease spillovers (Carlson et al. 2022).

There is some evidence that climate change could also affect macroeconomic growth. Empirical investigations of the causal relationship between temperature fluctuations and gross domestic product (GDP) generally find negative effects from hotter temperatures, particularly in poor and hot countries, with some indications that this heat depresses growth rates (Dell, Jones, and Olken 2012; Burke, Hsiang, and Miguel 2015; Bastien-Olvera, Granella, and Moore 2022). According to modeling and simulation studies of the macroeconomy, negative effects of climate change on growth greatly increase both the magnitude and uncertainty of aggregate climate costs (Moore and Diaz 2015; Newell, Prest, and Sexton 2021), but little is currently understood about the mechanisms connecting weather shocks and long-term climate trends to macroeconomic variables. Plausible mechanisms include faster depreciation of the capital stock resulting from more intense extremes (Hallegatte, Hourcade, and Dumas 2007; Otto et al. 2023), effects to productivity growth (Ortiz-Bobea et al. 2021), or effects on the labor force that either depress the supply of labor or slow the accumulation of human capital via effects on learning (Graff Zivin and Neidell 2014; Park et al. 2020). Improving empirical evidence and modeling capabilities in this area should be a high priority for future research.

Because climate change affects many aspects of well-being, including those not traded in traditional markets, the costs of climate change and losses of other natural capital are mismeasured by GDP (Coyle 2015; Brunetti et al. 2021; Svartzman et al. 2021; NGFS-INSPIRE 2022). For example, production that emits climate-change-causing greenhouse gases adds to GDP, and so too do expenditures to adapt to climate damage or reduce emissions. Meanwhile, many important services that nature provides, including reducing risks to health and protection from climate-driven extreme weather events, are not reflected in GDP or are misattributed. Examples include the role urban trees play in providing shade and lowering heat extremes or the value of intact wetlands in reducing coastal storm damage. A more complete accounting system than GDP that tracks national wealth—the stock of multiple forms of capital that produce flows of both market and nonmarket benefits—could provide clearer macroeconomic information on climate change than exclusive reliance on GDP (Agarwala and Coyle 2021; Dasgupta 2021). Including natural capital in measures of wealth would help track climate change costs and nature loss in ways that complement GDP and fill in important blind spots. This is why the Biden-Harris Administration has begun the process of rigorously measuring natural capital in a way that could inform a more complete picture of economic progress and climate change costs (White House 2022c).

Climate Change and Financial Stability

Climate change risks have historically been unpriced in private markets, but as these risks become increasingly apparent and investors become more cognizant of the threat, price adjustments for exposed assets would be expected. Property and long-lived physical infrastructure are particularly exposed, and risk becoming stranded as climate conditions shift beyond their design standard, thus causing investments to underperform or fail altogether. There is substantial evidence that *current* natural hazard risks are undercapitalized in property markets, a setting that could produce sudden price shocks in response to new information that reveals underlying risks to buyers (Bakkensen and Barrage 2022; Baldauf, Garlappi, and Yannelis 2020; Hino and Burke 2021; Gibson and Mullins 2020).

Certain financial instruments—such as insurance contracts, catastrophe bonds, and mortgages—that directly or indirectly price weather-related risks are also highly exposed to climate change. Rapid changes in asset prices or reassessments of the risks in response to a shifting climate could produce volatility and cascading instability in financial markets if not anticipated by regulators. Because of the interaction of long-lived investments and direct exposure to weather extremes, property insurance against catastrophic natural hazards is at the forefront of climate change risk exposure and is already showing signs of strain in several states (box 9-3).

Governments have typically stepped in to provide coverage when private insurers pull out from particularly risky areas or hazards. More than 95 percent of flood policies in the United States are insured through the Federal National Flood Insurance Program (NFIP), and the number of policies in State-run insurance plans has more than doubled since 1990 (Kousky et al. 2018). Figure 9-2 shows the long-run growth in State-run disaster insurance plans combined with a sharp rise following major hurricane strikes in 2004 and 2005, after which the largest insurance companies pulled out of Florida (Leefeldt 2022). Although the State was able to move policies off its rolls and back into the private market in the 2012–15 period, Florida's public insurer, Florida Citizens, is once again the largest property insurer in

Figure 9-2. Count of Policies under U.S. Residual Property Insurance Market, 1990–2021, with Geographic Breakdown for 2021

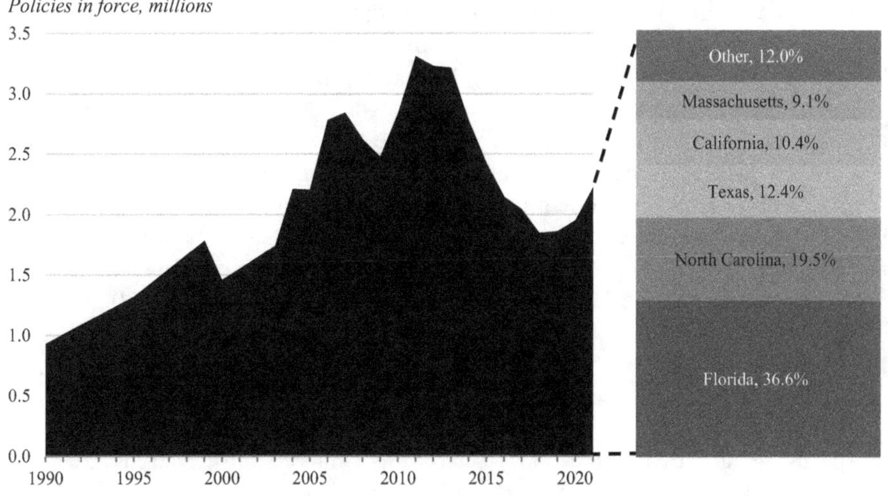

Sources: Insurance Information Institute, n.d.; Citizens Property Insurance Corporation of Florida, n.d.
Note: Data are linearly interpolated for the years 1991–94, 1996–98, and 2001–2. Policies from North Carolina are included only for 2011 (2.2 percent of total policies in that year) and later.

Box 9-3. Disaster Insurance in the Changing Climate: Challenges and Opportunities for Reform

Even in the absence of climate change, weather-related extremes—such as flooding, hurricanes, and wildfires—pose particular challenges to the insurance industry. Losses due to natural disasters are highly concentrated in space and time, leaving insurers financially vulnerable to a major weather event (Wagner 2020). Moreover, the distribution of losses from these events is "thick-tailed," a statistical property meaning that expected losses are heavily influenced by extremely rare events, the risks of which are difficult to quantify and price (Conte and Kelly 2018; Kousky 2022, 38–42). In the face of these challenges, insurers must limit exposure by either exiting from or limiting activity in certain markets or by purchasing reinsurance, which raises costs.

For these reasons, even without climate change, natural disasters hover on the edge of insurability. Without reforms to improve the functioning of insurance markets and reduce the costs of extremes (for instance through zoning changes and building code improvements), climate change could well make many more hazards uninsurable as the frequency and intensity of extremes increase. Climate change increases uncertainty, particularly in the tails of the distribution that drive expected losses, and raises the risk of completely unprecedented events for which there is no historical analog (figure 9-1). In the absence of high-quality, trusted information on quickly evolving climate risks, ambiguity in how to price extreme weather risks could lead insurers to leave certain markets altogether. Major insurers have already stopped offering hurricane wind coverage along the Gulf Coast and are increasingly exiting high fire-risk areas in California (Sadasivam 2020; Elliott 2022; Schuppe 2022; Querolo and Sullivan 2019). Moreover, the increasing likelihood that multiple catastrophic events could occur concurrently could raise costs or limit the availability of reinsurance.

A lack of access to insurance makes extreme events more costly because it slows economic recovery in affected communities and raises the probability of cascading financial hardships, such as mortgage defaults and debt delinquencies (Billings, Gallagher, and Ricketts 2022; Kousky 2019; Kousky, Palim, and Pan 2020; Otto et al. 2023). Therefore, reforms to address challenges in hazard insurance markets should be a high priority for adaptation policy. A major issue in the U.S. disaster insurance system is that although climate change presents a systemic threat that simultaneously raises the risk of multiple perils (wind, fires, and floods) across the United States, hazards are insured on a peril-by-peril basis and are regulated at the State level. Alternative models—such as those used in France, Spain, and New Zealand—instead create broad, diversified risk pools by mandating comprehensive, multiperil catastrophe insurance while also providing an explicit public reinsurance backstop that limits the exposure of private insurers (Kousky 2022, 53–55). These kinds of reforms will likely be increasingly important to stabilize insurance markets and expand access in the face of climate change.

the State after seeing a 48 percent growth in policies during 2022 (Florida Citizens 2023; Insurance Journal 2022). Other sharp growth in State insurance rolls in recent years has come from California, where wildfire risk has led private insurers to pull out and the number of policies on the State's FAIR plan to increase by over 80 percent since 2018 (State of California 2018; Insurance Information Institute, n.d.–a). These programs strain government finances because premiums generally do not cover payouts, meaning that losses are covered with general tax revenue or debt issuance (Hartwig and Wilkinson 2016).

Even with these implicit public subsidies that effectively transfer risks to general State and Federal taxpayers, the penetration of natural hazard insurance is low; for instance, only one-third of homes within FEMA-defined 100-year flood zones have flood insurance while fewer than 3 percent outside these flood zones have it, despite still being at risk of flooding (Evan et al. 2020). Increased risks of delinquencies and defaults after disasters can have subsequent implications for property and mortgage markets, particularly in the absence of insurance (Kousky 2019; Billings, Gallagher, and Ricketts 2022; Kousky, Palim, and Pan 2020). Sastry (2022) suggests that mortgage lenders respond to the availability of federally backed flood insurance by requiring higher down payments when public insurance is either limited or not required, changing the demographics of eligible home buyers.

Climate-change-driven weather extremes can have subsequent effects on State and municipal finances through several pathways beyond public insurance plans. First, responding to climate change places additional burdens on local budgets, which could cause serious financial hardships, particularly in communities with smaller budgets. The need to either rebuild damaged infrastructure after disasters or upgrade existing infrastructure to prepare for climate change raises the cost burden for cities, States, and Tribes. Second, repeated occurrences of climate extremes can threaten the property tax base and cause a decrease in revenues. For instance, the McKinsey Global Institute has estimated that an extreme storm surge event in 2050 would cause damage equivalent to 10 percent of the total market value of properties in Miami–Dade County and as much as 30 percent in Lee County, which was recently inundated by 18 feet of storm surge from Hurricane Ian (Woetzel et al. 2020b; Paquette and Kornfield 2022). Residential real estate construction has been an important driver of growth in some U.S. coastal communities, and declines in response to emerging climate risks could have serious implications for local economies, employment, and tax revenue (Brunetti et al. 2022).

Several researchers have found evidence that the municipal bond market is beginning to account for these risks in its pricing of loans to municipalities. Bonds for cities and towns in areas exposed to sea-level rise carry a premium, with significantly larger effects on longer-maturing bonds, implying that investors expect either a decline in cash flow or increasing volatility in exposed cities (Painter 2020; Goldsmith-Pinkham, Gustafson, and Lewis 2021). Acharya and others (2022) find evidence for the pricing of extreme heat in municipal and corporate bonds, beginning in about 2013–15, and also larger effects on longer-term bonds. Higher borrowing costs strain municipal finances and make it even more challenging for cities to finance disaster reconstruction or adaptive infrastructure investments without either raising taxes or diverting resources from other public services. In areas with local declines in tax revenue and rising climate change costs, municipal bankruptcies may be increasingly likely. Jerch, Kahn, and Lin (2023) find evidence that hurricane strikes decrease tax revenues and raise the risk of municipal default over the following decade, with the largest effects being felt in disadvantaged communities. In addition to losses to creditors, bankruptcy costs are borne by current and future residents in the form of higher taxes and service fees (Chapman, Lu, and Timmerhoff 2020).

The Federal Fiscal Implications of Physical Climate Risk

Climate change affects the Federal fiscal outlook via numerous pathways. On the revenue side, it threatens economic output, leading to a lower tax base. One estimate by the White House's Office of Management and Budget (White House 2022b) suggests that the Federal Government could see 7.1 percent lower annual tax revenue by 2100 as a result of the adverse effect of climate change on macroeconomic growth. Though some of this could be offset by increasing taxes on income or capital, Barrage (2020) points out that the distortionary effects of these revenue-raising mechanisms can be substantial, increasing climate change costs by up to about 30 percent. Ongoing research within the Biden-Harris Administration is expanding the capacity of the Federal Government to integrate the modeling of both the physical and transition risks of climate change into macroeconomic forecasting in order to better explain and plan for these effects (White House 2022f).

On the expenditure side, many Federal operations are being affected by the changing climate. Though these effects are too extensive to enumerate in detail here, this section briefly reviews four primary pathways by which the Federal Government is exposed to physical climate risk: risk assumption, the operation and financing of climate-exposed assets, the provision of national public goods, and social safety net programs.

Risk Assumption

By fully or partially assuming certain types of risk, the Federal Government is able to attract private investment and support production across broad sections of the economy. One of the most significant examples of this is the Federal role in housing: Through the government-sponsored enterprises (GSEs)—Fannie Mae and Freddie Mac, which are privately owned but federally chartered and are currently in conservatorship—and Federal agencies (e.g., the Department of Housing and Urban Development, Ginnie Mae, and the Department of Veterans Affairs), the Federal Government guarantees mortgages and securities backed by mortgages. Together, the GSEs and Ginnie Mae accounted for more than 65 percent ($7.7 trillion) of total outstanding mortgage debt in 2022 (Urban Institute 2022). The growing damage from hurricanes, storm surges, and wildfires has implications for defaults, recoveries, and other key cost drivers—and, by extension, for Federal loss exposure (Kousky, Palim, and Pan 2020; Rossi 2020; Woetzel et al. 2020b). There is evidence that private lenders are shifting climate-exposed loans into the GSEs, which may bear a substantial share of the increasing climate risk in the absence of policies that manage Federal exposure (Ouazad and Kahn 2022).

In addition to its support for the housing finance system, the Federal Government also directly assumes risk through various insurance programs. Flooding is the most frequent and most costly natural disaster in the United States, and the Federal Government underwrites essentially all home flood insurance policies via the NFIP (Federal Emergency Management Agency 2010; Kousky et al. 2018; Federal Insurance and Mitigation Administration 2022). Climate change will increase costs from flooding due to both more intense rainfall and higher sea levels, which worsen flooding from storm surges and slow drainage in low-lying coastal areas. The NFIP is already at risk of financial insolvency; it has a debt to the Treasury of $18.1 billion, despite the fact that Congress canceled $17 billion of its debt in 2017 (Federal Emergency Management Agency, n.d.; Environmental Law Institute 2022, 702). Without fundamental reforms of the U.S. disaster insurance system and of the Federal Government's role in managing these risks (box 9-3), these losses will continue to grow (White House 2022b).

Climate-Exposed Assets

The Federal Government owns and operates critical climate-sensitive infrastructure, most significantly dams, irrigation systems, and major flood defenses such as river and coastal levees, along with buildings, military installations, and other physical assets that may be at risk from climate change (White House 2022b; U.S. Department of Defense 2021a). These assets were built over many decades at substantial cost and are now critical foundations for communities and regional economies across the United States.

The Bureau of Reclamation (2022) is the Nation's largest wholesale water supplier, operating 338 reservoirs and maintaining 487 dams that supply water to about 10 percent of U.S. residents, as well as supplying hydropower and water for agricultural irrigation. The functioning of some of these systems will be challenged by the changing hydroclimate, which is already bringing both more intense rainfall and more droughts, including the persistent megadrought currently hitting western States (Kao et al. 2022). The Central Valley Project, which supplies water to cities and farmers in California, has slashed its water deliveries to cities and has completely cut water to many farmers in 4 of the last 10 years (James 2022). The project's long-term operation is further threatened by sea-level rise, which will increase the salinity of the California Delta and eventually render its water unfit for drinking and irrigation (State of California 2018; Fleenor et al. 2008). Water levels in Lake Meade and Lake Powell reservoirs are close to the critical threshold, below which they will cease to produce electricity (Wheeler et al. 2022). The costs of either maintaining water and power services from Federal facilities in the changing climate or decommissioning projects and finding alternative solutions for dependent communities has not been fully estimated.

The U.S. Army Corps of Engineers (n.d.) is tasked with building certain public infrastructure projects that manage the risks of flooding, including riverine and coastal levees and flood control dams throughout the country. More intense rainfall events, higher sea levels, and stronger storms are expected to increase the costs of maintaining existing flood protection and expanding it to newly at-risk areas. The costs resulting from climate change for Federal flood control could be extremely high. Future expenditures will depend on high-level strategic decisions that have yet to be made regarding what role flood protection infrastructure will play in managing growing coastal and inland flood risks. For example, the Corps of Engineers has released a feasibility study for a plan to protect the New York metropolitan area from coastal storms. This plan—which includes storm surge barriers, floodwalls, levees, seawalls, and other measures—would cost upward of $52 billion, with 65 percent borne by the Federal Government (New York District 2022).

The Provision of National Public Goods

A central function of the Federal Government is to provide national public goods, most critically national defense, which accounted for about 45 percent of Federal discretionary spending in 2021 (CBO 2022a). Climate change poses threats to U.S. national security, which raises questions about its implications for defense spending and the Federal budget (U.S. Government Accountability Office 2022; National Intelligence Council 2021). The Department of Defense has identified climate change as a factor in national security planning and as an urgent and growing threat to U.S. security (White House 2015b; Department of Defense 2021b). Climate change effects are expected to increase global tensions, as nations compete for scarcer resources—threatening health and human rights and triggering conflict and mass migration (White House 2022e).

A second aspect of Federal public goods provision that is substantively affected by climate change is the stewardship of natural resources, public lands, and biodiversity. By altering the climatic environment to which ecosystems are adapted, climate change threatens to degrade ecosystem functioning and species survival (U.S. Global Change Research Program 2018). The additional costs of managing public lands in this rapidly shifting environment are not fully known. An example of costs that have been partially quantified are annual Federal wildland fire suppression expenditures, which, on average, have more than tripled since 1989, partly driven by intense, climate-change-driven droughts in the West (CBO 2022b). Moore and others (2022) estimate that direct spending on biodiversity conservation via the Endangered Species Act could increase by 75 percent (roughly $34 billion) by 2100, as unmitigated climate change pushes an estimated one in six species toward extinction (Urban 2015).

The Programs of the Social Safety Net

The various Federal programs known as the social safety net provide benefits and assistance to maintain a minimum level of well-being for the U.S. population. Climate change could increase the burden on these programs through a number of pathways, most notably health-related expenditures and assistance for disaster response and recovery.

Federal health programs—namely, Medicare and Medicaid—represented 38 percent of total national health expenditures in 2021, or about $1.6 trillion (Centers for Medicare & Medicaid Services 2022). Several studies have estimated that health-related risks constitute the largest fraction of climate-change-related damage, with particularly severe effects on those over 65 years of age, who are much more likely to be treated through government programs (Rennert et al. 2022; Hsiang et al. 2017; Carleton et al. 2022). A White House study estimated annual Federal health care costs from the effects of climate change on air quality, Valley Fever, southwestern dust, and wildfires by 2100 at between $835 million and $22 billion (White House 2022b). An additional unquantified, but likely much higher, cost would arise from hospitalizations resulting from extreme heat conditions, such as dehydration, renal failure, and stroke (Green et al. 2010; Wondmagegn et al. 2021).

Federal programs play a critical role in supporting communities affected by natural disasters. The Congressional Budget Office (CBO) estimates that the expected annual loss from hurricane winds and storm-related flooding is $56 billion, or 0.3 percent of 2019 GDP, with annual costs to the Federal budget of $18 billion through disaster assistance and NFIP claims (CBO 2019). However, Deryugina (2017) shows that disasters have far larger fiscal implications due to increases in social insurance payments—such as Medicaid, disability insurance, and income maintenance programs—which persist for 10 years after a storm hits. The Federal Government supports postdisaster response and recovery, not just through the immediate FEMA response but also through low-interest loans from the Small Business Administration and Community Development Block Grant Disaster Recovery funding from the Department of Housing and Urban Development to aid rebuilding disaster-affected communities (Howe et al. 2022, 700–704; U.S. Small Business Administration, n.d.).

Market Failures and Distortions That Slow Adaptive Adjustments and Policy Responses

As described above, shifting weather risks present incentives to private actors to adjust so as to reduce the negative effects of climate change and take advantage of any opportunities it offers. Indeed, there is evidence that these adjustments are already happening, in prices that seem to be starting to account for climate change risks (Keys and Mulder 2020; Bernstein, Gustafson, and Lewis 2019; Baldauf, Garlappi, and Yannelis 2020; Severen, Costello, and Deschênes 2018), as well as other evidence that households and local governments are altering practices in response to or in anticipation of the changing climate (Berrang-Ford et al. 2021).

Private adaptive adjustments occurring in the United States are subject to market imperfections—along with informational, institutional, legal, and financial constraints—that could limit or slow adaptation. Public adaptation policy should target these barriers to enable faster and more effective private action. This section reviews major market failures, imperfections, and distortions that are relevant to managing physical climate risks and describes the policy tools that can address them.

Imperfect Information on Physical Climate Risks

Adaptation to the changing climate requires incorporating information about how shifting weather patterns will alter the distribution of future weather risks. This is particularly important for decisions that are highly sensitive to climate change through long-lived investments or exposure to low-probability, high-consequence tail risks. A substantial body of literature indicates that individuals consistently underestimate or discount the probabilities of catastrophic events, a phenomenon that can lead to low rates of disaster insurance coverage and underinvestment in risk reduction (Wagner 2022; Bakkensen and Barrage 2022; Royal and Walls 2018). Information on climate risks that is of high quality and is trusted, decision-relevant, and widely disseminated is foundational for adaptation planning and is urgently needed. Yet it is now largely missing. Modeling tools used to understand the global climate system, termed general circulation models, are most accurate over large spatial scales and long time frames. Different, more fine-tuned tools are needed to make information on specific risks in particular places over short to medium time frames widely available to stakeholders making adaptation decisions (Fiedler et al. 2021; Pitman et al. 2022; American Society of Civil Engineers 2018, 7).

Governments already support a global network of satellites, in situ observing systems, weather stations, modeling facilities, and technical workforces that produce public weather forecasts. Similarly, as climate change information becomes an essential complement of weather data, governments will need to play a role in funding the production of and access to this essential public good to support climate-informed decisionmaking by many actors. This includes not just developing the ability of climate science to provide better information at the spatial and temporal scale at which decisions are made but also supporting the training of highly skilled workers who can translate and disseminate this information to the public and private actors seeking to use it (Fiedler et al. 2021; Kopp 2021). The Biden-Harris Administration has begun this work through development of the Climate Mapping for Resilience and Adaptation tool (CMRA, n.d.).

Information Asymmetries

Information asymmetries occur when one party in a transaction has more information than another, which can lead to price distortions and market failure (Akerlof 1970). In the climate risk context, information asymmetries could arise when buyers and sellers have varying knowledge about an asset's climate change exposure, such as a property's propensity to flood or wildfire risk. In this regard, Keenan and Bradt (2020) and Ouazad and Kahn (2022) find evidence of information asymmetries operating in coastal mortgage markets, with lenders shifting risks of flooding-exposed properties onto Fannie Mae and Freddie Mac or to other lenders that have less knowledge of local risk exposure.

Mandatory disclosure laws are one tool governments can use to correct information asymmetries. These require parties to share particular types of information relevant to asset valuation. A proposed rule by the U.S. Securities and Exchange Commission (2022) would add climate-related risks to the required disclosures of publicly traded companies. Disclosure laws related to property transactions are governed at the State level and vary widely in the degree to which they require sellers to disclose climate-related risks (particularly flooding) to buyers (Hino and Burke 2021; Natural Resources Defense Council, n.d.). Only a handful of States—notably, Louisiana and Texas—have strong flood disclosure regulations to protect buyers, while 16 have no disclosure requirements at all (Federal Emergency Management Agency 2022).

Building codes and standards can be another way to protect buyers from information asymmetries in property markets. Details of building construction that determine how vulnerable a structure is to water, wind, and wildfire hazards can be highly technical and not easily understood by home buyers. This creates a market failure, if more resilient but also more expensive construction cannot command a premium because these qualities are not easily observable. By setting common minimum standards for all construction, governments can prevent a race to the bottom in building quality (White House 2022f).

Adverse selection in insurance markets—where buyers know more about their risk than providers, leading more risky individuals to opt into insurance at a given price—is another form of information asymmetry. There is some evidence of adverse selection operating in U.S. disaster insurance markets, where those with a lower flood risk (e.g., from an elevated house) are less likely to purchase coverage (Wagner 2022; Bradt, Kousky, and Wing 2021). In the absence of corrective policies, adverse selection can lead to an unraveling of insurance markets as insurers raise rates to cover the higher risk, driving lower-risk individuals from the marketplace and further concentrating insured risks. This market failure historically has been addressed through purchase mandates that solve the adverse selection problem by requiring everyone to participate in insurance markets thereby pooling the risk. Insurance mandates can also improve welfare in settings without adverse selection but where individuals systematically underestimate their exposure to a catastrophic loss (Wagner 2022).

Externalities and Public Goods

Although many adaptation actions are private goods that result from individual households and firms weighing their own costs and benefits, important public adaptation goods will also be underprovided without government action (Mendelsohn 2000). Examples include building infrastructure for coastal protection; expanding the tree cover for urban cooling and other nature-based forms of climate adaptation; basic research relevant to adaptation, such as developing improved crop varieties; and the protection of species or ecosystems threatened by the changing climate. But unlike greenhouse gas mitigation, which is a global public good, many public adaptation benefits are more local and therefore may be best provided by State, Tribal, and local governments. The Federal Government may still have a role to play in coordinating, supplying information, and reducing transaction costs.

In addition to pure public goods, some private adaptations may involve externalities that require collective action by communities or higher levels of government. This is particularly the case for environmental goods and natural resource management, where preexisting inefficiencies related to the lack of established property rights can be exacerbated by climate change. Examples include the spillover effects of coastal protection onto neighbors, and the increasing drawing down of open-access aquifers to meet higher crop water requirements resulting from warmer temperatures (Beasley and Dundas 2021; Gopalakrishnan et al. 2017; Rosa et al. 2020). Threats to biodiversity are similarly characterized by market failures and problems of public good provision. Though habitat conversion, pollution, and invasive species are primary drivers of species endangerment, climate change further stresses threatened species and exacerbates these drivers (Tilman et al. 2017; Moore et al. 2022; Hashida et al. 2020). In these settings, reforms to more sustainably manage natural resources will have ancillary benefits in reducing climate damage and can be thought of as an important tool for managing climate risks.

Credit Constraints

A number of adaptive actions require upfront capital investments that will pay off gradually. Examples range from homeowners installing air-conditioners to farmers adopting irrigation to manage increasing heat and droughts to major community projects to slow or prevent coastal erosion. If actors are unable to finance these investments at competitive interest rates, they will be underprovided relative to an optimal level, meaning that governments may play an important role in alleviating credit constraints to enable adaptation. Examples of relevant government programs include targeted subsidies for home efficiency upgrades such as certain provisions in the Bipartisan Infrastructure Law and the Inflation Reduction Act (box 9-1). This will be particularly compelling for populations that have been historically underserved by financial institutions and for financing adaptations where there is a strong social interest in ensuring adaptation to alleviate climate-related risks.

Credit constraints do not just apply to individuals and business but may also limit the ability of States and municipalities to fund major public adaptation projects. Most States require voter approval for general obligation bonds backed by future tax revenues or have other constitutional limits on long-term debt issuance, constraints that do not apply to the Federal Government (Kiewiet and Szakaty 1996). The costs of major infrastructure projects to manage growing climate risks may be beyond the fiscal reach of many local governments, particularly if climate risks are simultaneously jeopardizing future tax revenue. Low-cost loans or grants from the Federal Government may therefore be important sources of financing for municipalities and States seeking to make major investments to reduce climate risks, a recent example being pilot grants for voluntary relocation of Tribal communities made by the U.S. Department of the Interior (2022).

Moral Hazard

"Moral hazard" refers to a phenomenon in insurance markets whereby access to insurance lowers incentives for risk-reducing or risk-avoiding behavior, increasing overall hazard costs. Settings with pervasive moral hazard can see higher insurance premiums or an unraveling of private insurance markets. Other programs that shift the costs of hazards—whether through subsidized insurance, publicly provided protection, or loan guarantees—can, unless carefully structured, also create moral hazard distortions. Annan and Schlenker (2015) estimate that the moral hazard associated with subsidized crop insurance has reduced the incentives of farmers to adapt to extreme heat and has led to a higher sensitivity to heat in insured crops. Baylis and Boomhower (2023) find that the implicit subsidy from public wildland fire fighting can reach 20 percent of home values in low-density, wildfire-prone areas. Similar indirect subsidies for building in flood-prone areas have likely led to more people and property in these risky areas (Panjwani 2022).

The moral hazard problem does not only apply to individuals; it can also apply to State and local governments. Many decisions relevant to reducing the costs of weather-related disasters—including zoning, building codes, and land-use management—are made at the State or local level (figure 9-3). State and local governments making these decisions see benefits in growth and tax revenues, but they are shielded from the full costs of risky development because of the Federal Government's assumption of disaster risk through the NFIP and disaster relief programs. Several States have seen rapid development in areas exposed to coastal flooding by sea-level rise, with local governments permitting two or three times more construction in these risky areas than in safer regions (Climate Central and Zillow 2018).

Reforming Federal programs and private insurance contracts to incentivize or require risk-reducing activities or to place a higher share of costs on those undertaking the risk (e.g., through higher deductibles) can help mitigate issues of moral hazard (Kousky 2022, 38).

Four Potential Pillars of the Federal Adaptation Strategy and Major Policy Opportunities

Adaptation to climate change is characterized by complex governance across multiple scales, with relevant decisionmaking operating at the national, State, Tribal, and local levels (figure 9-3). Given the complex regulatory and planning processes relevant to managing climate risks and the local nature of many adaptation benefits, this nested governance structure may be appropriate (Dietz, Ostrom, and Stern 2003). Federal adaptation policy needs to be developed with an appreciation of the multilayered, complex regulatory systems that characterize adaptation-relevant policy areas. This final section outlines four broad, cross-cutting roles for further Federal adaptation efforts to support specific policymaking across these many issue areas, and it highlights major opportunities for action in each area.

Producing and Disseminating Knowledge about Climate Risk

As firms, local governments, and individuals increasingly seek to account for climate change in their planning and investments, actionable information will be a necessary input. From home buyers deciding where to move to local governments planning new stormwater drainage to businesses looking to disclose their climate risk exposure, actors across the economy will

Figure 9-3. Governance of Climate Risk Is Complex and Multiscale

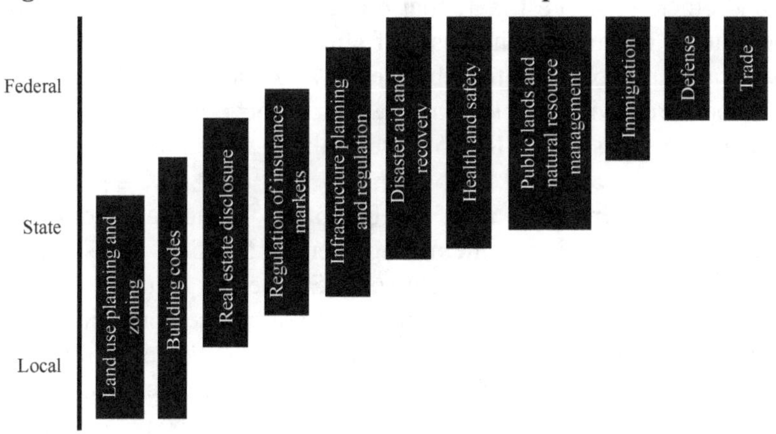

Sources: Howe et al. (2002); CEA calculations.

require high-quality, trusted, and accessible climate impact information. This is essential "informational infrastructure"—technical information produced at high fixed costs but with broad applicability and value. Thanks to strong Federal support, the United States is a global leader in climate science. But the modeling tools used to understand the global climate system are not yet designed to deliver the decision-specific information needed by most stakeholders to manage climate risk (Fiedler et al. 2021; Pitman et al. 2022; ASCE 2018, 7).

Major opportunity: invest in the Federal capacity for catastrophic climate risk modeling. The U.S. government has an opportunity to lead the world in developing a high-performance public capability for catastrophic climate risk modeling. Managing evolving climate risks will require new scientific approaches that combine insights from climate models with other tools, such as statistical modeling and detailed engineering data to produce decision-relevant climate information tailored to the needs of stakeholders across the United States (Pitman et al. 2022). Catastrophe modeling is used in the insurance industry to understand the risks of extreme events, but it is done by just a few companies, is expensive to access, and can be difficult to evaluate (ModEx, n.d.). Given both the growing role of the public sector in absorbing climate risk and the need for many actors—ranging from State and local governments to homeowners to general businesses—to understand their exposure, information that is publicly available, credible, and from trusted sources is urgently needed. The U.S. government has the opportunity to build on its existing foundation of excellence in climate modeling and Earth system sciences to develop this critical capacity.

Long-Term Planning for the Climate Transition

Long-term, forward-looking planning that anticipates coming climate change is necessary to avoid unnecessary losses and destabilizing effects. Neumann and others (2021) estimate that proactive adaptations that anticipate future climate can reduce the costs of climate change for the United States' road, rail, and coastal infrastructure by a factor of between 3 and 6 by 2090, compared with purely reactive adaptation; Diaz (2016) finds a similar magnitude of savings for forward-looking adaptation for global coastal defenses.

The Federal Government, in a number of its capacities, from the Social Security Administration to the management of National Parks, has a particular role in the long-term stewardship of U.S. assets. It regularly makes decisions that will have consequences for decades if not centuries into the future. Planning across all affected Federal agencies should recognize the effects of climate change that are already apparent and are expected to intensify well into the future. Exposure to climate hazards should be incorporated into an agency's enterprise risk management process. For example, the U.S. Department of Defense (2021b) is planning to integrate climate risk into all relevant hazard threat assessments.

In addition, high-level strategic planning will be essential to identify critical risks that climate change poses for agencies' missions, high-priority opportunities to address these risks, and the additional resources or legislative changes that may be required to realize these opportunities. Current and future climate change effects may necessitate difficult trade-offs involving many stakeholders with conflicting interests. Timely work to identify principles and priorities that will guide agencies will improve coordination, identify necessary reforms that may take a long time to implement, and ultimately lower costs and improve effectiveness, a motivation behind the ongoing agency climate adaptation planning process (box 9-1).

Clarity at the Federal level regarding priorities for funding public adaptation efforts is important for driving action by State and local governments. Estimated costs just for protection from sea-level rise are large, and are likely far beyond the means of many coastal communities (Diaz 2016). Other costs of responding to droughts, wildfires, and inland floods will further strain government budgets. As described above, Federal loans and grants will be essential to alleviate credit constraints for State and local governments, but these resources are necessarily limited. Establishing clear funding priorities and resolving uncertainty over which protection costs the Federal Government will finance can assist State and local actors in their own planning for the climate transition.

Major opportunity: use access to Federal funds to incentivize subnational adaptive reforms. Many policies critical to building long-term resilience to natural disasters are controlled at the State or local level (figure 9-3). However, Federal funds flowing through States both directly and indirectly finance long-lived, climate-exposed infrastructure and development projects (CBO 2018). If physical climate risks are not fully integrated into agency enterprise risk management, these investments risk underperforming and becoming stranded. Similarly, decisions to convert land subject to wildfires or flooding to developed uses implicates the Federal Government via its various risk-absorbing functions, such as mortgage guarantees, flood insurance, and disaster management and response. Reforms to zoning, building codes, insurance markets, and residential disclosures can all have major benefits in reducing the costs of disasters.

Climate-relevant Federal investments can be tied to the enactment of adaptive reforms that will protect both affected communities and the Federal budget. For example, FEMA has proposed reforms of the NFIP to Congress that would, if enacted, condition participation in the program on the development of community-level flood disclosure requirements for property transactions (U.S. Department of Homeland Security 2022), while provisions of the Bipartisan Infrastructure Law lower the non-Federal share of certain grants for transportation projects prioritized in a State's Resilience Improvement Plan (U.S. Department of Transportation 2022).

Ensuring the Accurate Pricing of Climate Risk

Provided that actionable and credible information on climate risk is available, prices would be expected to adjust, sending accurate signals to actors to reallocate investment and production in response to and in anticipation of the changing climate. However, market failures arising from information asymmetries or misaligned incentives can distort these signals and require a policy response. One role of the Federal adaptation strategy should be to identify and correct these market failures to enable stronger market signals that would guide adaptive decisions over the longer term. Specific market failures relevant to adaptation and policy tools to address them were discussed in the previous section; they include information provision, disclosure requirements, building standards, and insurance purchase mandates. An important example is the recent reform of pricing in the NFIP, termed Risk Rating 2.0, which prices policies based on individualized flood risk assessments while continuing to provide discounts for investments by individuals or communities that lower flood costs (CRS 2022).

Market mechanisms can play an important role in allocating resources efficiently and sending price signals to market actors on the scarcity of resources. In places where markets are missing or incomplete, climate-change-induced scarcity could exacerbate existing distortions—meaning that reforms to expand market access or establish property rights over common-pool resources could lower total costs, one example being the allocation of water use in California (Arellano-Gonzalez et al. 2021). Even in the absence of markets, using mechanisms such as auctions to allocate resources cost-effectively could be a useful strategy to manage scarcity under climate change (Hagerty and Leonard 2022).

Major opportunity: develop quality and transparency standards for climate data and the modeling used in market transactions. An important part of supporting the integration of physical climate risks into market prices will be oversight of the quality of climate information being used. Pricing climate risk requires the use of specialized modeling tools, and evaluating the quality of this information is a technical and highly specialized skill. Use of proprietary models of natural hazard risk that cannot be evaluated by the expert community as an input into significant regulatory decisions has caused tensions in the past, particularly in the insurance industry (Xu, Webb, and Evans 2019). Developing minimum standards and reporting requirements for the climate data used to inform significant investment decisions could help build trust, ensure quality, and enable broader adoption.

This is particularly important when insurance contracts are leveraged into more complex financial instruments, such as catastrophe bonds and other insurance-linked securities, or when used as input into scenario exercises central banks are beginning to use to evaluate climate risks to the financial system (Insurance Information Institute, n.d.–b; Braun and Kousky 2021; U.S. Federal Reserve 2023; Financial Stability Board 2022). Oversight and evaluation of the Earth system models used for significant economic or regulatory decisionmaking could be important in preventing natural disasters from triggering more systemic failures across the financial system.

Protecting the Vulnerable

Climate change is expected to increase weather-related hazards for many Americans, but its effects will not likely be felt equally (see box 9-2 above). Low-income and disadvantaged communities are both more exposed to climate effects (e.g., through working in industries exposed to extreme heat, such as agriculture and construction) and lack assets that can be drawn on to smooth the costs of weather-related disasters. In the absence of policies addressing the needs of low-income and marginalized communities, pre-existing vulnerabilities—such as inadequate health care, poor-quality or overcrowded housing, and food insecurity—will likely interact with climate change effects to worsen inequalities. Addressing these underlying vulnerabilities and developing policies targeted at disadvantaged populations should be a critical part of an effective U.S. adaptation strategy, building on the robust set of existing programs within the Biden-Harris Administration targeted at low-income and disadvantaged communities (boxes 9-1 and 9-2).

As prices adjust to reflect changing climate risks, this could present challenges for low-income communities, for whom higher prices are particularly burdensome. For instance, low-income households are already less likely to have flood insurance and almost 9 percent of policyholders in FEMA-defined 100 year floodplains pay more than 5 percent of their income for flood insurance premiums and fees (U.S. Department of Homeland Security 2018). To the extent possible, rather than restricting price adjustments, which would blunt the incentive for private risk reduction and increase risks over the long term, policies should seek to address these adverse distributional effects via targeted lump sum transfers. More generally, policies that seek to accelerate income growth and increase access to wealth-building opportunities for the poorest Americans should be thought of as broadly adaptive. Although by no means the main goal of programs that may be primarily focused on educational opportunities, housing affordability, or poverty alleviation, by increasing resources available to the most vulnerable that can be drawn on to manage the effects of climate shocks, they should lower overall vulnerability and decrease climate costs over the long term.

Major opportunity: develop criteria for public adaptation funding that reflect the social value of investments. Criteria for the prioritization and evaluation of public adaptation projects that accurately reflect the social benefits of these investments should be developed. Historically, public investments in flood defenses or community risk reductions have used the value of protected property as a key metric in evaluating project benefits (McGee 2021). However, inequality in property values and ownership in the United States reflects decades of exclusion of racial minorities from homeownership and public investment (Rothstein 2017). Evaluating the benefits of climate protections solely using property values is unlikely to capture the full, multidimensional benefits of these projects and risks perpetuating these historical injustices and exacerbating differences in vulnerability (Martinich et al. 2013). Additional criteria that capture differential vulnerability and variations in the extent to which communities are able to self-insure and recover from damage could be developed to assess project outcomes.

Major opportunity: reenvisioning social insurance under climate change. The increasing frequency and intensity of climate-change-related disasters, along with the disruptions and dislocations required to adjust to changing conditions, will likely challenge the policies and programs that spread risks and protect the vulnerable as never before. Understanding the burden this will place on traditional social insurance programs in the United States and identifying reforms to strengthen the social safety net is essential in this era of climate change. In addition, a process for reimagining the public role in catastrophe management and social solidarity in the face of rising risks is also urgently needed. The United States' current approach—managing catastrophic perils in a piecemeal way with fiscally unstable public insurance programs—will only become more problematic as climate change continues. U.S. policymakers should seriously consider models from other countries, where governments act as backstop reinsurers, capping catastrophic losses in the private sector to crowd in private financing while also spreading the risk broadly through mandated natural disaster coverage (Kousky 2022, 53–56).

Conclusion

The United States is making historic investments that will transform the American energy system to address the challenge of climate change and meet President Biden's goal of halving U.S. greenhouse gas emissions by 2030. These investments are central to the global effort to rein in emissions and limit the effects of climate change.

Even with the massive shift already under way in global energy production, models show the climate will continue changing for decades (IPCC 2021; Meinshausen et al. 2022). Shifting weather patterns will likely subject communities to unprecedented extremes making the management of weather risks and natural disasters increasingly difficult. A large body of literature, as well as the mounting costs of climate-change-associated extreme events, shows that the U.S. economy is sensitive to the effects of climate change. Without forward-looking adaptive planning that anticipates changing conditions, climate costs will very likely keep growing, compounding risks to infrastructural, social, economic, and financial systems across the United States.

Managing the risks of climate change is a complex challenge across multiple policy areas, characterized by varying market failures and nested governance structures. However, the particular capacities, authorities, and interests of the Federal Government mean that it should play an essential role in leading adaptation policy development and structuring the responses of subnational and private actors to emerging climate risk. An effective Federal adaptation strategy includes producing and disseminating knowledge about climate risk, long-term planning for the climate transition, ensuring accurate pricing of climate risks, and protecting the vulnerable. Managing the risks and consequences of the warming planet, along with continued efforts to reduce greenhouse gas emissions, will allow the Nation to face the climate challenges of the 21st century.

References

Chapter 1

Acemoglu, D., D. Autor, and D. Lyle. 2004. "Women, War, and Wages: The Effect of Female Labor Supply on the Wage Structure at Midcentury." *Journal of Political Economy* 112, no. 3: 497–551. https://doi.org/10.1086/383100.

ACLU (American Civil Liberties Union). 2021. "How Artificial Intelligence Can Deepen Racial and Economic Inequities." By Olga Akselrod. https://www.aclu.org/news/privacy-technology/how-artificial-intelligence-can-deepen-racial-and-economic-inequities.

Armstrong, M. 2022. "The Market for Smart Home Devices Is Expected to Boom Over the Next 5 Years." World Economic Forum. https://www.weforum.org/agenda/2022/04/homes-smart-tech-market.

Atasoy, H. 2013. "The Effects of Broadband Internet Expansion on Labor Market Outcomes." *ILR Review* 66, no. 2. https://doi.org/10.1177/001979391306600202.

Auffhammer, M., P. Baylis, and C. Hausman. 2017. "Climate Change Is Projected to Have Severe Impacts on the Frequency and Intensity of Peak Electricity Demand Across the United States." *Proceedings of the National Academy of Sciences* 114, no. 8. https://doi.org/10.1073/pnas.1613193114.

Bank of England. 2021. "Key Elements of the 2021 Biennial Exploratory Scenario: Financial Risks from Climate Change." https://www.bankofengland.co.uk/stress-testing/2021/key-elements-2021-biennial-exploratory-scenario-financial-risks-climate-change.

Bastien-Olvera, B., and F. Moore. 2021. "Use and Non-Use Value of Nature and the Social Cost of Carbon." *Nature Sustainability* 4, no. 1: 101–8. https://doi.org/10.1038/s41893-020-00615-0.

Blau, F., and L. Kahn. 2013. "Female Labor Supply: Why Is the United States Falling Behind?" *American Economic Review* 103, no. 3: 251–56. https://doi.org/10.1257/aer.103.3.251.

BLS (U.S. Bureau of Labor Statistics). 2019. "Number and Percent of Eldercare Providers Who Were Parents of Household Children Under Age 18 by Sex and Selected Characteristics, Averages for the Combined Years 2017–2018." https://www.bls.gov/news.release/elcare.t09.htm.

———. 2021. "Employment by Detailed Occupation." https://www.bls.gov/emp/tables/emp-by-detailed-occupation.htm.

———. 2022a. “Employee Benefits in the United States.” https://www.bls.gov/ncs/ebs/benefits/2022/home.htm.

———. 2022b. “Computer and Information Technology Occupations.” https://www.bls.gov/ooh/computer-and-information-technology/home.htm.

Blunden, J. 2014. “2013 State of the Climate: Carbon Dioxide Tops 400 PPM.” National Oceanic and Atmospheric Administration. https://www.climate.gov/news-features/understanding-climate/2013-state-climate-carbon-dioxide-tops-400-ppm.

Bolt, J., and J. van Zanden. 2020. “Maddison Style Estimates of the Evolution of the World Economy.” Groningen Growth and Development Centre. http://reparti.free.fr/maddi2020.pdf.

Botzen, W., J. van den Bergh, and L. Bouwer. 2010. “Climate Change and Increased Risk for the Insurance Sector: A Global Perspective and an Assessment for the Netherlands.” *Natural Hazards* 52: 577–98. https://doi.org/10.1007/s11069-009-9404-1.

Brunetti, C., B. Dennis, D. Gates, D. Hancock, D. Ignell, E. Kiser, G. Kotta, A. Kovner, R. Rosen, and N. Tabor. 2021. “Climate Change and Financial Stability.” Board of Governors of the Federal Reserve System. https://www.federalreserve.gov/econres/notes/feds-notes/climate-change-and-financial-stability-20210319.html.

Brynjolfsson, E., and G. Petropoulos. 2021. “The Coming Productivity Boom.” *MIT Technology Review*. https://www.technologyreview.com/2021/06/10/1026008/the-coming-productivity-boom/.

Burke, A., A. Okrent, and K. Hale. 2022. “The State of U.S. Science and Engineering 2022.” National Science Foundation. https://ncses.nsf.gov/pubs/nsb20221/u-s-and-global-research-and-development.

Burke, M., S. Hsiang, and E. Miguel. 2015. “Global Non-Linear Effect of Temperature on Economic Production.” *Nature* 527: 235–39. https://doi.org/10.1038/nature15725.

Capka, J. 2006. “Celebrating 50 Years: The Eisenhower Interstate Highway System.” U.S. Department of Transportation. https://www7.transportation.gov/testimony/celebrating-50-years-eisenhower-interstate-highway-system.

Carleton, T., A. Jina, M. Delgado, M. Greenstone, T. Houser, S. Hsiang, A. Hultgren, R. Kopp, K. McCusker, I. Nath, J. Rising, A. Rode, H. Kwon Seo, A. Viaene, J. Yuan, and A. Tianbo Zhang. 2022. “Valuing the Global Mortality Consequences of Climate Change Accounting for Adaptation Costs and Benefits.” *Quarterly Journal of Economics* 137, no. 4: 2037–105. https://doi.org/10.1093/qje/qjac020.

Carter, S., S. Gartner, M. Haines, A. Olmstead, R. Sutch, and G. Wright, eds. 2006. *Historical Statistics of the United States*. Cambridge: Cambridge University Press. https://hsus.cambridge.org/HSUSWeb/HSUSEntryServlet.

Climate Central and Zillow. 2018. "Ocean at the Door: New Homes and the Rising Sea." http://assets.climatecentral.org/pdfs/Nov2018_Report_OceanAtTheDoor.pdf?pdf=OceanAtTheDoor-Report.

Council of Economic Advisers. 2015. *Economic Report of the President*. https://www.whitehouse.gov/wp-content/uploads/2021/07/2015-ERP.pdf.

Council of Economic Advisers and Office of Management and Budget. 2022. "Climate-Related Macroeconomic Risks and Opportunities." https://www.whitehouse.gov/wp-content/uploads/2022/04/CEA_OMB_Climate_Macro_WP_2022-430pm.pdf.

Czernich, N., O. Falck, T. Kretschmer, and L. Woessmann. 2011. "Broadband Infrastructure and Economic Growth." *Economic Journal* 121, no. 552: 505–32. https://doi.org/10.1111/j.1468-0297.2011.02420.x.

DeLong, B. 2022. *Slouching Towards Utopia: An Economic History of the Twentieth Century*. New York: Basic Books. https://www.basicbooks.com/titles/j-bradford-delong/slouching-towards-utopia/9780465019595/.

Dieppe, A. 2020. "The Broad-Based Productivity Slowdown, in Seven Charts." World Bank Blogs. https://blogs.worldbank.org/developmenttalk/broad-based-productivity-slowdown-seven-charts.

Digital Competition Expert Panel. 2019. "Unlocking Digital Competition." https://assets.publishing.service.gov.uk/government/uploads/system/uploads/attachment_data/file/785547/unlocking_digital_competition_furman_review_web.pdf.

Elliott, D. 2022. "Insurances Woes in Coastal Louisiana Make Hurricane Recovery Difficult." National Public Radio, July 27. https://www.npr.org/2022/07/27/1113639292/insurances-woes-in-coastal-louisiana-make-hurricane-recovery-difficult.

File, T. 2013. "Computer and Internet Use in the United States: Population Characteristics." U.S. Census Bureau. https://www.census.gov/content/dam/Census/library/publications/2013/demo/p20-569.pdf.

Financial Stability Oversight Council. 2021. "Report on Climate-Related Financial Risk." U.S. Department of the Treasury. https://home.treasury.gov/system/files/261/FSOC-Climate-Report.pdf.

FRED (Federal Reserve Economic Data). 2022. "Gross Private Domestic Investment (GPDI)." Federal Reserve Bank of St. Louis. https://fred.stlouisfed.org/series/GPDI.

Gelzinis, G., and G. Steele. 2019. "Climate Change Threatens the Stability of the Financial System." Center for American Progress. https://www.americanprogress.org/article/climate-change-threatens-stability-financial-system/.

Goldin, C. 2006. "The Quiet Revolution That Transformed Women's Employment, Education, and Family." *AEA Papers and Proceedings*, 1–21. https://scholar.harvard.edu/files/goldin/files/the_quiet_revolution_that_transformed_womens_employment_education_and_family.pdf.

Goldin, C., and L. Katz. 2009. "Why the United States Led in Education: Lessons from Secondary School Expansion, 1910 to 1940." In *Human Capital and Institutions*, edited by D. Eltis, F. Lewis, and K. Sokoloff. Cambridge: Cambridge University Press. https://scholar.harvard.edu/lkatz/publications/why-united-states-led-education-lessons-secondary-school-expansion-1910-1940.

Goodwin, D. 2001. "The Way We Won: America's Economic Breakthrough During World War II." *American Prospect*. https://prospect.org/health/way-won-america-s-economic-breakthrough-world-war-ii/.

Gordon, R. 2016. *The Rise and Fall of American Growth*. Princeton, NJ: Princeton University Press. https://press.princeton.edu/books/hardcover/9780691147727/the-rise-and-fall-of-american-growth.

Graff Zivin, J., and M. Neidell. 2012. "The Impact of Pollution on Worker Productivity." *American Economic Review* 102, no. 7: 3652–73. https://doi.org/10.1257/aer.102.7.3652.

Groningen Growth and Development Centre. No date. "Maddison Database 2010." https://www.rug.nl/ggdc/historicaldevelopment/maddison/releases/maddison-database-2010.

Guiso, L., Sapienza, P., and L. Zingales. 2006. "Does Culture Affect Economic Outcomes?" *Journal of Economic Perspectives* 20, no. 2: 23–48. https://pubs.aeaweb.org/doi/pdfplus/10.1257/jep.20.2.23.

Hernandez, R. 2017. "Online Job Search: The New Normal." U.S. Bureau of Labor Statistics. https://www.bls.gov/opub/mlr/2017/beyond-bls/online-job-search-the-new-normal.htm.

Herrnstadt, E., and T. Dinan. 2020. "CBO's Projection of the Effect of Climate Change on U.S. Economic Output." Working paper, Congressional Budget Office. https://www.cbo.gov/system/files/2020-09/56505-Climate-Change.pdf.

Hsieh, C., E. Hurst, C. Jones, and P. Klenow. 2019. "The Allocation of Talent and U.S. Economic Growth." *Econometrica* 87, no. 5: 1439–74. https://doi.org/10.3982/ECTA11427.

Iglesias, V., A. Braswell, M. Rossi, M. Joseph, C. McShane, M. Cattau, M. Koontz, J. McGlinchy, R. Nagy, J. Balch, S. Leyk, and W. Travis. 2021. "Risky Development: Increasing Exposure to Natural Hazards in the United States." *Earth's Future* 9, no. 7. https://doi.org/10.1029/2020EF001795.

IPCC (Intergovernmental Panel on Climate Change). 2014. *Climate Change 2014 (Assessment Review 5): Synthesis Report*, edited by R. Pachauri, L. Mayer, and Core Writing Team. Geneva: IPCC. https://www.ipcc.ch/site/assets/uploads/2018/02/SYR_AR5_FINAL_full.pdf.

Jessoe, K., D. Manning, and J. Taylor. 2018. "Climate Change and Labour Allocation in Rural Mexico: Evidence from Annual Fluctuations in Weather." *Economic Journal* 128, no. 608: 230–61. https://doi.org/10.1111/ecoj.12448.

Kalkuhl, M., and L. Wenz. 2020. "The Impact of Climate Conditions on Economic Production. Evidence from a Global Region of Panels." *Journal of Environmental Economics and Management* 103. https://doi.org/10.1016/j.jeem.2020.102360.

Kao, S., M. Ashfaq, D. Rastogi, S. Gangrade, R. Uría Martínez, A. Fernandez, G. Konapala, N. Voisin, T. Zhou, W. Xu, H. Gao, B. Zhao, and G. Zhao. 2022. "The Third Assessment of the Effects of Climate Change on Federal Hydropower." Oak Ridge National Laboratory. https://info.ornl.gov/sites/publications/Files/Pub168510.pdf.

Kober, N., and D. Rentner. 2020. "History and Evolution of Public Education in the U.S." Center on Education Policy. https://files.eric.ed.gov/fulltext/ED606970.pdf.

Lan, X., P. Tans, and K. Thoning. 2022. "Trends in Globally-Averaged CO2 Determined from NOAA Global Monitoring Laboratory Measurements." Global Monitoring Laboratory. https://gml.noaa.gov/ccgg/trends/gl_data.html.

Lara, R. 2019. "Fact Sheet: Impact of Wildfires on Insurance Non-Renewals and Availability." California Department of Insurance. http://www.insurance.ca.gov/0400-news/0100-press-releases/2019/upload/nr063_factsheetwildfire.pdf.

Lebergott, S. 1966. "Labor Force and Employment, 1800–1960." In *Output, Employment, and Productivity in the United States after 1800*, edited by D. Brady, 117–204. Cambridge, MA: National Bureau of Economic Research. https://www.nber.org/system/files/chapters/c1567/c1567.pdf.

Lee, J. 2019. "Lessons of East-Asia's Human Capital Development." Project Syndicate. https://www.project-syndicate.org/commentary/human-capital-east-asia-development-strategy-education-by-lee-jong-wha-2019-01

Lüthi, D., M. Le Floch, B. Bereiter, T. Blunier, J. Barnola, U. Siegenthaler, D. Raynaud, J. Jouzel, H. Fischer, K. Kawamura, and T. Stocker. 2008. "High-Resolution Carbon Dioxide Concentration Record 650,000–800,000 Years Before Present." *Nature* 453: 379–82. https://doi.org/10.1038/nature06949.

Maiello, M. 2017. "Diagnosing William Baumol's Cost Disease." *Chicago Booth Review*. https://www.chicagobooth.edu/review/diagnosing-william-baumols-cost-disease.

Mankiw, N. 2010. *Macroeconomics*, 7th ed. New York: Worth. https://jollygreengeneral.typepad.com/files/n.-gregory-mankiw-macroeconomics-7th-edition-2009.pdf.

Mauro, P. 1995. "Corruption and Growth." *Quarterly Journal of Economics* 110, no. 3: 681–712. https://www.jstor.org/stable/pdf/2946696.pdf.

Mazzucato, M. 2013. *The Entrepreneurial State: Debunking Public vs. Private Sector Myths*. New York: Anthem Press. https://marianamazzucato.com/books/the-entrepreneurial-state.

Migration Policy Institute. No date. "U.S. Immigrant Population and Share over Time, 1850–Present." https://www.migrationpolicy.org/programs/data-hub/charts/immigrant-population-over-time.

Missirian, A., and W. Schlenker. 2017. "Asylum Applications Respond to Temperature Fluctuations." Science 358, no. 6370: 1610–14. https://www.science.org/doi/10.1126/science.aao0432.

Morrissey, T. 2017. "Child Care and Parent Labor Force Participation: A Review of the Research Literature." *Review of Economics of the Household* 15, no. 1: 1–24. https://doi.org/10.1007/s11150-016-9331-3.

Muro, M., S. Liu, J. Whiton, and S. Kulkarni. 2017. "Digitalization and the American Workforce." Brookings Institution. https://www.brookings.edu/research/digitalization-and-the-american-workforce/.

National Archives. No date. "Executive Order 8802: Prohibition of Discrimination in the Defense Industry (1941)." https://www.archives.gov/milestone-documents/executive-order-8802.

National Center for Education Statistics. 1993. "120 Years of American Education: A Statistical Portrait." https://nces.ed.gov/pubs93/93442.pdf.

National Centers for Environmental Education. 2022. "United States Billion Dollar Disaster Events 1980–2022 (CPI-Adjusted)." https://www.ncei.noaa.gov/access/billions/time-series.

National Partnership for Women and Families. 2022. "State Paid Family and Medical Leave Insurance Laws." https://www.nationalpartnership.org/our-work/resources/economic-justice/paid-leave/state-paid-family-leave-laws.pdf.

National World War II Museum. No date. "Research Starters: U.S. Military by the Numbers." https://www.nationalww2museum.org/students-teachers/student-resources/research-starters/research-starters-us-military-numbers.

Newell, R., B. Prest, and S. Sexton. 2021. "The GDP–Temperature Relationship: Implications for Climate Change Damages." *Journal of Environmental Economics and Management* 108. https://doi.org/10.1016/j.jeem.2021.102445.

OECD (Organization for Economic Cooperation and Development). 2022a. "Gross Domestic Spending on R&D." https://data.oecd.org/rd/gross-domestic-spending-on-r-d.htm.

———. 2022b. "LFS by Sex and Age: Indicators." https://stats.oecd.org/index.aspx?r=967539#.

Park, R., A. Behrer, and J. Goodman. 2021. "Learning Is Inhibited by Heat Exposure, Both Internationally and Within the United States." *Nature Human Behavior* 5: 19–27. https://doi.org/10.1038/s41562-020-00959-9.

Park, R., J. Goodman, M. Hurwitz, and J. Smith. 2020. "Heat and Learning." *American Economic Journal: Economic Policy* 12, no. 2: 306–39. https://doi.org/10.1257/pol.20180612.

Partlow, J. 2022. "Disaster Scenarios Raise the Stakes for Colorado River Negotiations." *Washington Post*, December 17. https://www.washingtonpost.com/climate-environment/2022/12/17/colorado-river-crisis-conference/.

Pew Research Center. 2021a. "Internet/Broadband Fact Sheet." https://www.pewresearch.org/internet/fact-sheet/internet-broadband/.

———. 2021b. "Digital Divide Persists Even as Americans with Lower Incomes Make Gains in Tech Adoption." https://www.pewresearch.org/fact-tank/2021/06/22/digital-divide-persists-even-as-americans-with-lower-incomes-make-gains-in-tech-adoption/.

———. 2021c. "Home Broadband Adoption, Computer Ownership Vary by Race, Ethnicity in the U.S." https://www.pewresearch.org/fact-tank/2021/07/16/home-broadband-adoption-computer-ownership-vary-by-race-ethnicity-in-the-u-s/.

Pfeiffer, D. 1995. "Ike's Interstates at 50: Anniversary of the Highway System Recalls Eisenhower's Role as Catalyst." *Prologue Magazine* 38, no. 2. https://www.archives.gov/publications/prologue/2006/summer/interstates.html.

Ramirez, R. 2022. "The West's Historic Drought Is Threatening Hydropower at Hoover Dam." CNN. https://www.cnn.com/2022/08/16/us/hoover-dam-hydropower-drought-climate/index.html.

Ranson, M. 2014. "Crime, Weather, and Climate Change." *Journal of Environmental Economics and Management* 67, no. 3: 274–302. https://doi.org/10.1016/j.jeem.2013.11.008.

Rennert, K., F. Errickson, B. Prest, L. Rennels, R. Newell, W. Pizer, C. Kingdon, J. Wingenroth, R. Cooke, B. Parthum, D. Smith, K. Cromar, D. Diaz, F. Moore, U. Müller, R. Plevin, A. Raftery, H. Sevcikova, H. Sheets, J. Stock, T. Tan, M. Watson, T. Wong, and D. Anthoff. 2022. "Comprehensive Evidence Implies a Higher Social Cost of CO2." *Nature* 610, no. 1: 687–92. https://doi.org/10.1038/s41586-022-05224-9.

Sablik, T. 2020. "Electrifying Rural America." Federal Reserve Bank of Richmond. https://www.richmondfed.org/publications/research/econ_focus/2020/q1/economic_history.

Shen, K. 2021. "Who Benefits from Public Financing of Home Care for Low-Income Seniors?" Working paper, Harvard University. https://scholar.harvard.edu/files/kshen/files/caregivers.pdf.

Siminski, P., and R. Yetsenga. 2022. "Specialization, Comparative Advantage, and the Sexual Division of Labor." *Journal of Labor Economics* 40, no. 4. https://doi.org/10.1086/718430.

Smith, A. 2023. "2022 U.S. Billion-Dollar Weather and Climate Disasters in Historical Context." U.S. Department of Commerce. https://www.climate.gov/news-features/blogs/2022-us-billion-dollar-weather-and-climate-disasters-historical-context.

Spruk, R. 2019. "The Rise and Fall of Argentina." *Latin American Economic Review* 28. https://doi.org/10.1186/s40503-019-0076-2.

U.S. Census Bureau. 1975. "Energy." In *Historical Statistics of the United States, Colonial Times to 1970*, 811–33. Washington: U.S. Government Publishing

Office. https://www2.census.gov/library/publications/1975/compendia/hist_stats_colonial-1970/hist_stats_colonial-1970p2-chS.pdf.

———. 2021. "Selected Social Characteristics in the United States." https://data.census.gov/table?q=DP02:+SELECTED+SOCIAL+CHARACTERISTICS+IN+THE+UNITED+STATES&g=0100000US&tid=ACSDP1Y2021.DP02.

———. 2023. "Quarterly Retail E-Commerce Sales, 3rd Quarter 2022." https://www.census.gov/retail/mrts/www/data/pdf/ec_current.pdf.

U.S. Securities and Exchange Commission. 2023. "Meta Platforms, Inc.: Form 10-K for Fiscal Year Ended December 31, 2022." EDGAR Database. https://www.sec.gov/ix?doc=/Archives/edgar/data/1326801/000132680123000013/meta-20221231.htm#i6df229dad1864210ab76200083e26819_79.

Weiss, T. 1999. "Estimates of White and Nonwhite Gainful Workers in the United States by Age Group, Race, and Sex Decennial Census Years, 1800–1900." *Historical Methods: A Journal of Quantitative and Interdisciplinary History* 32, no. 1: 21–36. https://doi.org/10.1080/01615449909598924.

Weller, C. 2002. "Learning Lessons from the 1990s." Economic Policy Institute. https://www.epi.org/publication/webfeatures_viewpoints_l-t_growth_lessons/.

White House. 2022. "Fact Sheet: White House Releases First-Ever Comprehensive Framework for Responsible Development of Digital Assets." https://www.whitehouse.gov/briefing-room/statements-releases/2022/09/16/fact-sheet-white-house-releases-first-ever-comprehensive-framework-for-responsible-development-of-digital-assets/.

———. 2023. "Fact Sheet: Biden-Harris Administration Releases National Strategy to Put Nature on the Nation's Balance Sheet." https://www.whitehouse.gov/ostp/news-updates/2023/01/19/fact-sheet-biden-harris-administration-releases-national-strategy-to-put-nature-on-the-nations-balance-sheet/.

Woetzel, J., D. Pinner, H. Samandari, H. Engel, M. Krishnan, B. Boland, and C. Powis. 2020. "Climate Risk and Response: Physical Hazards and Socioeconomic Impacts." McKinsey Global Institute. https://www.mckinsey.com/~/media/mckinsey/business%20functions/sustainability/our%20insights/climate%20risk%20and%20response%20physical%20hazards%20and%20socioeconomic%20impacts/mgi-climate-risk-and-response-full-report-vf.pdf.

World Bank. 1993. *The East Asian Miracle: Economic Growth and Public Policy*. New York: Oxford University Press. https://documents1.worldbank.org/curated/en/975081468244550798/pdf/multi-page.pdf.

World Economic Forum. 2020. "Nature Risk Rising: Why the Crisis Engulfing Nature Matters for Business and the Economy." https://www3.weforum.org/docs/WEF_New_Nature_Economy_Report_2020.pdf.

Chapter 2

Aladangady, A., D. Cho, L. Feiveson, and E. Pinto. 2022. "Excess Savings during the COVID-19 Pandemic." Board of Governors of the Federal Reserve System. https://www.federalreserve.gov/econres/notes/feds-notes/excess-savings-during-the-covid-19-pandemic-20221021.html.

Ascari, G., and A. Sbordone. 2014. "The Macroeconomics of Trend Inflation." *Journal of Economic Literature* 52: 679–739. https://www.aeaweb.org/articles?id=10.1257/jel.52.3.679.

Banerjee R., V. Boctor, A. Mehrotra, and F, Zampolli. 2022. "Fiscal Deficits and Inflation Risks: The Role of Fiscal and Monetary Regimes." Working paper, Bank for International Settlements. https://www.bis.org/publ/work1028.pdf.

Bassetto, M. 2008. "Fiscal Theory of Price Level." In *The New Palgrave Dictionary of Economics*, edited by S. Durlauf and L. Blume. London: Palgrave. http://users.nber.org/~bassetto/research/palgrave/ftheorypost.pdf.

Belz, S., L. Scheiner, and S. Campbell. 2022. "A Guide to the Hutchins Center Fiscal Impact Measure." Brookings Institution. https://www.brookings.edu/2022/02/17/a-guide-to-the-hutchins-center-fiscal-impact-measure/.

Bernanke, B. 2007. "Inflation Expectations and Inflation Forecasting." Transcript of speech delivered at Monetary Economics Workshop of the National Bureau of Economic Research Summer Institute, Cambridge, MA, July 10. https://www.federalreserve.gov/newsevents/speech/Bernanke20070710a.htm.

———. 2022. "Inflation Expectations and Monetary Policy." Speech delivered at Inflation Expectations: Determinants and Consequences Conference, May 19. https://www.nber.org/lecture/2022-inflation-expectations-determinants-and-consequence-keynote-ben-bernanke-inflation-expectations.

Biden, J. 2022. "Joe Biden: My Plan for Fighting Inflation." *Wall Street Journal*, May 30. https://www.wsj.com/articles/my-plan-for-fighting-inflation-joe-biden-gas-prices-economy-unemployment-jobs-covid-11653940654?mod=opinion_major_pos5.

Bilbiie, F., G. Eggertsson, G. Primiceri, and A. Tambalotti. 2021. "'Excess Savings' Are Not Excessive." *Liberty Street Economics*, Federal Reserve Bank of New York. https://libertystreeteconomics.newyorkfed.org/2021/04/excess-savings-are-not-excessive/.

Blanchard, O., E. Cerutti, and L. Summers. 2015. *Inflation and Activity: Two Explorations and Their Monetary Policy Implications*. NBER Working Paper 21726. Cambridge, MA: National Bureau of Economic Research. https://www.nber.org/papers/w21726.

Boehm, C., and N. Pandalai-Nayar. 2022. "Convex Supply Curves." *American Economic Review* 112, no. 12: 3941–69. https://www.aeaweb.org/articles/pdf/doi/10.1257/aer.20210811.

Bordo, M., and M. Levy. 2021. "Do Enlarged Fiscal Deficits Cause Inflation? The Historical Record." *Economic Affairs* 41, no. 1: 59–83. https://onlinelibrary.wiley.com/doi/abs/10.1111/ecaf.12446.

Bräuning, F., J. Fillat, and G. Joaquim. 2022. "Cost–Price Relationships in a Concentrated Economy." Federal Reserve Bank of Boston. https://www.bostonfed.org/publications/current-policy-perspectives/2022/cost-price-relationships-in-a-concentrated-economy.aspx.

Catão, L., and M. Terrones. 2005. "Fiscal Deficits and Inflation." *Journal of Monetary Economics* 52, no. 3: 529–54. https://www.sciencedirect.com/science/article/abs/pii/S0304393205000139.

CBO (Congressional Budget Office). 2019. "The Budget and Economic Outlook: 2019 to 2029." https://www.cbo.gov/system/files/2019-03/54918-Outlook-3.pdf.

———. 2022. "Chapter 2: The Economic Outlook." https://www.cbo.gov/system/files?file=2022-05/57950-Chapter-2.pdf.

CEA (Council of Economic Advisers). 2016. "The Year in Review and the Years Ahead." https://www.govinfo.gov/content/pkg/ERP-2016/pdf/ERP-2016-chapter2.pdf.

———. 2022. *Economic Report of the President.* https://www.whitehouse.gov/wp-content/uploads/2022/04/ERP-2022.pdf.

Chetty, R., J. Friedman, M. Stepner, and Opportunity Insights Team. 2022. *The Economic Impacts of COVID-19: Evidence from a New Public Database Built Using Private Sector Data.* NBER Working Paper 27431. Cambridge, MA: National Bureau of Economic Research. https://www.nber.org/system/files/working_papers/w27431/w27431.pdf.

Clark, T., and S. Terry. 2010. "Time Variation in the Inflation Passthrough of Energy Prices." *Journal of Money, Credit and Banking* 42, no. 7: 1419–33. http://www.jstor.org/stable/40925694.

Cochrane, J. 2023. *The Fiscal Theory of the Price Level.* Princeton, NJ: Princeton University Press. https://press.princeton.edu/books/hardcover/9780691242248/the-fiscal-theory-of-the-price-level.

Congressional Research Service. 2022. "An Excise Tax on Stock Repurchases and Tax Advantages of Buybacks over Dividends." https://crsreports.congress.gov/product/pdf/IF/IF11960.

Crawley, E., and E. Gagnon. 2022. "Substitutability between Balance Sheet Reductions and Policy Rate Hikes: Some Illustrations and a Discussion." Board of Governors of the Federal Reserve System. https://doi.org/10.17016/2380-7172.3147.

Detmeister, A. 2011. "The Usefulness of Core PCE Inflation Measures." Finance and Economics Discussion Series, Federal Reserve Board. https://www.federalreserve.gov/pubs/feds/2011/201156/201156abs.html.

Donaldson, D., and R. Hornbeck. 2016. "Railroads and American Economic Growth: A 'Market Access' Approach." *Quarterly Journal of Economics* 131, no. 2: 799–858. https://doi.org/10.1093/qje/qjw002.

Federal Reserve (Board of Governors of the Federal Reserve System). 2012. "Federal Reserve Issues FOMC Statement of Longer-Run Goals and Policy Strategy." https://www.federalreserve.gov/newsevents/pressreleases/monetary20120125c.htm.

———. 2020. "2020 Statement on Longer-Run Goals and Monetary Policy Strategy." https://www.federalreserve.gov/monetarypolicy/review-of-monetary-policy-strategy-tools-and-communications-statement-on-longer-run-goals-monetary-policy-strategy.htm.

———. 2022a. "Summary of Economic Projections." https://www.federalreserve.gov/monetarypolicy/files/fomcprojtabl20221214.pdf.

———. 2022b. "Federal Reserve Issues FOMC Statement." https://www.federalreserve.gov/monetarypolicy/files/monetary20221214a1.pdf.

Federal Reserve Bank of Atlanta, Center for Human Capital Studies. No date. "Wage Growth Tracker." https://www.atlantafed.org/chcs/wage-growth-tracker.

Federal Reserve Bank of Cleveland. 2023. "Median CPI." https://www.clevelandfed.org/indicators-and-data/median-cpi.

Federal Reserve Bank of Dallas. No date. "Trimmed Mean MCE Inflation Rate." https://www.dallasfed.org/research/pce.

Federal Reserve Bank of Philadelphia. 2020. "Fourth Quarter 2020 Survey of Professional Forecasters." https://www.philadelphiafed.org/surveys-and-data/real-time-data-research/spf-q4-2020.

Friedman, M. 1970. "The Counter-Revolution in Monetary Theory." Institute of Economic Affairs, Occasional Paper 33. https://onlinelibrary.wiley.com/doi/pdf/10.1002/9781119205814.app2.

Furman, J., and W. Powell. 2021. "What Is the Best Measure of Labor Market Tightness?" Peterson Institute for International Economics. https://www.piie.com/blogs/realtime-economic-issues-watch/what-best-measure-labor-market-tightness.

Galí, J. 2015. *Monetary Policy, Inflation, and the Business Cycle: An Introduction to the New Keynesian Framework and Its Applications—Second Edition. Princeton,* NJ: Princeton University Press. https://press.princeton.edu/books/hardcover/9780691164786/monetary-policy-inflation-and-the-business-cycle.

Gleckman, H., and J. Holtzblatt. 2022. "Cutting Through the Misinformation About the IRS's Plan to Spend $80 Billion." Tax Policy Center. https://www.taxpolicycenter.org/taxvox/cutting-through-misinformation-about-irss-plan-spend-80-billion.

Gordon, R. 1975. "Alternative Reponses of Policy to External Supply Shocks." *Brookings Papers on Economic Activity*, no 1: 183–206. https://www.brookings.edu/wp-content/uploads/1975/01/1975a_bpea_gordon.pdf.

Gross, D., and B. Sampat. 2020. *America, Jump-Started: World War II R&D and the Takeoff of the U.S. Innovation System*. NBER Working Paper 27375. Cambridge, MA: National Bureau of Economic Research. https://doi.org/10.3386/w27375.

Guerrieri, V., G. Lorenzoni, L. Straub, and I. Werning. 2021. "Monetary Policy in Times of Structural Reallocation." Working paper, Jackson Hole Economic Policy Symposium. https://www.kansascityfed.org/documents/8322/JH_Guerrieri.pdf.

Hicks, J. 1937. "Mr. Keynes and the 'Classics': A Suggested Interpretation." *Econometrica* 5, no. 2: 147–59. https://doi.org/10.2307%2F1907242.

Jordà, Ò., C. Liu, F. Nechio, and F. Rivera-Reyes. 2022. "Wage Growth When Inflation Is High." Federal Reserve Bank of San Francisco. https://www.frbsf.org/economic-research/publications/economic-letter/2022/september/wage-growth-when-inflation-is-high/.

Jordà, Ò., and A. Taylor. 2019. "Riders on the Storm." Working paper, Federal Reserve Bank of San Francisco. https://doi.org/10.24148/wp2019-20.

Jørgensen, P., and S. Ravn. 2022. "The Inflation Response to Government Spending Shocks: A Fiscal Price Puzzle?" *European Economic Review* 141. https://doi.org/10.1016/j.euroecorev.2021.103982.

Keynes, J. 1936. *The General Theory of Employment, Interest, and Money*. Boston: Houghton Mifflin. https://archive.org/details/generaltheoryofe00keyn_0/page/n9/mode/2u.

Klein, L., and A. Goldberger. 1955. *An Econometric Model of the United States, 1929–1952*. Amsterdam: North Holland. https://doi.org/10.2307/2227976.

Michaillat, P., and E. Saez. 2022. $u^* = \sqrt{uv}$. NBER Working Paper 30211. Cambridge, MA: National Bureau of Economic Research. https://doi.org/10.3386/w30211.

Miranda-Agrippino, S., and G. Ricco. 2021. "The Transmission of Monetary Policy Shocks." *American Economic Journal: Macroeconomics* 5, no. 3: 74–107. https://doi.org/10.1257/mac.20180124.

Phillips, A. 1958. "The Relation Between Unemployment and the Rate of Change of Money Wage Rates in the United Kingdom, 1861–1957." *Economica* 25, no. 100: 289–99. https://doi.org/10.2307/2550759.

Powell, J. 2018. "Monetary Policy in a Changing Economy." Transcript of speech at Changing Market Structure and Implications for Monetary Policy Symposium,Jackson Hole, WY, August 24. https://www.federalreserve.gov/newsevents/speech/powell20180824a.htm.

———. 2022a. "Inflation and the Labor Market." Transcript of a speech at the Hutchins Center of Fiscal and Monetary Policy, Brookings Institution, Washington, November 30. https://www.federalreserve.gov/newsevents/speech/powell20221130a.htm.

———. 2022b. "Monetary Policy and Price Stability." Transcript of speech at Reassessing Constraints on the Economy and Policy Symposium, Jackson Hole,

WY, August 26. https://www.federalreserve.gov/newsevents/speech/powell20220826a.htm.

Ramey, V. 2019. "Ten Years After the Financial Crisis: What Have We Learned from the Renaissance in Fiscal Research?" *Journal of Economic Perspectives* 33, no. 2: 89–144. https://doi.org/10.1257/jep.33.2.89.

Rankin, E., and M. Idil. 2014. "A Century of Stock-Bond Correlations." Reserve Bank of Australia. https://www.rba.gov.au/publications/bulletin/2014/sep/pdf/bu-0914-8.pdf.

Rudd, J. 2020. "Underlying Inflation: Its Measurement and Significance." *FEDS Notes*. Washington: Board of Governors of the Federal Reserve System, September 18. https://doi.org/10.17016/2380-7172.2624.

———. 2021. "Why Do We Think That Inflation Expectations Matter for Inflation? (And Should We?)" Finance and Economics Discussion Series. https://doi.org/10.17016/FEDS.2021.062.

Social Security Administration. 2022a. "Table V.A2: Immigration Assumptions." https://www.ssa.gov/oact/TR/2022/lr5a2.html.

———. 2022b. "The 2022 Annual Report of The Board of Trustees of The Federal Old-Age and Survivors Insurance and Federal Disability Insurance Trust Funds." https://www.ssa.gov/oact/tr/2022/tr2022.pdf.

Stigum, M., and A. Crescenzi. 2007. "Stigum's Money Market, 4E." https://www.mhprofessional.com/stigum-s-money-market-4e-9780071448451-usa.

Syverson, C. 2019. "Macroeconomics and Market Power: Context, Implications, and Open Questions." *Journal of Economic Perspectives* 33, no. 3: 23–43. https://doi.org/10.1257/jep.33.3.23.

U.S. Bureau of Labor Statistics. 2020. "Consumer Price Index: Overview." https://www.bls.gov/opub/hom/cpi/home.htm.

Werning, I. 2022. *Expectations and the Rate of Inflation*. NBER Working Paper 30260. Cambridge, MA: National Bureau of Economic Research. https://doi.org/10.3386/w30260.

White House. 2021. "Remarks by President Biden on the State of the Economy and the Need for the American Rescue Plan." https://www.whitehouse.gov/briefing-room/speeches-remarks/2021/02/05/remarks-by-president-biden-on-the-state-of-the-economy-and-the-need-for-the-american-rescue-plan/.

Yellen, J. 2015. "Inflation Dynamics and Monetary Policy." Transcript of Philip Gamble Memorial Lecture, University of Massachusetts, Amherst, September 24. https://www.federalreserve.gov/newsevents/speech/yellen20150924a.htm.

Chapter 3

Ahmed, U. 2019. "The Importance of Cross-Border Regulatory Cooperation in an Era of Digital Trade." *World Trade Review* 18, no. S1: S99–S120. https://doi.org/10.1017/S1474745618000514.

Alfaro, L. 2016. "Gains from Foreign Direct Investment: Macro and Micro Approaches." *World Bank Economic Review* 30, no. S1: S2–S15. https://academic.oup.com/wber/article/30/Supplement_1/S2/2897332.

Amiti, M., and S. Wei. 2006. *Service Offshoring, Productivity, and Employment: Evidence from the United States*. IMF Working Paper 05/238. Washington, DC: International Monetary Fund. https://papers.ssrn.com/sol3/papers.cfm?abstract_id=888107.

Aslund, A., and M. Snegovaya. 2021. "The Impact of Western Sanctions on Russia and How They Can Be Made Even More Effective." Atlantic Council. https://www.atlanticcouncil.org/wp-content/uploads/2021/05/The-impact-of-Western-sanctions-on-Russia-and-how-they-can-be-made-even-more-effective-5.2.pdf.

Autor, D., D. Dorn, and G. Hanson. 2013. "The Geography of Trade and Technology Shocks in the United States." *American Economic Review* 103, no. 3: 220–25. https://doi.org/10.1257/aer.103.3.220.

———. 2016. "The China Shock: Learning from Labor-Market Adjustment to Large Changes in Trade." *Annual Review of Economics* 8: 205–40. https://doi.org/10.1146/annurev-economics-080315-015041.

———. 2021. *On the Persistence of the China Shock*. NBER Working Paper 29401. Cambridge, MA: National Bureau of Economic Research. https://doi.org/10.3386/w29401.

Autor, D., D. Dorn, G. Hanson, and J. Song. 2014. "Trade Adjustment: Worker-Level Evidence." *Quarterly Journal of Economics* 129, no. 4: 1799–1806. https://doi.org/10.1093/qje/qju026.

Baldwin, R. 2022. "The Peak Globalisation Myth: Part 4—Services Trade Did Not Peak." Center for Economic and Policy Research. https://cepr.org/voxeu/columns/peak-globalisation-myth-part-4-services-trade-did-not-peak.

Baldwin, R., and R. Freeman. 2022. "Risks and Global Supply Chains: What We Know and What We Need to Know." *Annual Review of Economics* 14: 153–80. https://doi.org/10.1146/annurev-economics-051420-113737.

Bapat, N., and T. Morgan. 2009. "Multilateral Versus Unilateral Sanctions Reconsidered: A Test Using New Data." *International Studies Quarterly* 53, no. 4: 1075–94. https://doi.org/10.1111/j.1468-2478.2009.00569.x.

Bauer, M., H. Lee-Makiyama, E. van der Marel, and B. Verschelde. 2014. "The Costs of Data Localisation: Friendly Fire on Economic Recovery." European Centre for International Political Economy, Occasional Paper 3/2014. https://ecipe.org/wp-content/uploads/2014/12/OCC32014__1.pdf.

BEA (U.S. Bureau of Economic Analysis). 2022. "International Data." https://www.bea.gov/itable/international-transactions-services-and-investment-position.

———. 2023a. "Real Gross Domestic Product, Chained Dollars." https://apps.bea.gov/iTable/?reqid=19&step=3&isuri=1&select_all_years=0&nipa_table_list=6&series=q&first_year=2018&last_year=2020&scale=-9&categories=survey.

———. 2023b. "Real Exports and Imports of Goods and Services by Type of Product, Chained Dollars." https://apps.bea.gov/iTable/?reqid=19&step=4&isuri=1&192-1=flatfiles#eyJhcHBpZCI6MTksInN0ZXBzIjpbMSwyLDNdLCJkYXRhIjpbWyJDYXRlZ29yaWVzIiwiU3VydmV5Il0sWyJOSVBBX1RhYmxlX0xpc3QiLCIxMzQiXV19.

———. 2023c. "International Trade in Goods and Services." https://www.bea.gov/data/intl-trade-investment/international-trade-goods-and-services.

———. 2023d. "Price Indexes for Gross Domestic Product." https://apps.bea.gov/iTable/?reqid=19&step=2&isuri=1&categories=survey#eyJhcHBpZCI6MTksInN0ZXBzIjpbMSwyLDNdLCJkYXRhIjpbWyJjYXRlZ29yaWVzIiwiU3VydmV5Il0sWyJOSVBBX1RhYmxlX0xpc3QiLCI0Il1dfQ.

Berner, R., S. Cecchetti, and K. Schoenholtz. 2022. "Russian Sanctions: Some Questions and Answers." Center for Economic and Policy Research. https://cepr.org/voxeu/columns/russian-sanctions-some-questions-and-answers.

Birshan, M., T. Devesa, H. Samandari, J. Seong, S. Smit, O. White, and J. Woetzel. 2022. "Global Flows: The Ties That Bind an Interconnected World." MicKinsey Global Institute. https://www.mckinsey.com/capabilities/strategy-and-corporate-finance/our-insights/global-flows-the-ties-that-bind-in-an-interconnected-world.

BLS (U.S. Bureau of Labor Statistics). 2023. "Import/Export Price Indexes (MXP)." https://www.bls.gov/mxp/.

Bonadio, B., Z. Huo, A. Levchenko, and N. Pandalai-Nayar. 2021. "Global Supply Chains in the Pandemic." *Journal of International Economics* 133. https://doi.org/10.1016/j.jinteco.2021.103534.

Borusyak, K., and X. Jaravel. 2021. *The Distributional Effects of Trade: Theory and Evidence from the United States*. NBER Working Paper 28957. Cambridge, MA: National Bureau of Economic Research. https://www.nber.org/system/files/working_papers/w28957/w28957.pdf.

Bown, C. 2022a. "Four Years into the Trade War, Are the US and China Decoupling?" Peterson Institute for International Economics. https://www.piie.com/blogs/realtime-economics/four-years-trade-war-are-us-and-china-decoupling.

———. 2022b. "First Trade War, Now Russia's Real War. Why U.S. Exports to China Continue to Suffer." Peterson Institute for International Economics. https://www.piie.com/blogs/realtime-economics/first-trade-war-now-russias-real-war-why-us-exports-china-continue-suffer.

———. 2022c. "The WTO and Vaccine Supply Chain Resilience during a Pandemic." Peterson Institute for International Economics, Working Paper 22-15. https://

www.piie.com/publications/working-papers/wto-and-vaccine-supply-chain-resilience-during-pandemic.

Bown, C., and J. Hillman. 2019. "WTO'ing a Resolution to the China Subsidy Problem." *Journal of International Economic Law* 22, no. 4: 557–78. https://doi.org/10.1093/jiel/jgz035.

Brynjolfsson, E., J. Horton, A. Ozimek, D. Rock, G. Sharma, and H. TuYe. 2020. *COVID-19 and Remote Work: An Early Look at U.S. Data*. NBER Working Paper 27344. Cambridge, MA: National Bureau of Economic Research. https://doi.org/10.3386/w27344.

Capri, A., and W. Lehmacher. 2021. "How COVID-19 Accelerated the Shift Towards TradeTech." World Economic Forum. https://www.weforum.org/agenda/2021/01/how-covid-19-has-accelerated-the-shift-towards-tradetech/.

Carr, B., C. French, and C. Lowery. 2020. "Data Localization: Costs, Tradeoffs, and Impacts Across the Economy." Institute of International Finance. https://www.iif.com/portals/0/Files/content/Innovation/12_22_2020_data_localization.pdf.

Caselli, F., M. Koren, M. Lisicky, and S. Tenreyro. 2020. "Diversification Through Trade." *Quarterly Journal of Economics* 135, no. 1: 449–502. https://doi.org/10.1093/qje/qjz028.

Casalini, F., and J. González. 2019. *Trade and Cross-Border Data Flows*. OECD Trade Policy Paper 220. Paris: OECD Publishing. https://doi.org/10.1787/b2023a47-en.

Casalini, F., J. González, and E. Moïsé. 2019. *Approaches to Market Openness in the Digital Age*. OECD Trade Policy Paper 219. Paris: OECD Publishing. https://doi.org/10.1787/818a7498-en.

CEA (Council of Economic Advisers). 2022. *Economic Report of the President*. Washington: U.S. Government Publishing Office. https://www.whitehouse.gov/wp-content/uploads/2022/04/ERP-2022.pdf.

Cerdeiro, D., and A. Komaromi. 2020. *Supply Spillovers During the Pandemic: Evidence from High-Frequency Shipping Data*. IMF Working Paper 20/284. https://www.imf.org/en/Publications/WP/Issues/2020/12/18/Supply-Spillovers-During-the-Pandemic-Evidence-from-High-Frequency-Shipping-Data-49966.

CFR (Council on Foreign Relations). 2022. "Confronting Reality in Cyberspace: Foreign Policy for a Fragmented Internet." Independent Task Force Report 80. https://www.cfr.org/report/confronting-reality-in-cyberspace.

Chetty, R., J. Friedman, N. Hendren, M. Stepner, and Opportunity Insights Team. 2022. *The Economic Impacts of COVID-19: Evidence from a New Public Database Built Using Private Sector Data*. NBER Working Paper 27431. Cambridge, MA: National Bureau of Economic Research. https://doi.org/10.3386/w27431.

Chetverikov, D., B. Larsen, and C. Palmer. 2016. "IV Quantile Regression for Group-Level Treatments, with an Application to the Distributional Effects of Trade." *Econometrica* 84, no. 2: 809–33. https://doi.org/10.3982/ECTA12121.

Chivvis, C., and E. Kapstein. 2022. "U.S. Strategy and Economic Statecraft: Understanding the Trade-Offs." Carnegie Endowment for International Peace. https://carnegieendowment.org/2022/04/28/u.s.-strategy-and-economic-statecraft-understanding-tradeoffs-pub-86995.

Choi, S., D. Furceri, and C. Yoon. 2020. "Policy Uncertainty and Foreign Direct Investment." *Review of International Economics* 29, no. 2: 195–227. https://doi.org/10.1111/roie.12495.

Clausing, K. 2019. *Open: The Progressive Case for Free Trade, Immigration, and Global Capital.* Cambridge, MA: Harvard University Press.

Comini, N., V. Foster, and S. Srinivasan. 2021. "Improving Data Infrastructure Helps Ensure Equitable Access for Poor People in Poor Countries." World Bank Data Blog. https://blogs.worldbank.org/opendata/improving-data-infrastructure-helps-ensure-equitable-access-poor-people-poor-countries.

Cooke, B., G. Nigatu, K. Heerman, M. Landes, and R. Seely. 2016. "Global Macroeconomic Developments Drive Downturn in U.S. Agricultural Exports." U.S. Department of Agriculture. https://www.ers.usda.gov/webdocs/outlooks/35809/59822_aes-94.pdf?v=203.4.

Corbeau, A. 2022. "How Deep Is Europe's Dependence on Russian Oil?" Columbia Climate School, State of the Planet. https://news.climate.columbia.edu/2022/03/14/qa-how-deep-is-europes-dependence-on-russian-oil/.

CRS (Congressional Research Service). 2022a. "Russia's War on Ukraine: Financial and Trade Sanctions." https://crsreports.congress.gov/product/pdf/IF/IF12062.

———. 2022b. "Biden Administration Plans for an Indo-Pacific Economic Framework." https://crsreports.congress.gov/product/pdf/IN/IN11814.

———. 2023. "U.S. Trade Policy: Background and Current Issues." https://crsreports.congress.gov/product/pdf/IF/IF10156.

D'Aguanno, L., O. Davies, A. Dogan, R. Freeman, S. Lloyd, D. Reinhardt, R. Sajedi, and R. Zymek. 2021. "Global Value Chains, Volatility and Safe Openness: Is Trade a Double-Edged Sword?" Bank of England Financial Stability Paper 46. https://www.bankofengland.co.uk/financial-stability-paper/2021/global-value-chains-volatility-and-safe-openness-is-trade-a-double-edged-sword.

De Loecker, J., P. Goldberg, A. Khandelwal, and N. Pavcnik. 2016. "Prices, Markups, and Trade Reform." *Econometrica* 84, no 2: 445–510. https://doi.org/10.3982/ECTA11042.

Demertzis, M., B. Hilgenstock, B. McWilliams, E. Ribakova, and S. Tagliapietra. 2022. "How Have Sanctions Impacted Russia?" Bruegel Policy Contribution 18/22. https://www.bruegel.org/sites/default/files/2022-10/PC%2018%202022_1.pdf.

Dingel, J., and B. Neiman. 2020. "How Many Jobs Can Be Done at Home?" *Journal of Public Economics* 189. https://doi.org/10.1016/j.jpubeco.2020.104235.

DOE (U.S. Department of Energy). 2022. "Poland and U.S. Announce Strategic Partnership to Launch Poland's Civil Nuclear Program." https://www.energy.

gov/articles/poland-and-us-announce-strategic-partnership-launch-polands-civil-nuclear-program.

DOL (U.S. Department of Labor). 2022. “U.S. Department of Labor Joins U.S. Trade Representative, European Commission to Host First Principals’ Meeting of the U.S.-EU Trade and Labor Dialogue.” https://www.dol.gov/newsroom/releases/ilab/ilab20221205.

Drury, A. 1998. “Revisiting Economic Sanctions Reconsidered.” *Journal of Peace Research* 35, no. 4: 497–509. https://doi.org/10.1177/0022343398035004006.

Economist Intelligence Unit. 2022. “Russia: Forecast Summary.” http://country.eiu.com/article.aspx?articleid=1802639163&Country=Russia&topic=Economy&subtopic=Forecast&subsubtopic=Forecast+summary.

Eppinger, P. 2019. “Service Offshoring and Firm Employment.” *Journal of International Economics* 117: 209–28. https://doi.org/10.1016/j.jinteco.2019.01.007.

Eppinger, P., G. Felbermayr, O. Krebs, and B. Kukharskyy. 2021. “Decoupling Global Value Chains.” Center for Economic Studies and Ifo Institute, Working Paper 6079. https://www.econstor.eu/bitstream/10419/235449/1/cesifo1_wp9079.pdf.

Eriksson, K., K. Russ, J. Shambaugh, and M. Xu. 2021. “Reprint: Trade Shocks and the Shifting Landscape of U.S. Manufacturing.” *Journal of International Money and Finance* 114. https://www.sciencedirect.com/science/article/pii/S0261560621000589.

Espitia, A., A. Mattoo, N. Rocha, M. Ruta, and D. Winkler. 2021. “Pandemic Trade: COVID-19, Remote Work, and Global Value Chains.” World Bank Working Paper 9508. https://documents1.worldbank.org/curated/en/843301610630752625/pdf/Pandemic-Trade-Covid-19-Remote-Work-and-Global-Value-Chains.pdf.

Espitia, A., N. Rocha, and M. Ruta. 2022. “How Export Restrictions Are Impacting Global Food Prices.” World Bank Private Sector Development Blog. https://blogs.worldbank.org/psd/how-export-restrictions-are-impacting-global-food-prices.

Fan, H., Y. Li, and S. Yeaple. 2015. “Trade Liberalization, Quality, and Export Prices.” *Review of Economics and Statistics* 95, no. 5: 1033–51. https://doi.org/10.1162/REST_a_00524.

Feenstra, R., H. Ma, and Y. Xu. 2019. “U.S. Exports and Employment.” *Journal of International Economics* 120: 46–58. https://doi.org/10.1016/j.jinteco.2019.05.002.

Flanagan, M., A. Kammer, A. Pescatori, and M. Stuermer. 2022. “How a Russian Natural Gas Cutoff Could Weigh on Europe’s Economies.” International Monetary Fund Blog. https://www.imf.org/en/Blogs/Articles/2022/07/19/blog-how-a-russias-natural-gas-cutoff-could-weigh-on-european-economies.

Foggo, J., and B. Mainardi. 2022. “Boiling the Frog: Russia’s Black Sea Aggression Part II, the War.” Center for European Policy Analysis. https://cepa.org/article/boiling-the-frog-russias-black-sea-aggression-part-ii-the-war/.

Freund, C., A. Mulabdic, and M. Ruta. 2022. "Is 3D Printing a Threat to Global Trade? The Trade Effects You Didn't Hear About." *Journal of International Economics* 138. https://doi.org/10.1016/j.jinteco.2022.103646.

Georgieva, K., G. Gopinath, and C. Pazarbasioglu. 2022. "Why We Must Resist Geoeconomic Fragmentation—and How." International Monetary Fund Blog. https://www.imf.org/en/Blogs/Articles/2022/05/22/blog-why-we-must-resist-geoeconomic-fragmentation.

Glauber, J., and D. Laborde. 2022. "How Sanctions on Russia and Belarus Are Impacting Exports of Agricultural Products and Fertilizer." International Food Policy Research Institute Blog. https://www.ifpri.org/blog/how-sanctions-russia-and-belarus-are-impacting-exports-agricultural-products-and-fertilizer..

Goldberg, L., and K. Crockett. 1998. "The Dollar and U.S. Manufacturing." *Current Issues in Economics and Finance* (Federal Reserve Bank of New York) 4, no. 12. https://www.newyorkfed.org/research/current_issues/ci4-12.html.

Goldberg, P., A. Khandelwal, N. Pavcnik, and P. Topalova. 2010. "Imported Intermediate Inputs and Domestic Product Growth: Evidence from India." *Quarterly Journal of Economics* 125, no. 4: 1727–67. https://doi.org/10.1162/qjec.2010.125.4.1727.

Goldfarb, A., and C. Tucker. 2019. "Digital Economics." *Journal of Economic Literature* 57, no. 1: 3–43. https://doi.org/10.1257/jel.20171452.

Gopinath, G., and O. Itskhoki. 2021. *Dominant Currency Paradigm: A Review*. NBER Working Paper 29556. Cambridge, MA: National Bureau of Economic Research. https://doi.org/10.3386/w29556.

Gopinath, G., O. Itskhoki, and R. Rigobon. 2010. "Currency Choice and Exchange Rate Pass-Through." *American Economic Review* 100, no. 1: 304–36. https://doi.org/10.1257/aer.100.1.304.

Grossman, G., E. Helpman, and H. Lhuillier. 2021. *Supply Chain Resilience: Should Policy Promote Diversification or Reshoring?* NBER Working Paper 29330. Cambridge, MA: National Bureau of Economic Research. https://doi.org/10.3386/w29330.

Grossman, G., and E. Rossi-Hansberg. 2008. "Trading Tasks: A Simple Theory of Offshoring." *American Economic Review* 98, no. 5: 1978–97. https://doi.org/10.1257/aer.98.5.1978.

Gulen, H., and M. Ion. 2016. "Policy Uncertainty and Corporate Investment." *Review of Financial Studies* 29, no. 3: 523–64. https://doi.org/10.1093/rfs/hhv050.

Harrell, P., E. Rosenberg, and E. Saravelle. 2018. "China's Use of Coercive Economic Measures." Center for a New American Security. https://www.cnas.org/publications/reports/chinas-use-of-coercive-economic-measures.

Higgins, M., and T. Klitgaard. 2021. "How Much Have Consumers Spent on Imports during the Pandemic?" *Liberty Street Economics*, Federal Reserve Bank of New York. https://libertystreeteconomics.newyorkfed.org/2021/10/how-much-have-consumers-spent-on-imports-during-the-pandemic/.

Huang, K., S. Madnick, and S. Johnson. 2019. "Framework for Understanding Cybersecurity Impacts on International Trade." Working Paper 2019-23, Cybersecurity Interdisciplinary Systems Laboratory, Sloan School of Management, Massachusetts Institute of Technology. https://papers.ssrn.com/sol3/papers.cfm?abstract_id=3555341.

IBM. 2022. "Cost of a Data Breach 2022." https://www.ibm.com/reports/data-breach.

IDC (International Data Corporation). 2021. "Digital Transformation Investments to Represent More Than Half of All ICT Investment by 2024, According to IDC FutureScape." https://www.idc.com/getdoc.jsp?containerId=prUS48333121.

IEA (International Energy Agency). 2022a. "Frequently Asked Questions on Energy Security." https://www.iea.org/articles/frequently-asked-questions-on-energy-security.

———. 2022b. "How to Avoid Gas Shortages in the European Union in 2023: The Need for Action." https://www.iea.org/reports/how-to-avoid-gas-shortages-in-the-european-union-in-2023/the-need-for-action#abstract.

IMF (International Monetary Fund). 2022a. "World Economic Outlook, April 2022: War Sets Back the Global Recovery." https://www.imf.org/en/Publications/WEO/Issues/2022/04/19/world-economic-outlook-april-2022#Global-Trade-and-Value-Chains-in-the-Pandemic.

———. 2022b. "World Economic Outlook, October 2022: Countering the Cost-of-Living Crisis." https://www.imf.org/en/Publications/WEO/Issues/2022/10/11/world-economic-outlook-october-2022.

Irwin, D. 2022a. *The Trade Reform Wave of 1985–1995*. NBER Working Paper 29973. Cambridge, MA: National Bureau for Economic Research. https://doi.org/10.3386/w29973.

———. 2022b. "Globalization Enabled Nearly All Countries to Grow Richer in Recent Decades." Peterson Institute for International Economics. https://www.piie.com/blogs/realtime-economic-issues-watch/globalization-enabled-nearly-all-countries-grow-richer-recent.

Jaravel, X., and E. Sager. 2019. "What Are the Price Effects of Trade? Evidence from the U.S. and Implications for Quantitative Trade Models." Board of Governors of the Federal Reserve System, Finance and Economics Discussion Series, Working Paper 2019-68. https://papers.ssrn.com/sol3/papers.cfm?abstract_id=3473054.

Jiang, H., B. Kenner, D. Russell, and J. Kaufman. 2022. "Outlook for U.S. Agricultural Trade: November 2022." U.S. Department of Agriculture. https://www.ers.usda.gov/webdocs/outlooks/105356/aes-122.pdf?v=5558.3.

Julio, B., and Y. Yook. 2016. "Policy Uncertainty, Irreversibility, and Cross-Border Flows of Capital." *Journal of International Economics* 103: 13–26. https://www.sciencedirect.com/science/article/abs/pii/S0022199616300915.

Keller, W., and S. Yeaple. 2009. "Multinational Enterprises, International Trade, and Productivity Growth: Firm-Level Evidence from the United States." *Review of*

Economics and Statistics 91, no. 4: 821–31. https://direct.mit.edu/rest/article/91/4/821/57821/Multinational-Enterprises-International-Trade-and.

Klapper, L., and M. Miller. 2021. "The Impact of COVID-19 on Digital Financial Inclusion." World Bank. https://www.gpfi.org/sites/gpfi/files/sites/default/files/5_WB%20Report_The%20impact%20of%20COVID-19%20on%20digital%20financial%20inclusion.pdf.

Krugman, P. 1980. "Scale Economies, Product Differentiation, and the Pattern of Trade." *American Economic Review* 70, no 5: 950–59. https://www.jstor.org/stable/1805774#metadata_info_tab_contents.

Lagarde, C. 2022. "A New Global Map: European Resilience in a Changing World." Transcript of speech at Peterson Institute for International Economics Event, Washington, April 22. https://www.ecb.europa.eu/press/key/date/2022/html/ecb.sp220422~c43af3db20.en.html.

Mattoo, A., P. Mishra, and A. Subramanian. 2017. "Beggar-Thy-Neighbor Effects of Exchange Rates: A Study of the Renminbi." *American Economic Journal: Economic Policy* 9, no. 4: 344–66. https://doi.org/10.1257/pol.20150293.

Meltzer, J. 2019. "A WTO Reform Agenda: Data Flows and International Regulatory Cooperation." Brookings Global Economy and Development, Working Paper 130. https://www.brookings.edu/wp-content/uploads/2019/09/WTO-Reform-Agenda_final.pdf.

———. 2020. "Cybersecurity, Digital Trade, and Data Flows: Rethinking a Role for International Trade Rules." Brookings Global Economy and Development, Working Paper 123. https://papers.ssrn.com/sol3/papers.cfm?abstract_id=3595175.

Meltzer, J., and C. Kerry. 2019. "Cybersecurity and Digital Trade: Getting It Right." Brookings Institution. https://www.brookings.edu/research/cybersecurity-and-digital-trade-getting-it-right/.

Miroudot, S. 2021. "Lessons from the Pandemic for Trade Cooperation on Cross-Border Supply Chains." In *Revitalizing Multilateralism: Pragmatic Ideas for the New WTO Director-General*, edited by S. Evenett and R. Baldwin, 141–54. Washington: Center for Economic and Policy Research. http://ciwto.uibe.edu.cn/docs/2021-07/492701afda8648478dc08aca4231d0bb.pdf#page=140.

Mollenkopf, D., S. Peinkofer, and Y. Chu. 2022. "Supply Chain Transparency: Consumer Reactions to Incongruent Signals." *Journal of Operations Management* 68, no. 4: 306–27. https://doi.org/10.1002/joom.1180.

Morcos, P., and C. Wall. 2021. "Invisible and Vital: Undersea Cables and Transatlantic Security." Center for Strategic and International Studies. https://www.csis.org/analysis/invisible-and-vital-undersea-cables-and-transatlantic-security.

National Academies of Sciences, Engineering, and Medicine. 2022. *Building Resilience into the Nation's Medical Product Supply Chains*. Washington: National Academies Press. https://doi.org/10.17226/26420.

National Security Council. 2022. "National Security Strategy." https://www.whitehouse.gov/wp-content/uploads/2022/10/Biden-Harris-Administrations-National-Security-Strategy-10.2022.pdf.

OECD (Organization for Economic Cooperation and Development). 2015. *Digital Security Risk Management for Economic and Social Prosperity: OECD Recommendation and Companion Document*. Paris: OECD Publishing. https://doi.org/10.1787/9789264245471-en.

———. 2020a. "Foreign Direct Investment Flows in the Time of COVID-19." https://read.oecd-ilibrary.org/view/?ref=132_132646-g8as4msdp9&title=Foreign-direct-investment-flows-in-the-time-of-COVID-19.

———. 2020b. "COVID-19 and Global Value Chains: Policy Options to Build More Resilient Production Networks." https://www.oecd.org/coronavirus/policy-responses/covid-19-and-global-value-chains-policy-options-to-build-more-resilient-production-networks-04934ef4/.

———. 2022a. "FDI in Figures." https://www.oecd.org/investment/investment-policy/FDI-in-Figures-October-2022.pdf.

———. 2022b. "International Investment Implications of Russia's War Against Ukraine (Abridged Version)." https://www.oecd.org/ukraine-hub/policy-responses/international-investment-implications-of-russia-s-war-against-ukraine-abridged-version-6224dc77/.

———. 2022c. "Paying the Price of War: OECD Economic Outlook, Interim Report, September 2022." https://www.oecd.org/economic-outlook/september-2022/.

———. 2022d. *Cross-Border Data Flows: Taking Stock of Key Policies and Initiatives*. Paris: OECD Publishing. https://doi.org/10.1787/5031dd97-en.

———. 2023a. "The Impact of Digitalisation on Trade." https://www.oecd.org/trade/topics/digital-trade/.

———. 2023b. "FDI Flows." https://data.oecd.org/fdi/fdi-flows.htm.

Oldenski, L. 2011. "The Task Composition of Offshoring by U.S. Multinationals." Forum for Research in Empirical International Trade Working Paper. https://www.freit.org/WorkingPapers/Papers/ForeignInvestment/FREIT262.pdf.

Pei, J., G. de Vries, and M. Zhang. 2021 "International Trade and COVID-19: City-Level Evidence from China's Lockdown Policy." *Journal of Regional Science* 62, no. 3: 670–95. https://doi.org/10.1111/jors.12559.

Peksen, D. 2019. "When Do Imposed Economic Sanctions Work? A Critical Review of the Sanctions Effectiveness Literature." *Defence and Peace Economics* 30, no. 6: 635–47. https://doi.org/10.1080/10242694.2019.1625250.

Riker, D. 2015. "Export-Intensive Industry Pay More on Average: An Update." U.S. International Trade Commission, Office of Economics, Research Note 2015-04A. https://www.usitc.gov/publications/332/ec201504a.pdf.

Shivakumar, S., C. Wessner, and T. Howell. 2022. "Opportunities and Pitfalls for U.S.-EU Collaboration on Semiconductor Value Chain Resilience." Center for Strategic and International Studies. https://www.csis.org/analysis/opportunities-and-pitfalls-us-eu-collaboration-semiconductor-value-chain-resilience.

Staiger, R. 2021a. *Does Digital Trade Change the Purpose of a Trade Agreement?* NBER Working Paper 29578. Cambridge, MA: National Bureau for Economic Research. https://doi.org/10.3386/w29578.

———. 2021b. *A World Trading System for the Twenty-First Century*. NBER Working Paper 28947. Cambridge, MA: National Bureau for Economic Research. https://doi.org/10.3386/w28947.

Sykes, A. 2015. "The Limited Economic Case for Subsidies Regulation." Stanford Law and Economics, Olin Working Paper 472. https://papers.ssrn.com/sol3/papers.cfm?abstract_id=2531051.

Tai, K. 2021a. "Remarks from Ambassador Katherine Tai on Trade, Policy, the Environment and Climate Change." https://ustr.gov/about-us/policy-offices/press-office/speeches-and-remarks/2021/april/remarks-ambassadaor-katherine-tai-trade-policy-environment-and-climate-change.

———. 2021b. "Remarks of Ambassador Katherine Tai Outlining the Biden-Harris Administration's 'Worker-Centered' Trade Policy." https://ustr.gov/about-us/policy-offices/press-office/speeches-and-remarks/2021/june/remarks-ambassador-katherine-tai-outlining-biden-harris-administrations-worker-centered-trade-policy.

———. 2022. "Statement from Ambassador Katherine Tai on the Announcement of Additional Economic Actions Against Russia." https://ustr.gov/about-us/policy-offices/press-office/press-releases/2022/march/statement-ambassador-katherine-tai-announcement-additional-economic-actions-against-russia.

UNCDF (United Nations Capital Development Fund). 2022. "The Role of Cybersecurity and Data Security in the Digital Economy." https://policyaccelerator.uncdf.org/policy-tools/brief-cybersecurity-digital-economy.

United Nations. 2022. "The Black Sea Grain Initiative: What It Is, and Why It's Important for the World." *UN News*, September 16. https://news.un.org/en/story/2022/09/1126811.

U.S. Census Bureau. 2022. "Quarterly Retail E-Commerce Sales." https://www.census.gov/retail/ecommerce.html.

———. 2023a. "Country and Product Trade Data." https://www.census.gov/foreign-trade/statistics/country/index.html.

———. 2023b. "U.S. International Trade in Goods and Services, December and Annual 2022." https://www.census.gov/foreign-trade/Press-Release/ft900/ft900_2212.pdf.

U.S. Department of Commerce. 2021. "Jobs Supported by U.S. Exports." https://www.trade.gov/data-visualization/jobs-supported-us-exports.

———. 2022. "Commerce Department Expands Restrictions on Exports to Russia and Belarus in Response to Ongoing Aggression in Ukraine." https://www.

commerce.gov/news/press-releases/2022/04/commerce-department-expands-restrictions-exports-russia-and-belarus.

U.S. Department of State. 2022a. "The Passage of the CHIPS and Science Act of 2022." https://www.state.gov/the-passage-of-the-chips-and-science-act-of-2022/.

———. 2022b. "Fact Sheet: The Impact of Sanctions and Export Controls on the Russian Federation." https://www.state.gov/the-impact-of-sanctions-and-export-controls-on-the-russian-federation/.

———. 2022c. "United States Takes Next Step in Supporting Innovative Clean Nuclear Technology in Europe." https://www.state.gov/united-states-takes-next-step-in-supporting-innovative-clean-nuclear-technology-in-europe/.

———. 2022d. "Special Presidential Envoy for Climate Kerry and Ukraine Minster of Energy Galushchenko Announce Cooperation on a Clean Fuels from Small Modular Reactors Pilot, COP27 Climate Conference." https://www.state.gov/special-presidential-envoy-for-climate-kerry-and-ukraine-minister-of-energy-galushchenko-announce-cooperation-on-a-clean-fuels-from-small-modular-reactors-pilot-cop27-climate-conference/.

U.S. Department of the Treasury. 2022a. "Updates Related to Price Cap on Russian Oil." https://home.treasury.gov/policy-issues/financial-sanctions/recent-actions/20220902_33.

———. 2022b. "Fact Sheet: Limiting Kremlin Revenues and Stabilizing Global Energy Supply with a Price Cap on Russian Oil." https://home.treasury.gov/news/press-releases/jy1141.

———. 2022c. "OFAC Food Security Fact Sheet: Russia Sanctions and Agricultural Trade." https://home.treasury.gov/system/files/126/russia_fact_sheet_20220714.pdf.

USTR (Office of the U.S. Trade Representative). 2021. "Joint Statement on the Results of the Council Meeting of the U.S.–Central Asia Trade and Investment Framework Agreement (TIFA)." https://ustr.gov/about-us/policy-offices/press-office/press-releases/2021/march/joint-statement-results-council-meeting-us-central-asia-trade-and-investment-framework-agreement.

———. 2022a. "Joint Statement on the U.S./U.K. Dialogues on the Future of Atlantic Trade." https://ustr.gov/about-us/policy-offices/press-office/press-releases/2022/march/joint-statement-usuk-dialogues-future-atlantic-trade.

———. 2022b. "Ministerial Text for the Trade Pillar of the Indo-Pacific Economic Framework for Prosperity." https://ustr.gov/sites/default/files/2022-09/IPEF%20Pillar%201%20Ministerial%20Text%20(Trade%20Pillar)_FOR%20PUBLIC%20RELEASE%20(1).pdf.

———. 2022c. "United States and Kenya Announce the Launch of the U.S.–Kenya Strategic Trade and Investment Partnership." https://ustr.gov/about-us/policy-offices/press-office/press-releases/2022/july/united-states-and-kenya-announce-launch-us-kenya-strategic-trade-and-investment-partnership.

———. 2022d. "United States and Taiwan Commence Formal Negotiations on U.S.–Taiwan Initiative on 21st Century Trade." https://ustr.gov/about-us/

policy-offices/press-office/press-releases/2022/august/united-states-and-taiwan-commence-formal-negotiations-us-taiwan-initiative-21st-century-trade.

———. 2022e. "2022 Trade Policy Agenda and 2021 Annual Report of the President of the United States on the Trade Agreements Program." https://ustr.gov/sites/default/files/2022%20Trade%20Policy%20Agenda%20and%202021%20Annual%20Report%20(1).pdf.

Valero, P. 2016. "This Is Why We Should Care About the Free Flow of Data Between Countries." World Economic Forum. https://www.weforum.org/agenda/2016/07/free-flow-of-data-between-countries/.

Wharton School. 2019. "Your Data Is Shared and Sold; . . . What's Being Done About It?" Knowledge at Wharton, October 28. https://knowledge.wharton.upenn.edu/article/data-shared-sold-whats-done/.

White House. 2021a. "Executive Order on America's Supply Chains." https://www.whitehouse.gov/briefing-room/presidential-actions/2021/02/24/executive-order-on-americas-supply-chains/.

———. 2021b. "Fact Sheet: Prioritizing Climate in Foreign Policy and National Security." https://www.whitehouse.gov/briefing-room/statements-releases/2021/10/21/fact-sheet-prioritizing-climate-in-foreign-policy-and-national-security/.

———. 2022a. "Fact Sheet: President Biden and G7 Leaders Formally Launch the Partnership for Global Infrastructure and Investment." https://www.whitehouse.gov/briefing-room/statements-releases/2022/06/26/fact-sheet-president-biden-and-g7-leaders-formally-launch-the-partnership-for-global-infrastructure-and-investment/.

———. 2022b. "Fact Sheet: In Asia, President Biden and a Dozen Indo-Pacific Partners Launch the Indo-Pacific Economic Framework for Prosperity." https://www.whitehouse.gov/briefing-room/statements-releases/2022/05/23/fact-sheet-in-asia-president-biden-and-a-dozen-indo-pacific-partners-launch-the-indo-pacific-economic-framework-for-prosperity/.

———. 2022c. "Joint Readout of U.S.-EU Task Force Meeting on Energy Security." https://www.whitehouse.gov/briefing-room/statements-releases/2022/11/07/joint-readout-of-u-s-eu-task-force-meeting-on-energy-security/.

———. 2022d. "Joint Statement between the United States and the European Commission on European Energy Security." https://www.whitehouse.gov/briefing-room/statements-releases/2022/03/25/joint-statement-between-the-united-states-and-the-european-commission-on-european-energy-security/.

———. 2022e. "A Declaration for the Future of the Internet." https://www.whitehouse.gov/wp-content/uploads/2022/04/Declaration-for-the-Future-for-the-Internet_Launch-Event-Signing-Version_FINAL.pdf

———. 2022f. "Fact Sheet: President Biden Announces the Americas Partnership for Economic Prosperity." https://www.whitehouse.gov/briefing-room/statements-releases/2022/06/08/fact-sheet-president-biden-announces-the-americas-partnership-for-economic-prosperity/.

World Bank. 2020. *World Development Report 2020: Trading for Development in the Age of Global Value Chains*. Washington: World Bank. https://doi.org/10.1596/978-1-4648-1457-0.

World Economic Forum. 2020. "A Roadmap for Cross-Border Data Flows: Future-Proofing Readiness and Cooperation in the New Data Economy." https://www3.weforum.org/docs/WEF_A_Roadmap_for_Cross_Border_Data_Flows_2020.pdf.

WTO (World Trade Organization). 2022. "The Carbon Content of International Trade." Trade and Climate Change, Information Brief 4. https://www.wto.org/english/news_e/news21_e/clim_03nov21-4_e.pdf.

Yale School of Public Health, Humanitarian Research Lab. 2022. "Ukraine's Crop Storage Infrastructure: Post-Invasion Impact Assessment." *Conflict Observatory*, September 15. https://hub.conflictobservatory.org/portal/apps/sites/#/home/pages/grain-1.

Yellen, J. 2022a. "Remarks by Secretary of the Treasury Janet L. Yellen on Way Forward for the Global Economy." Transcript of speech delivered to Atlantic Council, Washington, April 13. https://home.treasury.gov/news/press-releases/jy0714.

———. 2022b. "Remarks by Secretary of the Treasury Janet L. Yellen at LG Sciencepark." Transcript of speech delivered at LG Sciencepark, Seoul, July 19. https://home.treasury.gov/news/press-releases/jy0880.

Chapter 4

Aizer, A., H. Hoynes, and A. Lleras-Muney. 2022. "Children and the U.S. Social Safety Net: Balancing Disincentives for Adults and Benefits for Children." *Journal of Economic Perspectives* 36, no. 2: 149–74. https://www.aeaweb.org/articles?id=10.1257/jep.36.2.149.

Alaimo, K., C. Olson, and E. Frongillo Jr. 2001. "Food Insufficiency and American School-Aged Children's Cognitive, Academic, and Psychosocial Development." *Pediatrics* 108, no. 1: 44–53. https://doi.org/10.1542/peds.108.1.44.

Almond, D., H. Hoynes, and D. Schanzenbach. 2011. "Inside the War on Poverty: The Impact of Food Stamps on Birth Outcomes." *Review of Economics and Statistics* 93, no. 2: 387–403. https://doi.org/10.1162/REST_a_00089.

Asiedu, E., J. Freeman, and A. Nti-Addae. 2012. "Access to Credit by Small Businesses: How Relevant Are Race, Ethnicity, and Gender." *American Economic Review* 102, no. 3: 532–37. https://doi.org/10.1257/aer.102.3.532.

Athey, S., R. Chetty, G. Imbens, and H. Kang. 2019. *The Surrogate Index: Combining Short- Term Proxies to Estimate Long-Term Treatment Effects More Rapidly and Precisely*. NBER Working Paper 26463. Cambridge, MA: National Bureau of Economic Research. https://www.nber.org/papers/w26463.

Bailey, M., H. Hoynes, M. Rossin-Slater, and R. Walker. 2020. *Is the Social Safety Net a Long-Term Investment? Large-Scale Evidence from the Food Stamps Program.* NBER Working Paper 26942. Cambridge, MA: National Bureau of Economic Research. https://www.nber.org/papers/w26942.

Bailey, M., S. Sun, and B. Timpe. 2021. "Prep School for Poor Kids: The Long-Run Impacts of Head Start on Human Capital and Economic Self-Sufficiency." *American Economic Review* 111, no. 12: 3963–4001. https://doi.org/10.1257/aer.20181801.

Baker, M., J. Gruber, and K. Milligan. 2008. "Universal Child Care, Maternal Labor Supply, and Family Well Being." *Journal of Political Economy* 116, no. 4: 709–45. https://www.journals.uchicago.edu/doi/abs/10.1086/591908.

Banerjee, A., E. Gould, and M. Sawo. 2021. "Setting Higher Wages for Child Care and Home Health Care Workers Is Long Overdue." Economic Policy Institute. https://files.epi.org/uploads/237703.pdf.

Barr, A., and C. Gibbs. 2022. "Breaking the Cycle? Intergenerational Effects of an Antipoverty Program in Early Childhood." *Journal of Political Economy* 130, no. 12: 3253–85. https://doi.org/10.1086/720764.

Bassok, D., T. Dee, and S. Latham. 2019. "The Effects of Accountability Incentives in Early Childhood Education." *Journal of Policy Analysis and Management* 38, no. 4: 838–66. https://onlinelibrary.wiley.com/doi/10.1002/pam.22149.

Bassok, D., J. Doromal, M. Michie, and V. Wong, 2021b. "The Effects of Financial Incentives on Teacher Turnover in Early Childhood Settings: Experimental Evidence from Virginia." University of Virginia EdPolicyWorks. https://files.elfsightcdn.com/022b8cb9-839c-4bc2-992e-cefccb8e877e/6de6fd54-e921-4c88-a452-ad7cabccc362.pdf.

Bassok, D., M. Fitzpatrick, E. Greenberg, and S. Loeb. 2016. "Within- and Between-Sector Quality Differences in Early Childhood Education and Care." *Child Development* 87, no. 5. https://doi.org/10.1111/cdev.12551.

Bassok, D., A. Markowitz, L. Bellows, and K. Sadowski. 2021a. "New Evidence on Teacher Turnover in Early Childhood." *Educational Evaluation and Policy Analysis* 43, no. 1: 172–80. https://doi.org/10.3102/0162373720985340.

Bauernschuster, S., and M. Schlotter. 2015. "Public Child Care and Mothers' Labor Supply: Evidence from Two Quasi-Expirements." *Journal of Public Economics* 123: 1–16. https://doi.org/10.1016/j.jpubeco.2014.12.013.

Bhattacharya, J., J. Currie, and S. Haider. 2006. "Breakfast of Champions? The School Breakfast Program and the Nutrition of Children and Families." *Journal of Human Resources* 41, no. 3: 445–66. http://jhr.uwpress.org/content/XLI/3/445.short.

Bigelow, J., A. Pennington, K. Schaberg, and D. Jones. 2021. "A Guide for Using Administrative Data to Examine Long-Term Outcomes in Program Evaluation." OPRE Report 145. https://www.acf.hhs.gov/sites/default/files/documents/opre/T2P%20Guide_sept-2021.pdf.

Blau, D. 1993. "The Supply of Child Care Labor." *Journal of Labor Economics* 11, no. 2: 324–47. https://www.journals.uchicago.edu/doi/abs/10.1086/298299.

Blau, D., and J. Currie. 2006. "Pre-School, Day Care, and After-School Care: Who's Minding the Kids?" *Handbook of the Economics of Education* 2: 1163–1278. https://doi.org/10.1016/S1574-0692(06)02020-4.

Blau, D., and E. Tekin. 2007. "The Determinants and Consequences of Child Care Subsidies for Single Mothers in the USA." *Journal of Population Economics* 20: 719–41. https://doi.org/10.1007/s00148-005-0022-2.

Blau, F., and L. Kahn. 2013. "Female Labor Supply: Why Is the United States Falling Behind?" *American Economic Review* 103, no. 3: 251–56. https://www.aeaweb.org/articles?id=10.1257/aer.103.3.251.

BLS (U.S. Bureau of Labor Statistics). 2021a. "Occupational Employment and Wage Statistics." https://www.bls.gov/oes/current/oes_stru.htm.

———. 2021b. "National Compensation Survey: Employee Benefits in the United States." https://www.bls.gov/ebs/home.htm.

———. 2022. "Table 4: Families with Own Children: Employment Status of Parents by Age of Youngest Child and Family Type, 2020–2021 Annual Averages." https://www.bls.gov/news.release/famee.t04.htm.

———. 2023. "Table B-8: Average Hourly and Weekly Earnings of Production and Nonsupervisory Employees on Private Nonfarm Payrolls by Industry Sector, Seasonally Adjusted." https://www.bls.gov/news.release/empsit.t24.htm.

Bodéré, P. 2023. "Dynamic Spatial Competition in Early Education: An Equilibrium Analysis of the Preschool Market in Pennsylvania." Working paper, New York University, Department of Economics. https://pierrebodere.github.io/content/bodere_jmp.pdf.

Boesch, T., R. Grunewald, R. Nunn, and V. Palmer. 2021. "Pandemic Pushes Mother of Young Children Out of the Labor Force." Federal Reserve Bank of Minneapolis. https://www.minneapolisfed.org/article/2021/pandemic-pushes-mothers-of-young-children-out-of-the-labor-force .

Borowsky, J., J. Brown, E. Davis, C. Gibbs, C. Herbst, A. Sojourner, E. Tekin, and M. Wiswall. 2022. An *Equilibrium Model of the Impact of Increased Public Investment in Early Childhood Education.* NBER Working Paper 30140. Cambridge, MA: National Bureau of Economic Research. https://doi.org/10.3386/w30140.

Bradley, V., S. Kuriwaki, M. Isakov, D. Sejdinovic, X. Meng, and S. Flaxman. 2021. "Unrepresentative Big Surveys Significantly Overestimated U.S. Vaccine Uptake." *Nature* 600: 695–700. https://www.nature.com/articles/s41586-021-04198-4?s=03.

Brown, J., and C. Herbst. 2022. "Childcare over the Business Cycle." *Journal of Labor Economics* 40, no. 1: 429–68. https://www.journals.uchicago.edu/doi/full/10.1086/718189 .

Burnham, L., and N. Theodore. 2012. "Home Economics: The Invisible and Unregulated World of Domestic Work." National Domestic Workers Alliance. https://www.domesticworkers.org/reports-and-publications/home-economics-the-invisible-and-unregulated-world-of-domestic-work/.

Cajner, T., L. Feiveson, C. Kurz, and S. Tevlin. 2022. "Lessons Learned from the Use of Nontraditional Data during COVID-19." Hamilton Project and Hutchins Center on Fiscal & Monetary Policy at Brookings. https://www.hamiltonproject.org/assets/files/Lessons_Learned_from_the_Use_of_Nontraditional_Data_during_COVID-19.pdf.

Campbell, F., G. Conti, J. Heckman, S. Moon, R. Pinto, E. Pungello, and Y. Pan. 2014. "Early Childhood Investments Substantially Boost Adult Health." *Science* 343, no. 6178: 4178–85. https://doi.org/10.1126/science.1248429.

Cannon, J., G. Zellman, L. Karoly, and H. Schwartz. 2017. *Quality Rating and Improvement Systems for Early Care and Education Programs: Making the Second Generation Better*. Santa Monica, CA: RAND Corporation. https://doi.org/10.7249/PE235.

Carson, J., and M. Mattingly. 2020. "COVID-19 Didn't Create a Child Care Crisis, but Hastened and Inflamed It." Federal Reserve Bank of Boston and Carsey School of Public Policy. https://carsey.unh.edu/publication/child-care-crisis-COVID-19.

Cascio, E. 2009. "Maternal Labor Supply and the Introduction of Kindergartens into American Public Schools." *Journal of Human Resources* 44, no. 1: 140–70. https://doi.org/10.3368/jhr.44.1.140.

Cascio, E., and D. Schanzenbach. 2013. "The Impacts of Expanding Access to High-Quality Preschool Education." Brookings Institution. https://www.brookings.edu/bpea-articles/the-impacts-of-expanding-access-to-high-quality-preschool-education/.

Caven, M., N. Khanani, X. Zhang, and C. Parker. 2021. "Center- and Program-Level Factors Associated with Turnover in the Early Childhood Education Workforce." U.S. Department of Education, Institute of Education Sciences, National Center for Education Evaluation and Regional Assistance. https://ies.ed.gov/ncee/edlabs/regions/northeast/pdf/REL_2021069.pdf.

Center for American Progress. 2020. "U.S. Child Care Deserts." https://childcaredeserts.org/.

Chetty, R., J. Friedman, N. Hilger, E. Saez, D. Schanzenbach, and D. Yagan. 2011. "How Does Your Kindergarten Classroom Affect Your Earnings? Evidence from Project Star." *Quarterly Journal of Economics* 126, no. 4: 1593–1660. https://doi.org/10.1093/qje/qjr041.

Chien, N. 2022. "Factsheet: Estimates of Child Care Eligibility & Receipt for Fiscal Year 2019." Office of the Assistant Secretary for Planning and Evaluation, U.S. Department of Health and Human Services. https://aspe.hhs.gov/sites/default/files/documents/1d276a590ac166214a5415bee430d5e9/cy2019-child-care-subsidy-eligibility.pdf.

Child Care Aware of America. 2022. "State Session Round Up, Summer 2022." https://info.childcareaware.org/blog/state-session-round-up-summer-2022.

Collins, C., L. Landivar, L. Ruppanner, and W. Scarborough. 2021. "COVID-19 and the Gender Gap in Work Hours." *Gender Work Organ* 28: 549–60. https://onlinelibrary.wiley.com/doi/full/10.1111/gwao.12506.

Davis, E., C. Carlin, C. Krafft, and N. Forry. 2018. "Do Child Care Subsidies Increase Employment Among Low-Income Parents?" *Journal of Family and Economic Issues* 39: 662–82. https://doi.org/10.1007/s10834-018-9582-7.

Davis, E., and A. Sojourner. 2021. "Increasing Federal Investment in Children's Early Care and Education to Raise Quality, Access, and Affordability." Brookings Institution. https://www.brookings.edu/research/increasing-federal-investment-in-childrens-early-care-and-education-to-raise-quality-access-and-affordability/.

de Brey, C., L. Musu, J. McFarland, S. Wilkinson-Flicker, M. Diliberti, A. Zhang, C. Branstetter, and X. Wang. 2019. "Status and Trends in the Education of Racial and Ethnic Groups 2018." U.S. Department of Education, NCES 2019-038. https://nces.ed.gov/pubs2019/2019038.pdf.

Deming, D. 2009. "Early Childhood Intervention and Life-Cycle Skill Development: Evidence from Head Start." *American Economic Journal: Applied Economics* 1, no. 3: 111–34. https://doi.org/10.1257/app.1.3.111.

Doromal, J., D. Bassok, L. Bellows, and A. Markowitz. 2022. "Hard-to-Staff Centers: Exploring Center-Level Variation in the Persistence of Child Care Teacher Turnover." *Early Childhood Research Quarterly* 61: 170–78. https://doi.org/10.1016/j.ecresq.2022.07.007.

Duncan, G., and K. Magnuson. 2013. "Investing in Preschool Programs." *Journal of Economic Perspectives* 27, no. 2: 109–32. http://dx.doi.org/10.1257/jep.27.2.109.

ECLKC (Early Childhood Learning & Knowledge Center). 2022. "Head Start Program Facts: Fiscal Year 2021." https://eclkc.ohs.acf.hhs.gov/about-us/article/head-start-program-facts-fiscal-year-2021.

———. 2019. "Head Start Timeline." https://eclkc.ohs.acf.hhs.gov/about-us/article/head-start-timeline.

Finseraas, H., I. Hardoy, and P. Schøne. 2016. "School Enrolment and Mothers' Labor Supply: Evidence from a Regression Discontinuity Approach." *Review of Economics of the Household* 15: 621–38. https://doi.org/10.1007/s11150-016-9350-0.

Fitzpatrick, M. 2010. "Preschoolers Enrolled and Mothers at Work? The Effects of Universal Prekindergarten." *Journal of Labor Economics* 28, no. 1: 51–85. https://www.journals.uchicago.edu/doi/full/10.1086/648666#_i2.

———. 2012. "Revising Our Thinking About the Relationship Between Maternal Labor Supply and Preschool." *Journal of Human Resources* 47, no. 3: 583–612. https://doi.org/10.3368/jhr.47.3.583.

Flood, S., J. McMurry, A. Sojourner, and M. Wiswall. 2022. "Inequality in Early Care Experienced by U.S. Children." *Journal of Economic Perspectives* 36, no. 2: 199–222. https://doi.org/10.1257/jep.36.2.199.

Frisvold, D. 2015. "Nutrition and Cognitive Achievement: An Evaluation of the School Breakfast Program." *Journal of Public Economics* 124: 91–204. https://doi.org/10.1016/j.jpubeco.2014.12.003.

García, J., F. Bennhoff, D. Leaf, and J. Heckman. 2021. *The Dynastic Benefits of Early Childhood Education.* NBER Working Paper 29004. Cambridge, MA: National Bureau of Economic Research. https://doi.org/10.3386/w29004.

García, J., J. Heckman, D. Leaf, and M. Prados. 2020. "Quantifying the Life-Cycle Benefits of an Influential Early-Childhood Program." *Journal of Political Economy* 128, no. 7: 2502–41. https://doi.org/10.1086/705718.

García, J., J. Heckman, and V. Ronda. 2021. *The Lasting Effects of Early Childhood Education on Promoting the Skills and Social Mobility of Disadvantaged African Americans.* NBER Working Paper 29057. Cambridge, MA: National Bureau of Economic Research. https://doi.org/10.3386/w29057.

Gelbach, J. 2002. "Public Schooling for Young Children and Maternal Labor Supply." *American Economic Review* 92, no. 1: 307–22. https://www.jstor.org/stable/3083335.

Ghertner, R., and A. Schreier. 2022. "*Young Children's Geographic Access to Head Start Preschool, 2022.*" Office of the Assistant Secretary for Planning and Evaluation, U.S. Department of Health and Human Services. https://aspe.hhs.gov/sites/default/files/documents/73453cd79dfe28592a0396ca2a0c75ee/Geographic-Access-Head-Start-Brief.pdf.

Glenn, E. 2012. *Forced to Care: Coercion and Caregiving in America.* Cambridge, MA: Harvard University Press. https://www.hup.harvard.edu/catalog.php?isbn=9780674064157.

Goldstein, D. 2022. "With Child Care Scarce, States Try to Fix 'a Broken Market.'" *New York Times*, June 18. https://www.nytimes.com/2022/06/18/us/child-care-state-regulations.html.

Gould, E. 2015. "Child Care Workers Aren't Paid Enough to Make Ends Meet." Economic Policy Institute. https://www.epi.org/publication/child-care-workers-arent-paid-enough-to-make-ends-meet/.

Gould, E., M. Sawo, and A. Banerjee. 2021. "Care Workers Are Deeply Undervalued and Underpaid." Economic Policy Institute, Working Economics Blog. https://www.epi.org/blog/care-workers-are-deeply-undervalued-and-underpaid-estimating-fair-and-equitable-wages-in-the-care-sectors/.

Gray-Lobe, G., P. Pathak, and C. Walters. 2023. "The Long-Term Effects of Universal Preschool in Boston." *Quarterly Journal of Economics* 138, no. 1: 363–411. https://doi.org/10.1093/qje/qjac036.

Grunewald, R., and P. Davies. 2011. "Hardly Child's Play: Times Have Been Even Tougher than Usual for District Childcare Providers." Federal Reserve Bank of Minneapolis. https://www.minneapolisfed.org/article/2011/hardly-childs-play.

Grunewald, R., R. Nunn, and V. Palmer. 2022. "Examining Teacher Turnover in Early Care and Education." Federal Reserve Bank of Minneapolis. https://www.minneapolisfed.org/article/2022/examining-teacher-turnover-in-early-care-and-education.

Gundersen, C., B. Kreider, and J. Pepper. 2012. "The Impact of the National School Lunch Program on Child Health: A Nonparametric Bounds Analysis." *Journal of Econometrics* 166, no. 1: 79–91. https://doi.org/10.1016/j.jeconom.2011.06.007.

Hatfield, B., M. Burchinal, R. Pianta, and J. Sideris. 2016. "Thresholds in the Association Between Quality of Teacher–Child Interactions and Preschool Children's School Readiness Skills." *Early Childhood Research Quarterly* 36: 561–71. https://www.sciencedirect.com/science/article/abs/pii/S0885200615300053.

Heckman, J. 2008. "Schools, Skills, and Synapses." *Economic Inquiry* 46, no. 3: 289–324. https://doi.org/10.1111/j.1465-7295.2008.00163.x.

Heckman, J., and T. Kautz. 2014. "Fostering and Measuring Skills Interventions that Improve Character and Cognition." In *The Myth of Achievement Tests: The GED and the Role of Character in American Life*, edited by J. Heckman, J. Humphries, and T. Kautz. Chicago: University of Chicago Press. https://doi.org/10.7208/chicago/9780226100128.003.0009.

Heckman, J., and D. Masterov. 2007. "The Productivity Argument for Investing in Young Children." Review of Agricultural Economics 29, no. 3: 446–93. https://doi.org/10.1111/j.1467-9353.2007.00359.x.

Heckman, J., S. Moon, R. Pinto, P. Savelyev, and A. Yavitz. 2010. "The Rate of Return to the HighScope Perry Preschool Program." *Journal of Public Economics* 94, no. 1: 114–28. https://doi.org/10.1016/j.jpubeco.2009.11.001.

Heflin, C., I. Arteaga, and S. Gable. 2015. "The Child and Adult Care Food Program and Food Insecurity." *Social Service Review* 89, no. 1: 77–98. https://www.journals.uchicago.edu/doi/abs/10.1086/679760.

Heggeness, M. 2020. "Estimating the Immediate Impact of the COVID-19 Shock on Parental Attachment to the Labor Market and the Double Bind of Mothers." *Review of Economics of the Household* 18: 1053–78. https://link.springer.com/article/10.1007/s11150-020-09514-x.

Hendren, N., and B. Sprung-Keyser. 2020. "A Unified Welfare Analysis of Government Policies." *Quarterly Journal of Economics* 135, no. 3: 1209–1318. https://doi.org/10.1093/qje/qjaa006.

Herbst, C. 2017. "Universal Child Care, Maternal Employment, and Children's Long-Run Outcomes: Evidence from the U.S. Lanham Act of 1940." *Journal of Labor Economics* 35, no. 2. https://doi.org/10.1086/689478.

———. 2022. "Child Care in the United States: Markets, Policy, and Evidence." *Journal of Policy Analysis and Management*. https://doi.org/10.1002/pam.22436.

Herbst, C., and E. Tekin, 2011. "Do Child Care Subsidies Influence Single Mothers' Decision to Invest in Human Capital?" *Economics of Education Review* 30, no. 5: 901–12. https://doi.org/10.1016/j.econedurev.2011.03.006.

Hinrichs, P. 2010. "The Effects of the National School Lunch Program on Education and Health." *Journal of Policy Analysis and Management* 29, no. 3: 479–505. https://doi.org/10.1002/pam.20506.

Hoynes, H., M. Page, and A. Stevens. 2011. "Can Targeted Transfers Improve Birth Outcomes? Evidence from the Introduction of the WIC Program." *Journal of Public Economics* 95, nos. 7–8: 813–27. https://doi.org/10.1016/j.jpubeco.2010.12.006.

Hoynes, H., D. Schanzenbach, and D. Almond. 2016. "Long-Run Impacts of Childhood Access to the Safety Net." *American Economic Review* 106, no. 4: 903–34. https://www.aeaweb.org/articles?id=10.1257/aer.20130375.

Imberman, S., and A. Kugler. 2014. "The Effect of Providing Breakfast in Class on Student Performance." *Journal of Policy Analysis and Management* 33, no. 3: 669–99. https://doi.org/10.1002/pam.21759.

IRS (Internal Revenue Service). 2022. "Child and Dependent Care Credit FAQs." https://www.irs.gov/newsroom/child-and-dependent-care-credit-faqs.

Jessen-Howard, S., R. Malik, and M. Falgout. 2020. "Costly and Unavailable: America Lacks Sufficient Child Care Supply for Infants and Toddlers." Center for American Progress. https://www.americanprogress.org/article/costly-unavailable-america-lacks-sufficient-child-care-supply-infants-toddlers/.

Johnson, R., and C. Jackson. 2019. "Reducing Inequality through Dynamic Complementarity: Evidence from Head Start and Public School Spending." *American Economic Journal: Economic Policy* 11, no. 4: 310–49. https://doi.org/10.1257/pol.20180510.

King, E., A. Johnson, D. Cassidy, Y. Wang, J. Lower, and V. Kintner-Duffy. 2016. "Preschool Teachers' Financial Well-Being and Work Time Supports: Associations with Children's Emotional Expressions and Behaviors in Classrooms." *Early Childhood Education Journal* 44: 545–53. https://link.springer.com/article/10.1007/s10643-015-0744-z.

Knudsen, E., J. Heckman, J. Cameron, and J. Shonkoff. 2006. "Economic, Neurobiological, and Behavioral Perspectives on Building America's Future Workforce." *Proceedings of the National Academy of Sciences* 103, no. 27: 10155–62. https://doi.org/10.1073/pnas.0600888103.

Korenman, S., K. Abner, R. Kaestner, and R. Gordon. 2013. "The Child and Adult Care Food Program and the Nutrition of Preschoolers." *Early Childhood Research Quarterly* 28, no. 2: 325–36. https://doi.org/10.1016/j.ecresq.2012.07.007.

Landivar, L., N. Graf, and G. Rayo. 2023. "Childcare Prices in Local Areas: Initial Findings from the National Database of Childcare Prices." U.S. Department of

Labor, Women's Bureau Issue Brief. https://www.dol.gov/sites/dolgov/files/WB/NDCP/WB_IssueBrief-NDCP-final.pdf.

Lefebvre, P., and P. Merrigan. 2008. "Child Care Policy and the Labor Supply of Mothers with Young Children: A Natural Experiment from Canada." *Journal of Labor Economics* 26, no. 3: 519–48. https://doi.org/10.1086/587760.

Livingston, G. 2018. "Stay-at-Home Moms and Dads Account for About One-in-Five U.S. Parents." Pew Research Center. https://www.pewresearch.org/fact-tank/2018/09/24/stay-at-home-moms-and-dads-account-for-about-one-in-five-u-s-parents/.

Malik, R., K. Hamm, L. Schochet, C. Novoa, S. Workman, and S. Jessen-Howard. 2018. "America's Child Care Deserts in 2018." Center for American Progress. https://www.americanprogress.org/article/americas-child-care-deserts-2018/.

Mocan, N. 2007. "Can Consumers Detect Lemons? An Empirical Analysis of Information Asymmetry in the Market for Child Care." *Journal of Population Economics* 20: 743–80. http://www.jstor.org/stable/40344407.

Moloney, M. 2021. "Ireland's Reform Agenda: Transforming the Early Childhood Education and Care Sector into One of the Best in the World." *International Perspectives on Early Childhood Teacher Education in the 21st Century*, 93–109. https://doi.org/10.1007/978-981-16-5739-9_7.

Morrissey, T. 2017. "Child Care and Parent Labor Force Participation: A Review of the Research Literature." *Review of Economics of the Household* 15: 1–24. https://doi.org/10.1007/s11150-016-9331-3.

Mueller, E. 2020. "'Crashing Down': How the Child Care Crisis Is Magnifying Racial Disparities." *Politico*. https://www.politico.com/news/2020/07/22/coronavirus-child-care-racial-disparities-377058.

National Household Education Surveys Program. 2019. "Young Children's Care and Education Before Kindergarten." National Center for Education Statistics. https://nces.ed.gov/nhes/young_children.asp.

National Women's Business Council. 2020. "Annual Report 2020." https://cdn.www.nwbc.gov/wp-content/uploads/2020/12/21113833/pdf/NWBC-2020-Annual-Report-Final.pdf.

National Women's Law Center. 2018. "Family, Friend, and Neighbor Care: Facts and Figures." https://d3n8a8pro7vhmx.cloudfront.net/rrnetwork/pages/103/attachments/original/1522790259/family_friend___neighbor_care_fact_sheet-final.pdf?1522790259.

NCES (National Center for Education Statistics). 2016. "Teacher Turnover: Stayers, Movers, and Leavers." Condition of Education, U.S. Department of Education, Institute of Education Sciences. https://nces.ed.gov/programs/coe/pdf/coe_slc.pdf.

———. 2018. "Early Childhood Care Arrangements: Choices and Costs." Condition of Education, U.S. Department of Education, Institute of Education Sciences. https://nces.ed.gov/programs/coe/indicator/tca.

———. 2022. "Enrollment Rates of Young Children." Condition of Education, U.S. Department of Education, Institute of Education Sciences. https://nces.ed.gov/programs/coe/indicator/cfa.

NSECE (National Survey of Early Care and Education). 2019. "Home-Based Public-Use Data File." https://www.childandfamilydataarchive.org/cfda/archives/cfda/studies/37941/datadocumentation.

———. 2020. "National Survey of Early Care and Education 2019: Household Questionnaire." https://www.acf.hhs.gov/opre/report/national-survey-early-care-and-education-2019-household-questionnaire.

OECD (Organization for Economic Cooperation and Development). 2011. "Encouraging Quality in Early Childhood Education and Care." OECD Network on Early Childhood Education and Care, Survey for the Quality Toolbox and ECE Portal. https://www.oecd.org/education/school/48483436.pdf.

———. 2016. "Parental Leave: Where Are the Fathers?" https://www.oecd.org/policy-briefs/parental-leave-where-are-the-fathers.pdf.

———. 2019. "Education at a Glance 2019: OECD Indicators." https://www.oecd-ilibrary.org/sites/f8d7880d-en/1/2/3/2/index.html?itemId=/content/publication/f8d7880d-en&mimeType=text/html&_csp_=b2d87f13821f45339443c7ca94aafe46&itemIGO=oecd&itemContentType=book.

———. 2021. "Public Spending on Childcare and Early Education?" https://www.oecd.org/els/soc/PF3_1_Public_spending_on_childcare_and_early_education.pdf.

———. No date. "OECD.stat Enrollment Rates by Age." https://stats.oecd.org/Index.aspx?datasetcode=EAG_ENRL_RATE_AGE.

Office of Child Care. 2011. "A Foundation for Quality Improvement Systems: State Licensing, Preschool, and QRIS Program Quality Standards." U.S. Department of Health and Human Services, Administration for Children and Families. https://childcareta.acf.hhs.gov/sites/default/files/public/a_foundation_for_quality.pdf.

———. 2022. "Child Care and Development Fund Reauthorization." U.S. Department of Health and Human Services, Administration for Children and Families. https://www.acf.hhs.gov/occ/ccdf-reauthorization.

———. No date. "Ratios and Group Sizes." U.S. Department of Health and Human Services, Administration for Children and Families. https://childcare.gov/consumer-education/ratios-and-group-sizes.

Office of Early Childhood Development. 2022. "Preschool Development Birth through Five (PDG B–5)." https://www.acf.hhs.gov/ecd/early-learning/preschool-development-grants.

OESE (Office of Elementary and Secondary Education). 2023. "Preschool Development Grant–Birth through Five." https://oese.ed.gov/offices/office-of-discretionary-grants-support-services/innovation-early-learning/preschool-development-grants/.

Olivetti, C., and B. Petrongolo. 2017. "The Economic Consequences of Family Policies: Lessons from a Century of Legislation in High-Income Countries." *Journal of Economic Perspectives* 31, no. 1: 205–50. https://pubs.aeaweb.org/doi/pdfplus/10.1257/jep.31.1.205.

Parker, M. 2015. "Women More Than Men Adjust Their Careers for Family Life." Pew Research Center. https://www.pewresearch.org/fact-tank/2015/10/01/women-more-than-men-adjust-their-careers-for-family-life/.

Pew Research Center. 2022. "Working Mothers Are More Likely Than Working Fathers to Say They Felt Like They Could Not Give 100% At Work, Needed to Reduce Their Hours During the Pandemic." https://www.pewresearch.org/fact-tank/2022/05/06/working-moms-in-the-u-s-have-faced-challenges-on-multiple-fronts-during-the-pandemic/ft_2021-01-26_workingparents_04-2/.

Pianta, R. 1997. "Adult–Child Relationship Processes and Early Schooling." *Early Education and Development* 8, no. 1: 11–26. https://doi.org/10.1207/s15566935eed0801_2.

Porter, T., D. Paulsell, P. Del Grosso, S. Avellar, R. Hass, and L. Vuong. 2010. *A Review of the Literature on Home-Based Child Care: Implications for Future Directions*. Princeton, NJ: Mathematica Policy Research. https://mathematica.org/publications/a-review-of-the-literature-on-homebased-child-care-implications-for-future-directions.

Ritchie, L., M. Boyle, K. Chandran, P. Spector, S. Whaley, P. James, S. Samuels, K. Hecht, and P. Crawford. 2012. "Participation in the Child and Adult Care Food Program Is Associated with More Nutritious Foods and Beverages in Child Care." *Childhood Obesity* 8, no. 3. https://doi.org/10.1089/chi.2011.0061.

Ritchie, L., S. Sharma, G. Gildengorin, S. Yoshida, E. Braff-Guajardo, and P. Crawford. 2015. "Policy Improves What Beverages Are Served to Young Children in Child Care." *Journal of the Academy of Nutrition and Dietetics* 115, no. 5: 724–30. https://doi.org/10.1016/j.jand.2014.07.019.

Sabol, T., and R. Pianta. 2012. "Recent Trends in Research on Teacher–Child Relationships." *Attachment & Human Development* 14, no. 3: 213–31. https://doi.org/10.1080/14616734.2012.672262.

Schanzenbach, D., and M. Zaki. 2014. *Expanding the School Breakfast Program: Impacts on Children's Consumption, Nutrition, and Health.* NBER Working Paper 20308. Cambridge, MA: National Bureau of Economic Research. https://www.nber.org/system/files/working_papers/w20308/w20308.pdf.

Schlieber, M., and C. McLean. 2020. "Educator Work Environments Are Children's Learning Environments: How and Why They Should be Improved." Center for the Study of Child Care Employment. https://cscce.berkeley.edu/blog/educator-work-environments-are-childrens-learning-environments-how-and-why-they-should-be-improved/.

Shonkoff, J., and D. Phillips. 2000. *From Neurons to Neighborhoods: The Science of Early Childhood Development.* Washington: National Academies Press. https://doi.org/10.17226/9824

Smith, L., K. McHenry, and H. Mullaly. 2021. "What Is the Employer-Provided Child Care Credit (45F)?" Bipartisan Policy Center. https://bipartisanpolicy.org/blog/what-is-employer-provided-child-care-credit-45f/.

Tekin, E. 2005. "Child Care Subsidy Receipt, Employment, and Child Care Choices of Single Mothers." *Economics Letters* 89, no. 1: 1–6. https://doi.org/10.1016/j.econlet.2005.03.005.

———. 2007. "Childcare Subsidies, Wages, and Employment of Single Mothers." *Journal of Human Resources* 42, no. 2: 453–87. https://doi.org/10.3368/jhr.XLII.2.453.

Tüzemen, D. 2021. "Women Without a College Degree, Especially Minority Mothers, Face a Steeper Road to Recovery." Federal Reserve Bank of Kansas City. https://www.kansascityfed.org/Economic%20Review/documents/8243/EconomicReviewV106N3Tuzemen.pdf.

U.S. Census Bureau. 2018. "CBP and NES Combined Report." https://www.census.gov/data/tables/2018/econ/cbp/2018-combined-report.html.

———. 2021a. "Food Security." https://www.census.gov/data/datasets/time-series/demo/cps/cps-supp_cps-repwgt/cps-food-security.html.

———. 2021b. "School Enrollment in the United States: October 2019: Detailed Tables." https://www.census.gov/data/tables/2019/demo/school-enrollment/2019-cps.html.

USDA (U.S. Department of Agriculture). 2022a. "Key Statistics & Graphics." https://www.ers.usda.gov/topics/food-nutrition-assistance/food-security-in-the-u-s/key-statistics-graphics/#children.

———. 2022b. "Summer Electronic Benefit Transfer for Children (SEBTC)." https://www.fns.usda.gov/ops/summer-electronic-benefit-transfer-children-sebtc.

U.S. Department of Health and Human Services. 2005. "Head Start Impact Study: First Year Findings." Administration for Children and Families. https://files.eric.ed.gov/fulltext/ED543015.pdf.

———. 2020. "National Survey of Early Care and Education 2019: Household Questionnaire." Administration for Children and Families. https://www.acf.hhs.gov/opre/report/national-survey-early-care-and-education-2019-household-questionnaire.

———. 2022. "ARP Child Care Stabilization Funding State Fact Sheets." https://www.acf.hhs.gov/occ/map/arp-act-stabilization-funding-state-fact-sheets.

U.S. Department of the Treasury. 2021. "The Economics of Child Care Supply in the United States." https://home.treasury.gov/system/files/136/The-Economics-of-Childcare-Supply-09-14-final.pdf.

Vinovskis, M. 2005. *The Birth of Head Start: Preschool Education Policies in the Kennedy and Johnson Administrations*. Chicago: University Chicago Press. https://press.uchicago.edu/ucp/books/book/chicago/B/bo3533726.html.

Weiland, C., and H. Yoshikawa. 2013. "Impacts of a Prekindergarten Program on Children's Mathematics, Language, Literacy, Executive Function, and Emotional Skills." *Child Development* 84, no. 6: 2112–30. https://doi.org/10.1111/cdev.12099.

Wesnes, K., C. Pincock, D. Richardson, G. Helm, and S. Hails. 2003. "Breakfast Reduces Declines in Attention and Memory Over the Morning in Schoolchildren." *Appetite* 41, no. 3: 329–31. https://doi.org/10.1016/j.appet.2003.08.009.

Whitebook, M., C. McLean, L. Austin, and B. Edwards. 2018. "Early Childhood Workforce Index 2018." Center for the Study of Child Care Employment. https://cscce.berkeley.edu/wp-content/uploads/2022/04/Early-Childhood-Workforce-Index-2018.pdf.

White House. 2022. "Fact Sheet: American Rescue Plan Funds Provided a Critical Lifeline to 200,000 Child Care Providers—Helping Millions of Families to Work." https://www.whitehouse.gov/briefing-room/statements-releases/2022/10/21/fact-sheet-american-rescue-plan-funds-provided-a-critical-lifeline-to-200000-child-care-providers-helping-millions-of-families-to-work/.

Wikle, J., and R. Wilson. 2022. "Access to Head Start and Maternal Labor Supply: Experimental and Quasi-Experimental Evidence." *Journal of Labor Economics*. https://doi.org/10.1086/720980.

Workman, S. 2018. "Where Does Your Child Care Dollar Go?" Center for American Progress. https://www.americanprogress.org/article/child-care-dollar-go/.

Yellen, J. 2020. "The History of Women's Work and Wages and How It Has Created Success for Us All." Brookings Institution. https://www.brookings.edu/essay/the-history-of-womens-work-and-wages-and-how-it-has-created-success-for-us-all/.

Chapter 5

Acton, R. 2021. "Effects of Reduced Community College Tuition on College Choices and Degree Completion." *Education Finance and Policy* 16, no. 3: 388–417. https://doi.org/10.1162/edfp_a_00313.

Agarwal, S., J. Driscoll, X. Gabaix, and D. Laibson. 2009. "The Age of Reason: Financial Decisions over the Life Cycle and Implications for Regulation." *Brookings Papers on Economic Activity*, no. 2. https://www.brookings.edu/wp-content/uploads/2016/07/2009b_bpea_agarwal-1.pdf.

Aghion, P., L. Boustan, C. Hoxby, and J. Vandenbussche. 2009. "The Causal Impact of Education on Economic Growth: Evidence from the U.S." *Brookings Papers on Economic Activity*, no. 1: 1–73. https://scholar.harvard.edu/files/aghion/files/causal_impact_of_education.pdf.

Alsan, M., O. Garrick, and G. Graziani. 2019. "Does Diversity Matter for Health? Experimental Evidence from Oakland." *American Economic Review* 109, no. 12: 4071–111. https://doi.org/10.1257/aer.20181446.

Alpert, W., K. Couch, and O. Harmon. 2016. "A Randomized Assessment of Online Learning." *American Economic Review* 106: 378–82. https://doi.org/10.1257/aer.p20161057.

An, B., and J. Taylor. 2019. "A Review of Empirical Studies on Dual Enrollment: Assessing Educational Outcomes." *Higher Education: Handbook of Theory and Research* 34: 99–151. https://nacep.org/docs/briefs/An%20&%20Taylor%20(2019).pdf.

Andrews, R., J. Li, and M. Lovenheim. 2016. "Quantile Treatment Effects of College Quality on Earnings." *Journal of Human Resources* 51, no. 1: 200–238. https://doi.org/10.3368/jhr.51.1.200.

Armona, L., and S. Cao. 2022. "Redesigning Federal Student Aid in Sub-Baccalaureate Education." Social Science Research Network. https://ssrn.com/abstract=4300755.

Armona, L., R. Chakrabarti, and M. Lovenheim. 2022. "Student Debt and Default: The Role of For-Profit Colleges." *Journal of Financial Economics* 144, no. 1: 67–92. https://doi.org/10.1016/j.jfineco.2021.12.008.

Bahr, P. 2016. "The Earnings of Community College Graduates in California." Working paper, Center for Analysis of Postsecondary Education and Employment. https://capseecenter.org/wp-content/uploads/2016/12/the-earnings-of-community-college-graduates-in-california.pdf.

Bahr, P., S. Dynarski, B. Jacob, D. Kreisman, A. Sosa, and M. Wiederspan. 2015. "Labor Market Returns to Community College Awards: Evidence from Michigan." Working paper, Center for Analysis of Postsecondary Education and Employment. https://capseecenter.org/labor-market-returns-michigan/.

Bailey, M., and S. Dynarski. 2011. *Gains and Gaps: Changing Inequality in U.S. College Entry and Completion*. NBER Working Paper 17633. Cambridge, MA: National Bureau of Economic Research. https://doi.org/10.3386/w17633.

Baird, M., M. Kofoed, T. Miller, and J. Wenger. 2022. "Veteran Educators or For-Profiteers? Tuition Responses to Changes in the Post-9/11 GI Bill." *Journal of Policy Analysis and Management* 41, no. 4: 1012–39. https://doi.org/10.1002/pam.22408.

Baker, D. 2020. "'Name and Shame': An Effective Strategy for College Tuition Accountability?" *Educational Evaluation and Policy Analysis* 42, no. 3: 393–416. https://doi.org/10.3102/0162373720937672.

Baker, R., E. Bettinger, B. Jacob, and I. Marinescu. 2018. "The Effect of Labor Market Information on Community College Students' Major Choice." *Economics of Education Review* 65: 18–30. https://doi.org/10.1016/j.econedurev.2018.05.005.

Barnes, M., L. Bauer, W. Edelberg, S. Estep, R. Greenstein, and M. Macklin. 2021. "The Social Insurance System in the U.S.: Policies to Protect Workers and Families."

Brookings Institution. https://www.brookings.edu/wp-content/uploads/2021/06/Social-Insurance-FP_v4.5.pdf.

Barr, A., L. Kawano, B. Sacerdote, W. Skimmyhorn, and M. Stevens. 2021. *You Can't Handle the Truth: The Effects of the Post-9/11 G.I. Bill on Higher Education and Earnings*. NBER Working Paper 29024. Cambridge, MA: National Bureau of Economic Research. https://doi.org/10.3386/w29024.

Barr, A., and S. Turner. 2015. "Out of Work and Into School: Labor Market Policies and College Enrollment during the Great Recession." *Journal of Public Economics* 124: 63–73. https://doi.org/10.1016/j.jpubeco.2014.12.009.

———. 2018. "A Letter and Encouragement: Does Information Increase Postsecondary Enrollment of UI Recipients?" *American Economic Journal: Economic Policy* 10, no. 3: 42–68. https://www.jstor.org/stable/26529036.

Barr, N. 2004. "Higher Education Funding." *Oxford Review of Economic Policy* 20, no. 2: 264–83. https://doi.org/10.1093/oxrep/grh015.

Barr, N., B. Chapman, L. Dearden, and S. Dynarski. 2019. "The U.S. College Loans System: Lessons from Australia and England." *Economics of Education Review* 71: 32–48. https://doi.org/10.1016/j.econedurev.2018.07.007.

Barrow, L., and O. Malamud. 2015. "Is College a Worthwhile Investment?" *Annual Review of Economics* 7: 519–55. https://doi.org/10.1146/annurev-economics-080614-115510.

Baum, S., K. Payea, and P. Steele. 2009. "Trends in Student Aid." College Board. https://research.collegeboard.org/media/pdf/trends-student-aid-2009-full-report.pdf.

Belfield, C. 2015. "Weathering the Great Recession with Human Capital? Evidence on Labor Market Returns to Education from Arkansas." Working paper, Center for Analysis of Postsecondary Education and Employment. https://files.eric.ed.gov/fulltext/ED562519.pdf.

Belfield, C., and T. Bailey. 2017. "The Labor Market Returns to Sub-Baccalaureate College: A Review." Working paper, Center for Analysis of Postsecondary Education and Employment. https://capseecenter.org/wp-content/uploads/2017/04/labor-market-returns-sub-baccalaureate-college-review.pdf.

Beshears, J., J. Choi, D. Laibson, and B. Madrian. 2008. "How Are Preferences Revealed?" *Journal of Public Economics* 92, nos. 8–9: 1787–94. https://doi.org/10.1016/j.jpubeco.2008.04.010.

Bettinger, E., and R. Baker. 2014. "The Effects of Student Coaching: An Evaluation of a Randomized Experiment in Student Advising." *Educational Evaluation and Policy Analysis* 36, no. 1. https://doi.org/10.3102/0162373713500523.

Bettinger, E., L. Fox, S. Loeb, and E. Taylor. 2017. "Virtual Classrooms: How Online College Courses Affect Student Success." *American Economic Review* 107, no. 9: 2855–75. https://www.aeaweb.org/articles?id=10.1257/aer.20151193.

Bettinger, E., B. Long, P. Oreopoulos, and L. Sanbonmatsu. 2012. "The Role of Application Assistance and Information in College Decisions: Results from the

H&R Block Fafsa Experiment." *Quarterly Journal of Economics* 127, no. 3: 1205–42. https://doi.org/10.1093/qje/qjs017.

Bettinger, E., and A. Soliz. 2016. "Returns to Vocational Credentials: Evidence from Ohio's Community and Technical Colleges." Working paper, Center for Analysis of Postsecondary Education and Employment. https://www.capseecenter.org/wp-content/uploads/2016/10/returns-to-vocational-credentials.pdf.

Betts, J., and L. McFarland. 1995. "Safe Port in a Storm: The Impact of Labor Market Conditions on Community College Enrollments." *Journal of Human Resources* 30, no. 4: 741–65. https://doi.org/10.2307/146230.

Bird, K., B. Castleman, and G. Lohner. 2022. "Negative Impacts from the Shift to Online Learning during the COVID-19 Crisis: Evidence from a Statewide Community College System." Annenberg Institute, EdWorkingPaper 20-299. https://www.edworkingpapers.com/sites/default/files/ai20-299.pdf.

Birdsall, C. 2018. "Performance Management in Public Higher Education: Unintended Consequences and Implications of Organizational Diversity." *Public Performance & Management Review* 41, no. 4: 669–95. https://doi.org/10.1080/15309576.2018.1481116.

Black, S., J. Denning, and J. Rothstein. 2020. *Winners and Losers? The Effect of Gaining and Losing Access to Selective Colleges on Education and Labor Market Outcomes*. NBER Working Paper 26821. Cambridge, MA: National Bureau of Economic Research. https://doi.org/10.3386/w26821.

Blagg, K., and M. Chingos. 2016. "Choice Deserts: How Geography Limits the Potential Impact of Earnings Data on Higher Education." Urban Institute. https://www.urban.org/sites/default/files/publication/86581/choice_deserts_3.pdf.

Bleemer, Z. 2021. "Top Percent Policies and the Return to Postsecondary Selectivity." Working paper, University of California. https://zacharybleemer.com/wp-content/uploads/2020/10/ELC_Paper.pdf.

Blume, G., E. Meza, D. Bragg, and I. Love. 2019. "Estimating the Impact of Nation's Largest Single Investment in Community Colleges." Center on Education and Labor Education Policy. https://www.newamerica.org/education-policy/reports/estimating-impact-taaccct/.

Boatman, A., B. Evans, and A. Soliz. 2017. "Understanding Loan Aversion in Education: Evidence from High School Seniors, Community College Students, and Adults." *Aera Open* 3, no. 1: 1–16. https://journals.sagepub.com/doi/pdf/10.1177/2332858416683649.

Bound, J., B. Braga, G. Khanna, and S. Turner. 2021. *The Globalization of Postsecondary Education: The Role of International Students in the U.S. Higher Education System*. NBER Working Paper 28342. Cambridge, MA: National Bureau of Economic Research. https://www.nber.org/papers/w28342.

Bound, J., M. Lovenheim, and S. Turner. 2010. "Why Have College Completion Rates Declined? An Analysis of Changing Student Preparation and Collegiate

Resources." *American Economic Journal: Applied Economics* 2, no. 3: 129–57. https://doi.org/10.1257/app.2.3.129.

———. 2012. "Increasing Time to Baccalaureate Degree in the United States." *Education Finance and Policy* 7, no. 4: 375–424. https://doi.org/10.1162/EDFP_a_00074.

Bound, J., and S. Turner. 2007. "Cohort Crowding: How Resources Affect Collegiate Attainment." *Journal of Public Economics* 91, no. 5: 877–99. https://doi.org/10.1016/j.jpubeco.2006.07.006.

Bowen, W., M. Chingos, K. Lack, and T. Nygren. 2014. "Interactive Learning Online at Public Universities: Evidence from a Six-Campus Randomized Trial." *Journal of Policy Analysis and Management* 33: 94–111. https://doi.org/10.1002/pam.21728.

Bowen, W., M. Chingos, and M. McPherson. 2009. *Crossing the Finish Line: Completing College at America's Public Universities*. Princeton, NJ: Princeton University Press. https://press.princeton.edu/books/paperback/9780691149905/crossing-the-finish-line.

Cellini, R. 2009. "Crowded Colleges and College Crowd-Out: The Impact of Public Subsidies on the Two-Year College Market." *American Economic Journal: Economic Policy*, no. 2: 1–30. https://www.aeaweb.org/articles?id=10.1257/pol.1.2.1.

Cellini, S., and L. Chaudhary. 2020. "Commercials for College? Advertising in Higher Education." Brookings Institution. https://www.brookings.edu/research/commercials-for-college-advertising-in-higher-education/.

Cellini, S., R. Darolia, and L. Turner. 2020. "Where Do Students Go When For-Profit Colleges Lose Federal Aid?" *American Economic Journal: Economic Policy* 12, no. 2: 46–83. https://doi.org/10.1257/pol.20180265.

Cellini, S., and C. Koedel. 2017. "The Case for Limiting Federal Student Aid to For-Profit Colleges." *Journal of Policy Analysis and Management* 36, no. 4: 934–42. https://doi.org/10.1002/pam.22008.

Cellini, S., and N. Turner. 2019. "Gainfully Employed? Assessing the Employment and Earnings of For-Profit College Students Using Administrative Data." *Journal of Human Resources* 54, no. 2: 342–70. https://doi.org/10.3368/jhr.54.2.1016.8302R1.

Century Foundation. 2021. "Voters Overwhelmingly Support Guardrails on For-Profit Colleges, Finds TCF and Data for Progress Poll." https://tcf.org/content/about-tcf/voters-overwhelmingly-support-guardrails-profit-colleges-finds-tcf-data-progress-poll/.

Chakrabarti, R., N. Gorton, and M. Lovenheim. 2020. *State Investment in Higher Education: Effects on Human Capital Formation, Student Debt, and Long-Term Financial Outcomes of Students*. NBER Working Paper 27885. Cambridge, MA: National Bureau of Economic Research. https://www.nber.org/papers/w27885.

Chetty, R., J. Friedman, E. Saez, N. Turner, and D. Yagan. 2017. *Mobility Report Cards: The Role of Colleges in Intergenerational Mobility*. NBER Working Paper 23618. Cambridge, MA: National Bureau of Economic Research. https://www.nber.org/papers/w23618.

Chetty, R., J. Friedman, E. Saez, N. Turner, and D. Yagan. 2020. "Income Segregation and Intergenerational Mobility Across Colleges in the United States." *Quarterly Journal of Economics* 135, no. 3: 1567–633. https://doi.org/10.1093/qje/qjaa005.

Cohen, A., F. Brawer, and C. Kisker. 2013. *The American Community College*. Hoboken, NJ: John Wiley & Sons. https://www.wiley.com/en-us/The+American+Community+College,+6th+Edition-p-9781118449813.

Cohodes, S., and J. Goodman. 2014. "Merit Aid, College Quality, and College Completion: Massachusetts' Adams Scholarship as an In-Kind Subsidy." *American Economic Journal: Applied Economics* 6, no. 4: 251–85. https://doi.org/10.1257/app.6.4.251.

College Scorecard. 2022. U.S. Department of Education. https://collegescorecard.ed.gov/.

CUNY (City University of New York). No date. "ASAP [Accelerated Study in Associated Programs]." https://www1.cuny.edu/sites/asap/about/.

Currie, J., and E. Moretti. 2003. "Mother's Education and the Intergenerational Transmission of Human Capital: Evidence from College Openings." *Quarterly Journal of Economics* 118, no. 4: 1495–532. https://doi.org/10.1162/003355303322552856.

Dadgar, M., and M. Trimble. 2015. "Labor Market Returns to Sub-Baccalaureate Credentials: How Much Does a Community College Degree or Certificate Pay?" *Educational Evaluation and Policy* 37, no. 4. https://files.eric.ed.gov/fulltext/ED533520.pdf.

Darolia, R. 2013. "Integrity Versus Access? The Effect of Federal Financial Aid Availability on Postsecondary Enrollment." *Journal of Public Economics* 106: 101–14. https://doi.org/10.1016/j.jpubeco.2013.08.001.

Darolia, R., C. Koedel, P. Martorell, K. Wilson, and F. Perez-Arce. 2015. "Do Employers Prefer Workers Who Attend For-Profit Colleges? Evidence from a Field Experiment." *Journal of Policy Analysis and Management* 34, no. 4: 881–903. https://doi.org/10.1002/pam.21863.

Dee, T. 2003. *Are There Civic Returns to Education?* NBER Working Paper 9588. Cambridge, MA: National Bureau of Economic Research. https://doi.org/10.3386/w9588.

Deming, D. 2017. "Increasing College Completion with a Federal Higher Education Matching Grant." Hamilton Project. https://www.hamiltonproject.org/assets/files/increasing_college_completion_with_federal_higher_education_matching_grant_pp.pdf.

Deming, D., C. Goldin, and L. Katz. 2012. "The For-Profit Postsecondary School Sector: Nimble Critters or Agile Predators?" *Journal of Economic Perspectives* 26, no. 1: 139–64. https://www.aeaweb.org/articles?id=10.1257/jep.26.1.139.

Deming, D., and C. Walters. 2017. *The Impact of Price Caps and Spending Cuts on U.S. Postsecondary Attainment*. NBER Working Paper 23736. Cambridge, MA: National Bureau of Economic Research. https://doi.org/10.3386/w23736.

Deming, D., N. Yuchtman, A. Abulafi, C. Goldin, and L. Katz. 2016. "The Value of Postsecondary Credentials in the Labor Market: An Experimental Study." *American Economic Review* 106, no. 3: 778–806. https://doi.org/10.1257/aer.20141757.

Denning, J., E. Eide, K. Mumford, R. Patterson, and M. Warnick. 2022. "Why Have College Completion Rates Increased?" *American Economic Journal: Applied Economics* 14, no. 3: 1–29. https://pubs.aeaweb.org/doi/pdfplus/10.1257/app.20200525.

Dinerstein, M., C. Hoxby, J. Meer, and P. Villanueva. 2014. "Did the Fiscal Stimulus Work for Universities?" In *How the Financial Crisis and Great Recession Affected Higher Education*, 263–320. Chicago: University of Chicago Press. https://www.nber.org/system/files/chapters/c12864/c12864.pdf.

Dynarski, S., C. Libassi, K. Michelmore, and S. Owen. 2021. "Closing the Gap: The Effect of Reducing Complexity and Uncertainty in College Pricing on the Choices of Low-Income Students." *American Economic Review* 111, no.6: 1721–56. https://www.aeaweb.org/articles?id=10.1257/aer.20200451.

Dynarski, S., A. Nurshatayeva, L. Page, and J. Scott-Clayton. 2022. *Addressing Non-Financial Barriers to College Access and Success: Evidence and Policy Implications*. NBER Working Paper 30054. Cambridge, MA: National Bureau of Economic Research. https://doi.org/10.3386/w30054.

Dynarski, S., L. Page, and J. Scott-Clayton. 2022. *College Costs, Financial Aid, and Student Decisions*. NBER Working Paper 30275. Cambridge, MA: National Bureau of Economic Research. https://doi.org/10.3386/w30275.

Education Commission of the States. 2022. "State Information Request: College Promise Programs." https://www.ecs.org/wp-content/uploads/State-Information-Request_College-Promise-Programs.pdf.

Edmunds, J., F. Unlu, J. Furey, E. Glennie, and N. Arshavsky. 2020. "What Happens When You Combine High School and College? The Impact of the Early College Model on Postsecondary Performance and Completion." *Sage Journals* 42, no. 2. https://doi.org/10.3102/0162373720912249.

Emmons, W., and L. Ricketts. 2017. "College Is Not Enough: Higher Education Does Not Eliminate Racial Wealth Gaps." *Federal Reserve Bank of St. Louis Review* 99, no. 1: 7–39. https://doi.org/10.20955/r.2017.7-39.

Evans, W., M. Kearney, B. Perry, and J. Sullivan. 2020. "Increasing Community College Completion Rates among Low-Income Students: Evidence from a Randomized Controlled Trial Evaluation of a Case-Management Intervention." *Journal of*

Policy Analysis and Management 39, no. 4: 930–65. https://doi.org/10.1002/pam.22256.

Fairlie, R., F. Hoffman, and P. Oreopoulous. 2014. "A Community College Instructor Like Me: Race and Ethnicity Interactions in the Classroom." *American Economic Review* 104, no. 8: 2567–91. https://doi.org/10.1257/aer.104.8.2567.

Figlio, D., M. Rush, and L. Yin. 2013. "Is It Live or Is It Internet? Experimental Estimates of the Effects of Online Instruction on Student Learning." *Journal of Labor Economics* 31, no. 4: 763–84. https://www.journals.uchicago.edu/doi/epdf/10.1086/669930.

Fishman, R. 2015. "2015 College Decisions Survey: Part I: Deciding to Go to College." New America. https://static.newamerica.org/attachments/3248-deciding-to-go-to-college/CollegeDecisions_PartI.148dcab30a0e414ea2a52f0d8fb04e7b.pdf.

Fountain, J. 2017. "The Campus-Based Financial Aid Programs: Background and Issues." Congressional Research Service, Report R45024. https://sgp.fas.org/crs/misc/R45024.pdf.

Gándara, D., and A. Rutherford. 2018. "Mitigating Unintended Impacts? The Effects of Premiums for Underserved Populations in Performance Funding Policies for Higher Education." *Research in Higher Education* 59, no. 6, 681–703. https://doi.org/10.1007/s11162-017-9483-x.

Gallup, Lumina Foundation, and Strada Education Network. 2019. "Some College and No Degree: How Individuals Who Attend and Don't Graduate Feel About Education." https://www.luminafoundation.org/wp-content/uploads/2019/12/some-college-no-degree.pdf.

GAO (U.S. Government Accountability Office). 2010. "For-Profit Colleges: Undercover Testing Finds Colleges Encouraged Fraud and Engaged in Deceptive and Questionable Marketing Practices." https://www.gao.gov/assets/gao-10-948t.pdf.

———. 2022. "Financial Aid Offers: Action Needed to Improve Information on College Costs and Student Aid." https://www.gao.gov/assets/gao-23-104708.pdf.

Gershenson, S., M. Hansen, and C. Lindsay. 2021. *Teacher Diversity and Student Success: Why Racial Representation Matters in the Classroom*. Cambridge, MA: Harvard Education Press. https://eric.ed.gov/?id=ED611696.

Gershenson, S., C. Hart, J. Hyman, C. Lindsay, and N. Papageorge. 2022. "The Long-Run Impacts of Same-Race Teachers." *American Economic Journal: Economic Policy* 14, no. 4: 300–342. https://www.aeaweb.org/articles?id=10.1257/pol.20190573.

Goldin, C., and L. Katz. 2008. *The Race Between Education and Technology*. Cambridge, MA: Harvard University Press. https://www.hup.harvard.edu/catalog.php?isbn=9780674035300.

Goodman, J., M. Hurwitz, and J. Smith. 2017. "Access to 4-Year Public Colleges and Degree Completion." *Journal of Labor Economics* 35, no. 3: 829–67. https://doi.org/10.1086/690818.

Goodman, S., and A. Henriques Volz. 2020. "Attendance Spillovers between Public and For-Profit Colleges: Evidence from Statewide Variation in Appropriations for Higher Education." *Education Finance and Policy*, no. 15: 428–56. https://doi.org/10.1162/edfp_a_00281.

Goolsbee, A., G. Hubbard, and A. Ganz. 2019. "A Policy Agenda to Develop Human Capital for the Modern Economy." Aspen Institute. https://www.aspeninstitute.org/wp-content/uploads/2019/01/1.1-Pgs-16-39-A-Policy-Agenda-to-Develop-Human-Capital-for-the-Modern-Economy.pdf.

Greenwood, B., R. Hardeman, L. Huang, and A. Sojourner. 2020. "Physician-Patient Racial Concordance and Disparities in Birthing Mortality for Newborns." *Proceedings of the National Academy of Sciences* 117, no. 35: 21194–200. https://www.pnas.org/doi/10.1073/pnas.1913405117.

Grosz, M. 2020. "The Returns to a Large Community College Program: Evidence from Admissions Lotteries." *American Economic Journal: Economic Policy* 12, no. 1: 226–53. https://www.aeaweb.org/articles?id=10.1257/pol.20170506.

Hemelt, S., N. Schwartz, and S. Dynarski. 2020. "Dual Credit Courses and the Road to College: Experimental Evidence from Tennessee." *Journal of Policy Analysis and Management* 39, no. 3: 686–719. https://doi.org/10.1002/pam.22180.

Hemelt, S., and K. Stange. 2020. "Why the Move to Online Instruction Won't Reduce College Costs." Brookings Institution. https://www.brookings.edu/blog/brown-center-chalkboard/2020/07/28/why-the-move-to-online-instruction-wont-reduce-college-costs/.

Herbst, D. 2023. "The Impact of Income-Driven Repayment on Student Borrower Outcomes." *American Economic Journal: Applied Economics* 15, no. 1: 1–25. https://www.aeaweb.org/articles?id=10.1257/app.20200362.

Hiler, T., and W. Whistle. 2018. "Creating a 'Title I' for Higher Ed." Third Way. https://www.thirdway.org/memo/creating-a-title-i-for-higher-ed.

Hillman, N. 2016. "Geography of College Opportunity: The Case of Education Deserts." *American Educational Research Journal* 53, no. 4. https://doi.org/10.3102/0002831216653204.

Hillman, N., and E. Orians. 2013. "Community Colleges and Labor Market Conditions: How Does Enrollment Demand Change Relative to Local Unemployment Rates?" *Research in Higher Education* 54, no. 7: 765–80. https://www.jstor.org/stable/24571744.

Hoekstra, M. 2009. "The Effect of Attending the Flagship State University on Earnings: A Discontinuity-Based Approach." *Review of Economics and Statistics* 91, no. 4: 717–24. https://doi.org/10.1162/rest.91.4.717.

Holzer, H. 2008. "Workforce Training: What Works? Who Benefits?" Wisconsin Family Impact Seminars. https://www.purdue.edu/hhs/hdfs/fii/wp-content/uploads/2015/07/s_wifis28c02.pdf.

———. 2015. "Sector-Based Training Strategies: The Challenges of Matching Workers and Their Skills to Well-Paying Jobs." U.S. Department of Labor, Future of

Work Paper Series. https://www.dol.gov/sites/dolgov/files/OASP/legacy/files/Future_of_work_sector_based_training_strategies.pdf.

——— 2021. "After COVID-19: Building a More Coherent and Effective Workforce Development System in the United States." Hamilton Project. https://tacc.org/sites/default/files/2021-02/holzer_coherent_effective_workforce.pdf.

Hout, M. 2012. "Social and Economic Returns to College Education in the United States." *Annual Review of Sociology* 38: 379–400. https://doi.org/10.1146/annurev.soc.012809.102503.

Hoxby, C. 2018. "Online Postsecondary Education and Labor Productivity." In *Education, Skills, and Technical Change: Implications for Future U.S. GDP Growth*, edited by C. Hulten and V. Ramey, 401–60. Chicago: University of Chicago Press. https://www.nber.org/system/files/chapters/c13709/c13709.pdf.

Hoxby, C., and C. Avery. 2013. "The Missing 'One-Offs': The Hidden Supply of High-Achieving, Low-Income Students." *Brookings Papers on Economic Activity*, no. 1: 1–65. https://www.brookings.edu/wp-content/uploads/2016/07/2013a_hoxby.pdf.

Huntington-Klein, N. 2016. "The Search: The Effect of the College Scorecard on Interest in Colleges." Unpublished manuscript. https://nickchk.com/Huntington-Klein_2017_The_Search.pdf.

Hurwitz, M., and J. Smith. 2017. "Student Responsiveness to Earnings Data in the College Scorecard." *Economic Inquiry* 56, no. 2: 1220–43. https://doi.org/10.1111/ecin.12530.

Hyman, B. 2018. "Can Displaced Labor Be Retrained? Evidence from Quasi-Random Assignment to Trade Adjustment Assistance." *Proceedings, Annual Conference on Taxation and Minutes of the Annual Meeting of the National Tax Association* 111: 1–70. https://www.jstor.org/stable/26939524.

Hyman, J. 2017. "Does Money Matter in the Long Run? Effects of School Spending on Educational Attainment." *American Economic Journal: Economic Policy* 9, no. 4: 256–80. https://doi.org/10.1257/pol.20150249.

Institute of International Education. 2020. "Project Atlas 2020 Release: A Quick Look at Global Mobility Trends." https://iie.widen.net/s/g2bqxwkwqv/project-atlas-infographics-2020.

IPEDS (Integrated Postsecondary Education Data System). 2020. "Table 1. Number and Percentage Distribution of Students Enrolled at Title IV Institutions, by Control of Institution, Student Level, Level of Institution, Enrollment Status, and Other Selected Characteristics: United States, Fall 2020." National Center for Education Statistics. https://nces.ed.gov/ipeds/search/ViewTable?tableId=29448.

Jackson, C., R. Johnson, and C. Persico. 2015. *The Effects of School Spending on Educational and Economic Outcomes: Evidence from School Finance Reforms*. NBER Working Paper 20847. Cambridge, MA: National Bureau of Economic Research. https://doi.org/10.3386/w20847.

Jacobson, L., R. LaLonde, and D. Sullivan. 2005. "Estimating the Returns to Community College Schooling for Displaced Workers." *Journal of Econometrics* 125, nos. 1–2: 271–304. https://doi.org/10.1016/j.jeconom.2004.04.010.

Jepsen, C., K. Troske, and P. Coomes. 2014. "The Labor-Market Returns to Community College Degrees, Diplomas, and Certificates." *Journal of Labor Economics* 32, no. 1: 95–121. https://doi.org/10.1086/671809.

Joyce, T., S. Crockett, D. Jaeger, O. Altindag, and S. O'Connell. 2015. "Does Classroom Time Matter?" *Economics of Education Review* 46: 64–77. https://www.sciencedirect.com/science/article/abs/pii/S0272775715000254.

Kane, T., P. Orszag, E. Apostolov, R. Inman, and A. Reschovsky. 2005. "Higher Education Appropriations and Public Universities: Role of Medicaid and the Business Cycle." *Brookings-Wharton Papers on Urban Affairs*, 99–146. http://www.jstor.org/stable/25067418.

Kane, T., and C. Rouse. 1995. "Labor-Market Returns to Two- and Four-Year College." *American Economic Review* 85, no 3: 600–614. https://www.jstor.org/stable/2118190.

Katz, L., J. Roth, R. Hendra, and K. Schaberg. 2022. "Why Do Sectoral Employment Programs Work? Lessons from WorkAdvance." *Journal of Labor Economics* 40, no. S1: 249–91. https://doi.org/10.1086/717932.

Kelchen, R., and Z. Liu. 2022. "Did Gainful Employment Regulations Result in College and Program Closures?" *Education Finance and Policy* 17, no. 3: 454–78. https://doi.org/10.1162/edfp_a_00340.

Klasik, D., K. Blagg, and Z. Pekor. 2018. "Out of the Education Desert: How Limited Local College Options Are Associated with Inequity in Postsecondary Opportunities." *Social Sciences* 7, no. 9: 165. https://www.mdpi.com/2076-0760/7/9/165.

Kinser, K. 2016. "Paying for For-Profit Higher Education: Implications of the United States Case." In *Student Financing of Higher Education: A Comparative Perspective*, edited by D. Heller and C. Callender, 98–114. London: Routledge. https://www.routledge.com/Student-Financing-of-Higher-Education-A-Comparative-Perspective/Heller-Callender/p/book/9781138645417.

Kofoed, M., L. Gebhart, D. Gilmore, and R. Moschitto. 2021. "Zooming to Class? Experimental Evidence on College Students' Online Learning during COVID-19." Institute of Labor Economics. https://docs.iza.org/dp14356.pdf.

Kozakowski, W. 2023. "Are Four-Year Public Colleges Engines for Economic Mobility? Evidence from Statewide Admissions Thresholds." Annenberg Institute, EdWorkingPaper 23-727. https://doi.org/10.26300/vapt-4e25.

Krieg, J., and S. Henson. 2016. "The Educational Impact of Online Learning: How Do University Students Perform in Subsequent Courses?" *Education Finance and Policy* 11, no. 4: 426–48. https://doi.org/10.1162/EDFP_a_00196.

Kuehn, D., S. Mills De La Rosa, R. Lerman, and K. Hollenbeck. 2022. *Do Employers Earn Positive Returns to Investments in Apprenticeship? Evidence from*

Registered Programs under the American Apprenticeship Initiative. Report prepared for U.S. Department of Labor, Employment and Training Administration. Rockville, MD: Abt Associates. https://www.abtassociates.com/files/insights/reports/2022/aai-roi-final-report-508c_9-16-22.pdf.

Labaree, D. 2017. *A Perfect Mess: The Unlikely Ascendancy of American Higher Education.* Chicago: University of Chicago Press. https://press.uchicago.edu/ucp/books/book/chicago/P/bo19995111.html.

Lavecchia, A., H. Liu, and P. Oreopoulos. 2016. "Behavioral Economics of Education: Progress and Possibilities." *Handbook of the Economics of Education* 5: 1–74. https://doi.org/10.1016/B978-0-444-63459-7.00001-4.

Leslie, L., and G. Johnson. 1974. "The Market Model and Higher Education." *Journal of Higher Education* 45, no. 1: 1–20. https://doi.org/10.1080/00221546.1974.1177 6918.

Levin, H., and E. Garcia. 2013. "Benefit-Cost Analysis of Accelerated Study in Associated Programs (ASAP) of the City University of New York (CUNY)." Center for Benefit-Cost Studies in Education. https://www1.nyc.gov/assets/opportunity/pdf/Levin_ASAP_Benefit_Cost_Report_FINAL_05212013.pdf.

Levine, P., J. Ma, and L. Russell. 2022. "Do College Applicants Respond to Changes in Sticker Prices Even When They Don't Matter?" *Education Finance and Policy*, 1–30. https://doi.org/10.1162/edfp_a_00372.

Levy, D. 2019. "Juxtaposing Global and U.S. Private Higher Education: What Is to Be Learned?" In *International Perspectives in Higher Education: Balancing Access, Equity, and Cost*, edited by J. Delisle and A. Usher, 49–66. https://www.routledge.com/Student-Financing-of-Higher-Education-A-Comparative-Perspective/Heller-Callender/p/book/9781138645417?utm_source=cjaffiliates&utm_medium=affiliates&cjevent=5a91649a9cc411ed82b6abb90a82b832.

Linkow, T., E. Bumgarner, H. Didriksen, K. Lack, A. Nichols, E. Dastrup, S. Dastrup, and B. Gamse. 2019. "The Story of Scaling Up: Interim Report on the Impact of Success Boston's Coaching for Completion." Abt Associates. https://files.eric.ed.gov/fulltext/ED602748.pdf.

Linkow, T., B. Gamse, F. Unlu, E. Bumgarner, H. Didriksen, J. Furey, M. Meneses, M. Sami, and A. Nichols. 2017. "The Power of Coaching: Highlights from the Interim Report on the Impact of Success Boston's Transition Coaching on College Success." Abt Associates. https://files.eric.ed.gov/fulltext/ED582090.pdf.

Liu, V., C. Belfield, and M. Trimble. 2015. "The Medium-Term Labor Market Returns to Community College Awards: Evidence from North Carolina." *Economics of Education Review* 44: 42–55. https://doi.org/10.1016/j.econedurev.2014.10.009.

Lochner, L. 2011. *Non-Production Benefits of Education: Crime, Health, and Good Citizenship.* NBER Working Paper 16722. Cambridge, MA: National Bureau of Economic Research. https://doi.org/10.3386/w16722.

Lochner, L., and E. Moretti. 2004. "The Effect of Education on Crime: Evidence from Prison Inmates, Arrests, and Self-Reports." *American Economic Review* 94, no. 1: 155–89. https://doi.org/10.1257/000282804322970751.

Long, M. 2008. "College Quality and Early Adult Outcomes." *Economics of Education Review* 27, no. 5: 588–602. https://doi.org/10.1016/j.econedurev.2007.04.004.

Love, I. 2022. "Why Community College Bachelor's Degrees? Similarities and Differences Across Urban and Rural Settings." New America. https://www.newamerica.org/education-policy/briefs/why-community-college-bachelors-degrees/.

Lovenheim, M., and J. Smith. 2022. *Returns to Different Postsecondary Investments: Institution Type, Academic Programs, and Credentials*. NBER Working Paper 29933. Cambridge, MA: National Bureau of Economic Research. https://doi.org/10.3386/w29933.

Lusher, L., D. Campbell, and S. Carrell. 2018. "TAs Like Me: Racial Interactions between Graduate Teaching Assistants and Undergraduates." *Journal of Public Economics* 159: 203–24. https://doi.org/10.1016/j.jpubeco.2018.02.005.

Ma, J., and M. Pender. 2021. "Trends in College Pricing and Student Aid 2021." College Board. https://research.collegeboard.org/media/pdf/trends-college-pricing-student-aid-2021.pdf.

———. 2022a. "Trends in College Pricing 2022: Data in Excel." College Board. https://research.collegeboard.org/media/xlsx/trends-college-pricing-excel-data-2022.xlsx.

———.2022b. "Trends in College Pricing and Student Aid 2022." College Board. https://research.collegeboard.org/media/pdf/trends-in-college-pricing-student-aid-2022.pdf.

Ma, J., M. Pender, and M. Welch. 2019. "Education Pays 2019." College Board. https://research.collegeboard.org/media/pdf/education-pays-2019-full-report.pdf.

Marcucci, P. 2013. "The Politics of Student Funding Policies from a Comparative Perspective." In *Student Financing of Higher Education: A Comparative Perspective*, edited by D. Heller and C. Callender, 9–31. London: Routledge. https://www.routledge.com/Student-Financing-of-Higher-Education-A-Comparative-Perspective/Heller-Callender/p/book/9781138645417.

Marken, S., L. Gray, and L. Lewis. 2013. "Dual Enrollment Programs and Courses for High School Students at Postsecondary Institutions: 2010–11." National Center for Education Statistics. http://nces.ed.gov/pubs2013/2013002.pdf.

McMillan-Cottom, T. 2017. *Lower Ed: The Troubling Rise of For-Profits*. New York: New Press. https://thenewpress.com/books/lower-ed.

Meyer, K., and K. Rosinger. 2019. "Applying Behavioral Insights to Improve Postsecondary Education Outcomes: A Review of Obama Administration Efforts and Next Steps Under the Trump Administration." *Journal of Policy Analysis and Management* 38, no. 2: 481–99. https://doi.org/10.1002/pam.22123.

Miller, B. 2017. "Who Are Student Loan Defaulters?" Center for American Progress. https://www.americanprogress.org/article/student-loan-defaulters/.

Miller, C., C. Headlam, M. Manno, and D. Cullinan. 2020. "Increasing Community College Graduation Rates with a Proven Model: Three-Year Results from the Accelerated Study in Associate Programs (ASAP) Ohio Demonstration." MDRC. https://www.mdrc.org/publication/increasing-community-college-graduation-rates-proven-model.

Minaya, V., and J. Scott-Clayton. 2022. "Labor Market Trajectories for Community College Graduates: How Returns to Certificates and Associate's Degrees Evolve over Time." *Education Finance and Policy* 17, no. 1: 53–80. https://doi.org/10.1162/edfp_a_00325.

Mishory, J. 2018. "The Future of Statewide College Promise Programs." Century Foundation. https://tcf.org/content/report/future-statewide-college-promise-programs/.

Mountjoy, J. 2022. "Community Colleges and Upward Mobility." *American Economic Review* 112, no. 8: 2580–2630. https://www.aeaweb.org/articles?id=10.1257/aer.20181756.

Mountjoy, J., and B. Hickman. 2021. *The Returns to College(s): Relative Value-Added and Match Effects in Higher Education.* NBER Working Paper 29276. Cambridge, MA: National Bureau of Economic Research. https://doi.org/10.3386/w29276.

Mueller, H., and C. Yannelis. 2019. "The Rise in Student Loan Defaults." *Journal of Financial Economics* 131, no. 1: 1–19. https://doi.org/10.1016/j.jfineco.2018.07.013.

Murphy, R., J. Scott-Clayton, and G. Wyness. 2019. "The End of Free College in England: Implications for Enrolments, Equity, and Quality." *Economics of Education Review* 71: 7–22. https://www.sciencedirect.com/science/article/abs/pii/S0272775717306404.

National Student Clearinghouse Research Center. 2022a. "Completing College: National and State Reports." https://nscresearchcenter.org/completing-college/.

_______. 2022b. "Overview: Spring 2022 Enrollment Estimates." https://nscresearchcenter.org/wp-content/uploads/CTEE_Report_Spring_2022.pdf.

NCES (National Center for Education Statistics). 2019. "Number and Percentage of Students Enrolled in Degree-Granting Postsecondary Institutions, by Distance Education Participation, Location of Student, Level of Enrollment, and Control and Level of Institution: Fall 2017 and Fall 2018." https://nces.ed.gov/programs/digest/d19/tables/dt19_311.15.asp.

———.2020a. "Percent of Undergraduate Students Receiving Pell Grants." https://nces.ed.gov/ipeds/TrendGenerator/app/answer/8/35.

———.2020b. "Percent of Undergraduate Students Receiving Pell Grants, by Level of Institution: 2020–21." https://nces.ed.gov/ipeds/TrendGenerator/app/build-table/8/35?cid=5.

———.2020c. “Percent of Undergraduate Students Receiving Pell Grants (Limited by Control of Institution).” https://nces.ed.gov/ipeds/TrendGenerator/app/answer/8/35?f=4%3D3.

———. 2021. “Percentage of the Population 25 to 64 Years Old Who Attained a Postsecondary Degree, by Highest Degree Attained, Age Group, and Country: 2020.” U.S. Department of Education. https://nces.ed.gov/programs/digest/d21/tables/dt21_603.30.asp?current=yes.

———. 2022a. “Age at Start of Postsecondary Education by NPSAS Institution Sector (4 with Multiple).” U.S. Department of Education, Quick Launch qquayy. https://nces.ed.gov/datalab/powerstats/121-national-postsecondary-student-aid-study-2016-undergraduates/percentage-distribution.

———. 2022b. “Residence While Enrolled by Age at Start of Postsecondary Education.” U.S. Department of Education, Quick Launch hgtstb. https://nces.ed.gov/datalab/powerstats/121-national-postsecondary-student-aid-study-2016-undergraduates/percentage-distribution.

———. 2022c. “NPSAS Institution Level by Age at Start of Postsecondary Education and Residence While Enrolled.” U.S. Department of Education, Quick Launch rgcflp. https://nces.ed.gov/datalab/powerstats/121-national-postsecondary-student-aid-study-2016-undergraduates/percentage-distribution.

———. 2022d. “NPSAS Institution Level by Age as of 12/31/2015.” U.S. Department of Education, Quick Launch ljkiep. https://nces.ed.gov/datalab/powerstats/121-national-postsecondary-student-aid-study-2016-undergraduates/percentage-distribution.

———. 2022e. “Residence While Enrolled by Age as of 12/31/2015. Filtered by NPSAS Institution Level (4-year).” U.S. Department of Education, Quick Launch krdscg. https://nces.ed.gov/datalab/powerstats/121-national-postsecondary-student-aid-study-2016-undergraduates/percentage-distribution.

———. 2022f. “Age as of 12/31/2015 by NPSAS Institution Sector (4 with Multiple).” U.S. Department of Education, Quick Launch vppist. https://nces.ed.gov/datalab/powerstats/121-national-postsecondary-student-aid-study-2016-undergraduates/percentage-distribution.

———. 2022g. “Institution Sector (4 with Multiple) by Enrollment Pattern. Year 2016.” U.S. Department of Education, Quick Launch: heqmyc. https://nces.ed.gov/datalab/powerstats/121-national-postsecondary-student-aid-study-2016-undergraduates/percentage-distribution/trend.

———. 2022h. “Distance from Student’s Home (in Miles) to NPSAS Institution by Institution Sector (4 with Multiple); Years 2004, 2008, 2012 and 2016.” U.S. Department of Education, Quick Launch: lqtmop. https://nces.ed.gov/datalab/powerstats/121-national-postsecondary-student-aid-study-2016-undergraduates/percentage-distribution/trend.

———. 2022i. “Distance from Student’s Home (in Miles) to NPSAS Institution by Race/Ethnicity (with Multiple) without Foreign Students; Years 1996, 2008, 2012 and

2016." U.S. Department of Education, Quick Launch: ubmvzr. https://nces.ed.gov/datalab/powerstats/121-national-postsecondary-student-aid-study-2016-undergraduates/percentage-distribution/trend.

———. 2022j. "Distance from Student's Home (in Miles) to NPSAS Institution by Income Percentile Rank for All Students. Years 2004, 2008, 2012 and 2016." U.S. Department of Education, Quick Launch: svljuv. https://nces.ed.gov/datalab/powerstats/121-national-postsecondary-student-aid-study-2016-undergraduates/percentage-distribution/trend.

Neelakantan, U., and J. Romero. 2017. "Falling Short: Why Isn't the U.S. Producing More College Graduates?" Federal Reserve Bank of Richmond. https://www.richmondfed.org/-/media/RichmondFedOrg/publications/research/annual_report/2017/article.pdf.

OECD (Organization for Economic Cooperation and Development). 2021. *Education at a Glance 2021: OECD Indicators*. Paris: OECD Publishing. https://doi.org/10.1787/b35a14e5-en.

———. 2022. *Education at a Glance 2022*: OECD Indicators. Paris: OECD Publishing. https://doi.org/10.1787/3197152b-en.

Oreopoulos, P., and U. Petronijevic. 2018. "Student Coaching: How Far Can Technology Go?" *Journal of Human Resources* 53, no. 2: 299–329. https://doi.org/10.3368/jhr.53.2.1216-8439R.

Oreopoulos, P., and K. Salvanes. 2011. "Priceless: The Nonpecuniary Benefits of Schooling." *Journal of Economic Perspectives* 25, no. 1: 159–84. https://doi.org/10.1257/jep.25.1.159.

Ortagus, J., R. Kelchen, K. Rosinger, and N. Voorhees. 2020. "Performance-Based Funding in American Higher Education: A Systematic Synthesis of the Intended and Unintended Consequences." *Educational Evaluation and Policy Analysis* 42, no. 4. https://doi.org/10.3102/0162373720953128.

Ost, B., W. Pan, and D. Webber. 2018. "The Returns to College Persistence for Marginal Students: Regression Discontinuity Evidence from University Dismissal Policies." *Journal of Labor Economics* 36, no. 3: 779–805. http://doi.org/10.1086/696204.

Protopsaltis, S., and S. Parrott. 2017. "Pell Grants: A Key Tool for Expanding College Access and Economic Opportunity—Need Strengthening, Not Cuts." Center on Budget and Policy Priorities. https://www.cbpp.org/research/federal-budget/pell-grants-a-key-tool-for-expanding-college-access-and-economic.

Redden, E. 2010. "The 'Community College' Internationally." *Inside Higher Ed*. https://www.insidehighered.com/news/2010/06/16/community-college-internationally.

Ross, R., S. White, J. Wright, and L. Knapp. 2013. "Using Behavioral Economics for Postsecondary Success." ideas42. http://www.ideas42.org/wp-content/uploads/2015/05/Using-Behavioral-Economics-for-Postsecondary-Success_ideas42_2013.pdf.

Rothstein, J., R. Santillano, T. von Wachter, W. Khan, and M. Yang. 2022. "Identifying the Impacts of Job Training Programs in California." California Policy Lab. https://www.capolicylab.org/identifying-the-impacts-of-job-training-programs-in-california/.

Rouse, C. 1995. "Democratization or Diversion? The Effect of Community Colleges on Educational Attainment." *Journal of Business and Economic Statistics* 13, no. 2: 217–24. https://www.tandfonline.com/doi/abs/10.1080/07350015.1995.10524596.

Salto, D. 2019. "Brazil: Expanding Access Through Private Institutions." In *International Perspectives in Higher Education: Balancing Access, Equity, and Cost*, edited by J. Delisle and A. Usher, 149–68. https://www.aei.org/research-products/book/international-perspectives-in-higher-education-balancing-access-equity-and-cost/.

Schanzenbach, D., and S. Turner. 2022. "Limited Supply and Lagging Enrollment: Production Technologies and Enrollment Changes at Community Colleges during the Pandemic." *Journal of Public Economics* 212. https://doi.org/10.1016/j.jpubeco.2022.104703.

Scott-Clayton, J. 2012. *Information Constraints and Financial Aid Policy*. NBER Working Paper 17811. Cambridge, MA: National Bureau of Economic Research. https://doi.org/10.3386/w17811.

———. 2018a. "What Accounts for Gaps in Student Loan Default, and What Happens After." Brookings Institution. https://www.brookings.edu/wp-content/uploads/2018/06/Report_Final.pdf.

———. 2018b. "The Looming Student Loan Default Crisis Is Worse Than We Thought." Brookings Institution. https://www.brookings.edu/wp-content/uploads/2018/01/scott-clayton-report.pdf.

Scrivener S., M. Weiss, A. Ratledge, T. Rudd, C. Sommo, and H. Fresques. 2015. "Doubling Graduation Rates: Three-Year Effects of CUNY's Accelerated Study in Associate Programs (ASAP) for Developmental Education Students." MDRC. https://www.mdrc.org/sites/default/files/doubling_graduation_rates_fr.pdf.

Skinner, R., and C. Cooper. 2020. "FY2019 State Grants Under Title I-A of the Elementary and Secondary Education Act (ESEA)." Congressional Research Service. https://www.everycrsreport.com/files/20200311_R46269_eb6aebd236181eef9c73e8ec2f3b932a3e244798.pdf.

Smith, J. 2013. "Ova and Out: Using Twins to Estimate the Educational Returns to Attending a Selective College." *Economics of Education Review* 36: 166–80. https://doi.org/10.1016/j.econedurev.2013.06.008.

Smith, J., J. Goodman, and M. Hurwitz. 2020. *The Economic Impact of Access to Public Four-Year Colleges*. NBER Working Paper 27177. Cambridge, MA: National Bureau of Economic Research. https://doi.org/10.3386/w27177.

Sommo, C., D. Cullinan, M. Manno, S. Blake, and E. Alonzo. 2018. "Doubling Graduation Rates in a New State: Two-Year Findings from the ASAP Ohio Demonstration." MDRC. https://files.eric.ed.gov/fulltext/ED592008.pdf.

Song, M., K. Zeiser, D. Atchison, and I. Brodziak de los Reyes. 2021. "Early College, Continued Success: Longer-Term Impact of Early College High Schools." *Journal of Research on Educational Effectiveness* 14, no.1: 116–42. https://doi.org/10.1080/19345747.2020.1862374.

Stolzenberg, E., M. Aragon, E. Romo, V. Couch, D. McLennan, M. Eagan, and N. Kang. 2020. *The American Freshman: National Norms Fall 2019*. Los Angeles: Higher Education Research Institute of the University of California, Los Angeles. https://www.heri.ucla.edu/monographs/TheAmericanFreshman2019.pdf.

Student Loans Company. 2022. *Student Loans in England: Financial Year 2021–22*. Statistical Publication SP01/2022. Glasgow: Student Loans Company. https://assets.publishing.service.gov.uk/government/uploads/system/uploads/attachment_data/file/1092922/slcsp012022.pdf.

Turner, L. 2021. "The Importance of 'Choice Architecture' for Student Loan Repayment Decisions and Outcomes." Postsecondary Equity and Economics Research Project. https://www.peerresearchproject.org/peer/research/body/Turner-Paper-Choice-Architecture.pdf.

U.S. Department of Education. 2014. "Fact Sheet on Final Gainful Employment Regulations." https://www2.ed.gov/policy/highered/reg/hearulemaking/2012/gainful-employment-fact-sheet-10302014.pdf.

———. 2020. "Cover Letter." https://www2.ed.gov/about/offices/list/ope/heerfinstitutionalcoverletter.pdf.

———. 2022a. "Federal Student Loan Portfolio." https://studentaid.gov/data-center/student/portfolio.

———. 2022b. "During 'Raise the B.A.R.' Summit, Education Department Announces College Completion Fund Competition to Support Postsecondary Student Success." https://www.ed.gov/news/press-releases/during-%E2%80%98raise-bar%E2%80%99-summit-education-department-announces-college-completion-fund-competition-support-postsecondary-student-success.

———. 2022c. "ARP: American Rescue Plan (HEERF III)." https://www2.ed.gov/about/offices/list/ope/arp.html.

———. 2022d. "Gainful Employment Information." https://studentaid.gov/data-center/school/ge.

———. 2022e. "Issue Paper 3: Gainful Employment." https://d1y8sb8igg2f8e.cloudfront.net/documents/Issue_Paper_3_Gainful_Employment_FINAL_3-8-22.pdf.

———. 2023a. "The U.S. Department of Education Offers Low-Interest Loans to Eligible Students to Help Cover the Cost of College or Career School." https://studentaid.gov/understand-aid/types/loans/subsidized-unsubsidized.

———. 2023b. "Department Awards Grants to Improve Opportunities and Outcomes for Nation's Postsecondary Students." https://www.ed.gov/news/press-releases/department-awards-grants-improve-opportunities-and-outcomes-nations-postsecondary-students.

———. 2023c. "Higher Education Emergency Relief Fund: 2021 Annual Performance Report." https://www2.ed.gov/about/offices/list/ope/heerf-2021-annual-performance-report.pdf.

U.S. Department of Labor. 2022a. "Trade Adjustment Assistance Community College and Career Training (TAACCCT) Grant Program Evaluation." https://www.dol.gov/agencies/oasp/evaluation/currentstudies/14.

———. 2022b. "ApprenticeshipUSA: A Proven Solution for Employers." https://www.apprenticeship.gov/sites/default/files/dol-industry-factsheet-employer-v10.pdf.

U.S. Department of the Treasury. 2022. "American Rescue Plan State and Local Fiscal Recovery Funds: Project Highlights." https://home.treasury.gov/system/files/136/American-Rescue-Plan-Anniversary-SLFRF-Examples.pdf.

Usher, A. 2019. "The Architecture of Student Loan Systems." In *International Perspectives in Higher Education: Balancing Access, Equity, and Cost*, edited by J. Delisle and A. Usher, 87–106. https://www.aei.org/research-products/book/international-perspectives-in-higher-education-balancing-access-equity-and-cost/.

Walton, D., K. Gardiner, and B. Barnow. 2022. *Expanding Apprenticeship to New Sectors and Populations: The Experiences and Outcomes of Apprentices in the American Apprenticeship Initiative*. Prepared for the U.S. Department of Labor, Employment and Training Administration. Rockville, MD: Abt Associates. https://www.abtassociates.com/files/insights/reports/2022/aai-outcomes-study-final-report-508.pdf.

Webb, M. 2014. *Early College Expansion: Propelling Students to Postsecondary Success, at a School Near You.* Washington: Jobs for the Future. https://eric.ed.gov/?id=ED559689.

Webber, D., and R. Ehrenberg. 2010. "Do Expenditures Other Than Instructional Expenditures Affect Graduation and Persistence Rates in American Higher Education?" *Economics of Education Review* 29, no. 6: 947–58. https://doi.org/10.1016/j.econedurev.2010.04.006.

Weiss, M., A. Ratledge, C. Sommo, and H. Gupta. 2019. "Supporting Community College Students from Start to Degree Completion: Long-Term Evidence from a Randomized Trial of CUNY's ASAP." *American Economic Journal: Applied Economics* 11, no. 3: 253–97. https://doi.org/10.1257/app.20170430.

White House. 2021. "Fact Sheet: The American Families Plan." https://www.whitehouse.gov/briefing-room/statements-releases/2021/04/28/fact-sheet-the-american-families-plan/.

———. 2022. "Fact Sheet: Biden-Harris Administration Launches the Apprenticeship Ambassador Initiative to Create Equitable, Debt-Free Pathways to High-Paying

Jobs." https://www.whitehouse.gov/briefing-room/statements-releases/2022/09/01/fact-sheet-biden-harris-administration-launches-the-apprenticeship-ambassador-initiative-to-create-equitable-debt-free-pathways-to-high-paying-jobs/

Wiswall, M., and B. Zafar. 2015. "How Do College Students Respond to Public Information About Earnings?" *Journal of Human Capital* 9, no. 2: 117–69. https://doi.org/10.1086/681542.

World Higher Education Database. No date. "The World of Higher Education at Your Fingertips." https://www.whed.net/home.php.

Xu, D., and S. Jaggars. 2013. "The Impact of Online Learning on Students' Course Outcomes: Evidence from a Large Community and Technical College System." *Economics of Education Review* 37: 46–57. https://doi.org/10.1016/j.econedurev.2013.08.001.

Xu, D., S. Jaggars, and J. Fletcher. 2016. "How and Why Does Two-Year College Entry Influence Baccalaureate Aspirants' Academic and Labor Market Outcomes." Working paper, Center for Analysis of Postsecondary Education and Employment. https://ccrc.tc.columbia.edu/media/k2/attachments/CAPSEE-how-and-why-two-year-college-entry-influence-outcomes.pdf.

Zimmerman, S. 2014. "The Returns to College Admission for Academically Marginal Students." *Journal of Labor Economics* 32, no. 4: 711–54. https://doi.org/10.1086/676661.

Chapter 6

Aaronson, S., T. Cajner, B. Fallick, F. Galbis-Reig, C. Smith, and W. Wascher. 2014. "Labor Force Participation: Recent Developments and Future Prospects." *Brookings Papers on Economic Activity* 2: 197–275. https://doi.org/10.1353/eca.2014.0015.

Abraham, K., and M. Kearney. 2020. "Examining the Decline in the U.S. Employment-to-Population Ratio: A Review of the Evidence." *Journal of Economic Literature* 58, no. 3: 585–643. https://doi.org/10.1257/jel.20191480.

Acemoglu, D., and D. Autor. 2010. *Skills, Tasks and Technologies: Implications for Employment and Earnings*. NBER Working Paper 16982. Cambridge, MA: National Bureau of Economic Research. https://doi.org/10.3386/w16082.

Acemoglu, D., D. Autor, D. Dorn, G. Hanson, and B. Price. 2015. "Import Competition and the Great U.S. Employment Sag of the 2000s." *Journal of Labor Economics* 34, no. S1: 141–98. https://doi.org/10.1086/682384.

Acemoglu, D., and P. Restrepo. 2017. "Secular Stagnation? The Effect of Aging on Economic Growth in the Age of Automation." *American Economic Review* 107, no. 5: 174–79. https://doi.org/10.1257/aer.p20171101.

Aiken, L., D. Sloane, M. McHugh, C. Pogue, and K. Lasater. 2022. "A Repeated Cross-Sectional Study of Nurses Immediately Before and During the COVID-19

Pandemic: Implications for Action." *Nursing Outlook* 71, no. 2: 1–10. https://doi.org/10.1016/j.outlook.2022.11.007.

Akee, R., D. Feir, M. Gorzig, and S. Myers Jr. 2022. "Native American 'Deaths of Despair' and Economic Conditions." IZA Discussion Paper 15546. https://www.econstor.eu/bitstream/10419/265767/1/dp15546.pdf.

Alesina, A., E. Glaeser, and B. Sacerdote. 2005. *Work and Leisure in the U.S. and Europe: Why So Different?* NBER Working Paper 11278. Cambridge, MA: National Bureau of Economic Research. https://doi.org/10.3386/w11278.

Anand, P., L. Dague, and K. Wagner. 2021. *The Role of Paid Family Leave in Labor Supply Responses to a Spouse's Disability or Health Shock*. NBER Working Paper 28808. Cambridge, MA: National Bureau of Economic Research. https://doi.org/10.3386/w28808.

Autor, D. 2019. *Work of the Past, Work of the Future*. NBER Working Paper 25588. Cambridge, MA: National Bureau of Economic Research. https://doi.org/10.3386/w25588.

Autor, D., and D. Dorn. 2013. "The Growth of Low-Skill Service Jobs and the Polarization of the U.S. Labor Market." *American Economic Review* 103, no. 5: 1553–97. https://doi.org/10.1257/aer.103.5.1553.

Autor, D., D. Dorn, and G. Hanson. 2013. "The China Syndrome: Local Labor Market Effects of Import Competition in the United States." *American Economic Review* 103, no. 6: 2121–68. https://doi.org/10.1257/aer.103.6.2121.

———. 2021. *On the Persistence of the China Shock*. NBER Working Paper 29401. Cambridge, MA: National Bureau of Economic Research. https://doi.org/10.3386/w29401.

Autor, D., D. Dorn., G. Hanson, and J. Song. 2014. "Trade Adjustment: Worker-Level Evidence." *Quarterly Journal of Economics* 129, no. 4: 1799–860. https://doi.org/10.1093/qje/qju026.

Autor, D., and M. Duggan. 2003. "The Rise in the Disability Rolls and the Decline in Unemployment." *Quarterly Journal of Economics* 118, no. 1: 157–206. https://doi.org/10.1162/00335530360535171.

Bacher-Hicks, A., O. Chi, and A. Orellana. 2021. "COVID-19 and the Composition of the Massachusetts Teacher Workforce." Boston University, Wheelock College of Education and Human Development. https://wheelockpolicycenter.org/wp-content/uploads/2021/10/TeacherWorkforce_PolicyBrief_Final.pdf.

Baker, M., J. Gruber, and K. Milligan. 2008. "Universal Child Care, Maternal Labor Supply, and Family Well-Being." *Journal of Political Economy* 116, no. 4: 709–45. https://doi.org/10.1086/591908.

Barkin, T. 2022. "Is a Labor Challenge Coming?" Speech to Virginia Economic Summit and Forum on International Trade, December 2. https://www.richmondfed.org/press_room/speeches/thomas_i_barkin/2022/barkin_speech_20221202

Basso, G., and G. Peri. 2020. "Internal Mobility: The Greater Responsiveness of Foreign-Born to Economic Conditions." *Journal of Economic Perspectives* 34, no. 3: 77–98. https://doi.org/10.1257/jep.34.3.77.

Bastian, J. 2020. "The Rise of Working Mothers and the 1975 Earned Income Tax Credit." *American Economic Journal: Economic Policy* 12, no. 3: 44–75. https://doi.org/10.1257/pol.20180039.

Bauernschuster, S., and M. Schlotter. 2015. "Public Child Care and Mothers' Labor Supply—Evidence from Two Quasi-Experiments." *Journal of Public Economics* 123: 1–16. https://doi.org/10.1016/j.jpubeco.2014.12.013.

Baum, C., and C. Ruhm. 2016. "The Effects of Paid Family Leave in California on Labor Market Outcomes." *Journal of Policy Analysis and Management* 35, no. 2: 333–56. https://doi.org/10.1002/pam.21894.

Bernstein, S., R. Diamond, A. Jiranaphawiboon, T. McQuade, and B. Pousada. 2022. *The Contribution of High-Skilled Immigrants to Innovation in the United States.* NBER Working Paper 30797. Cambridge, MA: National Bureau of Economic Research. https://doi.org/10.3386/w30797.

Binder, A., and J. Bound. 2019. "The Declining Labor Market Prospects of Less-Educated Men." *Journal of Economic Perspectives* 33, no. 2: 163–90. https://doi.org/10.1257/jep.33.2.163.

Black, S., and C. Juhn. 2000. "The Rise of Female Professionals: Are Women Responding to Skill Demand?" *American Economic Review* 90, no. 2; 450–55. http://www.jstor.org/stable/117267.

Black, S., D. Schanzenbach, and A. Breitwieser. 2017. "The Recent Decline in Women's Labor Force Participation." Hamilton Project. https://www.brookings.edu/wp-content/uploads/2017/10/es_10192017_decline_womens_labor_force_participation_blackschanzenbach.pdf.

Blanchard, O., and L. Katz. 1992. "Regional Evolutions." *Brookings Papers on Economic Activity*, no. 1. https://www.brookings.edu/bpea-articles/regional-evolutions/.

Blau, F., and L. Kahn. 2007. "Changes in the Labor Supply Behavior of Married Women: 1980–2000." *Journal of Labor Economics* 25 no. 3: 393–438. https://www.journals.uchicago.edu/doi/full/10.1086/513416.

———. 2013. "Female Labor Supply: Why Is the United States Falling Behind?" *American Economic Review* 103, no. 3: 251–56. https://doi.org/10.1257/aer.103.3.251.

Blau, F., and C. Mackie, eds. 2017. *The Economic and Fiscal Consequences of Immigration.* National Academies of Sciences, Engineering, and Medicine. Washington: National Academies Press. https://doi.org/10.17226/23550.

Bloom, N., A. Kurmann, K. Handley, and P. Luck. 2019. "The Impact of Chinese Trade on U.S. Employment: The Good, The Bad, and The Apocryphal." Society for Economic Dynamics. https://www.gsb.stanford.edu/faculty-research/publications/impact-chinese-trade-us-employment-good-bad-apocryphal.

BLS (U.S Bureau of Labor Statistics). 2022. "Current Population Survey: Concepts and Definitions." https://www.bls.gov/cps/definitions.htm.

Bound, J. 1989. "The Health and Earnings of Rejected Disability Insurance Applicants." *American Economic Review* 79, no. 3: 482–503. https://doi.org/10.3386/w2816.

Boyd, D., H. Lankford, S. Loeb, and J. Wyckoff. 2005. "Explaining the Short Careers of High-Achieving Teachers in Schools with Low-Performing Students." *American Economic Review* 95, no. 2: 166–71. https://doi.org/10.1257/000282805774669628.

Buerhous, P., D. Auerbach, and D. Staiger. 2017. "How Should We Prepare for the Wave of Retiring Baby Boomer Nurses?" *Health Affairs*. https://doi.org/10.1377/forefront.20170503.059894.

Cajner, T., J. Coglianese, and J. Montes. 2021. "The Long-Lived Cyclicality of the Labor Force Participation Rate." Working paper, Federal Reserve Board of Governors. https://www.johncoglianese.com/publication/lfpr-cyclicality/lfpr-cyclicality.pdf.

Cajner, T., L. Crane, R. Decker, J. Grigsby, A. Hamins-Puertolas, E. Hurst, C. Kurz, and A. Yildirmaz. *The U.S. Labor Market during the Beginning of the Pandemic Recession*. NBER Working Paper 27159. Cambridge, MA: National Bureau of Economic Research. https://doi.org/10.3386/w27159.

Card, D. 1996. "The Effect of Unions on the Structure of Wages: A Longitudinal Analysis." *Econometrica* 64, no. 4: 957–79. https://doi.org/10.2307/2171852.

Case, A., and A. Deaton. 2015. "Rising Morbidity and Mortality in Midlife among White Non-Hispanic Americans in the 21st Century." *Proceedings of the National Academy of Sciences* 112, no. 49: 15078–83. https://doi.org/10.1073/pnas.1518393112.

———. 2020. *Deaths of Despair and the Future of Capitalism*. Princeton, NJ: Princeton University Press. https://press.princeton.edu/books/hardcover/9780691190785/deaths-of-despair-and-the-future-of-capitalism.

———. 2021. "Life Expectancy in Adulthood Is Falling for Those Without a B.A. Degree, but as Educational Gaps Have Widened, Racial Gaps Have Narrowed." *Proceedings of the National Academy of Sciences* 118, no. 11: e2024777118. https://www.pnas.org/content/118/11/e2024777118.

Cassar, L., and S. Meier. 2018. "Nonmonetary Incentives and the Implications of Work as a Source of Meaning." *Journal of Economic Perspectives* 32, no. 3: 215–38. https://doi.org/10.1257/jep.32.3.215.

CEA (Council of Economic Advisers). 2016. "The Long-Term Decline in Prime-Age Male Labor Force Participation." https://obamawhitehouse.archives.gov/sites/default/files/page/files/20160620_cea_primeage_male_lfp.pdf.

Center on Budget and Policy Priorities. 2021. "Social Security Disability Insurance." https://www.cbpp.org/research/social-security/social-security-disability-insurance-0.

Charles, K., E. Hurst, and M. Schwartz. 2018. *The Transformation of Manufacturing and the Decline in U.S. Employment*. NBER Working Paper 24468. Cambridge, MA: National Bureau of Economic Research. https://doi.org/10.3386/w24468.

Clark, A. 2015. "What Makes a Good Job? Job Quality and Job Satisfaction." *IZA World of Labor*. https://wol.iza.org/articles/what-makes-good-job-job-quality-and-job-satisfaction.

Clemens, M., and E. Lewis. 2022. *The Effect of Low-Skill Immigration Restrictions on U.S. Firms and Workers: Evidence from a Randomized Lottery*. NBER Working Paper 30589. Cambridge, MA: National Bureau of Economic Research. https://doi.org/10.3386/w30589.

Coglianese, J. 2018. "The Rise of In-and-Outs: Declining Labor Force Participation of Prime Age Men." Working paper, Harvard University. https://www.johncoglianese.com/publication/in-and-outs/in-and-outs.pdf.

Coile, C., and P. Levine. 2011. "Recessions, Retirement, and Social Security." *American Economic Review* 101, no. 2: 23–28. https://doi.org/10.1257/aer.101.3.23.

Coile, C., and H. Zhang. 2022. *Recessions and Retirement: New Evidence from the COVID-19 Pandemic*. PRC Working Paper 20. Philadelphia: Pension Research Council, Wharton School, University of Pennsylvania. http://dx.doi.org/10.2139/ssrn.4199666.

Cowan, J., D. Goldhaber, K. Hayes, and R. Theobald. 2016. "Missing Elements in the Discussion of Teacher Shortages." *Educational Researcher* 45, no. 8: 460–62. https://doi.org/10.3102/0013189X16679145.

Cutler, D., J. Poterba, L. Sheiner, and L. Summers. 1990. "An Aging Society: Opportunity or Challenge?" *Brookings Papers on Economic Activity* 1: 1–73. https://doi.org/10.2307/2534525.

Dao, M., D. Furceri, and P. Loungani. 2017. "Regional Labor Market Adjustment in the United States: Trend and Cycle." *Review of Economics and Statistics* 99, no. 2: 243–57. https://doi.org/10.1162/REST_a_00642.

Dee, T., and D. Goldhaber. 2017. "Understanding and Addressing Teacher Shortages in the United States." Hamilton Project. https://www.hamiltonproject.org/assets/files/understanding_and_addressing_teacher_shortages_in_us_pp.pdf.

Doleac, J. 2016. "Increasing Employment for Individuals with Criminal Records." Hamilton Project. https://www.brookings.edu/wp-content/uploads/2016/10/es_20161021_prisoner_reentry_doleac.pdf.

Eggertsson, G., M. Lancastre, and L. Summers. 2019. "Aging, Output Per Capita, and Secular Stagnation." *American Economic Review: Insights* 1, no. 3: 325–42. https://doi.org/10.1257/aeri.20180383.

Eissa, N., and J. Liebman. 1996. "Labor Supply Response to the Earned Income Tax Credit." *Quarterly Journal of Economics* 111, no. 2: 605–37. https://doi.org/10.2307/2946689.

Farber, H. 2005. "Nonunion Wage Rates and the Threat of Unionization." *Industrial Labor and Relations Review* 58, no. 3: 335–52. https://journals.sagepub.com/doi/abs/10.1177/001979390505800302?journalCode=ilra.

Farber, H., D. Herbst, I. Kuziemko, and S. Naidu. 2021. "Unions and Inequality over the Twentieth Century: New Evidence from Survey Data." *Quarterly Journal of Economics* 136, no. 3: 1325–85. https://doi.org/10.1093/qje/qjab012.

Favilukis, J., and G. Li. 2023. "The Great Resignation Was Caused by the COVID-19 Housing Boom." Social Science Research Network. https://ssrn.com/abstract=4335860.

Feldman, M. 2022. "Place-Based Economic Development." *Issues in Science and Technology* 39, no. 1: 44–46. https://issues.org/place-based-economic-development-feldman/.

Foote, C., and R. Ryan. 2015. *Labor Market Polarization Over the Business Cycle.* NBER Working Paper 21030. Cambridge, MA: National Bureau of Economic Research. https://doi.org/10.3386/w21030.

Forsythe, E., L. Kahn, F. Lange, and D. Wiczer 2022. *Where Have All the Workers Gone? Recalls, Retirements, and Reallocation in the COVID Recovery.* NBER Working Paper 30387. Cambridge, MA: National Bureau of Economic Research. https://doi.org/10.3386/w30387.

Fry, R., J. Passel, and D. Cohn. 2020. "A Majority of Young Adults in the U.S. Live with Their Parents for the First Time since the Great Depression." Pew Research Center. https://www.pewresearch.org/fact-tank/2020/09/04/a-majority-of-young-adults-in-the-u-s-live-with-their-parents-for-the-first-time-since-the-great-depression/.

Gagnon, E., B. Johannsen, and D. López-Salido. 2021. "Understanding the New Normal: The Role of Demographics." *IMF Economic Review* 69: 357–90. https://doi.org/10.1057/s41308-021-00138-4.

Ganong, P., and D. Shoag. 2017. "Why Has Regional Income Convergence in the U.S. Declined?" *Journal of Urban Economics* 102: 76–90. https://doi.org/10.1016/j.jue.2017.07.002.

GAO (U.S. Government Accountability Office). 2021. "Physician Workforce: Caps on Medicare-Funded Graduate Medical Education at Teaching Hospitals." https://www.gao.gov/products/gao-21-391.

Garcia, K., and B. Cowan. 2022. *The Impact of U.S. School Closures on Labor Market Outcomes during the COVID-19 Pandemic.* NBER Working Paper 29641. Cambridge, MA: National Bureau of Economic Research. https://doi.org/10.3386/w29641.

Galvin, G. 2021. "Nearly 1 in 5 Health Care Workers Have Quit Their Jobs during the Pandemic." *Morning Consult.* https://morningconsult.com/2021/10/04/health-care-workers-series-part-2-workforce/.

Garin, A., D. Koustas, C. McPherson, S. Norris, M. Pecenco, E. Rose, Y. Shem-Tov, and J. Weaver. 2022. "The Impact of Incarceration on Employment, Earnings, and

Tax Filing." Working paper, Joint Statistical Research Program of the Statistics of Income Division, U.S. Internal Revenue Service. https://www.irs.gov/pub/irs-soi/07-2022-impact-incarceration-employment-earnings-tax-filing.pdf.

Gelbach, J. 2002. "Public Schooling for Young Children and Maternal Labor Supply." *American Economic Review* 92, no. 1: 307–22. https://doi.org/10.1257/000282802760015748.

Gelber, A., T. Moore, and A. Strand. 2017. "The Effect of Disability Insurance Payments on Beneficiaries' Earnings." *American Economic Journal: Economic Policy* 9, no. 3: 229–61. https://doi.org/10.1257/pol.20160014.

Goda, G., and E. Soltas. 2022. *The Impacts of COVID-19 Illnesses on Workers*. NBER Working Paper 30435. Cambridge, MA: National Bureau of Economic Research. https://doi.org/10.3386/w30435.

Goldhaber, D., C. Grout, K. Holden, and N. Brown. 2015. "Crossing the Border? Exploring the Cross-State Mobility of the Teacher Workforce." *Educational Researcher* 44, no. 8: 421–31. https://doi.org/10.3102/0013189X15613981.

Goldin, C., and L. Katz. 2002. "The Power of the Pill: Oral Contraceptives and Women's Career and Marriage Decisions." *Journal of Political Economy* 110, no. 4: 730–70. https://doi.org/10.1086/340778.

Gorodnichenko Y., J. Song, and D. Stolyarov. 2013. *Macroeconomic Determinants of Retirement Timing*. NBER Working Paper 19638. Cambridge, MA: National Bureau of Economic Research. https://doi.org/10.3386/w19638.

Gottlieb, J., and A. Zenilman. 2020. *When Workers Travel: Nursing Supply During COVID-19 Surges*. NBER Working Paper 28240. Cambridge, MA: National Bureau of Economic Research. https://doi.org/10.3386/w28240.

Greene, J., and M. Mauer. 2010. "Downscaling Prisons." Sentencing Project. https://www.justicestrategies.org/sites/default/files/publications/inc_DownscalingPrisons2010.pdf.

Grossman, G., and E. Oberfield. 2022. "The Elusive Explanation for the Declining Labor Share." *Annual Review of Economics* 14: 93–124. https://dx.doi.org/10.1146/annurev-economics-080921-103046.

Haeck, C., P. Lefebvre, and P. Merrigan. 2015. "Canadian Evidence on Ten Years of Universal Preschool Policies: The Good and the Bad." *Labour Economics* 36: 137–57. https://doi.org/10.1016/j.labeco.2015.05.002.

Ham, J., C. Swenson, A. İmrohoroğlu, and H. Song. 2011. "Government Programs Can Improve Local Labor Markets: Evidence from State Enterprise Zones, Federal Empowerment Zones and Federal Enterprise Community." *Journal of Public Economics* 95, nos. 7–8: 779–97. https://doi.org/10.1016/j.jpubeco.2010.11.027.

Hansen, B., J. Sabia, and J. Schaller 2022. *Schools, Job Flexibility, and Married Women's Labor Supply*. NBER Working Paper 29660. Cambridge, MA: National Bureau of Economic Research. https://doi.org/10.3386/w29660.

Hoynes, H., J. Rothstein, and K. Ruffini. 2017. "Making Work Pay Better Through an Expanded Earned Income Tax Credit." Hamilton Project. https://www.hamiltonproject.org/assets/files/making_work_pay_expanded_eitc_Hoynes_Rothstein_Ruffini.pdf.

Hsieh, C., and E. Moretti. 2019. "Housing Constraints and Spatial Misallocation." *American Economic Journal: Macroeconomics* 11, no. 2: 1–39. https://doi.org/10.1257/mac.20170388.

Hunt, J., and M. Gauthier-Loiselle. 2010. "How Much Does Immigration Boost Innovation?" *American Economic Journal: Macroeconomics* 2: 31–56. https://doi.org/10.1257/mac.2.2.31.

James, J., and J. Wyckoff. 2022. "School Segregation, Teacher Sorting, and the Distribution of Teachers." Working paper, Annenberg Institute at Brown University. https://doi.org/10.26300/tv5x-6t21.

Johnson, J., and M. Kleiner. 2020. "Is Occupational Licensing a Barrier to Interstate Migration?" *American Economic Journal: Economic Policy* 12, no. 3: 347–73. https://pubs.aeaweb.org/doi/pdfplus/10.1257/pol.20170704.

Juhn, C., and S. Potter. 2006. "Changes in Labor Force Participation in the United States." *Journal of Economic Perspectives* 20, no. 3: 27–46. https://doi.org/10.1257/jep.20.3.27.

Kaplan, G., and S. Schulhofer-Wohl. 2017. "Understanding the Long-Run Decline in Interstate Migration." *International Economic Review* 58, no. 1: 57–94. https://doi.org/10.1111/iere.12209.

Katz, B., W. Congdon, and J. Shakesprere. 2022. "Measuring Job Quality: Current Measures, Gaps, and New Approaches." Urban Institute Research Report. https://www.urban.org/sites/default/files/2022-04/Measuring%20Job%20Quality.pdf.

Keynes, J. 2010. "Economic Possibilities for Our Grandchildren." *Essays in Persuasion*, 321–32. Orig. pub. 1930. https://doi.org/10.1007/978-1-349-59072-8_25.

Kline, P., and E. Moretti. 2014. "Local Economic Development, Agglomeration Economies, and the Big Push: 100 Years of Evidence from the Tennessee Valley Authority." *Quarterly Journal of Economics* 129, no. 1: 275–331. https://doi.org/10.1093/qje/qjt034.

Krueger, A. 2017. "Where Have All the Workers Gone? An Inquiry into the Decline of the U.S. Labor Force Participation Rate." *Brookings Papers on Economic Activity*, no. 2. https://www.brookings.edu/wp-content/uploads/2018/02/kruegertextfa17bpea.pdf.

Levy, F., and P. Temin. 2007. *Inequality and Institutions in 20th-Century America*. NBER Working Paper 13106. Cambridge, MA: National Bureau of Economic Research. https://doi.org/10.3386/w13106.

Lofstrom, M., and S. Raphael. 2013. "Impact of Realignment on County Jail Populations." Public Policy Institute of California. https://gspp.berkeley.edu/assets/uploads/research/pdf/p73.pdf.

Looney, A., and N. Turner. 2018. *Work and Opportunity Before and After Incarceration.* Economic Studies at Brookings. Washington: Brookings Institution. https://www.brookings.edu/wp-content/uploads/2018/03/es_20180314_looneyincarceration_final.pdf.

Maestas, N., K. Mullen, and D. Powell. 2022. *The Effect of Population Aging on Economic Growth, the Labor Force, and Productivity.* NBER Working Paper 22452. Cambridge, MA: National Bureau of Economic Research. https://doi.org/10.3386/w22452.

Maestas, N., K. Mullen, D. Powell, R. von Wachter, and J. Wenger. 2017. "Working Conditions in the United States: Results of the 2015 American Working Conditions Survey." RAND Corporation Research Report. https://doi.org/10.7249/RR2014.

Maestas, N., K. Mullen, and A. Strand. 2013. "Does Disability Insurance Receipt Discourage Work? Using Examiner Assignment to Estimate Causal Effects of SSDI Receipt." *American Economic Review* 103, no. 5: 1797–829. https://doi.org/10.1257/aer.103.5.1797.

Matsudaira, J. 2015. "Economic Conditions and the Living Arrangements of Young Adults: 1960 to 2011." *Journal of Population Economics* 29: 167–95. https://doi.org/10.1007/s00148-015-0555-y.

McEntarfer, E. 2022. *Older Workers, Retirement, and Macroeconomic Shocks.* PRC Working Paper 2022-13. Philadelphia: Pension Research Council, Wharton School, University of Pennsylvania. http://dx.doi.org/10.2139/ssrn.4169082.

Meyer, B., and D. Rosenbaum. 2001. "Welfare, the Earned Income Tax Credit, and the Labor Supply of Single Mothers." *Quarterly Journal of Economics* 116, no. 3: 1063–1114. https://doi.org/10.1162/00335530152466313.

Migration Policy Institute. 2022. "What Has Been the Impact of the Pandemic on Immigrant Communities and U.S. Immigration Trends and Policies Two Years On? New Report Assesses." https://www.migrationpolicy.org/news/pandemic-impact-immigrants-us-immigration-two-years-on.

Montes, J., C. Smith, and J. Dajon. 2022. *"The Great Retirement Boom": The Pandemic-Era Surge in Retirements and Implications for Future Labor Force Participation.* Finance and Economics Discussion Series, Working Paper 081. Washington: Federal Reserve Board. https://doi.org/10.17016/FEDS.2022.081.

Morrissey, T. 2017. "Child Care and Parent Labor Force Participation: A Review of the Research Literature." *Review of Economics of the Household* 15: 1–24. https://doi.org/10.1007/s11150-016-9331-3.

Mueller-Smith, M. 2015. "The Criminal and Labor Market Impacts of Incarceration." Working paper, University of Michigan. https://www.irp.wisc.edu/newsevents/workshops/2015/participants/papers/10-Mueller-Smith-IRP-draft.pdf.

Murnane, R., and J. Steele. 2007. "What Is the Problem? The Challenge of Providing Effective Teachers for All Children." *Future of Children* 17, no. 1: 15–43. https://doi.org/10.1353/foc.2007.0010.

Ne'eman, A., and N. Maestas 2022. *How Has COVID-19 Impacted Disability Employment?* NBER Working Paper 30640. Cambridge, MA: National Bureau of Economic Research. https://doi.org/10.3386/w30640.

Neumark, D., and J. Kolko. 2010. "Do Enterprise Zones Create Jobs? Evidence from California's Enterprise Zone Program." *Journal of Urban Economics* 68, no. 1: 1–19. https://doi.org/10.1016/j.jue.2010.01.002.

Neumark, D., and H. Simpson. 2015. "Place-Based Policies." *Handbook of Regional and Urban Economics* 5: 1197–287. http://dx.doi.org/10.1016/B978-0-444-59531-7.00018-1.

Nguyen, T., C. Lam, and P. Bruno. 2022. "Is There a National Teacher Shortage? A Systematic Examination of Reports of Teacher Shortages in the United States." Working paper, Annenberg Institute at Brown University. https://doi.org/10.26300/76eq-hj32.

Nikolova, M., and F. Cnossen. 2020. "What Makes Work Meaningful and Why Economists Should Care About It." *Labour Economics* 65: 101847. https://doi.org/10.1016/j.labeco.2020.101847.

Nunn, R., J. Parsons, and J. Shambaugh. 2019. "Labor Force Nonparticipation: Trends, Causes, and Policy Solutions." Hamilton Project. https://www.brookings.edu/wp-content/uploads/2019/10/ES_THP_labor-force-nonparticipation_final.pdf.

OECD (Organization for Economic Cooperation and Development). 2019. "Public Spending on Childcare and Early Education." OECD Family Database. https://www.oecd.org/els/soc/PF3_1_Public_spending_on_childcare_and_early_education.pdf.

Pager, D. 2003. "The Mark of Criminal Record." *American Journal of Sociology* 108, no. 5: 937–75. https://www.jstor.org/stable/pdf/10.1086/374403.

Petterson, S., W. Liaw, R. Phillips, D. Rabin, D. Meyers, and A. Bazemore. 2012. "Projecting U.S. Primary Care Physician Workforce Needs: 2010–25." *Annals of Family Medicine* 10, no. 6: 503–9. https://doi.org/10.1370/afm.1431.

Piehl, A. 2016. "Putting Time Limits on the Punitiveness of the Criminal Justice System." Hamilton Project. https://www.hamiltonproject.org/assets/files/reducing_punitiveness_piehl_policymemo.pdf.

Pierce, J., and P. Schott. 2016. "The Surprisingly Swift Decline of U.S. Manufacturing Employment." *American Economic Review* 106, no. 7: 1632–62. https://doi.org/10.1257/aer.20131578.

Ricketts, T. 2005. "Workforce Issues in Rural Areas: A Focus on Policy Equity." *American Journal of Public Health* 95, no. 1: 42–48. https://doi.org10.2105/AJPH.2004.047597.

Rodriguez, M., and B. Avery. 2016. "Unlicensed & Untapped: Removing Barriers to State Occupational Licenses for People with Records." National Employment Law Project. https://s27147.pcdn.co/wp-content/uploads/Unlicensed-Untapped-Removing-Barriers-State-Occupational-Licenses.pdf.

Satiani, A., J. Niedermier, B. Satiani, and D. Svendsen. 2018. "Projected Workforce of Psychiatrists in the United States: A Population Analysis." *Psychiatric Services* 69, no. 6: 710–13. https://doi.org/10.1176/appi.ps.201700344.

Schmitt, J., and A. Mitukiewicz. 2012. "Politics Matter: Changes in Unionisation Rates in Rich Countries, 1960–2010." *Industrial Relations Journal* 43, no. 3: 260–80. https://doi.org/10.1111/j.1468-2338.2012.00675.x.

Schor, J. 1993. *The Overworked American: The Unexpected Decline of Leisure*. New York: Basic Books. https://www.basicbooks.com/titles/juliet-b-schor/the-overworked-american/9780465054343/.

Sheiner, L. 2014. "The Determinants of the Macroeconomic Implications of Aging." *American Economic Review* 104, no. 5: 218–23. https://doi.org/10.1257/aer.104.5.218.

Stansbury, A., and L. Summers. 2020. *The Declining Worker Power Hypothesis: An Explanation for the Recent Evolution of the American Economy*. NBER Working Paper 27193. Cambridge, MA: National Bureau of Economic Research. https://doi.org/10.3386/w27193.

U.S. Department of Education. 2022. "2022 School Pulse Panel." Institute of Education Sciences. https://ies.ed.gov/schoolsurvey/spp/.

Vahey, D., L. Aiken, D. Sloane, S. Clarke, and D. Vargas. 2004. "Nurse Burnout and Patient Satisfaction." *Med Care* 42 (2 Suppl.): 1157–66. https://www.ncbi.nlm.nih.gov/pmc/articles/PMC2904602/.

Volk, J., D. Palanker, M. O'Brien, and C. Goe. 2021. "States' Actions to Expand Telemedicine Access During COVID-19 and Future Policy Considerations." Commonwealth Fund. https://www.commonwealthfund.org/publications/issue-briefs/2021/jun/states-actions-expand-telemedicine-access-covid-19.

White House. 2021. "Statement by President Joe Biden on the House Taking up the PRO Act." https://www.whitehouse.gov/briefing-room/statements-releases/2021/03/09/statement-by-president-joe-biden-on-the-house-taking-up-the-pro-act/.

Wikle, J., and R. Wilson. 2022. "Access to Head Start and Maternal Labor Supply: Experimental and Quasi-Experimental Evidence." Working paper, Brigham Young University. https://economics.byu.edu/00000173-9aea-d2bd-a9f7-fbeb30dd0000/hs-laborsupply-wikle-wilson-july2020-pdf.

World Prison Brief. 2021. "World Prison Population List." Institute for Crime & Justice Policy Research. https://www.prisonstudies.org/sites/default/files/resources/downloads/world_prison_population_list_13th_edition.pdf.

Wu, P. 2022. *Wage Inequality and the Rise in Labor Force Exit: The Case of U.S. Prime-Age Men*. Research Department Working Paper 22-16. Boston: Federal Reserve Bank of Boston. https://doi.org/10.29412/res.wp.2022.16.

Ziliak, J. 2014. "Supporting Low-Income Workers through Refundable Child-Care Credits." Brookings Institution. https://www.brookings.edu/research/supporting-low-income-workers-through-refundable-child-care-credits/.

Chapter 7

Acemoglu, D., A. Makhdoumi, A. Malekian, and A. Ozdaglar. 2022. "Too Much Data: Prices and Inefficiencies in Data Markets." *American Economic Journal: Microeconomics* 14, no. 4: 218–56. https://doi.org/10.1257/mic.20200200.

Acquisti, A., C. Taylor, and L. Wagman. 2016. "The Economics of Privacy." *Journal of Economic Literature* 54, no. 2: 442–92. http://doi.org/10.1257/jel.54.2.442.

Aday, S., H. Farrell, D. Freelon, M. Lynch, J. Sides, and M. Dewar. 2013. "Watching from Afar: Media Consumption Patterns Around the Arab Spring." *Sage Journals* 57, no. 7: 899–919. https://doi.org/10.1177/0002764213479373.

Allcott, H., L. Braghieri, S. Eichmeyer, and M. Gentzkow. 2020. "The Welfare Effects of Social Media." *American Economic Review* 110, no. 3: 629–76. https://doi.org/10.1257/aer.20190658.

Allcott, H., and M. Gentzkow. 2017. "Social Media and Fake News in the 2016 Election." *Journal of Economic Perspectives* 31, no. 2: 211–36. https://doi.org/10.1257/jep.31.2.211.

Amazon. 2021. "The Evolution of Amazon's Inventory Planning System." https://www.amazon.science/latest-news/the-evolution-of-amazons-inventory-planning-system.

Armstrong, M. 2006. "Competition in Two-Sided Markets." *RAND Journal of Economics* 37, no. 3: 668–91. https://www.jstor.org/stable/pdf/25046266.pdf.

Athey, S., and F. Scott Morton. 2022. "Platform Annexation." *Antitrust Law Journal* 84, no. 3: 677–703. https://siepr.stanford.edu/publications/working-paper/platform-annexation.

Ayres, I., M. Banaji, and C. Jolls. 2015. "Race Effects on eBay." *RAND Journal of Economics* 46, no. 4: 891–917. https://doi.org/10.1111/1756-2171.12115.

Ayers, J., B. Chu, Z. Zhu, E. Leas, D. Smith, M. Dredze, and D. Broniatowski. 2021. "Spread of Misinformation About Face Masks and COVID-19 by Automated Software on Facebook." *JAMA Internal Medicine* 181, no. 9: 1251–53. https://doi.org/10.1001/jamainternmed.2021.2498.

Bail, C., L. Argyle, T. Brown, J. Bumpus, H. Chen, M. Hunzaker, J. Lee, M. Mann, F. Merhout, and A. Volfovsky. 2018. "Exposure to Opposing Views on Social Media Can Increase Political Polarization." *PNAS* 115, no. 37: 9216–21. https://doi.org/10.1073/pnas.1804840115.

Baker, J., and J. Chevalier. 2013. "The Competitive Consequences of Most-Favored-Nation Provisions." *Antitrust Magazine* 27, no. 2. https://papers.ssrn.com/sol3/papers.cfm?abstract_id=2251165.

Baye, M., J. Morgan, and P. Scholten. 2003. "The Value of Information in an Online Consumer Electronics Market." *Journal of Public Policy and Marketing* 22, no. 1: 17–25. https://www.jstor.org/stable/30000838.

Barrett, B. 2021. "Commercial Companies in Party Networks: Digital Advertising Firms in U.S. Elections from 2006–2016." *Political Communication* 39, no. 2: 147–65. https://doi.org/10.1080/10584609.2021.1978021.

Beknazar-Yuzbashev, G., and M. Stalinski. 2022. "Do Social Media Ads Matter for Political Behavior? A Field Experiment." *Journal of Public Economics* 214. https://doi.org/10.1016/j.jpubeco.2022.104735.

Bergemann, D., and A. Bonatti. 2019. "Markets for Information: An Introduction." *Annual Review of Economics* 11: 85–107. https://doi.org/10.1146/annurev-economics-080315-015439.

Berkshire Hathaway Inc. 2007. "Letter to Shareholders of Berkshire Hathaway Inc." https://www.berkshirehathaway.com/letters/2007ltr.pdf.

Blake, T., S. Moshary, K. Sweeney, and S. Tadelis. 2021. "Price Salience and Product Choice." *Marketing Science* 40, no. 4: 619–36. https://pubsonline.informs.org/doi/10.1287/mksc.2020.1261.

Boik, A., and K. Corts. 2016. "The Effects of Platform Most-Favored-Nation Clauses on Competition and Entry." *Journal of Law and Economics* 59, no. 1: 105–34. https://doi.org/10.1086/686971.

Bonbright, J. 1961. *Principles of Public Utility Rates*. New York: Columbia University Press.

Bond, R., C. Fariss, J. Jones, A. Kramer, C. Marlow, J. Settle, and J. Fowler. 2012. "A 61-Million-Person Experiment in Social Influence and Political Mobilization." *Nature* 489: 295–98. https://doi.org/10.1038/nature11421.

Boxell, L., M. Gentzkow, and J. Shapiro. 2017. "Greater Internet Use Is Not Associated with Faster Growth in Political Polarization among U.S. Demographic Groups." *PNAS* 114, no. 40: 10612–17. https://doi.org/10.1073/pnas.1706588114.

Bresnahan, T. 2002. "The Economics of the Microsoft Case." Working Paper 232, Stanford Law School. http://dx.doi.org/10.2139/ssrn.304701.

Brown, J., and A. Goolsbee. 2002. "Does the Internet Make Markets More Competitive? Evidence from the Life Insurance Industry." *Journal of Political Economy* 110, no. 3: 481–507. https://doi.org/10.1086/339714.

Brown, S. 2021. "Machine Learning, Explained." Massachusetts Institute of Technology, Sloan School of Management. https://mitsloan.mit.edu/ideas-made-to-matter/machine-learning-explained.

Brown, Z., and A. MacKay. Forthcoming. "Competition in Pricing Algorithms." *American Economic Journal: Microeconomics*. https://www.aeaweb.org/articles?id=10.1257/mic.20210158.

Brynjolfsson, E., A. Collis, E. Diewert, F. Eggers, and K. Fox. 2019. *GDP-B: Accounting for the Value of New and Free Goods in the Digital Economy*. NBER Working Paper 25695. Cambridge, MA: National Bureau of Economic Research. https://doi.org/10.3386/w25695.

Brynjolfsson, E., Y. Hu, and M. Smith. 2003. "Consumer Surplus in the Digital Economy: Estimating the Value of Increased Product Variety at Online Booksellers." *Management Science* 49, no. 11: 1580–96. https://www.jstor.org/stable/4134002.

Brynjolfsson, E., and M. Smith. 2000. "Frictionless Commerce? A Comparison of Internet and Conventional Retailers." *Management Science* 46, no. 4: 563–85. https://www.jstor.org/stable/2661602.

Byrne, D., and N. de Roos. 2019. "Learning to Coordinate: A Study in Retail Gasoline." *American Economic Review* 109, no. 2: 591–619. https://pubs.aeaweb.org/doi/pdfplus/10.1257/aer.20170116.

Caillaud, B., and B. Jullien. 2003. "Chicken & Egg: Competition among Intermediation Service Providers." *RAND Journal of Economics* 34, no. 2: 309–28. https://www.jstor.org/stable/pdf/1593720.pdf.

Caliskan, A. 2021. "Detecting and Mitigating Bias in Natural Language Processing." Brookings Institution. https://www.brookings.edu/research/detecting-and-mitigating-bias-in-natural-language-processing/.

Carney, N. 2016. "All Lives Matter, but So Does Race: Black Lives Matter and the Evolving Role of Social Media." *Humanity & Society* 40, no. 2: 180–99. https://journals.sagepub.com/doi/abs/10.1177/0160597616643868.

Cavallo, C. 2017. "Are Online and Offline Prices Similar? Evidence from Large Multi-Channel Retailers." *American Economic Review* 107, no. 1: 283–303. https://www.aeaweb.org/articles?id=10.1257/aer.20160542.

CFPB (Consumer Financial Protection Bureau). 2022. "Credit Card Late Fees." https://files.consumerfinance.gov/f/documents/cfpb_credit-card-late-fees_report_2022-03.pdf.

Chan, J., A. Ghose, and R. Seamans. 2016. "The Internet and Racial Hate Crimes: Offline Spillovers from Online Access." *MIS Quarterly* 40, no. 2: 381–403. http://dx.doi.org/10.2139/ssrn.2335637.

Chandra, A., and A. Collard-Wexler. 2009. "Mergers in Two-Sided Markets: An Application to the Canadian Newspaper Industry." *Journal of Economics & Management Strategy* 18, no. 4: 1045–70. https://doi.org/10.1111/j.1530-9134.2009.00237.x.

Chapman, P., and S. Bodoni. 2022. "Twitter Probed in EU for Pre-Musk Data Leak of 5.4 Million Users." Bloomberg. https://www.bloomberg.com/news/articles/2022-12-23/twitter-probed-by-top-eu-privacy-watchdog-for-pre-musk-era-leak?leadSource=uverify%20wall.

Chin, C. 2019. "Assessing Employer Intent When AI Hiring Tools Are Biased." Brookings Institution. https://www.brookings.edu/research/assessing-employer-intent-when-ai-hiring-tools-are-biased/.

Chiou, L., and C. Tucker. 2017. *Search Engines and Data Retention: Implications for Privacy and Antitrust*. NBER Working Paper 23815. Cambridge, MA: National Bureau for Economic Research. https://doi.org/10.3386/w23815.

Choi, J., D. Jeon, and B. Kim. 2019. "Privacy and Personal Data Collection with Information Externalities." *Journal of Public Economics* 173: 113–24. https://doi.org/10.1016/j.jpubeco.2019.02.001.

Competition Bureau Canada. 2017. "Big Data and Innovation: Implications for Competition Policy in Canada." https://www.competitionbureau.gc.ca/eic/site/cb-bc.nsf/eng/04304.html.

Connecticut, State of. 2022. "An Act Concerning Personal Data Privacy and Online Monitoring, Senate Bill No. 6, February Session, Connecticut General Assembly, 2022." https://www.cga.ct.gov/2022/amd/S/pdf/2022SB-00006-R00SA-AMD.pdf.

Council of the European Union. 2022. "Digital Markets Act (DMA): Agreement Between the Council and the European Parliament." https://www.consilium.europa.eu/en/press/press-releases/2022/03/25/council-and-european-parliament-reach-agreement-on-the-digital-markets-act/.

Crain, M. 2018. "The Limits of Transparency: Data Brokers and Commodification." *New Media and Society* 20, no. 1: 88–104. https://journals.sagepub.com/doi/abs/10.1177/1461444816657096.

Dastin, J. 2018. "Amazon Scraps Secret AI Recruiting Tool That Showed Bias Against Women." Reuters. https://www.reuters.com/article/us-amazon-com-jobs-automation-insight/amazon-scraps-secret-ai-recruiting-tool-that-showed-bias-against-women-idUSKCN1MK08G.

DeLuca, K., S. Lawson, and Y. Sun. 2012. "Occupy Wall Street on the Public Screens of Social Media: The Many Framings of the Birth of a Protest Movement." *Communication, Culture and Critique* 5, no. 4: 483–509. https://doi.org/10.1111/j.1753-9137.2012.01141.x.

Digital Regulation Cooperation Forum. 2022. "Auditing Algorithms: The Existing Landscape, Role of Regulators and Future Outlook." https://www.gov.uk/government/publications/findings-from-the-drcf-algorithmic-processing-workstream-spring-2022/auditing-algorithms-the-existing-landscape-role-of-regulators-and-future-outlook.

DiGrazia, J., K. McKelvey, J. Bollen, and F. Rojas. 2013. "More Tweets, More Votes: Social Media as a Quantitative Indicator of Political Behavior." *PLoS ONE* 8, no. 11. https://doi.org/10.1371/journal.pone.0079449.

DOJ (U.S. Department of Justice). 2020. "Justice Department Sues to Block Visa's Proposed Acquisition of Plaid." https://www.justice.gov/opa/pr/justice-department-sues-block-visas-proposed-acquisition-plaid.

Doleac, J., and L. Stein. 2013. "The Visible Hand: Race and Online Market Outcomes." *Economic Journal* 123, no. 572: 469–92. https://doi.org/10.1111/ecoj.12082.

Dubé, J., and S. Misra. 2023. "Personalized Pricing and Consumer Welfare." *Journal of Political Economy* 131, no. 1: 131–89. https://doi.org/10.1086/720793.

Eeckhout, J., and L. Veldkamp. 2022. *Data and Market Power*. NBER Working Paper 30022. Cambridge, MA: National Bureau of Economic Research. https://www.nber.org/system/files/working_papers/w30022/w30022.pdf.

Ellison, G., and S. Ellison. 2009. "Search, Obfuscation, and Price Elasticities on the Internet." *Econometrica* 77, no. 2: 427–52. https://doi.org/10.3982/ECTA5708.

Ellison, G., and D. Fudenberg. 2003. *Knife Edge of Plateau: When Do Market Models Tip?* NBER Working Paper 9528. Cambridge, MA: National Bureau of Economic Research. https://www.nber.org/papers/w9528.

Engler, A. 2021. "Auditing Employment Algorithms for Discrimination." Brookings Institution. https://www.brookings.edu/research/auditing-employment-algorithms-for-discrimination/.

European Parliament. 2022. "European Parliament Legislative Resolution of 5 July 2022 on the Proposal for a Regulation of the European Parliament and of the Council on a Single Market for Digital Services (Digital Services Act) and Amending Directive 2000/31/EC." https://www.europarl.europa.eu/doceo/document/TA-9-2022-0269_EN.html#title2.

European Parliament and Council of the European Union. 2022. "Regulation (EU) 2022/2065 of the European Parliament and of the Council of 19 October 2022 on a Single Market for Digital Services and Amending Directive 2000/31/EC (Digital Services Act)." https://eur-lex.europa.eu/legal-content/EN/TXT/PDF/?uri=CELEX:32022R2065&from=EN.

European Parliament and European Commission. 2022. "On Contestable and Fair Markets in the Digital Sector and Amending Directives (EU) 2019/1937 and (EU) 2020/1828 (Digital Markets Act)." https://eur-lex.europa.eu/legal-content/EN/TXT/PDF/?uri=CELEX:32022R1925&from=EN.

Evans, D. 2003. "The Antitrust Economics of Multi-Sided Platform Markets." *Yale Journal on Regulation* 20, no. 2. https://www.semanticscholar.org/paper/The-Antitrust-Economics-of-Multi-Sided-Platform-Evans/aef4ba3a170b9863f305c8562ad0ce1726ae2f98.

Farronato, C., J. Fong, and A. Fradkin. Forthcoming. "Dog Eat Dog: Balancing Network Effects and Differentiation in a Digital Platform Merger." *Management Science*. https://www.hbs.edu/faculty/Pages/item.aspx?num=62569.

FTC (U.S. Federal Trade Commission). 2014. "Data Brokers: A Call for Transparency and Accountability." https://www.ftc.gov/system/files/documents/reports/data-brokers-call-transparency-accountability-report-federal-trade-commission-may-2014/140527databrokerreport.pdf/.

———. 2017. "Economic Analysis of Hotel Resort Fees." https://www.ftc.gov/system/files/documents/reports/economic-analysis-hotel-resort-fees/p115503_hotel_resort_fees_economic_issues_paper.pdf.

———. 2019. "FTC Imposes $5 Billion Penalty and Sweeping New Privacy Restrictions on Facebook." https://www.ftc.gov/news-events/news/press-releases/2019/07/ftc-imposes-5-billion-penalty-sweeping-new-privacy-restrictions-facebook.

———. 2022. "Case No. 2:22-cv-377: Complaint for Permanent Injunction and Other Relief." https://www.ftc.gov/system/files/ftc_gov/pdf/1.%20Complaint.pdf.

Fiorina, M., and S. Abrams. 2008. "Political Polarization in the American Public." *Annual Review of Political Science* 11: 563–88. https://doi.org/10.1146/annurev.polisci.11.053106.153836.

Furl, N., P. Phillips, and A. O'Toole. 2002. "Face Recognition Algorithms and the Other-Race Effect: Computational Mechanisms for a Developmental Contact Hypothesis." *Cognitive Science* 26, no. 6: 797–815. https://doi.org/10.1016/S0364-0213(02)00084-8.

Gandal, N. 1994. "Hedonic Price Indexes for Spreadsheets and an Empirical Test for Network Externalities." *RAND Journal of Economics* 25, no. 1: 160–70. https://www.jstor.org/stable/2555859#metadata_info_tab_contents.

———. 1995. "Competing Compatibility Standards and Network Externalities in the PC Software Market." *Review of Economics and Statistics* 77, no. 4: 599–608. https://www.jstor.org/stable/2109809#metadata_info_tab_contents.

Garett, R., and S. Young. 2021. "Online Misinformation and Vaccine Hesitancy." *Translational Behavioral Medicine* 11, no. 12: 2194–99. https://doi.org/10.1093/tbm/ibab128.

Gentzkow, M. 2007. "Valuing New Goods in a Model with Complementarity: Online Newspapers." *American Economic Review* 97, no. 3: 713–44. https://www.jstor.org/stable/30035018.

Goldfarb, A., and C. Tucker. 2019. "Digital Economics." *Journal of Economic Literature* 57, no. 1: 3–43. https://doi.org/10.1257/jel.20171452.

Gorodnichenko, Y., T. Pham, and O. Talavera. 2021. "Social Media, Sentiment and Public Opinions: Evidence from #Brexit and #USElection." *European Economic Review* 136. https://doi.org/10.1016/j.euroecorev.2021.103772.

Gu, Y., L. Madio, and C. Reggiani. 2022. "Data Brokers Co-Opetition." *Oxford Economic Papers* 74, no. 3: 820–39. https://doi.org/10.1093/oep/gpab042.

Gu, Y., L. Madio, and C. Reggiani. 2022. "Data Brokers Co-Opetition." *Oxford Economic Papers* 74, no. 3: 820–39. https://doi.org/10.1093/oep/gpab042.

Guszcza, J., I. Rahwan, W. Bible, M. Cebrian, and V. Katyal. 2018. "Why We Need to Audit Algorithms." *Harvard Business Review*. https://hbr.org/2018/11/why-we-need-to-audit-algorithms.

Harrington, J. 2018. "Developing Competition Law for Collusion by Autonomous Artificial Agents." *Journal of Competition Law and Economics* 14, no. 3: 331–63. https://doi.org/10.1093/joclec/nhy016.

Highfill, T., and C. Surfield. 2022. "New and Revised Statistics of the U.S. Digital Economy, 2005–2021." U.S. Bureau of Economic Analysis. https://www.bea.gov/system/files/2022-11/new-and-revised-statistics-of-the-us-digital-economy-2005-2021.pdf.

Himelein-Wachowiak, M., S. Giorgi, A. Devoto, M. Rahman, L. Ungar, A. Schwartz, D. Epstein, L. Leggio, and B. Curtis. 2021. "Bots and Misinformation Spread on Social Media: Implications for COVID-19." *JMIR Publications* 23, no. 5. https://doi.org/10.2196/26933.

Ichihashi, S. 2020. "Online Privacy and Information Disclosure by Consumers." *American Economic Review* 110, no. 2: 569–95. https://doi.org/10.1257/aer.20181052.

Jones, J., R. Bond, E. Bakshy, D. Eckles, and J. Fowler. 2017. "Social Influence and Political Mobilization: Further Evidence from a Randomized Experiment in the 2012 U.S. Presidential Election." *PLoS ONE* 12, no. 4. https://pubmed.ncbi.nlm.nih.gov/28445476/.

Joskow, P. 2007. "Chapter 16 Regulation of Natural Monopoly." *Handbook of Law and Economics* 2: 1227–1348. https://doi.org/10.1016/S1574-0730(07)02016-6.

Joskow, P., and N. Rose. 1989. "The Effects of Economic Regulation." *Handbook of Industrial Organization* 2: 1449–1506. https://doi.org/10.1016/S1573-448X(89)02013-3.

Jullien, B., A. Pavan, and M. Rysman. 2021. "Chapter 7: Two-Sided Markets, Pricing, and Network Effects." *Handbook of Industrial Organization* 4, no. 1: 485–592. https://www.sciencedirect.com/science/article/abs/pii/S1573448X21000078?via%3Dihub.

Kades, M., and F. Scott Morton. 2020. "Interoperability as a Competition Remedy for Digital Networks." Working paper, Washington Center for Equitable Growth. https://equitablegrowth.org/working-papers/interoperability-as-a-competition-remedy-for-digital-networks/.

Kahn, A. 1988. *The Economics of Regulation.* Cambridge, MA: MIT Press. https://mitpress.mit.edu/9780262610520/the-economics-of-regulation/.

Kirpalani, R., and T. Philippon. 2020. *Data Sharing and Market Power with Two-Sided Platforms.* NBER Working Paper 28023. Cambridge, MA: National Bureau for Economic Research. https://doi.org/10.3386/w28023.

Kroll, J. 2021. "Why AI Is Just Automation." Brookings Institution. https://www.brookings.edu/research/why-ai-is-just-automation/.

Lajevardi, N., K. Oskooii, and H. Walker. 2022. "Hate, Amplified? Social Media News Consumption and Support for Anti-Muslim Policies." *Journal of Public Policy,* 1–28. https://doi.org/10.1017/S0143814X22000083.

Lambrecht, A., and C. Tucker. 2019. "Algorithmic Bias? An Empirical Study of Apparent Gender-Based Discrimination in the Display of STEM Career Ads." *Management Science* 65, no. 7: 2966–81. https://doi.org/10.1287/mnsc.2018.3093.

Lee, N., and S. Lai. 2021. "Why New York City Is Cracking Down on AI in Hiring." Brookings Institution. https://www.brookings.edu/blog/techtank/2021/12/20/why-new-york-city-is-cracking-down-on-ai-in-hiring/.

Levy, R. 2021. "Social Media, News Consumption, and Polarization: Evidence from a Field Experiment." *American Economic Review* 113, no. 3: 831–70. https://doi.org/10.1257/aer.20191777.

Liu, Y., R. Jia, J. Ye, and X. Qu. 2022. "How Machine Learning Informs Ride-Hailing Services: A Survey." *Communications in Transportation Research* 2. https://doi.org/10.1016/j.commtr.2022.100075.

Luco, F. 2019. "Who Benefits from Information Disclosure? The Case of Retail Gasoline." *American Economic Journal: Microeconomics* 11, no. 2: 277–305. https://www.jstor.org/stable/pdf/26641423.pdf.

McCurry, J. 2021. "South Korean AI Chatbot Pulled from Facebook After Hate Speech Towards Minorities." *Guardian*, January 13. https://www.theguardian.com/world/2021/jan/14/time-to-properly-socialise-hate-speech-ai-chatbot-pulled-from-facebook.

Mickle, T. 2019. "Apple Dominates App Store Search Results, Thwarting Competitors." *Wall Street Journal*, July 23. https://www.wsj.com/articles/apple-dominates-app-store-search-results-thwarting-competitors-11563897221.

Mishra, S. 2021. "The Dark Industry of Data Brokers: Need for Regulation?" *International Journal of Law and Information Technology* 29, no. 4: 395–410. https://doi.org/10.1093/ijlit/eaab012.

Möhlmann, M., and O. Henfridsson. 2019. "What People Hate About Being Managed by Algorithms, According to a Study of Uber Drivers." *Harvard Business Review*. https://hbr.org/2019/08/what-people-hate-about-being-managed-by-algorithms-according-to-a-study-of-uber-drivers.

Mundt, M., K. Ross, and C. Burnett. 2018. "Scaling Social Movements Through Social Media: The Case of Black Lives Matter." *Social Media + Society* 4, no. 4. https://journals.sagepub.com/doi/full/10.1177/2056305118807911.

NCSL (National Conference of State Legislatures). 2022. "State Laws Related to Digital Privacy." https://www.ncsl.org/research/telecommunications-and-information-technology/state-laws-related-to-internet-privacy.aspx.

Neely, S., C. Eldredge, R. Ersing, and C. Remington. 2022. "Vaccine Hesitancy and Exposure to Misinformation: A Survey Analysis." *Journal of General Internal Medicine* 37, no. 1: 179–87. https://doi.org/10.1007/s11606-021-07171-z.

Obermeyer, Z., B. Powers, C. Vogeli, and S. Mullainathan. 2019. "Dissecting Racial Bias in an Algorithm Used to Manage the Health of Populations." *Science* 366, no. 6464: 447–53. https://doi.org/10.1126/science.aax2342.

O'Connor, J., and N. Wilson. 2021. "Reduced Demand Uncertainty and the Sustainability of Collusion: How AI Could Affect Competition." *Information Economics and Policy* 54. https://doi.org/10.1016/j.infoecopol.2020.100882.

OECD (Organization for Economic Cooperation and Development). 2019. "OECD AI Principles Overview." https://oecd.ai/en/ai-principles.

O'Sullivan, D. "Half a Billion Facebook Users' Information Posted on Hacking Website, Cyber Experts Say." CNN Business. https://www.cnn.com/2021/04/04/tech/facebook-user-info-leaked/index.html.

Pierri, F., B. Perry, M. DeVerna, K. Yang, A. Flammini, F. Menczer, and J. Bryden. 2022. "Online Misinformation Is Linked to Early COVID-19 Vaccination Hesitancy and Refusal." *Scientific Reports* 12, no.1. https://doi.org/10.1038/s41598-022-10070-w.

Prior, M. 2013. "Media and Polarization." *Annual Review of Political Science* 16: 101–27. https://doi.org/10.1146/annurev-polisci-100711-135242.

Prüfer, J., and C. Schottmüller. 2022. "Competing with Big Data." *Journal of Industrial Economics* 69, no. 4: 967–1008. https://doi.org/10.1111/joie.12259.

Quan, T., and K. Williams. 2018. "Product Variety, Across-Market Demand Heterogeneity, and the Value of Online Retail." *RAND Journal of Economics* 49, no. 4: 877–913. https://www.jstor.org/stable/45147416.

Rochet, J., and J. Tirole. 2003. "Platform Competition in Two-Sided Markets." *Journal of the European Economic Association* 1, no. 4: 990–1029. https://doi.org/10.1162/154247603322493212.

Rysman, M. 2004. "Competition between Networks: A Study of the Market for Yellow Pages." *Review of Economic Studies* 71, no. 2: 483–512. https://doi.org/10.1111/0034-6527.00512.

Saloner, G., and A. Shepard. 1995. "Adoption of Technologies with Network Effects: An Empirical Examination of the Adoption of Automated Teller Machines." *RAND Journal of Economics* 26, no. 3: 479–501. https://www.jstor.org/stable/2555999.

Schmalensee, R. 1978. "A Note on Economies of Scale and Natural Monopoly in the Distribution of Public Utility Services." *Bell Journal of Economics* 9, no. 1: 207–76. https://doi.org/10.2307/3003626.

Scott Morton, F., P. Bouvier, A. Ezrachi, B. Jullien, R. Katz, G. Kimmelman, A. Melamed, and J. Morgenstern. 2019. "Committee for the Study of Digital Platforms Market Structure and Antitrust Subcommittee." Chicago Booth Stigler Center for the Study of the Economy and the State. https://research.chicagobooth.edu/-/media/research/stigler/pdfs/market-structure-report.pdf.

Scott Morton, F., G. Crawford, J. Crémer, D. Dinielli, A. Fletcher, P. Heidhues, M. Schnitzer, and K. Seim. 2021. "Equitable Interoperability: The 'Super Tool' of Digital Platform Governance." Yale Tobin Center for Economic Policy, Digital Regulation Policy. https://tobin.yale.edu/sites/default/files/Equitable%20 Interoperability.pdf.

Scott Morton, F., F. Zettelmeyer, and J. Silva-Risso. 2001. "Internet Car Retailing." *Journal of Industrial Economics* 49, no. 4: 501–19. https://www.jstor.org/stable/3569793.

Sherman, J. 2021. "Data Brokers and Sensitive Data on U.S. Individuals: Threats to American Civil Rights, National Security, and Democracy." Duke University, Sanford School of Public Policy. https://techpolicy.sanford.duke.edu/

wp-content/uploads/sites/4/2021/08/Data-Brokers-and-Sensitive-Data-on-US-Individuals-Sherman-2021.pdf.

Sinai, T., and J. Waldfogel. 2004. "Geography and the Internet: Is the Internet a Substitute or a Complement for Cities?" *Journal of Urban Economics* 56, no. 1: 1–24. https://doi.org/10.1016/j.jue.2004.04.001.

Sisson, P. 2022. "Robots Aren't Done Reshaping Warehouses." *New York Times*, July 12. https://www.nytimes.com/2022/07/12/business/warehouse-technology-robotics.html.

Smiley, R., and W. Greene. 1983. "Determinants of the Effectiveness of Electric Utility Regulation." *Resources and Energy* 5, no. 1: 65–81. https://doi.org/10.1016/0165-0572(83)90018-X.

Smith, B. 2021. "How TikTok Reads Your Mind." *New York Times*, December 5. https://www.nytimes.com/2021/12/05/business/media/tiktok-algorithm.html.

Song, M. 2021. "Estimating Platform Market Power in Two-Sided Markets with an Application to Magazine Advertising." *American Economic Journal: Microeconomics* 13, no. 2: 35–67. https://doi.org/10.1257/mic.20160052.

Spence, A. 1975. "Monopoly, Quality, and Regulation." *Bell Journal of Economics* 6, no. 2: 417–29. https://doi.org/10.2307/3003237.

State of New York et al. v. Facebook, Inc. 2020. New York State, Attorney General's Office. https://ag.ny.gov/sites/default/files/state_of_new_york_et_al._v._facebook_inc._-_filed_public_complaint_12.11.2020.pdf.

Stigler, G. 1961. "The Economics of Information." *Journal of Political Economy* 69, no. 3: 213–25. https://www.jstor.org/stable/1829263.

Suh, C., I. Vasi, and P. Chang. 2017. "How Social Media Matter: Repression and the Diffusion of the Occupy Wall Street Movement." *Social Science Research* 65: 282–93. https://doi.org/10.1016/j.ssresearch.2017.01.004.

Teh, T., C. Liu, J. Wright, and J. Zhou. Forthcoming. "Multi-Homing and Oligopolistic Platform Competition." *American Economic Journal: Microeconomics*. https://www.aeaweb.org/articles?id=10.1257/mic.20210324.

U.S. Census Bureau. 2022. "Quarterly Retail E-Commerce Sales, 2nd Quarter 2022." https://www.census.gov/retail/mrts/www/data/pdf/ec_current.pdf.

U.S. Senate. 2013. "What Information Do Data Brokers Have on Consumers, and How Do They Use It?" https://www.govinfo.gov/content/pkg/CHRG-113shrg95838/pdf/CHRG-113shrg95838.pdf.

U.S. Surgeon General's Advisory. 2021. "Protecting Youth Mental Health." U.S. Department of Health and Human Services. https://www.hhs.gov/sites/default/files/surgeon-general-youth-mental-health-advisory.pdf.

Victor, D. 2016. "Microsoft Created a Twitter Bot to Learn from Users; It Quickly Became a Racist Jerk." *New York Times*, March 24. https://www.nytimes.com/2016/03/25/technology/microsoft-created-a-twitter-bot-to-learn-from-users-it-quickly-became-a-racist-jerk.html.

Wall Street Journal. 2021. "Inside TikTok's Algorithm: A WSJ Video Investigation." July 21. https://www.wsj.com/articles/tiktok-algorithm-video-investigation-11626877477.

Wang, C., and J. Wright. Forthcoming. "Platform Investment and Price Parity Clauses." *Journal of Industrial Economics*. https://app.scholarsite.io/julian-wright/articles/platform-investment-and-price-parity-clauses-3.

Weyl, E. 2010. "A Price Theory of Multi-Sided Platforms." *American Economic Review* 100, no. 4: 1642–72. https://doi.org/10.1257/aer.20180478.

White House. 2021. "Executive Order on Promoting Competition in the American Economy." https://www.whitehouse.gov/briefing-room/presidential-actions/2021/07/09/executive-order-on-promoting-competition-in-the-american-economy/.

———. 2022. "Blueprint for an AI Bill of Rights: Making Automated Systems Work for the American People." https://www.whitehouse.gov/wp-content/uploads/2022/10/Blueprint-for-an-AI-Bill-of-Rights.pdf.

White House, National Economic Council. 2016. "The Competition Initiative and Hidden Fees." https://obamawhitehouse.archives.gov/sites/whitehouse.gov/files/documents/hiddenfeesreport_12282016.pdf.

Williams, C., and G. Gulati. 2017. "Digital Advertising Expenditures in the 2016 Presidential Election." *Sage Journals* 36, no. 4: 406–21. https://doi.org/10.1177/0894439317726751.

Wright, J. 2004. "One-Sided Logic in Two-Sided Markets." *Review of Network Economics* 3, no. 1: 1–21. https://doi.org/10.2202/1446-9022.1042.

Xu, W., and K. Sasahara. 2022. "Characterizing the Roles of Bots on Twitter during the COVID-19 Infodemic." *Journal of Computational Social Science* 5: 591–609. https://doi.org/10.1007/s42001-021-00139-3.

Zang, J. 2021. "How Facebook's Advertising Algorithms Can Discriminate by Race and Ethnicity." *Tech Science*. https://techscience.org/a/2021101901/.

Zhang, S., N. Mehta, P. Singh, and K. Srinivasan. 2021. "Frontiers: Can an Artificial Intelligence Algorithm Mitigate Racial Economic Inequality? An Analysis in the Context of Airbnb." *Management Science* 40: no. 5: 813–20. https://doi.org/10.1287/mksc.2021.1295.

Chapter 8

Acemoglu, D. 2021. "The Bitcoin Fountainhead." https://www.project-syndicate.org/commentary/bitcoin-an-appealing-distraction-by-daron-acemoglu-2021-10.

Adams, A., and M. Ibert. 2022. "Runs on Algorithmic Stablecoins: Evidence from Iron, Titan, and Steel." https://www.federalreserve.gov/econres/notes/feds-notes/runs-on-algorithmic-stablecoins-evidence-from-iron-titan-and-steel-20220602.html.

Amazon. 2017. "Amazon Aurora PostgreSQL-Compatible Edition Benchmarking Guide." https://d1.awsstatic.com/product-marketing/Aurora/RDS_Aurora_PostgreSQL_Performance_Assessment_Benchmarking_V1-0.pdf.

Anadu, K., M. Cipriani, R. Craver, and G. La Spada. 2021. "COVID Response: The Money Market Mutual Fund Liquidity Facility." Federal Reserve Bank of New York, Staff Report 980. https://www.newyorkfed.org/medialibrary/media/research/staff_reports/sr980.pdf.

Atlantic Council. 2022. "Central Bank Digital Currency Tracker." https://www.atlanticcouncil.org/cbdctracker/.

Bank of Canada, European Central Bank, Bank of Japan, Sveriges Riksbank, Swiss National Bank, Bank of England, Board of Governors the Federal Reserve System, and Bank for International Settlements. 2021. "Central Bank Digital Currencies: Financial Stability Implications." https://www.bis.org/publ/othp42_fin_stab.pdf.

Bank of England. 2020. "Why Does Money Depend on Trust?" https://www.bankofengland.co.uk/knowledgebank/why-does-money-depend-on-trust.

Baughman, G., F. Carapella, J. Gerszten, and D. Mills. 2022. "The Stable in Stablecoins." https://www.federalreserve.gov/econres/notes/feds-notes/the-stable-in-stablecoins-20221216.html.

Bech, M., J. Hancock, T. Rice, and A. Wadsworth. 2020. "On the Future of Securities Settlement." *BIS Quarterly Review*, March. https://www.bis.org/publ/qtrpdf/r_qt2003i.pdf.

Benetton, M., G. Compiani, and A. Morse. 2021. "When Cryptomining Comes to Town: High-Electricity-Use Spillovers to the Local Economy." http://dx.doi.org/10.2139/ssrn.3779720.

Berentsen, A., and F. Schär. 2018. "A Short Introduction to the World of Cryptocurrencies." *Review of the Federal Reserve Bank of St. Louis* 100: 1–16. https://files.stlouisfed.org/files/htdocs/publications/review/2018/01/10/a-short-introduction-to-the-world-of-cryptocurrencies.pdf.

Borri, N., Y. Liu, and A. Tsyvinski. 2022. "The Economics of Non-Fungible Tokens." Working paper. https://papers.ssrn.com/sol3/papers.cfm?abstract_id=4052045.

Bowman, M. 2022. "Technology, Innovation, and Financial Services." Federal Reserve Board. https://www.federalreserve.gov/newsevents/speech/bowman20220817a.htm.

Briola, A., D. Vidal-Tomás, Y. Wang, and T. Aste. 2023. "Anatomy of a Stablecoin's Failure: The Terra-Luna Case." *Finance Research Letter* 51. https://www.sciencedirect.com/science/article/abs/pii/S1544612322005359.

Brown, K. 2002. "Announcing Approval of Federal Information Processing Standard (FIPS) 180-2, Secure Hash Standard; a Revision of FIPS 180-1." National Institute of Standards and Technology. *Federal Register*. https://www.federalregister.gov/documents/2002/08/26/02-21599/announcing-approval-of-federal-information-processing-standard-fips-180-2-secure-hash-standard-a.

Brunnermeier, M., and L. Pedersen. 2007. *Market Liquidity and Funding Liquidity*. NBER Working Paper 12939. Cambridge, MA: National Bureau of Economic Research. https://doi.org/10.3386/w12939.

BTC. 2022. "Difficulty." btc.com/stats/diff.

Calma, J. 2022. "Texas' Fragile Grid Isn't Ready for Crypto Mining's Explosive Growth." *The Verge*. https://www.theverge.com/2022/7/14/23206795/bitcoin-crypto-mining-electricity-texas-grid-energy-bills-emissions.

Carapella, F., E. Dumas, J. Gerszten, N. Swem, and L. Wall. 2022. "Decentralized Finance (DeFi): Transformative Potential & Associated Risks." Federal Reserve Board, Finance and Economics Discussion Series 2022-057. https://www.federalreserve.gov/econres/feds/files/2022057pap.pdf.

Cassidy, J. 2008. "The Minsky Moment: Subprime Mortgage Crisis and Possible Recession." *New Yorker*, February 4. https://www.newyorker.com/magazine/2008/02/04/the-minsky-moment.

Chaum, D. 1982. "Computer Systems Established, Maintained, and Trusted by Mutually Suspicious Groups." Ph.D. dissertation, University of California, Berkeley. https://evervault.com/papers/chaum.pdf.

Cheng, E. 2017. "$24 Million Iced Tea Company Says It's Pivoting to the Blockchain, and Its Stock Jumps 200%." CNBC. https://www.cnbc.com/2017/12/21/long-island-iced-tea-micro-cap-adds-blockchain-to-name-and-stock-soars.html.

Clearing House. No date. "Real-Time Payments for All Financial Institutions." https://www.theclearinghouse.org/payment-systems/rtp.

Coindesk. 2022. "Bitcoin." https://www.coindesk.com/price/bitcoin/.

CoinMarketCap. 2022. "Helium." https://coinmarketcap.com/currencies/helium/.

———. 2023. "Top Stablecoin Tokens by Market Capitalization." https://coinmarketcap.com/view/stablecoin/.

CPFB (Consumer Protection Financial Bureau). 2022. "Complaint Bulletin." https://files.consumerfinance.gov/f/documents/cfpb_complaint-bulletin_crypto-assets_2022-11.pdf.

CRS (Congressional Research Service). 2022 "The U.S. Dollar as the World's Dominant Reserve Currency." https://crsreports.congress.gov/product/pdf/IF/IF11707.

Damalas, G., R. Abouseif, K. O'Brien, and A. Stafford. 2022. "Crypto Derivatives Are Becoming a Major Digital Asset Class." EY. https://www.ey.com/en_us/financial-services/crypto-derivatives-are-becoming-a-major-digital-asset-class.

de Vries, A. and C. Stoll. 2021. "Bitcoin's Growing E-Waste Problem." *Resources, Conservation, and Recycling* 175. https://www.sciencedirect.com/science/article/abs/pii/S0921344921005103.

Diamond., D., and P. Dybvig. 1983. "Bank Runs, Deposit Insurance, and Liquidity." *Journal of Political Economy* 91, no. 3: 401–19. https://www.jstor.org/stable/1837095.

Digiconomist. 2022. "Bitcoin Electronic Waste Monitor." https://digiconomist.net/bitcoin-electronic-waste-monitor/.

Dixon, C. 2021. "Why Web3 Matters." *Future*. https://future.com/why-web3-matters/.

Dowling, M. 2022. "Fertile LAND: Pricing Non-Fungible Tokens." *Finance Research Letters* 44. https://doi.org/10.1016/j.frl.2021.102096.

Emerson, S., D. Jeans, and P. Liu. 2022. "Crypto Darling Helium Promised a 'People's Network'; Instead, Its Executives Got Rich." *Forbes*, September 23. https://www.forbes.com/sites/sarahemerson/2022/09/23/helium-crypto-tokens-peoples-network/?sh=234bb5087316.

Emsisoft Malware Lab. 2021. "The Cost of Ransomware in 2021: A Country-by-Country Analysis." https://www.emsisoft.com/en/blog/38426/the-cost-of-ransomware-in-2021-a-country-by-country-analysis/.

Etherscan. 2022. "Ethereum Daily Transactions Chart." https://etherscan.io/chart/tx.

Faverio, M., and N. Massarat. 2022. "46% of Americans Who Have Invested in Cryptocurrency Say It's Done Worse Than Expected." Pew Research Center. pewresearch.org/fact-tank/2022/08/23/46-of-americans-who-have-invested-in-cryptocurrency-say-its-done-worse-than-expected/.

FCA (U.K. Financial Conduct Authority). 2021. "First Supervisory Notice." Reference 688849. https://www.fca.org.uk/publication/supervisory-notices/first-supervisory-notice-binance-markets-limited.pdf.

FDIC (Federal Deposit Insurance Corporation). 2022. "2021 FDIC National Survey of Unbanked and Underbanked Households." https://www.fdic.gov/analysis/household-survey/index.html.

Federal Register. 2019. "Notices." Vol. 84, no. 154: 39297–322. https://www.govinfo.gov/content/pkg/FR-2019-08-09/pdf/2019-17027.pdf.

Federal Reserve Board. 1988. "The Federal Reserve in the Payments Mechanism." https://www.federalreserve.gov/boarddocs/press/general/1998/19980105/19980105.pdf.

———. 2020. "Federal Reserve Board: Automated Clearinghouse Services." https://www.federalreserve.gov/paymentsystems/fedach_about.htm.

———. 2022a. "Developments in Noncash Payments for 2019 and 2020: Findings from the Federal Reserve Payments Study." https://www.federalreserve.gov/paymentsystems/december-2021-findings-from-the-federal-reserve-payments-study.htm.

———. 2022b. "FedNow Service." https://www.federalreserve.gov/paymentsystems/fednow_about.htm.

———. 2022c. "FedNow Service: Frequently Asked Questions." https://www.federalreserve.gov/paymentsystems/files/fednow_faq.pdf.

———. 2022d. "Money and Payments: The U.S. Dollar in the Age of Digital Transformation." https://www.federalreserve.gov/publications/files/money-and-payments-20220120.pdf.

———. 2023. "Policy Statement on Section 9(13) of the Federal Reserve Act." https://www.federalreserve.gov/newsevents/pressreleases/files/bcreg20230127a1.pdf.

———. No date. "Fostering Payment and Settlement System Safety and Efficiency." https://www.federalreserve.gov/aboutthefed/files/pf_6.pdf.

Federal Reserve Bank of Minneapolis. 1988. "Developing an Efficient Payments System." https://www.minneapolisfed.org/article/1988/developing-an-efficient-payments-system.

Federal Reserve Bank of San Francisco. No date. "What Is the Fed? Payment Services." https://www.frbsf.org/education/teacher-resources/what-is-the-fed/payment-services/.

Fletcher, E. 2021. "Crypto-Assets Buzz Drives Record Investment Scam Losses." Federal Trade Commission. https://www.ftc.gov/news-events/data-visualizations/data-spotlight/2021/05/cryptocurrency-buzz-drives-record-investment-scam-losses.

Flood, J. 2012. "Bank Runs." *New York*, May 25. https://nymag.com/news/intelligencer/topic/banks-2012-6/.

Ge Huang, V., A. Osipovich, and P. Kowsmann. 2022. "FTX Tapped into Customer Accounts to Fund Risky Bets, Setting Up Its Downfall." *Wall Street Journal*. https://www.wsj.com/articles/ftx-tapped-into-customer-accounts-to-fund-risky-bets-setting-up-its-downfall-11668093732.

Gibson, M., and E. Belsky. 2022. "SR 22-6 / CA 22-6: Engagement in Crypto-Asset-Related Activities by Federal Reserve–Supervised Banking Organizations." Board of Governors of the Federal Reserve System. https://www.federalreserve.gov/supervisionreg/srletters/SR2206.htm.

Goldstein, J., and D. Kestenbaum. 2010. "The Island of Stone Money." NPR. https://www.npr.org/sections/money/2011/02/15/131934618/the-island-of-stone-money.

Goldstein, M., A. Stevenson, M. Farrell, and D. Yaffe-Bellany. 2022. "How FTX's Sister Firm Brought the Crypto Exchange Down." *New York Times*, November 18. https://www.nytimes.com/2022/11/18/business/ftx-alameda-ties.html.

Gorton, G. 2012. *Misunderstanding Financial Crises: Why We Don't See Them Coming*. Oxford: Oxford University Press. https://global.oup.com/academic/product/misunderstanding-financial-crises-9780199922901.

Gorton, G., and J. Zhang. 2021. "Taming Wildcat Stablecoins." Working paper. https://papers.ssrn.com/sol3/papers.cfm?abstract_id=3888752.

———. 2022. "Protecting the Sovereign's Money Monopoly." Working paper, University of Michigan. https://papers.ssrn.com/sol3/papers.cfm?abstract_id=4162884.

Government Accountability Office. 2021. "Virtual Currencies: Additional Information Could Improve Federal Agency Efforts to Counter Human and Drug Trafficking." https://www.gao.gov/assets/gao-22-105462.pdf.

Griffith, E. 2018. "Is Your Startup Stalled? Pivot to Blockchain." *Wired*. https://www.wired.com/story/is-your-startup-stalled-pivot-to-blockchain/.

Hoffman, A. No date. "Taking the Cryptic Out of Crypto Assets." Federal Reserve Bank of Dallas. https://www.dallasfed.org/-/media/Documents/educate/events/2022/22econsummit/22econsummit_Hoffman.pdf.

Howden. 2023. "The Great Realignment." https://www.howdengroup.com/sites/g/files/mwfley566/files/2023-01/the-great-realignment-report-2023.pdf.

Huang, J., C. O'Neill, and H. Tabuchi. 2021. "Bitcoin Uses More Electricity Than Many Countries; How Is That Possible?" *New York Times*, September 3. https://www.nytimes.com/interactive/2021/09/03/climate/bitcoin-carbon-footprint-electricity.html.

Hudson's Bay Company History Foundation. 2016. "Currency." https://www.hbcheritage.ca/history/fur-trade/currency.

Humphrey, T. 1975. "The Classical Concept of the Lender of Last Resort." *Federal Reserve Bank of Richmond Economic Review* 61: 2–9. https://www.richmondfed.org/~/media/richmondfedorg/publications/research/economic_review/1975/pdf/er610101.pdf.

Hyperledger Foundation. No date. "Case Study: DLT Labs and Walmart Canada Transform Freight Invoice Management with Hyperledger Fabric." https://www.hyperledger.org/learn/publications/dltlabs-case-study.

Iansiti, M., and K. Lakhani. 2017. "The Truth About Blockchain." *Harvard Business Review*. https://hbr.org/2017/01/the-truth-about-blockchain.

Jordan, L. 1997. "Wampum: Introduction." University of Notre Dame. https://coins.nd.edu/colcoin/colcoinintros/Wampum.intro.html.

Kamin, D. 2021. "Investors Snap Up Metaverse Real Estate in a Virtual Land Boom." *New York Times*, November 30. https://www.nytimes.com/2021/11/30/business/metaverse-real-estate.html.

Klein, A. 2019. "The Fastest Way to Address Income Inequality? Implement a Real Time Payment System." Brookings Institution. https://www.brookings.edu/research/the-fastest-way-to-address-income-inequality-implement-a-real-time-payment-system/.

Laaper, S. No date. "Using Blockchain to Drive Supply Chain Transparency: Future Trends in Supply Chain." Deloitte. https://www2.deloitte.com/us/en/pages/operations/articles/blockchain-supply-chain-innovation.html.

Liao, G., and J. Caramichael. "Stablecoins: Growth Potential and Impact on Banking." *Federal Reserve Board, International Finance Discussion Paper* 1334. https://www.federalreserve.gov/econres/ifdp/files/ifdp1334.pdf.

Lankenau, S. 2007. "Smoke 'Em If You Got 'Em: Cigarette Black Markets in U.S. Prisons and Jails." *National Library of Medicine, National Center for Biotechnology Information* 81, no. 2: 142–61. https://www.ncbi.nlm.nih.gov/pmc/articles/PMC2117377/.

Levine, M. 2022. "Gary Gensler Wants to Regulate Crypto." Bloomberg. https://www.bloomberg.com/opinion/articles/2022-09-08/gary-gensler-wants-to-regulate-crypto#xj4y7vzkg?leadSource=uverify%20wall.

Locke, T. 2021. "Jack Dorsey Sells His First Tweet Ever as NFT for Over $2.9 Million." CNBC. https://www.cnbc.com/2021/03/22/jack-dorsey-sells-his-first-tweet-ever-as-an-nft-for-over-2point9-million.html.

Maniff, J. 2020. "Inclusion by Design: Crafting a Central Bank Digital Currency to Reach All Americans." Federal Reserve Bank of Kansas City. https://www.kansascityfed.org/research/payments-system-research-briefings/inclusion-by-design-crafting-central-bank-digital-currency/.

Marlinspike, M. 2022. "My First Impressions of Web3." Blog. https://moxie.org/2022/01/07/web3-first-impressions.html.

Mickens, J. 2018. "Blockchains Are a Bad Idea." HBS Digital Initiative. https://www.youtube.com/watch?v=15RTC22Z2xI.

Minsky, H. 1992. "The Financial Instability Hypothesis." Working paper, Levy Economics Institute. https://www.levyinstitute.org/pubs/wp74.pdf.

———. 2008. *Stabilizing an Unstable Economy*, rev. ed. New York: McGraw-Hill. Orig. pub. 1986. https://www.amazon.com/Stabilizing-Unstable-Economy-Hyman-Minsky/dp/0071592997.

Mnuchin, S., and C. Phillips. 2018. "A Financial System That Creates Economic Opportunities: Nonbank Financials, Fintech, and Innovation." U.S. Department of the Treasury. https://home.treasury.gov/sites/default/files/2018-08/A-Financial-System-that-Creates-Economic-Opportunities---Nonbank-Financials-Fintech-and-Innovation_0.pdf.

Modderman, G. 2022. "Who Accepts Bitcoin as Payment?" *Coin Telegraph*, June 5. https://cointelegraph.com/explained/who-accepts-bitcoin-as-payment.

Moen, J., and E. Tallman. 2015. "The Panic of 1907." Federal Reserve History. https://www.federalreservehistory.org/essays/panic-of-1907.

Nacha. 2021. "Payments Myth Busting." https://www.nacha.org/content/payments-myth-busting.

Nakamoto, S. 2008. "Bitcoin: A Peer-to-Peer Electronic Cash System." https://bitcoin.org/bitcoin.pdf.

National Association of Federally-Insured Credit Unions. 2022. "Re: Money and Payments: The U.S. Dollar in the Age of Digital Transformation." https://www.nafcu.org/system/files/files/5.20.22%20Letter%20to%20Federal%20Reserve%20re%20Central%20Bank%20Digital%20Currency.pdf.

NIST (National Institute of Standards and Technology). No date. "Non-Repudiation." https://csrc.nist.gov/glossary/term/non_repudiation.

Nogrady, B. 2016. "There's Gold, Platinum and Other Valuable Materials in Every Phone—the Hard Part Is Getting It Out." https://www.bbc.com/future/article/20161017-your-old-phone-is-full-of-precious-metals.

Noko, J. 2011. "Dollarization: The Case of Zimbabwe." Cato Institute. https://www.cato.org/sites/cato.org/files/serials/files/cato-journal/2011/5/cj31n2-9.pdf.

OCC (U.S. Office of the Comptroller of the Currency). 2020. "Federally Chartered Banks and Thrifts May Provide Custody Services for Crypto Assets." https://www.occ.gov/news-issuances/news-releases/2020/nr-occ-2020-98.html.

OpenSea. 2022. "@jack 2006-03-21 20:50:14." https://opensea.io/assets/matic/0x28009881f0ffe85c90725b8b02be55773647c64a/20.

Oracle. 2022. "Permissioned Blockchain." https://developer.oracle.com/learn/technical-articles/permissioned-blockchain.

Orosz, G. 2022. Twitter post. https://twitter.com/GergelyOrosz/status/1516422295186722824.

Outten, S. 2021. "Bitcoin Transaction Validation, What Exactly Goes on Under the Hood?" Deltec Bank. https://www.deltecbank.com/2021/10/05/bitcoin-transaction-validation-what-exactly-goes-on-under-the-hood/.

Pechman, M. 2021. "Here's How Bitcoin's Intraday Volatility Complicates Leverage Trading." CoinTelegraph. https://cointelegraph.com/news/here-s-how-bitcoin-s-intraday-volatility-complicates-leverage-trading.

Putzier, K. 2021. "Metaverse Real Estate Piles Up Record Sales in Sandbox and Other Virtual Realms." *Wall Street Journal*, November 30. https://www.wsj.com/articles/metaverse-real-estate-piles-up-record-sales-in-sandbox-and-other-virtual-realms-11638268380.

Rathjen, J. 2022. "ACH Improvements, FedNow Represent Future of Electronic Payments." *Bloomberg Tax*, March 23. https://news.bloombergtax.com/payroll/ach-improvements-fednow-represent-future-of-electronic-payments.

Roose, K. 2022. "Maybe There's a Use for Crypto After All." *New York Times*, February 6. https://www.nytimes.com/2022/02/06/technology/helium-cryptocurrency-uses.html.

Rybarczyk, R. 2020. "Understanding the Bitcoin Blockchain Header." Medium. https://medium.com/fcats-blockchain-incubator/understanding-the-bitcoin-blockchain-header-a2b0db06b515.

Samford, H., and L. Domingo. "The Political Geography and Environmental Impacts of Cryptocurrency Mining." University of Washington. https://jsis.washington.edu/news/the-political-geography-and-environmental-impacts-of-cryptocurrency-mining/.

Schmidt, L., A. Timmermann, and R. Wermers. 2016. "Runs on Money Market Mutual Funds." *American Economic Review* 106, no. 9: 2625–57. https://pubs.aeaweb.org/doi/pdfplus/10.1257/aer.20140678.

Schneier, B. 2019. "There's No Good Reason to Trust Blockchain Technology." *Wired.* https://www.wired.com/story/theres-no-good-reason-to-trust-blockchain-technology/.

SEC (U.S. Securities and Exchange Commission). 2021a. "SEC Charges Global Crypto Lending Platform and Top Executives in $2 Billion Fraud." https://www.sec.gov/news/press-release/2021-172.

———. 2021b. "SEC Charges Three Individuals with Insider Trading." https://www.sec.gov/news/press-release/2021-121.

———. 2022. "Crypto Assets and Cyber Enforcement Actions." https://www.sec.gov/spotlight/cybersecurity-enforcement-actions.

Siegel, R. 2008. "Zimbabwe's Hyperinflation Poses Unique Challenges." NPR. https://www.npr.org/templates/story/story.php?storyId=89123990.

Seward, Z. 2021. "A16z Leads $111M Token Sale for Helium's HNT." CoinDesk. https://www.coindesk.com/business/2021/08/10/a16z-leads-111m-token-sale-for-heliums-hnt/.

Smilyanets, D. 2021. "'I Scrounged Through the Trash Heaps; . . . Now I'm a Millionaire: An Interview with REvil's Unknown." *Record.* https://therecord.media/i-scrounged-through-the-trash-heaps-now-im-a-millionaire-an-interview-with-revils-unknown/.

Tabuchi, H. 2022. "Cryptomining Capacity in U.S. Rivals Energy Use of Houston, Findings Show." *New York Times*, July 15. https://www.nytimes.com/2022/07/15/climate/cryptocurrency-bitcoin-mining-electricity.html.

Tian, R. 2021. "A Deep Dive into Leverages in DeFi Borrowing, Margin Trading, Leveraged Tokens and Options: FinNexus." Alexandria. https://coinmarketcap.com/alexandria/article/a-deep-dive-into-leverages-in-defi-borrowing-margin-trading-leveraged-tokens-and-options-finnexus.

Tikkanen, A. No date. "A Brief (and Fascinating) History of Money." *Britannica.* https://www.britannica.com/story/a-brief-and-fascinating-history-of-money.

Timón, J. 2016. "Amount.h." Code commit. https://github.com/bitcoin/bitcoin/blob/08a7316c144f9f2516db8fa62400893f4358c5ae/src/amount.h.

Tortorelli, P., and K. Rooney. 2022. "Sam Bankman-Fried's Alameda Quietly Used FTX Customer Funds for Trading, Say Sources." CNBC. https://www.cnbc.com/2022/11/13/sam-bankman-frieds-alameda-quietly-used-ftx-customer-funds-without-raising-alarm-bells-say-sources.html.

University of Cambridge. 2022. "Cambridge Bitcoin Electricity Consumption Index." https://ccaf.io/cbeci/index/comparisons.

U.S. Commercial Code. No date. "§ 1-201: General Definitions." https://www.law.cornell.edu/ucc/1/1-201.

U.S. Department of Labor. 2022. "Compliance Assistance Release No. 2022-01." https://www.dol.gov/agencies/ebsa/employers-and-advisers/plan-administration-and-compliance/compliance-assistance-releases/2022-01.

U.S. Department of Justice. 2022. "The Role of Law Enforcement in Detecting, Investigating, and Prosecuting Criminal Activity Related to Digital Assets." https://www.justice.gov/ag/page/file/1535236/download.

U.S. Department of the Treasury. 2022a. "Crypto-Assets: Implications for Consumers, Investors, and Businesses." https://home.treasury.gov/system/files/136/CryptoAsset_EO5.pdf.

———. 2022b. "The Future of Money and Payments: Report Pursuant to Section 4(b) of Executive Order 14067." https://home.treasury.gov/system/files/136/Future-of-Money-and-Payments.pdf.

———. 2022c. "Report on Digital Asset Financial Stability Risks and Regulation." https://home.treasury.gov/system/files/261/FSOC-Digital-Assets-Report-2022.pdf.

———. 2022d. "Action Plan to Address Illicit Financing Risks of Digital Assets." https://home.treasury.gov/system/files/136/Digital-Asset-Action-Plan.pdf.

———. 2022e. "Fact Sheet: Framework for International Engagement on Digital Assets." https://home.treasury.gov/news/press-releases/jy0854.

Velde, F. 2012. "On the Origin of Specie." Federal Reserve Bank of Chicago. https://www.atlantafed.org/-/media/documents/news/conferences/2012/monetary-economics/papers/velde.pdf.

Venmo. No date. "Bank Transfer Timeline." https://help.venmo.com/hc/en-us/articles/221083888-Bank-Transfer-Timeline.

Vitasek, K., J. Bayliss, L. Owen, and N. Srivastava. 2022. "How Walmart Canada Uses Blockchain to Solve Supply-Chain Challenges." *Harvard Business Review*. https://hbr.org/2022/01/how-walmart-canada-uses-blockchain-to-solve-supply-chain-challenges.

Warren, E. 2019. "Warren, Van Hollen, Pressley, García Introduce Legislation to Require the Fed to Act on Faster Payments." Press release. https://www.warren.senate.gov/newsroom/press-releases/warren-van-hollen-pressley-garca-introduce-legislation-to-require-the-fed-to-act-on-faster-payments.

Wheatley, J. 2013. "Six Things You Need to Know About Raghuram Rajan." *Financial Times*, August 6. https://www.ft.com/content/6b12ca6a-e993-3021-b774-7228934ba322.

White House. 2022a. "Technical Evaluation for a U.S. Central Bank Digital Currency System." https://www.whitehouse.gov/wp-content/uploads/2022/09/09-2022-Technical-Evaluation-US-CBDC-System.pdf.

———. 2022b. "Executive Order on Ensuring Responsible Development of Digital Assets." https://www.whitehouse.gov/briefing-room/presidential-actions/2022/03/09/executive-order-on-ensuring-responsible-development-of-digital-assets/.

———. 2022c. “Fact Sheet: White House Releases First-Ever Comprehensive Framework for Responsible Development of Digital Assets.” https://www.whitehouse.gov/briefing-room/statements-releases/2022/09/16/fact-sheet-white-house-releases-first-ever-comprehensive-framework-for-responsible-development-of-digital-assets/.

———. 2022d. “Energy Implications of Crypto-Assets in the United States.” https://www.whitehouse.gov/wp-content/uploads/2022/09/09-2022-Crypto-Assets-and-Climate-Report.pdf.

———. 2022e. “Policy Objectives for a U.S. Central Bank Digital Currency System.” https://www.whitehouse.gov/wp-content/uploads/2022/09/09-2022-Policy-Objectives-US-CBDC-System.pdf.

Williams. 2022. “A Neighborhood’s Cryptocurrency Mine: ‘Like a Jet That Never Leaves.’” *Washington Post*. https://www.washingtonpost.com/business/interactive/2022/cryptocurrency-mine-noise-homes-nc/.

Wong, R. 2022. Why Stablecoins Fail: An Economist’s Post-Mortem on Terra.” Federal Reserve Bank of Richmond, Economic Brief 22-24. https://www.richmondfed.org/publications/research/economic_brief/2022/eb_22-24.

World Bank. No date. “Tamper-Proof Logs.” https://id4d.worldbank.org/guide/tamper-proof-logs.

Yaffe-Bellany, D. 2022. “They Made Millions on Luna, Solana and Polygon: Crypto’s Boom Beyond Bitcoin.” *New York Times*, February 7. https://www.nytimes.com/2022/02/07/technology/cryptocurrency-luna-solana-polygon.html.

Yaga, D., P. Mell, N. Roby, and K. Scarfone. 2018. “Blockchain Technology Overview.” National Institute for Standards and Technology, Report 8202. https://nvlpubs.nist.gov/nistpubs/ir/2018/nist.ir.8202.pdf.

Yang, Y. 2022. “JPMorgan Finds New Use for Blockchain in Trading and Lending.” https://www.bloomberg.com/news/articles/2022-05-26/jpmorgan-finds-new-use-for-blockchain-in-collateral-settlement.

Chapter 9

Acharya, V., T. Johnson, S. Sundaresan, and T. Tomunen. 2022. *Is Physical Climate Risk Priced? Evidence from Regional Variation in Exposure to Heat Stress*. NBER Working Paper 30445. Cambridge, MA: National Bureau of Economic Research. https://doi.org/10.3386/w30445.

Agarwala, M., and D. Coyle. 2021. “Natural Capital in Climate Models.” *Nature Sustainability* 4: 81–82. https://doi.org/10.1038/s41893-020-00618-x.

Agarwala, M., and D. Zenghelis. 2020. “Natural Capital Accounting for Sustainable Macroeconomic Strategies.” U.N. Department of Economic and Social Affairs, System of Environmental and Economic Accounting. https://seea.un.org/content/natural-capital-accounting-sustainable-macroeconomic-strategies.

Ahmedzade, T., J. Horton, P. Mwai, and W. Song. 2022. "China, Europe, U.S. Drought: Is 2022 the Driest Year Recorded?" British Broadcasting Center, September 17. https://www.bbc.com/news/62751110.

Akerlof, G. 1970. "The Market for 'Lemons': Quality Uncertainty and the Market Mechanism." *Quarterly Journal of Economics* 84, no. 3: 488–500. https://doi.org/10.1016/B978-0-12-214850-7.50022-X.

American Society of Civil Engineers. 2018. *Climate-Resilient Infrastructure: Adaptive Design and Risk Management*, edited by B. Ayyub. Reston, VA: American Society of Civil Engineers.

———. 2021. "Investment Gap 2020–2029." 2021 Report Card for America's Infrastructure. https://infrastructurereportcard.org/resources/investment-gap-2020-2029/.

Annan, F., and W. Schlenker. 2015. "Federal Crop Insurance and the Disincentive to Adapt to Extreme Heat." *American Economic Review* 105, no. 5: 262–66. https://doi.org/10.1257/aer.p20151031.

Arellano-Gonzalez, J., A. AghaKouchak, M. Levy, Y. Qin, J. Burney, S. Davis, and F. Moore. 2021. "The Adaptive Benefits of Agricultural Water Markets in California." *Environmental Research Letters* 16, no. 4. https://doi.org/10.1088/1748-9326/abde5b.

Ash, K., and N. Obradovich. 2019. "Climatic Stress, Internal Migration, and Syrian Civil War Onset." *Journal of Conflict Resolution* 64, no. 1: 3–31. https://doi.org/10.1177/0022002719864140.

Auffhammer, M. 2022. "Climate Adaptive Response Estimation: Short- and Long-Run Impacts of Climate Change on Residential Electricity and Natural Gas Consumption." *Journal of Environmental Economics and Management* 114. https://doi.org/10.1016/j.jeem.2022.102669.

Bakkensen, L., and L. Barrage. 2022. "Going Underwater? Flood Risk Belief Heterogeneity and Coastal Home Price Dynamics." *Review of Financial Studies* 35, no. 8: 3666–709. https://doi.org/10.1093/rfs/hhab122.

Baldauf, M., L. Garlappi, and C. Yannelis. 2020. "Does Climate Change Affect Real Estate Prices? Only If You Believe in It." *Review of Financial Studies* 33, no. 3: 1256–95. https://doi.org/10.1093/rfs/hhz073.

Barrage, L. 2020. "The Fiscal Costs of Climate Change." *AEA Papers and Proceedings* 110: 107–12. https://doi.org/10.1093/restud/rdz055.

Barrage, L., and J. Furst. 2019. "Housing Investment, Sea Level Rise, and Climate Change Beliefs." *Economics Letters* 177: 105–8. https://doi.org/10.1016/j.econlet.2019.01.023.

Barreca, A., and J. Schaller. 2020. "The Impact of High Ambient Temperatures on Delivery Timing and Gestational Lengths." *Nature Climate* Change 10: 77–82. https://doi.org/10.1038/s41558-019-0632-4.

Bastien-Olvera, B., F. Granella, and F. Moore. 2022. "Persistent Effect of Temperature on GDP Identified from Lower Frequency Temperature Variability." *Environmental Research Letters* 17, no. 8. https://doi.org/10.1088/1748-9326/ac82c2.

Baylis, P., and J. Boomhower. 2023. "The Economic Incidence of Wildfire Suppression in the United States." *American Economic Journal: Applied Economics*. https://www.aeaweb.org/articles?id=10.1257/app.20200662.

Beasley, W., and S. Dundas. 2021. "Hold the Line: Modeling Private Coastal Adaptation Through Shoreline Armoring Decisions." *Journal of Environmental Economics and Management* 105: 102397. https://doi.org/10.1016/j.jeem.2020.102397.

Benveniste, H., M. Oppenheimer, and M. Fleurbaey. 2020. "Effect of Border Policy on Exposure and Vulnerability to Climate Change." *Proceedings of the National Academy of Sciences* 117, no. 43: 26692–702. https://doi.org/10.1073/pnas.2007597117.

Benz, S., and J. Burney. 2021. "Widespread Race and Class Disparities in the Surface Urban Heat Extremes Across the United States." *Earth's Future* 9. https://agupubs.onlinelibrary.wiley.com/doi/pdf/10.1029/2021EF002016.

Bercos-Hickey, E., T. O'Brien, M. Wehner, L. Zhang, C. Patriciola, H. Huang, and M. Risser. 2022. "Anthropogenic Contributions to the 2021 Pacific Northwest Heatwave." *Geophysical Research Letters* 49, no. 23. https://doi.org/10.1029/2022GL099396.

Berrang-Ford, L., et al. 2021. "A Systematic Global Stocktake of Evidence on Human Adaptation to Climate Change." *Nature Climate Change* 11: 989–1000. https://www.nature.com/articles/s41558-021-01170-y.

Bernstein, A., M. Gustafson, and R. Lewis. 2019. "Disaster on the Horizon: The Price Effect of Sea Level Rise." *Journal of Financial Economics* 134, no. 2: 253–72. https://doi.org/10.1016/j.jfineco.2019.03.013.

Bhutta, N., A. Chang, L. Dettling, and J. Hsu. 2020. "Disparities in Wealth by Race and Ethnicity in the 2019 Survey of Consumer Finances." Finance and Economics Discussion Series Notes, Board of Governors of the Federal Reserve System. https://www.federalreserve.gov/econres/notes/feds-notes/disparities-in-wealth-by-race-and-ethnicity-in-the-2019-survey-of-consumer-finances-20200928.html.

Billings, S., E. Gallagher, and L. Ricketts. 2022. "Let the Rich Be Flooded: The Distribution of Financial Aid and Distress After Hurricane Harvey." *Journal of Financial Economics*. https://doi.org/10.1016/j.jfineco.2021.11.006.

Borunda, A. 2021. "'Megadrought' Persists in Western U.S., as Another Extremely Dry Year Develops." *National Geographic*. https://www.nationalgeographic.com/environment/article/megadrought-persists-in-western-us-as-another-extremely-dry-year-develops.

Bradsher, K., and J. Dong. 2022. "China's Record Drought Is Drying Rivers and Feeding Its Coal Habit." *New York Times*, August 29. https://www.nytimes.com/2022/08/26/business/economy/china-drought-economy-climate.html.

Bradt, J., C. Kousky, and O. Wing. 2021. "Voluntary Purchases and Adverse Selection in the Market for Flood Insurance." *Journal of Environmental Economics and Management* 110: 102515. https://doi.org/10.1016/j.jeem.2021.102515.

Braun, A., and C. Kousky. 2021. "Catastrophe Bonds." *Wharton Risk Center Primer*, July. https://riskcenter.wharton.upenn.edu/wp-content/uploads/2021/07/Cat-Bond-Primer-July-2021.pdf.

Brunetti, C., J. Caramichael, M. Crosignani, B. Dennis, G. Kotta, D. Morgan, C. Shin, and I. Zer. 2022. "Climate-Related Financial Stability Risks for the United States: Methods and Applications." Finance and Economics Discussion Series, Board of Governors of the Federal Reserve System. https://www.federalreserve.gov/econres/feds/climate-related-financial-stability-risks-for-the-united-states.htm.

Brunetti, C., B. Dennis, D. Gates, D. Hancock, D. Ignell, E. Kiser, G. Kotta, A. Kovner, R. Rosen, and N. Tabor. 2021. "Climate Change and Financial Stability." *FEDS Notes*, Board of Governors of the Federal Reserve System. https://www.federalreserve.gov/econres/notes/feds-notes/climate-change-and-financial-stability-20210319.html.

Bureau of Reclamation. 2022. "About Us: Fact Sheet." https://www.usbr.gov/main/about/fact.html.

Burke, M., A. Driscoll, S. Heft-Neal, and M. Wara. 2021. "The Changing Risk and Burden of Wildfire in the United States." *Proceedings of the National Academy of Sciences* 118, no. 2. https://doi.org/10.1073/pnas.2011048118.

Burke, M., F. González, P. Baylis, S. Heft-Neal, C. Baysan, S. Basu, and S. Hsiang. 2018. "Higher Temperatures Increase Suicide Rates in the United States and Mexico." *Nature Climate Change* 8: 723–29. https://doi.org/10.1038/s41558-018-0222-x.

Burke, M., S. Heft-Neal, J. Li, A. Driscoll, P. Baylis, M. Stigler, J. Weill, J. Burney, J. Wen, M. Childs, and C. Gould. 2022. "Exposures and Behavioral Responses to Wildfire Smoke." *Nature Human Behavior* 6: 1351–61. https://doi.org/10.1038/s41562-022-01396-6.

Burke, M., S. Hsiang, and E. Miguel. 2015. "Global Non-Linear Effect of Temperature on Economic Production." *Nature* 527, no. 7577: 235–39. https://doi.org/10.1038/nature15725.

Carleton, T., A. Jina, M. Delgado, M. Greenstone, T. Houser, S. Hsiang, A. Hultgren, R. Kopp, K. McCusker, I. Nath, J. Rising, A. Rode, H. Seo, A. Viaene, J. Yuan, and A. Zhang. 2022. "Valuing the Global Mortality Consequences of Climate Change Accounting for Adaptation Costs and Benefits." *Quarterly Journal of Economics* 137, no. 4: 2037–2105. https://doi.org/10.1093/qje/qjac020.

Carlson, C., G. Albery, C. Merow, C. Trisos, C. Zipfel, E. Eskew, K. Olival, N. Ross, and S. Bansal. 2022. "Climate Change Increases Cross-Species Viral Transmission Risk." *Nature* 607: 555–62. https://doi.org/10.1038/s41586-022-04788-w.

CBO (Congressional Budget Office). 2018. "Federal Support for Financing State and Local Transportation and Water Infrastructure." http://www.cbo.gov/publication/54549.

———. 2019. "Expected Costs of Damage from Hurricane Winds and Storm-Related Flooding." https://www.cbo.gov/system/files/2019-04/55019-ExpectedCostsFromWindStorm.pdf.

———. 2022a. "Discretionary Spending in Fiscal Year 2021: An Infographic." https://www.cbo.gov/publication/58269.

———. 2022b. "Wildfires." https://www.cbo.gov/publication/58212.

Centers for Medicare & Medicaid Services. 2022. "NHE Fact Sheet." https://www.cms.gov/Research-Statistics-Data-and-Systems/Statistics-Trends-and-Reports/NationalHealthExpendData/NHE-Fact-Sheet.

Chapman, J., A. Lu, and L. Timmerhoff. 2020. "By the Numbers: A Look at Municipal Bankruptcies Over the Past 20 Years." Pew Research Institute. https://www.pewtrusts.org/en/research-and-analysis/articles/2020/07/07/by-the-numbers-a-look-at-municipal-bankruptcies-over-the-past-20-years.

Chediak, M. 2019. "Unprecedented California Blackout Ending as PG&E Restores Power." Bloomberg News, October 9. https://www.bloomberg.com/news/articles/2019-10-10/unprecedented-california-blackout-spreads-with-millions-in-dark?leadSource=uverify%20wall#xj4y7vzkg.

Childs, M., J. Li, J. Wen, S. Heft-Neal, A. Driscoll, S. Wang, C. Gould, M. Qiu, J. Burney, and M. Burke. 2022. "Daily Local-Level Estimates of Ambient Wildfire Smoke PM2.5 for the Contiguous U.S." *Environmental Science & Technology* 56, no. 19: 13607–21. https://doi.org/10.1021/acs.est.2c02934.

Climate Central and Zillow. 2018. "Ocean at the Door: New Homes and the Rising Sea: Recent Housing Growth Rates are Faster in High Flood Risk Zones for Most Coastal States." http://assets.climatecentral.org/pdfs/Nov2018_Report_OceanAtTheDoor.pdf?pdf=OceanAtTheDoor-Report.

CMRA. No date. "Climate Mapping for Resilience and Adaptation." https://resilience.climate.gov/#assessment-tool.

Cong, S., D. Nock, Y. Qiu, and B. Xing. 2022. "Unveiling Hidden Energy Poverty Using the Energy/Equity Gap." *Nature Communications* 13. https://doi.org/10.1038/s41467-022-30146-5.

Congressional Research Service. 2022. "National Flood Insurance Program Risk Rating 2.0: Frequently Asked Questions." https://crsreports.congress.gov/product/pdf/IN/IN11777.

Conte, M., and D. Kelly. 2018. "An Imperfect Storm: Fat-Tailed Tropical Cyclone Damages, Insurance, and Climate Policy." *Journal of Environmental Economics and Management* 92: 677–706. https://doi.org/10.1016/j.jeem.2017.08.010.

Cook, L. 2014. "Violence and Economic Activity: Evidence from African American Patents, 1870–1940." *Journal of Economic Growth* 19: 221–57. https://doi.org/10.1007/s10887-014-9102-z.

CoreLogic. 2022. "CoreLogic Analysis Shows Final Estimated Insured and Uninsured Damages for Hurricane Ian to Be Between $41 Billion and $70 Billion." https://

www.corelogic.com/press-releases/corelogic-analysis-shows-final-estimated-insured-and-uninsured-damages-for-hurricane-ian-to-be-between-41-billion-and-70-billion/.

Coyle, D. 2015. *GDP: A Brief but Affectionate History*. Princeton, NJ: Princeton University Press. https://press.princeton.edu/books/paperback/9780691169859/gdp.

Dasgupta, P. 2021. "The Economics of Biodiversity: The Dasgupta Review." Her Majesty's Treasury. https://www.gov.uk/government/publications/final-report-the-economics-of-biodiversity-the-dasgupta-review.

Davenport, F., M. Burke, and N. Diffenbaugh. 2021. "Contribution of Historical Precipitation Change to U.S. Flood Damages." *Proceedings of the National Academy of Sciences* 118, no. 4. https://doi.org/10.1073/pnas.2017524118.

Dell, M., B. Jones, and B. Olken. 2012. "Temperature Shocks and Economic Growth: Evidence from the Last Half Century." *American Economic Journal: Macroeconomics* 4, no. 3: 66–95. http://dx.doi.org/10.1257/mac.4.3.66.

Deng, H., D. Aldrich, M. Danziger, J. Gao, N. Phillips, S. Cornelius, and Q. Wang. 2021. "High-Resolution Human Mobility Data Reveal Race and Wealth Disparities in Disaster Evacuation Patterns." *Humanities and Social Sciences Communications* 8. https://doi.org/10.1057/s41599-021-00824-8.

Denholm, P., P. Brown, W. Cole, T. Mai, B. Sergi, M. Brown, P. Jadun, J. Ho, J. Mayernik, C. McMillan, and R. Sreenath. 2022. "Examining Supply-Side Options to Achieve 100% Clean Electricity by 2035." National Renewable Energy Laboratory. https://www.nrel.gov/docs/fy22osti/81644.pdf.

Derenoncourt, E., C. Kim, M. Kuhn, and M. Schularick. 2022. *Wealth of Two Nations: The U.S. Racial Wealth Gap, 1860–2020*. NBER Working Paper 30101. Cambridge, MA: National Bureau of Economic Research. https://doi.org/10.3386/w30101.

Deryugina, T. 2017. "The Fiscal Cost of Hurricanes: Disaster Aid Versus Social Insurance." *American Economic Journal: Economic Policy* 9, no. 3: 168–98. https://doi.org/10.1257/pol.20140296.

Deschênes, O. 2022. *The Impact of Climate Change on Mortality in the United States: Benefits and Costs of Adaptation*. NBER Working Paper 30282. Cambridge, MA: National Bureau of Economic Research. https://doi.org/10.3386/w30282.

Deschênes, O., and M. Greenstone. 2011. "Climate Change, Mortality, and Adaptation: Evidence from Annual Fluctuations in Weather in the U.S." *American Economic Journal: Applied Economics* 3, no. 4: 152–85. https://doi.org/10.1257/app.3.4.152.

Deschênes, O., M. Greenstone, and J. Guryan. 2009. "Climate Change and Birth Weight." *American Economic Review: Papers and Proceedings* 99, no. 2: 211–17. https://doi.org/10.1257/aer.99.2.211.

Diaz, D. 2016. "Estimating Global Damages from Sea Level Rise with the Coastal Impact and Adaptation Model (CIAM)." *Climatic Change* 137: 143–56. https://doi.org/10.1007/s10584-016-1675-4.

Dietz, T., E. Ostrom, and P. Stern. 2003. "The Struggle to Govern the Commons." *Science* 302, no. 5652: 1907–12. https://doi.org/10.1126/science.1091015.

Diffenbaugh, N., D. Swain, and D. Touma. 2015. "Anthropogenic Warming Has Increased Drought Risk in California." *Proceedings of the National Academy of Sciences* 112, no. 13: 3931–36. https://doi.org/10.1073/pnas.1422385112.

Dixon, L., N. Clancy, B. Bender, A. Kofner, D. Manheim, and L. Zakaras. 2013. *Flood Insurance in New York City Following Hurricane Sandy*. Santa Monica, CA: RAND Corporation. https://www.rand.org/pubs/research_reports/RR328.html.

Dundas, S., and R. von Haefen. 2020. "The Effects of Weather on Recreational Fishing Demand and Adaptation: Implications for a Changing Climate." *Journal of the Association of Environmental and Resource Economists* 7, no. 2. https://doi.org/10.1086/706343.

Electric Power Research Institute. 2022. "Costs and Benefits of Proactive Adaptation in the Electric Sector." https://www.epri.com/research/products/000000003002025872.

Elliott, D. 2022. "Insurance Woes in Coastal Louisiana Make Hurricane Recovery Difficult." National Public Radio, July 27. https://www.npr.org/2022/07/27/1113639292/insurances-woes-in-coastal-louisiana-make-hurricane-recovery-difficult.

Environmental and Energy Study Institute. 2017. "The National Security Impacts of Climate Change." https://www.eesi.org/files/IssueBrief_Climate_Change_Security_Implications.pdf.

Environmental Law Institute. 2022. *Law of Environmental Protection*. Blue Springs, MO: Aspen Publishing. https://www.eli.org/law-environmental-protection.

Evans, D., C Webb, E. Braunstein, J. Glowacki, A. Netter, B. Katz, and D. Lohmann. 2020. "Residential Flood Risk in the United States: Quantifying Flood Losses, Mortgage Risk and Sea Level Rise." Society of Actuaries. https://www.soa.org/globalassets/assets/files/resources/research-report/2020/soa-flood-report.pdf.

Farrell, J., P. Burow, K. McConnell, J. Bayham, K. Whyte, and G. Koss. 2021. "Effects of Land Dispossession and Forced Migration on Indigenous Peoples in North America." *Science* 374, no. 6567. https://doi.org/10.1126/science.abe4943.

Federal Emergency Management Agency. 2010. "Flooding: Our Nation's Most Frequent and Costly Natural Disaster." https://www.fbiic.gov/public/2010/mar/FloodingHistoryandCausesFS.PDF.

———. 2022. "Flood Risk Disclosure: Model State Requirements for Disclosing Flood Risk During Real Estate Transactions." https://www.fema.gov/sites/default/files/documents/fema_state-flood-risk-disclosure-best-practices_07142022.pdf.

———. No date. "The Watermark: National Flood Insurance Program Financial Statements." https://www.fema.gov/flood-insurance/work-with-nfip/watermark-financial-statements.

Federal Insurance and Mitigation Administration. 2022. "The Watermark: Fiscal Year 2022, Second Quarter, Volume 18." Federal Emergency Management Agency. https://www.fema.gov/sites/default/files/documents/fema_fy22-q2-watermark.pdf.

Fiedler, T., A. Pitman, K. Mackenzie, N. Wood, C. Jakob, and S. Perkins-Kirkpatrick. 2021. "Business Risk and the Emergence of Climate Analytics." *Nature Climate Change* 11: 87–94. https://doi.org/10.1038/s41558-020-00984-6.

Financial Stability Board. 2022. "Climate Scenario Analysis by Jurisdictions: Initial Findings and Lessons." https://www.ngfs.net/sites/default/files/medias/documents/climate_scenario_analysis_by_jurisdictions_initial_findings_and_lessons.pdf.

Fisher, E., S. Sippel, and R. Knutti. 2021. "Increasing Probability of Record-Shattering Climate Extremes." *Nature Climate Change* 11: 689–95. https://doi.org/10.1038/s41558-021-01092-9.

Fitch Ratings. 2022. "Fitch Downgrades Pakistan to 'CCC+.'" https://www.fitchratings.com/research/sovereigns/fitch-downgrades-pakistan-to-ccc-21-10-2022.

Fleenor, W., E. Hanak, J. Lund, and J. Mount. 2008. "Delta Hydrodynamics and Water Salinity with Future Conditions: Technical Appendix C." Public Policy Institute of California. https://www.ppic.org/wp-content/uploads/content/pubs/other/708EHR_appendixC.pdf.

Florida Citizens. 2023. "Policies in Force." https://www.citizensfla.com/policies-in-force.

Fothergill, A., and L. Peek. 2004. "Poverty and Disasters in the United States: A Review of Recent Sociological Findings." *Natural Hazards* 32: 89–110. https://doi.org/10.1023/B:NHAZ.0000026792.76181.d9.

Frame, D., M. Wehner, I. Noy, and S. Rosier. 2020. "The Economic Costs of Hurricane Harvey Attributable to Climate Change." *Climatic Change* 160: 271–81. https://doi.org/10.1007/s10584-020-02692-8.

George Washington University. 2018. "Ascertainment of the Estimated Excess Mortality for Hurricane Maria in Puerto Rico." Milken Institute School of Public Health. https://publichealth.gwu.edu/content/gw-report-delivers-recommendations-aimed-preparing-puerto-rico-hurricane-season.

Gibson, M., and J. Mullins. 2020. "Climate Risk and Beliefs in New York Floodplains." *Journal of the Association of Environmental and Resource Economists* 7, no. 6. https://doi.org/10.1086/710240.

Goldsmith-Pinkham, P., M. Gustafson, and R. Lewis. 2021. "Sea Level Rise Exposure and Municipal Bond Yields." Working paper, Jacobs Levy Equity Management Center for Quantitative Financial Research. http://dx.doi.org/10.2139/ssrn.3478364.

Gopalakrishnan, S., D. McNamara, M. Smith, and B. Murray. 2017. "Decentralized Management Hinders Coastal Climate Adaptation: The Spatial-Dynamics of Beach Nourishment." *Environmental and Resource Economics* 67: 761–87. https://doi.org/10.1007/s10640-016-0004-8.

Goss, M., D. Swain, J. Abatzoglou, A. Sarhadi, C. Kolden, A. Williams, and N. Diffenbaugh. 2020. "Climate Change Is Increasing the Likelihood of Extreme Autumn Wildfire Conditions Across California." *Environmental Research Letters* 15, no. 9. https://doi.org/10.1088/1748-9326/ab83a7.

Graff Zivin, J., and M. Neidell. 2014. "Temperature and the Allocation of Time: Implications for Climate Change." *Journal of Labor Economics* 32, no. 1. https://doi.org/10.1086/671766.

Green, R., R. Basu, B. Malig, R. Broadwin, J. Kim, and B. Ostro. 2010. "The Effect of Temperature on Hospital Admissions in Nine California Counties." *International Journal of Public Health* 55: 113–21. https://doi.org/10.1007/s00038-009-0076-0.

Gulev, S., P. Thorne, J. Ahn, F. Dentener, C. Domingues, S. Gerland, D. Gong, D. Kaufman, H. Nnamchi, J. Quaas, J. Rivera, S. Sathyendranath, S. Smith, B. Trewin, K. von Schuckmann, and R. Vose. 2021. "Changing State of the Climate System." In *Climate Change 2021: The Physical Science Basis*, edited by V. Masson-Delmotte, P. Zhai, A. Pirani, S. Connors, C. Péan, S. Berger, N. Caud, Y. Chen, L. Goldfarb, M. Gomis, M. Huang, K. Leitzell, E. Lonnoy, J. Matthews, T. Maycock, T. Waterfield, O. Yelekçi, R. Yu, and B. Zhou, 287–422. Cambridge: Cambridge University Press. https://doi.org/10.1017/9781009157896.004.

Gutiérrez, J., R. Jones, G. Narisma, L. Alves, M. Amjad, I. Gorodetskaya, M. Grose, N. Klutse, S. Krakovska, J. Li, D. Martínez-Castro, L. Mearns, S. Mernild, T. Ngo-Duc, B. van den Hurk, and J. Yoon. 2021. "Atlas." In *Climate Change 2021: The Physical Science Basis*, edited by V. Masson-Delmotte, P. Zhai, A. Pirani, S. Connors, C. Péan, S. Berger, N. Caud, Y. Chen, L. Goldfarb, M. Gomis, M. Huang, K. Leitzell, E. Lonnoy, J. Matthews, T. Maycock, T. Waterfield, O. Yelekçi, R. Yu, and B. Zhou, 1927–2058. Cambridge: Cambridge University Press. https://doi.org/10.1017/9781009157896.021.

Hagerty, N., and B. Leonard. 2022. "Interior's Plan Won't Solve the Colorado River Crisis. Here's What Will." *High Country News*, October 19. https://www.hcn.org/articles/opinion-colorado-river-interiors-plan-wont-solve-the-colorado-river-crisis-heres-what-will.

Hallegatte, S., J. Hourcade, and P. Dumas. 2007. "Why Economic Dynamics Matter in Assessing Climate Change Damages: Illustration on Extreme Events." *Ecological Economics* 62, no. 2: 330–40. https://doi.org/10.1016/j.ecolecon.2006.06.006.

Hartwig, R., and C. Wilkinson. 2016. "Residual Market Property Plans: From Markets of Last Resort to Markets of First Choice." Insurance Information Institute. https://www.iii.org/sites/default/files/docs/pdf/residual_markets_wp_051616.pdf.

Hashida, Y., J. Withey, D. Lewis, T. Newman, and J. Kline. 2020. "Anticipating Changes in Wildlife Habitat Induced by Private Forest Owners' Adaptation to Climate Change and Carbon Policy." Public Library of Science. https://doi.org/10.1371/journal.pone.0230525.

Hausfather, Z., and F. Moore. 2022. "Net-Zero Commitments Could Limit Warming to Below 2°C." *Nature* 604: 247–48. https://doi.org/10.1038/d41586-022-00874-1.

Hino, M., S. Belanger, C. Field, A. Davies, and K. Mach. 2019. 'High-Tide Flooding Disrupts Local Economic Activity." *Science Advances* 5, no. 2. https://doi.org/10.1126/sciadv.aau2736.

Hino, M., and M. Burke. 2021. "The Effect of Information About Climate Risk on Property Values." *Proceedings of the National Academy of Sciences* 118, no. 17. https://doi.org/10.1073/pnas.2003374118.

Hippe, A., A. Becker, M. Fischer, and B. Schwegler. 2015. "Estimation of Cost Required to Elevate U.S. Ports in Response to Climate Change: A Thought Exercise for Climate Critical Resources." Working paper, Stanford University. https://stacks.stanford.edu/file/druid:rm328fb1292/WP138.pdf.

Hoffman, J., V. Shandas, and N. Pendleton. 2020. "The Effects of Historical Housing Policies on Resident Exposure to Intra-Urban Heat: A Study of 108 U.S. Urban Areas." *Climate* 8, no. 1. https://doi.org/10.3390/cli8010012.

Howe, C., K. Anderson, A. R. Siders, B. Ristroph, K. Spidalieri, J. Li, W. Burns, E. Kronk Warner, H. Tanana, H. Vizcarra, N. Kuyumjian, and Z. Schiffer. 2002. "Chapter 24: Climate Change." In *Law of Environmental Protection*, 651–822. Washington: Environmental Law Institute.

Howell, J., and J. Elliott. 2019. "Damages Done: The Longitudinal Impacts of Natural Hazards on Wealth Inequality in the United States." *Social Problems* 66, no. 3. 448–67. https://doi.org/10.1093/socpro/spy016.

Hsiang, S., R. Kopp, A. Jina, J. Rising, M. Delgado, S. Mohan, D. Rasmussen, R. Muir-Wood, P. Wilson, M. Oppenheimer, K. Larsen, and T. Houser. 2017. "Estimating Economic Damage from Climate Change in the United States." *Science* 356, no. 6345: 1362–69. https://doi.org/10.1126/science.aal4369.

Insurance Information Institute. No date–a. "Current Table." https://www.iii.org/table-archive/20793.

———. No date–b. "Facts + Statistics: Catastrophe Bonds and Other Insurance-Linked Securities." https://www.iii.org/fact-statistic/facts-statistics-catastrophe-bonds.

Insurance Journal. 2022. "Florida Citizens Tops 1 Million Policies, Making It Largest in State by a Third." August 12. https://www.insurancejournal.com/news/southeast/2022/08/12/680306.htm.

IPCC (Intergovernmental Panel on Climate Change). 2021. "Summary for Policymakers." In *Climate Change 2021: The Physical Science Basis*, edited by V. Masson-Delmotte, P. Zhai, A. Pirani, S. Connors, C. Péan, S. Berger, N. Caud, Y. Chen, L. Goldfarb, M. Gomis, M. Huang, K. Leitzell, E. Lonnoy, J. Matthews, T. Maycock, T. Waterfield, O. Yelekçi, R. Yu, and B. Zhou, 1927–2058. Cambridge: Cambridge University Press. https://doi.org/10.1017/9781009157896.001.

Issler, P., R. Stanton, C. Vergara-Alert, and N. Wallace. 2020. "Mortgage Markets with Climate-Change Risk: Evidence from Wildfires in California." Working paper. http://dx.doi.org/10.2139/ssrn.3511843.

James, I. 2022. "As Drought Persists, Minimal Water Deliveries Announced for the Central Valley Project." *Los Angeles Times*, February 24. https://www.latimes.com/california/story/2022-02-24/minimal-water-allocations-for-the-central-valley-project.

Jenkins, J., J. Farbes, R. Jones, N. Patankar, and G. Schivley. 2022. "Electricity Transmission Is Key to Unlock the Full Potential of the Inflation Reduction Act." Rapid Energy Policy Evaluation and Analysis Toolkit. https://repeatproject.org/docs/REPEAT_IRA_Transmission_2022-09-22.pdf.

Jerch, R., M. Kahn, and G. Lin. 2023. "Local Public Finance Dynamics and Hurricane Shocks." *Journal of Urban Economics* 134. doi.org/10.1016/j.jue.2022.103516.

Kahn, M. 2021. *Adapting to Climate Change: Markets and the Management of an Uncertain Future*. New Haven, CT: Yale University Press. https://yalebooks.yale.edu/book/9780300246711/adapting-climate-change/.

Kao, S., M. Ashfaq, D. Rastogi, S. Gangrade, R. Martinez, A. Fernandez, G. Konapala, N. Voisin, T. Zhou, W. Xu, H. Gao, B. Zhao, and G. Zhao. 2022. *The Third Assessment of the Effects of Climate Change on Federal Hydropower*. Oak Ridge, TN: National Laboratory. https://info.ornl.gov/sites/publications/Files/Pub168510.pdf.

Keenan, J., and J. Bradt. 2020. "Underwaterwriting: From Theory to Empiricism in Regional Mortgage Markets in the U.S." *Climatic Change* 162: 2043–67. https://doi.org/10.1007/s10584-020-02734-1.

Kelley, C., S. Mohtadi, M. Cane, R. Seager, and Y. Kushnir. 2015. "Climate Change in the Fertile Crescent and Implications of the Recent Syrian Drought." *Proceedings of the National Academy of Sciences* 112, no. 11: 3241–46. https://doi.org/10.1073/pnas.1421533112.

Keys, B., and P. Mulder. 2020. Neglected *No More: Housing Markets, Mortgage Lending, and Sea Level Rise*. NBER Working Paper 27930. Cambridge, MA: National Bureau of Economic Research. https://doi.org/10.3386/w27930.

Kiewiet, R., and K. Szakaty. 1996. "Constitutional Limitations on Borrowing: An Analysis of State Bonded Indebtedness." *Journal of Law, Economics, and Organization* 12, no. 1: 62–97.

Kolstad, C., and F. Moore. 2020. "Estimating the Economic Impacts of Climate Change Using Weather Observations." *Review of Environmental Economics and Policy*. https://scholar.google.com/citations?view_op=view_citation&hl=en&user=ysvd9c0AAAAJ&citation_for_view=ysvd9c0AAAAJ:L8Ckcad2t8MC.

Kopp, R. 2021. "Land-Grant Lessons for Anthropocene Universities." *Climatic Change* 165, no. 28. https://doi.org/10.1007/s10584-021-03029-9.

Kousky, C. 2019. "The Role of Natural Disaster Insurance in Recovery and Risk Reduction." *Annual Review of Resource Economics* 11: 399–418.

———. 2022. *Understanding Disaster Insurance*. Washington: Island Press. https://islandpress.org/books/understanding-disaster-insurance.

Kousky, C., H. Kunreuther, B. Lingle, and L. Shabman. 2018. "The Emerging Private Residential Flood Insurance Market in the United States." Wharton Risk Management and Decision Processes Center, University of Pennsylvania. https://riskcenter.wharton.upenn.edu/wp-content/uploads/2018/07/Emerging-Flood-Insurance-Market-Report.pdf.

Kousky, C., M. Palim, and Y. Pan. 2020. "Flood Damage and Mortgage Credit Risk: A Case Study of Hurricane Harvey." *Journal of Housing Research* 29, no. 1: 86–120. https://doi.org/10.1080/10527001.2020.1840131.

Landers, J. 2021. "California Utility to Underground 10,000 Miles of Power Lines." American Society of Civil Engineers. https://www.asce.org/publications-and-news/civil-engineering-source/civil-engineering-magazine/article/2021/09/california-utility-to-underground-10000-mi-of-power-lines.

Leefeldt, E. 2022. "Why Is Homeowners Insurance in Florida Such a Disaster?" *Forbes*, November 22. https://www.forbes.com/advisor/homeowners-insurance/why-is-homeowners-insurance-in-florida-such-a-disaster/.

Lipton, D., M. Rubenstein, S. Weiskopf, S. Carter, J. Peterson, L. Crozier, M. Fogarty, S. Gaichas, K. Hyde, T. Morelli, J. Morisette, H. Moustahfid, R. Muñoz, R. Poudel, M. Staudinger, C. Stock, L. Thompson, R. Waples, and J. Weltzin, 2018. "Ecosystems, Ecosystem Services, and Biodiversity." In *Impacts, Risks, and Adaptation in the United States: Fourth National Climate Assessment, Volume II*, edited by D. Reidmiller, C. Avery, D. Easterling, K. Kunkel, K. Lewis, T. Maycock, and B. Stewart, 268–321. Washington: U.S. Global Change Research Program. https://doi.org/10.7930/NCA4.2018.CH7.

Lu, C. 2022. "The Lingering Impact of Pakistan's Floods." *Foreign Policy*, September 15. https://foreignpolicy.com/2022/09/15/pakistan-floods-humanitarian-disease-food-crisis-climate/.

Lustgarten, A. 2020. "The Great Climate Migration." *New York Times Magazine*, July 23. https://www.nytimes.com/interactive/2020/07/23/magazine/climate-migration.html.

Mach, K., C. Kraan, W. Adger, H. Buhaug, M. Burke, J. Fearon, C. Field, C. Hendrix, J. Maystadt, J. O'Loughlin, P. Roessler, J. Scheffran, K. Schultz, and N. von

Uexkull. 2019. "Climate as a Risk Factor for Armed Conflict." *Nature* 571: 193–97. https://doi.org/10.1038/s41586-019-1300-6.

Mack, K., C. Kraan, M. Hino, E. Johnston, and C. Field. 2019b. "Managed Retreat Through Voluntary Buyouts of Flood-Prone Properties." *Science Advances* 5, no. 10. https://doi.org/10.1126/sciadv.aax8995.

Marder, J. 2020. "Beating Back the Tides." National Aviation and Space Administration. https://sealevel.nasa.gov/news/203/beating-back-the-tides.

Martinich, J., J. Neumann, L. Ludwig, and L. Jantarasami. 2013. "Risks of Sea Level Rise to Disadvantaged Communities in the United States." *Mitigation and Adaptation Strategies for Global Change* 18: 169–85. https://doi.org/10.1007/s11027-011-9356-0.

McGee, K. 2021. "A Place Worth Protecting: Rethinking Cost-Benefit Analysis under FEMA's Flood-Mitigation Programs." *University of Chicago Law Review* 88, no. 8: 1925–70. https://heinonline.org/HOL/Page?handle=hein.journals/uclr88&div=64&g_sent=1&casa_token=nFrduvaQRJUAAAAA:M3P21KHCgkoPC6eTZJHTRHIf8L6uHFSy-vSGXG8GbJAntCQ9mAa34WUOPQ9OvtQ5F0u8sGjb&collection=journals.

Meinshausen, M., J. Lewis, C. McGlade, J. Gütschow, Z. Nicholls, R. Burdon, L. Cozzi, and B. Hackmann. 2022. "Realization of Paris Agreement Pledges May Limit Warming Just Below 2°C." *Nature* 604: 304–9. https://doi.org/10.1038/s41586-022-04553-z.

Mendelsohn, R. 2000. "Efficient Adaptation to Climate Change." *Climatic Change* 45: 583–600. https://doi.org/10.1023/A:1005507810350.

Mendelsohn, R., W. Nordhaus, and D. Shaw. 1994. "The Impact of Global Warming on Agriculture: A Ricardian Analysis." *American Economic Review* 84, no. 4: 753–71. https://doi.org/10.1257/aer.89.4.1046.

Milly, P., J. Betancourt, M. Falkenmark, R. Hirsch, Z. Kundzewicz, D. Lettenmaier, and R. Stouffer. 2018. "Stationarity Is Dead: Whither Water Management?" *Science* 319: 573–74. https://www.science.org/doi/10.1126/science.1151915

Missirian, A., and W. Schlenker. 2017. "Asylum Applications Respond to Temperature Fluctuations." *Science* 358, no. 6370: 1610–14. https://doi.org/10.1126/science.aao0432.

ModEx. No date. "The Catastrophe Risk Modeling Market: From Laggards to Leaders: Barriers, Consequences and Strategic Considerations." https://www.nasdaq.com/docs/1617-Q19%20ModEx%20Brochure%20rebrand%20to%20Nasdaq_MT_v2.pdf.

Moore, F., and D. Diaz. 2015. "Temperature Impacts on Economic Growth Warrant Stringent Mitigation Policy." *Nature Climate Change* 5: 127–35. https://doi.org/10.1038/nclimate2481.

Moore, F., A. Stokes, M. Conte, and X. Dong. 2022. "Noah's Ark in a Warming World: Climate Change, Biodiversity Loss, and Public Adaptation Costs in the United

States." *Journal of the Association of Environmental and Resource Economists* 9, no. 5: 981–1015. https://doi.org/10.1086/716662.

Mukherjee, A., and N. Sanders. 2021. *The Causal Effect of Heat on Violence: Social Implications of Unmitigated Heat Among the Incarcerated.* NBER Working Paper 28987. Cambridge, MA: National Bureau of Economic Research. https://www.nber.org/system/files/working_papers/w28987/w28987.pdf.

National Advisory Council. 2020. "Report to the FEMA Administrator." Federal Emergency Management Agency. https://www.fema.gov/sites/default/files/documents/fema_nac-report_11-2020.pdf.

National Intelligence Council. 2021. "Climate Change and International Responses Increasing Challenges to U.S. National Security through 2040." https://www.dni.gov/files/ODNI/documents/assessments/NIE_Climate_Change_and_National_Security.pdf.

National Oceanic and Atmospheric Administration. 2021. "What Percentage of the American Population Lives Near the Coast?" https://oceanservice.noaa.gov/facts/population.html.

———. No date. "Weather-Related Fatality and Injury Statistics." https://www.weather.gov/hazstat/.

Natural Resources Defense Council. No date. "Climate Resilience: How States Stack Up on Flood Disclosure." https://www.nrdc.org/flood-disclosure-map.

Neumann, J., P. Chinowsky, J. Helman, M. Black, C. Fant, K. Strzepek, and J. Martinich. 2021. "Climate Effects on U.S. Infrastructure: The Economics of Adaptation for Rail, Roads, and Coastal Development." *Climatic Change* 167, no. 44. https://doi.org/10.1007/s10584-021-03179-w.

New York District, North Atlantic Division of the U.S. Army Corps of Engineers, New Jersey Department of Environmental Protection, New York State Department of Environmental Conservation, New York State Department of State, and New York City Mayor's Office of Climate and Environmental Justice. 2022. "New York–New Jersey Harbor and Tributaries Coastal Storm Risk Management Feasibility Study: Draft Integrated Feasibility Report and Tier 1 Environmental Impact Statement." https://www.nan.usace.army.mil/Portals/37/NYNJHATS%20Draft%20Integrated%20Feasibility%20Report%20Tier%201%20EIS.pdf.

Newell, R., B. Prest, and S. Sexton. 2021. "The GDP-Temperature Relationship: Implications for Climate Change Damages." *Journal of Environmental Economics and Management* 108. https://doi.org/10.1016/j.jeem.2021.102445.

NGFS-INSPIRE. 2022. "Central Banking and Supervision in the Biosphere: An Agenda for Action on Biodiversity Loss, Financial Risk, and System Stability." NGFS Occasional Paper. https://www.ngfs.net/sites/default/files/medias/documents/central_banking_and_supervision_in_the_biosphere.pdf.

Nordhaus, W. 1991. "To Slow or Not to Slow: The Economics of The Greenhouse Effect." *Economic Journal* 101, no. 407: 920–37. https://doi.org/10.2307/2233864.

———. 2015. "Climate Clubs: Overcoming Free-Riding in International Policy." *American Economic Review* 105, no. 4: 1339-70. https://www.aeaweb.org/articles?id=10.1257/aer.15000001.

Ortiz-Bobea, A., T. Ault, C. Carrillo, R. Chambers, and D. Lobell. 2021. "Anthropogenic Climate Change Has Slowed Global Agricultural Productivity Growth." *Nature Climate Change* 11: 306–12. https://doi.org/10.1038/s41558-021-01000-1.

Otto, C., K. Kuhla, T. Geiger, J. Schewe, and K. Frieler. 2023. "Better Insurance Could Effectively Mitigation the Increase in Economic Growth Losses from U.S. Hurricanes Under Global Warming." *Science Advances* 9. https://www.science.org/doi/pdf/10.1126/sciadv.add6616.

Ouazad, A., and M. Kahn. 2022. "Mortgage Finance and Climate Change: Securitization Dynamics in the Aftermath of Natural Disasters." *Review of Financial Studies* 35, no. 8: 3617–65. https://doi.org/10.1093/rfs/hhab124.

Painter, M. 2020. "An Inconvenient Cost: The Effects of Climate Change on Municipal Bonds." *Journal of Financial Economics* 135, no. 2: 468–82. https://doi.org/10.1016/j.jfineco.2019.06.006.

Panjwani, A. 2022. "Underwater: The Effect of Federal Policies on Households' Exposure to Climate Change Risk." Working paper. https://static1.squarespace.com/static/595f21a5f7e0abb30f55b693/t/6324bffe703add302692d00f/1663352831153/Panjwani_Ahyan_Underwater.pdf.

Pankratz, N., and C. Schiller. 2022. *Climate Change and Adaptation in Global Supply-Chain Networks*. Finance and Economics Discussion Series, Working Paper 56. Washington: Board of Governors of the Federal Reserve System. https://doi.org/10.17016/FEDS.2022.056.

Paquette, D., and M. Kornfield. 2022. "Ian Is Florida's Deadliest Hurricane Since 1935; Most Victims Drowned." *Washington Post*, October 5. https://www.washingtonpost.com/nation/2022/10/05/hurricane-ian-florida-victims/.

Park, J., J. Goodman, M. Hurwitz, and J. Smith. 2020. "Heat and Learning." *American Economic Journal: Economic Policy* 12, no. 2: 306–39. https://doi.org/10.1257/pol.20180612.

Park Williams, A., B. Cook, and J. Smerdon. 2022. "Rapid Intensification of the Emerging Southwestern North American Megadrought in 2020–2021." *Nature Climate Change* 12: 232–34. https://doi.org/10.1038/s41558-022-01290-z.

Pitman, A., T. Fiedler, N. Ranger, C. Jakob, N. Ridder, S. Perkins-Kirkpatrick, N. Wood, and G. Abramowitz. 2022. "Acute Climate Risks in the Financial System: Examining the Utility of Climate Model Projections." *Environmental Research: Climate* 1, no. 2. https://doi.org/10.1088/2752-5295/ac856f.

Plume, K. 2022. "U.S. Barge Backlog Swells on Parched Mississippi River." Reuters. https://www.reuters.com/world/us/us-barge-backlog-swells-parched-mississippi-river-2022-10-04/.

Querolo, N., and B. Sullivan. 2019. "California Fire Damage Estimated at $25.4 Billion." Bloomberg News, October 28. https://www.bloomberg.com/news/

articles/2019-10-28/california-fire-damages-already-at-25-4-billion-and-counting#xj4y7vzkg.

Rennert, K., F. Errickson, B. Prest, L. Rennels, R. Newell, W. Pizer, C. Kingdon, J. Wingenroth, R. Cooke, B. Parthum, D. Smith, K. Cromar, D. Diaz, F. Moore, U. Müller, R. Plevin, A. Raftery, H. Sevčíková, H. Sheets, J. Stock, T. Tan, M. Watson, T. Wong, and D. Anthoff. 2022. "Comprehensive Evidence Implies a Higher Social Cost of CO2." *Nature* 610: 687–92. https://doi.org/10.1038/s41586-022-05224-9.

Robles, F., and J. Bidgood. 2017. "Three Months After Maria, Roughly Half of Puerto Ricans Still Without Power." New York Times, December 29. https://www.nytimes.com/2017/12/29/us/puerto-rico-power-outage.html.

Rosa, L., D. Chiarelli, M. Sangiorgio, A. Beltran-Peña, M. Rulli, P. D'Odorico, and I. Fung. 2020. "Potential for Sustainable Irrigation Expansion in a 3°C Warmer Climate." *Proceedings of the National Academy of Sciences* 117, no. 47: 29526–34. https://doi.org/10.1073/pnas.2017796117.

Rossi, C. 2020. "Assessing the Impact of Hurricane Frequency and Intensity on Mortgage Delinquency." *Journal of Risk Management in Financial Institutions* 14, no. 4: 426–42. https://www.newswise.com/pdf_docs/159438407991822_Assessing%20the%20Impact%20of%20Hurricane%20Frequency%20and%20Intensity%20on%20Mortgage%20Default%20Ris1%20(2).pdf.

Rothstein, R. 2017. *The Color of Law: A Forgotten History of How Our Government Segregated America*. New York: Liveright. https://www.epi.org/publication/the-color-of-law-a-forgotten-history-of-how-our-government-segregated-america/.

Royal, A., and M. Walls. 2018. "Flood Risk Perceptions and Insurance Choice: Do Decisions in the Floodplain Reflect Overoptimism?" *Risk Analysis* 39, no. 5. 1088–1104. https://doi.org/10.1111/risa.13240

Sadasivam, N. 2020. "Holding the Bill." *Grist*, March 4. https://grist.org/climate/insurance-companies-and-lenders-are-responding-to-climate-change-by-shifting-risk-to-taxpayers/.

Sastry, P. 2022. "Who Bears Flood Risk? Evidence from Mortgage Markets in Florida." https://papers.ssrn.com/sol3/papers.cfm?abstract_id=4306291.

Schlenker, W., and M. Roberts. 2009. "Nonlinear Temperature Effects Indicate Severe Damages to U.S. Crop Yields Under Climate Change." *Proceedings of the National Academy of Sciences* 106, no. 37: 15594–98. https://doi.org/10.1073/pnas.0906865106.

Schuppe, J. 2022. "Louisiana Faces an Insurance Crisis, Leaving People Afraid They Can't Afford Their Homes." *U.S. News & World Report*, September 16. https://www.nbcnews.com/news/us-news/louisiana-homeowners-insurance-crisis-hurricanes-rcna46746.

Seneviratne, S., X. Zhang, M. Adnan, W. Badi, C. Dereczynski, A. Di Luca, S. Ghosh, I. Iskander, J. Kossin, S. Lewis, F. Otto, I. Pinto, M. Satoh, S. M.

Vicente-Serrano, M. Wehner, and B. Zhou. 2021. "Weather and Climate Extreme Events in a Changing Climate." In *Climate Change 2021: The Physical Science Basis. Contribution of Working Group I to the Sixth Assessment Report of the Intergovernmental Panel on Climate Change*, edited by V. Masson-Delmotte, P. Zhai, A. Pirani, S. Connors, C. Pean, S. Berger, N. Caud, Y. Chen, L. Goldfarb, M. Gomis, M. Huang, K. Leitzell, E. Lonnoy, J. Matthews, T. Maycock, T. Waterfield, O. Yelekci, R. Yi, and B. Zhou, 1513–1766. Cambridge: Cambridge University Press. https://doi.org/10.1017/9781009157896.013.

Severen, C., C. Costello, and O. Deschênes. 2018. "A Forward-Looking Ricardian Approach: Do Land Markets Capitalize Climate Change Forecasts?" *Journal of Environmental Economics and Management* 89: 235–54. https://doi.org/10.1016/j.jeem.2018.03.009.

State of California, Governor's Office of Planning and Research. 2018. "California's Changing Climate 2018: A Summary of Key Findings from California's Fourth Climate Change Assessment." California Natural Resources Agency and California Energy Commission. https://www.energy.ca.gov/sites/default/files/2019-11/20180827_Summary_Brochure_ADA.pdf.

Stern, N. 2006. *The Economics of Climate Change: The Stern Review*. Cambridge: Cambridge University Press. https://www.lse.ac.uk/granthaminstitute/publication/the-economics-of-climate-change-the-stern-review/.

Stevens, H., and J. Samenow. 2022. "Maps Show Where Extreme Heat Shattered 7,000 Records This Summer." *Washington Post*, September 13. https://www.washingtonpost.com/climate-environment/interactive/2022/temperature-records-summer/.

Svartzman, R., E. Espagne, J. Gauthey, P. Hadji-Lazaro, M. Salin, T. Allen, J. Berger, J. Calas, A. Godin, and A. Vallier. 2021. "A 'Silent Spring' for the Financial System? Exploring Biodiversity-Related Financial Risks in France." Working Paper 826, Banque of France. https://publications.banque-france.fr/en/silent-spring-financial-system-exploring-biodiversity-related-financial-risks-france.

Thomas, K. 2017. "U.S. Hospitals Wrestle with Shortages of Drug Supplies Made in Puerto Rico." *New York Times*, October 23. https://www.nytimes.com/2017/10/23/health/puerto-rico-hurricane-maria-drug-shortage.html.

Tilman, D., M. Clare, D. Williams, K. Kimmel, S. Polasky, and C. Packer. 2017. "Future Threats to Biodiversity and Pathways to their Prevention." *Nature* 546: 73–81. https://doi.org/10.1038/nature22900.

Tran, B., and D. Wilson. 2022. *The Local Economic Impact of Natural Disasters*. Working Paper 34. San Francisco: Federal Reserve Bank of San Francisco. https://doi.org/10.24148/wp2020-34.

UN Framework Convention on Climate Change. 2021. *Adaptation Communication of the United States*. https://unfccc.int/sites/default/files/resource/USA%20Full%20 Adaptation%20Communication%202021.11.2%209am_.pdf.

Urban Institute. 2022. "Housing Finance at a Glance: A Monthly Chartbook." https:// www.urban.org/sites/default/files/2022-11/Housing%20Finance-%20At%20 A%20Glance%20Monthly%20Chartbook%2C%20November%202022.pdf.

U.S. Army Corps of Engineers. No date. "Flood Risk Management." https://www.usace. army.mil/Missions/Civil-Works/Flood-Risk-Management/.

U.S. Department of Agriculture, Office of Communications. 2022. "Secretary Vilsack Announces New 10-Year Strategy to Confront the Wildfire Crisis." U.S. Forest Service. https://www.fs.usda.gov/news/releases/ secretary-vilsack-announces-new-10-year-strategy-confront-wildfire-crisis.

U.S. Department of Commerce. 2022. "Biden Administration Announces Historic Coastal and Climate Resilience Funding." June 29. https://www.noaa.gov/news-release/ biden-administration-announces-historic-coastal-and-climate-resilience-funding.

U.S. Department of Defense. 2021a. *DOD Installation Exposure to Climate Change at Home and Abroad*. Office of the Deputy Assistant Secretary of Defense, Environment and Resilience. https://media.defense.gov/2021/ Apr/20/2002624613/-1/-1/1/DOD-INSTALLATION-EXPOSURE-TO-CLIMATE-CHANGE-AT-HOME-AND-ABROAD.PDF.

———. 2021b. *Department of Defense Climate Risk Analysis*. Office of the Undersecretary for Policy–Strategy, Plans, and Capabilities. https://media. defense.gov/2021/Oct/21/2002877353/-1/–1/0/DOD-CLIMATE-RISK-ANALYSIS-FINAL.PDF.

U.S. Department of Energy. 2022. "The Inflation Reduction Act Drives Significant Emissions Reductions and Positions America to Reach Our Climate Goals." Office of Policy. https://www.energy.gov/sites/default/files/2022-08/8.18%20 InflationReductionAct_Factsheet_Final.pdf.

U.S. Department of Homeland Security. 2018. "An Affordability Framework for the National Flood Insurance Program." Federal Emergency Management Agency. https://www.fema.gov/sites/default/files/2020-05/Affordability_april_2018.pdf.

———. 2022. "Summary of Proposed Reforms." Federal Emergency Management Agency. https://www.fema.gov/sites/default/files/documents/fema_flood-insurance-reform-proposal_5242022.pdf.

U.S. Department of the Interior. 2022. "Biden-Harris Administration Makes $135 Million Commitments to Support Relocation of Tribal Communities Affected by Climate Change." https://www.doi.gov/pressreleases/ biden-harris-administration-makes-135-million-commitment-support-relocation-tribal.

U.S. Department of State and Executive Office of the President. 2021. "The Long-Term Strategy of the United States: Pathways to Net-Zero Greenhouse Gas Emissions by 2050." https://www.whitehouse.gov/wp-content/uploads/2021/10/US-Long-Term-Strategy.pdf.

U.S. Department of Transportation. 2022. "Bipartisan Infrastructure Law: Promoting Resilient Operations for Transformative, Efficient, and Cost-Saving Transportation (PROTECT) Formula Program." Fact sheet, Federal Highway Administration, July 29. https://www.fhwa.dot.gov/bipartisan-infrastructure-law/protect_fact_sheet.cfm.

U.S. Environmental Protection Agency. 2021. "Climate Change and Social Vulnerability in the United States: A Focus on Six Impacts." https://www.epa.gov/cira/social-vulnerability-report.

———. 2022. "Greenhouse Gas Reduction Fund." https://www.epa.gov/inflation-reduction-act/greenhouse-gas-reduction-fund.

———. No date. "About the Office of Environmental Justice and External Civil Rights." https://www.epa.gov/aboutepa/about-office-environmental-justice-and-external-civil-rights.

U.S. Federal Reserve. 2023. "Pilot Climate Scenario Analysis Exercise: Participant Instructions." https://www.federalreserve.gov/publications/files/csa-instructions-20230117.pdf.

U.S. Global Change Research Program. 2018. "Fourth National Climate Assessment." https://nca2018.globalchange.gov.

U.S. Government Accountability Office. 2022. "National Security Snapshot: Climate Change Risks to National Security." https://www.gao.gov/products/gao-22-105830.

U.S. Securities and Exchanges Commission. 2022. "SEC Proposes Rules to Enhance and Standardize Climate-Related Disclosures for Investors." https://www.sec.gov/news/press-release/2022-46.

U.S. Small Business Administration. No date. "Disaster Assistance." https://www.sba.gov/funding-programs/disaster-assistance.

United Nations Climate Change. No date. "Paris Agreement: Status of Ratification." https://unfccc.int/process/the-paris-agreement/status-of-ratification.

Urban, M. 2015. "Accelerating Extinction Risk from Climate Change." *Science* 348, no. 6234: 571–73. https://doi.org/10.1126/science.aaa4984.

van der Wiel, K., S. Kapnick, G. vsn Oldenborgh, K. Whan, S. Philip, G. Vecchi, R. Singh, J. Arrighi, and H. Cullen. 2017. "Rapid Attribution of the August 2016 Flood-Inducing Extreme Precipitation in South Louisiana to Climate Change." *Hydrology and Earth System Sciences* 21: 897–921. https://hess.copernicus.org/articles/21/897/2017/hess-21-897-2017.pdf.

Vose, R., D. Easterling, A. LeGrande, and M. Wehner. 2017. "Temperature Changes in the United States." In *Climate Science Special Report: Fourth National Climate Assessment*, edited by D. Wuebbles, D. Fahey, K. Hibbard, D. Dokken, B.

Stewart, and T. Maycock, 185–206. Washington: U.S. Global Change Research Program. https://doi.org/10.7930/J0N29V45.

Wagner, K. 2020. "Why Is Reforming Natural Disaster Insurance Markets So Hard?" Policy Brief, Stanford Institute for Economic Policy Research. https://siepr.stanford.edu/publications/policy-brief/why-reforming-natural-disaster-insurance-markets-so-hard.

———. 2022. "Adaptation and Adverse Selection in Markets for Natural Disaster Insurance." *American Economic Journal: Economic Policy* 14, no. 3: 380–421. https://doi.org/10.1257/pol.20200378.

Wheeler, K., B. Udall, J. Wang, E. Kuhn, H. Salehabadi, and J. Schmidt. 2022. "What Will It Take to Stabilize the Colorado River?" *Science* 377, no. 6604: 373–75. https://doi.org/10.1126/science.abo4452.

White House. 2015a. "Findings from Select Federal Reports: The National Security Implications of a Changing Climate." https://obamawhitehouse.archives.gov/sites/default/files/docs/National_Security_Implications_of_Changing_Climate_Final_051915.pdf.

———. 2015b. "National Security Strategy." https://obamawhitehouse.archives.gov/sites/default/files/docs/2015_national_security_strategy_2.pdf.

———. 2021. "Fact Sheet: Historic Bipartisan Infrastructure Deal." https://www.whitehouse.gov/briefing-room/statements-releases/2021/07/28/fact-sheet-historic-bipartisan-infrastructure-deal/.

———. 2022a. "Fact Sheet: The Inflation Reduction Act Supports Workers and Families." https://www.whitehouse.gov/briefing-room/statements-releases/2022/08/19/fact-sheet-the-inflation-reduction-act-supports-workers-and-families/.

———. 2022b. "Federal Budget Exposure to Climate Risk." Office of Management and Budget. https://www.whitehouse.gov/wp-content/uploads/2022/04/ap_21_climate_risk_fy2023.pdf.

———. 2022c. "National Strategy to Develop Statistics for Environmental-Economic Decisions: A U.S. System of Natural Capital Accounting and Associated Environmental-Economic Statistics." Office of Science and Technology Policy, Office of Management and Budget, and Department of Commerce. https://www.whitehouse.gov/wp-content/uploads/2022/08/Natural-Capital-Accounting-Strategy.pdf.

———. 2022d. "OMB Analysis: The Social Benefits of the Inflation Reduction Act's Greenhous Gas Emission Reductions." Office of Management and Budget. https://www.whitehouse.gov/wp-content/uploads/2022/08/OMB-Analysis-Inflation-Reduction-Act.pdf.

———. 2022e. "National Security Strategy." https://www.whitehouse.gov/wp-content/uploads/2022/10/Biden-Harris-Administrations-National-Security-Strategy-10.2022.pdf.

———. 2022f. "Climate-Related Macroeconomic Risks and Opportunities." https://www.whitehouse.gov/wp-content/uploads/2022/04/CEA_OMB_Climate_Macro_WP_2022-430pm.pdf.

———. 2022g. "Fact Sheet: 10 Ways the Biden-Harris Administration Is Making America Resilient to Climate Change." https://www.whitehouse.gov/briefing-room/statements-releases/2022/08/01/fact-sheet-10-ways-the-biden-harris-administration-is-making-america-resilient-to-climate-change/.

———. 2022h. "Biden-Harris Administration Announces New Actions to Lower Energy Costs for Families." https://www.whitehouse.gov/briefing-room/statements-releases/2022/11/02/fact-sheet-biden-harris-administration-announces-new-actions-to-lower-energy-costs-for-families/.

———. 2022i. "Building a Clean Energy Economy: A Guidebook to the Inflation Reduction Act's Investments in Clean Energy and Climate Action." https://www.whitehouse.gov/wp-content/uploads/2022/12/Inflation-Reduction-Act-Guidebook.pdf.

———. 2022j. "Executive Order on Catalyzing Clean Energy Industries and Jobs through Federal Sustainability." https://www.whitehouse.gov/briefing-room/presidential-actions/2021/12/08/executive-order-on-catalyzing-clean-energy-industries-and-jobs-through-federal-sustainability/.

———. No date. "Justice40." https://www.whitehouse.gov/environmentaljustice/justice40/.

Wing, O., W. Lehman, P. Bates, C. Sampson, N. Quinn, A. Smith, J. Neal, J. Porter, and C. Kousky. 2022. "Inequitable Patterns of U.S. Flood Risk in the Anthropocene." *Nature Climate Change* 12: 156–62. https://doi.org/10.1038/s41558-021-01265-6.

Winter, J., H. Huang, E. Osterberg, and J. Mankin. 2020. "Anthropogenic Impacts on the Exceptional Precipitation of 2018 in the Mid-Atlantic United States." In *Explaining Extreme Events of 2018 from a Climate Perspective*, edited by S. Herring, N. Christidis, A. Hoell, M. Hoerling, and P. Stott, S5–S16. Washington: American Meteorological Society. https://doi.org/10.1175/BAMS-ExplainingExtremeEvents2018.1.

Woetzel, J., D. Pinner, H. Samandari, H. Engel, M. Krishnan, C. Kampel, and J. Graabak. 2020a. "Could Climate Become the Weak Link in Your Supply Chain?" McKinsey Global Institute. https://www.mckinsey.com/capabilities/sustainability/our-insights/could-climate-become-the-weak-link-in-your-supply-chain.

Woetzel, J., D. Pinner, H. Samandari, H. Engel, M. Krishnan, C. Kampel, and M. Vasmel. 2020b. "Will Mortgages and Markets Stay Afloat in Florida?" McKinsey Global Institute. https://www.mckinsey.com/~/media/mckinsey/business%20functions/sustainability/our%20insights/will%20mortgages%20and%20markets%20stay%20afloat%20in%20florida/mgi_climate%20risk_case%20studies_florida_may2020.pdf.

Wondmagegn, B., J. Xiang, K. Dear, S. Williams, A. Hansen, D. Pisaniello, M. Nitschke, J. Nairn, B. Scalleye, A. Xiao, L. Jian, M. Tong, H. Bambrick, J. Karnonh, and P. Bia. 2021. "Increasing Impacts of Temperature on Hospital Admissions, Length of Stay, and Related Healthcare Costs in the Context of Climate Change in Adelaide, South Australia." *Science of the Total Environment* 773, no. 15. https://doi.org/10.1016/j.scitotenv.2021.145656.

World Weather Attribution. 2017. "Climate Change Fingerprints Confirmed in Hurricane Harvey's Rainfall, August 2017." https://www.worldweatherattribution.org/hurricane-harvey-august-2017/.

Xu, E., C. Webb, and D. Evans. 2019. "Wildfire Catastrophe Models Could Spark the Changes California Needs." Milliman. https://www.milliman.com/-/media/milliman/importedfiles/uploadedfiles/wildfire_catastrophe_models_could_spark_the_changes_california_needs.ashx.

Yu, Y., J. Dunne, E. Sheviakova, P. Ginoux, S. Malyshev, J. John, and J. Krasting. 2021. "Increased Risk of the 2019 Alaskan July Fires Due to Anthropogenic Activity." In *Explaining Extreme Events of 2019 from a Climate Perspective*, edited by S. Herring, N. Christidis, A. Hoell, M. Hoerling, and P. Stott, S1–S8. Washington: American Meteorological Society. https://doi.org/10.1175/BAMS-D-20-0154.1.

Appendix A

Report to the President on the Activities of the Council of Economic Advisers during 2022

Letter of Transmittal

Council of Economic Advisers
Washington, December 31, 2022

Mr. President:

The Council of Economic Advisers submits this report on its activities during calendar year 2022 in accordance with the requirements of Congress, as set forth by Section 10(d) of the Employment Act of 1946, as amended by the Full Employment and Balanced Growth Act of 1978.

Sincerely yours,

Cecilia Elena Rouse
Chair

Jared Bernstein
Member

Heather Boushey
Member

Council Members and Their Dates of Service

Name	Position	Oath of office date	Separation date
Edwin G. Nourse	Chairman	August 9, 1946	November 1, 1949
Leon H. Keyserling	Vice Chairman	August 9, 1946	
	Acting Chairman	November 2, 1949	
	Chairman	May 10, 1950	January 20, 1953
John D. Clark	Member	August 9, 1946	
	Vice Chairman	May 10, 1950	February 11, 1953
Roy Blough	Member	June 29, 1950	August 20, 1952
Robert C. Turner	Member	September 8, 1952	January 20, 1953
Arthur F. Burns	Chairman	March 19, 1953	December 1, 1956
Neil H. Jacoby	Member	September 15, 1953	February 9, 1955
Walter W. Stewart	Member	December 2, 1953	April 29, 1955
Raymond J. Saulnier	Member	April 4, 1955	
	Chairman	December 3, 1956	January 20, 1961
Joseph S. Davis	Member	May 2, 1955	October 31, 1958
Paul W. McCracken	Member	December 3, 1956	January 31, 1959
Karl Brandt	Member	November 1, 1958	January 20, 1961
Henry C. Wallich	Member	May 7, 1959	January 20, 1961
Walter W. Heller	Chairman	January 29, 1961	November 15, 1964
James Tobin	Member	January 29, 1961	July 31, 1962
Kermit Gordon	Member	January 29, 1961	December 27, 1962
Gardner Ackley	Member	August 3, 1962	
	Chairman	November 16, 1964	February 15, 1968
John P. Lewis	Member	May 17, 1963	August 31, 1964
Otto Eckstein	Member	September 2, 1964	February 1, 1966
Arthur M. Okun	Member	November 16, 1964	
	Chairman	February 15, 1968	January 20, 1969
James S. Duesenberry	Member	February 2, 1966	June 30, 1968
Merton J. Peck	Member	February 15, 1968	January 20, 1969
Warren L. Smith	Member	July 1, 1968	January 20, 1969
Paul W. McCracken	Chairman	February 4, 1969	December 31, 1971
Hendrik S. Houthakker	Member	February 4, 1969	July 15, 1971
Herbert Stein	Member	February 4, 1969	
	Chairman	January 1, 1972	August 31, 1974
Ezra Solomon	Member	September 9, 1971	March 26, 1973
Marina v.N. Whitman	Member	March 13, 1972	August 15, 1973
Gary L. Seevers	Member	July 23, 1973	April 15, 1975
William J. Fellner	Member	October 31, 1973	February 25, 1975
Alan Greenspan	Chairman	September 4, 1974	January 20, 1977
Paul W. MacAvoy	Member	June 13, 1975	November 15, 1976
Burton G. Malkiel	Member	July 22, 1975	January 20, 1977
Charles L. Schultze	Chairman	January 22, 1977	January 20, 1981
William D. Nordhaus	Member	March 18, 1977	February 4, 1979
Lyle E. Gramley	Member	March 18, 1977	May 27, 1980
George C. Eads	Member	June 6, 1979	January 20, 1981
Stephen M. Goldfeld	Member	August 20, 1980	January 20, 1981
Murray L. Weidenbaum	Chairman	February 27, 1981	August 25, 1982
William A. Niskanen	Member	June 12, 1981	March 30, 1985
Jerry L. Jordan	Member	July 14, 1981	July 31, 1982

Council Members and Their Dates of Service

Name	Position	Oath of office date	Separation date
Martin Feldstein	Chairman	October 14, 1982	July 10, 1984
William Poole	Member	December 10, 1982	January 20, 1985
Beryl W. Sprinkel	Chairman	April 18, 1985	January 20, 1989
Thomas Gale Moore	Member	July 1, 1985	May 1, 1989
Michael L. Mussa	Member	August 18, 1986	September 19, 1988
Michael J. Boskin	Chairman	February 2, 1989	January 12, 1993
John B. Taylor	Member	June 9, 1989	August 2, 1991
Richard L. Schmalensee	Member	October 3, 1989	June 21, 1991
David F. Bradford	Member	November 13, 1991	January 20, 1993
Paul Wonnacott	Member	November 13, 1991	January 20, 1993
Laura D'Andrea Tyson	Chair	February 5, 1993	April 22, 1995
Alan S. Blinder	Member	July 27, 1993	June 26, 1994
Joseph E. Stiglitz	Member	July 27, 1993	
	Chairman	June 28, 1995	February 10, 1997
Martin N. Baily	Member	June 30, 1995	August 30, 1996
Alicia H. Munnell	Member	January 29, 1996	August 1, 1997
Janet L. Yellen	Chair	February 18, 1997	August 3, 1999
Jeffrey A. Frankel	Member	April 23, 1997	March 2, 1999
Rebecca M. Blank	Member	October 22, 1998	July 9, 1999
Martin N. Baily	Chairman	August 12, 1999	January 19, 2001
Robert Z. Lawrence	Member	August 12, 1999	January 12, 2001
Kathryn L. Shaw	Member	May 31, 2000	January 19, 2001
R. Glenn Hubbard	Chairman	May 11, 2001	February 28, 2003
Mark B. McClellan	Member	July 25, 2001	November 13, 2002
Randall S. Kroszner	Member	November 30, 2001	July 1, 2003
N. Gregory Mankiw	Chairman	May 29, 2003	February 18, 2005
Kristin J. Forbes	Member	November 21, 2003	June 3, 2005
Harvey S. Rosen	Member	November 21, 2003	
	Chairman	February 23, 2005	June 10, 2005
Ben S. Bernanke	Chairman	June 21, 2005	January 31, 2006
Katherine Baicker	Member	November 18, 2005	July 11, 2007
Matthew J. Slaughter	Member	November 18, 2005	March 1, 2007
Edward P. Lazear	Chairman	February 27, 2006	January 20, 2009
Donald B. Marron	Member	July 17, 2008	January 20, 2009
Christina D. Romer	Chair	January 29, 2009	September 3, 2010
Austan D. Goolsbee	Member	March 11, 2009	
	Chairman	September 10, 2010	August 5, 2011
Cecilia Elena Rouse	Member	March 11, 2009	February 28, 2011
Katharine G. Abraham	Member	April 19, 2011	April 19, 2013
Carl Shapiro	Member	April 19, 2011	May 4, 2012
Alan B. Krueger	Chairman	November 7, 2011	August 2, 2013
James H. Stock	Member	February 7, 2013	May 19, 2014
Jason Furman	Chairman	August 4, 2013	January 20, 2017
Betsey Stevenson	Member	August 6, 2013	August 7, 2015
Maurice Obstfeld	Member	July 21, 2014	August 28, 2015
Sandra E. Black	Member	August 10, 2015	January 20, 2017
Jay C. Shambaugh	Member	August 31, 2015	January 20, 2017

Council Members and Their Dates of Service

Name	Position	Oath of office date	Separation date
Kevin A. Hassett	Chairman	September 13, 2017	June 30, 2019
Richard V. Burkhauser	Member	September 28, 2017	May 18, 2019
Tomas J. Philipson	Member	August 31, 2017	
	Acting Chairman	July 1, 2019	
	Vice Chairman	July 24, 2019	June 22, 2020
Tyler B. Goodspeed	Member	May 22, 2019	
	Acting Chairman	June 23, 2020	
	Vice Chairman	June 23, 2020	January 6, 2021
Cecilia Elena Rouse	Chair	March 2, 2021	
Jared Bernstein	Member	January 20, 2021	
Heather Boushey	Member	January 20, 2021	

Report to the President on the Activities of the Council of Economic Advisers during 2022

Established by the Employment Act of 1946, the Council of Economic Advisers is charged with advising the President on economic policy based on data, research, and evidence. The Council is composed of three members: a Chair, who is appointed by the President with the advice and consent of the Senate; and two members, who are appointed by the President. Along with a team of economists, they analyze and interpret economic developments and formulate and recommend economic policies that advance the interests of the American people.

The Chair of the Council

Cecilia Elena Rouse was confirmed by the Senate on March 2, 2021, as the 30th Chair of the Council of Economic Advisers. She is the first African American to hold this position. In this role, she serves as President Biden's Chief Economist and a Member of the Cabinet. She is the Katzman-Ernst Professor in the Economics of Education and Professor of Economics and Public Affairs at Princeton University.

From 2012 to 2021, Rouse was Dean of Princeton University's School of Public and International Affairs. Rouse served as a Member of President Barack Obama's Council of Economic Advisers from 2009 to 2011. She also worked at the National Economic Council in the Clinton Administration as a Special Assistant to the President from 1998 to 1999. Her academic research has focused on the economics of education, including the economic benefits of community college attendance and impact of student loan debt on postgraduation outcomes, as well as other issues in labor economics, such as discrimination.

The Members of the Council

Heather Boushey was appointed to the Council by the President on January 20, 2021. Before assuming this position, Boushey cofounded the Washington Center for Equitable Growth, where she was President and CEO from 2013 to 2020. She previously served as Chief Economist for Secretary Hillary Clinton's 2016 transition team and as an economist at the

Center for American Progress, the Joint Economic Committee of the U.S. Congress, the Center for Economic and Policy Research, and the Economic Policy Institute.

Jared Bernstein was appointed to the Council by the President on January 20, 2021. Before this appointment, Bernstein spent 16 years in senior roles at the Economic Policy Institute, and worked at the Department of Labor. He was a Senior Fellow at the Center on Budget and Policy Priorities from 2011 to 2020. From 2009 to 2011, he was Chief Economist and Economic Adviser to then–Vice President Biden.

Areas of Activity

A central function of the Council is to advise the President on all economic issues and developments, including preparing almost-daily memos for the President, the Vice President, and White House senior staff on key economic data releases and policy issues. The Council works closely with officials at various government entities—including the National Economic Council, the Domestic Policy Council, the Office of Management and Budget, and Administrative Agencies—to engage in discussions on numerous policy matters. The Council, the Department of the Treasury, and the Office of Management and Budget are responsible for producing the economic forecasts that underlie the Administration's Budget proposals. Finally, the Council is a leading participant in the Organization for Economic Cooperation and Development (OECD), historically chairing the Economic Policy Committee and participating in OECD working meetings.

The Council produces economic analyses in a series of blogs and issue briefs. This past year, these included:

- "The Employment Situation," a monthly blog analyzing the employment situation that corresponds to the monthly Jobs Report (January–December 2022).
- "Looking Back, Moving Forward: Year One of President Biden's Economic Agenda," a blog analyzing how government support during the pandemic helped boost personal income and spending, thus contributing to economic growth (January 2022).
- "New Data Show that Economic Growth Was Broadly Shared in 2021," a blog on how government support during the pandemic helped boost personal income and spending, thus leading to economic growth (February 2022).
- "Climate-Related Macroeconomic Risks and Opportunities," an issue brief, cowritten with OMB, on how the President's policy proposals

can reduce greenhouse gas emissions while keeping energy costs low for consumers (April 2022).

- "Blocking the Low Road and Paving the High Road: Management Practices to Improve Productivity," an issue brief on how employment policies could increase worker productivity, thus leading to increased labor market outcomes (April 2022).
- "Care Businesses: A Model That Doesn't Work for Providers, Workers, or Families," an issue brief outlining the supports that meet the needs of workers' families—such as affordable, high-quality childcare, home health care, and paid family and medical leave—that can increase the U.S. labor supply and boost economic growth (April 2022).
- "Summary of the 2022 *Economic Report of the President*," a blog outlining the reflections of the Administration's economic accomplishments and challenges (April 2022).
- "Expanding Economic Opportunity for Formerly Incarcerated Persons," a blog focusing on the President's comprehensive strategy to support formerly incarcerated persons (May 2022).
- "Using Additive Manufacturing to Improve Supply Chain Resilience and Bolster Small and Mid-Size Firms," a blog outlining the use of additive manufacturing as a way to boost the supply chain capability in many industries (May 2022).
- "Reducing the Economic Burden of Unmet Mental Health Needs," an issue brief outlining how the social and economic consequences of mental health disorders can be reduced (May 2022).
- "Juneteenth: Reflecting on Some of the Progress and Challenges for Black Americans During the Pandemic," an issue brief highlighting the policies that increase economic capacity for Black students and workers (June 2022).
- "Excess Mortality during the Pandemic: The Role of Health Insurance," an issue brief identifying the President's policies to increase health insurance coverage to combat mortality across States (July 2022).
- "How Do Economists Determine Whether the Economy Is in a Recession?" a blog on the indicators used to assess significant declines in economic activity (July 2022).
- "The Economics Behind the President's Economic Agenda," a blog on how the President's policies can reduce inflationary pressure and increase economic capacity through long-term investments in physical

infrastructure, human capital, clean energy, housing, and health care (August 2022).

- "Pandemic Shifts in Black Employment and Wages," a blog assessing the pandemic's effect on wage growth and employment for Black Americans, presenting both short-run and long-run challenges (August 2022).
- "The Rising Costs of Extreme Weather Events," a blog on the importance of incorporating climate change into the economic projections that underlie assessments of financial risk and government finances (September 2022).
- "The State of Our Unions," a blog that examines the current uptick in union organizing efforts due to a tight labor market coming out the pandemic (September 2022).
- "Affordable Health Care for Individuals with Cancer," a blog on the importance of expanding health coverage and disability benefits for individuals living with cancer (September 2022).
- "The Impact of Artificial Intelligence on the Future of Workforces in the European Union and the United States of America," a report prepared by the CEA and the European Commission (December 2022).

Public Information

The *Economic Report of the President*, together with the Annual Report of the Council of Economic Advisers, is an important vehicle for presenting the Administration's domestic and international economic policies. It is available for purchase through the Government Publishing Office, and is viewable at no cost at www.gpo.gov/erp. All the Council's written materials noted above, including this *Report*, can be found at www.whitehouse.gov/cea. All links provided in this *Report* are active as of the date of publication.

The Staff of the Council of Economic Advisers

Front Office

Elisabeth Hirschhorn Donahue .... Chief of Staff & General Counsel
Martha Gimbel .... Senior Advisor
Katherine Harris .... Special Assistant to the Chair
Megan Bell .... Special Assistant to a Member
Julien Rosenbloom .... Special Assistant to a Member

Senior Economists

Randy Akee .... Social Insurance, Labor
Steven Braun .... Director of Macroeconomic Forecasting
Chloe Gibbs .... Education, Labor
Joshua Goodman................ Education
Kari Heerman .... International Trade
Sandile Hlatshwayo .... International
Margaret Loudermilk .... Industrial Organization, Supply Chains
Erika McEntarfer .... Labor
David Miller .... Macroeconomics
Frances Moore .... Climate, Environment
Judith Scott-Clayton .... Higher Education, Tax, Regulation
Michael Sinkinson .... Industrial Organization, Technology
Ernie Tedeschi .... Macroeconomics
Tugkan Tuzun .... Finance, Energy, Housing
Victoria Udalova .... Health

National Security Economist

Meghan Greene................. Senior Advisor for National Security

Staff Economists

Ryan Cummings .... Finance, Macroeconomics, Energy
Melanie Friedrichs .... Macroeconomics
John Iselin .... Tax, Regulation
Andrew Wilson................. Climate, Environment
Joe Winkelmann .... Applied Microeconomics, International

Research Assistants

Erin Deal . . . . Macroeconomics
Aiden Lee . . . . Industrial Organization, Technology
Shawdi Mehrvarzan . . . . Health, Labor, International
Yailin Navarro . . . . Education, Health
Stephen Nyarko. . . . . International, Finance, OECD
Anna Pasnau . . . . Care, Labor, Climate
Natalie Tomeh. . . . . Housing, Care, Social Insurance
Sarah Wheaton . . . . Labor, Macroeconomics

Statistical Office

Brian Amorosi . . . . Director of Statistical Office
Madison Fox . . . . Statistical Office Associate

Administrative Office

Megan Packer . . . . Director of Finance and Administration

Interns

Sofia Bletnitsky, Caleb Brobst, Sylvia Brown, Saumya Gunampalli, Emma Hussey, Osamwonyi Igbineweka, Roushda Khan, Aarti Kumar, Christian Mira, Ester Muzychuk, Alaina Neuburger, Lauren Ottley, Irena Petryk, Daniel Posthumus, Ali Sait, and Lauren Taylor

ERP Production

Alfred Imhoff . . . . Editor

Appendix B

Statistical Tables Relating to Income, Employment, and Production

Contents

National Income or Expenditure

Labor Market Indicators

Production and Business Activity

Prices

Money Stock, Credit, and Finance

Government Finance

Corporate Profits and Finance

International Statistics

General Notes

Detail in these tables may not add to totals due to rounding.

Because of the formula used for calculating real gross domestic product (GDP), the chained (2012) dollar estimates for the detailed components do not add to the chained-dollar value of GDP or to any intermediate aggregate. The Department of Commerce (Bureau of Economic Analysis) no longer publishes chained-dollar estimates prior to 2002, except for selected series.

Because of the method used for seasonal adjustment, the sum or average of seasonally adjusted monthly values generally will not equal annual totals based on unadjusted values.

Unless otherwise noted, all dollar figures are in current dollars.

Symbols used:

^{p} Preliminary.
... Not available (also, not applicable).
NSA Not seasonally adjusted.

Data in these tables reflect revisions made by source agencies through March 2, 2023.

Excel versions of these tables are available at www.gpo.gov/erp.

Table B–1. Percent changes in real gross domestic product, 1972–2022

[Percent change, fourth quarter over fourth quarter; quarterly changes at seasonally adjusted annual rates]

Year or quarter	Gross domestic product	Personal consumption expenditures			Gross private domestic investment							
						Fixed investment						Change in private inventories
							Nonresidential				Residential	
		Total	Goods	Services	Total	Total	Total	Structures	Equipment	Intellectual property products		
1972	6.9	7.3	8.5	6.2	15.0	12.0	11.5	5.1	17.0	6.2	12.9	....
1973	4.0	1.8	.4	3.2	10.2	3.5	10.6	7.9	13.5	5.1	−10.5	....
1974	−1.9	−1.6	−5.6	2.4	−10.4	−9.9	−3.9	−6.4	−3.7	1.6	−24.6	....
1975	2.6	5.1	6.1	4.1	−9.8	−2.6	−5.9	−8.1	−6.7	2.8	7.8	....
1976	4.3	5.4	6.4	4.5	15.2	12.1	7.8	3.8	9.0	11.8	23.8	....
1977	5.0	4.2	4.9	3.7	14.9	12.1	11.9	5.7	17.2	4.8	12.6	....
1978	6.7	4.0	3.5	4.4	14.3	13.1	16.0	21.7	14.5	10.3	6.8	....
1979	1.3	1.7	.3	2.9	−3.4	1.1	5.5	8.8	2.7	9.4	−9.1	....
1980	.0	.0	−2.5	2.2	−7.2	−4.8	−.9	2.7	−4.4	4.7	−15.3	....
1981	1.3	.1	−.2	.3	6.7	1.5	9.0	14.1	4.6	12.1	−22.0	....
1982	−1.4	3.5	3.6	3.4	−17.3	−8.0	−9.5	−13.5	−10.0	3.4	−1.7	....
1983	7.9	6.6	8.3	5.3	31.3	18.3	10.4	−3.9	19.9	13.0	49.7	....
1984	5.6	4.3	5.3	3.6	14.2	11.3	13.9	15.7	13.4	12.6	3.7	....
1985	4.2	4.8	4.6	5.0	1.9	3.7	3.2	3.3	1.7	7.7	5.2	....
1986	2.9	4.4	6.5	3.0	−4.1	.6	−3.2	−14.3	.8	5.4	11.8	....
1987	4.5	2.8	.4	4.6	9.8	1.5	2.2	4.9	.1	4.2	−.5	....
1988	3.8	4.6	4.5	4.7	−.5	3.7	5.1	−3.3	8.2	9.8	.1	....
1989	2.7	2.4	1.8	2.7	.7	1.5	4.5	3.3	2.5	11.3	−6.5	....
1990	.6	.8	−1.6	2.3	−6.5	−4.2	−.9	−3.2	−2.7	6.2	−13.6	....
1991	1.2	.9	−.8	2.0	2.1	−1.9	−3.4	−12.8	−3.2	7.2	2.9	....
1992	4.4	4.9	5.3	4.7	7.7	8.7	7.1	1.0	11.3	4.8	13.6	....
1993	2.6	3.3	4.4	2.7	7.6	8.4	7.6	.2	13.1	2.9	10.6	....
1994	4.1	3.8	5.5	2.8	11.5	6.6	8.5	1.6	12.5	5.8	1.6	....
1995	2.2	2.8	2.3	3.0	.8	5.5	7.4	4.7	8.1	8.3	.1	....
1996	4.4	3.4	4.8	2.7	11.2	9.9	11.3	10.9	11.1	12.1	5.6	....
1997	4.5	4.5	5.3	4.0	11.4	8.3	9.7	4.4	10.7	12.4	4.0	....
1998	4.9	5.6	8.1	4.3	9.7	11.5	11.6	4.3	14.8	11.5	11.3	....
1999	4.8	5.2	6.6	4.5	8.5	7.2	8.4	−.1	9.5	13.3	3.5	....
2000	2.9	4.3	4.0	4.5	4.3	5.9	8.5	10.8	8.5	6.6	−1.5	....
2001	.2	2.5	4.9	1.3	−11.1	−4.7	−6.8	−10.6	−7.7	−2.1	2.0	....
2002	2.0	2.0	1.7	2.1	4.4	−1.5	−5.1	−15.7	−3.7	.9	8.1	....
2003	4.3	3.8	6.6	2.3	8.7	8.6	6.8	1.9	9.6	5.8	12.7	....
2004	3.4	3.8	4.3	3.6	8.0	6.5	6.5	.3	9.8	5.7	6.6	....
2005	3.0	2.8	3.0	2.7	6.1	5.8	6.1	1.5	8.7	5.1	5.2	....
2006	2.6	3.2	4.6	2.5	−1.5	.0	8.1	9.0	7.1	9.3	−15.2	....
2007	2.2	2.0	1.8	2.0	−1.8	−1.1	7.3	17.7	3.9	4.0	−21.2	....
2008	−2.5	−1.5	−6.8	1.2	−15.3	−11.1	−7.0	−.8	−15.9	.9	−24.7	....
2009	.1	−.2	.6	−.6	−9.2	−10.5	−10.3	−27.1	−8.4	3.8	−11.5	....
2010	2.8	2.8	4.3	2.1	12.1	6.1	8.9	−3.6	22.6	1.6	−5.7	....
2011	1.5	1.0	.9	1.0	10.4	9.2	10.0	8.6	12.7	7.2	5.3	....
2012	1.6	1.5	2.4	1.1	4.0	7.2	5.6	4.0	7.8	3.7	15.4	....
2013	2.5	1.9	3.5	1.1	9.3	5.7	5.4	6.7	5.4	4.5	7.1	....
2014	2.6	3.5	5.0	2.7	5.3	7.0	6.9	9.3	5.6	6.9	7.7	....
2015	1.9	2.6	3.8	2.1	2.3	1.7	−.1	−7.3	1.5	3.3	9.2	....
2016	2.0	2.3	3.4	1.8	1.8	2.8	2.5	3.6	−2.2	8.4	4.0	....
2017	2.8	2.8	5.2	1.7	4.6	5.0	5.2	.8	7.0	5.8	4.6	....
2018	2.3	2.5	2.7	2.4	4.8	3.5	5.7	1.7	5.1	9.3	−3.8	....
2019	2.6	2.2	3.5	1.6	.1	2.4	2.6	6.6	−3.1	6.9	2.0	....
2020	−1.5	−1.4	8.6	−5.8	2.4	1.0	−3.5	−16.0	−2.7	3.8	16.4	....
2021	5.7	7.2	7.1	7.2	8.6	3.7	5.0	−5.2	4.7	10.8	−.3	....
2022 p	.9	1.8	−.9	3.2	−4.0	−2.1	4.3	−3.3	4.0	8.5	−19.0	....
2019: I	2.2	.4	.0	.6	4.0	.8	1.8	.8	.9	3.6	−2.5	....
II	2.7	2.6	5.5	1.3	2.4	6.2	6.2	15.4	.8	7.3	6.5	....
III	3.6	3.4	5.8	2.3	2.6	4.1	4.1	17.9	−5.5	7.3	4.2	....
IV	1.8	2.4	2.8	2.1	−8.0	−1.3	−1.6	−5.8	−8.3	9.3	.0	....
2020: I	−4.6	−6.2	.0	−8.9	−5.1	−3.0	−8.2	−3.4	−23.9	7.9	17.4	....
II	−29.9	−32.1	−10.7	−40.4	−48.8	−28.9	−29.4	−42.9	−38.0	−9.3	−27.4	....
III	35.3	43.0	55.2	37.1	91.8	29.2	20.2	−10.4	57.1	9.5	61.6	....
IV	3.9	3.9	.3	5.7	18.0	16.8	11.5	.9	21.1	8.3	33.4	....
2021: I	6.3	10.8	25.3	4.0	−5.4	9.7	8.9	1.9	6.1	15.6	11.6	....
II	7.0	12.1	11.6	12.3	.9	5.8	9.9	−2.5	14.0	12.6	−4.9	....
III	2.7	3.0	−7.9	9.2	10.4	−1.1	.6	−6.7	−2.2	7.4	−5.8	....
IV	7.0	3.1	2.3	3.5	32.0	.6	1.1	−12.7	1.6	8.1	−1.1	....
2022: I	−1.6	1.3	−.1	2.1	5.4	4.8	7.9	−4.3	11.4	10.8	−3.1	....
II	−.6	2.0	−2.6	4.6	−14.1	−5.0	.1	−12.7	−2.0	8.9	−17.8	....
III	3.2	2.3	−.4	3.7	−9.6	−3.5	6.2	−3.6	10.6	6.8	−27.1	....
IV p	2.7	1.4	−.5	2.4	3.7	−4.6	3.3	8.5	−3.2	7.4	−25.9	....

See next page for continuation of table.

Table B–1. Percent changes in real gross domestic product, 1972–2022—*Continued*

[Percent change, fourth quarter over fourth quarter; quarterly changes at seasonally adjusted annual rates]

Year or quarter	Net exports of goods and services			Government consumption expenditures and gross investment					Final sales of domestic product	Gross domestic pur- chases [1]	Final sales to private domestic pur- chasers [2]	Gross domestic income (GDI) [3]	Average of GDP and GDI
	Net exports	Exports	Imports	Total	Federal			State and local					
					Total	National defense	Non- defense						
1972	....	19.5	17.9	−0.1	−2.6	−5.8	6.1	2.3	6.4	6.8	8.3	7.1	7.0
1973	....	18.4	−.5	−.3	−3.6	−5.0	−.3	2.9	2.8	2.8	2.2	3.8	3.9
1974	....	3.1	−1.0	3.0	3.7	1.2	9.5	2.4	−1.7	−2.3	−3.5	−2.9	−2.4
1975	....	1.6	−5.6	3.0	.8	.5	1.4	4.9	3.9	2.0	3.4	2.7	2.6
1976	....	4.3	19.2	−1.3	−1.0	−2.1	1.3	−1.6	3.8	5.4	6.7	3.8	4.1
1977	....	−1.4	5.7	1.9	2.3	.1	6.8	1.7	4.5	5.6	5.9	6.0	5.5
1978	....	18.8	9.9	4.4	3.5	2.9	4.8	5.2	6.4	6.0	6.1	5.4	6.0
1979	....	10.5	.9	.9	1.2	2.4	−1.1	.7	2.2	.5	1.5	.8	1.0
1980	....	3.9	−9.3	.3	4.0	3.7	4.6	−2.9	.4	−1.4	−1.2	1.3	.6
1981	....	.7	6.2	2.5	6.0	7.9	2.0	−.7	.3	1.8	.4	1.2	1.2
1982	....	−12.2	−3.9	2.6	4.5	7.3	−1.6	.8	.4	−.7	.8	−1.3	−1.3
1983	....	5.5	24.6	1.9	2.7	6.5	−6.6	1.1	6.0	9.5	9.1	6.6	7.3
1984	....	9.1	18.9	6.3	7.1	5.6	11.5	5.4	5.0	6.5	5.9	6.7	6.1
1985	....	1.5	5.6	6.1	6.7	8.2	2.8	5.5	4.6	4.5	4.6	3.4	3.8
1986	....	10.6	7.9	4.7	5.3	4.7	6.8	4.1	3.9	2.9	3.5	2.7	2.8
1987	....	12.8	6.3	3.0	3.6	5.3	−1.0	2.4	3.0	4.1	2.5	5.5	5.0
1988	....	14.0	3.8	1.4	−1.4	−.8	−3.0	4.1	4.6	3.0	4.4	4.7	4.2
1989	....	10.2	2.6	2.5	.5	−1.3	5.8	4.3	2.9	2.1	2.2	1.0	1.9
1990	....	7.4	−.2	2.6	1.5	.0	5.4	3.6	1.0	−.1	−.3	1.0	.8
1991	....	9.2	5.7	.0	−2.3	−4.9	4.3	1.9	.5	.9	.3	.7	.9
1992	....	4.5	6.5	1.3	1.6	−.4	6.2	1.1	4.5	4.6	5.6	3.9	4.1
1993	....	4.4	9.9	−.7	−4.5	−5.4	−2.5	2.2	2.7	3.2	4.3	3.0	2.8
1994	....	10.8	12.2	.0	−4.2	−6.7	1.1	3.1	3.3	4.3	4.4	4.3	4.2
1995	....	9.4	4.8	−.6	−4.8	−5.0	−4.3	2.2	3.0	1.8	3.3	2.9	2.6
1996	....	10.1	11.1	2.6	1.1	.3	2.6	3.6	4.2	4.6	4.8	4.8	4.6
1997	....	8.3	14.2	1.7	.2	−.8	1.9	2.7	3.9	5.2	5.3	5.5	5.0
1998	....	2.6	11.0	2.8	−.3	−2.4	3.3	4.6	5.2	5.9	6.9	4.9	4.9
1999	....	6.2	12.4	3.9	3.3	3.9	2.4	4.2	4.6	5.6	5.7	4.4	4.6
2000	....	6.0	11.1	.5	−1.9	−3.3	.4	1.8	3.2	3.7	4.7	3.6	3.2
2001	....	−12.2	−7.6	4.9	5.5	4.7	6.8	4.6	1.5	.4	.9	−.4	−.1
2002	....	4.0	9.6	3.8	8.1	8.1	8.2	1.5	.9	2.7	1.3	3.2	2.6
2003	....	7.2	5.9	1.8	6.5	8.9	2.6	−.8	4.3	4.2	4.8	2.7	3.5
2004	....	7.2	10.9	.9	2.6	2.8	2.3	−.2	3.1	4.0	4.4	3.8	3.6
2005	....	7.4	6.1	.9	1.8	1.8	1.9	.3	2.9	3.0	3.4	4.2	3.6
2006	....	9.9	4.0	1.9	2.4	3.1	1.3	1.6	2.9	2.1	2.5	2.5	2.6
2007	....	9.2	1.6	2.3	3.6	3.9	3.1	1.5	2.3	1.3	1.3	−.3	.9
2008	....	−2.0	−5.4	2.6	6.4	7.4	4.5	.3	−1.8	−3.1	−3.5	−2.6	−2.6
2009	....	1.4	−5.1	3.1	6.2	4.9	8.9	1.1	−.2	−.9	−2.1	.6	.3
2010	....	10.6	11.5	−1.5	1.8	1.3	2.7	−3.7	2.0	3.2	3.4	3.3	3.1
2011	....	4.7	3.3	−3.4	−3.6	−3.6	−3.5	−3.2	1.3	1.4	2.4	2.0	1.8
2012	....	3.0	.5	−2.1	−2.6	−4.7	1.2	−1.7	2.0	1.2	2.5	3.1	2.3
2013	....	5.2	2.9	−2.4	−6.1	−6.5	−5.4	.2	1.9	2.2	2.6	1.3	1.9
2014	....	2.4	6.5	.3	−1.0	−3.4	2.8	1.2	2.8	3.2	4.2	4.0	3.3
2015	....	−1.5	3.3	2.2	1.2	−.4	3.7	2.8	1.8	2.5	2.5	1.2	1.5
2016	....	1.3	2.2	1.6	.1	−.6	1.1	2.5	2.2	2.1	2.4	1.2	1.6
2017	....	6.2	5.3	.7	1.3	2.0	.2	.3	2.9	2.8	3.3	2.9	2.8
2018	....	.2	3.3	1.6	3.2	4.5	1.4	.6	2.1	2.7	2.7	2.9	2.6
2019	....	.8	−2.0	4.0	4.0	4.1	3.9	4.0	3.0	2.1	2.2	2.1	2.3
2020	....	−10.0	.4	1.0	5.4	4.2	7.4	−1.6	−1.8	−.3	−.9	.1	−.7
2021	....	6.5	10.1	.5	.4	−5.0	8.2	.6	4.8	6.2	6.4	4.1	4.9
2022 [p]	....	5.2	1.8	.8	.1	−.2	.5	1.3	1.3	.6	.9	....	....
2019: I	....	4.8	1.3	4.9	2.9	7.9	−4.1	6.1	1.6	1.8	.5	2.0	2.1
II	....	−2.3	.7	5.3	6.3	.0	16.6	4.7	3.4	3.0	3.3	1.2	2.0
III	....	.0	−1.7	3.4	4.9	6.8	2.2	2.4	3.9	3.3	3.6	1.6	2.6
IV	....	.8	−8.0	2.4	1.8	1.8	1.8	2.7	3.1	.5	1.6	3.6	2.7
2020: I	....	−15.3	−12.2	3.3	3.7	2.1	6.1	3.0	−4.3	−4.4	−5.5	−.4	−2.5
II	....	−60.9	−53.7	7.3	31.5	1.8	86.5	−5.5	−25.9	−29.4	−31.4	−30.6	−30.3
III	....	59.5	88.2	−5.9	−10.9	1.3	−24.7	−2.5	26.6	38.7	40.0	23.8	29.4
IV	....	24.2	32.9	−.1	1.8	11.8	−10.8	−1.3	3.7	5.5	6.5	17.2	10.4
2021: I	....	.4	7.6	6.5	17.3	−9.0	64.8	.1	9.1	7.1	10.6	2.0	4.1
II	....	4.9	7.9	−3.0	−6.9	−2.6	−11.9	−.4	7.9	7.4	10.7	3.1	5.0
III	....	−1.1	6.6	−.2	−7.2	−3.2	−12.1	4.5	.7	3.6	2.1	4.6	3.6
IV	....	23.5	18.6	−1.0	.0	−5.3	7.4	−1.6	1.9	6.9	2.6	6.7	6.8
2022: I	....	−4.6	18.4	−2.3	−5.3	−8.5	−1.1	−.4	−1.8	1.4	2.1	.8	−.4
II	....	13.8	2.2	−1.6	−3.4	1.4	−9.2	−.6	1.3	−1.6	.5	−.8	−.7
III	....	14.6	−7.3	3.7	3.7	4.7	2.5	3.7	4.5	.3	1.1	2.8	3.0
IV [p]	....	−1.6	−4.2	3.6	5.9	2.2	10.8	2.3	1.2	2.1	.1	....	....

[1] Gross domestic product (GDP) less exports of goods and services plus imports of goods and services.
[2] Personal consumption expenditures plus gross private fixed investment.
[3] Gross domestic income is deflated by the implicit price deflator for GDP.

Note: Percent changes based on unrounded GDP quantity indexes.

Source: Department of Commerce (Bureau of Economic Analysis).

TABLE B–2. Contributions to percent change in real gross domestic product, 1972–2022

[Percentage points, except as noted; annual average to annual average, quarterly data at seasonally adjusted annual rates]

Year or quarter	Gross domestic product (percent change)	Personal consumption expenditures			Gross private domestic investment							
						Fixed investment						
							Nonresidential					
		Total	Goods	Services	Total	Total	Total	Structures	Equipment	Intellectual property products	Residential	Change in private inventories
1972	5.3	3.66	1.90	1.76	1.90	1.85	0.97	0.12	0.75	0.11	0.87	0.06
1973	5.6	2.97	1.52	1.45	1.95	1.47	1.51	.30	1.12	.08	–.04	.48
1974	–.5	–.50	–1.08	.58	–1.24	–.98	.10	–.08	.14	.05	–1.08	–.26
1975	–.2	1.36	.20	1.16	–2.91	–1.68	–1.13	–.42	–.73	.01	–.54	–1.24
1976	5.4	3.41	2.03	1.38	2.91	1.54	.66	.09	.39	.18	.88	1.37
1977	4.6	2.59	1.26	1.33	2.47	2.23	1.26	.15	1.01	.11	.97	.24
1978	5.5	2.68	1.19	1.49	2.22	2.10	1.72	.52	1.08	.12	.38	.12
1979	3.2	1.44	.45	.99	.72	1.11	1.34	.51	.62	.20	–.22	–.40
1980	–.3	–.19	–.72	.53	–2.07	–1.18	.00	.26	–.35	.09	–1.19	–.89
1981	2.5	.85	.33	.52	1.64	.50	.87	.39	.28	.21	–.37	1.13
1982	–1.8	.88	.19	.69	–2.46	–1.16	–.43	–.09	–.47	.12	–.72	–1.31
1983	4.6	3.51	1.69	1.82	1.60	1.32	–.06	–.56	.32	.17	1.38	.28
1984	7.2	3.30	1.91	1.39	4.73	2.83	2.18	.58	1.29	.30	.65	1.90
1985	4.2	3.20	1.38	1.83	–.01	1.02	.91	.31	.39	.21	.11	–1.03
1986	3.5	2.58	1.45	1.13	.03	.34	–.24	–.49	.08	.17	.58	–.31
1987	3.5	2.15	.47	1.67	.53	.11	.01	–.11	.03	.10	.10	.41
1988	4.2	2.65	.96	1.69	.45	.59	.63	.02	.43	.18	–.05	–.13
1989	3.7	1.86	.64	1.21	.72	.55	.71	.07	.35	.29	–.16	.17
1990	1.9	1.28	.16	1.12	–.45	–.25	.14	.05	–.14	.22	–.38	–.21
1991	–.1	.12	–.49	.61	–1.09	–.84	–.48	–.38	–.28	.18	–.35	–.26
1992	3.5	2.36	.76	1.60	1.11	.83	.33	–.18	.34	.17	.49	.28
1993	2.8	2.24	.99	1.26	1.24	1.17	.84	–.01	.73	.12	.32	.07
1994	4.0	2.51	1.26	1.26	1.90	1.29	.91	.05	.75	.11	.38	.61
1995	2.7	1.91	.71	1.20	.55	.99	1.15	.16	.78	.20	–.15	–.44
1996	3.8	2.26	1.06	1.20	1.49	1.48	1.13	.15	.65	.33	.35	.02
1997	4.4	2.45	1.12	1.33	2.01	1.49	1.38	.21	.76	.41	.11	.52
1998	4.5	3.42	1.54	1.88	1.76	1.82	1.44	.16	.91	.37	.38	–.07
1999	4.8	3.49	1.83	1.66	1.62	1.65	1.36	.01	.89	.45	.29	–.03
2000	4.1	3.29	1.23	2.06	1.31	1.34	1.31	.24	.71	.36	.03	–.03
2001	1.0	1.63	.72	.92	–1.11	–.27	–.31	–.04	–.31	.04	.04	–.84
2002	1.7	1.70	.92	.78	–.16	–.64	–.94	–.56	–.35	–.03	.29	.48
2003	2.8	2.13	1.15	.98	.76	.77	.30	–.09	.26	.14	.47	–.02
2004	3.9	2.54	1.21	1.34	1.64	1.23	.67	.00	.49	.18	.57	.41
2005	3.5	2.38	.98	1.40	1.26	1.33	.92	.06	.60	.26	.41	–.07
2006	2.8	1.95	.87	1.08	.60	.50	1.00	.22	.57	.21	–.50	.10
2007	2.0	1.63	.65	.98	–.48	–.24	.89	.42	.25	.23	–1.13	–.25
2008	.1	.10	–.71	.81	–1.52	–1.05	.08	.23	–.29	.14	–1.14	–.46
2009	–2.6	–.88	–.70	–.18	–3.51	–2.69	–1.95	–.71	–1.21	–.02	–.74	–.82
2010	2.7	1.31	.62	.68	1.85	.43	.52	–.50	.91	.11	–.08	1.42
2011	1.5	1.16	.49	.68	.94	.99	.99	.07	.69	.24	.00	–.05
2012	2.3	.94	.48	.46	1.64	1.47	1.16	.34	.62	.20	.31	.17
2013	1.8	1.01	.70	.31	1.10	.87	.53	.04	.28	.22	.33	.23
2014	2.3	1.82	.89	.93	.95	1.06	.95	.33	.42	.20	.12	–.12
2015	2.7	2.20	1.03	1.18	.95	.64	.32	–.03	.19	.16	.33	.31
2016	1.7	1.67	.73	.94	–.18	.35	.12	–.14	–.11	.37	.23	–.53
2017	2.2	1.62	.82	.80	.70	.69	.54	.13	.16	.25	.15	.00
2018	2.9	1.95	.83	1.12	.99	.84	.86	.13	.37	.36	–.02	.15
2019	2.3	1.34	.66	.69	.49	.44	.48	.07	.07	.34	–.04	.05
2020	–2.8	–2.01	1.07	–3.08	–.95	–.40	–.67	–.32	–.59	.23	.28	–.55
2021	5.9	5.54	2.72	2.83	1.55	1.30	.83	–.19	.52	.50	.47	.24
2022 [p]	2.1	1.86	–.12	1.99	.71	–.04	.50	–.19	.22	.46	–.53	.74
2019: I	2.2	.26	.00	.27	.72	.15	.25	.02	.05	.17	–.10	.57
II	2.7	1.73	1.11	.61	.44	1.07	.83	.45	.04	.34	.24	–.62
III	3.6	2.27	1.18	1.09	.48	.71	.55	.53	–.32	.35	.16	–.24
IV	1.8	1.55	.57	.98	–1.48	–.24	–.24	–.19	–.49	.44	.00	–1.24
2020: I	–4.6	–4.25	–.02	–4.23	–.88	–.54	–1.16	–.11	–1.44	.38	.63	–.35
II	–29.9	–23.07	–2.07	–21.01	–9.65	–5.30	–4.12	–1.60	–2.05	–.46	–1.18	–4.35
III	35.3	26.34	10.85	15.50	12.69	5.12	2.91	–.32	2.69	.53	2.21	7.57
IV	3.9	2.53	.06	2.47	3.07	2.76	1.46	.02	1.02	.42	1.30	.30
2021: I	6.3	6.98	5.26	1.71	–.82	1.70	1.18	.04	.36	.78	.52	–2.52
II	7.0	7.84	2.65	5.19	.30	1.05	1.29	–.08	.73	.64	–.24	–.75
III	2.7	1.98	–1.96	3.94	1.78	–.18	.10	–.18	–.09	.38	–.29	1.96
IV	7.0	2.14	.55	1.58	5.14	.12	.17	–.35	.10	.42	–.05	5.01
2022: I	–1.6	.91	–.02	.93	.98	.83	.98	–.11	.55	.54	–.15	.15
II	–.6	1.38	–.61	1.99	–2.83	–.92	.01	–.34	–.11	.46	–.93	–1.91
III	3.2	1.54	–.08	1.63	–1.80	–.62	.80	–.09	.53	.36	–1.42	–1.19
IV [p]	2.7	.93	–.13	1.06	.66	–.81	.43	.21	–.17	.39	–1.24	1.47

See next page for continuation of table.

TABLE B–2. Contributions to percent change in real gross domestic product, 1972–2022—*Continued*

[Percentage points, except as noted; annual average to annual average, quarterly data at seasonally adjusted annual rates]

Year or quarter	Net exports of goods and services							Government consumption expenditures and gross investment					Final sales of domestic product
	Net exports	Exports			Imports			Total	Federal			State and local	
		Total	Goods	Services	Total	Goods	Services		Total	National defense	Non-defense		
1972	−0.19	0.42	0.43	−0.01	−0.61	−0.55	−0.06	−0.12	−0.37	−0.60	0.22	0.25	5.20
1973	.80	1.08	1.05	.02	−.28	−.33	.05	−.07	−.39	−.40	.01	.32	5.16
1974	.73	.56	.49	.08	.17	.17	.00	.47	.06	−.07	.14	.41	−.28
1975	.86	−.05	−.14	.09	.91	.85	.06	.49	.05	−.07	.13	.43	1.03
1976	−1.05	.36	.34	.02	−1.41	−1.31	−.10	.12	.01	−.04	.06	.10	4.01
1977	−.70	.19	.12	.07	−.89	−.82	−.07	.26	.21	.06	.15	.05	4.38
1978	.05	.80	.64	.17	−.76	−.66	−.10	.60	.23	.04	.19	.37	5.42
1979	.64	.80	.69	.11	−.16	−.13	−.02	.36	.20	.15	.05	.16	3.56
1980	1.64	.95	.88	.07	.69	.66	.03	.36	.38	.22	.16	−.02	.63
1981	−.15	.12	−.05	.17	−.26	−.18	−.09	.20	.43	.40	.03	−.23	1.41
1982	−.59	−.71	−.63	−.08	.12	.20	−.08	.37	.35	.47	−.11	.01	−.50
1983	−1.32	−.22	−.21	.00	−1.10	−.98	−.12	.79	.65	.51	.14	.14	4.31
1984	−1.54	.61	.41	.20	−2.16	−1.78	−.38	.74	.33	.38	−.04	.41	5.34
1985	−.39	.24	.20	.05	−.63	−.50	−.13	1.37	.78	.62	.16	.59	5.20
1986	−.29	.53	.27	.25	−.82	−.80	−.02	1.14	.61	.52	.09	.53	3.77
1987	.17	.77	.62	.15	−.60	−.39	−.21	.62	.38	.38	.01	.24	3.05
1988	.81	1.23	.99	.24	−.41	−.35	−.07	.26	−.15	−.04	−.12	.42	4.31
1989	.51	.97	.72	.26	−.46	−.37	−.09	.58	.15	−.02	.18	.43	3.51
1990	.40	.78	.56	.22	−.37	−.25	−.13	.65	.20	.02	.18	.45	2.09
1991	.62	.61	.45	.16	.01	−.04	.05	.25	.01	−.06	.07	.24	.15
1992	−.04	.66	.52	.14	−.70	−.76	.05	.10	−.15	−.31	.16	.25	3.24
1993	−.56	.31	.22	.09	−.87	−.82	−.05	−.17	−.32	−.32	.00	.15	2.68
1994	−.41	.84	.65	.19	−1.25	−1.15	−.10	.02	−.31	−.28	−.02	.32	3.41
1995	.12	1.02	.83	.19	−.90	−.84	−.06	.10	−.21	−.21	.00	.31	3.13
1996	−.15	.86	.68	.18	−1.01	−.91	−.10	.18	−.09	−.08	−.01	.27	3.76
1997	−.31	1.26	1.10	.16	−1.57	−1.40	−.17	.30	−.06	−.13	.07	.36	3.92
1998	−1.14	.26	.17	.08	−1.39	−1.18	−.21	.44	−.06	−.09	.03	.50	4.55
1999	−.90	.52	.32	.20	−1.42	−1.31	−.11	.59	.12	.06	.06	.47	4.82
2000	−.85	.86	.72	.13	−1.71	−1.45	−.26	.33	.02	−.04	.06	.31	4.11
2001	−.24	−.59	−.49	−.10	.35	.39	−.04	.67	.24	.13	.12	.43	1.80
2002	−.67	−.19	−.24	.05	−.48	−.41	−.07	.82	.47	.30	.18	.35	1.21
2003	−.49	.19	.19	.01	−.68	−.67	−.01	.39	.45	.35	.10	−.06	2.81
2004	−.63	.88	.58	.30	−1.51	−1.28	−.22	.30	.31	.26	.05	−.01	3.45
2005	−.31	.67	.52	.15	−.98	−.88	−.09	.15	.15	.11	.04	.00	3.56
2006	−.06	.95	.71	.24	−1.01	−.81	−.20	.30	.17	.07	.10	.13	2.68
2007	.52	.94	.53	.41	−.42	−.27	−.15	.34	.14	.13	.01	.20	2.26
2008	1.04	.67	.48	.19	.37	.47	−.10	.49	.46	.33	.14	.03	.58
2009	1.07	−1.00	−1.00	.00	2.07	2.10	−.03	.72	.48	.29	.20	.24	−1.77
2010	−.43	1.43	1.13	.30	−1.86	−1.73	−.13	−.02	.34	.16	.18	−.36	1.29
2011	.12	.90	.65	.26	−.79	−.74	−.05	−.67	−.23	−.12	−.12	−.44	1.60
2012	.12	.54	.37	.17	−.42	−.38	−.04	−.42	−.16	−.18	.02	−.26	2.11
2013	.20	.40	.27	.13	−.20	−.28	.07	−.47	−.44	−.33	−.10	−.03	1.61
2014	−.31	.52	.41	.11	−.84	−.75	−.09	−.17	−.19	−.19	.00	.02	2.41
2015	−.78	.04	−.03	.07	−.81	−.75	−.07	.33	.00	−.09	.09	.33	2.40
2016	−.17	.05	.05	.00	−.22	−.14	−.08	.35	.03	−.02	.06	.31	2.20
2017	−.15	.51	.32	.19	−.66	−.53	−.13	.08	.03	.04	−.01	.05	2.24
2018	−.29	.35	.34	.01	−.63	−.62	−.01	.29	.19	.13	.07	.10	2.80
2019	−.11	.06	.01	.05	−.17	−.06	−.11	.58	.25	.20	.05	.32	2.25
2020	−.26	−1.54	−.76	−.78	1.28	.67	.61	.45	.41	.12	.30	.04	−2.22
2021	−1.25	.64	.52	.12	−1.89	−1.61	−.28	.11	.17	−.05	.22	−.06	5.71
2022 ^p^	−.40	.80	.49	.31	−1.20	−.86	−.35	−.10	−.17	−.11	−.07	.07	1.32
2019: I	.37	.55	.42	.13	−.19	−.04	−.15	.83	.19	.30	−.11	.65	1.62
II	−.37	−.27	−.59	.31	−.09	.06	−.15	.92	.41	.00	.41	.51	3.34
III	.28	.02	.16	−.14	.26	.20	.06	.58	.32	.26	.06	.26	3.84
IV	1.30	.13	.01	.12	1.18	1.14	.04	.41	.12	.07	.05	.29	3.02
2020: I	−.05	−1.82	−.23	−1.59	1.77	.89	.88	.57	.25	.08	.16	.32	−4.27
II	1.30	−8.66	−6.48	−2.18	9.95	7.23	2.73	1.57	2.07	.11	1.96	−.50	−25.51
III	−2.74	4.98	4.87	.12	−7.72	−7.27	−.45	−.97	−.77	.09	−.86	−.20	27.75
IV	−1.68	2.20	1.57	.64	−3.88	−2.96	−.92	−.01	.13	.47	−.34	−.14	3.61
2021: I	−1.02	.03	−.05	.08	−1.06	−1.27	.22	1.18	1.17	−.38	1.55	.02	8.84
II	−.60	.51	.26	.25	−1.11	−.49	−.61	−.54	−.50	−.10	−.40	−.04	7.76
III	−1.08	−.13	−.28	.15	−.95	−.05	−.90	−.02	−.51	−.12	−.39	.49	.69
IV	−.16	2.37	1.62	.74	−2.53	−2.20	−.33	−.16	.01	−.20	.21	−.17	1.94
2022: I	−3.13	−.53	−.58	.06	−2.60	−2.38	−.22	−.40	−.36	−.33	−.03	−.04	−1.78
II	1.16	1.51	1.18	.33	−.35	.05	−.41	−.29	−.22	.05	−.28	−.06	1.33
III	2.86	1.65	1.38	.26	1.21	1.19	.02	.65	.24	.17	.07	.41	4.43
IV ^p^	.46	−.19	−.62	.43	.65	.71	−.06	.63	.37	.08	.29	.25	1.21

Source: Department of Commerce (Bureau of Economic Analysis).

Table B–3. Gross domestic product, 2007–2022

[Quarterly data at seasonally adjusted annual rates]

Year or quarter	Gross domestic product	Personal consumption expenditures			Gross private domestic investment							
						Fixed investment						Change in private inventories
							Nonresidential					
		Total	Goods	Services	Total	Total	Total	Structures	Equipment	Intellectual property products	Residential	
	Billions of dollars											
2007	14,474.2	9,746.6	3,367.0	6,379.6	2,673.0	2,639.1	1,948.6	510.3	893.4	544.8	690.5	34.0
2008	14,769.9	10,050.1	3,363.2	6,686.9	2,477.6	2,506.9	1,990.9	571.1	845.4	574.4	516.0	–29.2
2009	14,478.1	9,891.2	3,180.0	6,711.2	1,929.7	2,080.4	1,690.4	455.8	670.3	564.4	390.0	–150.8
2010	15,049.0	10,260.3	3,317.8	6,942.4	2,165.5	2,111.6	1,735.0	379.8	777.0	578.2	376.6	53.9
2011	15,599.7	10,698.9	3,518.1	7,180.7	2,332.6	2,286.3	1,907.5	404.5	881.3	621.7	378.8	46.3
2012	16,254.0	11,047.4	3,637.7	7,409.6	2,621.8	2,550.5	2,118.5	479.4	983.4	655.7	432.0	71.2
2013	16,843.2	11,363.5	3,730.0	7,633.6	2,826.0	2,721.5	2,211.5	492.5	1,027.0	691.9	510.0	104.5
2014	17,550.7	11,847.7	3,863.0	7,984.8	3,044.2	2,960.2	2,400.1	577.6	1,091.9	730.5	560.2	84.0
2015	18,206.0	12,263.5	3,923.0	8,340.5	3,237.2	3,100.4	2,466.6	584.4	1,119.5	762.7	633.8	136.8
2016	18,695.1	12,693.3	3,991.8	8,701.4	3,205.0	3,168.8	2,469.3	560.4	1,087.8	821.2	699.4	36.3
2017	19,477.3	13,233.6	4,159.4	9,074.2	3,385.6	3,353.4	2,593.2	599.5	1,118.3	875.3	760.3	32.2
2018	20,533.1	13,905.0	4,355.2	9,549.8	3,642.4	3,583.3	2,784.7	633.6	1,193.2	957.9	798.6	59.1
2019	21,381.0	14,392.7	4,473.5	9,919.2	3,807.1	3,734.4	2,921.1	674.7	1,209.8	1,036.6	813.2	72.8
2020	21,060.5	14,116.2	4,670.1	9,446.0	3,642.9	3,698.7	2,797.9	614.4	1,077.8	1,105.7	900.8	–55.8
2021	23,315.1	15,902.6	5,496.5	10,406.1	4,113.5	4,132.6	3,025.0	598.2	1,194.0	1,232.7	1,107.6	–19.1
2022 p	25,464.5	17,360.4	5,939.6	11,420.8	4,631.0	4,472.0	3,345.1	648.2	1,322.5	1,374.3	1,126.9	159.0
2019: I	21,013.1	14,145.9	4,382.5	9,763.4	3,778.8	3,659.4	2,867.0	635.6	1,226.9	1,004.4	792.4	119.4
II	21,272.4	14,323.7	4,461.4	9,862.4	3,820.0	3,733.7	2,924.9	668.0	1,228.2	1,028.7	808.9	86.3
III	21,531.8	14,482.2	4,508.5	9,973.7	3,849.4	3,778.6	2,955.2	701.0	1,206.2	1,047.9	823.4	70.8
IV	21,706.5	14,619.0	4,541.6	10,077.5	3,780.3	3,765.6	2,937.5	694.2	1,178.1	1,065.2	828.2	14.7
2020: I	21,538.0	14,440.2	4,532.2	9,907.9	3,737.6	3,751.2	2,884.4	691.6	1,103.2	1,089.6	866.9	–13.7
II	19,636.7	13,049.8	4,344.3	8,705.5	3,161.4	3,459.0	2,657.1	599.7	979.4	1,078.0	802.0	–297.6
III	21,362.4	14,388.7	4,897.0	9,491.7	3,743.3	3,706.4	2,781.9	583.6	1,089.9	1,108.4	924.5	36.9
IV	21,704.7	14,586.0	4,907.1	9,679.0	3,929.4	3,878.3	2,868.3	582.7	1,138.8	1,146.8	1,010.0	51.1
2021: I	22,313.9	15,131.5	5,265.3	9,866.2	3,902.3	4,004.1	2,934.6	587.5	1,166.1	1,181.0	1,069.5	–101.8
II	23,046.9	15,813.5	5,529.9	10,283.6	3,943.4	4,102.8	3,007.3	595.4	1,191.5	1,220.4	1,095.6	–159.4
III	23,550.4	16,147.3	5,517.1	10,630.2	4,109.1	4,164.3	3,046.3	599.7	1,197.3	1,249.2	1,118.0	–55.2
IV	24,349.1	16,518.0	5,673.7	10,844.3	4,499.2	4,259.2	3,111.8	610.3	1,221.2	1,280.4	1,147.3	240.0
2022: I	24,740.5	16,874.8	5,843.2	11,031.6	4,671.0	4,413.6	3,225.0	627.3	1,277.8	1,319.9	1,188.6	257.4
II	25,248.5	17,261.3	5,953.6	11,307.7	4,609.9	4,464.6	3,292.2	631.2	1,299.5	1,361.4	1,172.4	145.4
III	25,723.9	17,542.7	5,988.6	11,554.1	4,579.1	4,508.2	3,403.4	654.8	1,352.0	1,396.6	1,104.8	70.9
IV p	26,145.0	17,762.7	5,972.9	11,789.9	4,663.8	4,501.6	3,459.7	679.6	1,360.8	1,419.4	1,041.9	162.2
	Billions of chained (2012) dollars											
2007	15,623.9	10,638.7	3,607.6	7,027.0	2,684.1	2,653.5	1,982.1	568.6	865.8	554.3	665.8	40.6
2008	15,643.0	10,654.7	3,498.9	7,154.9	2,462.9	2,499.4	1,994.2	605.4	824.4	575.3	504.6	–32.7
2009	15,236.3	10,515.6	3,389.8	7,125.8	1,942.0	2,099.8	1,704.3	492.2	649.7	572.4	395.3	–177.3
2010	15,649.0	10,716.0	3,485.7	7,230.4	2,216.5	2,164.2	1,781.0	412.8	781.2	588.1	383.0	57.3
2011	15,891.5	10,898.3	3,561.8	7,336.7	2,362.1	2,317.8	1,935.4	424.1	886.2	624.8	382.5	46.7
2012	16,254.0	11,047.4	3,637.7	7,409.6	2,621.8	2,550.5	2,118.5	479.4	983.4	655.7	432.0	71.2
2013	16,553.3	11,211.7	3,752.2	7,460.3	2,801.5	2,692.1	2,206.0	485.5	1,029.2	691.4	485.5	108.7
2014	16,932.1	11,515.3	3,905.1	7,613.2	2,959.2	2,869.2	2,365.3	538.8	1,101.1	724.8	504.1	86.3
2015	17,390.3	11,892.9	4,090.9	7,809.8	3,121.8	2,979.0	2,420.3	534.1	1,134.6	752.4	555.4	137.6
2016	17,680.3	12,187.7	4,231.7	7,968.5	3,089.9	3,041.0	2,442.0	511.0	1,114.6	818.8	592.1	35.7
2017	18,076.7	12,478.2	4,395.8	8,104.4	3,216.0	3,165.4	2,542.5	533.3	1,146.0	864.9	615.8	36.3
2018	18,609.1	12,837.3	4,568.4	8,299.1	3,398.9	3,320.0	2,708.3	555.2	1,221.2	935.2	612.3	66.1
2019	19,036.1	13,092.3	4,711.6	8,421.0	3,492.7	3,404.2	2,804.6	567.9	1,236.5	1,003.2	606.2	73.1
2020	18,509.1	12,700.7	4,955.7	7,863.0	3,306.5	3,326.8	2,666.0	510.4	1,107.3	1,051.2	649.8	–54.6
2021	19,609.8	13,754.1	5,561.9	8,361.1	3,603.0	3,574.6	2,835.4	477.5	1,221.8	1,153.0	719.4	–19.4
2022 p	20,015.4	14,133.3	5,534.2	8,737.7	3,745.1	3,567.6	2,943.5	444.4	1,274.2	1,255.5	642.7	124.9
2019: I	18,835.4	12,955.7	4,623.6	8,365.1	3,484.3	3,351.5	2,762.1	543.4	1,250.1	975.7	596.0	134.6
II	18,962.2	13,038.9	4,685.5	8,392.5	3,504.9	3,402.6	2,803.8	563.3	1,252.4	993.0	605.4	81.1
III	19,130.9	13,148.9	4,752.0	8,441.2	3,527.2	3,437.0	2,832.1	586.9	1,235.0	1,010.7	611.7	71.9
IV	19,215.7	13,225.6	4,785.2	8,485.4	3,454.4	3,425.7	2,820.4	578.1	1,208.7	1,033.5	611.7	4.8
2020: I	18,989.9	13,016.8	4,785.0	8,290.7	3,409.9	3,399.5	2,760.6	573.1	1,129.1	1,053.3	636.8	–34.4
II	17,378.7	11,817.1	4,651.1	7,284.5	2,884.2	3,121.3	2,530.6	498.1	1,001.8	1,027.8	587.8	–279.1
III	18,743.7	12,922.4	5,191.3	7,883.0	3,394.1	3,327.4	2,649.9	484.6	1,121.7	1,051.3	662.7	36.8
IV	18,924.3	13,046.6	5,195.5	7,993.9	3,537.6	3,459.2	2,723.0	485.7	1,176.6	1,072.4	712.2	58.3
2021: I	19,216.2	13,386.8	5,496.5	8,072.4	3,489.3	3,540.4	2,781.4	488.0	1,194.3	1,112.0	732.0	–83.0
II	19,544.2	13,773.7	5,649.9	8,309.5	3,496.9	3,590.9	2,847.7	484.9	1,234.0	1,145.4	723.0	–143.6
III	19,672.6	13,874.4	5,534.6	8,494.3	3,584.1	3,581.1	2,852.2	476.6	1,227.1	1,166.0	712.2	–48.6
IV	20,006.2	13,981.5	5,566.7	8,568.2	3,841.8	3,586.2	2,860.2	460.7	1,232.0	1,188.8	710.3	197.6
2022: I	19,924.1	14,028.4	5,565.7	8,613.0	3,892.5	3,628.6	2,915.0	455.6	1,265.7	1,219.6	704.7	214.5
II	19,895.3	14,099.5	5,529.6	8,709.6	3,747.0	3,581.9	2,915.5	440.4	1,259.1	1,245.9	671.0	110.2
III	20,054.7	14,178.6	5,524.5	8,788.4	3,653.9	3,550.5	2,959.7	436.4	1,291.3	1,266.7	620.0	38.7
IV p	20,187.5	14,226.8	5,516.9	8,839.9	3,687.0	3,509.2	2,983.6	445.4	1,280.7	1,289.5	575.3	136.3

See next page for continuation of table.

TABLE B–3. Gross domestic product, 2007–2022—*Continued*

[Quarterly data at seasonally adjusted annual rates]

Year or quarter	Net exports of goods and services			Government consumption expenditures and gross investment					Final sales of domestic product	Gross domestic purchases [1]	Final sales to private domestic purchasers [2]	Gross domestic income (GDI) [3]	Average of GDP and GDI
	Net exports	Exports	Imports	Total	Federal			State and local					
					Total	National defense	Non-defense						
	Billions of dollars												
2007	−735.9	1,659.3	2,395.2	2,790.6	1,051.0	679.3	371.8	1,739.5	14,440.3	15,210.2	12,385.7	14,454.4	14,464.3
2008	−740.9	1,835.3	2,576.2	2,983.0	1,152.0	750.3	401.6	1,831.1	14,799.1	15,510.7	12,556.9	14,572.9	14,671.4
2009	−419.2	1,582.8	2,001.9	3,076.3	1,220.8	787.6	433.2	1,855.6	14,628.8	14,897.2	11,971.7	14,276.0	14,377.0
2010	−532.3	1,857.2	2,389.6	3,155.6	1,300.2	828.0	472.2	1,855.4	14,995.1	15,581.3	12,371.8	14,966.4	15,007.7
2011	−579.6	2,115.9	2,695.5	3,147.9	1,299.8	834.0	465.8	1,848.2	15,553.5	16,179.3	12,985.2	15,612.0	15,605.9
2012	−551.6	2,217.7	2,769.3	3,136.5	1,287.0	814.2	472.8	1,849.5	16,182.8	16,805.6	13,597.9	16,442.8	16,348.4
2013	−479.4	2,287.0	2,766.4	3,133.0	1,227.2	764.2	462.9	1,905.9	16,738.7	17,322.6	14,085.0	16,958.0	16,900.6
2014	−510.0	2,377.4	2,887.4	3,168.8	1,216.0	743.4	472.6	1,952.8	17,466.7	18,060.7	14,807.9	17,807.9	17,679.3
2015	−526.2	2,268.7	2,794.9	3,231.6	1,221.8	729.7	492.0	2,009.8	18,069.2	18,732.2	15,363.9	18,440.5	18,323.3
2016	−506.3	2,232.1	2,738.4	3,303.1	1,234.5	727.9	506.6	2,068.5	18,658.8	19,201.4	15,862.0	18,788.5	18,741.8
2017	−536.7	2,388.3	2,925.0	3,394.8	1,262.4	746.1	516.3	2,132.4	19,445.1	20,014.1	16,587.0	19,592.6	19,535.0
2018	−593.1	2,538.1	3,131.2	3,578.8	1,337.9	792.3	545.6	2,240.8	20,474.0	21,126.1	17,488.3	20,647.0	20,590.1
2019	−578.8	2,538.5	3,117.2	3,759.9	1,415.4	847.8	567.6	2,344.5	21,308.2	21,959.8	18,127.1	21,486.5	21,433.7
2020	−627.5	2,148.6	2,776.1	3,928.9	1,520.6	882.4	638.1	2,408.3	21,116.3	21,688.0	17,814.9	21,275.4	21,167.9
2021	−861.7	2,539.6	3,401.4	4,160.7	1,609.2	904.0	705.1	2,551.6	23,334.2	24,176.8	20,035.2	23,444.0	23,379.6
2022 p	−974.3	2,979.6	3,953.9	4,447.4	1,646.7	924.9	721.7	2,800.7	25,305.5	26,438.8	21,832.4	....	....
2019: I	−599.9	2,542.7	3,142.6	3,688.3	1,393.0	835.6	557.4	2,295.3	20,893.7	21,613.0	17,805.3	21,204.7	21,108.9
II	−615.7	2,549.6	3,165.3	3,744.4	1,405.2	838.4	566.8	2,339.2	21,186.1	21,888.2	18,057.5	21,388.0	21,330.2
III	−584.8	2,533.3	3,118.2	3,785.1	1,425.7	854.9	570.8	2,359.4	21,461.0	22,116.7	18,260.8	21,541.5	21,536.7
IV	−514.7	2,528.2	3,042.9	3,821.9	1,437.7	862.4	575.3	2,384.2	21,691.9	22,221.2	18,384.7	21,811.6	21,759.1
2020: I	−522.7	2,412.7	2,935.4	3,883.0	1,455.6	869.0	586.6	2,427.4	21,551.7	22,060.8	18,191.4	21,880.0	21,709.0
II	−526.3	1,817.5	2,343.7	3,951.8	1,560.0	870.6	689.4	2,391.8	19,934.3	20,163.0	16,508.8	19,892.5	19,764.6
III	−692.4	2,106.6	2,799.0	3,922.9	1,525.3	879.9	645.4	2,397.6	21,325.6	22,054.8	18,095.1	21,165.9	21,264.2
IV	−768.6	2,257.8	3,026.4	3,957.8	1,541.3	910.3	631.0	2,416.5	21,653.6	22,473.3	18,464.3	22,163.2	21,933.9
2021: I	−808.6	2,369.1	3,177.7	4,088.7	1,620.3	900.7	719.6	2,468.4	22,415.6	23,122.5	19,135.6	22,547.6	22,430.7
II	−834.4	2,503.1	3,337.5	4,124.4	1,608.0	904.3	703.7	2,516.4	23,206.4	23,881.3	19,916.4	23,071.2	23,059.1
III	−889.1	2,553.3	3,442.5	4,183.1	1,595.5	906.8	688.8	2,587.6	23,605.6	24,439.6	20,311.6	23,683.9	23,617.2
IV	−914.7	2,733.0	3,647.7	4,246.7	1,612.8	904.4	708.4	2,633.9	24,109.1	25,263.8	20,777.1	24,473.3	24,411.2
2022: I	−1,116.7	2,811.2	3,927.9	4,311.4	1,613.1	898.7	714.4	2,698.2	24,483.1	25,857.2	21,288.4	25,017.5	24,879.0
II	−1,035.6	3,038.8	4,074.4	4,412.8	1,622.7	918.3	704.4	2,790.0	25,103.1	26,284.0	21,725.9	25,517.8	25,383.1
III	−890.8	3,065.0	3,955.8	4,493.0	1,657.1	935.3	721.8	2,836.0	25,653.0	26,614.8	22,050.8	25,967.6	25,845.8
IV p	−854.1	3,003.2	3,857.4	4,572.5	1,693.8	947.4	746.4	2,878.7	25,982.8	26,999.1	22,264.4	....	....
	Billions of chained (2012) dollars												
2007	−847.9	1,816.9	2,664.8	3,116.9	1,147.3	740.3	407.0	1,972.7	15,586.7	16,476.2	13,317.3	15,602.5	15,613.2
2008	−685.7	1,921.9	2,607.6	3,195.8	1,220.0	791.5	428.6	1,977.6	15,678.0	16,332.6	13,169.7	15,434.4	15,538.7
2009	−516.3	1,762.5	2,278.8	3,310.7	1,296.0	836.7	459.4	2,015.9	15,400.3	15,757.9	12,613.3	15,023.6	15,130.0
2010	−589.4	1,989.5	2,578.9	3,308.0	1,348.4	861.3	487.0	1,959.8	15,596.8	16,238.4	12,878.7	15,563.2	15,606.1
2011	−571.0	2,132.1	2,703.1	3,202.7	1,312.0	842.9	469.1	1,890.8	15,847.4	16,462.7	13,215.8	15,904.1	15,897.8
2012	−551.6	2,217.7	2,769.3	3,136.5	1,287.0	814.2	472.8	1,849.5	16,182.8	16,805.6	13,597.9	16,442.8	16,348.4
2013	−519.3	2,283.6	2,802.9	3,060.7	1,215.8	759.6	456.2	1,844.4	16,444.1	17,073.1	13,903.7	16,666.2	16,609.8
2014	−575.3	2,372.3	2,947.6	3,033.2	1,184.7	728.4	456.1	1,847.6	16,842.3	17,505.4	14,384.4	17,180.2	17,056.1
2015	−721.7	2,378.7	3,100.4	3,088.4	1,184.5	713.1	471.0	1,902.2	17,248.3	18,100.1	14,871.9	17,614.3	17,502.3
2016	−757.1	2,388.4	3,145.4	3,148.8	1,190.5	709.1	480.8	1,956.3	17,630.6	18,423.5	15,228.6	17,768.6	17,724.5
2017	−796.9	2,490.3	3,287.2	3,162.3	1,195.5	715.6	479.4	1,964.8	18,025.6	18,852.7	15,643.5	18,183.6	18,130.1
2018	−865.4	2,560.1	3,425.5	3,215.3	1,231.3	739.5	491.4	1,982.5	18,530.8	19,446.0	16,157.1	18,712.4	18,660.7
2019	−892.6	2,572.1	3,464.7	3,321.7	1,279.3	778.5	500.7	2,041.1	18,948.5	19,901.7	16,496.2	19,130.0	19,083.0
2020	−922.6	2,231.7	3,154.3	3,406.7	1,358.9	801.1	556.6	2,048.5	18,527.2	19,415.5	16,027.3	18,698.0	18,603.6
2021	−1,233.4	2,366.8	3,600.2	3,426.3	1,390.5	791.3	597.0	2,037.9	19,581.3	20,774.8	17,328.4	19,718.3	19,664.0
2022 p	−1,356.6	2,537.8	3,894.4	3,406.2	1,355.3	769.3	583.8	2,050.8	19,843.4	21,268.3	17,699.4	....	....
2019: I	−903.6	2,582.3	3,485.9	3,271.0	1,255.6	771.3	484.5	2,014.0	18,704.8	19,705.4	16,307.0	19,007.2	18,921.3
II	−924.5	2,567.3	3,491.8	3,313.8	1,275.0	771.3	503.5	2,037.5	18,861.4	19,852.4	16,441.2	19,065.2	19,013.7
III	−909.4	2,567.0	3,476.4	3,341.2	1,290.4	784.0	506.2	2,049.7	19,041.9	20,012.1	16,585.6	19,139.6	19,135.2
IV	−832.8	2,571.8	3,404.7	3,360.9	1,296.1	787.5	508.5	2,063.4	19,186.0	20,037.0	16,651.1	19,308.7	19,262.2
2020: I	−828.2	2,467.3	3,295.5	3,387.9	1,307.9	791.6	516.0	2,078.7	18,977.9	19,812.9	16,416.0	19,291.4	19,140.6
II	−767.3	1,951.4	2,718.6	3,448.0	1,400.5	795.2	603.0	2,049.3	17,606.7	18,162.1	14,938.2	17,605.1	17,491.9
III	−991.1	2,193.0	3,184.2	3,395.9	1,360.6	797.6	561.7	2,036.2	18,677.0	19,711.4	16,249.4	18,571.3	18,657.5
IV	−1,104.0	2,315.0	3,419.0	3,394.8	1,366.6	820.2	545.8	2,029.6	18,847.1	19,975.5	16,505.6	19,324.0	19,124.1
2021: I	−1,164.5	2,317.5	3,482.0	3,448.7	1,422.1	801.2	618.5	2,030.2	19,264.2	20,321.7	16,926.8	19,417.6	19,316.9
II	−1,203.9	2,345.1	3,549.0	3,422.4	1,397.1	795.8	599.1	2,028.0	19,633.3	20,686.1	17,364.3	19,564.8	19,554.5
III	−1,267.5	2,338.8	3,606.3	3,421.0	1,371.4	789.5	580.0	2,050.7	19,668.6	20,870.2	17,455.3	19,784.1	19,728.4
IV	−1,297.6	2,465.7	3,763.3	3,412.9	1,371.5	778.8	590.5	2,042.7	19,759.2	21,221.1	17,567.4	20,108.2	20,057.2
2022: I	−1,488.7	2,436.9	3,925.6	3,393.4	1,353.0	761.7	588.9	2,040.7	19,669.8	21,297.3	17,656.9	20,147.2	20,035.6
II	−1,430.5	2,516.9	3,947.5	3,379.5	1,341.3	764.5	574.8	2,037.8	19,735.9	21,208.9	17,680.5	20,107.5	20,001.4
III	−1,268.8	2,604.1	3,872.9	3,410.6	1,353.7	773.3	578.3	2,056.5	19,954.2	21,227.1	17,727.2	20,244.6	20,149.6
IV p	−1,238.4	2,593.4	3,831.7	3,441.1	1,373.2	777.5	593.4	2,068.3	20,013.7	21,339.9	17,733.1	....	....

[1] Gross domestic product (GDP) less exports of goods and services plus imports of goods and services.
[2] Personal consumption expenditures plus gross private fixed investment.
[3] For chained dollar measures, gross domestic income is deflated by the implicit price deflator for GDP.

Source: Department of Commerce (Bureau of Economic Analysis).

TABLE B–4. Percentage shares of gross domestic product, 1972–2022

[Percent of nominal GDP]

Year or quarter	Gross domestic product (percent)	Personal consumption expenditures			Gross private domestic investment							
		Total	Goods	Services	Total	Fixed investment						Change in private inventories
						Total	Nonresidential				Residential	
							Total	Structures	Equipment	Intellectual property products		
1972	100.0	60.1	29.2	30.8	17.8	17.1	11.5	3.7	6.2	1.6	5.7	0.7
1973	100.0	59.6	29.2	30.4	18.7	17.6	12.1	3.9	6.7	1.6	5.5	1.1
1974	100.0	60.2	29.2	31.0	17.8	16.9	12.4	4.0	6.8	1.7	4.5	.9
1975	100.0	61.2	29.2	32.0	15.3	15.6	11.7	3.6	6.4	1.7	4.0	–.4
1976	100.0	61.3	29.2	32.1	17.3	16.3	11.7	3.5	6.5	1.7	4.6	.9
1977	100.0	61.2	28.8	32.4	19.1	18.0	12.4	3.6	7.1	1.7	5.5	1.1
1978	100.0	60.5	28.2	32.3	20.3	19.2	13.4	4.0	7.7	1.7	5.9	1.1
1979	100.0	60.3	28.1	32.3	20.5	19.9	14.2	4.5	7.9	1.8	5.6	.7
1980	100.0	61.3	28.0	33.3	18.6	18.8	14.2	4.8	7.6	1.9	4.5	–.2
1981	100.0	60.3	27.1	33.2	19.7	18.8	14.7	5.2	7.5	2.0	4.0	.9
1982	100.0	61.9	26.9	35.0	17.4	17.8	14.5	5.3	7.0	2.2	3.3	–.4
1983	100.0	62.8	26.8	36.0	17.5	17.7	13.3	4.2	6.8	2.2	4.4	–.2
1984	100.0	61.7	26.3	35.4	20.3	18.7	14.0	4.4	7.2	2.4	4.7	1.6
1985	100.0	62.5	26.2	36.3	19.1	18.6	14.0	4.5	7.1	2.4	4.6	.5
1986	100.0	63.0	26.1	36.9	18.5	18.4	13.3	3.9	6.9	2.5	5.1	.1
1987	100.0	63.4	25.9	37.5	18.4	17.8	12.7	3.6	6.6	2.5	5.1	.6
1988	100.0	63.6	25.5	38.1	17.9	17.5	12.6	3.5	6.6	2.5	4.9	.4
1989	100.0	63.4	25.2	38.2	17.7	17.2	12.7	3.4	6.6	2.7	4.5	.5
1990	100.0	63.9	25.0	38.9	16.7	16.4	12.4	3.4	6.2	2.8	4.0	.2
1991	100.0	64.0	24.3	39.7	15.3	15.3	11.8	3.0	5.9	2.9	3.6	.0
1992	100.0	64.4	24.0	40.4	15.5	15.3	11.4	2.6	5.9	2.9	3.9	.3
1993	100.0	64.9	23.9	41.0	16.1	15.8	11.7	2.6	6.2	2.9	4.2	.3
1994	100.0	64.8	24.0	40.8	17.2	16.4	11.9	2.6	6.5	2.8	4.4	.9
1995	100.0	65.0	23.8	41.2	17.2	16.8	12.6	2.7	6.9	3.0	4.2	.4
1996	100.0	65.0	23.8	41.2	17.7	17.4	12.9	2.8	7.0	3.1	4.4	.4
1997	100.0	64.5	23.4	41.2	18.6	17.8	13.4	2.9	7.1	3.4	4.4	.8
1998	100.0	64.9	23.3	41.6	19.2	18.5	13.8	3.0	7.3	3.5	4.6	.7
1999	100.0	65.2	23.7	41.5	19.6	19.0	14.2	3.0	7.4	3.8	4.8	.6
2000	100.0	66.0	23.9	42.1	19.9	19.4	14.6	3.1	7.5	4.0	4.7	.5
2001	100.0	66.8	23.9	43.0	18.3	18.6	13.8	3.2	6.7	3.9	4.8	–.4
2002	100.0	67.2	23.8	43.5	17.7	17.5	12.4	2.6	6.0	3.7	5.1	.2
2003	100.0	67.6	23.8	43.8	17.7	17.6	12.0	2.5	5.9	3.7	5.6	.1
2004	100.0	67.4	23.8	43.6	18.7	18.1	12.0	2.5	5.9	3.6	6.1	.5
2005	100.0	67.3	23.6	43.6	19.4	19.0	12.4	2.7	6.1	3.6	6.6	.4
2006	100.0	67.2	23.4	43.7	19.6	19.1	13.0	3.1	6.2	3.7	6.1	.5
2007	100.0	67.3	23.3	44.1	18.5	18.2	13.5	3.5	6.2	3.8	4.8	.2
2008	100.0	68.0	22.8	45.3	16.8	17.0	13.5	3.9	5.7	3.9	3.5	–.2
2009	100.0	68.3	22.0	46.4	13.3	14.4	11.7	3.1	4.6	3.9	2.7	–1.0
2010	100.0	68.2	22.0	46.1	14.4	14.0	11.5	2.5	5.2	3.8	2.5	.4
2011	100.0	68.6	22.6	46.0	15.0	14.7	12.2	2.6	5.6	4.0	2.4	.3
2012	100.0	68.0	22.4	45.6	16.1	15.7	13.0	2.9	6.1	4.0	2.7	.4
2013	100.0	67.5	22.1	45.3	16.8	16.2	13.1	2.9	6.1	4.1	3.0	.6
2014	100.0	67.5	22.0	45.5	17.3	16.9	13.7	3.3	6.2	4.2	3.2	.5
2015	100.0	67.4	21.5	45.8	17.8	17.0	13.5	3.2	6.1	4.2	3.5	.8
2016	100.0	67.9	21.4	46.5	17.1	16.9	13.2	3.0	5.8	4.4	3.7	.2
2017	100.0	67.9	21.4	46.6	17.4	17.2	13.3	3.1	5.7	4.5	3.9	.2
2018	100.0	67.7	21.2	46.5	17.7	17.5	13.6	3.1	5.8	4.7	3.9	.3
2019	100.0	67.3	20.9	46.4	17.8	17.5	13.7	3.2	5.7	4.8	3.8	.3
2020	100.0	67.0	22.2	44.9	17.3	17.6	13.3	2.9	5.1	5.3	4.3	–.3
2021	100.0	68.2	23.6	44.6	17.6	17.7	13.0	2.6	5.1	5.3	4.8	–.1
2022 p	100.0	68.2	23.3	44.9	18.2	17.6	13.1	2.5	5.2	5.4	4.4	.6
2019: I	100.0	67.3	20.9	46.5	18.0	17.4	13.6	3.0	5.8	4.8	3.8	.6
II	100.0	67.3	21.0	46.4	18.0	17.6	13.7	3.1	5.8	4.8	3.8	.4
III	100.0	67.3	20.9	46.3	17.9	17.5	13.7	3.3	5.6	4.9	3.8	.3
IV	100.0	67.3	20.9	46.4	17.4	17.3	13.5	3.2	5.4	4.9	3.8	.1
2020: I	100.0	67.0	21.0	46.0	17.4	17.4	13.4	3.2	5.1	5.1	4.0	–.1
II	100.0	66.5	22.1	44.3	16.1	17.6	13.5	3.1	5.0	5.5	4.1	–1.5
III	100.0	67.4	22.9	44.4	17.5	17.4	13.0	2.7	5.1	5.2	4.3	.2
IV	100.0	67.2	22.6	44.6	18.1	17.9	13.2	2.7	5.2	5.3	4.7	.2
2021: I	100.0	67.8	23.6	44.2	17.5	17.9	13.2	2.6	5.2	5.3	4.8	–.5
II	100.0	68.6	24.0	44.6	17.1	17.8	13.0	2.6	5.2	5.3	4.8	–.7
III	100.0	68.6	23.4	45.1	17.4	17.7	12.9	2.5	5.1	5.3	4.7	–.2
IV	100.0	67.8	23.3	44.5	18.5	17.5	12.8	2.5	5.0	5.3	4.7	1.0
2022: I	100.0	68.2	23.6	44.6	18.9	17.8	13.0	2.5	5.2	5.3	4.8	1.0
II	100.0	68.4	23.6	44.8	18.3	17.7	13.0	2.5	5.1	5.4	4.6	.6
III	100.0	68.2	23.3	44.9	17.8	17.5	13.2	2.5	5.3	5.4	4.3	.3
IV p	100.0	67.9	22.8	45.1	17.8	17.2	13.2	2.6	5.2	5.4	4.0	.6

See next page for continuation of table.

Table B–4. Percentage shares of gross domestic product, 1972–2022—*Continued*

[Percent of nominal GDP]

Year or quarter	Net exports of goods and services							Government consumption expenditures and gross investment				
	Net exports	Exports			Imports			Total	Federal			State and local
		Total	Goods	Services	Total	Goods	Services		Total	National defense	Non-defense	
1972	–0.3	5.5	4.1	1.4	5.8	4.5	1.4	22.4	11.1	7.9	3.2	11.3
1973	.3	6.7	5.3	1.4	6.4	5.0	1.4	21.4	10.3	7.2	3.1	11.1
1974	–.1	8.2	6.7	1.5	8.2	6.8	1.5	22.1	10.3	7.1	3.2	11.8
1975	.9	8.2	6.7	1.6	7.3	5.9	1.4	22.6	10.3	7.0	3.3	12.3
1976	–.1	8.0	6.5	1.5	8.1	6.7	1.4	21.6	9.9	6.7	3.2	11.7
1977	–1.1	7.7	6.2	1.5	8.8	7.3	1.4	20.9	9.6	6.5	3.2	11.2
1978	–1.1	7.9	6.4	1.6	9.0	7.5	1.5	20.3	9.3	6.2	3.1	10.9
1979	–.9	8.8	7.1	1.6	9.6	8.1	1.5	20.0	9.2	6.1	3.0	10.8
1980	–.5	9.8	8.1	1.8	10.3	8.7	1.6	20.6	9.6	6.4	3.2	11.0
1981	–.4	9.5	7.6	1.9	9.9	8.4	1.6	20.4	9.8	6.7	3.1	10.6
1982	–.6	8.5	6.7	1.8	9.1	7.5	1.6	21.3	10.4	7.3	3.1	10.9
1983	–1.4	7.6	5.9	1.7	9.0	7.5	1.5	21.1	10.5	7.5	3.0	10.6
1984	–2.5	7.5	5.7	1.8	10.0	8.3	1.7	20.5	10.2	7.4	2.8	10.3
1985	–2.6	7.0	5.2	1.7	9.6	7.9	1.7	21.0	10.4	7.6	2.8	10.5
1986	–2.9	7.0	5.1	2.0	9.9	8.1	1.8	21.3	10.5	7.7	2.8	10.8
1987	–3.0	7.5	5.5	2.0	10.5	8.5	1.9	21.2	10.4	7.7	2.7	10.9
1988	–2.1	8.5	6.3	2.1	10.6	8.6	1.9	20.6	9.8	7.3	2.5	10.8
1989	–1.5	8.9	6.6	2.3	10.5	8.6	1.9	20.4	9.5	6.9	2.5	11.0
1990	–1.3	9.3	6.8	2.5	10.6	8.5	2.0	20.8	9.4	6.8	2.6	11.3
1991	–.5	9.7	7.0	2.7	10.1	8.1	2.0	21.1	9.5	6.7	2.7	11.6
1992	–.5	9.7	7.0	2.7	10.2	8.4	1.9	20.6	9.0	6.2	2.8	11.6
1993	–1.0	9.5	6.8	2.7	10.5	8.6	1.9	19.9	8.5	5.7	2.7	11.4
1994	–1.3	9.9	7.1	2.8	11.2	9.3	1.9	19.2	7.9	5.2	2.6	11.4
1995	–1.2	10.6	7.8	2.9	11.8	9.9	1.9	19.0	7.5	4.9	2.6	11.4
1996	–1.2	10.7	7.8	3.0	11.9	10.0	1.9	18.5	7.2	4.7	2.5	11.3
1997	–1.2	11.1	8.2	3.0	12.3	10.3	2.0	18.0	6.8	4.3	2.5	11.2
1998	–1.8	10.5	7.6	2.9	12.3	10.3	2.0	17.8	6.5	4.1	2.4	11.3
1999	–2.7	10.3	7.4	2.9	13.0	10.9	2.1	17.9	6.3	4.0	2.4	11.5
2000	–3.7	10.7	7.8	2.9	14.4	12.2	2.2	17.8	6.2	3.8	2.3	11.6
2001	–3.6	9.7	7.0	2.7	13.3	11.1	2.1	18.4	6.3	3.9	2.4	12.1
2002	–4.0	9.1	6.5	2.7	13.2	11.0	2.2	19.1	6.8	4.2	2.6	12.3
2003	–4.6	9.0	6.4	2.6	13.6	11.3	2.3	19.3	7.2	4.5	2.7	12.1
2004	–5.2	9.6	6.8	2.9	14.8	12.4	2.4	19.1	7.3	4.7	2.6	11.8
2005	–5.7	10.0	7.1	2.9	15.7	13.2	2.4	19.0	7.3	4.7	2.6	11.7
2006	–5.7	10.6	7.6	3.1	16.3	13.8	2.6	19.0	7.2	4.6	2.6	11.7
2007	–5.1	11.5	8.0	3.5	16.5	13.8	2.7	19.3	7.3	4.7	2.6	12.0
2008	–5.0	12.4	8.7	3.7	17.4	14.5	2.9	20.2	7.8	5.1	2.7	12.4
2009	–2.9	10.9	7.3	3.6	13.8	11.0	2.9	21.2	8.4	5.4	3.0	12.8
2010	–3.5	12.3	8.5	3.9	15.9	12.9	2.9	21.0	8.6	5.5	3.1	12.3
2011	–3.7	13.6	9.4	4.2	17.3	14.3	3.0	20.2	8.3	5.3	3.0	11.8
2012	–3.4	13.6	9.4	4.2	17.0	14.1	2.9	19.3	7.9	5.0	2.9	11.4
2013	–2.8	13.6	9.3	4.3	16.4	13.6	2.8	18.6	7.3	4.5	2.7	11.3
2014	–2.9	13.5	9.2	4.3	16.5	13.6	2.8	18.1	6.9	4.2	2.7	11.1
2015	–2.9	12.5	8.2	4.2	15.4	12.6	2.8	17.8	6.7	4.0	2.7	11.0
2016	–2.7	11.9	7.7	4.2	14.6	11.9	2.8	17.7	6.6	3.9	2.7	11.1
2017	–2.8	12.3	7.9	4.3	15.0	12.2	2.8	17.4	6.5	3.8	2.7	10.9
2018	–2.9	12.4	8.1	4.2	15.2	12.5	2.8	17.4	6.5	3.9	2.7	10.9
2019	–2.7	11.9	7.7	4.2	14.6	11.8	2.8	17.6	6.6	4.0	2.7	11.0
2020	–3.0	10.2	6.7	3.5	13.2	10.9	2.2	18.7	7.2	4.2	3.0	11.4
2021	–3.7	10.9	7.5	3.4	14.6	12.2	2.4	17.8	6.9	3.9	3.0	10.9
2022 p	–3.8	11.7	8.1	3.6	15.5	12.9	2.7	17.5	6.5	3.6	2.8	11.0
2019: I	–2.9	12.1	7.9	4.2	15.0	12.1	2.8	17.6	6.6	4.0	2.7	10.9
II	–2.9	12.0	7.7	4.2	14.9	12.0	2.8	17.6	6.6	3.9	2.7	11.0
III	–2.7	11.8	7.6	4.2	14.5	11.7	2.8	17.6	6.6	4.0	2.7	11.0
IV	–2.4	11.6	7.5	4.1	14.0	11.3	2.8	17.6	6.6	4.0	2.7	11.0
2020: I	–2.4	11.2	7.4	3.8	13.6	11.1	2.6	18.0	6.8	4.0	2.7	11.3
II	–2.7	9.3	5.8	3.4	11.9	9.9	2.1	20.1	7.9	4.4	3.5	12.2
III	–3.2	9.9	6.6	3.2	13.1	11.1	2.0	18.4	7.1	4.1	3.0	11.2
IV	–3.5	10.4	7.0	3.4	13.9	11.7	2.3	18.2	7.1	4.2	2.9	11.1
2021: I	–3.6	10.6	7.2	3.4	14.2	12.1	2.2	18.3	7.3	4.0	3.2	11.1
II	–3.6	10.9	7.5	3.4	14.5	12.2	2.3	17.9	7.0	3.9	3.1	10.9
III	–3.8	10.8	7.4	3.4	14.6	12.1	2.5	17.8	6.8	3.9	2.9	11.0
IV	–3.8	11.2	7.7	3.5	15.0	12.4	2.5	17.4	6.6	3.7	2.9	10.8
2022: I	–4.5	11.4	7.8	3.5	15.9	13.3	2.6	17.4	6.5	3.6	2.9	10.9
II	–4.1	12.0	8.5	3.6	16.1	13.4	2.7	17.5	6.4	3.6	2.8	11.1
III	–3.5	11.9	8.3	3.6	15.4	12.7	2.7	17.5	6.4	3.6	2.8	11.0
IV p	–3.3	11.5	7.8	3.7	14.8	12.1	2.7	17.5	6.5	3.6	2.9	11.0

Source: Department of Commerce (Bureau of Economic Analysis).

TABLE B–5. Chain-type price indexes for gross domestic product, 1972–2022

[Index numbers, 2012=100, except as noted; quarterly data seasonally adjusted]

Year or quarter	Gross domestic product	Personal consumption expenditures			Gross private domestic investment						
						Fixed investment					
							Nonresidential				
		Total	Goods	Services	Total	Total	Total	Structures	Equipment	Intel-lectual property products	Residential
1972	23.745	22.542	33.926	17.441	32.388	31.420	39.297	13.674	64.686	40.490	17.975
1973	25.045	23.756	35.949	18.284	34.153	33.169	40.882	14.734	65.780	42.494	19.571
1974	27.292	26.229	40.436	19.833	37.559	36.449	44.857	16.770	70.713	46.461	21.593
1975	29.827	28.415	43.703	21.533	42.059	40.874	50.766	18.773	81.484	50.190	23.590
1976	31.469	29.974	45.413	23.027	44.384	43.232	53.562	19.692	86.486	52.408	25.117
1977	33.424	31.923	47.837	24.770	47.655	46.550	57.111	21.401	91.800	54.709	27.683
1978	35.775	34.145	50.773	26.674	51.517	50.444	60.930	23.468	96.900	57.557	31.082
1979	38.741	37.178	55.574	28.911	56.141	54.977	65.830	26.194	103.167	61.382	34.593
1980	42.251	41.182	61.797	31.918	61.395	60.105	71.641	28.629	112.249	66.123	38.325
1981	46.240	44.871	66.389	35.187	67.123	65.624	78.453	32.566	120.463	71.058	41.425
1982	49.099	47.363	68.198	37.949	70.679	69.311	82.911	35.136	125.415	75.093	43.646
1983	51.018	49.378	69.429	40.280	70.896	69.575	82.774	34.241	125.776	77.898	44.680
1984	52.860	51.243	70.742	42.376	71.661	70.253	83.036	34.540	124.748	80.081	46.003
1985	54.533	53.031	71.877	44.450	72.548	71.277	83.893	35.361	124.748	81.413	47.267
1986	55.638	54.184	71.541	46.276	74.178	73.021	85.365	36.039	127.254	82.047	49.351
1987	57.004	55.855	73.842	47.660	75.723	74.506	86.339	36.618	128.083	83.518	51.486
1988	59.018	58.038	75.788	49.939	77.627	76.586	88.514	38.171	129.854	86.129	53.278
1989	61.331	60.572	78.704	52.293	79.606	78.561	90.572	39.666	132.337	87.240	55.020
1990	63.636	63.231	81.927	54.690	81.270	80.278	92.516	40.948	135.042	88.147	56.288
1991	65.777	65.345	83.930	56.829	82.648	81.683	94.267	41.689	137.330	90.271	57.021
1992	67.278	67.087	84.943	58.850	82.647	81.728	93.960	41.699	137.121	89.373	57.723
1993	68.874	68.758	85.681	60.885	83.627	82.711	94.161	42.922	135.518	89.998	60.074
1994	70.342	70.193	86.552	62.540	84.875	83.983	94.904	44.437	135.277	90.468	62.247
1995	71.819	71.671	87.361	64.288	86.240	85.378	95.849	46.362	133.796	93.134	64.473
1996	73.132	73.204	88.321	66.051	86.191	85.450	95.267	47.540	130.762	93.544	65.856
1997	74.399	74.478	88.219	67.914	86.241	85.599	94.735	49.355	127.156	94.052	67.444
1998	75.219	75.070	86.893	69.351	85.608	85.133	93.248	51.612	121.451	93.595	69.223
1999	76.272	76.164	87.349	70.731	85.690	85.277	92.314	53.198	116.763	95.105	71.816
2000	78.016	78.090	89.082	72.740	86.815	86.486	92.718	55.283	114.224	97.814	75.004
2001	79.814	79.656	89.015	75.063	87.555	87.241	92.346	58.178	110.858	97.684	78.564
2002	81.013	80.702	88.166	77.004	87.841	87.500	91.863	60.603	108.531	96.376	80.510
2003	82.635	82.398	88.054	79.574	88.561	88.265	91.156	62.769	105.725	95.647	84.325
2004	84.842	84.443	89.292	82.018	91.148	90.843	92.055	67.416	104.841	95.335	90.243
2005	87.490	86.876	91.084	84.774	94.839	94.597	94.443	75.733	104.598	95.952	96.706
2006	90.212	89.322	92.306	87.844	98.176	97.958	96.745	84.749	103.560	97.088	102.355
2007	92.653	91.614	93.331	90.786	99.656	99.456	98.310	89.748	103.191	98.284	103.708
2008	94.397	94.325	96.122	93.458	100.474	100.296	99.832	94.335	102.542	99.834	102.249
2009	95.019	94.062	93.812	94.182	99.331	99.076	99.184	92.613	103.169	98.589	98.671
2010	96.164	95.747	95.183	96.017	97.687	97.568	97.416	92.006	99.471	98.306	98.317
2011	98.157	98.170	98.773	97.875	98.704	98.641	98.559	95.362	99.447	99.517	99.049
2012	100.000	100.000	100.000	100.000	100.000	100.000	100.000	100.000	100.000	100.000	100.000
2013	101.769	101.354	99.407	102.322	100.979	101.091	100.251	101.455	99.787	100.081	105.054
2014	103.662	102.887	98.920	104.880	102.922	103.172	101.469	107.198	99.169	100.791	111.118
2015	104.662	103.116	95.896	106.796	103.535	104.075	101.909	109.403	98.671	101.374	114.114
2016	105.703	104.148	94.332	109.197	103.516	104.202	101.119	109.670	97.592	100.302	118.127
2017	107.743	106.054	94.621	111.966	105.243	105.939	101.992	112.411	97.579	101.202	123.454
2018	110.344	108.317	95.334	115.070	107.191	107.932	102.824	114.116	97.711	102.423	130.417
2019	112.303	109.933	94.948	117.791	108.918	109.698	104.155	118.805	97.841	103.327	134.144
2020	113.814	111.145	94.237	120.133	110.342	111.179	104.948	120.380	97.340	105.183	138.622
2021	118.924	115.621	98.824	124.458	114.329	115.608	106.688	125.276	97.726	106.913	153.963
2022 p	127.225	122.857	107.331	130.733	123.676	125.389	113.639	145.767	103.783	109.469	175.521
2019: I	111.560	109.188	94.785	116.721	108.426	109.189	103.802	116.992	98.154	102.943	132.927
II	112.184	109.857	95.216	117.519	108.978	109.733	104.321	118.629	98.069	103.596	133.581
III	112.558	110.144	94.877	118.159	109.156	109.942	104.347	119.483	97.674	103.689	134.623
IV	112.910	110.543	94.913	118.765	109.114	109.929	104.150	120.115	97.465	103.079	135.445
2020: I	113.427	110.946	94.727	119.509	109.613	110.357	104.481	120.717	97.694	103.447	136.277
II	113.053	110.445	93.416	119.511	109.899	110.832	104.994	120.425	97.735	104.891	136.613
III	114.032	111.366	94.345	120.416	110.562	111.401	104.978	120.434	97.151	105.445	139.674
IV	114.744	111.821	94.461	121.095	111.293	112.125	105.338	119.946	96.779	106.950	141.926
2021: I	116.199	113.059	95.803	122.248	112.200	113.107	105.513	120.332	97.641	106.220	146.120
II	117.974	114.838	97.882	123.791	112.977	114.265	105.612	122.702	96.560	106.556	151.487
III	119.763	116.413	99.688	125.185	114.847	116.290	106.818	125.729	97.577	107.156	156.862
IV	121.758	118.173	101.923	126.607	117.292	118.771	108.811	132.340	99.125	107.721	161.384
2022: I	124.209	120.323	104.987	128.126	120.103	121.640	110.646	137.535	100.963	108.238	168.513
II	126.914	122.459	107.670	129.875	122.982	124.647	112.932	143.194	103.211	109.282	174.587
III	128.276	123.760	108.402	131.516	125.266	126.981	115.006	149.909	104.707	110.267	178.040
IV p	129.502	124.888	108.266	133.418	126.353	128.287	115.972	152.430	106.252	110.090	180.945

See next page for continuation of table.

TABLE B–5. Chain-type price indexes for gross domestic product, 1972–2022—*Continued*

[Index numbers, 2012=100, except as noted; quarterly data seasonally adjusted]

Year or quarter	Exports and imports of goods and services		Government consumption expenditures and gross investment					Final sales of domestic product	Personal consumption expenditures excluding food and energy	Gross domestic purchases [1]	Percent change [2]			
				Federal							Gross domestic product	Personal consumption expenditures		Gross domestic purchases [1]
	Exports	Imports	Total	Total	National defense	Non-defense	State and local					Total	Excluding food and energy	
1972	32.187	22.593	18.664	22.488	21.883	23.589	16.163	23.609	23.856	23.147	4.3	3.4	3.2	4.5
1973	36.430	26.520	19.938	24.054	23.484	25.028	17.246	24.907	24.764	24.469	5.5	5.4	3.8	5.7
1974	44.865	37.942	21.854	25.975	25.404	26.916	19.158	27.136	26.726	26.954	9.0	10.4	7.9	10.2
1975	49.453	41.100	23.872	28.258	27.545	29.497	21.000	29.661	28.958	29.417	9.3	8.3	8.4	9.1
1976	51.076	42.338	25.183	30.016	29.345	31.137	22.025	31.305	30.718	31.033	5.5	5.5	6.1	5.5
1977	53.158	46.068	26.742	31.863	31.268	32.796	23.395	33.262	32.694	33.079	6.2	6.5	6.4	6.6
1978	56.391	49.315	28.510	34.012	33.561	34.627	24.915	35.614	34.861	35.431	7.0	7.0	6.6	7.1
1979	63.184	57.753	30.856	36.571	36.216	36.968	27.115	38.566	37.403	38.539	8.3	8.9	7.3	8.8
1980	69.594	71.945	34.048	40.104	39.919	40.124	30.082	42.056	40.840	42.551	9.1	10.8	9.2	10.4
1981	74.748	75.834	37.428	43.849	43.747	43.662	33.228	46.016	44.419	46.476	9.4	9.0	8.8	9.2
1982	75.104	73.281	39.973	46.950	47.039	46.309	35.403	48.889	47.306	49.154	6.2	5.6	6.5	5.8
1983	75.410	70.535	41.520	48.506	48.778	47.418	36.966	50.803	49.727	50.864	3.9	4.3	5.1	3.5
1984	76.116	69.925	43.322	50.644	51.013	49.300	38.546	52.637	51.789	52.585	3.6	3.8	4.1	3.4
1985	73.850	67.628	44.663	51.719	51.872	50.929	40.115	54.335	53.893	54.149	3.2	3.5	4.1	3.0
1986	72.618	67.627	45.413	51.964	51.894	51.770	41.271	55.456	55.752	55.278	2.0	2.2	3.4	2.1
1987	74.222	71.715	46.640	52.325	52.267	52.099	43.198	56.814	57.548	56.839	2.5	3.1	3.2	2.8
1988	78.022	75.146	48.181	54.033	53.904	53.997	44.642	58.851	59.994	58.850	3.5	3.9	4.3	3.5
1989	79.315	76.789	50.021	55.542	55.365	55.629	46.754	61.165	62.484	61.166	3.9	4.4	4.2	3.9
1990	79.762	78.991	52.118	57.258	57.162	57.118	49.156	63.477	65.016	63.586	3.8	4.4	4.1	4.0
1991	80.651	78.332	54.010	59.317	58.964	59.813	50.955	65.621	67.338	65.583	3.4	3.3	3.6	3.1
1992	80.259	78.396	55.647	60.832	60.678	60.851	52.692	67.125	69.384	67.108	2.3	2.7	3.0	2.3
1993	80.391	77.795	56.958	62.159	61.615	63.021	54.004	68.722	71.269	68.623	2.4	2.5	2.7	2.3
1994	81.325	78.526	58.468	63.870	63.229	64.926	55.397	70.194	72.864	70.062	2.1	2.1	2.2	2.1
1995	83.143	80.677	60.128	65.847	65.027	67.252	56.874	71.676	74.451	71.575	2.1	2.1	2.2	2.2
1996	82.039	79.271	61.361	66.946	66.114	68.373	58.180	73.009	75.863	72.820	1.8	2.1	1.9	1.7
1997	80.593	76.516	62.566	67.981	67.035	69.621	59.474	74.297	77.201	73.893	1.7	1.7	1.8	1.5
1998	78.685	72.396	63.630	68.850	67.871	70.548	60.633	75.152	78.183	74.386	1.1	.8	1.3	.7
1999	78.091	72.827	65.753	70.532	69.559	72.218	62.963	76.221	79.210	75.518	1.4	1.5	1.3	1.5
2000	79.592	76.013	68.577	72.898	71.908	74.616	65.989	77.983	80.625	77.480	2.3	2.5	1.8	2.6
2001	78.968	74.046	70.558	74.249	73.270	75.947	68.258	79.785	82.153	78.987	2.3	2.0	1.9	1.9
2002	78.287	73.164	72.386	76.648	75.714	78.272	69.792	80.978	83.526	80.070	1.5	1.3	1.7	1.4
2003	79.531	75.377	75.044	80.025	79.505	80.946	72.063	82.609	84.874	81.807	2.0	2.1	1.6	2.2
2004	82.435	78.971	78.169	82.777	82.263	83.689	75.382	84.814	86.544	84.151	2.7	2.5	2.0	2.9
2005	85.289	83.618	82.132	86.222	86.011	86.586	79.631	87.470	88.440	87.083	3.1	2.9	2.2	3.5
2006	88.006	86.854	85.695	88.969	89.022	88.858	83.659	90.195	90.558	89.885	3.1	2.8	2.4	3.2
2007	91.328	89.887	89.530	91.609	91.750	91.340	88.181	92.645	92.578	92.327	2.7	2.6	2.2	2.7
2008	95.493	98.795	93.334	94.397	94.801	93.647	92.590	94.392	94.393	94.947	1.9	3.0	2.0	2.8
2009	89.803	87.854	92.921	94.193	94.126	94.308	92.045	94.990	95.270	94.534	.7	–.3	.9	–.4
2010	93.350	92.655	95.391	96.425	96.128	96.951	94.674	96.142	96.651	95.951	1.2	1.8	1.4	1.5
2011	99.237	99.716	98.289	99.069	98.946	99.284	97.747	98.146	98.184	98.272	2.1	2.5	1.6	2.4
2012	100.000	100.000	100.000	100.000	100.000	100.000	100.000	100.000	100.000	100.000	1.9	1.9	1.8	1.8
2013	100.148	98.697	102.363	100.933	100.609	101.482	103.332	101.791	101.535	101.478	1.8	1.4	1.5	1.5
2014	100.216	97.961	104.470	102.643	102.056	103.621	105.698	103.707	103.187	103.181	1.9	1.5	1.6	1.7
2015	95.373	90.144	104.638	103.143	102.334	104.466	105.656	104.760	104.487	103.464	1.0	.2	1.3	.3
2016	93.458	87.058	104.899	103.695	102.650	105.370	105.739	105.832	106.138	104.187	1.0	1.0	1.6	.7
2017	95.903	88.980	107.353	105.592	104.260	107.697	108.534	107.875	107.938	106.155	1.9	1.8	1.7	1.9
2018	99.142	91.408	111.303	108.662	107.147	111.044	113.028	110.486	110.095	108.645	2.4	2.1	2.0	2.3
2019	98.692	89.972	113.192	110.639	108.903	113.360	114.864	112.453	111.973	110.326	1.8	1.5	1.7	1.5
2020	96.278	88.010	115.329	111.898	110.148	114.640	117.568	113.975	113.464	111.733	1.3	1.1	1.3	1.3
2021	107.304	94.481	121.436	115.724	114.240	118.111	125.206	119.165	117.388	116.403	4.5	4.0	3.5	4.2
2022 p	117.425	101.571	130.552	121.463	120.206	123.579	136.568	127.532	123.280	124.323	7.0	6.3	5.0	6.8
2019: I	98.435	90.138	112.763	110.943	108.341	115.011	113.974	111.706	111.230	109.678	1.5	.8	1.5	1.1
II	99.284	90.641	112.997	110.205	108.704	112.555	114.817	112.330	111.808	110.254	2.3	2.5	2.1	2.1
III	98.690	89.702	113.287	110.480	109.041	112.740	115.118	112.709	112.255	110.523	1.3	1.0	1.6	1.0
IV	98.357	89.406	113.719	110.926	109.525	113.133	115.545	113.068	112.597	110.850	1.3	1.5	1.2	1.2
2020: I	97.908	89.139	114.613	111.301	109.788	113.693	116.772	113.570	113.119	111.354	1.8	1.5	1.9	1.8
II	93.295	86.295	114.609	111.393	109.496	114.338	116.705	113.231	112.846	111.075	–1.3	–1.8	–1.0	–1.0
III	96.228	87.998	115.515	112.109	110.314	114.926	117.738	114.193	113.729	111.948	3.5	3.4	3.2	3.2
IV	97.680	88.608	116.580	112.788	110.993	115.605	119.056	114.905	114.163	112.555	2.5	1.6	1.5	2.2
2021: I	102.334	91.336	118.549	113.922	112.410	116.345	121.585	116.375	115.072	113.859	5.2	4.5	3.2	4.7
II	106.803	94.102	120.505	115.079	113.612	117.444	124.087	118.217	116.774	115.498	6.3	6.4	6.0	5.9
III	109.210	95.510	122.268	116.325	114.838	118.718	126.195	120.035	118.152	117.155	6.2	5.6	4.8	5.9
IV	110.868	96.977	124.423	117.568	116.100	119.938	128.957	122.034	119.555	119.101	6.8	6.2	4.8	6.8
2022: I	115.384	100.107	127.043	119.203	117.965	121.279	132.234	124.489	121.206	121.447	8.3	7.5	5.6	8.1
II	120.763	103.266	130.566	120.951	120.108	122.515	136.930	127.215	122.592	123.940	9.0	7.3	4.7	8.5
III	117.722	102.190	131.727	122.383	120.925	124.771	137.914	128.579	123.997	125.391	4.4	4.3	4.7	4.8
IV p	115.830	100.719	132.870	123.316	121.826	125.752	139.195	129.845	125.324	126.515	3.9	3.7	4.3	3.6

[1] Gross domestic product (GDP) less exports of goods and services plus imports of goods and services.
[2] Quarterly percent changes are at annual rates.

Source: Department of Commerce (Bureau of Economic Analysis).

Table B–6. Gross value added by sector, 1972–2022

[Billions of dollars; quarterly data at seasonally adjusted annual rates]

Year or quarter	Gross domestic product	Business[1]			Households and institutions			General government[3]			Addendum: Gross housing value added
		Total	Nonfarm[1]	Farm	Total	Households	Nonprofit institutions serving households[2]	Total	Federal	State and local	
1972	1,279.1	972.5	942.9	29.7	114.0	72.7	41.4	192.6	92.4	100.2	93.9
1973	1,425.4	1,094.0	1,047.2	46.8	124.6	78.5	46.1	206.8	96.4	110.4	101.4
1974	1,545.2	1,182.8	1,138.5	44.2	137.2	85.5	51.7	225.3	102.5	122.8	110.4
1975	1,684.9	1,284.8	1,239.2	45.6	151.6	93.7	58.0	248.4	110.5	138.0	121.3
1976	1,873.4	1,443.3	1,400.2	43.0	164.9	101.7	63.2	265.3	117.3	148.0	130.9
1977	2,081.8	1,616.2	1,572.7	43.5	179.9	110.7	69.2	285.7	125.2	160.6	144.2
1978	2,351.6	1,838.2	1,787.5	50.7	202.1	124.8	77.3	311.3	135.8	175.5	160.2
1979	2,627.3	2,062.8	2,002.7	60.1	226.3	139.5	86.9	338.2	145.4	192.8	177.7
1980	2,857.3	2,225.8	2,174.4	51.4	258.2	158.8	99.3	373.4	159.8	213.5	204.0
1981	3,207.0	2,502.0	2,437.0	65.0	291.6	179.2	112.4	413.5	178.3	235.2	231.6
1982	3,343.8	2,568.6	2,508.2	60.4	323.8	198.2	125.6	451.4	195.7	255.6	258.6
1983	3,634.0	2,801.9	2,757.0	44.9	352.5	213.6	138.9	479.7	207.1	272.6	280.6
1984	4,037.6	3,136.7	3,072.6	64.2	383.8	230.9	152.8	517.1	225.3	291.9	303.1
1985	4,339.0	3,369.6	3,305.9	63.7	411.8	248.2	163.6	557.5	240.0	317.6	333.8
1986	4,579.6	3,539.3	3,479.4	59.9	447.0	268.4	178.6	593.3	250.6	342.7	364.5
1987	4,855.2	3,735.2	3,673.2	62.0	489.5	289.8	199.7	630.4	261.0	369.4	392.1
1988	5,236.4	4,019.3	3,957.9	61.4	539.8	316.4	223.4	677.4	278.5	398.8	424.2
1989	5,641.6	4,326.7	4,252.8	73.9	586.0	341.4	244.6	728.8	292.8	436.1	452.7
1990	5,963.1	4,542.0	4,464.2	77.8	636.3	367.6	268.8	784.9	306.7	478.2	487.0
1991	6,158.1	4,645.0	4,574.7	70.4	677.3	386.6	290.7	835.8	323.5	512.2	515.3
1992	6,520.3	4,920.2	4,840.4	79.9	720.3	407.1	313.2	879.8	329.6	550.2	545.2
1993	6,858.6	5,177.4	5,106.2	71.3	772.8	437.6	335.1	908.3	331.5	576.9	578.4
1994	7,287.2	5,523.7	5,440.1	83.6	824.7	472.7	352.0	938.8	332.6	606.2	619.6
1995	7,639.7	5,795.1	5,726.7	68.4	877.8	506.9	370.9	966.9	333.0	633.9	662.6
1996	8,073.1	6,159.5	6,066.9	92.6	923.2	534.6	388.7	990.3	331.8	658.6	695.0
1997	8,577.6	6,578.8	6,490.6	88.1	975.9	565.7	410.2	1,022.9	333.5	689.3	731.9
1998	9,062.8	6,959.2	6,880.2	79.0	1,040.6	601.6	439.0	1,063.0	336.8	726.2	774.8
1999	9,631.2	7,401.8	7,330.9	70.9	1,111.2	644.0	467.2	1,118.1	345.0	773.1	825.1
2000	10,251.0	7,875.9	7,799.9	76.0	1,190.7	692.3	498.4	1,184.3	360.3	824.0	880.6
2001	10,581.9	8,057.7	7,979.6	78.1	1,271.7	748.9	522.8	1,252.6	370.3	882.3	947.7
2002	10,929.1	8,256.0	8,181.7	74.3	1,344.7	781.6	563.0	1,328.4	397.8	930.6	983.5
2003	11,456.5	8,642.9	8,551.1	91.8	1,408.8	814.1	594.6	1,404.8	434.7	970.1	1,014.8
2004	12,217.2	9,249.3	9,129.1	120.2	1,489.2	862.6	626.6	1,478.7	459.4	1,019.3	1,074.1
2005	13,039.2	9,911.0	9,805.4	105.6	1,572.8	922.3	650.5	1,555.4	488.4	1,067.0	1,149.7
2006	13,815.6	10,524.7	10,427.2	97.5	1,658.9	976.2	682.8	1,631.9	509.9	1,122.1	1,209.4
2007	14,474.2	10,997.8	10,880.7	117.1	1,749.5	1,035.9	713.6	1,726.9	535.7	1,191.2	1,279.3
2008	14,769.9	11,061.8	10,943.6	118.2	1,886.9	1,125.2	761.7	1,821.2	569.1	1,252.1	1,388.7
2009	14,478.1	10,659.6	10,557.4	102.2	1,934.9	1,136.8	798.2	1,883.5	603.0	1,280.5	1,415.5
2010	15,049.0	11,137.8	11,021.6	116.2	1,965.0	1,150.7	814.3	1,946.1	640.0	1,306.1	1,443.9
2011	15,599.7	11,614.9	11,464.5	150.4	2,012.0	1,164.0	848.0	1,972.9	659.8	1,313.1	1,471.0
2012	16,254.0	12,206.4	12,058.5	148.0	2,058.4	1,168.8	889.6	1,989.1	663.7	1,325.5	1,493.6
2013	16,843.2	12,689.6	12,506.4	183.3	2,114.2	1,196.5	917.7	2,039.3	658.4	1,380.9	1,536.3
2014	17,550.7	13,279.8	13,113.8	166.0	2,182.9	1,228.3	954.6	2,088.0	666.8	1,421.1	1,582.8
2015	18,206.0	13,804.8	13,659.6	145.2	2,260.2	1,258.8	1,001.4	2,141.0	673.7	1,467.3	1,633.1
2016	18,695.1	14,168.5	14,038.6	129.9	2,344.1	1,299.3	1,044.8	2,182.5	683.9	1,498.6	1,691.5
2017	19,477.3	14,801.8	14,663.0	138.9	2,436.3	1,352.8	1,083.5	2,239.2	697.8	1,541.3	1,753.3
2018	20,533.1	15,649.6	15,513.7	135.9	2,552.5	1,417.4	1,135.2	2,331.0	724.7	1,606.3	1,836.1
2019	21,381.0	16,305.7	16,185.8	119.8	2,671.2	1,482.0	1,189.2	2,404.1	748.1	1,655.9	1,924.0
2020	21,060.5	15,806.3	15,685.5	120.7	2,768.3	1,533.3	1,235.0	2,485.9	782.3	1,703.5	1,991.3
2021	23,315.1	17,855.9	17,691.2	164.7	2,873.2	1,582.0	1,291.2	2,585.9	819.3	1,766.6	2,052.9
2022 p	25,464.5	19,592.0	19,348.6	243.4	3,145.1	1,715.2	1,429.9	2,727.3	854.4	1,872.9	2,219.5
2019: I	21,013.1	16,016.6	15,899.0	117.6	2,626.5	1,460.5	1,166.0	2,370.0	740.4	1,629.5	1,893.9
II	21,272.4	16,233.6	16,117.1	116.6	2,653.0	1,474.6	1,178.3	2,385.8	744.7	1,641.1	1,914.4
III	21,531.8	16,432.6	16,311.7	120.9	2,683.5	1,488.6	1,194.9	2,415.7	751.1	1,664.6	1,933.8
IV	21,706.5	16,539.8	16,415.5	124.3	2,721.9	1,504.4	1,217.6	2,444.8	756.3	1,688.5	1,953.8
2020: I	21,538.0	16,284.0	16,148.5	135.5	2,767.8	1,522.4	1,245.3	2,486.3	765.0	1,721.2	1,976.1
II	19,636.7	14,450.1	14,355.8	94.3	2,731.3	1,531.5	1,199.8	2,455.4	776.6	1,678.8	1,988.6
III	21,362.4	16,093.3	15,976.1	117.1	2,771.1	1,539.1	1,232.0	2,498.1	792.0	1,706.1	1,998.8
IV	21,704.7	16,397.8	16,261.7	136.0	2,803.1	1,540.1	1,263.0	2,503.8	795.8	1,708.1	2,001.7
2021: I	22,313.9	16,979.2	16,847.6	131.6	2,806.1	1,549.7	1,256.4	2,528.6	806.2	1,722.4	2,013.8
II	23,046.9	17,644.4	17,472.5	171.9	2,839.4	1,569.2	1,270.1	2,563.2	816.2	1,747.0	2,037.1
III	23,550.4	18,039.8	17,860.1	179.7	2,896.9	1,591.2	1,305.7	2,613.7	823.8	1,789.8	2,063.7
IV	24,349.1	18,760.4	18,584.8	175.6	2,950.5	1,617.9	1,332.5	2,638.3	831.1	1,807.2	2,097.1
2022: I	24,740.5	19,030.9	18,810.5	220.5	3,036.7	1,651.0	1,385.8	2,672.8	841.8	1,831.0	2,137.4
II	25,248.5	19,438.7	19,190.8	247.9	3,104.1	1,690.2	1,414.0	2,705.7	850.1	1,855.6	2,187.5
III	25,723.9	19,793.7	19,543.5	250.2	3,182.0	1,736.8	1,445.1	2,748.2	859.8	1,888.4	2,246.8
IV p	26,145.0	20,104.8	19,849.8	255.0	3,257.6	1,782.8	1,474.8	2,782.5	866.0	1,916.5	2,306.2

[1] Gross domestic business value added equals gross domestic product excluding gross value added of households and institutions and of general government. Nonfarm value added equals gross domestic business value added excluding gross farm value added.

[2] Equals compensation of employees of nonprofit institutions, the rental value of nonresidential fixed assets owned and used by nonprofit institutions serving households, and rental income of persons for tenant-occupied housing owned by nonprofit institutions.

[3] Equals compensation of general government employees plus general government consumption of fixed capital.

Source: Department of Commerce (Bureau of Economic Analysis).

TABLE B–7. Real gross value added by sector, 1972–2022

[Billions of chained (2012) dollars; quarterly data at seasonally adjusted annual rates]

Year or quarter	Gross domestic product	Business[1]			Households and institutions			General government[3]			Addendum: Gross housing value added
		Total	Nonfarm[1]	Farm	Total	House-holds	Nonprofit institu-tions serving house-holds[2]	Total	Federal	State and local	
1972	5,386.7	3,619.3	3,577.2	48.2	718.4	425.8	289.6	1,226.9	487.2	724.6	546.8
1973	5,690.9	3,870.6	3,837.0	47.7	742.5	439.5	300.0	1,232.9	473.6	750.1	564.2
1974	5,660.1	3,811.6	3,779.4	46.6	772.8	459.1	310.4	1,257.1	473.8	777.4	591.9
1975	5,648.5	3,775.4	3,717.7	55.5	799.6	472.2	324.2	1,276.0	472.1	801.0	610.8
1976	5,952.8	4,030.5	3,984.3	52.8	810.0	478.4	328.4	1,286.8	473.3	811.7	616.9
1977	6,228.1	4,261.3	4,213.0	55.6	816.4	478.3	335.3	1,300.3	475.2	824.3	625.7
1978	6,572.8	4,533.1	4,494.3	53.5	846.9	501.3	342.2	1,325.1	481.5	843.7	648.2
1979	6,780.9	4,694.1	4,646.4	58.6	870.4	511.5	355.7	1,339.9	482.5	859.1	660.8
1980	6,763.5	4,651.7	4,606.8	56.9	896.6	526.1	367.4	1,359.9	490.3	871.1	684.1
1981	6,935.2	4,787.4	4,711.8	75.2	913.8	531.8	379.3	1,369.5	498.5	871.0	697.5
1982	6,810.1	4,650.0	4,567.7	78.8	941.5	539.1	401.1	1,385.7	507.7	876.9	713.7
1983	7,122.3	4,896.4	4,850.7	54.5	980.4	560.2	419.0	1,397.7	520.6	873.5	741.3
1984	7,637.7	5,330.7	5,261.1	72.7	1,002.9	570.7	431.4	1,418.3	534.1	879.0	755.5
1985	7,956.2	5,579.3	5,492.8	86.1	1,020.3	583.6	435.4	1,461.1	551.1	904.3	786.8
1986	8,231.7	5,782.0	5,700.6	82.4	1,052.2	595.3	456.5	1,500.5	564.4	930.7	808.2
1987	8,516.4	5,989.5	5,907.8	83.2	1,091.6	610.4	481.9	1,537.5	582.2	949.1	827.0
1988	8,872.2	6,246.0	6,176.9	73.9	1,147.8	635.7	513.6	1,580.7	593.4	981.6	854.3
1989	9,198.0	6,485.1	6,403.9	84.0	1,194.3	655.5	541.4	1,619.4	602.4	1,011.9	872.1
1990	9,371.5	6,589.0	6,499.6	90.7	1,232.6	668.2	568.4	1,659.8	612.9	1,042.2	889.6
1991	9,361.3	6,548.8	6,458.7	91.2	1,257.9	678.5	583.9	1,676.7	616.4	1,055.9	907.8
1992	9,691.1	6,826.1	6,721.2	105.3	1,289.8	693.9	600.8	1,683.9	606.3	1,073.9	929.9
1993	9,957.7	7,020.7	6,928.5	93.4	1,356.2	727.5	634.0	1,687.9	596.3	1,088.7	963.2
1994	10,358.9	7,359.3	7,247.4	113.0	1,401.9	764.4	641.5	1,689.5	579.7	1,107.7	1,004.4
1995	10,637.0	7,585.5	7,496.4	90.0	1,443.7	790.9	656.4	1,691.9	561.2	1,129.6	1,040.2
1996	11,038.3	7,937.6	7,833.7	104.1	1,472.5	807.1	669.0	1,695.2	547.8	1,147.1	1,058.1
1997	11,529.2	8,354.3	8,237.5	116.7	1,517.7	829.9	691.8	1,708.1	538.8	1,169.7	1,083.6
1998	12,045.8	8,813.8	8,700.2	112.6	1,537.4	851.5	688.8	1,726.8	533.1	1,194.6	1,109.0
1999	12,623.4	9,323.0	9,206.0	115.5	1,573.1	878.8	696.4	1,742.1	528.9	1,214.4	1,140.3
2000	13,138.0	9,741.3	9,607.5	136.6	1,633.7	917.7	717.7	1,770.3	531.7	1,240.0	1,179.4
2001	13,263.4	9,799.7	9,672.8	126.6	1,674.3	951.4	723.7	1,801.4	533.2	1,269.6	1,216.8
2002	13,488.4	9,966.6	9,835.1	132.3	1,698.4	956.4	743.6	1,835.6	542.6	1,294.4	1,215.6
2003	13,865.5	10,281.2	10,139.9	144.4	1,734.8	984.2	751.6	1,858.5	557.0	1,302.8	1,236.4
2004	14,399.7	10,733.3	10,578.9	159.2	1,798.6	1,020.5	779.3	1,871.5	565.1	1,307.5	1,280.1
2005	14,901.3	11,154.8	10,992.0	168.6	1,858.1	1,068.7	789.8	1,888.4	572.3	1,317.0	1,341.3
2006	15,315.9	11,520.2	11,357.8	165.5	1,888.4	1,097.0	791.4	1,903.9	576.7	1,328.3	1,367.7
2007	15,623.9	11,766.1	11,617.4	145.4	1,922.7	1,123.2	799.3	1,930.9	584.6	1,347.3	1,394.1
2008	15,643.0	11,663.6	11,514.9	145.7	2,007.0	1,185.0	821.5	1,970.9	606.3	1,365.3	1,467.0
2009	15,236.3	11,234.6	11,071.4	168.1	1,994.8	1,161.9	832.8	2,006.7	636.6	1,370.5	1,452.4
2010	15,649.0	11,597.6	11,436.4	162.7	2,035.1	1,186.5	848.4	2,016.3	658.0	1,358.5	1,492.0
2011	15,891.5	11,825.7	11,670.5	155.3	2,058.7	1,186.4	872.2	2,007.2	664.3	1,343.0	1,500.9
2012	16,254.0	12,206.4	12,058.5	148.0	2,058.4	1,168.8	889.6	1,989.1	663.7	1,325.5	1,493.6
2013	16,553.3	12,506.7	12,328.6	177.9	2,071.4	1,174.6	896.7	1,975.7	652.0	1,323.7	1,505.6
2014	16,932.1	12,874.0	12,695.2	178.3	2,088.0	1,182.5	905.5	1,971.9	646.9	1,324.7	1,516.6
2015	17,390.3	13,313.2	13,123.8	190.0	2,104.4	1,180.9	923.2	1,977.2	642.5	1,334.2	1,520.7
2016	17,680.3	13,564.1	13,364.9	203.0	2,126.4	1,186.6	939.5	1,995.5	645.4	1,349.5	1,528.9
2017	18,076.7	13,924.1	13,726.5	197.4	2,151.7	1,201.0	950.5	2,009.6	646.2	1,362.5	1,536.7
2018	18,609.1	14,412.5	14,209.4	202.1	2,185.7	1,221.4	964.0	2,024.4	649.7	1,373.9	1,559.9
2019	19,036.1	14,791.5	14,596.3	185.4	2,214.5	1,236.9	977.3	2,047.1	656.8	1,389.4	1,580.8
2020	18,509.1	14,285.3	14,090.9	189.4	2,189.5	1,239.5	950.2	2,042.3	675.5	1,367.1	1,584.2
2021	19,609.8	15,379.2	15,193.3	169.9	2,213.7	1,253.6	960.4	2,049.7	683.4	1,366.9	1,600.8
2022 p	20,015.4	15,719.0	15,541.5	161.4	2,255.3	1,274.4	981.0	2,076.1	687.6	1,388.8	1,624.9
2019: I	18,835.4	14,622.3	14,426.5	187.5	2,207.1	1,235.9	971.0	2,021.8	644.4	1,376.3	1,578.6
II	18,962.2	14,725.2	14,528.5	188.5	2,213.0	1,236.5	976.2	2,040.3	658.0	1,381.5	1,580.4
III	19,130.9	14,878.5	14,683.2	184.7	2,215.8	1,236.7	978.8	2,054.9	661.4	1,392.7	1,581.2
IV	19,215.7	14,940.1	14,747.1	180.7	2,222.1	1,238.3	983.3	2,071.5	663.3	1,407.1	1,583.2
2020: I	18,989.9	14,697.6	14,493.6	201.5	2,230.2	1,240.4	989.3	2,073.8	667.1	1,405.6	1,585.0
II	17,378.7	13,194.3	13,014.4	175.1	2,152.3	1,240.6	913.0	2,015.5	673.5	1,342.8	1,585.1
III	18,743.7	14,531.2	14,334.3	191.0	2,181.4	1,238.9	942.8	2,047.4	681.9	1,366.1	1,583.6
IV	18,924.3	14,718.3	14,521.1	189.8	2,194.0	1,238.1	955.7	2,032.6	679.4	1,353.9	1,583.2
2021: I	19,216.2	15,008.4	14,819.1	175.6	2,201.1	1,245.1	956.0	2,033.6	681.7	1,352.8	1,591.1
II	19,544.2	15,324.7	15,138.4	170.1	2,210.6	1,251.3	959.5	2,041.5	684.0	1,358.4	1,598.4
III	19,672.6	15,423.3	15,240.1	166.4	2,219.0	1,257.5	961.8	2,062.8	683.9	1,379.2	1,605.1
IV	20,006.2	15,760.5	15,575.8	167.4	2,224.3	1,260.5	964.2	2,060.8	684.2	1,377.0	1,608.8
2022: I	19,924.1	15,663.3	15,478.8	167.3	2,230.5	1,260.8	969.8	2,066.7	686.2	1,381.0	1,610.0
II	19,895.3	15,607.6	15,430.5	160.8	2,250.6	1,272.5	978.3	2,070.4	686.8	1,384.0	1,623.0
III	20,054.7	15,743.8	15,569.1	158.9	2,265.4	1,280.4	985.2	2,079.8	688.1	1,392.0	1,631.5
IV p	20,187.5	15,861.3	15,687.4	158.4	2,274.6	1,283.9	990.6	2,087.3	689.3	1,398.2	1,635.2

[1] Gross domestic business value added equals gross domestic product excluding gross value added of households and institutions and of general government. Nonfarm value added equals gross domestic business value added excluding gross farm value added.

[2] Equals compensation of employees of nonprofit institutions, the rental value of nonresidential fixed assets owned and used by nonprofit institutions serving households, and rental income of persons for tenant-occupied housing owned by nonprofit institutions.

[3] Equals compensation of general government employees plus general government consumption of fixed capital.

Source: Department of Commerce (Bureau of Economic Analysis).

TABLE B–8. Gross domestic product (GDP) by industry, value added, in current dollars and as a percentage of GDP, 1997–2021

[Billions of dollars; except as noted]

Year	Gross domestic product	Private industries									
		Total private industries	Agriculture, forestry, fishing, and hunting	Mining	Construction	Manufacturing			Utilities	Wholesale trade	Retail trade
						Total manufacturing	Durable goods	Nondurable goods			
	Value added										
1997	8,577.6	7,432.0	108.6	95.1	339.6	1,382.9	823.8	559.1	171.5	527.5	579.9
1998	9,062.8	7,871.5	99.8	81.7	379.8	1,430.6	850.7	579.9	163.7	563.7	626.9
1999	9,631.2	8,378.8	92.6	84.6	417.7	1,489.6	875.2	614.4	180.0	584.2	652.8
2000	10,251.0	8,927.9	98.3	110.5	461.2	1,549.8	924.6	625.2	180.1	622.5	685.4
2001	10,581.9	9,189.0	99.8	123.9	486.4	1,473.5	833.3	640.3	181.3	613.7	709.4
2002	10,929.1	9,454.7	95.9	112.4	493.5	1,468.3	832.8	635.6	177.6	613.1	732.6
2003	11,456.5	9,904.1	114.6	138.9	525.2	1,524.0	863.1	660.9	183.9	641.4	769.5
2004	12,217.2	10,585.9	143.8	166.4	584.6	1,607.8	905.0	702.8	199.1	697.1	795.5
2005	13,039.2	11,328.9	129.5	225.4	651.6	1,692.5	956.3	736.2	197.9	754.7	840.6
2006	13,815.6	12,023.6	126.4	273.1	697.1	1,793.5	1,004.2	789.3	226.7	811.4	869.8
2007	14,474.2	12,587.2	145.5	314.1	715.7	1,845.8	1,031.0	814.7	231.9	858.2	869.4
2008	14,769.9	12,788.3	146.0	392.5	649.3	1,802.1	1,000.2	801.8	241.7	884.8	848.8
2009	14,478.1	12,433.0	129.1	275.4	565.4	1,700.8	880.4	820.5	257.8	833.8	827.3
2010	15,049.0	12,941.0	144.9	306.4	525.7	1,799.8	965.5	834.3	279.1	890.0	852.1
2011	15,599.7	13,462.7	179.2	357.8	525.6	1,873.6	1,017.9	855.7	288.3	937.1	873.1
2012	16,254.0	14,094.5	178.7	360.5	554.9	1,934.7	1,065.2	869.5	280.7	1,000.3	910.0
2013	16,843.2	14,630.7	214.3	387.8	588.7	1,997.3	1,104.5	892.8	286.9	1,042.2	950.6
2014	17,550.7	15,279.3	198.9	417.0	637.7	2,053.5	1,135.6	917.9	298.3	1,089.6	975.1
2015	18,206.0	15,866.6	180.1	261.7	695.3	2,131.0	1,184.4	946.6	299.2	1,143.6	1,020.3
2016	18,695.1	16,310.9	165.8	218.1	747.7	2,102.9	1,187.8	915.1	302.0	1,135.8	1,053.0
2017	19,477.3	17,031.7	175.4	275.4	800.6	2,199.7	1,235.6	964.0	311.6	1,165.7	1,081.9
2018	20,533.1	17,987.5	174.4	321.6	847.3	2,335.0	1,299.3	1,035.7	319.0	1,217.4	1,119.9
2019	21,381.0	18,762.5	159.5	298.7	904.0	2,368.9	1,328.1	1,040.8	330.8	1,277.4	1,166.5
2020	21,060.5	18,360.2	162.2	201.1	894.4	2,241.8	1,273.9	967.8	338.0	1,264.9	1,205.1
2021	23,315.1	20,502.2	206.6	333.9	945.3	2,496.8	1,395.0	1,101.8	378.4	1,444.5	1,391.1
	Percent	Industry value added as a percentage of GDP (percent)									
1997	100.0	86.6	1.3	1.1	4.0	16.1	9.6	6.5	2.0	6.2	6.8
1998	100.0	86.9	1.1	.9	4.2	15.8	9.4	6.4	1.8	6.2	6.9
1999	100.0	87.0	1.0	.9	4.3	15.5	9.1	6.4	1.9	6.1	6.8
2000	100.0	87.1	1.0	1.1	4.5	15.1	9.0	6.1	1.8	6.1	6.7
2001	100.0	86.8	.9	1.2	4.6	13.9	7.9	6.1	1.7	5.8	6.7
2002	100.0	86.5	.9	1.0	4.5	13.4	7.6	5.8	1.6	5.6	6.7
2003	100.0	86.4	1.0	1.2	4.6	13.3	7.5	5.8	1.6	5.6	6.7
2004	100.0	86.6	1.2	1.4	4.8	13.2	7.4	5.8	1.6	5.7	6.5
2005	100.0	86.9	1.0	1.7	5.0	13.0	7.3	5.6	1.5	5.8	6.4
2006	100.0	87.0	.9	2.0	5.0	13.0	7.3	5.7	1.6	5.9	6.3
2007	100.0	87.0	1.0	2.2	4.9	12.8	7.1	5.6	1.6	5.9	6.0
2008	100.0	86.6	1.0	2.7	4.4	12.2	6.8	5.4	1.6	6.0	5.7
2009	100.0	85.9	.9	1.9	3.9	11.7	6.1	5.7	1.8	5.8	5.7
2010	100.0	86.0	1.0	2.0	3.5	12.0	6.4	5.5	1.9	5.9	5.7
2011	100.0	86.3	1.1	2.3	3.4	12.0	6.5	5.5	1.8	6.0	5.6
2012	100.0	86.7	1.1	2.2	3.4	11.9	6.6	5.3	1.7	6.2	5.6
2013	100.0	86.9	1.3	2.3	3.5	11.9	6.6	5.3	1.7	6.2	5.6
2014	100.0	87.1	1.1	2.4	3.6	11.7	6.5	5.2	1.7	6.2	5.6
2015	100.0	87.2	1.0	1.4	3.8	11.7	6.5	5.2	1.6	6.3	5.6
2016	100.0	87.2	.9	1.2	4.0	11.2	6.4	4.9	1.6	6.1	5.6
2017	100.0	87.4	.9	1.4	4.1	11.3	6.3	4.9	1.6	6.0	5.6
2018	100.0	87.6	.8	1.6	4.1	11.4	6.3	5.0	1.6	5.9	5.5
2019	100.0	87.8	.7	1.4	4.2	11.1	6.2	4.9	1.5	6.0	5.5
2020	100.0	87.2	.8	1.0	4.2	10.6	6.0	4.6	1.6	6.0	5.7
2021	100.0	87.9	.9	1.4	4.1	10.7	6.0	4.7	1.6	6.2	6.0

[1] Consists of agriculture, forestry, fishing, and hunting; mining; construction; and manufacturing.

[2] Consists of utilities; wholesale trade; retail trade; transportation and warehousing; information; finance, insurance, real estate, rental, and leasing; professional and business services; educational services, health care, and social assistance; arts, entertainment, recreation, accommodation, and food services; and other services, except government.

Note: Data shown in Tables B–8 and B–9 are consistent with the 2022 annual revision of the industry accounts released in September 2022. For details see *Survey of Current Business*, October 2022.

See next page for continuation of table.

TABLE B–8. Gross domestic product (GDP) by industry, value added, in current dollars and as a percentage of GDP, 1997–2021—*Continued*

[Billions of dollars; except as noted]

Year	Private industries—Continued							Government	Private goods-producing industries[1]	Private services-producing industries[2]
	Transportation and warehousing	Information	Finance, insurance, real estate, rental, and leasing	Professional and business services	Educational services, health care, and social assistance	Arts, entertainment, recreation, accommodation, and food services	Other services, except government			
	Value added									
1997	257.3	394.1	1,612.4	840.6	590.6	301.8	230.3	1,145.6	1,926.1	5,505.9
1998	280.0	434.6	1,710.1	914.0	615.8	322.1	248.7	1,191.3	1,991.8	5,879.7
1999	290.1	485.3	1,835.4	997.4	654.1	354.2	260.9	1,252.3	2,084.5	6,294.3
2000	307.8	471.2	1,974.7	1,104.9	695.4	386.5	279.7	1,323.0	2,219.9	6,708.0
2001	308.0	502.3	2,129.4	1,155.3	749.8	390.7	265.5	1,392.9	2,183.7	7,005.3
2002	305.6	550.5	2,210.0	1,189.8	807.0	413.5	284.9	1,474.4	2,170.2	7,284.6
2003	321.4	564.8	2,294.2	1,247.4	862.7	432.1	283.8	1,552.3	2,302.8	7,601.3
2004	352.0	620.3	2,392.8	1,340.9	927.2	461.1	297.2	1,631.3	2,502.7	8,083.2
2005	375.6	642.0	2,611.4	1,446.0	970.2	481.1	310.6	1,710.3	2,698.9	8,630.0
2006	410.3	651.9	2,745.2	1,546.5	1,035.3	511.4	325.0	1,792.0	2,890.1	9,133.5
2007	414.0	707.5	2,865.6	1,667.3	1,088.0	533.6	330.5	1,887.1	3,021.1	9,566.0
2008	427.0	743.8	2,816.1	1,777.9	1,185.0	542.9	330.3	1,981.6	2,989.8	9,798.4
2009	404.4	721.4	2,903.1	1,688.1	1,267.0	533.0	326.4	2,045.1	2,670.7	9,762.3
2010	433.5	754.9	2,990.4	1,768.5	1,311.3	556.2	328.2	2,108.0	2,776.8	10,164.2
2011	452.5	763.0	3,080.8	1,860.0	1,356.2	581.9	333.5	2,137.1	2,936.1	10,526.5
2012	473.3	762.7	3,289.2	1,968.9	1,409.3	622.7	348.6	2,159.5	3,028.8	11,065.7
2013	492.1	831.4	3,362.0	2,020.1	1,448.4	652.3	356.7	2,212.5	3,188.0	11,442.7
2014	522.5	844.4	3,560.7	2,120.2	1,492.6	691.9	376.8	2,271.4	3,307.1	11,972.2
2015	566.1	907.8	3,713.8	2,237.7	1,571.2	747.0	391.6	2,339.4	3,268.2	12,598.4
2016	582.4	970.3	3,883.2	2,306.2	1,652.6	790.5	400.5	2,384.2	3,234.5	13,076.4
2017	609.1	1,004.2	4,020.0	2,434.9	1,711.2	828.7	413.4	2,445.6	3,451.1	13,580.6
2018	648.7	1,067.4	4,258.3	2,588.4	1,784.8	868.8	436.4	2,545.5	3,678.3	14,309.2
2019	682.7	1,126.7	4,482.7	2,723.9	1,874.3	912.7	453.6	2,618.5	3,731.1	15,031.4
2020	588.3	1,171.8	4,592.7	2,717.1	1,869.7	684.6	428.6	2,700.3	3,499.4	14,860.8
2021	688.2	1,313.3	4,885.6	3,037.5	2,005.6	905.5	469.9	2,812.9	3,982.6	16,519.6
	Industry value added as a percentage of GDP (percent)									
1997	3.0	4.6	18.8	9.8	6.9	3.5	2.7	13.4	22.5	64.2
1998	3.1	4.8	18.9	10.1	6.8	3.6	2.7	13.1	22.0	64.9
1999	3.0	5.0	19.1	10.4	6.8	3.7	2.7	13.0	21.6	65.4
2000	3.0	4.6	19.3	10.8	6.8	3.8	2.7	12.9	21.7	65.4
2001	2.9	4.7	20.1	10.9	7.1	3.7	2.5	13.2	20.6	66.2
2002	2.8	5.0	20.2	10.9	7.4	3.8	2.6	13.5	19.9	66.7
2003	2.8	4.9	20.0	10.9	7.5	3.8	2.5	13.5	20.1	66.3
2004	2.9	5.1	19.6	11.0	7.6	3.8	2.4	13.4	20.5	66.2
2005	2.9	4.9	20.0	11.1	7.4	3.7	2.4	13.1	20.7	66.2
2006	3.0	4.7	19.9	11.2	7.5	3.7	2.4	13.0	20.9	66.1
2007	2.9	4.9	19.8	11.5	7.5	3.7	2.3	13.0	20.9	66.1
2008	2.9	5.0	19.1	12.0	8.0	3.7	2.2	13.4	20.2	66.3
2009	2.8	5.0	20.1	11.7	8.8	3.7	2.3	14.1	18.4	67.4
2010	2.9	5.0	19.9	11.8	8.7	3.7	2.2	14.0	18.5	67.5
2011	2.9	4.9	19.7	11.9	8.7	3.7	2.1	13.7	18.8	67.5
2012	2.9	4.7	20.2	12.1	8.7	3.8	2.1	13.3	18.6	68.1
2013	2.9	4.9	20.0	12.0	8.6	3.9	2.1	13.1	18.9	67.9
2014	3.0	4.8	20.3	12.1	8.5	3.9	2.1	12.9	18.8	68.2
2015	3.1	5.0	20.4	12.3	8.6	4.1	2.2	12.8	18.0	69.2
2016	3.1	5.2	20.8	12.3	8.8	4.2	2.1	12.8	17.3	69.9
2017	3.1	5.2	20.6	12.5	8.8	4.3	2.1	12.6	17.7	69.7
2018	3.2	5.2	20.7	12.6	8.7	4.2	2.1	12.4	17.9	69.7
2019	3.2	5.3	21.0	12.7	8.8	4.3	2.1	12.2	17.5	70.3
2020	2.8	5.6	21.8	12.9	8.9	3.3	2.0	12.8	16.6	70.6
2021	3.0	5.6	21.0	13.0	8.6	3.9	2.0	12.1	17.1	70.9

Note (cont'd): Value added is the contribution of each private industry and of government to GDP. Value added is equal to an industry's gross output minus its intermediate inputs. Current-dollar value added is calculated as the sum of distributions by an industry to its labor and capital, which are derived from the components of gross domestic income.

Value added industry data shown in Tables B–8 and B–9 are based on the 2012 North American Industry Classification System (NAICS).

Source: Department of Commerce (Bureau of Economic Analysis).

Table B–9. Real gross domestic product by industry, value added, and percent changes, 1997–2021

Year	Gross domestic product	Private industries: Total private industries	Agriculture, forestry, fishing, and hunting	Mining	Construction	Manufacturing: Total manufacturing	Durable goods	Nondurable goods	Utilities	Wholesale trade	Retail trade
	Chain-type quantity indexes for value added (2012=100)										
1997	70.931	70.046	77.781	72.719	124.354	73.447	54.511	107.960	81.637	67.499	76.759
1998	74.110	73.402	75.893	75.656	130.050	76.469	58.994	106.119	77.993	74.131	84.135
1999	77.663	77.229	78.203	73.421	135.421	80.746	63.131	109.889	90.800	76.606	87.240
2000	80.830	80.653	89.714	65.086	140.845	86.510	70.473	110.880	91.942	80.289	90.127
2001	81.601	81.255	86.605	75.515	138.221	83.058	66.103	109.949	76.548	81.714	93.502
2002	82.985	82.670	89.789	77.598	133.748	83.793	67.503	109.179	79.187	82.739	97.602
2003	85.305	84.993	97.128	68.794	136.061	88.483	72.557	112.634	77.791	87.144	102.667
2004	88.592	88.565	104.991	69.198	140.907	94.727	77.761	120.408	82.510	91.106	104.409
2005	91.678	91.949	109.754	70.313	141.526	97.591	83.117	118.265	78.281	95.261	107.790
2006	94.229	94.880	111.588	81.229	138.689	103.211	89.557	122.110	83.357	98.148	108.680
2007	96.123	96.595	99.272	87.622	134.513	106.720	93.800	124.218	85.179	101.407	105.184
2008	96.241	96.324	99.372	84.835	121.342	104.522	94.301	117.744	89.539	101.651	101.255
2009	93.739	93.332	110.461	97.011	103.961	94.688	80.569	114.123	84.369	89.214	96.810
2010	96.278	95.883	107.225	85.963	98.810	100.081	90.953	112.119	94.906	94.469	99.023
2011	97.770	97.540	103.127	89.386	97.298	100.599	97.223	104.835	98.679	96.638	99.257
2012	100.000	100.000	100.000	100.000	100.000	100.000	100.000	100.000	100.000	100.000	100.000
2013	101.842	101.880	116.130	103.744	102.401	102.945	102.358	103.671	98.755	102.072	103.046
2014	104.172	104.617	116.724	114.972	104.349	104.601	103.902	105.467	94.883	106.032	104.956
2015	106.991	107.828	124.160	125.161	109.037	105.768	105.519	106.067	94.918	110.553	108.872
2016	108.775	109.748	131.263	118.502	113.193	105.458	105.707	105.121	100.030	109.159	112.919
2017	111.214	112.362	128.547	120.220	117.148	108.889	109.965	107.504	101.045	109.560	116.565
2018	114.489	115.952	132.178	121.676	119.780	113.474	115.202	111.281	100.705	110.698	120.158
2019	117.116	118.900	124.392	136.969	121.509	115.310	116.094	114.274	101.127	110.195	122.726
2020	113.875	115.159	127.921	135.452	116.832	110.069	110.822	109.083	104.811	110.182	119.205
2021	120.646	122.856	117.076	113.426	119.698	117.424	121.576	112.321	100.553	116.297	122.324
	Percent change from year earlier										
1997	4.4	4.9	8.5	3.7	0.5	6.6	9.1	3.1	–5.2	10.9	7.5
1998	4.5	4.8	–2.4	4.0	4.6	4.1	8.2	–1.7	–4.5	9.8	9.6
1999	4.8	5.2	3.0	–3.0	4.1	5.6	7.0	3.6	16.4	3.3	3.7
2000	4.1	4.4	14.7	–11.4	4.0	7.1	11.6	.9	1.3	4.8	3.3
2001	1.0	.7	–3.5	16.0	–1.9	–4.0	–6.2	–.8	–16.7	1.8	3.7
2002	1.7	1.7	3.7	2.8	–3.2	.9	2.1	–.7	3.4	1.3	4.4
2003	2.8	2.8	8.2	–11.3	1.7	5.6	7.5	3.2	–1.8	5.3	5.2
2004	3.9	4.2	8.1	.6	3.6	7.1	7.2	6.9	6.1	4.5	1.7
2005	3.5	3.8	4.5	1.6	.4	3.0	6.9	–1.8	–5.1	4.6	3.2
2006	2.8	3.2	1.7	15.5	–2.0	5.8	7.7	3.3	6.5	3.0	.8
2007	2.0	1.8	–11.0	7.9	–3.0	3.4	4.7	1.7	2.2	3.3	–3.2
2008	.1	–.3	.1	–3.2	–9.8	–2.1	.5	–5.2	5.1	.2	–3.7
2009	–2.6	–3.1	11.2	14.4	–14.3	–9.4	–14.6	–3.1	–5.8	–12.2	–4.4
2010	2.7	2.7	–2.9	–11.4	–5.0	5.7	12.9	–1.8	12.5	5.9	2.3
2011	1.5	1.7	–3.8	4.0	–1.5	.5	6.9	–6.5	4.0	2.3	.2
2012	2.3	2.5	–3.0	11.9	2.8	–.6	2.9	–4.6	1.3	3.5	.7
2013	1.8	1.9	16.1	3.7	2.4	2.9	2.4	3.7	–1.2	2.1	3.0
2014	2.3	2.7	.5	10.8	1.9	1.6	1.5	1.7	–3.9	3.9	1.9
2015	2.7	3.1	6.4	8.9	4.5	1.1	1.6	.6	.0	4.3	3.7
2016	1.7	1.8	5.7	–5.3	3.8	–.3	.2	–.9	5.4	–1.3	3.7
2017	2.2	2.4	–2.1	1.4	3.5	3.3	4.0	2.3	1.0	.4	3.2
2018	2.9	3.2	2.8	1.2	2.2	4.2	4.8	3.5	–.3	1.0	3.1
2019	2.3	2.5	–5.9	12.6	1.4	1.6	.8	2.7	.4	–.5	2.1
2020	–2.8	–3.1	2.8	–1.1	–3.8	–4.5	–4.5	–4.5	3.6	.0	–2.9
2021	5.9	6.7	–8.5	–16.3	2.5	6.7	9.7	3.0	–4.1	5.5	2.6

[1] Consists of agriculture, forestry, fishing, and hunting; mining; construction; and manufacturing

[2] Consists of utilities; wholesale trade; retail trade; transportation and warehousing; information; finance, insurance, real estate, rental, and leasing; professional and business services; educational services, health care, and social assistance; arts, entertainment, recreation, accommodation, and food services; and other services, except government

See next page for continuation of table

Table B–9. Real gross domestic product by industry, value added, and percent changes, 1997–2021—*Continued*

Year	Private industries—Continued							Govern-ment	Private goods-producing industries[1]	Private services-producing industries[2]
	Transpor-tation and ware-housing	Information	Finance, insurance, real estate, rental, and leasing	Profes-sional and business services	Educational services, health care, and social assistance	Arts, entertain-ment, recreation, accommo-dation, and food services	Other services, except govern-ment			
	Chain-type quantity indexes for value added (2012=100)									
1997	84.687	45.514	64.047	63.505	65.087	78.592	115.380	87.664	81.001	67.082
1998	88.991	50.255	66.832	66.440	65.370	80.744	120.186	88.684	84.104	70.519
1999	89.731	56.341	71.072	69.573	67.564	85.167	120.996	89.743	88.164	74.287
2000	89.480	55.253	74.812	73.644	70.038	90.255	123.725	91.570	93.389	77.217
2001	83.650	58.676	78.601	75.849	71.815	87.220	111.631	92.529	91.021	78.624
2002	80.670	64.338	79.078	76.729	74.683	89.599	114.679	94.176	91.172	80.375
2003	83.579	66.391	79.608	79.196	77.657	91.907	111.481	95.338	94.634	82.397
2004	90.509	74.041	81.082	81.122	81.355	96.013	112.927	96.193	100.195	85.441
2005	94.860	78.974	86.517	84.732	82.879	96.269	113.691	97.080	102.577	89.093
2006	100.505	81.801	88.398	87.160	86.244	98.946	114.286	97.638	107.155	91.577
2007	99.790	89.943	90.254	90.088	86.927	98.432	111.693	98.590	108.829	93.305
2008	98.863	95.681	88.297	94.308	92.430	96.222	107.558	100.494	104.591	94.115
2009	92.702	93.038	92.938	88.066	95.531	90.582	101.117	100.556	97.383	92.247
2010	97.391	98.573	94.383	91.902	96.650	94.163	99.308	101.076	98.450	95.186
2011	99.295	100.202	95.951	95.650	98.364	97.550	98.489	100.755	98.726	97.215
2012	100.000	100.000	100.000	100.000	100.000	100.000	100.000	100.000	100.000	100.000
2013	101.389	108.867	99.486	101.208	101.220	102.051	99.174	99.296	103.727	101.376
2014	104.448	111.584	101.652	105.828	103.045	105.746	102.044	99.081	106.526	104.095
2015	107.144	123.147	102.770	109.409	106.918	109.018	102.620	99.199	109.624	107.334
2016	108.740	134.001	103.834	111.630	109.940	110.917	101.787	100.179	110.207	109.587
2017	113.329	142.355	104.183	116.793	111.831	113.696	102.344	101.136	113.401	112.056
2018	117.634	153.756	105.964	123.444	114.941	115.574	105.142	101.998	117.291	115.569
2019	118.854	162.823	108.719	128.766	118.266	117.763	105.478	102.603	119.754	118.636
2020	104.580	169.253	108.644	127.215	114.867	85.257	95.030	102.241	115.166	115.103
2021	112.400	192.824	113.824	142.051	120.115	109.348	100.187	102.794	118.736	123.803
	Percent change from year earlier									
1997	4.4	–1.3	4.2	7.3	1.8	5.7	4.7	1.3	5.4	4.7
1998	5.1	10.4	4.3	4.6	0.4	2.7	4.2	1.2	3.8	5.1
1999	.8	12.1	6.3	4.7	3.4	5.5	.7	1.2	4.8	5.3
2000	–.3	–1.9	5.3	5.9	3.7	6.0	2.3	2.0	5.9	3.9
2001	–6.5	6.2	5.1	3.0	2.5	–3.4	–9.8	1.0	–2.5	1.8
2002	–3.6	9.6	.6	1.2	4.0	2.7	2.7	1.8	.2	2.2
2003	3.6	3.2	.7	3.2	4.0	2.6	–2.8	1.2	3.8	2.5
2004	8.3	11.5	1.9	2.4	4.8	4.5	1.3	.9	5.9	3.7
2005	4.8	6.7	6.7	4.5	1.9	.3	.7	.9	2.4	4.3
2006	6.0	3.6	2.2	2.9	4.1	2.8	.5	.6	4.5	2.8
2007	–.7	10.0	2.1	3.4	.8	–.5	–2.3	1.0	1.6	1.9
2008	–.9	6.4	–2.2	4.7	6.3	–2.2	–3.7	1.9	–3.9	.9
2009	–6.2	–2.8	5.3	–6.6	3.4	–5.9	–6.0	.1	–6.9	–2.0
2010	5.1	5.9	1.6	4.4	1.2	4.0	–1.8	.5	1.1	3.2
2011	2.0	1.7	1.7	4.1	1.8	3.6	–.8	–.3	.3	2.1
2012	.7	–.2	4.2	4.5	1.7	2.5	1.5	–.7	1.3	2.9
2013	1.4	8.9	–.5	1.2	1.2	2.1	–.8	–.7	3.7	1.4
2014	3.0	2.5	2.2	4.6	1.8	3.6	2.9	–.2	2.7	2.7
2015	2.6	10.4	1.1	3.4	3.8	3.1	.6	.1	2.9	3.1
2016	1.5	8.8	1.0	2.0	2.8	1.7	–.8	1.0	.5	2.1
2017	4.2	6.2	.3	4.6	1.7	2.5	.5	1.0	2.9	2.3
2018	3.8	8.0	1.7	5.7	2.8	1.7	2.7	.9	3.4	3.1
2019	1.0	5.9	2.6	4.3	2.9	1.9	.3	.6	2.1	2.7
2020	–12.0	3.9	–.1	–1.2	–2.9	–27.6	–9.9	–.4	–3.8	–3.0
2021	7.5	13.9	4.8	11.7	4.6	28.3	5.4	.5	3.1	7.6

Note: Data are based on the 2012 North American Industry Classification System (NAICS).
See Note, Table B–8.

Source: Department of Commerce (Bureau of Economic Analysis).

Table B–10. Personal consumption expenditures, 1972–2022

[Billions of dollars; quarterly data at seasonally adjusted annual rates]

Year or quarter	Personal consumption expenditures	Goods						Services					Addendum: Personal consumption expenditures excluding food and energy[2]
		Total	Durable		Nondurable			Total	Household consumption expenditures				
			Total[1]	Motor vehicles and parts	Total[1]	Food and beverages purchased for off-premises consumption	Gasoline and other energy goods		Total[1]	Housing and utilities	Health care	Financial services and insurance	
1972	768.2	373.8	116.4	49.4	257.4	114.5	29.4	394.3	381.5	131.2	59.8	37.1	605.8
1973	849.6	416.6	130.5	54.4	286.1	126.7	34.3	432.9	419.2	143.5	67.2	39.9	668.5
1974	930.2	451.5	130.2	48.2	321.4	143.0	43.8	478.6	463.1	158.6	76.1	44.1	719.7
1975	1,030.5	491.3	142.2	52.6	349.2	156.6	48.0	539.2	522.2	176.5	89.0	51.8	797.3
1976	1,147.7	546.3	168.6	68.2	377.7	167.3	53.0	601.4	582.4	194.7	101.8	56.8	894.7
1977	1,274.0	600.4	192.0	79.8	408.4	179.8	57.8	673.6	653.0	217.8	115.7	65.1	998.6
1978	1,422.3	663.6	213.3	89.2	450.2	196.1	61.5	758.7	735.7	244.3	131.2	76.7	1,122.4
1979	1,585.4	737.9	226.3	90.2	511.6	218.4	80.4	847.5	821.4	273.4	148.8	83.6	1,239.7
1980	1,750.7	799.8	226.4	84.4	573.4	239.2	101.9	950.9	920.8	312.5	171.7	91.7	1,353.1
1981	1,934.0	869.4	243.9	93.0	625.4	255.3	113.4	1,064.6	1,030.4	352.1	201.9	98.5	1,501.5
1982	2,071.3	899.3	253.0	100.0	646.3	267.1	108.4	1,172.0	1,134.0	387.5	225.2	113.7	1,622.9
1983	2,281.6	973.8	295.0	122.9	678.8	277.0	106.5	1,307.8	1,267.1	421.2	253.1	141.0	1,817.2
1984	2,492.3	1,063.7	342.2	147.2	721.5	291.1	108.2	1,428.6	1,383.3	457.5	276.5	150.8	2,008.1
1985	2,712.8	1,137.6	380.4	170.1	757.2	303.0	110.5	1,575.2	1,527.3	500.6	302.2	178.2	2,210.3
1986	2,886.3	1,195.6	421.4	187.5	774.2	316.4	91.2	1,690.7	1,638.0	537.0	330.2	187.7	2,391.3
1987	3,076.3	1,256.3	442.0	188.2	814.3	324.3	96.4	1,820.0	1,764.3	571.6	366.0	189.5	2,566.6
1988	3,330.0	1,337.3	475.1	202.2	862.3	342.8	99.9	1,992.7	1,929.4	614.4	410.1	202.9	2,793.1
1989	3,576.8	1,423.8	494.3	207.8	929.5	365.4	110.4	2,153.0	2,084.9	655.2	451.2	222.3	3,002.1
1990	3,809.0	1,491.3	497.1	205.1	994.2	391.2	124.2	2,317.7	2,241.8	696.5	506.2	230.8	3,194.9
1991	3,943.4	1,497.4	477.2	185.7	1,020.3	403.0	121.1	2,446.0	2,365.9	735.2	555.8	250.1	3,314.4
1992	4,197.6	1,563.3	508.1	204.8	1,055.2	404.5	125.0	2,634.3	2,546.4	771.1	612.8	277.0	3,561.7
1993	4,452.0	1,642.3	551.5	224.7	1,090.8	413.5	126.9	2,809.6	2,719.6	814.9	648.8	314.0	3,796.6
1994	4,721.0	1,746.6	607.2	249.8	1,139.4	432.1	129.2	2,974.4	2,876.6	863.3	680.5	327.9	4,042.5
1995	4,962.6	1,815.5	635.7	255.7	1,179.8	443.7	133.4	3,147.1	3,044.7	913.7	719.9	347.0	4,267.2
1996	5,244.6	1,917.7	676.3	273.5	1,241.4	461.9	144.7	3,326.9	3,216.9	962.4	752.1	372.1	4,513.0
1997	5,536.8	2,006.5	715.5	293.1	1,291.0	474.8	147.7	3,530.3	3,424.7	1,009.8	790.9	408.9	4,787.8
1998	5,877.2	2,108.4	779.3	320.2	1,329.1	487.4	132.4	3,768.8	3,645.0	1,065.5	832.0	446.1	5,132.4
1999	6,283.8	2,287.1	855.6	350.7	1,431.5	515.5	146.5	3,996.7	3,858.5	1,123.1	863.6	484.6	5,495.9
2000	6,767.2	2,453.2	912.6	363.2	1,540.6	540.6	184.5	4,314.0	4,156.0	1,198.6	918.4	541.9	5,904.5
2001	7,073.8	2,525.6	941.5	383.3	1,584.1	564.0	178.0	4,548.2	4,369.1	1,287.5	996.6	529.3	6,182.2
2002	7,348.9	2,598.8	985.4	401.3	1,613.4	575.1	167.9	4,750.1	4,551.8	1,329.5	1,082.9	539.0	6,460.4
2003	7,740.7	2,722.6	1,017.8	401.5	1,704.8	599.6	196.4	5,018.2	4,812.6	1,391.1	1,154.0	574.2	6,784.4
2004	8,232.0	2,902.0	1,080.6	409.3	1,821.4	632.6	232.7	5,329.9	5,123.6	1,466.6	1,238.9	619.3	7,198.5
2005	8,769.1	3,082.9	1,128.6	410.0	1,954.3	668.2	283.8	5,686.1	5,475.9	1,580.1	1,320.5	676.8	7,627.2
2006	9,277.2	3,239.7	1,158.3	394.9	2,081.3	700.3	319.7	6,037.6	5,798.4	1,665.7	1,391.9	719.5	8,056.6
2007	9,746.6	3,367.0	1,188.0	400.6	2,179.0	737.3	345.5	6,379.6	6,130.8	1,759.6	1,478.2	762.7	8,453.5
2008	10,050.1	3,363.2	1,098.8	343.3	2,264.5	769.1	391.1	6,686.9	6,399.6	1,872.7	1,555.3	777.5	8,666.3
2009	9,891.2	3,180.0	1,012.1	318.6	2,167.9	772.9	287.0	6,711.2	6,422.0	1,900.0	1,632.7	720.5	8,616.1
2010	10,260.3	3,317.8	1,049.0	344.5	2,268.9	786.9	336.7	6,942.4	6,648.0	1,947.9	1,699.6	768.0	8,915.3
2011	10,698.9	3,518.1	1,093.5	365.2	2,424.6	819.5	413.8	7,180.7	6,868.9	1,983.3	1,757.1	811.1	9,246.6
2012	11,047.4	3,637.7	1,144.2	396.6	2,493.5	846.2	421.9	7,409.6	7,068.1	2,014.7	1,821.3	830.9	9,571.6
2013	11,363.5	3,730.0	1,189.4	417.5	2,540.6	864.0	418.2	7,633.6	7,281.0	2,083.5	1,858.2	869.3	9,861.4
2014	11,847.7	3,863.0	1,242.1	442.0	2,620.9	896.9	403.3	7,984.8	7,619.2	2,151.4	1,940.5	922.9	10,315.3
2015	12,263.5	3,923.0	1,307.6	475.3	2,615.4	921.0	309.4	8,340.5	7,968.9	2,206.6	2,057.3	974.4	10,807.4
2016	12,693.3	3,991.8	1,345.2	484.3	2,646.7	940.6	275.7	8,701.4	8,300.0	2,280.8	2,159.4	996.1	11,256.1
2017	13,233.6	4,159.4	1,398.2	502.2	2,761.1	972.9	309.9	9,074.2	8,659.8	2,363.6	2,237.6	1,064.8	11,726.1
2018	13,905.0	4,355.2	1,470.7	520.9	2,884.5	999.7	350.4	9,549.8	9,108.3	2,473.2	2,338.1	1,145.5	12,310.8
2019	14,392.7	4,473.5	1,510.5	517.0	2,963.0	1,030.8	337.1	9,919.2	9,480.3	2,572.7	2,462.8	1,142.3	12,784.7
2020	14,116.2	4,670.1	1,646.8	533.9	3,023.3	1,126.1	247.8	9,446.0	8,942.9	2,666.6	2,339.2	1,170.6	12,501.5
2021	15,902.6	5,496.5	2,060.2	688.7	3,436.3	1,205.0	369.4	10,406.1	9,940.5	2,775.4	2,583.5	1,275.0	14,069.3
2022 p	17,360.4	5,939.6	2,184.7	723.0	3,754.9	1,277.4	492.8	11,420.8	10,890.4	2,995.9	2,724.7	1,318.8	15,286.7
2019: I	14,145.9	4,382.5	1,470.5	505.9	2,912.1	1,016.8	324.8	9,763.4	9,328.4	2,536.9	2,412.4	1,138.5	12,559.2
II	14,323.7	4,461.4	1,498.1	513.1	2,963.3	1,027.4	348.4	9,862.4	9,421.6	2,554.4	2,452.8	1,139.4	12,714.7
III	14,482.2	4,508.5	1,527.7	519.5	2,980.8	1,039.6	334.2	9,973.7	9,531.8	2,587.1	2,472.2	1,144.0	12,868.1
IV	14,619.0	4,541.6	1,545.9	529.5	2,995.7	1,039.6	340.9	10,077.5	9,639.2	2,612.6	2,513.8	1,147.3	12,996.7
2020: I	14,440.2	4,532.2	1,495.3	480.1	3,036.9	1,113.0	308.3	9,907.9	9,400.9	2,620.8	2,429.4	1,165.5	12,794.5
II	13,049.8	4,344.3	1,486.5	474.1	2,857.8	1,131.3	188.2	8,705.5	8,156.0	2,663.8	2,046.9	1,138.3	11,483.8
III	14,388.7	4,897.0	1,796.5	583.9	3,100.4	1,132.6	247.3	9,491.7	9,011.9	2,682.0	2,397.3	1,175.0	12,763.1
IV	14,586.0	4,907.1	1,808.8	597.5	3,098.3	1,127.7	247.2	9,679.0	9,202.7	2,700.0	2,483.2	1,203.5	12,964.6
2021: I	15,131.5	5,265.3	1,990.9	666.9	3,274.4	1,175.2	305.6	9,866.2	9,403.8	2,727.2	2,496.2	1,237.3	13,396.5
II	15,813.5	5,529.9	2,113.5	736.8	3,416.4	1,194.2	354.0	10,283.6	9,835.0	2,752.8	2,571.7	1,263.5	14,010.7
III	16,147.3	5,517.1	2,035.0	656.3	3,482.2	1,211.7	387.6	10,630.2	10,167.6	2,792.4	2,615.1	1,287.0	14,284.3
IV	16,518.0	5,673.7	2,101.6	695.0	3,572.1	1,239.0	430.6	10,844.3	10,355.6	2,829.4	2,650.9	1,312.1	14,585.8
2022: I	16,874.8	5,843.2	2,183.9	737.1	3,659.3	1,248.5	474.5	11,031.6	10,525.4	2,896.1	2,673.4	1,309.8	14,863.6
II	17,261.3	5,953.6	2,181.8	724.5	3,771.9	1,260.4	541.0	11,307.7	10,779.2	2,958.4	2,684.8	1,309.1	15,158.2
III	17,542.7	5,988.6	2,195.8	713.1	3,792.7	1,289.9	492.3	11,554.1	11,015.6	3,027.3	2,742.8	1,320.9	15,452.7
IV p	17,762.7	5,972.9	2,177.2	717.3	3,795.6	1,310.6	463.3	11,789.9	11,241.5	3,101.8	2,797.6	1,335.6	15,672.4

[1] Includes other items not shown separately.

[2] Food consists of food and beverages purchased for off-premises consumption; food services, which include purchased meals and beverages, are not classified as food.

Source: Department of Commerce (Bureau of Economic Analysis).

TABLE B–11. Real personal consumption expenditures, 2002–2022

[Billions of chained (2012) dollars; quarterly data at seasonally adjusted annual rates]

Year or quarter	Personal consumption expenditures	Goods						Services					Addendum: Personal consumption expenditures excluding food and energy [2]
		Total	Durable		Nondurable			Total	Household consumption expenditures				
			Total [1]	Motor vehicles and parts	Total [1]	Food and beverages purchased for off-premises consumption	Gasoline and other energy goods		Total [1]	Housing and utilities	Health care	Financial services and insurance	
2002	9,106.2	2,947.6	820.2	416.9	2,157.5	744.5	455.2	6,168.7	5,983.7	1,705.6	1,440.7	710.3	7,734.5
2003	9,394.4	3,092.0	879.3	429.2	2,233.6	761.8	455.6	6,306.3	6,104.2	1,730.0	1,479.3	711.3	7,993.5
2004	9,748.6	3,250.0	952.1	441.1	2,306.5	779.5	459.4	6,498.5	6,294.1	1,774.1	1,531.2	736.0	8,317.8
2005	10,093.8	3,384.7	1,004.9	435.1	2,383.4	809.2	457.4	6,707.4	6,505.2	1,846.2	1,581.9	775.2	8,624.1
2006	10,386.2	3,509.7	1,049.3	419.0	2,461.6	834.0	456.3	6,873.1	6,641.7	1,867.5	1,618.2	790.5	8,896.6
2007	10,638.7	3,607.6	1,099.7	427.3	2,503.4	845.2	455.4	7,027.0	6,788.8	1,906.3	1,657.2	809.7	9,131.3
2008	10,654.7	3,498.9	1,036.4	373.1	2,463.9	831.0	437.5	7,154.9	6,877.4	1,959.9	1,697.9	829.4	9,181.1
2009	10,515.6	3,389.8	973.0	346.7	2,423.1	825.3	440.1	7,125.8	6,837.0	1,966.3	1,735.1	821.2	9,043.8
2010	10,716.0	3,485.7	1,027.3	360.0	2,461.3	837.7	437.9	7,230.4	6,932.0	2,011.3	1,761.7	820.0	9,224.2
2011	10,898.3	3,561.8	1,079.7	370.1	2,482.9	839.0	427.8	7,336.7	7,023.9	2,019.1	1,788.7	841.3	9,417.7
2012	11,047.4	3,637.7	1,144.2	396.6	2,493.5	846.2	421.9	7,409.6	7,068.1	2,014.7	1,821.3	830.9	9,571.6
2013	11,211.7	3,752.2	1,214.1	415.3	2,538.5	855.5	429.7	7,460.3	7,114.7	2,033.6	1,832.6	826.0	9,712.4
2014	11,515.3	3,905.1	1,301.6	439.4	2,605.3	871.4	430.0	7,613.2	7,267.9	2,039.3	1,892.8	828.7	9,996.8
2015	11,892.9	4,090.9	1,400.6	472.8	2,693.7	884.8	450.0	7,809.8	7,471.7	2,039.6	1,994.6	848.8	10,343.3
2016	12,187.7	4,231.7	1,476.0	487.2	2,760.5	913.2	453.0	7,968.5	7,614.8	2,049.4	2,070.0	830.7	10,605.2
2017	12,478.2	4,395.8	1,569.9	511.0	2,833.4	945.8	450.7	8,104.4	7,753.1	2,053.2	2,113.9	843.7	10,863.8
2018	12,837.3	4,568.4	1,677.0	530.1	2,903.7	966.8	448.3	8,299.1	7,932.8	2,083.5	2,168.3	855.2	11,182.0
2019	13,092.3	4,711.6	1,740.1	522.0	2,985.4	987.1	447.0	8,421.0	8,068.3	2,103.2	2,244.5	828.4	11,417.7
2020	12,700.7	4,955.7	1,914.2	530.3	3,066.7	1,043.1	387.9	7,863.0	7,460.9	2,123.1	2,079.1	841.3	11,018.0
2021	13,754.1	5,561.9	2,268.8	614.0	3,336.2	1,082.0	433.0	8,361.1	8,023.2	2,146.7	2,231.5	874.1	11,985.3
2022 p	14,133.3	5,534.2	2,258.2	574.6	3,318.7	1,038.1	435.3	8,737.7	8,390.8	2,171.2	2,299.2	894.1	12,402.0
2019: I	12,955.7	4,623.6	1,683.2	511.4	2,951.0	973.1	450.0	8,365.1	8,010.0	2,097.6	2,215.0	837.7	11,291.5
II	13,038.9	4,685.5	1,719.5	518.1	2,978.3	984.6	449.2	8,392.5	8,036.9	2,095.6	2,242.0	825.2	11,372.2
III	13,148.9	4,752.0	1,762.3	523.5	3,004.6	996.7	446.5	8,441.2	8,089.6	2,107.2	2,249.5	823.7	11,463.7
IV	13,225.6	4,785.2	1,795.3	535.2	3,007.8	993.8	442.4	8,485.4	8,136.8	2,112.6	2,271.5	826.9	11,543.3
2020: I	13,016.8	4,785.0	1,742.3	485.3	3,053.5	1,054.5	419.4	8,290.7	7,886.5	2,103.3	2,186.2	832.4	11,311.7
II	11,817.1	4,651.1	1,744.2	480.1	2,924.1	1,036.5	340.8	7,284.5	6,837.0	2,126.0	1,824.3	829.3	10,177.9
III	12,922.4	5,191.3	2,083.5	576.8	3,144.1	1,042.6	400.9	7,883.0	7,500.6	2,129.9	2,119.1	844.3	11,224.2
IV	13,046.6	5,195.5	2,086.6	579.0	3,145.1	1,038.7	390.3	7,993.9	7,619.5	2,133.0	2,186.7	859.4	11,358.4
2021: I	13,386.8	5,496.5	2,288.6	649.5	3,256.1	1,078.1	401.1	8,072.4	7,715.1	2,142.4	2,168.8	865.4	11,644.3
II	13,773.7	5,649.9	2,347.0	668.9	3,351.4	1,084.7	434.8	8,309.5	7,978.1	2,143.7	2,226.4	867.4	12,000.9
III	13,874.4	5,534.6	2,206.0	563.8	3,365.5	1,081.8	445.9	8,494.3	8,164.9	2,151.7	2,254.9	875.4	12,092.8
IV	13,981.5	5,566.7	2,233.5	573.6	3,371.7	1,083.3	450.2	8,568.2	8,234.9	2,149.1	2,276.1	888.4	12,203.1
2022: I	14,028.4	5,565.7	2,275.1	594.7	3,334.1	1,062.7	438.4	8,613.0	8,270.4	2,165.9	2,273.5	884.8	12,266.2
II	14,099.5	5,529.6	2,259.2	578.7	3,313.5	1,035.3	436.0	8,709.6	8,359.0	2,170.5	2,276.0	888.9	12,367.9
III	14,178.6	5,524.5	2,254.4	559.8	3,312.7	1,027.6	432.9	8,788.4	8,438.7	2,169.3	2,307.0	900.4	12,465.4
IV p	14,226.8	5,516.9	2,243.9	565.1	3,314.4	1,026.9	434.1	8,839.9	8,494.9	2,179.0	2,340.3	902.2	12,508.7

[1] Includes other items not shown separately.

[2] Food consists of food and beverages purchased for off-premises consumption; food services, which include purchased meals and beverages, are not classified as food.

Source: Department of Commerce (Bureau of Economic Analysis).

TABLE B–12. Private fixed investment by type, 1972–2022

[Billions of dollars; quarterly data at seasonally adjusted annual rates]

Year or quarter	Private fixed investment	Nonresidential												Residential		
		Total nonresidential	Structures	Equipment						Intellectual property products			Total residential[1]	Structures	
				Total[1]	Information processing equipment			Industrial equipment	Transportation equipment	Total[1]	Software	Research and development[2]		Total[1]	Single family
					Total	Computers and peripheral equipment	Other								
1972	219.0	146.6	47.2	78.9	16.7	3.5	13.2	21.4	21.8	20.6	2.8	12.9	72.4	70.9	32.8
1973	251.0	172.7	55.0	95.1	19.9	3.5	16.3	26.0	26.6	22.7	3.2	14.6	78.3	76.6	35.2
1974	260.5	191.1	61.2	104.3	23.1	3.9	19.2	30.7	26.3	25.5	3.9	16.4	69.5	67.6	29.7
1975	263.5	196.8	61.4	107.6	23.8	3.6	20.2	31.3	25.2	27.8	4.8	17.5	66.7	64.8	29.6
1976	306.1	219.3	65.9	121.2	27.5	4.4	23.1	34.1	30.0	32.2	5.2	19.6	86.8	84.6	43.9
1977	374.3	259.1	74.6	148.7	33.7	5.7	28.0	39.4	39.3	35.8	5.5	21.8	115.2	112.8	62.2
1978	452.6	314.6	93.6	180.6	42.3	7.6	34.8	47.7	47.3	40.4	6.3	24.9	138.0	135.3	72.8
1979	521.7	373.8	117.7	208.1	50.3	10.2	40.2	56.2	53.6	48.1	8.1	29.1	147.8	144.7	72.3
1980	536.4	406.9	136.2	216.4	58.9	12.5	46.4	60.7	48.4	54.4	9.8	34.2	129.5	126.1	52.9
1981	601.4	472.9	167.3	240.9	69.6	17.1	52.5	65.5	50.6	64.8	11.8	39.7	128.5	124.9	52.0
1982	595.9	485.1	177.6	234.9	74.2	18.9	55.3	62.7	46.8	72.7	14.0	44.8	110.8	107.2	41.5
1983	643.3	482.2	154.3	246.5	83.7	23.9	59.8	58.9	53.5	81.3	16.4	49.6	161.1	156.9	72.5
1984	754.7	564.3	177.4	291.9	101.2	31.6	69.6	68.1	64.4	95.0	20.4	56.9	190.4	185.6	86.4
1985	807.8	607.8	194.5	307.9	106.6	33.7	72.9	72.5	69.0	105.3	23.8	63.0	200.1	195.0	87.4
1986	842.6	607.8	176.5	317.7	111.1	33.4	77.7	75.4	70.5	113.5	25.6	66.5	234.8	229.3	104.1
1987	865.0	615.2	174.2	320.9	112.2	35.8	76.4	76.7	68.1	120.1	29.0	69.2	249.8	244.0	117.2
1988	918.5	662.3	182.8	346.8	120.8	38.0	82.8	84.2	72.9	132.7	33.3	76.4	256.2	250.1	120.1
1989	972.0	716.0	193.7	372.2	130.7	43.1	87.6	93.3	67.9	150.1	40.6	84.1	256.0	249.9	120.9
1990	978.9	739.2	202.9	371.9	129.6	38.6	90.9	92.1	70.0	164.4	45.4	91.5	239.7	233.7	112.9
1991	944.7	723.6	183.6	360.8	129.2	37.7	91.5	89.3	71.5	179.1	48.7	101.0	221.2	215.4	99.4
1992	996.7	741.9	172.6	381.7	142.1	44.0	98.1	93.0	74.7	187.7	51.1	105.4	254.7	248.8	122.0
1993	1,086.0	799.2	177.2	425.1	153.3	47.9	105.4	102.2	89.4	196.9	57.2	106.3	286.8	280.7	140.1
1994	1,192.7	868.9	186.8	476.4	167.0	52.4	114.6	113.6	107.7	205.7	60.4	109.2	323.8	317.6	162.3
1995	1,286.3	962.2	207.3	528.1	188.4	66.1	122.3	129.0	116.1	226.8	65.5	121.2	324.1	317.7	153.5
1996	1,401.3	1,043.2	224.6	565.3	204.7	72.8	131.9	136.5	123.2	253.3	74.5	134.5	358.1	351.7	170.8
1997	1,524.7	1,149.1	250.3	610.9	222.8	81.4	141.4	140.4	135.5	288.0	93.8	148.1	375.6	369.3	175.2
1998	1,673.0	1,254.1	276.0	660.0	240.1	87.9	152.2	147.4	147.1	318.1	109.2	160.6	418.8	412.1	199.4
1999	1,826.2	1,364.5	285.7	713.6	259.8	97.2	162.5	149.1	174.4	365.1	136.6	177.5	461.8	454.5	223.8
2000	1,983.9	1,498.4	321.0	766.1	293.8	103.2	190.6	162.9	170.8	411.3	156.8	199.0	485.4	477.7	236.8
2001	1,973.1	1,460.1	333.5	711.5	265.9	87.6	178.4	151.9	154.2	415.0	157.7	202.7	513.1	505.2	249.1
2002	1,910.4	1,352.8	287.0	659.6	236.7	79.7	157.0	141.7	141.6	406.2	152.5	196.1	557.6	549.6	265.9
2003	2,013.0	1,375.9	286.6	670.6	242.7	79.9	162.8	143.4	134.1	418.7	155.0	201.0	637.1	628.8	310.6
2004	2,217.2	1,467.4	307.7	721.9	255.8	84.2	171.6	144.2	159.2	437.8	166.3	207.4	749.8	740.8	377.6
2005	2,477.2	1,621.0	353.0	794.9	267.0	84.2	182.8	162.4	179.6	473.1	178.6	224.7	856.2	846.6	433.5
2006	2,632.0	1,793.8	425.2	862.3	288.5	92.6	195.9	181.6	194.3	506.3	189.5	245.6	838.2	828.1	416.0
2007	2,639.1	1,948.6	510.3	893.4	310.9	95.4	215.5	194.1	188.8	544.8	206.4	268.0	690.5	680.6	305.2
2008	2,506.9	1,990.9	571.1	845.4	306.3	93.9	212.4	194.3	148.7	574.4	223.8	284.2	516.0	506.4	185.8
2009	2,080.4	1,690.4	455.8	670.3	275.6	88.9	186.7	153.7	74.9	564.4	226.0	274.6	390.0	381.2	105.3
2010	2,111.6	1,735.0	379.8	777.0	307.5	99.6	207.9	155.2	135.8	578.2	226.4	282.4	376.6	367.4	112.6
2011	2,286.3	1,907.5	404.5	881.3	313.3	95.6	217.7	191.5	177.8	621.7	249.8	303.4	378.8	369.1	108.2
2012	2,550.5	2,118.5	479.4	983.4	331.2	103.5	227.7	211.2	215.3	655.7	272.1	313.4	432.0	421.5	132.0
2013	2,721.5	2,211.5	492.5	1,027.0	341.7	102.1	239.6	209.3	242.5	691.9	283.7	337.9	510.0	499.0	170.8
2014	2,960.2	2,400.1	577.6	1,091.9	346.0	101.9	244.1	218.8	272.8	730.5	297.5	359.5	560.2	548.8	193.6
2015	3,100.4	2,466.6	584.4	1,119.5	352.8	101.3	251.5	218.2	306.3	762.7	307.1	378.3	633.8	622.1	221.1
2016	3,168.8	2,469.3	560.4	1,087.8	353.0	99.4	253.6	213.9	292.3	821.2	334.8	404.4	699.4	687.3	242.5
2017	3,353.4	2,593.2	599.5	1,118.3	370.1	105.7	264.4	225.6	293.3	875.3	365.6	423.8	760.3	747.9	270.2
2018	3,583.3	2,784.7	633.6	1,193.2	391.6	120.3	271.2	243.6	309.2	957.9	402.4	465.5	798.6	785.6	289.6
2019	3,734.4	2,921.1	674.7	1,209.8	390.9	118.5	272.5	255.7	301.6	1,036.6	428.7	515.9	813.2	800.1	280.0
2020	3,698.7	2,797.9	614.4	1,077.8	389.3	128.9	260.3	237.0	207.2	1,105.7	460.9	556.8	900.8	886.4	309.4
2021	4,132.6	3,025.0	598.2	1,194.0	426.7	140.5	286.2	277.3	224.5	1,232.7	512.4	629.8	1,107.6	1,090.4	423.9
2022 p	4,472.0	3,345.1	648.2	1,322.5	457.9	149.0	308.9	316.9	250.7	1,374.3	567.6	696.3	1,126.9	1,109.1	445.3
2019: I	3,659.4	2,867.0	635.6	1,226.9	394.6	117.7	276.8	253.3	317.1	1,004.4	415.5	498.1	792.4	779.5	270.1
II	3,733.7	2,924.9	668.0	1,228.2	398.5	122.5	276.1	258.4	305.2	1,028.7	424.5	512.7	808.9	795.8	276.8
III	3,778.6	2,955.2	701.0	1,206.2	389.8	115.7	274.1	260.9	293.3	1,047.9	433.5	522.1	823.4	810.1	284.3
IV	3,765.6	2,937.5	694.2	1,178.1	380.9	118.0	262.9	250.3	290.8	1,065.2	441.2	530.7	828.2	815.0	288.7
2020: I	3,751.2	2,884.4	691.6	1,103.2	358.7	110.9	247.7	240.8	255.3	1,089.6	454.3	542.4	866.9	853.7	303.3
II	3,459.0	2,657.1	599.7	979.4	377.6	129.7	247.9	223.9	154.8	1,078.0	452.1	537.1	802.0	788.3	279.8
III	3,706.4	2,781.9	583.6	1,089.9	407.2	136.4	270.8	236.1	197.0	1,108.4	462.2	561.5	924.5	908.9	300.7
IV	3,878.3	2,868.3	582.7	1,138.8	413.6	138.7	274.9	247.0	221.5	1,146.8	475.2	586.2	1,010.0	994.7	353.7
2021: I	4,004.1	2,934.6	587.5	1,166.1	422.6	143.6	278.9	252.0	232.0	1,181.0	492.9	603.1	1,069.5	1,052.6	392.5
II	4,102.8	3,007.3	595.4	1,191.5	422.7	136.3	286.4	273.2	232.9	1,220.4	510.0	622.9	1,095.6	1,078.2	421.8
III	4,164.3	3,046.3	599.7	1,197.3	420.3	138.4	281.9	285.6	224.4	1,249.2	520.3	636.8	1,118.0	1,100.7	438.1
IV	4,259.2	3,111.8	610.3	1,221.2	441.3	143.5	297.8	298.4	208.8	1,280.4	526.5	656.4	1,147.3	1,130.2	443.2
2022: I	4,413.6	3,225.0	627.3	1,277.8	464.2	153.2	310.9	315.8	208.5	1,319.9	545.1	674.3	1,188.6	1,170.8	469.4
II	4,464.6	3,292.2	631.2	1,299.5	458.5	145.4	313.0	318.7	224.0	1,361.4	558.9	693.9	1,172.4	1,154.5	479.0
III	4,508.2	3,403.4	654.8	1,352.0	469.1	157.6	311.5	313.3	269.4	1,396.6	579.3	702.7	1,104.8	1,086.7	434.8
IV p	4,501.6	3,459.7	679.6	1,360.8	440.1	139.9	300.2	319.6	301.0	1,419.4	587.2	714.6	1,041.9	1,024.3	398.0

[1] Includes other items not shown separately.
[2] Research and development investment includes expenditures for software.

Source: Department of Commerce (Bureau of Economic Analysis).

TABLE B–13. Real private fixed investment by type, 2002–2022

[Billions of chained (2012) dollars; quarterly data at seasonally adjusted annual rates]

Year or quarter	Private fixed investment	Nonresidential: Total nonresidential	Nonresidential: Structures	Equipment: Total [2]	Information processing equipment: Total	Information processing equipment: Computers and peripheral equipment [1]	Information processing equipment: Other	Equipment: Industrial equipment	Equipment: Transportation equipment	Intellectual property products: Total [2]	Intellectual property products: Software	Intellectual property products: Research and development [3]	Residential: Total residential [2]	Residential structures: Total [2]	Residential structures: Single family
2002	2,183.4	1,472.7	473.5	607.8	133.3	35.9	98.3	181.4	162.4	421.5	125.5	244.1	692.6	685.1	327.1
2003	2,280.6	1,509.4	456.6	634.3	150.4	40.2	111.1	182.2	150.3	437.7	133.5	246.1	755.5	747.7	362.0
2004	2,440.7	1,594.0	456.3	688.6	169.4	45.7	124.7	178.8	171.2	459.2	149.3	248.1	830.9	822.1	405.4
2005	2,618.7	1,716.4	466.1	760.0	187.6	51.8	136.5	194.2	192.1	493.1	163.4	261.6	885.4	876.3	432.8
2006	2,686.8	1,854.2	501.7	832.6	217.0	64.7	152.4	210.6	206.4	521.5	173.5	279.6	818.9	809.5	390.4
2007	2,653.5	1,982.1	568.6	865.8	247.2	73.9	173.3	217.3	197.7	554.3	191.1	296.1	665.8	656.6	283.5
2008	2,499.4	1,994.2	605.4	824.4	260.6	79.7	180.9	208.3	155.0	575.3	206.7	304.8	504.6	495.7	178.1
2009	2,099.8	1,704.3	492.2	649.7	247.5	81.1	166.5	162.7	72.5	572.4	212.9	297.4	395.3	386.9	105.3
2010	2,164.2	1,781.0	412.8	781.2	289.1	94.1	195.1	162.5	141.5	588.1	220.9	298.5	383.0	373.8	114.3
2011	2,317.8	1,935.4	424.1	886.2	303.2	93.9	209.3	194.9	181.8	624.8	245.2	311.0	382.5	372.4	109.1
2012	2,550.5	2,118.5	479.4	983.4	331.2	103.5	227.7	211.2	215.3	655.7	272.1	313.4	432.0	421.5	132.0
2013	2,692.1	2,206.0	485.5	1,029.2	351.8	103.0	248.8	208.4	238.5	691.4	287.2	333.8	485.5	474.1	161.8
2014	2,869.2	2,365.3	538.8	1,101.1	370.2	102.9	267.7	216.5	265.0	724.8	305.3	346.9	504.1	491.8	171.8
2015	2,979.0	2,420.3	534.1	1,134.6	393.3	103.4	291.0	216.7	292.8	752.4	320.2	357.1	555.4	542.0	191.5
2016	3,041.0	2,442.0	511.0	1,114.6	410.5	103.0	309.3	213.4	276.3	818.8	354.0	387.1	592.1	577.7	201.3
2017	3,165.4	2,542.5	533.3	1,146.0	439.6	109.9	331.8	223.0	272.5	864.9	392.2	394.6	615.8	600.6	214.8
2018	3,320.0	2,708.3	555.2	1,221.2	473.7	124.8	349.7	236.2	286.5	935.2	437.7	418.9	612.3	596.9	220.7
2019	3,404.2	2,804.6	567.9	1,236.5	486.1	127.1	360.1	244.2	277.3	1,003.2	468.1	455.4	606.2	590.8	206.8
2020	3,326.8	2,666.0	510.4	1,107.3	492.4	141.8	348.7	224.3	192.5	1,051.2	509.0	470.9	649.8	633.3	219.7
2021	3,574.6	2,835.4	477.5	1,221.8	540.4	152.6	386.3	251.0	222.7	1,153.0	574.2	511.9	719.4	701.2	268.9
2022 p	3,567.6	2,943.5	444.4	1,274.2	569.0	156.2	412.4	264.8	233.4	1,255.5	644.1	539.7	642.7	625.6	242.3
2019: I	3,351.5	2,762.1	543.4	1,250.1	484.6	123.3	363.1	242.8	291.5	975.7	454.2	442.0	596.0	581.0	200.6
II	3,402.6	2,803.8	563.3	1,252.4	493.9	130.7	363.9	247.1	278.9	993.0	461.8	451.8	605.4	590.2	205.7
III	3,437.0	2,832.1	586.9	1,235.0	486.6	124.9	363.2	248.7	270.8	1,010.7	471.3	459.5	611.7	596.1	209.6
IV	3,425.7	2,820.4	578.1	1,208.7	479.5	129.4	350.1	238.2	268.1	1,033.5	485.2	468.2	611.7	595.9	211.2
2020: I	3,399.5	2,760.6	573.1	1,129.1	452.7	122.4	330.3	228.4	232.4	1,053.3	502.2	473.6	636.8	620.8	219.7
II	3,121.3	2,530.6	498.1	1,001.8	477.8	142.3	332.6	212.6	139.9	1,027.8	499.1	457.8	587.8	572.1	201.4
III	3,327.4	2,649.9	484.6	1,121.7	514.9	149.6	363.0	223.5	185.1	1,051.3	511.3	471.6	662.7	645.3	211.8
IV	3,459.2	2,723.0	485.7	1,176.6	524.1	152.9	368.7	232.8	212.4	1,072.4	523.6	480.8	712.2	695.0	245.8
2021: I	3,540.4	2,781.4	488.0	1,194.3	536.4	157.8	375.7	234.8	215.8	1,112.0	553.5	494.4	732.0	713.6	264.4
II	3,590.9	2,847.7	484.9	1,234.0	536.7	149.1	386.8	250.0	237.7	1,145.4	571.0	509.7	723.0	704.5	273.5
III	3,581.1	2,852.2	476.6	1,227.1	531.7	149.5	380.9	256.2	229.2	1,166.0	582.8	516.2	712.2	694.2	272.5
IV	3,586.2	2,860.2	460.7	1,232.0	556.7	154.2	401.8	263.0	208.2	1,188.8	589.7	527.3	710.3	692.6	265.4
2022: I	3,628.6	2,915.0	455.6	1,265.7	579.0	162.1	415.8	270.9	206.3	1,219.6	615.7	534.3	704.7	687.1	268.8
II	3,581.9	2,915.5	440.4	1,259.1	569.6	152.2	418.2	266.7	212.1	1,245.9	630.9	541.7	671.0	653.6	262.2
III	3,550.5	2,959.7	436.4	1,291.3	582.3	165.1	415.3	258.9	249.1	1,266.7	653.5	540.3	620.0	602.9	232.2
IV p	3,509.2	2,983.6	445.4	1,280.7	544.9	145.6	400.2	262.8	266.2	1,289.5	676.3	542.6	575.3	558.9	206.2

[1] Because computers exhibit rapid changes in prices relative to other prices in the economy, the chained-dollar estimates should not be used to measure the component's relative importance or its contribution to the growth rate of more aggregate series. The quantity index for computers can be used to accurately measure the real growth rate of this series. For information on this component, see *Survey of Current Business* Table 5.3.1 (for growth rates), Table 5.3.2 (for contributions), and Table 5.3.3 (for quantity indexes).

[2] Includes other items not shown separately.

[3] Research and development investment includes expenditures for software.

Source: Department of Commerce (Bureau of Economic Analysis).

Table B–14. Foreign transactions in the national income and product accounts, 1972–2022

[Billions of dollars; quarterly data at seasonally adjusted annual rates]

Year or quarter	Current receipts from rest of the world					Current payments to rest of the world									Balance on current account, NIPA[2]
	Total	Exports of goods and services			Income receipts	Total	Imports of goods and services			Income payments	Current taxes and transfer payments to rest of the world (net)				
		Total	Goods[1]	Services[1]			Total	Goods[1]	Services[1]		Total	From persons (net)	From government (net)	From business (net)	
1972	87.1	70.8	52.6	18.3	16.3	91.2	74.2	56.9	17.3	7.7	9.2	1.4	7.4	0.5	–4.0
1973	118.8	95.3	75.8	19.5	23.5	109.9	91.2	71.8	19.3	10.9	7.9	1.6	5.6	.7	8.9
1974	156.5	126.7	103.5	23.2	29.8	150.5	127.5	104.5	22.9	14.3	8.7	1.4	6.4	1.0	6.0
1975	166.7	138.7	112.5	26.2	28.0	146.9	122.7	99.0	23.7	15.0	9.1	1.3	7.1	.7	19.8
1976	181.9	149.5	121.5	28.0	32.4	174.8	151.1	124.6	26.5	15.5	8.1	1.4	5.7	1.1	7.1
1977	196.5	159.3	128.4	30.9	37.2	207.5	182.4	152.6	29.8	16.9	8.1	1.4	5.3	1.4	–10.9
1978	233.1	186.9	149.9	37.0	46.3	245.8	212.3	177.4	34.8	24.7	8.8	1.6	5.9	1.4	–12.6
1979	298.5	230.1	187.3	42.9	68.3	299.6	252.7	212.8	39.9	36.4	10.6	1.7	6.8	2.0	–1.2
1980	359.9	280.8	230.4	50.3	79.1	351.4	293.8	248.6	45.3	44.9	12.6	2.0	8.3	2.4	8.5
1981	397.3	305.2	245.2	60.0	92.0	393.9	317.8	267.8	49.9	59.1	17.0	5.6	8.3	3.2	3.4
1982	384.2	283.2	222.6	60.7	101.0	387.5	303.2	250.5	52.6	64.5	19.8	6.7	9.7	3.4	–3.3
1983	378.9	277.0	214.0	62.9	101.9	413.9	328.6	272.7	56.0	64.8	20.5	7.0	10.1	3.4	–35.1
1984	424.2	302.4	231.3	71.1	121.9	514.3	405.1	336.3	68.8	85.6	23.6	7.9	12.2	3.5	–90.1
1985	415.9	303.2	227.5	75.7	112.7	530.2	417.2	343.3	73.9	87.3	25.7	8.3	14.4	2.9	–114.3
1986	432.3	321.0	231.4	89.6	111.3	575.0	452.9	370.0	82.9	94.4	27.8	9.1	15.4	3.2	–142.7
1987	487.2	363.9	265.6	98.4	123.3	641.3	508.7	414.8	93.9	105.8	26.8	10.0	13.4	3.4	–154.1
1988	596.7	444.6	332.1	112.5	152.1	712.4	554.0	452.1	101.9	129.5	29.0	10.8	13.7	4.5	–115.7
1989	682.0	504.3	374.8	129.5	177.7	774.3	591.0	484.8	106.2	152.9	30.4	11.6	14.2	4.6	–92.4
1990	740.7	551.9	403.3	148.6	188.8	815.6	629.7	508.1	121.7	154.2	31.7	12.2	14.7	4.8	–74.9
1991	763.3	594.9	430.1	164.8	168.4	755.4	623.5	500.7	122.8	136.8	–4.9	14.1	–24.0	5.0	7.9
1992	785.1	633.1	455.3	177.7	152.1	830.7	667.8	544.9	122.9	121.0	41.9	14.5	22.0	5.4	–45.6
1993	810.4	654.8	467.7	187.1	155.6	889.8	720.0	592.8	127.2	124.4	45.4	17.1	22.9	5.4	–79.4
1994	905.5	720.9	518.4	202.6	184.5	1,021.1	813.4	676.8	136.6	161.6	46.1	18.9	21.1	6.0	–115.6
1995	1,042.6	812.8	592.4	220.4	229.8	1,148.5	902.6	757.4	145.1	201.9	44.1	20.3	15.6	8.2	–105.9
1996	1,114.0	867.6	628.8	238.8	246.4	1,229.0	964.0	807.4	156.5	215.5	49.5	22.6	20.0	6.9	–115.0
1997	1,233.9	953.8	699.9	253.9	280.1	1,364.0	1,055.8	885.7	170.1	256.8	51.4	25.7	16.7	9.1	–130.1
1998	1,239.8	953.0	692.6	260.4	286.8	1,445.1	1,115.7	930.8	184.9	269.4	60.0	29.7	17.4	13.0	–205.3
1999	1,355.2	992.9	711.7	281.2	324.6	1,631.9	1,252.5	1,051.2	201.3	293.7	85.7	36.3	25.0	24.4	–276.6
2000	1,527.8	1,096.1	795.1	301.1	390.6	1,924.7	1,477.2	1,251.2	226.0	352.2	95.4	38.6	26.8	29.9	–396.9
2001	1,411.6	1,026.8	739.6	287.2	339.6	1,803.0	1,403.6	1,176.2	227.4	289.3	110.2	42.5	26.7	41.1	–391.4
2002	1,390.6	998.0	706.6	291.4	335.8	1,846.0	1,437.7	1,198.9	238.9	290.0	118.3	44.4	29.3	44.6	–455.4
2003	1,478.5	1,035.2	733.9	301.3	377.4	2,006.2	1,557.1	1,299.0	258.1	318.9	130.1	46.1	32.0	52.0	–527.6
2004	1,705.6	1,176.4	828.0	348.4	464.7	2,343.4	1,810.5	1,513.6	296.9	388.0	144.9	49.5	34.0	61.4	–637.8
2005	1,940.9	1,301.6	919.3	382.2	569.3	2,692.0	2,041.5	1,722.8	318.7	494.5	156.1	54.4	39.9	61.8	–751.2
2006	2,247.7	1,470.2	1,043.1	427.1	702.6	3,067.0	2,256.6	1,900.6	356.0	656.2	154.2	57.1	41.7	55.3	–819.3
2007	2,584.4	1,659.3	1,159.7	499.6	850.2	3,325.2	2,395.2	2,002.7	392.5	754.5	175.5	65.3	49.1	61.0	–740.9
2008	2,779.9	1,835.3	1,291.0	544.3	855.2	3,484.1	2,576.2	2,148.7	427.5	710.0	198.0	71.1	54.3	72.5	–704.2
2009	2,362.1	1,582.8	1,057.4	525.4	689.3	2,745.3	2,001.9	1,588.1	413.8	539.0	204.3	69.8	62.9	71.6	–383.1
2010	2,714.1	1,857.2	1,272.9	584.3	760.0	3,153.8	2,389.6	1,947.0	442.5	554.3	209.9	72.1	63.3	74.6	–439.8
2011	3,049.8	2,115.9	1,468.5	647.4	827.9	3,510.1	2,695.5	2,231.1	464.3	589.9	224.7	74.7	66.8	83.2	–460.3
2012	3,161.8	2,217.7	1,529.6	688.1	827.4	3,585.8	2,769.3	2,293.3	476.1	594.7	221.8	75.7	67.3	78.7	–423.9
2013	3,265.2	2,287.0	1,563.9	723.1	847.2	3,617.2	2,766.4	2,293.9	472.5	616.9	233.9	77.8	66.6	89.6	–352.1
2014	3,404.8	2,377.4	1,617.0	760.5	881.6	3,781.0	2,887.4	2,389.3	498.1	646.4	247.2	83.7	65.3	98.1	–376.2
2015	3,267.5	2,268.7	1,496.7	772.0	860.8	3,692.2	2,794.9	2,289.6	505.3	640.4	257.0	89.5	65.2	102.3	–424.7
2016	3,272.2	2,232.1	1,447.6	784.5	893.5	3,675.9	2,738.4	2,218.7	519.7	661.5	276.0	90.6	69.2	116.3	–403.7
2017	3,585.1	2,388.3	1,546.7	841.6	1,031.1	3,956.5	2,925.0	2,369.9	555.1	738.2	293.4	95.7	67.8	129.8	–371.4
2018	3,830.7	2,538.1	1,669.3	868.8	1,138.7	4,271.8	3,131.2	2,559.1	572.1	848.4	292.3	98.7	74.3	119.3	–441.2
2019	3,872.7	2,538.5	1,644.8	893.7	1,172.2	4,325.3	3,117.2	2,516.7	600.5	894.2	313.9	102.3	74.3	137.3	–452.6
2020	3,290.1	2,148.6	1,420.0	728.6	971.3	3,882.5	2,776.1	2,304.5	471.6	774.3	332.1	104.1	87.7	140.3	–592.5
2021	3,803.5	2,539.6	1,741.5	798.2	1,087.0	4,664.9	3,401.4	2,844.7	556.7	913.9	349.6	109.4	93.6	146.6	–861.4
2022 p	....	2,979.6	2,063.9	915.6	....	....	3,953.9	3,277.6	676.3	....	382.6	115.0	117.6	149.9	....
2019: I	3,874.5	2,542.7	1,667.1	875.6	1,174.1	4,351.7	3,142.6	2,546.4	596.2	888.0	321.1	100.6	75.6	144.9	–477.1
II	3,906.3	2,549.6	1,646.3	903.3	1,198.9	4,384.4	3,165.3	2,559.7	605.5	909.0	310.1	101.9	70.0	138.2	–478.1
III	3,879.2	2,533.3	1,636.4	896.9	1,175.2	4,323.5	3,118.2	2,517.6	600.6	894.0	311.4	102.8	75.1	133.5	–444.3
IV	3,830.6	2,528.2	1,629.2	899.0	1,140.7	4,241.6	3,042.9	2,443.0	599.9	885.7	313.1	103.9	76.7	132.4	–411.0
2020: I	3,637.1	2,412.7	1,595.4	817.3	1,057.1	4,058.9	2,935.4	2,382.5	552.9	801.1	322.4	104.4	79.6	138.4	–421.8
II	2,853.0	1,817.5	1,143.1	674.4	871.3	3,377.7	2,343.7	1,936.8	406.9	702.1	331.9	105.0	95.4	131.5	–524.7
III	3,252.7	2,106.6	1,416.3	690.3	971.3	3,917.6	2,799.0	2,362.9	436.1	771.3	347.4	103.2	94.3	149.9	–665.0
IV	3,417.6	2,257.8	1,525.3	732.5	985.4	4,175.9	3,026.4	2,535.8	490.6	822.8	326.8	103.8	81.6	141.4	–758.3
2021: I	3,605.1	2,369.1	1,614.8	754.3	1,057.5	4,383.9	3,177.7	2,692.6	485.1	860.1	346.0	106.6	97.9	141.5	–778.7
II	3,739.9	2,503.1	1,721.3	781.8	1,062.8	4,584.1	3,337.5	2,806.6	530.9	917.0	329.5	107.9	82.4	139.3	–844.1
III	3,836.5	2,553.3	1,751.6	801.8	1,106.8	4,751.5	3,442.5	2,850.5	592.0	939.0	370.1	110.8	108.7	150.6	–915.0
IV	4,032.3	2,733.0	1,878.2	854.9	1,120.9	4,939.9	3,647.7	3,029.0	618.7	939.5	352.7	112.5	85.2	155.0	–907.6
2022: I	4,133.1	2,811.2	1,940.9	870.4	1,147.1	5,242.6	3,927.9	3,289.3	638.6	958.4	356.4	114.3	97.3	144.8	–1,109.5
II	4,450.5	3,038.8	2,134.7	904.2	1,231.3	5,471.0	4,074.4	3,394.8	679.6	1,023.3	373.2	115.8	108.6	148.8	–1,020.5
III	4,534.1	3,065.0	2,141.2	923.8	1,292.1	5,495.8	3,955.8	3,269.7	686.1	1,130.6	409.4	115.7	141.2	152.4	–961.7
IV p	....	3,003.2	2,039.0	964.3	....	....	3,857.4	3,156.6	700.8	....	391.3	114.3	123.5	153.6	....

[1] Certain goods, primarily military equipment purchased and sold by the Federal Government, are included in services. Beginning with 1986, repairs and alterations of equipment were reclassified from goods to services.

[2] National income and product accounts (NIPA).

Source: Department of Commerce (Bureau of Economic Analysis).

TABLE B–15. Real exports and imports of goods and services, 2002–2022

[Billions of chained (2012) dollars; quarterly data at seasonally adjusted annual rates]

Year or quarter	Exports of goods and services						Imports of goods and services					
	Total	Goods [1]				Services [1]	Total	Goods [1]				Services [1]
		Total	Durable goods	Nondurable goods	Nonagricultural goods			Total	Durable goods	Nondurable goods	Nonpetroleum goods	
2002	1,274.8	897.2	523.3	386.5	794.1	377.7	1,965.1	1,643.8	789.9	902.0	1,216.4	320.6
2003	1,301.6	923.1	540.7	394.0	818.1	378.5	2,065.8	1,744.1	837.0	959.0	1,289.8	321.8
2004	1,427.0	1,006.1	602.9	409.1	902.8	421.0	2,292.6	1,939.6	956.0	1,021.0	1,442.4	353.4
2005	1,526.1	1,082.6	662.0	421.7	973.1	443.6	2,441.4	2,075.8	1,042.2	1,061.9	1,555.7	366.6
2006	1,670.5	1,191.4	738.5	450.7	1,072.1	479.4	2,598.2	2,201.9	1,139.5	1,077.1	1,674.9	397.1
2007	1,816.9	1,274.7	795.9	475.0	1,147.0	542.1	2,664.8	2,244.4	1,171.4	1,084.5	1,722.4	420.6
2008	1,921.9	1,349.5	834.4	512.2	1,214.1	572.4	2,607.6	2,171.0	1,134.1	1,047.7	1,666.6	436.4
2009	1,762.5	1,189.3	694.1	499.3	1,059.1	572.7	2,278.8	1,835.1	904.2	951.7	1,380.4	441.3
2010	1,989.5	1,369.4	818.5	552.1	1,224.5	620.1	2,578.9	2,117.3	1,117.2	1,004.6	1,640.2	461.5
2011	2,132.1	1,471.5	896.8	574.7	1,327.9	660.6	2,703.1	2,234.1	1,222.7	1,012.0	1,761.4	469.1
2012	2,217.7	1,529.6	941.7	587.9	1,384.5	688.1	2,769.3	2,293.3	1,322.3	971.0	1,858.9	476.1
2013	2,283.6	1,574.6	962.5	612.1	1,427.5	709.0	2,802.9	2,339.3	1,384.4	954.9	1,929.8	463.9
2014	2,372.3	1,644.7	1,002.4	642.3	1,486.2	727.9	2,947.6	2,469.5	1,507.2	962.7	2,073.9	478.9
2015	2,378.7	1,638.9	980.3	660.5	1,477.5	739.2	3,100.4	2,612.4	1,607.7	1,004.4	2,206.1	490.6
2016	2,388.4	1,649.3	969.7	685.2	1,479.9	739.0	3,145.4	2,641.3	1,627.2	1,013.5	2,224.5	505.2
2017	2,490.3	1,717.4	1,000.6	724.7	1,545.0	772.5	3,287.2	2,759.6	1,741.5	1,010.6	2,335.1	528.7
2018	2,560.1	1,789.7	1,035.6	763.5	1,616.1	774.0	3,425.5	2,899.4	1,839.0	1,051.8	2,475.7	531.5
2019	2,572.1	1,791.5	1,011.4	793.3	1,619.2	783.1	3,464.7	2,913.5	1,843.3	1,061.9	2,503.4	552.9
2020	2,231.7	1,609.7	849.4	785.8	1,430.7	635.8	3,154.3	2,744.6	1,706.8	1,032.9	2,370.9	431.3
2021	2,366.8	1,728.9	948.6	802.2	1,559.2	656.9	3,600.2	3,143.0	2,013.9	1,119.1	2,730.7	484.2
2022 p	2,537.8	1,837.7	998.0	862.6	1,671.7	717.3	3,894.4	3,360.5	2,173.7	1,178.9	2,940.0	555.0
2019: I	2,582.3	1,813.0	1,039.8	784.1	1,642.7	774.5	3,485.9	2,939.7	1,868.9	1,061.6	2,524.2	549.8
II	2,567.3	1,779.2	1,006.5	785.5	1,602.9	788.9	3,491.8	2,936.8	1,856.3	1,071.9	2,523.0	557.0
III	2,567.0	1,787.4	1,001.3	800.4	1,610.8	782.0	3,476.4	2,924.6	1,848.3	1,068.0	2,515.2	553.8
IV	2,571.8	1,786.5	998.0	803.0	1,620.6	786.8	3,404.7	2,853.1	1,799.6	1,046.1	2,451.1	551.0
2020: I	2,467.3	1,770.4	968.6	819.9	1,598.7	710.1	3,295.5	2,796.1	1,737.7	1,053.6	2,401.2	505.9
II	1,951.4	1,350.2	661.3	727.3	1,183.7	599.8	2,718.6	2,359.0	1,380.7	986.6	2,032.1	376.7
III	2,193.0	1,612.0	857.6	776.4	1,426.0	601.9	3,184.2	2,818.3	1,777.5	1,031.1	2,441.7	398.8
IV	2,315.0	1,706.2	910.3	819.6	1,514.4	631.5	3,419.0	3,005.2	1,931.5	1,060.1	2,608.5	444.0
2021: I	2,317.5	1,703.0	930.0	794.1	1,520.5	635.4	3,482.0	3,083.9	1,981.6	1,090.5	2,683.1	433.9
II	2,345.1	1,717.5	954.8	783.8	1,551.9	647.3	3,549.0	3,114.0	2,000.6	1,103.0	2,703.4	464.9
III	2,338.8	1,701.5	941.7	781.7	1,546.2	654.7	3,606.3	3,115.9	1,985.4	1,121.5	2,699.9	510.5
IV	2,465.7	1,793.5	967.9	849.3	1,618.2	690.3	3,763.3	3,258.2	2,088.1	1,161.4	2,836.4	527.5
2022: I	2,436.9	1,760.2	974.0	810.3	1,592.3	693.0	3,925.6	3,412.7	2,208.3	1,196.2	2,985.8	539.0
II	2,516.9	1,824.9	991.0	856.9	1,645.8	709.5	3,947.5	3,409.5	2,215.3	1,186.8	2,997.9	560.1
III	2,604.1	1,901.0	1,014.9	908.0	1,737.8	722.5	3,872.9	3,333.4	2,171.1	1,155.6	2,912.4	559.0
IV p	2,593.4	1,864.7	1,012.0	875.1	1,711.1	744.1	3,831.7	3,286.6	2,100.1	1,176.9	2,863.8	562.0

[1] Certain goods, primarily military equipment purchased and sold by the Federal Government, are included in services. Repairs and alterations of equipment are also included in services.

Source: Department of Commerce (Bureau of Economic Analysis).

Table B–16. Sources of personal income, 1972–2022

[Billions of dollars; quarterly data at seasonally adjusted annual rates]

Year or quarter	Personal income	Compensation of employees							Proprietors' income with inventory valuation and capital consumption adjustments			Rental income of persons with capital consumption adjustment
		Total	Wages and salaries			Supplements to wages and salaries			Total	Farm	Nonfarm	
			Total	Private industries	Government	Total	Employer contributions for employee pension and insurance funds	Employer contributions for government social insurance				
1972	1,024.5	731.3	638.8	500.9	137.9	92.5	61.4	31.2	95.1	17.0	78.1	22.7
1973	1,140.8	812.7	708.8	560.0	148.8	103.9	64.1	39.8	112.5	29.1	83.4	23.1
1974	1,251.8	887.7	772.3	611.8	160.5	115.4	70.7	44.7	112.2	23.5	88.7	23.2
1975	1,369.4	947.2	814.8	638.6	176.2	132.4	85.7	46.7	118.2	22.0	96.2	22.3
1976	1,502.6	1,048.3	899.7	710.8	188.9	148.6	94.2	54.4	131.0	17.2	113.8	20.3
1977	1,659.2	1,165.8	994.2	791.6	202.6	171.7	110.6	61.1	144.5	16.0	128.5	15.9
1978	1,863.7	1,316.8	1,120.6	900.6	220.0	196.2	124.7	71.5	166.0	19.9	146.1	16.5
1979	2,082.7	1,477.2	1,253.3	1,016.2	237.1	223.9	141.3	82.6	179.4	22.2	157.3	16.1
1980	2,323.6	1,622.2	1,373.4	1,112.0	261.5	248.8	159.9	88.9	171.6	11.7	159.9	19.0
1981	2,605.1	1,792.5	1,511.4	1,225.5	285.8	281.2	177.5	103.6	179.7	19.0	160.7	23.8
1982	2,791.6	1,893.0	1,587.5	1,280.0	307.5	305.5	195.7	109.8	171.2	13.3	157.9	23.8
1983	2,981.1	2,012.5	1,677.5	1,352.7	324.8	335.0	215.1	119.9	186.3	6.2	180.1	24.4
1984	3,292.7	2,215.9	1,844.9	1,496.8	348.1	371.0	231.9	139.0	228.2	20.9	207.3	24.7
1985	3,524.9	2,387.3	1,982.6	1,608.7	373.9	404.8	257.0	147.7	241.1	21.0	220.1	26.2
1986	3,733.1	2,542.1	2,102.3	1,705.1	397.2	439.7	281.9	157.9	256.5	22.8	233.7	18.3
1987	3,961.6	2,722.4	2,256.3	1,833.2	423.1	466.1	299.9	166.3	286.5	28.9	257.6	16.6
1988	4,283.4	2,948.0	2,439.8	1,987.7	452.0	508.2	323.6	184.6	325.5	26.8	298.7	22.5
1989	4,625.6	3,139.6	2,583.1	2,101.9	481.1	556.6	362.9	193.7	341.1	33.0	308.1	21.5
1990	4,913.8	3,340.4	2,741.2	2,222.2	519.0	599.2	392.7	206.5	353.2	32.2	321.0	28.2
1991	5,084.9	3,450.5	2,814.5	2,265.7	548.8	636.0	420.9	215.1	354.2	26.8	327.4	38.6
1992	5,420.9	3,668.2	2,965.5	2,393.5	572.0	702.7	474.3	228.4	400.2	34.8	365.4	60.6
1993	5,657.9	3,817.3	3,079.3	2,490.3	589.0	737.9	498.3	239.7	428.0	31.4	396.6	90.1
1994	5,947.1	4,006.2	3,236.6	2,627.1	609.5	769.6	515.5	254.1	456.6	34.7	422.0	113.7
1995	6,291.4	4,198.1	3,418.0	2,789.0	629.0	780.1	515.9	264.1	481.2	22.0	459.2	124.9
1996	6,678.5	4,416.9	3,616.5	2,968.4	648.1	800.5	525.7	274.8	543.8	37.3	506.4	142.5
1997	7,092.5	4,708.8	3,876.8	3,205.0	671.9	832.0	542.4	289.6	584.0	32.4	551.6	147.1
1998	7,606.7	5,071.1	4,181.6	3,480.3	701.3	889.5	582.3	307.2	640.2	28.5	611.7	165.2
1999	8,006.8	5,402.7	4,457.9	3,724.2	733.8	944.8	621.4	323.3	696.4	28.1	668.3	178.5
2000	8,655.9	5,847.1	4,824.9	4,045.2	779.8	1,022.2	677.0	345.2	753.9	31.5	722.4	183.5
2001	9,012.8	6,038.3	4,953.6	4,131.6	822.0	1,084.7	726.7	358.0	831.0	32.1	798.9	202.4
2002	9,160.9	6,135.1	4,995.8	4,123.0	872.9	1,139.3	773.2	366.0	870.0	20.2	849.8	208.4
2003	9,498.5	6,353.6	5,138.3	4,224.3	914.0	1,215.3	832.8	382.5	897.5	37.1	860.4	227.1
2004	10,044.3	6,719.5	5,421.0	4,468.7	952.3	1,298.5	889.7	408.8	962.9	52.4	910.5	242.8
2005	10,604.9	7,066.1	5,691.4	4,700.1	991.3	1,374.7	946.7	428.1	979.1	47.9	931.2	221.1
2006	11,384.7	7,479.7	6,056.7	5,022.2	1,034.5	1,422.9	975.6	447.3	1,050.9	34.3	1,016.6	181.1
2007	12,021.4	7,878.5	6,396.4	5,307.8	1,088.5	1,482.1	1,020.4	461.7	995.5	41.7	953.8	186.3
2008	12,477.6	8,056.8	6,534.1	5,390.2	1,143.9	1,522.7	1,051.3	471.4	959.7	38.9	920.7	290.3
2009	12,080.4	7,759.0	6,249.1	5,073.9	1,175.2	1,509.9	1,051.8	458.1	937.6	27.2	910.5	347.6
2010	12,594.5	7,925.4	6,372.5	5,181.3	1,191.2	1,552.9	1,083.9	469.0	1,107.3	37.6	1,069.7	433.7
2011	13,339.3	8,226.2	6,626.2	5,431.3	1,194.9	1,600.0	1,107.3	492.7	1,227.4	63.0	1,164.4	506.5
2012	14,014.3	8,567.4	6,928.1	5,729.8	1,198.3	1,639.2	1,125.9	513.3	1,346.4	59.9	1,286.4	534.5
2013	14,193.6	8,835.0	7,114.0	5,906.0	1,208.0	1,721.0	1,194.7	526.3	1,402.2	87.0	1,315.3	577.4
2014	14,976.6	9,250.2	7,476.3	6,239.4	1,236.9	1,773.9	1,227.5	546.4	1,445.6	67.7	1,377.9	602.7
2015	15,685.2	9,699.4	7,859.5	6,583.7	1,275.8	1,839.9	1,270.6	569.4	1,420.8	54.1	1,366.7	609.5
2016	16,096.9	9,966.1	8,091.2	6,783.2	1,308.0	1,874.9	1,293.9	580.9	1,423.3	34.1	1,389.2	626.6
2017	16,839.8	10,424.4	8,474.4	7,126.2	1,348.2	1,950.0	1,345.3	604.7	1,504.6	39.1	1,465.5	650.6
2018	17,683.8	10,957.9	8,900.0	7,498.1	1,402.0	2,057.9	1,433.1	624.8	1,568.7	29.2	1,539.5	680.0
2019	18,587.0	11,448.1	9,324.6	7,874.1	1,450.5	2,123.5	1,472.9	650.7	1,601.4	29.1	1,572.3	698.2
2020	19,832.3	11,592.7	9,457.4	7,962.9	1,494.5	2,135.4	1,476.2	659.1	1,643.1	45.2	1,597.9	719.8
2021	21,294.8	12,538.5	10,290.1	8,746.0	1,544.1	2,248.4	1,550.3	698.1	1,753.6	51.3	1,702.2	723.8
2022 p	21,806.3	13,601.5	11,224.3	9,610.5	1,613.8	2,377.2	1,612.5	764.7	1,848.5	91.7	1,756.8	781.3
2019: I	18,345.4	11,329.6	9,222.0	7,797.6	1,424.4	2,107.6	1,463.3	644.3	1,583.4	25.1	1,558.3	689.6
II	18,504.9	11,389.4	9,272.7	7,836.7	1,436.0	2,116.7	1,469.2	647.5	1,575.2	15.6	1,559.6	696.1
III	18,655.5	11,455.2	9,328.7	7,869.4	1,459.2	2,126.5	1,475.7	650.8	1,615.3	37.3	1,578.0	699.1
IV	18,842.3	11,618.2	9,475.0	7,992.8	1,482.2	2,143.3	1,483.1	660.1	1,631.9	38.7	1,593.2	708.0
2020: I	19,033.7	11,781.8	9,624.7	8,111.4	1,513.3	2,157.1	1,489.5	667.6	1,643.2	38.2	1,605.0	722.6
II	20,479.4	11,053.4	8,995.7	7,529.8	1,466.0	2,057.7	1,420.6	637.1	1,475.6	25.3	1,450.3	717.9
III	20,019.2	11,563.4	9,425.4	7,926.3	1,499.1	2,138.0	1,478.9	659.1	1,751.6	42.5	1,709.2	722.6
IV	19,796.9	11,972.4	9,783.7	8,284.1	1,499.6	2,188.7	1,516.0	672.7	1,702.0	74.7	1,627.3	716.3
2021: I	22,095.5	12,058.5	9,851.2	8,340.8	1,510.4	2,207.3	1,532.7	674.6	1,655.0	26.4	1,628.6	719.4
II	20,916.4	12,369.8	10,138.5	8,609.3	1,529.3	2,231.3	1,542.4	688.9	1,776.9	71.2	1,705.7	713.5
III	21,005.2	12,681.3	10,422.3	8,858.2	1,564.2	2,259.0	1,554.6	704.4	1,792.7	63.8	1,728.9	722.7
IV	21,162.1	13,044.4	10,748.4	9,175.7	1,572.7	2,296.0	1,571.3	724.6	1,789.8	43.9	1,745.9	739.6
2022: I	21,319.8	13,259.7	10,925.5	9,337.8	1,587.8	2,334.2	1,589.6	744.6	1,811.4	74.4	1,737.0	744.9
II	21,578.3	13,415.2	11,058.0	9,457.7	1,600.4	2,357.1	1,603.6	753.6	1,835.4	95.7	1,739.7	775.9
III	21,969.5	13,755.0	11,361.0	9,737.3	1,623.8	2,394.0	1,620.0	774.0	1,863.5	95.9	1,767.6	794.9
IV p	22,357.6	13,975.9	11,552.5	9,909.4	1,643.1	2,423.4	1,636.8	786.6	1,883.5	100.6	1,782.9	809.4

See next page for continuation of table.

Table B–16. Sources of personal income, 1972–2022—*Continued*

[Billions of dollars; quarterly data at seasonally adjusted annual rates]

Year or quarter	Personal income receipts on assets			Personal current transfer receipts								Less: Contributions for government social insurance, domestic
					Government social benefits to persons						Other current transfer receipts, from business (net)	
	Total	Personal interest income	Personal dividend income	Total	Total [1]	Social security [2]	Medicare [3]	Medicaid	Unemployment insurance	Other		
1972	136.6	109.8	26.8	97.9	94.8	40.9	8.8	8.2	6.0	21.4	3.1	59.2
1973	155.4	125.5	29.9	112.6	108.6	50.7	10.2	9.6	4.6	23.3	3.9	75.5
1974	180.6	147.4	33.2	133.3	128.6	57.6	12.7	11.2	7.0	28.4	4.7	85.2
1975	201.0	168.0	32.9	170.0	163.1	65.9	15.6	13.9	18.1	35.7	6.8	89.3
1976	220.0	181.0	39.0	184.3	177.6	74.5	18.8	15.5	16.4	38.7	6.7	101.3
1977	251.6	206.9	44.7	194.6	189.5	83.2	22.1	16.7	13.1	40.9	5.1	113.1
1978	285.8	235.1	50.7	209.9	203.4	91.4	25.5	18.6	9.4	44.9	6.5	131.3
1979	327.1	269.7	57.4	235.6	227.3	102.6	29.9	21.1	9.7	49.9	8.2	152.7
1980	396.9	332.9	64.0	280.1	271.5	118.6	36.2	23.9	16.1	62.1	8.6	166.2
1981	485.8	412.2	73.6	319.0	307.8	138.6	43.5	27.7	15.9	66.3	11.2	195.7
1982	557.0	479.5	77.6	355.5	343.1	153.7	50.9	30.2	25.2	66.8	12.4	208.9
1983	599.5	516.3	83.3	384.3	370.5	164.4	57.8	33.9	26.4	71.5	13.8	226.0
1984	680.8	590.1	90.6	400.6	380.9	173.0	64.7	36.6	16.0	74.3	19.7	257.5
1985	726.3	628.9	97.4	425.4	403.1	183.3	69.7	39.7	15.9	78.0	22.3	281.4
1986	768.2	662.1	106.0	451.6	428.6	193.6	75.3	43.6	16.5	83.0	22.9	303.4
1987	791.1	679.0	112.2	468.1	447.9	201.0	81.6	47.8	14.6	86.4	20.2	323.1
1988	851.4	721.7	129.7	497.5	476.9	213.9	86.3	53.0	13.3	93.6	20.6	361.5
1989	964.3	806.5	157.8	544.2	521.1	227.4	98.2	60.8	14.4	103.1	23.2	385.2
1990	1,005.3	836.5	168.8	596.9	574.7	244.1	107.6	73.1	18.2	113.9	22.2	410.1
1991	1,003.7	823.5	180.2	668.1	650.5	264.2	117.5	96.9	26.8	127.0	17.6	430.2
1992	998.8	809.8	189.1	748.0	731.8	281.8	132.6	116.2	39.6	142.9	16.3	455.0
1993	1,007.0	802.3	204.7	793.0	778.9	297.9	146.8	130.1	34.8	150.0	14.1	477.4
1994	1,049.8	814.6	235.2	829.0	815.7	312.2	164.4	139.4	23.9	156.1	13.3	508.2
1995	1,136.6	878.6	258.0	883.5	864.7	327.7	181.2	149.6	21.7	164.0	18.7	532.8
1996	1,201.2	899.0	302.2	929.2	906.3	342.0	194.9	158.2	22.3	167.6	22.9	555.1
1997	1,285.0	947.1	337.9	954.9	935.4	356.6	206.9	163.1	20.1	166.4	19.4	587.2
1998	1,370.9	1,015.5	355.4	983.9	957.9	369.2	205.6	170.2	19.7	170.0	26.0	624.7
1999	1,364.3	1,017.7	346.6	1,026.2	992.2	379.9	208.7	184.6	20.5	174.4	34.0	661.3
2000	1,490.0	1,106.5	383.5	1,087.3	1,044.9	401.4	219.1	199.5	20.7	179.1	42.4	705.8
2001	1,481.7	1,112.3	369.3	1,192.6	1,145.8	425.1	242.6	227.3	31.9	192.4	46.8	733.2
2002	1,413.6	1,014.8	398.8	1,285.2	1,251.0	446.9	259.7	250.0	53.5	211.3	34.2	751.5
2003	1,452.3	1,020.2	432.1	1,347.3	1,321.0	463.5	276.7	264.5	53.2	231.2	26.3	779.3
2004	1,527.1	965.4	561.7	1,421.2	1,404.5	485.5	304.4	289.8	36.4	254.3	16.8	829.2
2005	1,695.2	1,117.4	577.8	1,516.7	1,490.9	512.7	332.1	304.4	31.8	273.5	25.8	873.3
2006	1,981.7	1,258.9	722.8	1,613.8	1,593.0	544.1	399.1	299.1	30.4	281.5	20.8	922.5
2007	2,194.5	1,379.2	815.3	1,728.1	1,697.3	575.7	428.2	324.2	32.7	294.9	30.8	961.4
2008	2,204.0	1,399.4	804.6	1,955.1	1,919.3	605.5	461.6	338.3	51.1	417.7	35.8	988.4
2009	1,853.7	1,300.7	553.0	2,146.7	2,107.7	664.5	493.0	369.6	131.2	398.0	39.0	964.3
2010	1,786.8	1,242.9	543.9	2,325.2	2,281.4	690.2	513.4	396.9	138.9	484.2	43.7	983.7
2011	1,937.1	1,255.6	681.5	2,358.7	2,310.1	713.3	535.6	406.0	107.2	484.8	48.5	916.7
2012	2,153.7	1,318.6	835.1	2,363.0	2,322.6	762.1	554.7	417.5	83.6	434.4	40.4	950.5
2013	2,058.9	1,265.6	793.3	2,424.3	2,385.9	799.0	572.8	440.0	62.5	432.5	38.4	1,104.3
2014	2,290.0	1,336.8	953.2	2,541.5	2,498.6	834.6	600.0	490.9	35.5	453.5	42.9	1,153.6
2015	2,474.9	1,441.8	1,033.1	2,685.4	2,635.1	871.8	634.9	535.9	32.5	467.4	50.3	1,204.7
2016	2,542.6	1,465.2	1,077.4	2,777.0	2,717.3	896.5	662.1	562.8	32.0	467.1	59.7	1,238.8
2017	2,703.5	1,549.0	1,154.6	2,855.7	2,807.4	926.1	691.8	573.7	30.2	474.2	48.3	1,298.9
2018	2,862.2	1,608.9	1,253.4	2,976.6	2,926.5	972.4	733.6	589.8	27.7	483.3	50.1	1,361.6
2019	3,119.0	1,658.1	1,460.9	3,144.8	3,089.7	1,030.7	787.1	614.0	27.6	499.3	55.1	1,424.6
2020	3,095.4	1,647.3	1,448.1	4,231.2	4,187.1	1,077.9	815.7	657.6	537.4	952.9	44.1	1,450.0
2021	3,202.4	1,658.6	1,543.9	4,617.3	4,546.4	1,114.6	880.6	735.6	320.9	1,340.5	71.0	1,540.8
2022 p	3,341.6	1,724.8	1,616.8	3,910.0	3,838.9	1,211.6	920.4	783.0	20.3	742.9	71.1	1,676.6
2019: I	3,047.7	1,647.3	1,400.4	3,105.7	3,048.6	1,019.2	772.6	598.7	29.4	503.1	57.1	1,410.6
II	3,121.8	1,664.0	1,457.8	3,140.3	3,082.7	1,026.6	785.8	614.4	26.9	500.1	57.6	1,418.0
III	3,148.6	1,655.5	1,493.1	3,162.7	3,107.3	1,034.4	793.7	622.4	26.4	498.0	55.4	1,425.4
IV	3,158.0	1,665.8	1,492.2	3,170.5	3,120.1	1,042.8	796.3	620.7	27.7	496.2	50.4	1,444.4
2020: I	3,144.3	1,660.2	1,484.1	3,212.4	3,169.8	1,068.2	795.3	606.6	40.7	518.4	42.6	1,470.6
II	3,076.3	1,638.6	1,437.7	5,556.4	5,512.0	1,074.9	808.0	654.7	1,007.5	1,822.6	44.4	1,400.3
III	3,043.8	1,643.2	1,400.6	4,385.7	4,344.3	1,080.3	822.1	690.7	792.9	811.0	41.4	1,447.8
IV	3,117.4	1,647.2	1,470.1	3,770.2	3,722.2	1,088.2	837.5	678.3	308.5	659.8	48.0	1,481.3
2021: I	3,132.0	1,655.7	1,476.3	6,022.3	5,962.9	1,105.7	857.6	704.4	556.2	2,587.1	59.5	1,491.6
II	3,196.3	1,665.4	1,530.9	4,381.6	4,305.7	1,109.4	875.4	744.8	448.6	974.2	76.0	1,521.7
III	3,222.9	1,655.7	1,567.3	4,139.6	4,064.4	1,116.8	889.5	748.2	245.1	909.6	75.2	1,554.0
IV	3,258.5	1,657.5	1,601.0	3,925.7	3,852.5	1,126.5	900.0	745.0	33.8	890.9	73.2	1,595.8
2022: I	3,269.9	1,670.8	1,599.1	3,868.7	3,797.7	1,198.7	908.0	763.1	23.6	746.6	71.1	1,634.7
II	3,323.0	1,708.6	1,614.4	3,883.2	3,809.1	1,206.9	911.8	789.5	18.6	722.7	74.1	1,654.4
III	3,358.8	1,738.1	1,620.7	3,892.8	3,823.0	1,214.6	920.3	786.1	18.5	721.7	69.8	1,695.6
IV p	3,414.8	1,781.7	1,633.1	3,995.4	3,925.9	1,226.0	941.6	793.3	20.4	780.5	69.5	1,721.6

[1] Includes Veterans' benefits, not shown seperately.

[2] Includes old-age, survivors, and disability insurance benefits that are distributed from the federal old-age and survivors insurance trust fund and the disability insurance trust fund.

[3] Includes hospital and supplementary medical insurance benefits that are distributed from the federal hospital insurance trust fund and the supplementary medical insurance trust fund.

Source: Department of Commerce (Bureau of Economic Analysis).

Table B–17. Disposition of personal income, 1972–2022

[Billions of dollars, except as noted; quarterly data at seasonally adjusted annual rates]

Year or quarter	Personal income	Less: Personal current taxes	Equals: Disposable personal income	Less: Personal outlays				Equals: Personal saving	Percent of disposable personal income [2]		
				Total	Personal consumption expenditures	Personal interest payments [1]	Personal current transfer payments		Personal outlays		Personal saving
									Total	Personal consumption expenditures	
1972	1,024.5	123.6	900.8	789.3	768.2	18.0	3.2	111.5	87.6	85.3	12.4
1973	1,140.8	132.4	1,008.4	872.6	849.6	19.6	3.4	135.8	86.5	84.3	13.5
1974	1,251.8	151.0	1,100.8	954.5	930.2	20.9	3.4	146.3	86.7	84.5	13.3
1975	1,369.4	147.6	1,221.8	1,057.8	1,030.5	23.4	3.8	164.0	86.6	84.3	13.4
1976	1,502.6	172.7	1,330.0	1,175.6	1,147.7	23.5	4.4	154.4	88.4	86.3	11.6
1977	1,659.2	197.9	1,461.4	1,305.4	1,274.0	26.6	4.8	155.9	89.3	87.2	10.7
1978	1,863.7	229.6	1,634.1	1,459.0	1,422.3	31.3	5.4	175.1	89.3	87.0	10.7
1979	2,082.7	268.9	1,813.8	1,627.0	1,585.4	35.5	6.0	186.8	89.7	87.4	10.3
1980	2,323.6	299.5	2,024.1	1,800.1	1,750.7	42.5	6.9	224.1	88.9	86.5	11.1
1981	2,605.1	345.8	2,259.3	1,993.9	1,934.0	48.4	11.5	265.5	88.3	85.6	11.8
1982	2,791.6	354.7	2,436.9	2,143.5	2,071.3	58.5	13.8	293.3	88.0	85.0	12.0
1983	2,981.1	352.9	2,628.2	2,364.2	2,281.6	67.4	15.1	264.0	90.0	86.8	10.0
1984	3,292.7	377.9	2,914.8	2,584.5	2,492.3	75.0	17.1	330.3	88.7	85.5	11.3
1985	3,524.9	417.8	3,107.1	2,822.1	2,712.8	90.6	18.8	284.9	90.8	87.3	9.2
1986	3,733.1	437.8	3,295.3	3,004.7	2,886.3	97.3	21.1	290.6	91.2	87.6	8.8
1987	3,961.6	489.6	3,472.0	3,196.6	3,076.3	97.1	23.2	275.4	92.1	88.6	7.9
1988	4,283.4	505.9	3,777.5	3,457.0	3,330.0	101.3	25.6	320.5	91.5	88.2	8.5
1989	4,625.6	567.7	4,057.8	3,717.9	3,576.8	113.1	28.0	340.0	91.6	88.1	8.4
1990	4,913.8	594.7	4,319.1	3,958.0	3,809.0	118.4	30.6	361.1	91.6	88.2	8.4
1991	5,084.9	588.9	4,496.0	4,100.0	3,943.4	119.9	36.7	396.0	91.2	87.7	8.8
1992	5,420.9	612.8	4,808.1	4,354.2	4,197.6	116.1	40.5	453.9	90.6	87.3	9.4
1993	5,657.9	648.8	5,009.2	4,611.5	4,452.0	113.9	45.6	397.7	92.1	88.9	7.9
1994	5,947.1	693.1	5,254.0	4,890.6	4,721.0	119.9	49.8	363.4	93.1	89.9	6.9
1995	6,291.4	748.4	5,543.0	5,155.9	4,962.6	140.4	52.9	387.1	93.0	89.5	7.0
1996	6,678.5	837.1	5,841.4	5,459.2	5,244.6	157.0	57.6	382.3	93.5	89.8	6.5
1997	7,092.5	931.8	6,160.7	5,770.4	5,536.8	169.7	63.9	390.3	93.7	89.9	6.3
1998	7,606.7	1,032.4	6,574.2	6,127.7	5,877.2	180.9	69.5	446.5	93.2	89.4	6.8
1999	8,006.8	1,111.9	6,894.9	6,550.9	6,283.8	190.8	76.3	344.0	95.0	91.1	5.0
2000	8,655.9	1,236.3	7,419.6	7,068.1	6,767.2	217.7	83.2	351.4	95.3	91.2	4.7
2001	9,012.8	1,239.0	7,773.8	7,390.9	7,073.8	225.6	91.5	382.8	95.1	91.0	4.9
2002	9,160.9	1,052.2	8,108.8	7,646.3	7,348.9	200.6	96.7	462.5	94.3	90.6	5.7
2003	9,498.5	1,003.5	8,495.0	8,038.3	7,740.7	196.5	101.1	456.7	94.6	91.1	5.4
2004	10,044.3	1,048.7	8,995.5	8,550.1	8,232.0	207.3	110.9	445.4	95.0	91.5	5.0
2005	10,604.9	1,212.5	9,392.5	9,124.5	8,769.1	237.3	118.1	268.0	97.1	93.4	2.9
2006	11,384.7	1,357.0	10,027.7	9,669.1	9,277.2	266.9	124.9	358.7	96.4	92.5	3.6
2007	12,021.4	1,492.5	10,528.9	10,176.2	9,746.6	291.2	138.4	352.7	96.7	92.6	3.3
2008	12,477.6	1,507.5	10,970.1	10,466.7	10,050.1	272.0	144.6	503.4	95.4	91.6	4.6
2009	12,080.4	1,152.4	10,928.0	10,288.4	9,891.2	252.8	144.3	639.7	94.1	90.5	5.9
2010	12,594.5	1,237.6	11,356.9	10,647.6	10,260.3	242.3	145.0	709.3	93.8	90.3	6.2
2011	13,339.3	1,453.7	11,885.6	11,079.6	10,698.9	229.9	150.8	806.0	93.2	90.0	6.8
2012	14,014.3	1,509.5	12,504.8	11,431.8	11,047.4	229.6	154.8	1,073.1	91.4	88.3	8.6
2013	14,193.6	1,676.4	12,517.3	11,751.3	11,363.5	229.5	158.3	766.0	93.9	90.8	6.1
2014	14,976.6	1,784.6	13,192.0	12,261.1	11,847.7	243.7	169.6	930.9	92.9	89.8	7.1
2015	15,685.2	1,939.9	13,745.3	12,710.4	12,263.5	263.5	183.5	1,034.9	92.5	89.2	7.5
2016	16,096.9	1,958.2	14,138.7	13,150.8	12,693.3	272.8	184.8	987.8	93.0	89.8	7.0
2017	16,839.8	2,048.6	14,791.2	13,717.5	13,233.6	290.4	193.5	1,073.8	92.7	89.5	7.3
2018	17,683.8	2,074.9	15,608.9	14,428.6	13,905.0	320.2	203.4	1,180.3	92.4	89.1	7.6
2019	18,587.0	2,198.4	16,388.6	14,942.0	14,392.7	339.5	209.7	1,446.6	91.2	87.8	8.8
2020	19,832.3	2,236.4	17,595.9	14,603.6	14,116.2	284.2	203.2	2,992.3	83.0	80.2	17.0
2021	21,294.8	2,661.7	18,633.1	16,389.8	15,902.6	274.4	212.8	2,243.4	88.0	85.3	12.0
2022 *p*	21,806.3	3,200.7	18,605.6	17,920.7	17,360.4	336.6	223.7	684.9	96.3	93.3	3.7
2019: I	18,345.4	2,160.2	16,185.2	14,679.9	14,145.9	328.5	205.5	1,505.3	90.7	87.4	9.3
II	18,504.9	2,221.6	16,283.3	14,872.7	14,323.7	337.2	211.8	1,410.6	91.3	88.0	8.7
III	18,655.5	2,195.8	16,459.6	15,037.8	14,482.2	346.8	208.8	1,421.8	91.4	88.0	8.6
IV	18,842.3	2,216.0	16,626.3	15,177.4	14,619.0	345.6	212.8	1,448.9	91.3	87.9	8.7
2020: I	19,033.7	2,249.1	16,784.6	14,983.4	14,440.2	337.4	205.8	1,801.2	89.3	86.0	10.7
II	20,479.4	2,098.2	18,381.2	13,529.1	13,049.8	273.0	206.3	4,852.1	73.6	71.0	26.4
III	20,019.2	2,237.5	17,781.7	14,857.8	14,388.7	272.5	196.6	2,923.9	83.6	80.9	16.4
IV	19,796.9	2,360.7	17,436.2	15,044.1	14,586.0	254.0	204.0	2,392.1	86.3	83.7	13.7
2021: I	22,095.5	2,509.0	19,586.5	15,597.8	15,131.5	258.3	208.1	3,988.7	79.6	77.3	20.4
II	20,916.4	2,638.5	18,277.8	16,299.3	15,813.5	275.5	210.2	1,978.6	89.2	86.5	10.8
III	21,005.2	2,693.2	18,312.0	16,643.0	16,147.3	281.1	214.5	1,669.1	90.9	88.2	9.1
IV	21,162.1	2,806.1	18,356.1	17,019.0	16,518.0	282.8	218.2	1,337.1	92.7	90.0	7.3
2022: I	21,319.8	3,145.5	18,174.4	17,389.5	16,874.8	293.5	221.3	784.9	95.7	92.8	4.3
II	21,578.3	3,188.5	18,389.8	17,798.7	17,261.3	313.1	224.2	591.1	96.8	93.9	3.2
III	21,969.5	3,236.5	18,733.0	18,124.5	17,542.7	357.1	224.7	608.5	96.8	93.6	3.2
IV *p*	22,357.6	3,232.5	19,125.1	18,370.1	17,762.7	382.7	224.7	755.0	96.1	92.9	3.9

[1] Consists of nonmortgage interest paid by households.
[2] Percents based on data in millions of dollars.

Source: Department of Commerce (Bureau of Economic Analysis).

TABLE B–18. Total and per capita disposable personal income and personal consumption expenditures, and per capita gross domestic product, in current and real dollars, 1972–2022

[Quarterly data at seasonally adjusted annual rates, except as noted]

Year or quarter	Disposable personal income				Personal consumption expenditures				Gross domestic product per capita (dollars)		Population (thou- sands)[1]
	Total (billions of dollars)		Per capita (dollars)		Total (billions of dollars)		Per capita (dollars)				
	Current dollars	Chained (2012) dollars	Current dollars	Chained (2012) dollars	Current dollars	Chained (2012) dollars	Current dollars	Chained (2012) dollars	Current dollars	Chained (2012) dollars	
1972	900.8	3,996.2	4,291	19,036	768.2	3,407.7	3,659	16,233	6,093	25,660	209,924
1973	1,008.4	4,244.8	4,758	20,028	849.6	3,576.3	4,009	16,874	6,725	26,851	211,939
1974	1,100.8	4,196.8	5,146	19,621	930.2	3,546.4	4,349	16,580	7,224	26,462	213,898
1975	1,221.8	4,299.8	5,657	19,908	1,030.5	3,626.8	4,771	16,792	7,801	26,153	215,981
1976	1,330.0	4,437.1	6,098	20,346	1,147.7	3,828.9	5,262	17,557	8,590	27,296	218,086
1977	1,461.4	4,577.7	6,634	20,780	1,274.0	3,990.7	5,783	18,116	9,450	28,272	220,289
1978	1,634.1	4,785.8	7,340	21,497	1,422.3	4,165.4	6,388	18,710	10,563	29,524	222,629
1979	1,813.8	4,878.6	8,057	21,672	1,585.4	4,264.4	7,043	18,944	11,672	30,123	225,106
1980	2,024.1	4,915.1	8,888	21,584	1,750.7	4,251.1	7,688	18,668	12,547	29,700	227,726
1981	2,259.3	5,035.2	9,823	21,891	1,934.0	4,310.0	8,408	18,739	13,943	30,152	230,008
1982	2,436.9	5,145.0	10,494	22,156	2,071.3	4,373.1	8,919	18,832	14,399	29,326	232,218
1983	2,628.2	5,322.6	11,216	22,714	2,281.6	4,620.7	9,737	19,718	15,508	30,394	234,333
1984	2,914.8	5,688.2	12,330	24,062	2,492.3	4,863.8	10,543	20,575	17,080	32,309	236,394
1985	3,107.1	5,859.0	13,027	24,565	2,712.8	5,115.6	11,374	21,449	18,192	33,358	238,506
1986	3,295.3	6,081.6	13,691	25,268	2,886.3	5,326.8	11,992	22,132	19,028	34,201	240,683
1987	3,472.0	6,216.1	14,297	25,597	3,076.3	5,507.6	12,668	22,680	19,993	35,070	242,843
1988	3,777.5	6,508.6	15,414	26,559	3,330.0	5,737.7	13,589	23,413	21,368	36,204	245,061
1989	4,057.8	6,699.2	16,403	27,080	3,576.8	5,905.0	14,458	23,869	22,805	37,181	247,387
1990	4,319.1	6,830.7	17,264	27,303	3,809.0	6,023.9	15,225	24,078	23,835	37,459	250,181
1991	4,496.0	6,880.4	17,734	27,138	3,943.4	6,034.8	15,554	23,803	24,290	36,924	253,530
1992	4,808.1	7,166.9	18,714	27,895	4,197.6	6,256.9	16,338	24,353	25,379	37,720	256,922
1993	5,009.2	7,285.2	19,245	27,990	4,452.0	6,474.8	17,104	24,876	26,350	38,258	260,282
1994	5,254.0	7,485.1	19,943	28,411	4,721.0	6,725.7	17,919	25,529	27,660	39,320	263,455
1995	5,543.0	7,733.9	20,792	29,011	4,962.6	6,924.1	18,615	25,973	28,658	39,900	266,588
1996	5,841.4	7,979.7	21,658	29,586	5,244.6	7,164.4	19,445	26,563	29,932	40,926	269,714
1997	6,160.7	8,271.8	22,570	30,304	5,536.8	7,434.2	20,284	27,236	31,424	42,238	272,958
1998	6,574.2	8,757.4	23,806	31,712	5,877.2	7,829.0	21,283	28,350	32,818	43,620	276,154
1999	6,894.9	9,052.7	24,684	32,409	6,283.8	8,250.3	22,496	29,536	34,480	45,192	279,328
2000	7,419.6	9,501.3	26,274	33,645	6,767.2	8,665.8	23,963	30,687	36,300	46,523	282,398
2001	7,773.8	9,759.2	27,255	34,216	7,073.8	8,880.4	24,801	31,135	37,100	46,502	285,225
2002	8,108.8	10,047.8	28,160	34,894	7,348.9	9,106.2	25,521	31,624	37,954	46,842	287,955
2003	8,495.0	10,309.7	29,230	35,474	7,740.7	9,394.4	26,635	32,325	39,420	47,709	290,626
2004	8,995.5	10,652.8	30,674	36,325	8,232.0	9,748.6	28,070	33,242	41,660	49,102	293,262
2005	9,392.5	10,811.4	31,732	36,526	8,769.1	10,093.8	29,626	34,101	44,052	50,343	295,993
2006	10,027.7	11,226.5	33,558	37,570	9,277.2	10,386.2	31,046	34,758	46,234	51,255	298,818
2007	10,528.9	11,492.6	34,899	38,093	9,746.6	10,638.7	32,306	35,263	47,976	51,787	301,696
2008	10,970.1	11,630.0	36,021	38,188	10,050.1	10,654.7	33,001	34,986	48,498	51,365	304,543
2009	10,928.0	11,617.9	35,568	37,814	9,891.2	10,515.6	32,194	34,226	47,123	49,591	307,240
2010	11,356.9	11,861.4	36,654	38,282	10,260.3	10,716.0	33,115	34,586	48,570	50,507	309,839
2011	11,885.6	12,107.2	38,059	38,769	10,698.9	10,898.3	34,259	34,898	49,952	50,886	312,295
2012	12,504.8	12,504.8	39,732	39,732	11,047.4	11,047.4	35,102	35,102	51,645	51,645	314,725
2013	12,517.3	12,350.0	39,474	38,947	11,363.5	11,211.7	35,836	35,357	53,117	52,202	317,099
2014	13,192.0	12,821.9	41,276	40,118	11,847.7	11,515.3	37,070	36,030	54,914	52,979	319,601
2015	13,745.3	13,330.0	42,672	41,383	12,263.5	11,892.9	38,072	36,922	56,521	53,988	322,113
2016	14,138.7	13,575.5	43,556	41,821	12,693.3	12,187.7	39,103	37,546	57,593	54,466	324,609
2017	14,791.2	13,946.9	45,252	42,669	13,233.6	12,478.2	40,487	38,176	59,589	55,304	326,860
2018	15,608.9	14,410.4	47,473	43,828	13,905.0	12,837.3	42,291	39,044	62,450	56,598	328,794
2019	16,388.6	14,907.8	49,585	45,105	14,392.7	13,092.3	43,547	39,612	64,690	57,596	330,513
2020	17,595.9	15,831.6	53,034	47,716	14,116.2	12,700.7	42,546	38,280	63,476	55,786	331,788
2021	18,633.1	16,115.7	56,065	48,490	15,902.6	13,754.1	47,849	41,384	70,152	59,003	332,351
2022 p	18,605.6	15,147.0	55,773	45,405	17,360.4	14,133.3	52,040	42,367	76,333	59,999	333,595
2019: I	16,185.2	14,823.4	49,066	44,937	14,145.9	12,955.7	42,883	39,275	63,701	57,100	329,868
II	16,283.3	14,822.6	49,307	44,884	14,323.7	13,038.9	43,373	39,482	64,414	57,418	330,245
III	16,459.6	14,944.2	49,768	45,186	14,482.2	13,148.9	43,789	39,757	65,104	57,845	330,729
IV	16,626.3	15,041.5	50,199	45,414	14,619.0	13,225.6	44,139	39,931	65,537	58,017	331,208
2020: I	16,784.6	15,130.1	50,627	45,636	14,440.2	13,016.8	43,556	39,262	64,965	57,279	331,534
II	18,381.2	16,645.0	55,415	50,181	13,049.8	11,817.1	39,342	35,626	59,200	52,393	331,699
III	17,781.7	15,969.6	53,580	48,120	14,388.7	12,922.4	43,356	38,938	64,370	56,479	331,872
IV	17,436.2	15,596.0	52,512	46,970	14,586.0	13,046.6	43,928	39,292	65,367	56,993	332,045
2021: I	19,586.5	17,328.1	58,998	52,195	15,131.5	13,386.8	45,578	40,323	67,213	57,882	331,989
II	18,277.8	15,920.1	55,029	47,931	15,813.5	13,773.7	47,610	41,468	69,387	58,842	332,149
III	18,312.0	15,734.4	55,077	47,324	16,147.3	13,874.4	48,566	41,730	70,833	59,169	332,480
IV	18,356.1	15,537.3	55,159	46,689	16,518.0	13,981.5	49,635	42,014	73,168	60,117	332,786
2022: I	18,174.4	15,108.8	54,581	45,375	16,874.8	14,028.4	50,678	42,130	74,301	59,836	332,978
II	18,389.8	15,021.2	55,171	45,065	17,261.3	14,099.5	51,786	42,300	75,748	59,688	333,321
III	18,733.0	15,140.6	56,121	45,359	17,542.7	14,178.6	52,554	42,476	77,064	60,080	333,799
IV p	19,125.1	15,318.0	57,212	45,823	17,762.7	14,226.8	53,137	42,559	78,212	60,391	334,282

[1] Population of the United States including Armed Forces overseas. Annual data are averages of quarterly data. Quarterly data are averages for the period.

Source: Department of Commerce (Bureau of Economic Analysis and Bureau of the Census).

Table B–19. Gross saving and investment, 1972–2022

[Billions of dollars, except as noted; quarterly data at seasonally adjusted annual rates]

Year or quarter	Gross saving										
	Total gross saving	Net saving							Consumption of fixed capital		
		Total net saving	Net private saving			Net government saving			Total	Private	Government
			Total	Personal saving	Undistributed corporate profits [1]	Total	Federal	State and local			
1972	277.6	116.6	159.6	111.5	48.0	–42.9	–49.0	6.1	161.0	117.5	43.5
1973	335.3	156.6	189.3	135.8	53.5	–32.7	–38.3	5.6	178.7	131.5	47.2
1974	349.2	142.3	186.0	146.3	39.7	–43.7	–41.3	–2.3	206.9	153.2	53.7
1975	348.1	109.6	218.3	164.0	54.3	–108.7	–97.9	–10.7	238.5	178.8	59.7
1976	399.3	139.1	224.4	154.4	70.0	–85.3	–80.9	–4.4	260.2	196.5	63.7
1977	459.4	169.6	242.5	155.9	86.6	–72.9	–73.4	.5	289.8	221.1	68.7
1978	548.0	220.8	278.0	175.1	102.9	–57.2	–62.0	4.9	327.2	252.1	75.1
1979	613.5	239.6	288.2	186.8	101.4	–48.6	–47.4	–1.2	373.9	290.7	83.1
1980	630.1	201.7	296.4	224.1	72.3	–94.7	–88.8	–5.9	428.4	335.0	93.5
1981	743.9	256.6	354.9	265.5	89.4	–98.2	–88.1	–10.2	487.2	381.9	105.3
1982	725.8	188.9	379.0	293.3	85.6	–190.1	–167.4	–22.8	537.0	420.4	116.6
1983	716.7	154.1	379.7	264.0	115.7	–225.6	–207.2	–18.4	562.6	438.8	123.8
1984	881.6	283.2	479.9	330.3	149.5	–196.7	–196.5	–.2	598.4	463.5	134.9
1985	881.0	240.8	442.5	284.9	157.5	–201.7	–199.2	–2.4	640.1	496.4	143.7
1986	864.5	179.2	399.1	290.6	108.5	–219.9	–215.9	–4.0	685.3	531.6	153.7
1987	948.9	218.5	398.6	275.4	123.2	–180.1	–165.7	–14.4	730.4	566.3	164.1
1988	1,076.6	292.1	463.4	320.5	142.9	–171.3	–160.0	–11.3	784.5	607.9	176.6
1989	1,109.8	271.5	450.2	340.0	110.3	–178.7	–159.4	–19.3	838.3	649.6	188.6
1990	1,113.4	224.8	464.4	361.1	103.2	–239.5	–203.3	–36.2	888.5	688.4	200.1
1991	1,153.4	221.0	529.5	396.0	133.5	–308.5	–248.4	–60.1	932.4	721.5	210.9
1992	1,147.6	187.4	592.8	453.9	139.0	–405.5	–334.5	–71.0	960.2	742.9	217.4
1993	1,163.4	159.9	545.9	397.7	148.2	–386.0	–313.5	–72.5	1,003.5	778.2	225.3
1994	1,295.1	239.5	559.0	363.4	195.7	–319.6	–255.6	–63.9	1,055.6	822.5	233.1
1995	1,426.3	303.9	616.5	387.1	229.4	–312.5	–242.1	–70.4	1,122.4	880.7	241.7
1996	1,578.9	403.6	636.8	382.3	254.5	–233.2	–179.4	–53.8	1,175.3	929.1	246.2
1997	1,780.5	541.2	675.1	390.3	284.9	–133.9	–92.0	–42.0	1,239.3	987.8	251.6
1998	1,930.6	620.8	649.5	446.5	203.0	–28.7	1.4	–30.1	1,309.7	1,052.2	257.6
1999	2,007.2	608.3	578.1	344.0	234.0	30.2	69.1	–38.9	1,398.9	1,132.2	266.7
2000	2,124.6	613.4	494.3	351.4	142.9	119.0	159.7	–40.6	1,511.2	1,231.5	279.7
2001	2,069.1	469.6	573.5	382.8	190.7	–104.0	15.0	–119.0	1,599.5	1,311.7	287.8
2002	1,996.0	338.0	788.7	462.5	326.2	–450.7	–267.8	–182.9	1,658.0	1,361.8	296.2
2003	1,983.5	264.5	843.1	456.7	386.5	–578.7	–397.4	–181.3	1,719.1	1,411.9	307.1
2004	2,153.4	331.6	874.1	445.4	428.6	–542.5	–393.5	–149.0	1,821.8	1,497.1	324.7
2005	2,349.4	378.3	774.9	268.0	506.9	–396.6	–293.8	–102.8	1,971.0	1,622.6	348.4
2006	2,636.9	512.8	819.7	358.7	461.1	–307.0	–221.9	–85.0	2,124.1	1,751.8	372.3
2007	2,504.4	251.6	640.5	352.7	287.9	–389.0	–259.7	–129.3	2,252.8	1,852.5	400.3
2008	2,206.0	–152.8	693.0	503.4	189.6	–845.8	–624.9	–220.9	2,358.8	1,931.8	427.0
2009	1,987.4	–384.1	1,200.5	639.7	560.8	–1,584.5	–1,243.2	–341.3	2,371.5	1,928.7	442.8
2010	2,287.7	–103.3	1,522.6	709.3	813.3	–1,625.8	–1,318.4	–307.5	2,390.9	1,933.8	457.2
2011	2,521.2	46.7	1,555.9	806.0	749.9	–1,509.2	–1,234.1	–275.1	2,474.5	1,997.3	477.2
2012	3,007.7	431.7	1,787.2	1,073.1	714.1	–1,355.5	–1,072.7	–282.8	2,576.0	2,082.4	493.6
2013	3,189.2	507.9	1,405.0	766.0	639.1	–897.1	–631.8	–265.3	2,681.2	2,176.6	504.6
2014	3,527.8	712.7	1,548.0	930.9	617.1	–835.3	–597.4	–237.9	2,815.0	2,298.5	516.6
2015	3,669.6	758.2	1,534.2	1,034.9	499.3	–776.0	–560.2	–215.8	2,911.4	2,388.5	522.9
2016	3,534.7	547.7	1,460.0	987.8	472.1	–912.3	–667.6	–244.7	2,987.1	2,459.9	527.1
2017	3,797.8	679.0	1,640.9	1,073.8	567.1	–961.8	–734.4	–227.4	3,118.7	2,576.8	542.0
2018	4,027.0	751.4	1,856.2	1,180.3	675.9	–1,104.7	–907.3	–197.4	3,275.6	2,710.5	565.1
2019	4,211.1	774.5	2,020.1	1,446.6	573.5	–1,245.6	–1,052.2	–193.4	3,436.6	2,850.1	586.5
2020	4,055.9	478.1	3,422.2	2,992.3	429.9	–2,944.1	–2,957.4	13.3	3,577.8	2,971.8	605.9
2021	4,188.1	356.5	2,966.9	2,243.4	723.6	–2,610.5	–2,835.3	224.9	3,831.6	3,184.5	647.1
2022 [p]				684.9					4,284.4	3,567.9	716.5
2019: I	4,238.9	858.5	2,085.4	1,505.3	580.1	–1,226.8	–1,028.2	–198.7	3,380.4	2,800.7	579.7
II	4,202.3	780.7	1,986.5	1,410.6	575.9	–1,205.8	–1,052.3	–153.5	3,421.6	2,837.2	584.3
III	4,169.5	711.2	1,998.8	1,421.8	577.0	–1,287.5	–1,087.6	–199.9	3,458.2	2,869.0	589.2
IV	4,233.9	747.7	2,010.0	1,448.9	561.1	–1,262.3	–1,041.0	–221.4	3,486.2	2,893.5	592.8
2020: I	4,439.3	914.2	2,201.1	1,801.2	399.9	–1,286.9	–1,090.2	–196.7	3,525.1	2,927.6	597.6
II	3,678.6	123.4	5,071.0	4,852.1	218.9	–4,947.6	–5,388.5	440.9	3,555.1	2,953.2	601.9
III	3,671.5	78.5	3,570.1	2,923.9	646.2	–3,491.6	–3,372.5	–119.1	3,593.0	2,984.0	608.9
IV	4,434.2	796.4	2,846.6	2,392.1	454.5	–2,050.2	–1,978.4	–71.8	3,637.9	3,022.5	615.4
2021: I	4,155.4	464.9	4,658.6	3,988.7	669.8	–4,193.7	–4,120.3	–73.3	3,690.5	3,064.4	626.1
II	3,920.6	145.2	2,734.6	1,978.6	756.0	–2,589.4	–3,382.7	793.3	3,775.4	3,136.0	639.4
III	4,137.7	262.1	2,431.7	1,669.1	762.6	–2,169.7	–2,314.4	144.7	3,875.7	3,222.5	653.2
IV	4,538.6	553.7	2,042.8	1,337.1	705.7	–1,489.1	–1,524.0	34.9	3,984.9	3,315.2	669.7
2022: I	4,667.8	554.2	1,415.9	784.9	631.0	–861.6	–929.0	67.4	4,113.6	3,422.4	691.2
II	4,697.7	455.6	1,373.3	591.1	782.2	–917.8	–879.9	–37.9	4,242.1	3,530.9	711.2
III	4,729.9	371.8	1,467.5	608.5	859.0	–1,095.7	–1,015.7	–80.0	4,358.1	3,631.8	726.3
IV [p]				755.0					4,423.9	3,686.6	737.3

[1] With inventory valuation and capital consumption adjustments.

See next page for continuation of table.

TABLE B–19. Gross saving and investment, 1972–2022—*Continued*

[Billions of dollars, except as noted; quarterly data at seasonally adjusted annual rates]

Year or quarter	Gross domestic investment, capital account transactions, and net lending, NIPA[2]						Statistical discrepancy	Addenda:						
	Total	Gross domestic investment			Capital account transactions (net)[3]	Net lending or net borrowing (−), NIPA[2, 4]		Gross private saving	Gross government saving			Net domestic investment	Gross saving as a percent of gross national income	Net saving as a percent of gross national income
		Total	Gross private domestic investment	Gross government investment					Total	Federal	State and local			
1972	284.8	288.8	228.1	60.7	0.0	−4.1	7.2	277.1	0.6	−18.8	19.4	127.8	21.7	9.1
1973	341.4	332.6	266.9	65.6	.0	8.8	6.1	320.8	14.5	−6.0	20.4	153.9	23.4	10.9
1974	356.6	350.7	274.5	76.2	.0	5.9	7.4	339.1	10.1	−6.0	16.0	143.8	22.5	9.2
1975	361.5	341.7	257.3	84.4	.1	19.8	13.3	397.1	−48.9	−59.2	10.3	103.1	20.7	6.5
1976	420.0	412.9	323.2	89.6	.1	7.0	20.7	420.9	−21.6	−39.2	17.6	152.6	21.4	7.4
1977	478.9	489.8	396.6	93.2	.1	−11.0	19.4	463.6	−4.2	−28.2	24.0	199.9	22.1	8.1
1978	571.3	583.9	478.4	105.6	.1	−12.7	23.3	530.1	17.9	−12.4	30.3	256.7	23.3	9.4
1979	658.6	659.8	539.7	120.1	.1	−1.3	45.1	579.0	34.6	7.2	27.3	285.9	23.5	9.2
1980	674.6	666.0	530.1	135.9	.1	8.4	44.4	631.4	−1.2	−28.4	27.1	237.6	22.1	7.1
1981	781.9	778.6	631.2	147.3	.1	3.3	38.1	736.8	7.1	−20.6	27.6	291.3	23.2	8.0
1982	734.7	738.0	581.0	156.9	.1	−3.4	8.8	799.4	−73.5	−92.0	18.4	201.0	21.5	5.6
1983	773.6	808.7	637.5	171.2	.1	−35.2	57.0	818.5	−101.8	−126.1	24.3	246.1	19.8	4.3
1984	923.2	1,013.3	820.1	193.2	.1	−90.2	41.6	943.4	−61.8	−105.9	44.1	414.9	21.9	7.0
1985	935.2	1,049.5	829.7	219.9	.1	−114.5	54.3	938.9	−57.9	−102.3	44.4	409.4	20.4	5.6
1986	944.6	1,087.2	849.1	238.1	.1	−142.8	80.1	930.7	−66.2	−112.4	46.2	401.9	19.1	4.0
1987	992.7	1,146.8	892.2	254.6	.1	−154.2	43.8	964.9	−16.0	−55.6	39.6	416.4	19.7	4.5
1988	1,079.6	1,195.4	937.0	258.4	.1	−115.9	3.0	1,071.3	5.3	−41.0	46.4	410.9	20.5	5.6
1989	1,177.8	1,270.1	999.7	270.4	.3	−92.7	68.0	1,099.9	9.9	−32.5	42.4	431.9	19.8	4.9
1990	1,208.9	1,283.8	993.4	290.4	7.4	−82.3	95.5	1,152.8	−39.4	−69.8	30.4	395.3	18.9	3.8
1991	1,246.3	1,238.4	944.3	294.1	5.3	2.6	93.0	1,250.9	−97.6	−108.3	10.8	306.0	18.9	3.6
1992	1,263.6	1,309.1	1,013.0	296.1	−1.3	−44.3	115.9	1,335.7	−188.1	−191.2	3.1	348.9	17.8	2.9
1993	1,319.3	1,398.7	1,106.8	291.9	.9	−80.2	156.0	1,324.1	−160.7	−166.5	5.8	395.2	17.3	2.4
1994	1,435.1	1,550.7	1,256.5	294.2	1.3	−116.9	140.0	1,381.6	−86.4	−105.3	18.8	495.0	18.1	3.3
1995	1,519.3	1,625.2	1,317.5	307.7	.4	−106.3	93.0	1,497.2	−70.9	−88.6	17.7	502.8	18.8	4.0
1996	1,637.0	1,752.0	1,432.1	320.0	.2	−115.2	58.1	1,565.9	13.0	−25.7	38.7	576.7	19.6	5.0
1997	1,792.1	1,922.2	1,595.6	326.6	.5	−130.6	11.6	1,662.9	117.6	62.3	55.3	682.9	20.7	6.3
1998	1,875.3	2,080.7	1,736.7	344.0	.2	−205.6	−55.2	1,701.7	228.9	156.8	72.1	770.9	21.1	6.8
1999	1,978.9	2,255.5	1,887.1	368.5	6.7	−283.3	−28.3	1,710.3	296.9	227.3	69.7	856.6	20.7	6.3
2000	2,030.4	2,427.3	2,038.4	388.9	4.6	−401.4	−94.2	1,725.9	398.8	322.8	76.0	916.0	20.5	5.9
2001	1,955.3	2,346.7	1,934.8	411.9	−11.9	−379.5	−113.8	1,885.2	183.8	179.5	4.4	747.2	19.3	4.4
2002	1,918.7	2,374.1	1,930.4	443.7	4.2	−459.6	−77.3	2,150.5	−154.5	−101.0	−53.5	716.1	18.1	3.1
2003	1,963.6	2,491.3	2,027.1	464.2	8.8	−536.4	−19.9	2,255.1	−271.6	−225.1	−46.4	772.2	17.2	2.3
2004	2,129.7	2,767.5	2,281.3	486.2	4.6	−642.4	−23.7	2,371.2	−217.8	−213.0	−4.8	945.6	17.5	2.7
2005	2,296.8	3,048.0	2,534.7	513.3	−.7	−750.5	−52.5	2,397.5	−48.1	−103.2	55.1	1,077.0	17.8	2.9
2006	2,432.5	3,251.8	2,701.0	550.9	7.7	−827.0	−204.3	2,571.5	65.4	−20.7	86.0	1,127.7	18.7	3.6
2007	2,524.2	3,265.0	2,673.0	592.0	6.4	−747.2	19.8	2,493.0	11.3	−46.9	58.2	1,012.2	17.2	1.7
2008	2,403.0	3,107.2	2,477.6	629.6	.8	−705.0	197.0	2,624.8	−418.8	−399.1	−19.7	748.4	15.0	−1.0
2009	2,189.5	2,572.6	1,929.7	642.9	6.3	−389.4	202.0	3,129.2	−1,141.8	−1,009.5	−132.2	201.1	13.8	−2.7
2010	2,370.2	2,810.0	2,165.5	644.5	7.4	−447.2	82.5	3,456.3	−1,168.7	−1,074.6	−94.1	419.1	15.1	−.7
2011	2,508.8	2,969.2	2,332.6	636.6	9.5	−469.8	−12.3	3,553.2	−1,032.1	−979.2	−52.9	494.7	15.9	.3
2012	2,818.8	3,242.8	2,621.8	621.0	−.5	−423.4	−188.9	3,869.6	−861.9	−811.0	−50.8	666.8	18.0	2.6
2013	3,074.3	3,426.4	2,826.0	600.4	7.0	−359.0	−114.8	3,581.6	−392.4	−365.9	−26.5	745.2	18.6	3.0
2014	3,270.6	3,646.7	3,044.2	602.6	6.9	−383.0	−257.2	3,846.5	−318.7	−327.1	8.4	831.7	19.6	4.0
2015	3,435.1	3,859.8	3,237.2	622.6	8.3	−433.0	−234.5	3,922.7	−253.1	−288.7	35.6	948.4	19.7	4.1
2016	3,441.3	3,845.0	3,205.0	639.9	7.0	−410.7	−93.4	3,919.9	−385.1	−396.9	11.7	857.9	18.6	2.9
2017	3,682.5	4,053.9	3,385.6	668.3	16.0	−387.4	−115.3	4,217.6	−419.9	−458.5	38.7	935.2	19.1	3.4
2018	3,913.1	4,354.2	3,642.4	711.8	4.7	−445.8	−114.0	4,566.7	−539.6	−622.3	82.6	1,078.6	19.2	3.6
2019	4,105.6	4,558.3	3,807.1	751.1	6.9	−459.5	−105.5	4,870.2	−659.1	−758.4	99.3	1,121.7	19.3	3.6
2020	3,841.0	4,433.4	3,642.9	790.5	6.0	−598.5	−214.9	6,394.0	−2,338.1	−2,652.6	314.5	855.7	18.9	2.2
2021	4,059.1	4,920.5	4,113.5	807.0	3.6	−865.0	−128.9	6,151.4	−1,963.4	−2,512.7	549.3	1,088.9	17.7	1.5
2022 [p]	....	5,487.7	4,631.0	856.8	....	....	....	....	....	....	....	1,203.3	....	....
2019: I	4,047.3	4,524.4	3,778.8	745.6	11.4	−488.5	−191.7	4,886.1	−647.1	−736.4	89.3	1,144.0	19.7	4.0
II	4,086.7	4,564.7	3,820.0	744.7	3.9	−481.9	−115.6	4,823.7	−621.4	−759.9	138.4	1,143.2	19.4	3.6
III	4,159.8	4,604.1	3,849.4	754.7	4.1	−448.4	−9.7	4,867.8	−698.3	−792.9	94.6	1,145.9	19.1	3.3
IV	4,128.8	4,539.8	3,780.3	759.5	8.2	−419.2	−105.1	4,903.4	−669.6	−744.3	74.7	1,053.6	19.2	3.4
2020: I	4,097.3	4,519.1	3,737.6	781.6	11.9	−433.8	−342.0	5,128.6	−689.3	−790.7	101.4	994.0	20.1	4.1
II	3,422.8	3,947.5	3,161.4	786.1	4.3	−529.0	−255.8	8,024.2	−4,345.7	−5,085.3	739.6	392.4	18.3	.6
III	3,868.0	4,533.0	3,743.3	789.7	2.7	−667.7	196.6	6,554.2	−2,882.7	−3,066.3	183.6	940.0	17.2	.4
IV	3,975.8	4,734.1	3,929.4	804.7	5.1	−763.4	−458.5	5,869.1	−1,434.8	−1,668.3	233.4	1,096.3	19.9	3.6
2021: I	3,921.6	4,700.3	3,902.3	798.0	14.1	−792.8	−233.8	7,722.9	−3,567.6	−3,805.5	237.9	1,009.8	18.3	2.0
II	3,896.3	4,740.4	3,943.4	797.0	4.0	−848.1	−24.3	5,870.6	−1,950.0	−3,063.2	1,113.1	965.1	16.9	.6
III	4,004.2	4,919.2	4,109.1	810.1	−11.5	−903.5	−133.5	5,654.2	−1,516.5	−1,989.2	472.8	1,043.5	17.3	1.1
IV	4,414.4	5,322.0	4,499.2	822.9	7.8	−915.5	−124.2	5,358.0	−819.4	−1,192.8	373.4	1,337.2	18.4	2.2
2022: I	4,390.8	5,500.3	4,671.0	829.3	8.0	−1,117.5	−277.0	4,838.3	−170.5	−590.8	420.3	1,386.7	18.5	2.2
II	4,428.3	5,448.8	4,609.9	838.9	16.1	−1,036.7	−269.3	4,904.2	−206.6	−534.2	327.7	1,206.7	18.3	1.8
III	4,486.2	5,447.9	4,579.1	868.8	−20.4	−941.3	−243.7	5,099.3	−369.4	−664.6	295.2	1,089.8	18.1	1.4
IV [p]	....	5,553.9	4,663.8	890.0	....	....	....	....	....	....	....	1,129.9	....	....

[2] National income and product accounts (NIPA).
[3] Consists of capital transfers and the acquisition and disposal of nonproduced nonfinancial assets.
[4] Prior to 1982, equals the balance on current account, NIPA.

Source: Department of Commerce (Bureau of Economic Analysis).

Table B–20. Median money income (in 2021 dollars) and poverty status of families and people, by race, 2014–2021

Race, Hispanic origin, and year	Families[1]						People below poverty level[2]		Median money income (in 2021 dollars) of people 15 years old and over with income[3]			
	Number (millions)	Median money income (in 2021 dollars)[3]	Below poverty level[2]: Total		Below poverty level[2]: Female householder, no husband present		Number (millions)	Percent	Males		Females	
			Number (millions)	Percent	Number (millions)	Percent			All people	Year-round full-time workers	All people	Year-round full-time workers
TOTAL (all races)[4]												
2014	81.7	$76,331	9.5	11.6	4.8	30.6	46.7	14.8	$41,586	$58,946	$25,477	$46,736
2015	82.2	80,849	8.6	10.4	4.4	28.2	43.1	13.5	42,471	59,749	27,182	47,750
2016	82.9	82,089	8.1	9.8	4.1	26.6	40.6	12.7	43,884	60,373	28,104	48,773
2017	83.1	83,931	7.8	9.3	4.0	25.7	39.7	12.3	44,646	61,711	28,169	49,050
2017[5]	83.5	84,149	7.8	9.3	4.0	26.2	39.6	12.3	44,647	61,344	28,623	50,655
2018	83.5	84,856	7.5	9.0	3.7	24.9	38.1	11.8	44,901	61,737	29,217	50,202
2019	83.7	91,151	6.6	7.8	3.3	22.2	34.0	10.5	46,957	64,514	31,164	53,125
2020[6]	83.7	88,286	7.3	8.7	3.6	23.5	37.5	11.5	44,691	67,971	30,785	55,065
2021	84.3	88,590	7.4	8.8	3.6	23.0	37.9	11.6	45,923	63,743	30,937	52,979
WHITE, non-Hispanic[7]												
2014	53.8	87,817	3.9	7.3	1.7	23.7	19.7	10.1	47,051	67,258	27,499	50,675
2015	53.8	92,090	3.5	6.4	1.6	21.7	17.8	9.1	48,268	69,473	29,309	52,255
2016	54.1	92,659	3.4	6.3	1.6	21.1	17.3	8.8	49,000	69,093	29,914	53,415
2017	53.9	94,889	3.2	6.0	1.4	19.8	17.0	8.7	50,661	68,993	29,970	54,113
2017[5]	54.2	96,119	3.2	5.9	1.4	20.2	16.6	8.5	51,054	68,880	30,738	55,880
2018	54.2	96,511	3.2	5.8	1.4	19.7	15.7	8.1	51,593	70,437	31,795	54,697
2019	54.3	102,904	2.7	5.0	1.1	17.1	14.2	7.3	53,587	74,498	33,211	56,944
2020[6]	53.5	101,111	3.1	5.8	1.3	18.8	16.0	8.2	52,530	75,661	32,963	59,945
2021	53.5	100,977	3.0	5.6	1.2	17.3	15.8	8.1	51,442	72,655	32,647	57,806
BLACK[7]												
2014	9.9	49,432	2.3	22.9	1.6	37.2	10.8	26.2	30,436	47,303	24,018	40,472
2015	9.8	52,355	2.1	21.1	1.5	33.9	10.0	24.1	31,339	47,699	24,717	42,439
2016	10.0	55,735	1.9	19.0	1.3	31.6	9.2	22.0	33,462	47,398	25,781	42,155
2017	10.0	55,923	1.8	18.2	1.3	30.8	9.0	21.2	33,282	48,299	26,127	41,503
2017[5]	10.0	55,980	1.9	18.9	1.4	31.9	9.2	21.7	32,468	46,885	26,446	42,621
2018	9.8	57,298	1.7	17.7	1.2	29.4	8.9	20.8	33,579	49,190	27,473	43,389
2019	10.0	62,015	1.6	16.3	1.1	27.3	8.1	18.8	33,129	49,537	28,635	44,499
2020[6]	10.2	60,259	1.7	16.8	1.2	28.2	8.6	19.6	32,733	53,858	27,977	48,200
2021	10.3	59,541	1.8	17.4	1.3	29.3	8.6	19.5	33,900	51,139	28,481	48,179
ASIAN[7]												
2014	4.5	94,775	.4	8.9	.1	18.9	2.1	12.0	46,855	69,076	29,087	55,613
2015	4.7	103,892	.4	8.0	.1	16.2	2.1	11.4	49,981	74,036	30,342	57,315
2016	4.7	105,562	.3	7.2	.1	19.4	1.9	10.1	52,602	75,909	30,225	58,011
2017	4.9	102,551	.4	7.8	.1	15.5	2.0	10.0	53,983	78,271	31,235	57,725
2017[5]	4.9	104,675	.4	7.4	.1	16.3	1.9	9.7	54,363	78,046	30,507	59,297
2018	5.1	109,238	.4	7.6	.1	19.6	2.0	10.1	55,877	77,426	33,650	62,635
2019	5.1	118,932	.3	5.7	.1	14.4	1.5	7.3	56,883	83,035	34,017	63,874
2020[6]	5.2	114,748	.3	6.4	.1	15.4	1.6	8.1	54,241	93,055	33,756	75,271
2021	5.3	118,386	.4	7.1	.1	14.7	1.9	9.3	56,682	86,198	34,270	68,834
HISPANIC (any race)[7]												
2014	12.5	51,681	2.7	21.5	1.3	37.9	13.1	23.6	30,558	40,225	20,145	35,317
2015	12.8	54,124	2.5	19.6	1.2	35.5	12.1	21.4	32,146	41,139	21,620	36,203
2016	13.0	57,699	2.3	17.3	1.1	32.7	11.1	19.4	34,449	43,110	22,475	36,171
2017	13.2	59,258	2.2	16.3	1.1	32.7	10.8	18.3	33,922	44,101	22,450	35,854
2017[5]	13.3	59,237	2.2	16.4	1.1	33.4	10.8	18.3	33,702	42,603	22,670	36,309
2018	13.3	59,443	2.1	15.5	1.0	30.8	10.5	17.6	33,898	43,547	23,399	37,946
2019	13.2	64,568	1.8	13.9	.9	26.8	9.5	15.7	34,215	44,501	24,820	39,110
2020[6]	13.7	62,865	2.0	14.8	1.0	28.6	10.5	17.0	33,574	47,983	23,978	42,190
2021	14.1	62,301	2.1	15.0	1.0	28.2	10.7	17.1	36,334	46,371	25,324	40,575

[1] The term "family" refers to a group of two or more persons related by birth, marriage, or adoption and residing together. Every family must include a reference person.
[2] Poverty thresholds are updated each year to reflect changes in the consumer price index for all urban consumers (CPI-U).
[3] Adjusted by consumer price index retroactive series (R-CPI-U-RS).
[4] Data for American Indians and Alaska natives, native Hawaiians and other Pacific Islanders, and those reporting two or more races are included in the total but not shown separately.
[5] Reflects implementation of an updated data processing system.
[6] Reflects implementation of Census 2020-based population controls comparable to succeeding years.
[7] The CPS allows respondents to choose more than one race. Data shown are for "white alone, non-Hispanic," "black alone," and "Asian alone" race categories. ("Black" is also "black or African American.") Family race and Hispanic origin are based on the reference person.

Note: For details see *Income and Poverty in the United States* in publication Series P–60 on the CPS ASEC.

Source: Department of Commerce (Bureau of the Census).

TABLE B–21. Real farm income, 1957–2023

[Billions of chained (2023) dollars]

Year	Income of farm operators from farming [1]							
	Gross farm income						Production expenses	Net farm income
	Total	Value of agricultural sector production				Direct Federal Government payments		
		Total	Crops [2, 3]	Animals and animal products [3]	Farm-related income [4]			
1957	287.0	278.6	112.6	149.8	16.1	8.4	195.5	91.4
1958	314.1	305.3	121.0	167.5	16.8	8.8	207.9	106.2
1959	301.5	296.1	117.5	160.6	18.0	5.4	216.2	85.2
1960	302.9	297.4	123.0	156.0	18.4	5.5	214.9	88.0
1961	314.9	303.3	122.9	161.4	19.0	11.6	222.0	92.9
1962	324.9	311.5	127.8	164.4	19.3	13.4	232.3	92.6
1963	329.0	316.1	136.0	160.0	20.1	12.9	239.7	89.3
1964	316.1	299.8	126.1	153.0	20.8	16.3	237.7	78.4
1965	341.6	323.5	139.6	162.9	21.0	18.1	246.9	94.7
1966	360.2	336.8	130.7	184.6	21.5	23.4	260.6	99.6
1967	350.4	329.1	133.3	173.4	22.4	21.4	264.9	85.6
1968	345.0	321.9	125.9	173.7	22.3	23.0	263.0	82.0
1969	357.8	333.7	124.8	186.0	22.9	24.1	267.1	90.7
1970	354.3	332.0	123.6	185.4	23.0	22.4	267.8	86.5
1971	356.2	338.1	134.3	180.4	23.4	18.0	270.1	86.1
1972	391.0	369.2	142.6	202.8	23.8	21.8	284.1	106.9
1973	515.4	501.8	224.3	252.0	25.5	13.6	336.4	179.0
1974	469.8	467.3	235.0	204.7	27.5	2.5	339.4	130.4
1975	440.0	436.4	220.5	188.1	27.8	3.5	328.3	111.6
1976	426.8	423.8	200.6	193.4	29.8	3.0	343.1	83.7
1977	424.7	417.6	199.7	184.8	33.1	7.1	347.0	77.6
1978	468.6	457.5	206.5	214.7	36.3	11.1	376.6	91.9
1979	507.7	503.1	224.5	239.8	38.7	4.6	415.4	92.3
1980	461.1	457.1	198.8	217.2	41.1	4.0	411.2	49.9
1981	469.4	464.0	222.7	198.7	42.5	5.5	393.6	75.9
1982	436.3	427.0	190.9	187.4	48.8	9.3	372.9	63.4
1983	393.6	369.8	145.5	179.2	45.1	23.8	357.1	36.5
1984	414.7	393.9	191.9	177.8	24.2	20.8	350.6	64.1
1985	385.5	367.0	176.3	165.1	25.7	18.4	317.2	68.2
1986	366.2	338.5	148.5	165.9	24.1	27.7	293.2	73.0
1987	385.6	347.2	147.6	173.4	26.2	38.3	298.5	87.0
1988	393.4	361.4	153.2	173.9	34.4	32.0	305.8	87.6
1989	407.7	384.5	173.4	177.6	33.5	23.2	308.8	98.9
1990	405.6	386.6	170.6	184.6	31.3	19.1	310.8	94.9
1991	381.0	364.7	161.1	173.1	30.6	16.3	301.2	79.8
1992	389.0	371.2	172.8	169.0	29.5	17.8	291.7	97.3
1993	388.5	363.1	156.6	174.3	32.2	25.4	299.9	88.5
1994	400.9	386.3	186.4	166.5	33.4	14.6	303.4	97.5
1995	383.1	369.9	174.3	159.5	36.1	13.2	310.8	72.3
1996	420.8	407.7	206.4	164.3	37.0	13.1	315.6	105.2
1997	417.5	404.4	197.3	169.0	38.1	13.1	327.5	90.0
1998	403.5	382.1	177.2	163.4	41.5	21.5	321.8	81.8
1999	402.0	365.2	158.7	162.9	43.5	36.8	320.4	81.6
2000	404.3	365.4	158.8	165.7	40.8	38.8	319.5	84.8
2001	408.6	371.9	155.4	173.9	42.6	36.7	318.9	89.7
2002	371.4	351.4	157.7	150.6	43.2	20.0	308.4	63.1
2003	408.6	382.5	171.5	165.8	45.2	26.1	312.3	96.3
2004	453.6	433.6	192.5	191.2	50.0	20.0	319.1	134.5
2005	445.3	408.9	170.6	188.7	49.6	36.4	327.8	117.5
2006	419.8	396.9	171.7	172.6	52.6	22.8	336.7	83.1
2007	478.3	461.5	212.8	195.0	53.7	16.8	379.7	98.6
2008	503.9	487.0	240.2	192.7	54.1	16.9	396.1	107.8
2009	462.2	445.5	226.1	164.3	55.2	16.7	376.8	85.4
2010	483.8	467.0	228.1	190.3	48.6	16.8	379.2	104.6
2011	558.9	545.1	265.0	217.7	62.4	13.9	408.0	151.0
2012	586.9	573.1	277.8	220.7	74.6	13.9	461.2	125.8
2013	620.7	606.6	299.8	232.2	74.6	14.1	462.1	158.6
2014	608.4	596.1	259.7	269.8	66.6	12.3	492.3	116.1
2015	549.6	536.2	229.8	242.1	64.2	13.5	447.8	101.8
2016	509.0	493.0	233.7	204.2	55.0	16.0	432.0	76.9
2017	515.3	501.3	227.6	214.3	59.4	14.0	424.3	91.0
2018	502.5	486.3	220.0	209.8	56.5	16.2	406.6	95.8
2019	497.0	470.9	206.3	203.5	61.1	26.1	405.0	92.0
2020	518.6	466.3	217.4	189.0	59.9	52.2	410.3	108.3
2021	563.2	534.8	264.5	212.7	57.5	28.5	408.6	154.6
2022 p	621.1	605.1	276.8	261.6	66.7	16.1	453.8	167.3
2023 p	596.4	586.2	276.4	242.4	67.4	10.2	459.5	136.9

[1] The GDP chain-type price index is used to convert the current-dollar statistics to 2023=100 equivalents.
[2] Crop receipts include proceeds received from commodities placed under Commodity Credit Corporation loans.
[3] The value of production equates to the sum of cash receipts, home consumption, and the value of the change in inventories.
[4] Includes income from forest products sold, the gross imputed rental value of farm dwellings, machine hire and custom work, and other sources of farm income such as commodity insurance indemnities.

Note: Data for 2022 and 2023 are forecasts.

Source: Department of Agriculture (Economic Research Service).

Labor Market Indicators

Table B–22. Civilian labor force, 1929–2022

[Monthly data seasonally adjusted, except as noted]

Year or month	Civilian noninstitutional population[1]	Civilian labor force					Not in labor force	Civilian labor force participation rate[2]	Civilian employment/population ratio[3]	Unemployment rate, civilian workers[4]
		Total	Employment			Unemployment				
			Total	Agricultural	Nonagricultural					
	Thousands of persons 14 years of age and over							Percent		
1929		49,180	47,630	10,450	37,180	1,550				3.2
1930		49,820	45,480	10,340	35,140	4,340				8.7
1931		50,420	42,400	10,290	32,110	8,020				15.9
1932		51,000	38,940	10,170	28,770	12,060				23.6
1933		51,590	38,760	10,090	28,670	12,830				24.9
1934		52,230	40,890	9,900	30,990	11,340				21.7
1935		52,870	42,260	10,110	32,150	10,610				20.1
1936		53,440	44,410	10,000	34,410	9,030				16.9
1937		54,000	46,300	9,820	36,480	7,700				14.3
1938		54,610	44,220	9,690	34,530	10,390				19.0
1939		55,230	45,750	9,610	36,140	9,480				17.2
1940	99,840	55,640	47,520	9,540	37,980	8,120	44,200	55.7	47.6	14.6
1941	99,900	55,910	50,350	9,100	41,250	5,560	43,990	56.0	50.4	9.9
1942	98,640	56,410	53,750	9,250	44,500	2,660	42,230	57.2	54.5	4.7
1943	94,640	55,540	54,470	9,080	45,390	1,070	39,100	58.7	57.6	1.9
1944	93,220	54,630	53,960	8,950	45,010	670	38,590	58.6	57.9	1.2
1945	94,090	53,860	52,820	8,580	44,240	1,040	40,230	57.2	56.1	1.9
1946	103,070	57,520	55,250	8,320	46,930	2,270	45,550	55.8	53.6	3.9
1947	106,018	60,168	57,812	8,256	49,557	2,356	45,850	56.8	54.5	3.9
	Thousands of persons 16 years of age and over									
1947	101,827	59,350	57,038	7,890	49,148	2,311	42,477	58.3	56.0	3.9
1948	103,068	60,621	58,343	7,629	50,714	2,276	42,447	58.8	56.6	3.8
1949	103,994	61,286	57,651	7,658	49,993	3,637	42,708	58.9	55.4	5.9
1950	104,995	62,208	58,918	7,160	51,758	3,288	42,787	59.2	56.1	5.3
1951	104,621	62,017	59,961	6,726	53,235	2,055	42,604	59.2	57.3	3.3
1952	105,231	62,138	60,250	6,500	53,749	1,883	43,093	59.0	57.3	3.0
1953	107,056	63,015	61,179	6,260	54,919	1,834	44,041	58.9	57.1	2.9
1954	108,321	63,643	60,109	6,205	53,904	3,532	44,678	58.8	55.5	5.5
1955	109,683	65,023	62,170	6,450	55,722	2,852	44,660	59.3	56.7	4.4
1956	110,954	66,552	63,799	6,283	57,514	2,750	44,402	60.0	57.5	4.1
1957	112,265	66,929	64,071	5,947	58,123	2,859	45,336	59.6	57.1	4.3
1958	113,727	67,639	63,036	5,586	57,450	4,602	46,088	59.5	55.4	6.8
1959	115,329	68,369	64,630	5,565	59,065	3,740	46,960	59.3	56.0	5.5
1960	117,245	69,628	65,778	5,458	60,318	3,852	47,617	59.4	56.1	5.5
1961	118,771	70,459	65,746	5,200	60,546	4,714	48,312	59.3	55.4	6.7
1962	120,153	70,614	66,702	4,944	61,759	3,911	49,539	58.8	55.5	5.5
1963	122,416	71,833	67,762	4,687	63,076	4,070	50,583	58.7	55.4	5.7
1964	124,485	73,091	69,305	4,523	64,782	3,786	51,394	58.7	55.7	5.2
1965	126,513	74,455	71,088	4,361	66,726	3,366	52,058	58.9	56.2	4.5
1966	128,058	75,770	72,895	3,979	68,915	2,875	52,288	59.2	56.9	3.8
1967	129,874	77,347	74,372	3,844	70,527	2,975	52,527	59.6	57.3	3.8
1968	132,028	78,737	75,920	3,817	72,103	2,817	53,291	59.6	57.5	3.6
1969	134,335	80,734	77,902	3,606	74,296	2,832	53,602	60.1	58.0	3.5
1970	137,085	82,771	78,678	3,463	75,215	4,093	54,315	60.4	57.4	4.9
1971	140,216	84,382	79,367	3,394	75,972	5,016	55,834	60.2	56.6	5.9
1972	144,126	87,034	82,153	3,484	78,669	4,882	57,091	60.4	57.0	5.6
1973	147,096	89,429	85,064	3,470	81,594	4,365	57,667	60.8	57.8	4.9
1974	150,120	91,949	86,794	3,515	83,279	5,156	58,171	61.3	57.8	5.6
1975	153,153	93,775	85,846	3,408	82,438	7,929	59,377	61.2	56.1	8.5
1976	156,150	96,158	88,752	3,331	85,421	7,406	59,991	61.6	56.8	7.7
1977	159,033	99,009	92,017	3,283	88,734	6,991	60,025	62.3	57.9	7.1
1978	161,910	102,251	96,048	3,387	92,661	6,202	59,659	63.2	59.3	6.1
1979	164,863	104,962	98,824	3,347	95,477	6,137	59,900	63.7	59.9	5.8
1980	167,745	106,940	99,303	3,364	95,938	7,637	60,806	63.8	59.2	7.1
1981	170,130	108,670	100,397	3,368	97,030	8,273	61,460	63.9	59.0	7.6
1982	172,271	110,204	99,526	3,401	96,125	10,678	62,067	64.0	57.8	9.7
1983	174,215	111,550	100,834	3,383	97,450	10,717	62,665	64.0	57.9	9.6
1984	176,383	113,544	105,005	3,321	101,685	8,539	62,839	64.4	59.5	7.5
1985	178,206	115,461	107,150	3,179	103,971	8,312	62,744	64.8	60.1	7.2
1986	180,587	117,834	109,597	3,163	106,434	8,237	62,752	65.3	60.7	7.0
1987	182,753	119,865	112,440	3,208	109,232	7,425	62,888	65.6	61.5	6.2
1988	184,613	121,669	114,968	3,169	111,800	6,701	62,944	65.9	62.3	5.5
1989	186,393	123,869	117,342	3,199	114,142	6,528	62,523	66.5	63.0	5.3

[1] Not seasonally adjusted.
[2] Civilian labor force as percent of civilian noninstitutional population.
[3] Civilian employment as percent of civilian noninstitutional population.
[4] Unemployed as percent of civilian labor force.

See next page for continuation of table.

TABLE B–22. Civilian labor force, 1929–2022—*Continued*

[Monthly data seasonally adjusted, except as noted]

Year or month	Civilian noninstitutional population [1]	Civilian labor force					Not in labor force	Civilian labor force participation rate [2]	Civilian employment/ population ratio [3]	Unemployment rate, civilian workers [4]
		Total	Employment			Unemployment				
			Total	Agricultural	Non-agricultural					
	Thousands of persons 16 years of age and over							Percent		
1990	189,164	125,840	118,793	3,223	115,570	7,047	63,324	66.5	62.8	5.6
1991	190,925	126,346	117,718	3,269	114,449	8,628	64,578	66.2	61.7	6.8
1992	192,805	128,105	118,492	3,247	115,245	9,613	64,700	66.4	61.5	7.5
1993	194,838	129,200	120,259	3,115	117,144	8,940	65,638	66.3	61.7	6.9
1994	196,814	131,056	123,060	3,409	119,651	7,996	65,758	66.6	62.5	6.1
1995	198,584	132,304	124,900	3,440	121,460	7,404	66,280	66.6	62.9	5.6
1996	200,591	133,943	126,708	3,443	123,264	7,236	66,647	66.8	63.2	5.4
1997	203,133	136,297	129,558	3,399	126,159	6,739	66,837	67.1	63.8	4.9
1998	205,220	137,673	131,463	3,378	128,085	6,210	67,547	67.1	64.1	4.5
1999	207,753	139,368	133,488	3,281	130,207	5,880	68,385	67.1	64.3	4.2
2000 [5]	212,577	142,583	136,891	2,464	134,427	5,692	69,994	67.1	64.4	4.0
2001	215,092	143,734	136,933	2,299	134,635	6,801	71,359	66.8	63.7	4.7
2002	217,570	144,863	136,485	2,311	134,174	8,378	72,707	66.6	62.7	5.8
2003	221,168	146,510	137,736	2,275	135,461	8,774	74,658	66.2	62.3	6.0
2004	223,357	147,401	139,252	2,232	137,020	8,149	75,956	66.0	62.3	5.5
2005	226,082	149,320	141,730	2,197	139,532	7,591	76,762	66.0	62.7	5.1
2006	228,815	151,428	144,427	2,206	142,221	7,001	77,387	66.2	63.1	4.6
2007	231,867	153,124	146,047	2,095	143,952	7,078	78,743	66.0	63.0	4.6
2008	233,788	154,287	145,362	2,168	143,194	8,924	79,501	66.0	62.2	5.8
2009	235,801	154,142	139,877	2,103	137,775	14,265	81,659	65.4	59.3	9.3
2010	237,830	153,889	139,064	2,206	136,858	14,825	83,941	64.7	58.5	9.6
2011	239,618	153,617	139,869	2,254	137,615	13,747	86,001	64.1	58.4	8.9
2012	243,284	154,975	142,469	2,186	140,283	12,506	88,310	63.7	58.6	8.1
2013	245,679	155,389	143,929	2,130	141,799	11,460	90,290	63.2	58.6	7.4
2014	247,947	155,922	146,305	2,237	144,068	9,617	92,025	62.9	59.0	6.2
2015	250,801	157,130	148,834	2,422	146,411	8,296	93,671	62.7	59.3	5.3
2016	253,538	159,187	151,436	2,460	148,976	7,751	94,351	62.8	59.7	4.9
2017	255,079	160,320	153,337	2,454	150,883	6,982	94,759	62.9	60.1	4.4
2018	257,791	162,075	155,761	2,425	153,336	6,314	95,716	62.9	60.4	3.9
2019	259,175	163,539	157,538	2,425	155,113	6,001	95,636	63.1	60.8	3.7
2020	260,329	160,742	147,795	2,349	145,446	12,947	99,587	61.7	56.8	8.1
2021	261,445	161,204	152,581	2,291	150,290	8,623	100,241	61.7	58.4	5.3
2022	263,973	164,287	158,291	2,290	156,001	5,996	99,686	62.2	60.0	3.6
2020: Jan	259,502	164,348	158,543	2,375	156,055	5,804	95,154	63.3	61.1	3.5
Feb	259,628	164,458	158,749	2,451	156,152	5,708	95,171	63.3	61.1	3.5
Mar	259,758	162,635	155,451	2,375	152,919	7,184	97,123	62.6	59.8	4.4
Apr	259,896	156,308	133,258	2,379	130,963	23,050	103,588	60.1	51.3	14.7
May	260,047	158,067	137,128	2,313	134,909	20,939	101,979	60.8	52.7	13.2
June	260,204	159,900	142,276	2,269	140,037	17,624	100,304	61.5	54.7	11.0
July	260,373	160,102	143,779	2,151	141,594	16,324	100,270	61.5	55.2	10.2
Aug	260,558	160,722	147,201	2,212	145,209	13,521	99,836	61.7	56.5	8.4
Sept	260,742	160,224	147,625	2,304	145,434	12,599	100,518	61.4	56.6	7.9
Oct	260,925	160,944	149,854	2,502	147,430	11,090	99,981	61.7	57.4	6.9
Nov	261,085	160,687	149,928	2,465	147,406	10,760	100,398	61.5	57.4	6.7
Dec	261,230	160,757	149,961	2,437	147,371	10,795	100,473	61.5	57.4	6.7
2021: Jan	260,851	160,025	149,871	2,442	147,284	10,155	100,826	61.3	57.5	6.3
Feb	260,918	160,187	150,205	2,287	147,751	9,982	100,732	61.4	57.6	6.2
Mar	261,003	160,463	150,751	2,213	148,304	9,712	100,540	61.5	57.8	6.1
Apr	261,103	160,908	151,171	2,268	148,889	9,737	100,195	61.6	57.9	6.1
May	261,210	160,740	151,482	2,282	149,261	9,257	100,470	61.5	58.0	5.8
June	261,338	161,192	151,684	2,312	149,552	9,508	100,146	61.7	58.0	5.9
July	261,469	161,486	152,782	2,267	150,636	8,704	99,984	61.8	58.4	5.4
Aug	261,611	161,535	153,211	2,342	151,082	8,324	100,076	61.7	58.6	5.2
Sept	261,766	161,544	153,867	2,277	151,706	7,677	100,222	61.7	58.8	4.8
Oct	261,908	161,740	154,395	2,313	152,236	7,345	100,167	61.8	59.0	4.5
Nov	262,029	162,315	155,535	2,225	153,310	6,780	99,714	61.9	59.4	4.2
Dec	262,136	162,410	156,081	2,297	153,650	6,329	99,726	62.0	59.5	3.9
2022: Jan	263,202	163,633	157,122	2,311	154,585	6,511	99,570	62.2	59.7	4.0
Feb	263,324	163,862	157,590	2,363	155,033	6,272	99,463	62.2	59.8	3.8
Mar	263,444	164,301	158,328	2,363	155,670	5,972	99,144	62.4	60.1	3.6
Apr	263,559	163,950	157,982	2,334	155,611	5,968	99,609	62.2	59.9	3.6
May	263,679	164,278	158,299	2,339	155,987	5,979	99,400	62.3	60.0	3.6
June	263,835	164,002	158,057	2,297	155,976	5,945	99,833	62.2	59.9	3.6
July	264,012	163,990	158,272	2,412	155,975	5,718	100,021	62.1	59.9	3.5
Aug	264,184	164,714	158,694	2,173	156,699	6,021	99,469	62.3	60.1	3.7
Sept	264,356	164,619	158,850	2,178	156,762	5,770	99,736	62.3	60.1	3.5
Oct	264,535	164,646	158,593	2,206	156,570	6,053	99,890	62.2	60.0	3.7
Nov	264,708	164,527	158,527	2,228	156,344	6,000	100,181	62.2	59.9	3.6
Dec	264,844	164,966	159,244	2,311	156,818	5,722	99,878	62.3	60.1	3.5

[5] Beginning in 2000, data for agricultural employment are for agricultural and related industries; data for this series and for nonagricultural employment are not strictly comparable with data for earlier years. Because of independent seasonal adjustment for these two series, monthly data will not add to total civilian employment.

Note: Labor force data in Tables B–22 through B–28 are based on household interviews and usually relate to the calendar week that includes the 12th of the month. Historical comparability is affected by revisions to population controls, changes in occupational and industry classification, and other changes to the survey. In recent years, updated population controls have been introduced annually with the release of January data, so data are not strictly comparable with earlier periods. Particularly notable changes were introduced for data in the years 1953, 1960, 1962, 1972, 1973, 1978, 1980, 1990, 1994, 1997, 1998, 2000, 2003, 2008 and 2012. For definitions of terms, area samples used, historical comparability of the data, comparability with other series, etc., see *Employment and Earnings* or concepts and methodology of the CPS at http://www.bls.gov/cps/documentation.htm#concepts.

Source: Department of Labor (Bureau of Labor Statistics).

Table B–23. Civilian employment by sex, age, and demographic characteristic, 1977–2022

[Thousands of persons 16 years of age and over, except as noted; monthly data seasonally adjusted]

Year or month	All civilian workers	By sex and age: Men 20 years and over	By sex and age: Women 20 years and over	By sex and age: Both sexes 16–19	White: Total	White: Men 20 years and over	White: Women 20 years and over	Black or African American: Total	Black or African American: Men 20 years and over	Black or African American: Women 20 years and over	Asian: Total	Hispanic or Latino ethnicity: Total	Hispanic or Latino ethnicity: Men 20 years and over	Hispanic or Latino ethnicity: Women 20 years and over
1977	92,017	50,555	33,775	7,688	81,700	45,326	29,306	8,540	4,273	3,758	....	4,079	2,335	1,370
1978	96,048	52,143	35,836	8,070	84,936	46,594	30,975	9,102	4,483	4,047	....	4,527	2,568	1,537
1979	98,824	53,308	37,434	8,083	87,259	47,546	32,357	9,359	4,606	4,174	....	4,785	2,701	1,638
1980	99,303	53,101	38,492	7,710	87,715	47,419	33,275	9,313	4,498	4,267	....	5,527	3,142	1,886
1981	100,397	53,582	39,590	7,225	88,709	47,846	34,275	9,355	4,520	4,329	....	5,813	3,325	2,029
1982	99,526	52,891	40,086	6,549	87,903	47,209	34,710	9,189	4,414	4,347	....	5,805	3,354	2,040
1983	100,834	53,487	41,004	6,342	88,893	47,618	35,476	9,375	4,531	4,428	....	6,072	3,523	2,127
1984	105,005	55,769	42,793	6,444	92,120	49,461	36,823	10,119	4,871	4,773	....	6,651	3,825	2,357
1985	107,150	56,562	44,154	6,434	93,736	50,061	37,907	10,501	4,992	4,977	....	6,888	3,994	2,456
1986	109,597	57,569	45,556	6,472	95,660	50,818	39,050	10,814	5,150	5,128	....	7,219	4,174	2,615
1987	112,440	58,726	47,074	6,640	97,789	51,649	40,242	11,309	5,357	5,365	....	7,790	4,444	2,872
1988	114,968	59,781	48,383	6,805	99,812	52,466	41,316	11,658	5,509	5,548	....	8,250	4,680	3,047
1989	117,342	60,837	49,745	6,759	101,584	53,292	42,346	11,953	5,602	5,727	....	8,573	4,853	3,172
1990	118,793	61,678	50,535	6,581	102,261	53,685	42,796	12,175	5,692	5,884	....	9,845	5,609	3,567
1991	117,718	61,178	50,634	5,906	101,182	53,103	42,862	12,074	5,706	5,874	....	9,828	5,623	3,603
1992	118,492	61,496	51,328	5,669	101,669	53,357	43,327	12,151	5,681	5,978	....	10,027	5,757	3,693
1993	120,259	62,355	52,099	5,805	103,045	54,021	43,910	12,382	5,793	6,095	....	10,361	5,992	3,800
1994	123,060	63,294	53,606	6,161	105,190	54,676	45,116	12,835	5,964	6,320	....	10,788	6,189	3,989
1995	124,900	64,085	54,396	6,419	106,490	55,254	45,643	13,279	6,137	6,556	....	11,127	6,367	4,116
1996	126,708	64,897	55,311	6,500	107,808	55,977	46,164	13,542	6,167	6,762	....	11,642	6,655	4,341
1997	129,558	66,284	56,613	6,661	109,856	56,986	47,063	13,969	6,325	7,013	....	12,726	7,307	4,705
1998	131,463	67,135	57,278	7,051	110,931	57,500	47,342	14,556	6,530	7,290	....	13,291	7,570	4,928
1999	133,488	67,761	58,555	7,172	112,235	57,934	48,098	15,056	6,702	7,663	....	13,720	7,576	5,290
2000	136,891	69,634	60,067	7,189	114,424	59,119	49,145	15,156	6,741	7,703	6,043	15,735	8,859	5,903
2001	136,933	69,776	60,417	6,740	114,430	59,245	49,369	15,006	6,627	7,741	6,180	16,190	9,100	6,121
2002	136,485	69,734	60,420	6,332	114,013	59,124	49,448	14,872	6,652	7,610	6,215	16,590	9,341	6,367
2003	137,736	70,415	61,402	5,919	114,235	59,348	49,823	14,739	6,586	7,636	5,756	17,372	10,063	6,541
2004	139,252	71,572	61,773	5,907	115,239	60,159	50,040	14,909	6,681	7,707	5,994	17,930	10,385	6,752
2005	141,730	73,050	62,702	5,978	116,949	61,255	50,589	15,313	6,901	7,876	6,244	18,632	10,872	6,913
2006	144,427	74,431	63,834	6,162	118,833	62,259	51,359	15,765	7,079	8,068	6,522	19,613	11,391	7,321
2007	146,047	75,337	64,799	5,911	119,792	62,806	51,996	16,051	7,245	8,240	6,839	20,382	11,827	7,662
2008	145,362	74,750	65,039	5,573	119,126	62,304	52,124	15,953	7,151	8,260	6,917	20,346	11,769	7,707
2009	139,877	71,341	63,699	4,837	114,996	59,626	51,231	15,025	6,628	7,956	6,635	19,647	11,256	7,649
2010	139,064	71,230	63,456	4,378	114,168	59,438	50,997	15,010	6,680	7,944	6,705	19,906	11,438	7,788
2011	139,869	72,182	63,360	4,327	114,690	60,118	50,881	15,051	6,765	7,906	6,867	20,269	11,685	7,918
2012	142,469	73,403	64,640	4,426	114,769	60,193	50,911	15,856	7,104	8,313	7,705	21,878	12,212	8,858
2013	143,929	74,176	65,295	4,458	115,379	60,511	51,198	16,151	7,304	8,408	8,136	22,514	12,638	9,056
2014	146,305	75,471	66,287	4,548	116,788	61,289	51,798	16,732	7,613	8,663	8,325	23,492	13,202	9,431
2015	148,834	76,776	67,323	4,734	117,944	61,959	52,161	17,472	7,938	9,032	8,706	24,400	13,624	9,853
2016	151,436	78,084	68,387	4,965	119,313	62,575	52,771	17,982	8,228	9,219	9,213	25,249	14,055	10,217
2017	153,337	78,919	69,344	5,074	120,176	63,009	53,179	18,587	8,500	9,514	9,448	25,938	14,355	10,543
2018	155,761	80,211	70,424	5,126	121,461	63,719	53,682	19,091	8,745	9,751	9,832	27,012	14,873	11,045
2019	157,538	80,917	71,470	5,150	122,441	64,070	54,304	19,381	8,883	9,910	10,179	27,805	15,204	11,516
2020	147,795	76,227	66,873	4,695	115,341	60,570	51,048	17,873	8,150	9,176	9,437	25,952	14,333	10,593
2021	152,581	78,216	69,099	5,266	118,291	61,737	52,389	18,726	8,597	9,525	10,016	27,429	15,138	11,165
2022	158,291	81,409	71,283	5,600	121,908	63,743	53,767	19,937	9,294	10,034	10,615	29,299	15,997	12,049
2021: Jan	149,871	77,088	67,766	5,017	116,582	60,892	51,712	18,321	8,458	9,273	9,611	26,427	14,561	10,762
Feb	150,205	77,000	68,045	5,159	116,822	60,869	51,847	18,160	8,372	9,225	9,860	26,679	14,677	10,829
Mar	150,751	77,107	68,468	5,176	117,124	60,882	52,136	18,397	8,497	9,291	9,796	26,910	14,774	11,006
Apr	151,171	77,380	68,408	5,383	117,400	61,142	52,012	18,520	8,488	9,416	9,778	26,889	14,876	10,925
May	151,482	77,478	68,571	5,433	117,652	61,314	52,067	18,583	8,531	9,447	9,871	27,070	15,000	11,014
June	151,684	77,742	68,729	5,213	117,476	61,306	52,064	18,771	8,648	9,472	9,818	27,191	15,008	11,115
July	152,782	78,248	69,235	5,299	118,390	61,807	52,423	18,764	8,620	9,504	10,082	27,622	15,268	11,205
Aug	153,211	78,617	69,341	5,254	118,622	62,052	52,397	18,902	8,637	9,658	10,125	27,657	15,341	11,238
Sept	153,867	78,975	69,569	5,323	119,024	62,265	52,575	19,037	8,653	9,710	10,201	27,762	15,424	11,255
Oct	154,395	79,228	69,865	5,302	119,451	62,390	52,835	18,988	8,716	9,681	10,317	27,994	15,426	11,383
Nov	155,535	79,851	70,354	5,330	120,258	62,936	53,085	19,169	8,800	9,817	10,382	28,479	15,707	11,549
Dec	156,081	79,958	70,831	5,292	120,775	63,055	53,506	19,086	8,740	9,806	10,346	28,463	15,606	11,689
2022: Jan	157,122	80,695	70,872	5,555	121,404	63,521	53,467	19,604	9,053	9,957	10,489	28,905	15,872	11,781
Feb	157,590	81,293	70,810	5,487	121,850	63,843	53,591	19,751	9,323	9,899	10,248	29,139	16,081	11,808
Mar	158,328	81,389	71,275	5,665	122,241	63,901	53,825	19,821	9,261	9,981	10,472	29,214	15,978	11,950
Apr	157,982	81,236	71,144	5,603	121,549	63,471	53,655	19,956	9,354	10,019	10,514	29,122	15,983	11,863
May	158,299	81,331	71,388	5,579	121,669	63,589	53,715	20,125	9,409	10,095	10,652	29,270	16,133	11,885
June	158,057	81,210	71,280	5,566	121,582	63,532	53,713	19,965	9,336	10,025	10,568	29,355	16,148	11,939
July	158,272	81,185	71,659	5,428	121,851	63,500	54,095	19,900	9,213	10,110	10,691	29,172	15,864	12,118
Aug	158,694	81,263	71,676	5,754	122,125	63,592	54,087	19,785	9,133	10,017	10,778	29,526	15,967	12,260
Sept	158,850	81,816	71,457	5,576	122,261	64,012	53,885	20,016	9,322	10,057	10,832	29,462	15,967	12,314
Oct	158,593	81,776	71,218	5,598	122,063	64,026	53,691	19,988	9,269	10,080	10,781	29,430	16,000	12,185
Nov	158,527	81,698	71,088	5,740	121,807	63,767	53,562	20,139	9,408	10,077	10,704	29,382	15,925	12,179
Dec	159,244	82,033	71,531	5,680	122,556	64,189	53,918	20,189	9,446	10,093	10,654	29,611	16,047	12,307

By race or ethnicity [1]

[1] Beginning in 2003, persons who selected this race group only. Persons whose ethnicity is identified as Hispanic or Latino may be of any race. Prior to 2003, persons who selected more than one race were included in the group they identified as the main race. Data for "black or African American" were for "black" prior to 2003. See *Employment and Earnings* or concepts and methodology of the Current Population Survey (CPS) at http://www.bls.gov/cps/documentation.htm#concepts for details.

Note: Detail will not sum to total because data for all race groups are not shown here.

See footnote 5 and Note, Table B–22.

Source: Department of Labor (Bureau of Labor Statistics).

TABLE B–24. Unemployment by sex, age, and demographic characteristic, 1977–2022

[Thousands of persons 16 years of age and over, except as noted; monthly data seasonally adjusted]

Year or month	All civilian workers	By sex and age: Men 20 years and over	By sex and age: Women 20 years and over	By sex and age: Both sexes 16–19	By race or ethnicity[1]: White: Total	White: Men 20 years and over	White: Women 20 years and over	Black or African American: Total	Black or African American: Men 20 years and over	Black or African American: Women 20 years and over	Asian: Total	Hispanic or Latino ethnicity: Total	Hispanic or Latino ethnicity: Men 20 years and over	Hispanic or Latino ethnicity: Women 20 years and over
1977	6,991	2,794	2,535	1,663	5,441	2,211	1,946	1,393	512	528	....	456	195	153
1978	6,202	2,328	2,292	1,583	4,698	1,797	1,713	1,330	462	510	....	452	175	168
1979	6,137	2,308	2,276	1,555	4,664	1,773	1,699	1,319	473	513	....	434	168	160
1980	7,637	3,353	2,615	1,669	5,884	2,629	1,964	1,553	636	574	....	620	284	190
1981	8,273	3,615	2,895	1,763	6,343	2,825	2,143	1,731	703	671	....	678	321	212
1982	10,678	5,089	3,613	1,977	8,241	3,991	2,715	2,142	954	793	....	929	461	293
1983	10,717	5,257	3,632	1,829	8,128	4,098	2,643	2,272	1,002	878	....	961	491	302
1984	8,539	3,932	3,107	1,499	6,372	2,992	2,264	1,914	815	747	....	800	393	258
1985	8,312	3,715	3,129	1,468	6,191	2,834	2,283	1,864	757	750	....	811	401	269
1986	8,237	3,751	3,032	1,454	6,140	2,857	2,213	1,840	765	728	....	857	438	278
1987	7,425	3,369	2,709	1,347	5,501	2,584	1,922	1,684	666	706	....	751	374	241
1988	6,701	2,987	2,487	1,226	4,944	2,268	1,766	1,547	617	642	....	732	351	234
1989	6,528	2,867	2,467	1,194	4,770	2,149	1,758	1,544	619	625	....	750	342	276
1990	7,047	3,239	2,596	1,212	5,186	2,431	1,852	1,565	664	633	....	876	425	289
1991	8,628	4,195	3,074	1,359	6,560	3,284	2,248	1,723	745	698	....	1,092	575	339
1992	9,613	4,717	3,469	1,427	7,169	3,620	2,512	2,011	886	800	....	1,311	675	418
1993	8,940	4,287	3,288	1,365	6,655	3,263	2,400	1,844	801	729	....	1,248	629	418
1994	7,996	3,627	3,049	1,320	5,892	2,735	2,197	1,666	682	685	....	1,187	558	431
1995	7,404	3,239	2,819	1,346	5,459	2,465	2,042	1,538	593	620	....	1,140	530	404
1996	7,236	3,146	2,783	1,306	5,300	2,363	1,998	1,592	639	643	....	1,132	495	438
1997	6,739	2,882	2,585	1,271	4,836	2,140	1,784	1,560	585	673	....	1,069	471	401
1998	6,210	2,580	2,424	1,205	4,484	1,920	1,688	1,426	524	622	....	1,026	436	376
1999	5,880	2,433	2,285	1,162	4,273	1,813	1,616	1,309	480	561	....	945	374	376
2000	5,692	2,376	2,235	1,081	4,121	1,731	1,595	1,241	499	512	227	954	388	371
2001	6,801	3,040	2,599	1,162	4,969	2,275	1,849	1,416	573	582	288	1,138	495	436
2002	8,378	3,896	3,228	1,253	6,137	2,943	2,269	1,693	695	738	389	1,353	636	496
2003	8,774	4,209	3,314	1,251	6,311	3,125	2,276	1,787	760	772	366	1,441	693	555
2004	8,149	3,791	3,150	1,208	5,847	2,785	2,172	1,729	733	755	277	1,342	635	504
2005	7,591	3,392	3,013	1,186	5,350	2,450	2,054	1,700	699	734	259	1,191	536	464
2006	7,001	3,131	2,751	1,119	5,002	2,281	1,927	1,549	640	656	205	1,081	497	414
2007	7,078	3,259	2,718	1,101	5,143	2,408	1,930	1,445	622	588	229	1,220	576	446
2008	8,924	4,297	3,342	1,285	6,509	3,179	2,384	1,788	811	732	285	1,678	860	567
2009	14,265	7,555	5,157	1,552	10,648	5,746	3,745	2,606	1,286	1,032	522	2,706	1,474	911
2010	14,825	7,763	5,534	1,528	10,916	5,828	3,960	2,852	1,396	1,165	543	2,843	1,519	1,001
2011	13,747	6,898	5,450	1,400	9,889	5,046	3,818	2,831	1,360	1,204	518	2,629	1,345	984
2012	12,506	5,984	5,125	1,397	8,915	4,347	3,564	2,544	1,152	1,119	483	2,514	1,195	995
2013	11,460	5,568	4,565	1,327	8,033	3,994	3,102	2,429	1,082	1,069	448	2,257	1,090	855
2014	9,617	4,585	3,926	1,106	6,540	3,141	2,623	2,141	973	943	436	1,878	864	764
2015	8,296	3,959	3,371	966	5,662	2,751	2,249	1,846	835	811	347	1,726	820	686
2016	7,751	3,675	3,151	925	5,345	2,594	2,100	1,655	737	724	349	1,548	720	627
2017	6,982	3,287	2,868	827	4,765	2,288	1,923	1,501	663	657	333	1,401	632	585
2018	6,314	2,976	2,578	759	4,354	2,094	1,743	1,322	582	573	304	1,323	591	547
2019	6,001	2,819	2,435	746	4,159	1,967	1,664	1,251	571	527	280	1,248	553	497
2020	12,947	6,118	5,804	1,025	9,090	4,334	4,013	2,304	1,069	1,062	894	3,018	1,451	1,291
2021	8,623	4,302	3,625	696	5,854	2,957	2,411	1,756	845	791	529	1,995	986	812
2022	5,996	2,867	2,453	675	4,049	1,995	1,585	1,300	572	596	306	1,302	626	513
2021: Jan	10,155	4,980	4,313	862	7,068	3,569	2,824	1,862	871	871	677	2,460	1,194	1,032
Feb	9,982	4,907	4,237	838	6,873	3,458	2,809	1,972	943	897	538	2,444	1,202	995
Mar	9,712	4,792	4,158	762	6,632	3,339	2,757	1,946	925	898	624	2,248	1,148	875
Apr	9,737	4,958	4,066	712	6,560	3,426	2,641	2,025	967	920	593	2,248	1,139	888
May	9,257	4,817	3,856	584	6,275	3,260	2,589	1,869	925	849	589	2,076	1,030	873
June	9,508	4,851	4,002	656	6,472	3,319	2,695	1,911	964	869	589	2,116	1,012	943
July	8,704	4,436	3,641	627	5,979	3,108	2,456	1,673	800	776	551	1,898	948	813
Aug	8,324	4,186	3,465	673	5,604	2,843	2,311	1,782	850	804	472	1,798	889	720
Sept	7,677	3,902	3,103	671	5,203	2,688	2,030	1,605	738	744	443	1,826	934	666
Oct	7,345	3,531	3,119	696	4,913	2,340	2,087	1,591	782	692	447	1,696	792	687
Nov	6,780	3,256	2,872	652	4,585	2,154	2,016	1,329	672	503	412	1,553	742	645
Dec	6,329	3,010	2,667	652	4,096	1,982	1,714	1,428	652	637	406	1,436	669	602
2022: Jan	6,511	3,190	2,645	676	4,293	2,137	1,711	1,450	685	611	382	1,479	705	603
Feb	6,272	2,971	2,672	628	4,175	1,990	1,734	1,388	637	637	318	1,357	622	595
Mar	5,972	2,877	2,462	634	4,021	2,023	1,573	1,304	554	586	299	1,274	648	526
Apr	5,968	2,963	2,365	640	4,074	2,026	1,561	1,249	608	540	332	1,278	633	478
May	5,979	2,834	2,489	656	4,052	2,029	1,585	1,339	567	630	263	1,352	592	587
June	5,945	2,818	2,441	686	4,121	2,022	1,598	1,245	527	599	326	1,331	603	554
July	5,718	2,720	2,297	701	3,885	1,958	1,448	1,274	553	573	285	1,218	605	403
Aug	6,021	2,929	2,422	670	4,022	2,024	1,538	1,344	582	624	305	1,395	666	546
Sept	5,770	2,786	2,272	712	3,856	1,871	1,463	1,244	570	579	274	1,211	569	457
Oct	6,053	2,829	2,534	690	4,117	2,006	1,649	1,259	514	616	325	1,295	653	469
Nov	6,000	2,827	2,444	729	4,094	1,992	1,611	1,226	539	556	291	1,218	601	458
Dec	5,722	2,661	2,398	662	3,852	1,856	1,543	1,229	510	586	265	1,281	677	478

[1] See footnote 1 and Note, Table B–23.

Note: See footnote 5 and Note, Table B–22.

Source: Department of Labor (Bureau of Labor Statistics).

Table B–25. Civilian labor force participation rate, 1977–2022

[Percent [1]; monthly data seasonally adjusted]

Year or month	All civilian workers	Men: 20 years and over	Men: 20–24 years	Men: 25–54 years	Men: 55 years and over	Women: 20 years and over	Women: 20–24 years	Women: 25–54 years	Women: 55 years and over	Both sexes 16–19 years	By race or ethnicity [2]: White	Black or African American	Asian	Hispanic or Latino ethnicity
1977	62.3	79.7	85.6	94.2	47.4	48.1	66.5	58.5	22.9	56.0	62.5	59.8	....	61.6
1978	63.2	79.8	85.9	94.3	47.2	49.6	68.3	60.6	23.1	57.8	63.3	61.5	....	62.9
1979	63.7	79.8	86.4	94.4	46.6	50.6	69.0	62.3	23.2	57.9	63.9	61.4	....	63.6
1980	63.8	79.4	85.9	94.2	45.6	51.3	68.9	64.0	22.8	56.7	64.1	61.0	....	64.0
1981	63.9	79.0	85.5	94.1	44.5	52.1	69.6	65.3	22.7	55.4	64.3	60.8	....	64.1
1982	64.0	78.7	84.9	94.0	43.8	52.7	69.8	66.3	22.7	54.1	64.3	61.0	....	63.6
1983	64.0	78.5	84.8	93.8	43.0	53.1	69.9	67.1	22.4	53.5	64.3	61.5	....	63.8
1984	64.4	78.3	85.0	93.9	41.8	53.7	70.4	68.2	22.2	53.9	64.6	62.2	....	64.9
1985	64.8	78.1	85.0	93.9	41.0	54.7	71.8	69.6	22.0	54.5	65.0	62.9	....	64.6
1986	65.3	78.1	85.8	93.8	40.4	55.5	72.4	70.8	22.1	54.7	65.5	63.3	....	65.4
1987	65.6	78.0	85.2	93.7	40.4	56.2	73.0	71.9	22.0	54.7	65.8	63.8	....	66.4
1988	65.9	77.9	85.0	93.6	39.9	56.8	72.7	72.7	22.3	55.3	66.2	63.8	....	67.4
1989	66.5	78.1	85.3	93.7	39.6	57.7	72.4	73.6	23.0	55.9	66.7	64.2	....	67.6
1990	66.5	78.2	84.4	93.4	39.4	58.0	71.3	74.0	22.9	53.7	66.9	64.0	....	67.4
1991	66.2	77.7	83.5	93.1	38.5	57.9	70.1	74.1	22.6	51.6	66.6	63.3	....	66.5
1992	66.4	77.7	83.3	93.0	38.4	58.5	70.9	74.6	22.8	51.3	66.8	63.9	....	66.8
1993	66.3	77.3	83.2	92.6	37.7	58.5	70.9	74.6	22.8	51.5	66.8	63.2	....	66.2
1994	66.6	76.8	83.1	91.7	37.8	59.3	71.0	75.3	24.0	52.7	67.1	63.4	....	66.1
1995	66.6	76.7	83.1	91.6	37.9	59.4	70.3	75.6	23.9	53.5	67.1	63.7	....	65.8
1996	66.8	76.8	82.5	91.8	38.3	59.9	71.3	76.1	23.9	52.3	67.2	64.1	....	66.5
1997	67.1	77.0	82.5	91.8	38.9	60.5	72.7	76.7	24.6	51.6	67.5	64.7	....	67.9
1998	67.1	76.8	82.0	91.8	39.1	60.4	73.0	76.5	25.0	52.8	67.3	65.6	....	67.9
1999	67.1	76.7	81.9	91.7	39.6	60.7	73.2	76.8	25.6	52.0	67.3	65.8	....	67.7
2000	67.1	76.7	82.6	91.6	40.1	60.6	73.1	76.7	26.1	52.0	67.3	65.8	67.2	69.7
2001	66.8	76.5	81.6	91.3	40.9	60.6	72.7	76.4	27.0	49.6	67.0	65.3	67.2	69.5
2002	66.6	76.3	80.7	91.0	42.0	60.5	72.1	75.9	28.5	47.4	66.8	64.8	67.2	69.1
2003	66.2	75.9	80.0	90.6	42.6	60.6	70.8	75.6	30.0	44.5	66.5	64.3	66.4	68.3
2004	66.0	75.8	79.6	90.5	43.2	60.3	70.5	75.3	30.5	43.9	66.3	63.8	65.9	68.6
2005	66.0	75.8	79.1	90.5	44.2	60.4	70.1	75.3	31.4	43.7	66.3	64.2	66.1	68.0
2006	66.2	75.9	79.6	90.6	44.9	60.5	69.5	75.5	32.3	43.7	66.5	64.1	66.2	68.7
2007	66.0	75.9	78.7	90.9	45.2	60.6	70.1	75.4	33.2	41.3	66.4	63.7	66.5	68.8
2008	66.0	75.7	78.7	90.5	46.0	60.9	70.0	75.8	33.9	40.2	66.3	63.7	67.0	68.5
2009	65.4	74.8	76.2	89.7	46.3	60.8	69.6	75.6	34.7	37.5	65.8	62.4	66.0	68.0
2010	64.7	74.1	74.5	89.3	46.4	60.3	68.3	75.2	35.1	34.9	65.1	62.2	64.7	67.5
2011	64.1	73.4	74.7	88.7	46.3	59.8	67.8	74.7	35.1	34.1	64.5	61.4	64.6	66.5
2012	63.7	73.0	74.5	88.7	46.8	59.3	67.4	74.5	35.1	34.3	64.0	61.5	63.9	66.4
2013	63.2	72.5	73.9	88.4	46.5	58.8	67.5	73.9	35.1	34.5	63.5	61.2	64.6	66.0
2014	62.9	71.9	73.9	88.2	45.9	58.5	67.7	73.9	34.9	34.0	63.1	61.2	63.6	66.1
2015	62.7	71.7	73.0	88.3	45.9	58.2	68.3	73.7	34.7	34.3	62.8	61.5	62.8	65.9
2016	62.8	71.7	73.0	88.5	46.2	58.3	68.0	74.3	34.7	35.2	62.9	61.6	63.2	65.8
2017	62.9	71.6	74.1	88.6	46.1	58.5	68.5	75.0	34.7	35.2	62.8	62.3	63.6	66.1
2018	62.9	71.6	73.2	89.0	46.2	58.5	69.0	75.3	34.7	35.1	62.8	62.3	63.5	66.3
2019	63.1	71.6	74.0	89.1	46.3	58.9	70.4	76.0	35.0	35.3	63.0	62.5	64.0	66.8
2020	61.7	70.1	71.0	87.9	45.1	57.6	67.5	75.1	34.0	34.5	61.8	60.5	62.7	65.6
2021	61.7	69.8	73.0	88.0	44.2	57.3	68.6	75.3	33.3	36.2	61.5	60.9	63.8	65.5
2022	62.2	70.3	73.2	88.6	44.7	58.1	68.7	76.4	33.6	36.8	62.0	62.2	64.5	66.3
2021: Jan	61.3	69.6	72.7	87.6	44.2	57.0	67.9	74.7	33.1	35.7	61.3	60.3	62.6	64.9
Feb	61.4	69.5	72.7	87.6	44.2	57.1	67.9	75.0	33.2	36.4	61.4	60.1	62.7	65.3
Mar	61.5	69.4	72.2	87.6	43.8	57.4	68.2	75.2	33.4	36.1	61.4	60.7	63.0	65.3
Apr	61.6	69.8	73.6	87.8	44.2	57.2	67.3	75.1	33.4	37.0	61.5	61.2	62.7	65.2
May	61.5	69.7	72.8	87.9	44.2	57.2	68.1	75.0	33.3	36.6	61.4	60.9	63.3	65.1
June	61.7	69.9	72.2	88.1	44.4	57.4	69.2	75.4	33.2	35.7	61.4	61.6	63.3	65.3
July	61.8	70.0	72.2	88.3	44.3	57.5	68.9	75.5	33.1	36.0	61.6	60.8	64.4	65.7
Aug	61.7	70.0	72.3	88.3	44.3	57.4	68.2	75.3	33.6	36.0	61.5	61.5	64.0	65.4
Sept	61.7	70.0	73.0	88.1	44.6	57.2	68.3	75.2	33.3	36.4	61.5	61.3	64.4	65.6
Oct	61.8	69.9	73.2	88.1	44.1	57.4	69.3	75.4	33.4	36.5	61.5	61.1	65.3	65.7
Nov	61.9	70.2	74.5	88.2	44.3	57.6	69.4	75.7	33.4	36.4	61.7	60.8	65.4	66.4
Dec	62.0	70.0	74.0	88.0	44.3	57.8	69.9	75.9	33.5	36.1	61.7	60.8	64.7	66.0
2022: Jan	62.2	70.1	73.9	88.2	45.0	58.1	68.3	76.0	33.9	36.6	62.0	62.0	64.3	66.4
Feb	62.2	70.4	73.6	88.8	45.3	58.0	69.7	75.9	33.7	35.9	62.1	62.2	63.0	66.6
Mar	62.4	70.4	73.3	88.6	45.0	58.2	69.4	76.5	33.5	37.0	62.2	62.1	64.1	66.4
Apr	62.2	70.3	72.7	88.7	44.6	58.0	68.0	76.3	33.6	36.7	61.9	62.3	64.5	66.1
May	62.3	70.2	72.5	88.7	44.6	58.3	69.0	76.6	33.7	36.6	61.9	63.0	64.9	66.5
June	62.2	70.1	73.7	88.4	44.2	58.1	68.8	76.4	33.7	36.6	61.9	62.2	64.4	66.5
July	62.1	69.9	72.9	88.5	44.1	58.3	69.4	76.4	33.8	35.9	61.9	62.0	64.9	65.8
Aug	62.3	70.1	72.2	88.6	44.3	58.3	68.5	77.1	33.5	37.6	62.0	61.8	65.2	66.8
Sept	62.3	70.4	73.3	88.7	44.8	58.0	68.1	76.6	33.4	36.8	62.0	62.2	64.8	66.1
Oct	62.2	70.4	73.8	88.5	44.9	58.0	67.8	76.5	33.5	36.8	62.0	62.1	64.8	66.1
Nov	62.2	70.3	73.4	88.4	44.7	57.8	67.8	76.3	33.2	37.8	61.8	62.3	64.8	65.7
Dec	62.3	70.4	73.2	88.5	44.9	58.1	69.4	76.4	33.5	37.0	62.1	62.4	64.2	66.3

[1] Civilian labor force as percent of civilian noninstitutional population in group specified.
[2] See footnote 1, Table B–23.

Note: Data relate to persons 16 years of age and over, except as noted.
See footnote 5 and Note, Table B–22.

Source: Department of Labor (Bureau of Labor Statistics).

Table B–26. Civilian employment/population ratio, 1977–2022

[Percent [1]; monthly data seasonally adjusted]

Year or month	All civilian workers	Men				Women				Both sexes 16–19 years	By race or ethnicity [2]			
		20 years and over	20–24 years	25–54 years	55 years and over	20 years and over	20–24 years	25–54 years	55 years and over		White	Black or African American	Asian	Hispanic or Latino ethnicity
1977	57.9	75.6	76.3	90.1	45.5	44.8	59.0	54.8	21.9	46.1	58.6	51.4	....	55.4
1978	59.3	76.4	78.0	91.0	45.7	46.6	61.4	57.3	22.3	48.3	60.0	53.6	....	57.2
1979	59.9	76.5	78.9	91.1	45.2	47.7	62.4	59.0	22.5	48.5	60.6	53.8	....	58.3
1980	59.2	74.6	75.1	89.4	44.1	48.1	61.8	60.1	22.1	46.6	60.0	52.3	....	57.6
1981	59.0	74.0	74.2	89.0	42.9	48.6	61.8	61.2	21.9	44.6	60.0	51.3	....	57.4
1982	57.8	71.8	71.0	86.5	41.6	48.4	60.6	61.2	21.6	41.5	58.8	49.4	....	54.9
1983	57.9	71.4	71.3	86.1	40.6	48.8	60.9	62.0	21.4	41.5	58.9	49.5	....	55.1
1984	59.5	73.2	74.9	88.4	39.8	50.1	62.7	63.9	21.3	43.7	60.5	52.3	....	57.9
1985	60.1	73.3	75.3	88.7	39.3	51.0	64.1	65.3	21.1	44.4	61.0	53.4	....	57.8
1986	60.7	73.3	76.3	88.5	38.8	52.0	64.9	66.6	21.3	44.6	61.5	54.1	....	58.5
1987	61.5	73.8	76.8	89.0	39.0	53.1	66.1	68.2	21.3	45.5	62.3	55.6	....	60.5
1988	62.3	74.2	77.5	89.5	38.6	54.0	66.6	69.3	21.7	46.8	63.1	56.3	....	61.9
1989	63.0	74.5	77.8	89.9	38.3	54.9	66.4	70.4	22.4	47.5	63.8	56.9	....	62.2
1990	62.8	74.3	76.7	89.1	38.0	55.2	65.2	70.6	22.2	45.3	63.7	56.7	....	61.9
1991	61.7	72.7	73.8	87.5	36.8	54.6	63.2	70.1	21.9	42.0	62.6	55.4	....	59.8
1992	61.5	72.1	73.1	86.8	36.4	54.8	63.6	70.1	21.8	41.0	62.4	54.9	....	59.1
1993	61.7	72.3	73.8	87.0	35.9	55.0	64.0	70.4	22.0	41.7	62.7	55.0	....	59.1
1994	62.5	72.6	74.6	87.2	36.2	56.2	64.5	71.5	23.1	43.4	63.5	56.1	....	59.5
1995	62.9	73.0	75.4	87.6	36.5	56.5	64.0	72.2	23.0	44.2	63.8	57.1	....	59.7
1996	63.2	73.2	74.7	87.9	37.0	57.0	64.9	72.8	23.1	43.5	64.1	57.4	....	60.6
1997	63.8	73.7	75.2	88.4	37.7	57.8	66.8	73.5	23.8	43.4	64.6	58.2	....	62.6
1998	64.1	73.9	75.4	88.8	38.0	58.0	67.3	73.6	24.4	45.1	64.7	59.7	....	63.1
1999	64.3	74.0	75.6	89.0	38.5	58.5	68.0	74.1	24.9	44.7	64.8	60.6	....	63.4
2000	64.4	74.2	76.6	89.0	39.1	58.4	67.9	74.2	25.5	45.2	64.9	60.9	64.8	65.7
2001	63.7	73.3	74.2	87.9	39.6	58.1	67.3	73.4	26.3	42.3	64.2	59.7	64.2	64.9
2002	62.7	72.3	72.5	86.6	40.3	57.5	65.6	72.3	27.5	39.6	63.4	58.1	63.2	63.9
2003	62.3	71.7	71.5	85.9	40.7	57.5	64.2	72.0	28.9	36.8	63.0	57.4	62.4	63.1
2004	62.3	71.9	71.6	86.3	41.5	57.4	64.3	71.8	29.4	36.4	63.1	57.2	63.0	63.8
2005	62.7	72.4	71.5	86.9	42.7	57.6	64.5	72.0	30.4	36.5	63.4	57.7	63.4	64.0
2006	63.1	72.9	72.7	87.3	43.5	58.0	64.2	72.5	31.4	36.9	63.8	58.4	64.2	65.2
2007	63.0	72.8	71.7	87.5	43.7	58.2	65.0	72.5	32.2	34.8	63.6	58.4	64.3	64.9
2008	62.2	71.6	69.7	86.0	44.2	57.9	63.8	72.3	32.7	32.6	62.8	57.3	64.3	63.3
2009	59.3	67.6	63.3	81.5	43.0	56.2	61.1	70.2	32.6	28.4	60.2	53.2	61.2	59.7
2010	58.5	66.8	61.3	81.0	42.8	55.5	59.4	69.3	32.9	25.9	59.4	52.3	59.9	59.0
2011	58.4	67.0	63.0	81.4	43.1	55.0	58.7	69.0	32.9	25.8	59.4	51.7	60.0	58.9
2012	58.6	67.5	63.8	82.5	43.8	55.0	59.2	69.2	33.1	26.1	59.4	53.0	60.1	59.5
2013	58.6	67.4	63.5	82.8	43.8	54.9	59.8	69.3	33.3	26.6	59.4	53.2	61.2	60.0
2014	59.0	67.8	64.9	83.6	43.9	55.2	60.9	70.0	33.4	27.3	59.7	54.3	60.4	61.2
2015	59.3	68.1	65.1	84.4	44.1	55.4	62.5	70.3	33.5	28.5	59.9	55.7	60.4	61.6
2016	59.7	68.5	66.2	85.0	44.4	55.7	63.0	71.1	33.5	29.7	60.2	56.4	60.9	62.0
2017	60.1	68.8	67.9	85.4	44.6	56.1	64.2	72.1	33.6	30.3	60.4	57.6	61.5	62.7
2018	60.4	69.0	67.6	86.2	44.7	56.4	64.7	72.8	33.7	30.6	60.7	58.3	61.6	63.2
2019	60.8	69.2	68.3	86.4	45.1	56.9	66.4	73.7	34.0	30.9	61.0	58.7	62.3	63.9
2020	56.8	64.8	61.3	81.8	42.2	53.0	58.2	69.6	31.5	28.3	57.3	53.6	57.3	58.7
2021	58.4	66.2	65.9	83.6	42.3	54.5	63.0	71.7	31.9	32.0	58.6	55.7	60.6	61.1
2022	60.0	67.9	67.5	85.9	43.5	56.2	64.4	74.0	32.7	32.8	60.0	58.4	62.7	63.5
2021: Jan	57.5	65.4	65.4	82.6	41.8	53.6	61.3	70.4	31.4	30.4	57.8	54.7	58.5	59.4
Feb	57.6	65.3	65.1	82.7	41.7	53.8	61.8	70.7	31.4	31.3	57.9	54.2	59.4	59.8
Mar	57.8	65.4	64.6	82.8	41.8	54.1	61.8	71.1	31.8	31.4	58.1	54.9	59.3	60.3
Apr	57.9	65.6	65.2	83.0	41.9	54.0	61.0	71.1	31.8	32.7	58.2	55.2	59.1	60.1
May	58.0	65.6	64.7	83.0	42.2	54.1	61.8	71.3	31.6	33.0	58.3	55.4	59.7	60.4
June	58.0	65.8	64.8	83.1	42.2	54.2	63.7	71.3	31.6	31.7	58.2	55.9	59.8	60.6
July	58.4	66.2	64.8	83.9	42.4	54.6	63.5	72.0	31.7	32.2	58.6	55.8	61.0	61.5
Aug	58.6	66.5	65.5	84.0	42.5	54.6	62.1	72.0	32.3	32.0	58.7	56.2	61.2	61.5
Sept	58.8	66.7	66.4	84.1	43.0	54.8	63.9	72.1	32.2	32.4	58.9	56.5	61.7	61.6
Oct	59.0	66.9	67.2	84.6	42.6	55.0	65.0	72.2	32.2	32.2	59.1	56.3	62.6	62.0
Nov	59.4	67.4	68.5	84.9	43.0	55.3	64.7	73.0	32.2	32.4	59.5	56.8	62.9	63.0
Dec	59.5	67.5	68.3	85.0	43.1	55.7	65.4	73.3	32.4	32.2	59.7	56.6	62.3	62.8
2022: Jan	59.7	67.5	67.6	85.1	43.5	56.0	64.3	73.4	32.9	32.6	59.9	57.7	62.1	63.2
Feb	59.8	67.9	67.8	85.9	43.8	55.9	64.8	73.3	32.8	32.2	60.1	58.1	61.1	63.6
Mar	60.1	68.0	67.0	86.0	43.9	56.3	65.0	74.1	32.6	33.3	60.2	58.2	62.3	63.7
Apr	59.9	67.8	66.9	86.0	43.4	56.1	64.1	74.0	32.6	32.9	59.9	58.6	62.5	63.4
May	60.0	67.9	67.4	86.1	43.5	56.3	64.5	74.1	32.8	32.7	59.9	59.1	63.4	63.6
June	59.9	67.7	68.1	85.8	42.9	56.2	64.7	73.9	32.8	32.6	59.9	58.5	62.5	63.7
July	59.9	67.7	67.5	85.9	43.0	56.4	65.7	74.1	33.0	31.8	60.0	58.3	63.2	63.1
Aug	60.1	67.7	66.4	85.9	43.1	56.4	64.5	74.7	32.6	33.7	60.1	57.9	63.4	63.8
Sept	60.1	68.1	67.5	86.1	43.7	56.2	64.1	74.4	32.6	32.6	60.1	58.5	63.2	63.5
Oct	60.0	68.0	68.5	85.7	43.8	56.0	63.3	74.0	32.7	32.7	60.0	58.4	62.9	63.3
Nov	59.9	67.9	67.8	85.7	43.5	55.9	63.8	73.8	32.4	33.5	59.8	58.8	63.0	63.1
Dec	60.1	68.2	67.9	86.1	43.6	56.2	64.4	74.1	32.6	33.1	60.2	58.9	62.7	63.5

[1] Civilian employment as percent of civilian noninstitutional population in group specified.
[2] See footnote 1, Table B–23.

Note: Data relate to persons 16 years of age and over, except as noted.
See footnote 5 and Note, Table B–22.

Source: Department of Labor (Bureau of Labor Statistics).

TABLE B–27. Civilian unemployment rate, 1977–2022

[Percent [1]; monthly data seasonally adjusted]

Year or month	All civilian workers	By sex and age: Men 20 years and over	Women 20 years and over	Both sexes 16–19	By race or ethnicity [2]: White	Black or African American	Asian	Hispanic or Latino ethnicity	U-6 measure of labor underutilization [3]	By educational attainment (25 years & over): Less than a high school diploma	High school graduates, no college	Some college or associate degree	Bachelor's degree and higher [4]
1977	7.1	5.2	7.0	17.8	6.2	14.0	......	10.1	......	......	......	......	......
1978	6.1	4.3	6.0	16.4	5.2	12.8	......	9.1	......	......	......	......	......
1979	5.8	4.2	5.7	16.1	5.1	12.3	......	8.3	......	......	......	......	......
1980	7.1	5.9	6.4	17.8	6.3	14.3	......	10.1	......	......	......	......	......
1981	7.6	6.3	6.8	19.6	6.7	15.6	......	10.4	......	......	......	......	......
1982	9.7	8.8	8.3	23.2	8.6	18.9	......	13.8	......	......	......	......	......
1983	9.6	8.9	8.1	22.4	8.4	19.5	......	13.7	......	......	......	......	......
1984	7.5	6.6	6.8	18.9	6.5	15.9	......	10.7	......	......	......	......	......
1985	7.2	6.2	6.6	18.6	6.2	15.1	......	10.5	......	......	......	......	......
1986	7.0	6.1	6.2	18.3	6.0	14.5	......	10.6	......	......	......	......	......
1987	6.2	5.4	5.4	16.9	5.3	13.0	......	8.8	......	......	......	......	......
1988	5.5	4.8	4.9	15.3	4.7	11.7	......	8.2	......	......	......	......	......
1989	5.3	4.5	4.7	15.0	4.5	11.4	......	8.0	......	......	......	......	......
1990	5.6	5.0	4.9	15.5	4.8	11.4	......	8.2	......	......	......	......	......
1991	6.8	6.4	5.7	18.7	6.1	12.5	......	10.0	......	......	......	......	......
1992	7.5	7.1	6.3	20.1	6.6	14.2	......	11.6	......	11.5	6.8	5.6	3.2
1993	6.9	6.4	5.9	19.0	6.1	13.0	......	10.8	......	10.8	6.3	5.2	2.9
1994	6.1	5.4	5.4	17.6	5.3	11.5	......	9.9	10.9	9.8	5.4	4.5	2.6
1995	5.6	4.8	4.9	17.3	4.9	10.4	......	9.3	10.1	9.0	4.8	4.0	2.4
1996	5.4	4.6	4.8	16.7	4.7	10.5	......	8.9	9.7	8.7	4.7	3.7	2.2
1997	4.9	4.2	4.4	16.0	4.2	10.0	......	7.7	8.9	8.1	4.3	3.3	2.0
1998	4.5	3.7	4.1	14.6	3.9	8.9	......	7.2	8.0	7.1	4.0	3.0	1.8
1999	4.2	3.5	3.8	13.9	3.7	8.0	......	6.4	7.4	6.7	3.5	2.8	1.8
2000	4.0	3.3	3.6	13.1	3.5	7.6	3.6	5.7	7.0	6.3	3.4	2.7	1.7
2001	4.7	4.2	4.1	14.7	4.2	8.6	4.5	6.6	8.1	7.2	4.2	3.3	2.3
2002	5.8	5.3	5.1	16.5	5.1	10.2	5.9	7.5	9.6	8.4	5.3	4.5	2.9
2003	6.0	5.6	5.1	17.5	5.2	10.8	6.0	7.7	10.1	8.8	5.5	4.8	3.1
2004	5.5	5.0	4.9	17.0	4.8	10.4	4.4	7.0	9.6	8.5	5.0	4.2	2.7
2005	5.1	4.4	4.6	16.6	4.4	10.0	4.0	6.0	8.9	7.6	4.7	3.9	2.3
2006	4.6	4.0	4.1	15.4	4.0	8.9	3.0	5.2	8.2	6.8	4.3	3.6	2.0
2007	4.6	4.1	4.0	15.7	4.1	8.3	3.2	5.6	8.3	7.1	4.4	3.6	2.0
2008	5.8	5.4	4.9	18.7	5.2	10.1	4.0	7.6	10.5	9.0	5.7	4.6	2.6
2009	9.3	9.6	7.5	24.3	8.5	14.8	7.3	12.1	16.2	14.6	9.7	8.0	4.6
2010	9.6	9.8	8.0	25.9	8.7	16.0	7.5	12.5	16.7	14.9	10.3	8.4	4.7
2011	8.9	8.7	7.9	24.4	7.9	15.8	7.0	11.5	15.9	14.1	9.4	8.0	4.3
2012	8.1	7.5	7.3	24.0	7.2	13.8	5.9	10.3	14.7	12.4	8.3	7.1	4.0
2013	7.4	7.0	6.5	22.9	6.5	13.1	5.2	9.1	13.8	11.0	7.5	6.4	3.7
2014	6.2	5.7	5.6	19.6	5.3	11.3	5.0	7.4	12.0	9.0	6.0	5.4	3.2
2015	5.3	4.9	4.8	16.9	4.6	9.6	3.8	6.6	10.4	8.0	5.4	4.5	2.6
2016	4.9	4.5	4.4	15.7	4.3	8.4	3.6	5.8	9.6	7.4	5.2	4.1	2.5
2017	4.4	4.0	4.0	14.0	3.8	7.5	3.4	5.1	8.5	6.5	4.6	3.8	2.3
2018	3.9	3.6	3.5	12.9	3.5	6.5	3.0	4.7	7.7	5.6	4.1	3.3	2.1
2019	3.7	3.4	3.3	12.7	3.3	6.1	2.7	4.3	7.2	5.4	3.7	3.0	2.1
2020	8.1	7.4	8.0	17.9	7.3	11.4	8.7	10.4	13.6	11.7	9.0	7.8	4.8
2021	5.3	5.2	5.0	11.7	4.7	8.6	5.0	6.8	9.4	8.3	6.2	5.1	3.1
2022	3.6	3.4	3.3	10.8	3.2	6.1	2.8	4.3	6.9	5.5	4.0	3.1	2.0
2021: Jan	6.3	6.1	6.0	14.7	5.7	9.2	6.6	8.5	11.1	9.0	7.0	6.1	4.0
Feb	6.2	6.0	5.9	14.0	5.6	9.8	5.2	8.4	11.1	10.2	7.1	5.7	3.8
Mar	6.1	5.9	5.7	12.8	5.4	9.6	6.0	7.7	10.7	8.4	6.7	5.9	3.7
Apr	6.1	6.0	5.6	11.7	5.3	9.9	5.7	7.7	10.3	9.4	7.0	6.0	3.5
May	5.8	5.9	5.3	9.7	5.1	9.1	5.6	7.1	10.1	9.0	6.9	6.0	3.1
June	5.9	5.9	5.5	11.2	5.2	9.2	5.7	7.2	9.8	10.3	7.0	5.8	3.4
July	5.4	5.4	5.0	10.6	4.8	8.2	5.2	6.4	9.2	9.3	6.3	4.9	3.1
Aug	5.2	5.1	4.8	11.4	4.5	8.6	4.5	6.1	8.8	7.7	6.0	5.0	2.8
Sept	4.8	4.7	4.3	11.2	4.2	7.8	4.2	6.2	8.5	7.6	5.7	4.5	2.5
Oct	4.5	4.3	4.3	11.6	4.0	7.7	4.2	5.7	8.2	7.1	5.3	4.3	2.4
Nov	4.2	3.9	3.9	10.9	3.7	6.5	3.8	5.2	7.7	5.7	5.1	3.6	2.2
Dec	3.9	3.6	3.6	11.0	3.3	7.0	3.8	4.8	7.3	5.3	4.5	3.5	2.1
2022: Jan	4.0	3.8	3.6	10.9	3.4	6.9	3.5	4.9	7.1	6.3	4.5	3.5	2.3
Feb	3.8	3.5	3.6	10.3	3.3	6.6	3.0	4.5	7.2	4.5	4.4	3.7	2.2
Mar	3.6	3.4	3.3	10.1	3.2	6.2	2.8	4.2	6.9	5.3	4.0	3.1	2.0
Apr	3.6	3.5	3.2	10.2	3.2	5.9	3.1	4.2	7.0	5.4	3.8	3.1	2.0
May	3.6	3.4	3.4	10.5	3.2	6.2	2.4	4.4	7.1	5.2	3.8	3.4	2.0
June	3.6	3.4	3.3	11.0	3.3	5.9	3.0	4.3	6.7	5.7	3.6	3.1	2.1
July	3.5	3.2	3.1	11.4	3.1	6.0	2.6	4.0	6.8	5.8	3.6	2.9	2.0
Aug	3.7	3.5	3.3	10.4	3.2	6.4	2.8	4.5	7.0	6.1	4.4	2.9	1.9
Sept	3.5	3.3	3.1	11.3	3.1	5.9	2.5	3.9	6.7	5.5	3.7	2.9	1.8
Oct	3.7	3.3	3.4	11.0	3.3	5.9	2.9	4.2	6.7	6.2	3.9	3.0	1.9
Nov	3.6	3.3	3.3	11.3	3.3	5.7	2.6	4.0	6.7	4.4	3.9	3.2	2.0
Dec	3.5	3.1	3.2	10.4	3.0	5.7	2.4	4.1	6.5	5.0	3.6	2.9	1.9

[1] Unemployed as percent of civilian labor force in group specified.
[2] See footnote 1, Table B–23.
[3] Total unemployed, plus all persons marginally attached to the labor force, plus total employed part time for economic reasons, as a percent of the civilian labor force plus all persons marginally attached to the labor force.
[4] Includes persons with bachelor's, master's, professional, and doctoral degrees.

Note: Data relate to persons 16 years of age and over, except as noted.
See Note, Table B–22.

Source: Department of Labor (Bureau of Labor Statistics).

Table B–28. Unemployment by duration and reason, 1977–2022

[Thousands of persons, except as noted; monthly data seasonally adjusted [1]]

Year or month	Un-employment	Duration of unemployment						Reason for unemployment					
		Less than 5 weeks	5–14 weeks	15–26 weeks	27 weeks and over	Average (mean) duration (weeks) [2]	Median duration (weeks)	Job losers [3]			Job leavers	Re-entrants	New entrants
								Total	On layoff	Other			
1977	6,991	2,919	2,132	913	1,028	14.3	7.0	3,166	865	2,300	909	1,963	953
1978	6,202	2,865	1,923	766	648	11.9	5.9	2,585	712	1,873	874	1,857	885
1979	6,137	2,950	1,946	706	535	10.8	5.4	2,635	851	1,784	880	1,806	817
1980	7,637	3,295	2,470	1,052	820	11.9	6.5	3,947	1,488	2,459	891	1,927	872
1981	8,273	3,449	2,539	1,122	1,162	13.7	6.9	4,267	1,430	2,837	923	2,102	981
1982	10,678	3,883	3,311	1,708	1,776	15.6	8.7	6,268	2,127	4,141	840	2,384	1,185
1983	10,717	3,570	2,937	1,652	2,559	20.0	10.1	6,258	1,780	4,478	830	2,412	1,216
1984	8,539	3,350	2,451	1,104	1,634	18.2	7.9	4,421	1,171	3,250	823	2,184	1,110
1985	8,312	3,498	2,509	1,025	1,280	15.6	6.8	4,139	1,157	2,982	877	2,256	1,039
1986	8,237	3,448	2,557	1,045	1,187	15.0	6.9	4,033	1,090	2,943	1,015	2,160	1,029
1987	7,425	3,246	2,196	943	1,040	14.5	6.5	3,566	943	2,623	965	1,974	920
1988	6,701	3,084	2,007	801	809	13.5	5.9	3,092	851	2,241	983	1,809	816
1989	6,528	3,174	1,978	730	646	11.9	4.8	2,983	850	2,133	1,024	1,843	677
1990	7,047	3,265	2,257	822	703	12.0	5.3	3,387	1,028	2,359	1,041	1,930	688
1991	8,628	3,480	2,791	1,246	1,111	13.7	6.8	4,694	1,292	3,402	1,004	2,139	792
1992	9,613	3,376	2,830	1,453	1,954	17.7	8.7	5,389	1,260	4,129	1,002	2,285	937
1993	8,940	3,262	2,584	1,297	1,798	18.0	8.3	4,848	1,115	3,733	976	2,198	919
1994	7,996	2,728	2,408	1,237	1,623	18.8	9.2	3,815	977	2,838	791	2,786	604
1995	7,404	2,700	2,342	1,085	1,278	16.6	8.3	3,476	1,030	2,446	824	2,525	579
1996	7,236	2,633	2,287	1,053	1,262	16.7	8.3	3,370	1,021	2,349	774	2,512	580
1997	6,739	2,538	2,138	995	1,067	15.8	8.0	3,037	931	2,106	795	2,338	569
1998	6,210	2,622	1,950	763	875	14.5	6.7	2,822	866	1,957	734	2,132	520
1999	5,880	2,568	1,832	755	725	13.4	6.4	2,622	848	1,774	783	2,005	469
2000	5,692	2,558	1,815	669	649	12.6	5.9	2,517	852	1,664	780	1,961	434
2001	6,801	2,853	2,196	951	801	13.1	6.8	3,476	1,067	2,409	835	2,031	459
2002	8,378	2,893	2,580	1,369	1,535	16.6	9.1	4,607	1,124	3,483	866	2,368	536
2003	8,774	2,785	2,612	1,442	1,936	19.2	10.1	4,838	1,121	3,717	818	2,477	641
2004	8,149	2,696	2,382	1,293	1,779	19.6	9.8	4,197	998	3,199	858	2,408	686
2005	7,591	2,667	2,304	1,130	1,490	18.4	8.9	3,667	933	2,734	872	2,386	666
2006	7,001	2,614	2,121	1,031	1,235	16.8	8.3	3,321	921	2,400	827	2,237	616
2007	7,078	2,542	2,232	1,061	1,243	16.8	8.5	3,515	976	2,539	793	2,142	627
2008	8,924	2,932	2,804	1,427	1,761	17.9	9.4	4,789	1,176	3,614	896	2,472	766
2009	14,265	3,165	3,828	2,775	4,496	24.4	15.1	9,160	1,630	7,530	882	3,187	1,035
2010	14,825	2,771	3,267	2,371	6,415	33.0	21.4	9,250	1,431	7,819	889	3,466	1,220
2011	13,747	2,677	2,993	2,061	6,016	39.3	21.4	8,106	1,230	6,876	956	3,401	1,284
2012	12,506	2,644	2,866	1,859	5,136	39.4	19.3	6,877	1,183	5,694	967	3,345	1,316
2013	11,460	2,584	2,759	1,807	4,310	36.5	17.0	6,073	1,136	4,937	932	3,207	1,247
2014	9,617	2,471	2,432	1,497	3,218	33.7	14.0	4,878	1,007	3,871	824	2,829	1,086
2015	8,296	2,399	2,302	1,267	2,328	29.2	11.6	4,063	974	3,089	819	2,535	879
2016	7,751	2,362	2,226	1,158	2,005	27.5	10.6	3,740	966	2,774	858	2,330	823
2017	6,982	2,270	2,008	1,017	1,687	25.0	10.0	3,434	956	2,479	778	2,079	690
2018	6,314	2,170	1,876	917	1,350	22.7	9.3	2,990	852	2,138	794	1,928	602
2019	6,001	2,086	1,789	860	1,266	21.6	9.1	2,786	823	1,963	814	1,810	591
2020	12,947	3,708	4,728	2,516	1,995	16.5	9.7	9,770	6,371	3,399	683	1,969	526
2021	8,623	2,140	1,981	1,164	3,337	28.7	16.5	5,099	1,582	3,516	803	2,204	518
2022	5,996	2,216	1,711	756	1,314	22.6	8.7	2,767	830	1,936	857	1,891	482
2021: Jan	10,155	2,250	2,484	1,321	4,055	25.9	15.7	6,932	2,705	4,227	654	2,055	563
Feb	9,982	2,211	2,254	1,370	4,146	27.5	17.7	6,596	2,259	4,337	707	2,178	594
Mar	9,712	2,178	1,950	1,336	4,216	29.6	19.7	6,284	2,086	4,198	769	2,258	506
Apr	9,737	2,377	2,011	1,137	4,170	28.3	19.8	6,263	2,072	4,191	819	2,118	580
May	9,257	2,018	2,199	1,243	3,761	29.7	19.3	5,827	1,829	3,998	786	2,174	506
June	9,508	2,005	2,240	1,353	3,970	32.0	19.9	5,737	1,814	3,923	944	2,253	501
July	8,704	2,246	1,763	1,200	3,446	29.8	14.6	4,924	1,220	3,705	926	2,297	470
Aug	8,324	2,116	1,885	1,245	3,124	29.4	14.2	4,444	1,213	3,230	827	2,439	524
Sept	7,677	2,240	1,740	1,041	2,682	28.6	13.6	4,027	1,094	2,933	789	2,262	498
Oct	7,345	2,075	1,852	1,021	2,327	26.9	12.9	3,690	1,026	2,664	844	2,175	532
Nov	6,780	1,985	1,708	906	2,156	28.9	13.0	3,353	870	2,482	839	2,142	422
Dec	6,329	1,989	1,593	799	1,989	28.1	12.3	3,089	801	2,288	725	2,024	508
2022: Jan	6,511	2,428	1,619	819	1,683	24.5	9.6	3,217	952	2,265	953	1,995	438
Feb	6,272	2,142	1,803	726	1,691	26.2	9.3	3,004	879	2,125	964	1,971	429
Mar	5,972	2,303	1,688	552	1,429	24.1	8.3	2,840	784	2,057	789	1,992	472
Apr	5,968	2,242	1,630	526	1,474	24.8	8.2	2,850	857	1,993	794	1,856	516
May	5,979	2,052	1,771	687	1,349	22.5	8.7	2,732	815	1,916	766	1,944	530
June	5,945	2,259	1,576	777	1,337	22.3	8.2	2,633	832	1,802	833	1,979	466
July	5,718	2,086	1,769	734	1,093	22.1	8.3	2,616	802	1,814	843	1,822	465
Aug	6,021	2,227	1,797	887	1,165	22.3	8.6	2,693	796	1,898	897	1,833	451
Sept	5,770	2,158	1,643	901	1,089	20.3	8.5	2,530	772	1,758	904	1,834	460
Oct	6,053	2,215	1,774	817	1,169	20.8	8.4	2,695	853	1,842	861	1,873	494
Nov	6,000	2,244	1,694	821	1,215	21.4	8.8	2,761	806	1,956	829	1,798	558
Dec	5,722	2,233	1,639	826	1,069	19.5	8.9	2,629	814	1,815	825	1,767	497

[1] Because of independent seasonal adjustment of the various series, detail will not sum to totals.
[2] Beginning with 2011, includes unemployment durations of up to 5 years; prior data are for up to 2 years.
[3] Beginning with 1994, job losers and persons who completed temporary jobs.

Note: Data relate to persons 16 years of age and over.
See Note, Table B–22.

Source: Department of Labor (Bureau of Labor Statistics).

TABLE B–29. Employees on nonagricultural payrolls, by major industry, 1977–2022

[Thousands of jobs; monthly data seasonally adjusted]

Year or month	Total nonagricultural employment	Private industries: Total private	Goods-producing industries: Total	Goods-producing industries: Mining and logging	Goods-producing industries: Construction	Manufacturing: Total	Manufacturing: Durable goods	Manufacturing: Nondurable goods	Private service-providing industries: Total	Trade, transportation, and utilities[1]: Total	Trade, transportation, and utilities[1]: Retail trade
1977	82,593	67,334	22,972	865	3,940	18,167	11,132	7,035	44,362	16,741	9,363
1978	86,826	71,014	24,156	902	4,322	18,932	11,770	7,162	46,858	17,633	9,882
1979	89,933	73,865	24,997	1,008	4,562	19,426	12,220	7,206	48,869	18,276	10,185
1980	90,533	74,158	24,263	1,077	4,454	18,733	11,679	7,054	49,895	18,387	10,249
1981	91,297	75,117	24,118	1,180	4,304	18,634	11,611	7,023	50,999	18,577	10,369
1982	89,689	73,706	22,550	1,163	4,024	17,363	10,610	6,753	51,156	18,430	10,377
1983	90,295	74,284	22,110	997	4,065	17,048	10,326	6,722	52,174	18,642	10,640
1984	94,548	78,389	23,435	1,014	4,501	17,920	11,050	6,870	54,954	19,624	11,227
1985	97,532	81,000	23,585	974	4,793	17,819	11,034	6,784	57,415	20,350	11,738
1986	99,500	82,661	23,318	829	4,937	17,552	10,795	6,757	59,343	20,765	12,082
1987	102,116	84,960	23,470	771	5,090	17,609	10,767	6,842	61,490	21,271	12,422
1988	105,378	87,838	23,909	770	5,233	17,906	10,969	6,938	63,929	21,942	12,812
1989	108,051	90,124	24,045	750	5,309	17,985	11,004	6,981	66,079	22,477	13,112
1990	109,527	91,112	23,723	765	5,263	17,695	10,737	6,958	67,389	22,632	13,185
1991	108,425	89,879	22,588	739	4,780	17,068	10,220	6,848	67,292	22,243	12,896
1992	108,799	90,012	22,095	689	4,608	16,799	9,946	6,853	67,917	22,085	12,826
1993	110,931	91,942	22,219	666	4,779	16,774	9,901	6,872	69,723	22,335	13,016
1994	114,393	95,118	22,774	659	5,095	17,020	10,132	6,889	72,344	23,081	13,485
1995	117,401	97,968	23,156	641	5,274	17,241	10,373	6,868	74,813	23,782	13,889
1996	119,828	100,289	23,409	637	5,536	17,237	10,486	6,751	76,880	24,183	14,133
1997	122,941	103,278	23,886	654	5,813	17,419	10,705	6,714	79,392	24,640	14,377
1998	126,146	106,237	24,354	645	6,149	17,560	10,911	6,649	81,883	25,122	14,596
1999	129,228	108,921	24,465	598	6,545	17,322	10,831	6,491	84,456	25,703	14,955
2000	132,011	111,222	24,649	599	6,787	17,263	10,877	6,386	86,573	26,153	15,262
2001	132,073	110,955	23,873	606	6,826	16,441	10,336	6,105	87,082	25,908	15,219
2002	130,634	109,121	22,557	583	6,716	15,259	9,485	5,774	86,564	25,417	15,003
2003	130,330	108,747	21,816	572	6,735	14,509	8,964	5,546	86,931	25,200	14,894
2004	131,769	110,148	21,882	591	6,976	14,315	8,925	5,390	88,266	25,440	15,033
2005	134,033	112,229	22,190	628	7,336	14,227	8,956	5,271	90,039	25,861	15,253
2006	136,435	114,462	22,530	684	7,691	14,155	8,981	5,174	91,931	26,172	15,325
2007	137,981	115,763	22,233	724	7,630	13,879	8,808	5,071	93,530	26,520	15,490
2008	137,224	114,714	21,334	766	7,162	13,406	8,463	4,943	93,380	26,181	15,251
2009	131,296	108,741	18,557	694	6,016	11,847	7,284	4,564	90,184	24,794	14,488
2010	130,345	107,854	17,751	705	5,518	11,528	7,064	4,464	90,104	24,523	14,404
2011	131,914	109,828	18,048	788	5,533	11,726	7,273	4,453	91,780	24,947	14,630
2012	134,157	112,237	18,420	848	5,646	11,927	7,470	4,457	93,817	25,353	14,801
2013	136,363	114,511	18,738	863	5,856	12,020	7,548	4,472	95,773	25,735	15,037
2014	138,939	117,058	19,226	891	6,151	12,185	7,674	4,512	97,831	26,253	15,313
2015	141,824	119,795	19,610	813	6,461	12,336	7,765	4,571	100,185	26,754	15,559
2016	144,335	122,111	19,749	668	6,728	12,354	7,714	4,640	102,362	27,124	15,777
2017	146,607	124,257	20,084	676	6,969	12,439	7,741	4,699	104,173	27,336	15,789
2018	148,908	126,454	20,704	727	7,288	12,688	7,946	4,742	105,750	27,549	15,728
2019	150,904	128,291	21,037	727	7,493	12,817	8,039	4,778	107,254	27,662	15,560
2020	142,186	120,200	20,023	600	7,257	12,167	7,573	4,594	100,177	26,624	14,809
2021	146,285	124,311	20,350	560	7,436	12,354	7,681	4,673	103,961	27,653	15,253
2022 p	152,576	130,404	21,178	605	7,749	12,825	7,975	4,850	109,226	28,643	15,475
2021: Jan	142,969	121,188	20,109	550	7,363	12,196	7,576	4,620	101,079	27,220	15,177
Feb	143,544	121,751	20,054	541	7,291	12,222	7,594	4,628	101,697	27,310	15,208
Mar	144,328	122,452	20,219	554	7,395	12,270	7,624	4,646	102,233	27,431	15,234
Apr	144,614	122,685	20,190	556	7,406	12,228	7,591	4,637	102,495	27,402	15,202
May	145,096	123,166	20,209	556	7,394	12,259	7,615	4,644	102,957	27,471	15,221
June	145,789	123,790	20,236	560	7,400	12,276	7,634	4,642	103,554	27,582	15,256
July	146,558	124,521	20,325	561	7,415	12,349	7,687	4,662	104,196	27,625	15,223
Aug	147,221	125,121	20,390	564	7,431	12,395	7,712	4,683	104,731	27,715	15,235
Sept	147,778	125,704	20,473	564	7,472	12,437	7,739	4,698	105,231	27,866	15,305
Oct	148,559	126,522	20,578	568	7,514	12,496	7,779	4,717	105,944	28,015	15,359
Nov	149,173	127,135	20,672	572	7,560	12,540	7,799	4,741	106,463	28,085	15,354
Dec	149,742	127,686	20,757	579	7,594	12,584	7,828	4,756	106,929	28,189	15,365
2022: Jan	150,106	128,031	20,785	578	7,590	12,617	7,849	4,768	107,246	28,289	15,395
Feb	151,010	128,928	20,906	583	7,669	12,654	7,859	4,795	108,022	28,561	15,564
Mar	151,424	129,351	20,997	589	7,692	12,716	7,902	4,814	108,354	28,600	15,542
Apr	151,678	129,577	21,064	598	7,698	12,768	7,935	4,833	108,513	28,621	15,505
May	152,042	129,920	21,125	600	7,736	12,789	7,943	4,846	108,795	28,634	15,453
June	152,412	130,302	21,175	607	7,749	12,819	7,954	4,865	109,127	28,671	15,467
July	152,980	130,795	21,246	613	7,773	12,860	7,987	4,873	109,549	28,717	15,477
Aug	153,332	131,101	21,283	611	7,781	12,891	8,018	4,873	109,818	28,777	15,513
Sept	153,682	131,445	21,327	613	7,797	12,917	8,032	4,885	110,118	28,784	15,502
Oct	154,006	131,744	21,384	616	7,814	12,954	8,059	4,895	110,360	28,815	15,497
Nov	154,296	131,972	21,425	624	7,833	12,968	8,073	4,895	110,547	28,731	15,451
Dec p	154,556	132,241	21,468	629	7,859	12,980	8,098	4,882	110,773	28,756	15,453

[1] Includes wholesale trade, transportation and warehousing, and utilities, not shown separately.

Note: Data in Tables B–29 and B–30 are based on reports from employing establishments and relate to full- and part-time wage and salary workers in nonagricultural establishments who received pay for any part of the pay period that includes the 12th of the month. Not comparable with labor force data (Tables B–22 through B–28), which include proprietors, self-employed persons, unpaid family workers, and private household workers; which count persons as

See next page for continuation of table.

TABLE B–29. Employees on nonagricultural payrolls, by major industry, 1977–2022—*Continued*

[Thousands of jobs; monthly data seasonally adjusted]

Year or month	Private industries—Continued						Government			
	Private service-providing industries—Continued									
	Information	Financial activities	Profes-sional and business services	Education and health services	Leisure and hospitality	Other services	Total	Federal	State	Local
1977	2,185	4,348	6,611	6,052	6,065	2,359	15,258	2,859	3,377	9,023
1978	2,287	4,599	6,997	6,427	6,411	2,505	15,812	2,893	3,474	9,446
1979	2,375	4,843	7,339	6,768	6,631	2,637	16,068	2,894	3,541	9,633
1980	2,361	5,025	7,571	7,077	6,721	2,755	16,375	3,000	3,610	9,765
1981	2,382	5,163	7,809	7,364	6,840	2,865	16,180	2,922	3,640	9,619
1982	2,317	5,209	7,875	7,526	6,874	2,924	15,982	2,884	3,640	9,458
1983	2,253	5,334	8,065	7,781	7,078	3,021	16,011	2,915	3,662	9,434
1984	2,398	5,553	8,493	8,211	7,489	3,186	16,159	2,943	3,734	9,482
1985	2,437	5,815	8,900	8,679	7,869	3,366	16,533	3,014	3,832	9,687
1986	2,445	6,128	9,241	9,086	8,156	3,523	16,838	3,044	3,893	9,901
1987	2,507	6,385	9,639	9,543	8,446	3,699	17,156	3,089	3,967	10,100
1988	2,585	6,500	10,121	10,096	8,778	3,907	17,540	3,124	4,076	10,339
1989	2,622	6,562	10,588	10,652	9,062	4,116	17,927	3,136	4,182	10,609
1990	2,688	6,614	10,882	11,024	9,288	4,261	18,415	3,196	4,305	10,914
1991	2,678	6,561	10,750	11,556	9,256	4,249	18,545	3,110	4,355	11,081
1992	2,641	6,559	11,007	11,948	9,437	4,240	18,787	3,111	4,408	11,267
1993	2,668	6,742	11,534	12,362	9,732	4,350	18,989	3,063	4,488	11,438
1994	2,738	6,910	12,216	12,872	10,100	4,428	19,275	3,018	4,576	11,682
1995	2,844	6,866	12,889	13,360	10,501	4,572	19,432	2,949	4,635	11,849
1996	2,940	7,018	13,510	13,761	10,777	4,690	19,539	2,877	4,606	12,056
1997	3,084	7,255	14,386	14,185	11,018	4,825	19,664	2,806	4,582	12,276
1998	3,218	7,566	15,200	14,570	11,232	4,976	19,909	2,772	4,612	12,525
1999	3,419	7,753	16,013	14,939	11,543	5,087	20,307	2,769	4,709	12,829
2000	3,630	7,783	16,725	15,252	11,862	5,168	20,790	2,865	4,786	13,139
2001	3,629	7,900	16,537	15,814	12,036	5,258	21,118	2,764	4,905	13,449
2002	3,395	7,956	16,041	16,398	11,986	5,372	21,513	2,766	5,029	13,718
2003	3,188	8,078	16,057	16,835	12,173	5,401	21,583	2,761	5,002	13,820
2004	3,118	8,105	16,470	17,230	12,493	5,409	21,621	2,730	4,982	13,909
2005	3,061	8,197	17,034	17,676	12,816	5,395	21,804	2,732	5,032	14,041
2006	3,038	8,367	17,652	18,154	13,110	5,438	21,974	2,732	5,075	14,167
2007	3,032	8,348	18,034	18,676	13,427	5,494	22,218	2,734	5,122	14,362
2008	2,984	8,206	17,830	19,228	13,436	5,515	22,509	2,762	5,177	14,571
2009	2,804	7,838	16,674	19,630	13,077	5,367	22,555	2,832	5,169	14,554
2010	2,707	7,695	16,824	19,975	13,049	5,330	22,490	2,977	5,137	14,376
2011	2,674	7,697	17,433	20,318	13,353	5,360	22,086	2,859	5,078	14,150
2012	2,676	7,783	18,037	20,769	13,768	5,430	21,920	2,820	5,055	14,045
2013	2,706	7,886	18,623	21,086	14,254	5,483	21,853	2,769	5,046	14,037
2014	2,726	7,977	19,174	21,439	14,696	5,567	21,882	2,733	5,050	14,098
2015	2,750	8,123	19,747	22,029	15,160	5,622	22,029	2,757	5,077	14,195
2016	2,794	8,287	20,168	22,639	15,660	5,691	22,224	2,795	5,110	14,319
2017	2,814	8,451	20,563	23,188	16,051	5,770	22,350	2,805	5,165	14,379
2018	2,839	8,590	21,008	23,638	16,295	5,831	22,455	2,800	5,173	14,481
2019	2,864	8,754	21,334	24,163	16,586	5,891	22,613	2,831	5,206	14,576
2020	2,721	8,704	20,376	23,275	13,148	5,329	21,986	2,930	5,135	13,921
2021	2,856	8,806	21,386	23,652	14,151	5,457	21,973	2,886	5,156	13,931
2022 p	3,074	9,045	22,571	24,350	15,836	5,708	22,171	2,869	5,091	14,211
2021: Jan	2,749	8,734	20,854	23,365	12,835	5,322	21,781	2,887	5,162	13,732
Feb	2,765	8,723	20,940	23,427	13,207	5,325	21,793	2,881	5,167	13,745
Mar	2,770	8,733	21,067	23,538	13,352	5,342	21,876	2,887	5,195	13,794
Apr	2,792	8,753	21,048	23,573	13,558	5,369	21,929	2,899	5,191	13,839
May	2,820	8,760	21,131	23,615	13,782	5,378	21,930	2,891	5,179	13,860
June	2,837	8,767	21,234	23,635	14,055	5,444	21,999	2,889	5,190	13,920
July	2,866	8,804	21,397	23,680	14,339	5,485	22,037	2,888	5,163	13,986
Aug	2,902	8,821	21,500	23,708	14,565	5,520	22,100	2,890	5,149	14,061
Sept	2,917	8,850	21,592	23,707	14,765	5,534	22,074	2,887	5,138	14,049
Oct	2,934	8,877	21,821	23,803	14,931	5,563	22,037	2,877	5,132	14,028
Nov	2,955	8,912	21,960	23,851	15,108	5,592	22,038	2,882	5,120	14,036
Dec	2,973	8,935	22,069	23,892	15,258	5,613	22,056	2,873	5,113	14,070
2022: Jan	2,985	8,941	22,164	23,887	15,374	5,606	22,075	2,874	5,101	14,100
Feb	2,992	8,982	22,306	23,996	15,536	5,649	22,082	2,874	5,088	14,120
Mar	3,018	8,997	22,439	24,050	15,590	5,660	22,073	2,873	5,063	14,137
Apr	3,035	9,034	22,421	24,105	15,626	5,671	22,101	2,871	5,077	14,153
May	3,067	9,040	22,493	24,181	15,699	5,681	22,122	2,868	5,092	14,162
June	3,089	9,043	22,582	24,277	15,774	5,691	22,110	2,851	5,090	14,169
July	3,102	9,057	22,659	24,404	15,887	5,723	22,185	2,867	5,103	14,215
Aug	3,110	9,066	22,707	24,496	15,935	5,727	22,231	2,865	5,109	14,257
Sept	3,113	9,068	22,755	24,576	16,074	5,748	22,237	2,867	5,115	14,255
Oct	3,116	9,086	22,791	24,661	16,135	5,756	22,262	2,871	5,104	14,287
Nov	3,129	9,097	22,791	24,756	16,258	5,785	22,324	2,873	5,116	14,335
Dec p	3,124	9,108	22,830	24,832	16,322	5,801	22,315	2,873	5,078	14,364

Note (cont'd): employed when they are not at work because of industrial disputes, bad weather, etc., even if they are not paid for the time off; which are based on a sample of the working-age population; and which count persons only once—as employed, unemployed, or not in the labor force. In the data shown here, persons who work at more than one job are counted each time they appear on a payroll.

Establishment data for employment, hours, and earnings are classified based on the 2022 North American Industry Classification System (NAICS).

For further description and details see *Employment and Earnings*.

Source: Department of Labor (Bureau of Labor Statistics).

TABLE B–30. Hours and earnings in private nonagricultural industries, 1977–2022

[Monthly data seasonally adjusted]

Year or month	All employees: Average weekly hours	All employees: Average hourly earnings: Current dollars	All employees: Average hourly earnings: 1982–84 dollars[2]	All employees: Average weekly earnings: Level: Current dollars	All employees: Average weekly earnings: Level: 1982–84 dollars[2]	All employees: Average weekly earnings: Percent change from year earlier: Current dollars	All employees: Average weekly earnings: Percent change from year earlier: 1982–84 dollars[2]	Production and nonsupervisory employees[1]: Average weekly hours	Production and nonsupervisory employees[1]: Average hourly earnings: Current dollars	Production and nonsupervisory employees[1]: Average hourly earnings: 1982–84 dollars[3]	Production and nonsupervisory employees[1]: Average weekly earnings: Level: Current dollars	Production and nonsupervisory employees[1]: Average weekly earnings: Level: 1982–84 dollars[3]	Production and nonsupervisory employees[1]: Average weekly earnings: Percent change from year earlier: Current dollars	Production and nonsupervisory employees[1]: Average weekly earnings: Percent change from year earlier: 1982–84 dollars[3]
1977	....	....	....	....	....	....	....	35.9	$5.44	$8.93	$195.34	$320.76	7.1	0.6
1978	....	....	....	....	....	....	....	35.8	5.88	8.96	210.17	320.38	7.6	–.1
1979	....	....	....	....	....	....	....	35.6	6.34	8.67	225.46	308.43	7.3	–3.7
1980	....	....	....	....	....	....	....	35.2	6.84	8.25	240.83	290.51	6.8	–5.8
1981	....	....	....	....	....	....	....	35.2	7.43	8.13	261.29	285.88	8.5	–1.6
1982	....	....	....	....	....	....	....	34.7	7.86	8.11	272.98	281.71	4.5	–1.5
1983	....	....	....	....	....	....	....	34.9	8.20	8.22	286.34	286.91	4.9	1.8
1984	....	....	....	....	....	....	....	35.1	8.49	8.22	298.08	288.56	4.1	.6
1985	....	....	....	....	....	....	....	34.9	8.73	8.17	304.37	284.72	2.1	–1.3
1986	....	....	....	....	....	....	....	34.7	8.92	8.21	309.69	285.17	1.7	.2
1987	....	....	....	....	....	....	....	34.7	9.14	8.12	317.33	282.07	2.5	–1.1
1988	....	....	....	....	....	....	....	34.6	9.44	8.07	326.50	279.06	2.9	–1.1
1989	....	....	....	....	....	....	....	34.5	9.81	8.00	338.42	276.04	3.7	–1.1
1990	....	....	....	....	....	....	....	34.3	10.20	7.91	349.63	271.03	3.3	–1.8
1991	....	....	....	....	....	....	....	34.1	10.51	7.83	358.46	266.91	2.5	–1.5
1992	....	....	....	....	....	....	....	34.2	10.77	7.79	368.17	266.40	2.7	–.2
1993	....	....	....	....	....	....	....	34.3	11.04	7.77	378.80	266.57	2.9	.1
1994	....	....	....	....	....	....	....	34.5	11.33	7.78	391.11	268.62	3.2	.8
1995	....	....	....	....	....	....	....	34.3	11.65	7.78	399.93	266.98	2.3	–.6
1996	....	....	....	....	....	....	....	34.3	12.04	7.81	413.17	268.12	3.3	.4
1997	....	....	....	....	....	....	....	34.5	12.51	7.94	431.67	273.90	4.5	2.2
1998	....	....	....	....	....	....	....	34.5	13.01	8.15	448.47	280.82	3.9	2.5
1999	....	....	....	....	....	....	....	34.3	13.48	8.26	463.07	283.74	3.3	1.0
2000	....	....	....	....	....	....	....	34.3	14.01	8.29	480.90	284.72	3.9	.3
2001	....	....	....	....	....	....	....	33.9	14.54	8.38	493.53	284.46	2.6	–.1
2002	....	....	....	....	....	....	....	33.9	14.96	8.50	506.48	287.94	2.6	1.2
2003	....	....	....	....	....	....	....	33.7	15.36	8.54	517.65	287.90	2.2	.0
2004	....	....	....	....	....	....	....	33.7	15.68	8.50	528.65	286.53	2.1	–.5
2005	....	....	....	....	....	....	....	33.8	16.11	8.43	543.91	284.77	2.9	–.6
2006	....	....	....	....	....	....	....	33.9	16.75	8.50	567.00	287.67	4.2	1.0
2007	34.4	$20.92	$10.09	$719.74	$347.13	....	....	33.8	17.41	8.59	589.09	290.53	3.9	1.0
2008	34.3	21.56	10.01	738.96	343.22	2.7	–1.1	33.6	18.06	8.56	607.10	287.65	3.1	–1.0
2009	33.8	22.17	10.33	749.92	349.55	1.5	1.8	33.1	18.60	8.87	615.82	293.77	1.4	2.1
2010	34.1	22.56	10.35	769.57	352.92	2.6	1.0	33.4	19.04	8.90	635.86	297.18	3.3	1.2
2011	34.3	23.03	10.24	790.79	351.56	2.8	–.4	33.6	19.43	8.77	652.75	294.60	2.7	–.9
2012	34.5	23.49	10.23	809.43	352.55	2.4	.3	33.7	19.73	8.72	665.56	294.20	2.0	–.1
2013	34.4	23.95	10.28	825.08	354.18	1.9	.5	33.7	20.13	8.78	677.62	295.49	1.8	.4
2014	34.5	24.46	10.33	844.77	356.84	2.4	.8	33.7	20.60	8.85	694.74	298.47	2.5	1.0
2015	34.5	25.02	10.56	864.10	364.57	2.3	2.2	33.7	21.03	9.07	708.73	305.74	2.0	2.4
2016	34.4	25.64	10.68	881.09	367.11	2.0	.7	33.6	21.53	9.20	723.20	308.96	2.0	1.1
2017	34.4	26.32	10.74	906.19	369.69	2.8	.7	33.7	22.05	9.22	742.42	310.57	2.7	.5
2018	34.5	27.11	10.80	936.37	372.90	3.3	.9	33.8	22.71	9.26	767.01	312.88	3.3	.7
2019	34.4	27.99	10.95	963.06	376.70	2.9	1.0	33.6	23.51	9.43	790.64	317.24	3.1	1.4
2020	34.6	29.35	11.34	1,014.38	391.94	5.3	4.0	33.9	24.68	9.78	837.39	331.97	5.9	4.6
2021	34.7	30.60	11.29	1,063.08	392.32	4.8	.1	34.2	25.90	9.75	886.54	333.90	5.9	.6
2022 [p]	34.5	32.25	11.02	1,113.99	380.65	4.8	–3.0	34.0	27.56	9.57	937.22	325.44	5.7	–2.5
2021: Jan	35.0	29.92	11.39	1,047.20	398.71	7.4	5.9	34.5	25.17	9.81	868.37	338.57	8.1	6.4
Feb	34.6	30.05	11.40	1,039.73	394.38	5.9	4.1	34.0	25.26	9.81	858.84	333.40	6.4	4.3
Mar	34.9	30.05	11.34	1,048.75	395.88	6.8	4.1	34.4	25.35	9.79	872.04	336.74	7.9	4.7
Apr	34.9	30.20	11.32	1,053.98	395.24	2.7	–1.4	34.4	25.51	9.78	877.54	336.44	4.2	–.4
May	34.9	30.38	11.32	1,060.26	394.97	2.8	–2.0	34.4	25.67	9.77	883.05	336.06	4.0	–1.5
June	34.8	30.53	11.28	1,062.44	392.68	4.6	–.7	34.3	25.81	9.73	885.28	333.88	5.1	–.9
July	34.8	30.66	11.28	1,066.97	392.61	4.9	–.3	34.3	25.94	9.74	889.74	333.99	6.1	.2
Aug	34.7	30.78	11.28	1,068.07	391.42	4.4	–.7	34.2	26.12	9.76	893.30	333.85	5.3	–.4
Sept	34.8	30.96	11.30	1,077.41	393.18	4.9	–.5	34.3	26.29	9.78	901.75	335.51	6.3	.4
Oct	34.7	31.14	11.26	1,080.56	390.77	5.1	–1.1	34.2	26.44	9.74	904.25	333.07	6.4	–.4
Nov	34.8	31.24	11.21	1,087.15	390.06	5.4	–1.4	34.2	26.57	9.70	908.69	331.80	6.2	–1.3
Dec	34.8	31.42	11.19	1,093.42	389.27	5.0	–2.0	34.1	26.76	9.69	912.52	330.33	6.0	–1.8
2022: Jan	34.6	31.63	11.19	1,094.40	387.26	4.5	–2.9	34.0	26.88	9.67	913.92	328.75	5.2	–2.9
Feb	34.7	31.63	11.11	1,097.56	385.64	5.6	–2.2	34.2	26.98	9.63	922.72	329.42	7.4	–1.2
Mar	34.7	31.83	11.07	1,104.50	384.21	5.3	–2.9	34.1	27.12	9.58	924.79	326.59	6.0	–3.0
Apr	34.6	31.94	11.07	1,105.12	382.91	4.9	–3.1	34.1	27.27	9.60	929.91	327.38	6.0	–2.7
May	34.6	32.06	11.01	1,109.28	380.85	4.6	–3.6	34.1	27.39	9.55	934.00	325.68	5.8	–3.1
June	34.6	32.18	10.92	1,113.43	377.78	4.8	–3.8	34.1	27.53	9.47	938.77	322.96	6.0	–3.3
July	34.6	32.33	10.97	1,118.62	379.67	4.8	–3.3	34.0	27.64	9.52	939.76	323.77	5.6	–3.1
Aug	34.5	32.43	10.98	1,118.84	378.86	4.8	–3.2	34.0	27.75	9.55	943.50	324.66	5.6	–2.8
Sept	34.6	32.53	10.97	1,125.54	379.56	4.5	–3.5	34.0	27.85	9.55	946.90	324.77	5.0	–3.2
Oct	34.6	32.66	10.96	1,130.04	379.22	4.6	–3.0	34.0	27.96	9.54	950.64	324.46	5.1	–2.6
Nov	34.5	32.80	10.98	1,131.60	378.97	4.1	–2.8	33.9	28.09	9.57	952.25	324.50	4.8	–2.2
Dec [p]	34.4	32.93	11.01	1,132.79	378.87	3.6	–2.7	33.9	28.19	9.60	955.64	325.59	4.7	–1.4

[1] Production employees in goods-producing industries and nonsupervisory employees in service-providing industries. These groups account for four-fifths of the total employment on private nonfarm payrolls.

[2] Current dollars divided by the consumer price index for all urban consumers (CPI-U) on a 1982–84=100 base.

[3] Current dollars divided by the consumer price index for urban wage earners and clerical workers (CPI-W) on a 1982–84=100 base.

Note: See Note, Table B–29.

Source: Department of Labor (Bureau of Labor Statistics).

TABLE B–31. Employment cost index, private industry, 2005–2022

Year and month	Total private			Goods-producing			Service-providing [1]			Manufacturing		
	Total compen- sation	Wages and salaries	Benefits [2]	Total compen- sation	Wages and salaries	Benefits [2]	Total compen- sation	Wages and salaries	Benefits [2]	Total compen- sation	Wages and salaries	Benefits [2]
	Indexes on NAICS basis, December 2005=100; not seasonally adjusted											
December:												
2005	100.0	100.0	100.0	100.0	100.0	100.0	100.0	100.0	100.0	100.0	100.0	100.0
2006	103.2	103.2	103.1	102.5	102.9	101.7	103.4	103.3	103.7	101.8	102.3	100.8
2007	106.3	106.6	105.6	105.0	106.0	103.2	106.7	106.8	106.6	103.8	104.9	101.7
2008	108.9	109.4	107.7	107.5	109.0	104.7	109.4	109.6	108.9	105.9	107.7	102.5
2009	110.2	110.8	108.7	108.6	110.0	105.8	110.8	111.1	109.9	107.0	108.9	103.6
2010	112.5	112.8	111.9	111.1	111.6	110.1	113.0	113.1	112.6	110.0	110.7	108.8
2011	115.0	114.6	115.9	113.8	113.5	114.4	115.3	114.9	116.4	113.1	112.7	113.9
2012	117.1	116.6	118.2	115.6	115.4	116.0	117.6	117.0	119.1	114.9	114.8	115.0
2013	119.4	119.0	120.5	117.7	117.6	118.0	120.0	119.4	121.5	117.0	117.2	116.6
2014	122.2	121.6	123.5	120.3	120.1	120.7	122.8	122.1	124.6	119.8	119.8	119.8
2015	124.5	124.2	125.1	123.2	123.2	123.1	124.9	124.5	125.9	122.8	123.0	122.5
2016	127.2	127.1	127.3	125.8	126.2	124.9	127.7	127.4	128.3	125.5	126.2	124.3
2017	130.5	130.6	130.2	128.9	129.3	128.0	131.0	131.0	131.2	128.9	129.3	128.0
2018	134.4	134.7	133.6	131.9	133.0	129.6	135.2	135.2	135.1	131.6	132.9	129.1
2019	138.0	138.7	136.2	135.8	137.5	132.5	138.7	139.1	137.6	135.3	137.1	131.9
2020	141.6	142.6	139.1	138.9	141.0	134.9	142.4	143.1	140.6	138.5	140.7	134.3
2021	147.8	149.7	143.2	144.0	146.6	138.7	148.9	150.5	144.8	143.5	146.4	138.2
2022	155.3	157.4	150.1	150.6	153.9	143.9	156.6	158.3	152.3	150.3	153.9	143.5
2022: Mar	150.2	151.8	146.1	146.2	148.3	141.8	151.3	152.8	147.8	146.2	148.7	141.7
June	152.4	154.2	148.2	148.2	150.8	143.0	153.7	155.1	150.0	148.0	150.7	142.8
Sept	154.0	155.9	149.2	149.4	152.4	143.3	155.3	156.9	151.3	149.1	152.5	142.8
Dec	155.3	157.4	150.1	150.6	153.9	143.9	156.6	158.3	152.3	150.3	153.9	143.5
	Indexes on NAICS basis, December 2005=100; seasonally adjusted											
2021: Mar	143.2	144.5	140.2	140.0	142.1	135.7	144.2	145.1	141.9	139.4	141.8	134.9
June	144.3	145.8	140.7	141.3	143.8	136.4	145.2	146.4	142.3	140.7	143.5	135.4
Sept	146.3	148.1	142.1	142.8	145.1	138.1	147.4	148.9	143.6	142.5	145.1	137.7
Dec	147.9	149.8	143.4	144.1	146.7	138.8	149.0	150.6	145.1	143.6	146.5	138.2
2022: Mar	150.0	151.7	146.1	146.2	148.5	141.7	151.1	152.5	147.7	146.2	148.7	141.6
June	152.3	154.1	148.0	148.0	150.5	142.8	153.5	155.0	149.8	147.8	150.5	142.7
Sept	153.9	155.9	149.2	149.3	152.4	143.2	155.2	156.8	151.3	149.2	152.5	142.8
Dec	155.4	157.5	150.3	150.6	153.9	144.0	156.7	158.4	152.5	150.4	154.0	143.6
	Percent change from 12 months earlier, not seasonally adjusted											
December:												
2005	2.9	2.5	4.0	3.2	2.9	3.8	2.8	2.4	4.1	3.2	2.7	4.2
2006	3.2	3.2	3.1	2.5	2.9	1.7	3.4	3.3	3.7	1.8	2.3	.8
2007	3.0	3.3	2.4	2.4	3.0	1.5	3.2	3.4	2.8	2.0	2.5	.9
2008	2.4	2.6	2.0	2.4	2.8	1.5	2.5	2.6	2.2	2.0	2.7	.8
2009	1.2	1.3	.9	1.0	.9	1.1	1.3	1.4	.9	1.0	1.1	1.1
2010	2.1	1.8	2.9	2.3	1.5	4.1	2.0	1.8	2.5	2.8	1.7	5.0
2011	2.2	1.6	3.6	2.4	1.7	3.9	2.0	1.6	3.4	2.8	1.8	4.7
2012	1.8	1.7	2.0	1.6	1.7	1.4	2.0	1.8	2.3	1.6	1.9	1.0
2013	2.0	2.1	1.9	1.8	1.9	1.7	2.0	2.1	2.0	1.8	2.1	1.4
2014	2.3	2.2	2.5	2.2	2.1	2.3	2.3	2.3	2.6	2.4	2.2	2.7
2015	1.9	2.1	1.3	2.4	2.6	2.0	1.7	2.0	1.0	2.5	2.7	2.3
2016	2.2	2.3	1.8	2.1	2.4	1.5	2.2	2.3	1.9	2.2	2.6	1.5
2017	2.6	2.8	2.3	2.5	2.5	2.5	2.6	2.8	2.3	2.7	2.5	3.0
2018	3.0	3.1	2.6	2.3	2.9	1.3	3.2	3.2	3.0	2.1	2.8	.9
2019	2.7	3.0	1.9	3.0	3.4	2.2	2.6	2.9	1.9	2.8	3.2	2.2
2020	2.6	2.8	2.1	2.3	2.5	1.8	2.7	2.9	2.2	2.4	2.6	1.8
2021	4.4	5.0	2.9	3.7	4.0	2.8	4.6	5.2	3.0	3.6	4.1	2.9
2022	5.1	5.1	4.8	4.6	5.0	3.7	5.2	5.2	5.2	4.7	5.1	3.8
2022: Mar	4.8	5.0	4.1	4.5	4.4	4.4	4.9	5.2	4.2	4.9	4.9	5.0
June	5.5	5.7	5.3	4.7	4.7	4.8	5.8	5.9	5.3	5.1	4.9	5.4
Sept	5.2	5.2	5.0	4.6	5.0	3.7	5.4	5.3	5.4	4.6	5.2	3.7
Dec	5.1	5.1	4.8	4.6	5.0	3.7	5.2	5.2	5.2	4.7	5.1	3.8
	Percent change from 3 months earlier, seasonally adjusted											
2021: Mar	1.1	1.2	0.6	0.7	0.8	0.5	1.2	1.3	0.7	0.6	0.7	0.4
June	.8	.9	.4	.9	1.2	.5	.7	.9	.3	.9	1.2	.4
Sept	1.4	1.6	1.0	1.1	.9	1.2	1.5	1.7	.9	1.3	1.1	1.7
Dec	1.1	1.1	.9	.9	1.1	.5	1.1	1.1	1.0	.8	1.0	.4
2022: Mar	1.4	1.3	1.9	1.5	1.2	2.1	1.4	1.3	1.8	1.8	1.5	2.5
June	1.5	1.6	1.3	1.2	1.3	.8	1.6	1.6	1.4	1.1	1.2	.8
Sept	1.1	1.2	.8	.9	1.3	.3	1.1	1.2	1.0	.9	1.3	.1
Dec	1.0	1.0	.7	.9	1.0	.6	1.0	1.0	.8	.8	1.0	.6

[1] On Standard Industrial Classification (SIC) basis, data are for service-producing industries.
[2] Employer costs for employee benefits.

Note: Changes effective with the release of March 2006 data (in April 2006) include changing industry classification to NAICS from SIC and rebasing data to December 2005=100. Historical SIC data are available through December 2005.

Data exclude farm and household workers.

Source: Department of Labor (Bureau of Labor Statistics).

Table B–32. Productivity and related data, business and nonfarm business sectors, 1972–2022

[Index numbers, 2012=100; quarterly data seasonally adjusted]

Year or quarter	Labor productivity (output per hour)		Output [1]		Hours of all persons [2]		Compensation per hour [3]		Real compensation per hour [4]		Unit labor costs		Value-added output price deflator [5]	
	Business sector	Nonfarm business sector	Business sector	Nonfarm business sector	Business sector	Nonfarm business sector	Business sector	Nonfarm business sector	Business sector	Nonfarm business sector	Business sector	Nonfarm business sector	Business sector	Nonfarm business sector
1972	45.574	46.924	29.651	29.666	65.061	63.222	13.662	13.835	68.518	69.385	29.978	29.484	26.870	26.357
1973	46.943	48.369	31.710	31.820	67.550	65.786	14.744	14.891	69.614	70.308	31.409	30.787	28.263	27.292
1974	46.130	47.560	31.226	31.342	67.691	65.900	16.116	16.294	68.529	69.284	34.937	34.259	31.031	30.125
1975	47.733	48.841	30.930	30.831	64.797	63.125	17.827	17.995	69.465	70.120	37.348	36.844	34.031	33.332
1976	49.320	50.547	33.019	33.041	66.948	65.366	19.251	19.396	70.925	71.459	39.032	38.372	35.809	35.144
1977	50.220	51.425	34.910	34.938	69.514	67.940	20.792	20.988	71.926	72.602	41.402	40.812	37.928	37.330
1978	50.820	52.142	37.137	37.271	73.075	71.480	22.541	22.785	72.869	73.660	44.354	43.699	40.551	39.773
1979	50.881	52.025	38.456	38.533	75.580	74.066	24.718	24.951	72.985	73.674	48.580	47.959	43.944	43.101
1980	50.861	51.997	38.108	38.204	74.926	73.473	27.361	27.627	72.655	73.361	53.797	53.133	47.850	47.200
1981	51.942	52.757	39.220	39.075	75.507	74.066	29.932	30.276	72.625	73.460	57.626	57.388	52.262	51.721
1982	51.648	52.323	38.094	37.879	73.757	72.394	32.148	32.483	73.559	74.325	62.244	62.080	55.240	54.913
1983	53.406	54.463	40.113	40.227	75.109	73.861	33.560	33.931	73.645	74.459	62.839	62.301	57.224	56.835
1984	54.931	55.683	43.671	43.630	79.502	78.354	35.045	35.393	73.830	74.564	63.798	63.561	58.842	58.401
1985	56.185	56.645	45.708	45.551	81.352	80.414	36.830	37.116	75.015	75.598	65.550	65.523	60.395	60.187
1986	57.766	58.335	47.368	47.275	82.000	81.041	38.909	39.253	77.886	78.575	67.356	67.289	61.213	61.035
1987	58.082	58.656	49.068	48.993	84.480	83.525	40.366	40.731	78.117	78.823	69.498	69.440	62.364	62.175
1988	58.956	59.625	51.170	51.225	86.793	85.912	42.507	42.822	79.392	79.980	72.100	71.819	64.349	64.075
1989	59.630	60.158	53.129	53.107	89.098	88.279	43.785	44.063	78.353	78.850	73.427	73.245	66.717	66.409
1990	60.812	61.172	53.979	53.901	88.764	88.114	46.516	46.699	79.328	79.641	76.491	76.341	68.933	68.683
1991	61.779	62.167	53.650	53.562	86.841	86.158	48.667	48.916	80.084	80.494	78.776	78.686	70.930	70.829
1992	64.649	64.948	55.922	55.738	86.501	85.820	51.658	51.956	82.943	83.421	79.905	79.997	72.080	72.017
1993	64.710	65.022	57.517	57.458	88.884	88.368	52.413	52.592	82.085	82.365	80.996	80.884	73.744	73.697
1994	65.080	65.468	60.290	60.102	92.640	91.803	52.794	53.106	80.991	81.469	81.122	81.117	75.058	75.063
1995	65.535	66.174	62.143	62.167	94.825	93.944	54.072	54.420	81.000	81.521	82.509	82.237	76.397	76.392
1996	67.131	67.564	65.028	64.964	96.867	96.152	55.997	56.295	81.708	82.143	83.415	83.322	77.600	77.447
1997	68.581	68.867	68.442	68.313	99.798	99.196	58.243	58.487	83.187	83.536	84.926	84.928	78.747	78.794
1998	70.924	71.182	72.206	72.150	101.808	101.360	61.677	61.871	86.915	87.188	86.963	86.919	78.959	79.081
1999	73.814	73.968	76.378	76.345	103.473	103.214	64.654	64.739	89.210	89.327	87.591	87.523	79.393	79.631
2000	76.104	76.167	79.805	79.675	104.863	104.605	69.136	69.278	92.264	92.453	90.845	90.956	80.850	81.185
2001	78.118	78.140	80.283	80.216	102.772	102.656	72.295	72.287	93.808	93.799	92.546	92.510	82.224	82.495
2002	81.413	81.478	81.651	81.562	100.292	100.103	73.900	73.946	94.403	94.462	90.772	90.755	82.836	83.189
2003	84.538	84.487	84.228	84.089	99.633	99.530	76.688	76.705	95.789	95.810	90.714	90.789	84.064	84.332
2004	87.180	87.006	87.932	87.730	100.862	100.832	80.260	80.197	97.613	97.537	92.062	92.174	86.174	86.295
2005	89.115	88.900	91.385	91.156	102.548	102.538	83.156	83.122	97.822	97.782	93.314	93.501	88.849	89.205
2006	90.030	89.782	94.378	94.190	104.829	104.910	86.360	86.320	98.402	98.356	95.924	96.144	91.359	91.806
2007	91.382	91.202	96.392	96.343	105.483	105.637	90.213	90.050	99.956	99.777	98.721	98.738	93.471	93.658
2008	92.755	92.636	95.552	95.492	103.015	103.083	93.007	92.929	99.241	99.158	100.271	100.316	94.841	95.039
2009	96.433	96.222	92.038	91.814	95.442	95.419	94.146	94.107	100.806	100.765	97.628	97.802	94.882	95.358
2010	99.644	99.491	95.012	94.841	95.352	95.327	95.803	95.846	100.916	100.961	96.145	96.337	96.036	96.373
2011	99.359	99.280	96.881	96.782	97.506	97.484	97.599	97.704	99.666	99.773	98.229	98.412	98.217	98.235
2012	100.000	100.000	100.000	100.000	100.000	100.000	100.000	100.000	100.000	100.000	100.000	100.000	100.000	100.000
2013	100.929	100.562	102.460	102.240	101.516	101.668	101.484	101.322	100.002	99.843	100.549	100.756	101.463	101.442
2014	101.354	101.112	105.469	105.280	104.060	104.122	104.018	104.024	100.793	100.799	102.628	102.880	103.152	103.298
2015	102.484	102.347	109.067	108.835	106.424	106.339	107.077	107.295	103.578	103.789	104.482	104.835	103.693	104.083
2016	103.156	102.987	111.123	110.834	107.724	107.620	108.551	108.777	103.668	103.883	105.231	105.622	104.455	105.041
2017	104.321	104.132	114.071	113.833	109.346	109.316	112.375	112.552	105.060	105.225	107.721	108.086	106.304	106.822
2018	105.926	105.639	118.073	117.838	111.468	111.548	116.183	116.340	106.035	106.178	109.684	110.129	108.583	109.179
2019	107.921	107.726	121.178	121.046	112.284	112.365	120.612	120.794	108.118	108.282	111.759	112.131	110.237	110.890
2020	112.652	112.545	117.031	116.855	103.887	103.830	130.314	130.634	115.375	115.659	115.678	116.073	110.647	111.317
2021	115.110	115.030	125.993	125.997	109.455	109.534	136.581	136.774	115.529	115.693	118.653	118.903	116.104	116.441
2022 p	113.244	113.108	128.776	128.884	113.715	113.947	143.216	143.230	112.492	112.503	126.467	126.631	124.640	124.497
2019: I	107.077	106.823	119.792	119.638	111.874	111.996	120.093	120.249	108.654	108.795	112.155	112.568	109.535	110.207
II	107.739	107.492	120.635	120.484	111.970	112.087	120.218	120.364	107.918	108.049	111.583	111.975	110.244	110.934
III	108.240	108.095	121.890	121.767	112.611	112.648	120.250	120.462	107.546	107.736	111.096	111.441	110.446	111.091
IV	108.840	108.711	122.395	122.297	112.454	112.497	122.149	122.371	108.593	108.790	112.228	112.565	110.708	111.313
2020: I	108.811	108.570	120.409	120.194	110.659	110.706	125.120	125.382	110.873	111.105	114.989	115.484	110.793	111.419
II	112.922	112.978	108.093	107.928	95.724	95.530	132.281	132.754	118.212	118.635	117.144	117.504	109.517	110.306
III	114.975	114.762	119.045	118.873	103.540	103.582	130.431	130.585	115.206	115.343	113.443	113.788	110.750	111.454
IV	113.760	113.739	120.578	120.423	105.994	105.877	133.342	133.737	117.134	117.481	117.213	117.582	111.411	111.986
2021: I	114.692	114.702	122.955	122.893	107.204	107.141	133.098	133.447	115.755	116.058	116.048	116.342	113.131	113.689
II	115.409	115.372	125.546	125.542	108.784	108.815	135.429	135.693	115.510	115.735	117.347	117.613	115.137	115.418
III	114.633	114.496	126.354	126.385	110.225	110.384	137.533	137.639	115.418	115.507	119.977	120.213	116.964	117.191
IV	115.489	115.336	129.116	129.169	111.800	111.994	139.859	139.902	115.156	115.191	121.102	121.300	119.034	119.318
2022: I	113.627	113.538	128.320	128.365	112.930	113.059	140.438	140.558	113.316	113.412	123.596	123.798	121.500	121.524
II	112.614	112.456	127.864	127.964	113.542	113.790	141.476	141.466	111.553	111.544	125.629	125.797	124.546	124.369
III	112.889	112.785	128.979	129.113	114.253	114.478	144.227	144.268	112.197	112.229	127.759	127.915	125.724	125.528
IV p	113.447	113.250	129.942	130.095	114.540	114.874	146.116	146.013	112.513	112.434	128.797	128.929	126.754	126.533

[1] Output refers to real gross domestic product in the sector.

[2] Hours at work of all persons engaged in sector, including hours of employees, proprietors, and unpaid family workers. Estimates based primarily on establishment data.

[3] Wages and salaries of employees plus employers' contributions for social insurance and private benefit plans. Also includes an estimate of wages, salaries, and supplemental payments for the self-employed.

[4] Hourly compensation divided by consumer price series. The trend for 1978-2021 is based on the consumer price index retroactive series (CPI-U-RS). The change for prior years and recent quarters is based on the consumer price index for all urban consumers (CPI-U).

[5] Current dollar output divided by the output index.

Source: Department of Labor (Bureau of Labor Statistics).

TABLE B–33. Changes in productivity and related data, business and nonfarm business sectors, 1972–2022

[Percent change from preceding period; quarterly data at seasonally adjusted annual rates]

Year or quarter	Labor productivity (output per hour)		Output [1]		Hours of all persons [2]		Compensation per hour [3]		Real compensation per hour [4]		Unit labor costs		Value-added output price deflator [5]	
	Business sector	Nonfarm business sector	Business sector	Nonfarm business sector	Business sector	Nonfarm business sector	Business sector	Nonfarm business sector	Business sector	Nonfarm business sector	Business sector	Nonfarm business sector	Business sector	Nonfarm business sector
1972	3.4	3.5	6.5	6.7	3.1	3.1	6.3	6.5	3.0	3.2	2.9	2.9	3.4	3.1
1973	3.0	3.1	6.9	7.3	3.8	4.1	7.9	7.6	1.6	1.3	4.8	4.4	5.2	3.5
1974	−1.7	−1.7	−1.5	−1.5	.2	.2	9.3	9.4	−1.6	−1.5	11.2	11.3	9.8	10.4
1975	3.5	2.7	−.9	−1.6	−4.3	−4.2	10.6	10.4	1.4	1.2	6.9	7.5	9.7	10.6
1976	3.3	3.5	6.8	7.2	3.3	3.6	8.0	7.8	2.1	1.9	4.5	4.1	5.2	5.4
1977	1.8	1.7	5.7	5.7	3.8	3.9	8.0	8.2	1.4	1.6	6.1	6.4	5.9	6.2
1978	1.2	1.4	6.4	6.7	5.1	5.2	8.4	8.6	1.3	1.5	7.1	7.1	6.9	6.5
1979	.1	−.2	3.6	3.4	3.4	3.6	9.7	9.5	.2	.0	9.5	9.7	8.4	8.4
1980	.0	−.1	−.9	−.9	−.9	−.8	10.7	10.7	−.5	−.4	10.7	10.8	8.9	9.5
1981	2.1	1.5	2.9	2.3	.8	.8	9.4	9.6	.0	.1	7.1	8.0	9.2	9.6
1982	−.6	−.8	−2.9	−3.1	−2.3	−2.3	7.4	7.3	1.3	1.2	8.0	8.2	5.7	6.2
1983	3.4	4.1	5.3	6.2	1.8	2.0	4.4	4.5	.1	.2	1.0	.4	3.6	3.5
1984	2.9	2.2	8.9	8.5	5.8	6.1	4.4	4.3	.3	.1	1.5	2.0	2.8	2.8
1985	2.3	1.7	4.7	4.4	2.3	2.6	5.1	4.9	1.6	1.4	2.7	3.1	2.6	3.1
1986	2.8	3.0	3.6	3.8	.8	.8	5.6	5.8	3.8	3.9	2.8	2.7	1.4	1.4
1987	.5	.6	3.6	3.6	3.0	3.1	3.7	3.8	.3	.3	3.2	3.2	1.9	1.9
1988	1.5	1.7	4.3	4.6	2.7	2.9	5.3	5.1	1.6	1.5	3.7	3.4	3.2	3.1
1989	1.1	.9	3.8	3.7	2.7	2.8	3.0	2.9	−1.3	−1.4	1.8	2.0	3.7	3.6
1990	2.0	1.7	1.6	1.5	−.4	−.2	6.2	6.0	1.2	1.0	4.2	4.2	3.3	3.4
1991	1.6	1.6	−.6	−.6	−2.2	−2.2	4.6	4.7	1.0	1.1	3.0	3.1	2.9	3.1
1992	4.6	4.5	4.2	4.1	−.4	−.4	6.1	6.2	3.6	3.6	1.4	1.7	1.6	1.7
1993	.1	.1	2.9	3.1	2.8	3.0	1.5	1.2	−1.0	−1.3	1.4	1.1	2.3	2.3
1994	.6	.7	4.8	4.6	4.2	3.9	.7	1.0	−1.3	−1.1	.2	.3	1.8	1.9
1995	.7	1.1	3.1	3.4	2.4	2.3	2.4	2.5	.0	.1	1.7	1.4	1.8	1.8
1996	2.4	2.1	4.6	4.5	2.2	2.4	3.6	3.4	.9	.8	1.1	1.3	1.6	1.4
1997	2.2	1.9	5.3	5.2	3.0	3.2	4.0	3.9	1.8	1.7	1.8	1.9	1.5	1.7
1998	3.4	3.4	5.5	5.6	2.0	2.2	5.9	5.8	4.5	4.4	2.4	2.3	.3	.4
1999	4.1	3.9	5.8	5.8	1.6	1.8	4.8	4.6	2.6	2.5	.7	.7	.5	.7
2000	3.1	3.0	4.5	4.4	1.3	1.3	6.9	7.0	3.4	3.5	3.7	3.9	1.8	2.0
2001	2.6	2.6	.6	.7	−2.0	−1.9	4.6	4.3	1.7	1.5	1.9	1.7	1.7	1.6
2002	4.2	4.3	1.7	1.7	−2.4	−2.5	2.2	2.3	.6	.7	−1.9	−1.9	.7	.8
2003	3.8	3.7	3.2	3.1	−.7	−.6	3.8	3.7	1.5	1.4	−.1	.0	1.5	1.4
2004	3.1	3.0	4.4	4.3	1.2	1.3	4.7	4.6	1.9	1.8	1.5	1.5	2.5	2.3
2005	2.2	2.2	3.9	3.9	1.7	1.7	3.6	3.6	.2	.3	1.4	1.4	3.1	3.4
2006	1.0	1.0	3.3	3.3	2.2	2.3	3.9	3.8	.6	.6	2.8	2.8	2.8	2.9
2007	1.5	1.6	2.1	2.3	.6	.7	4.5	4.3	1.6	1.4	2.9	2.7	2.3	2.0
2008	1.5	1.6	−.9	−.9	−2.3	−2.4	3.1	3.2	−.7	−.6	1.6	1.6	1.5	1.5
2009	4.0	3.9	−3.7	−3.9	−7.4	−7.4	1.2	1.3	1.6	1.6	−2.6	−2.5	.0	.3
2010	3.3	3.4	3.2	3.3	−.1	−.1	1.8	1.8	.1	.2	−1.5	−1.5	1.2	1.1
2011	−.3	−.2	2.0	2.0	2.3	2.3	1.9	1.9	−1.2	−1.2	2.2	2.2	2.3	1.9
2012	.6	.7	3.2	3.3	2.6	2.6	2.5	2.3	.3	.2	1.8	1.6	1.8	1.8
2013	.9	.6	2.5	2.2	1.5	1.7	1.5	1.3	.0	−.2	.5	.8	1.5	1.4
2014	.4	.5	2.9	3.0	2.5	2.4	2.5	2.7	.8	1.0	2.1	2.1	1.7	1.8
2015	1.1	1.2	3.4	3.4	2.3	2.1	2.9	3.1	2.8	3.0	1.8	1.9	.5	.8
2016	.7	.6	1.9	1.8	1.2	1.2	1.4	1.4	.1	.1	.7	.8	.7	.9
2017	1.1	1.1	2.7	2.7	1.5	1.6	3.5	3.5	1.3	1.3	2.4	2.3	1.8	1.7
2018	1.5	1.4	3.5	3.5	1.9	2.0	3.4	3.4	.9	.9	1.8	1.9	2.1	2.2
2019	1.9	2.0	2.6	2.7	.7	.7	3.8	3.8	2.0	2.0	1.9	1.8	1.5	1.6
2020	4.4	4.5	−3.4	−3.5	−7.5	−7.6	8.0	8.1	6.7	6.8	3.5	3.5	.4	.4
2021	2.2	2.2	7.7	7.8	5.4	5.5	4.8	4.7	.1	.0	2.6	2.4	4.9	4.6
2022 p	−1.6	−1.7	2.2	2.3	3.9	4.0	4.9	4.7	−2.6	−2.8	6.6	6.5	7.4	6.9
2019: I	3.3	3.4	2.7	3.0	−.5	−.3	9.9	9.7	8.9	8.6	6.4	6.1	1.2	1.3
II	2.5	2.5	2.8	2.9	.3	.3	.4	.4	−2.7	−2.7	−2.0	−2.1	2.6	2.7
III	1.9	2.3	4.2	4.3	2.3	2.0	.1	.3	−1.4	−1.2	−1.7	−1.9	.7	.6
IV	2.2	2.3	1.7	1.8	−.6	−.5	6.5	6.5	4.0	4.0	4.1	4.1	1.0	.8
2020: I	−.1	−.5	−6.3	−6.7	−6.2	−6.2	10.1	10.2	8.7	8.8	10.2	10.8	.3	.4
II	16.0	17.3	−35.1	−35.0	−44.0	−44.6	24.9	25.7	29.2	30.0	7.7	7.2	−4.5	−3.9
III	7.5	6.5	47.1	47.2	36.9	38.2	−5.5	−6.4	−9.8	−10.6	−12.1	−12.1	4.6	4.2
IV	−4.2	−3.5	5.3	5.3	9.8	9.2	9.2	10.0	6.9	7.6	14.0	14.0	2.4	1.9
2021: I	3.3	3.4	8.1	8.5	4.6	4.9	−.7	−.9	−4.6	−4.8	−3.9	−4.2	6.3	6.2
II	2.5	2.4	8.7	8.9	6.0	6.4	7.2	6.9	−.8	−1.1	4.6	4.4	7.3	6.2
III	−2.7	−3.0	2.6	2.7	5.4	5.9	6.4	5.9	−.3	−.8	9.3	9.1	6.5	6.3
IV	3.0	3.0	9.0	9.1	5.8	6.0	6.9	6.7	−.9	−1.1	3.8	3.7	7.3	7.5
2022: I	−6.3	−6.1	−2.4	−2.5	4.1	3.9	1.7	1.9	−6.2	−6.0	8.5	8.5	8.5	7.6
II	−3.5	−3.8	−1.4	−1.2	2.2	2.6	3.0	2.6	−6.1	−6.4	6.7	6.6	10.4	9.7
III	1.0	1.2	3.5	3.6	2.5	2.4	8.0	8.2	2.3	2.5	7.0	6.9	3.8	3.8
IV p	2.0	1.7	3.0	3.1	1.0	1.4	5.3	4.9	1.1	.7	3.3	3.2	3.3	3.2

[1] Output refers to real gross domestic product in the sector.
[2] Hours at work of all persons engaged in the sector. See footnote 2, Table B–32.
[3] Wages and salaries of employees plus employers' contributions for social insurance and private benefit plans. Also includes an estimate of wages, salaries, and supplemental payments for the self-employed.
[4] Hourly compensation divided by a consumer price index. See footnote 4, Table B–32.
[5] Current dollar output divided by the output index.

Note: Percent changes are calculated using index numbers to three decimal places and may differ slightly from percent changes based on indexes in Table B–32, which are rounded to one decimal place.

Source: Department of Labor (Bureau of Labor Statistics).

Table B–34. Industrial production indexes, major industry divisions, 1977–2022

[2017=100, except as noted; monthly data seasonally adjusted]

Year or month	Total industrial production [1]		Manufacturing					Mining	Utilities
	Index, 2017=100	Percent change from year earlier [2]	Total [1]	Percent change from year earlier [2]	Durable	Nondurable	Other (non-NAICS) [1]		
1977	47.6	7.6	45.8	8.6	28.8	73.0	154.4	86.3	54.3
1978	50.3	5.5	48.6	6.1	31.1	75.6	159.8	89.0	55.7
1979	51.8	3.0	50.1	3.1	32.6	76.1	163.1	91.7	56.9
1980	50.4	−2.6	48.3	−3.6	31.1	73.7	168.8	93.5	57.3
1981	51.1	1.3	48.8	1.0	31.5	74.4	172.8	96.0	58.1
1982	48.4	−5.2	46.2	−5.5	28.8	73.3	174.8	91.3	56.1
1983	49.8	2.7	48.4	4.8	30.2	76.7	179.8	86.5	56.5
1984	54.2	8.9	53.1	9.8	34.5	80.3	188.1	92.1	59.9
1985	54.9	1.2	54.0	1.6	35.2	80.7	195.5	90.3	61.4
1986	55.4	1.0	55.1	2.2	35.8	83.0	199.5	83.7	61.9
1987	58.3	5.2	58.3	5.7	37.9	87.5	210.9	84.6	64.9
1988	61.3	5.2	61.4	5.3	40.7	90.4	210.0	86.9	68.9
1989	61.9	.9	61.9	.8	41.2	91.0	207.1	85.9	71.0
1990	62.5	1.0	62.3	.8	41.3	92.4	204.6	87.1	72.4
1991	61.5	−1.5	61.2	−1.9	40.1	92.1	196.2	85.3	74.2
1992	63.3	2.9	63.4	3.7	42.2	94.6	192.2	83.7	74.2
1993	65.4	3.3	65.7	3.5	44.5	95.9	193.6	83.5	76.7
1994	68.9	5.3	69.6	5.9	48.4	99.2	191.9	85.0	78.3
1995	72.1	4.6	73.1	5.1	52.4	100.9	191.9	84.9	81.1
1996	75.3	4.5	76.7	4.9	57.1	101.3	190.0	86.4	83.4
1997	80.7	7.2	83.1	8.4	63.9	105.0	206.1	88.1	83.2
1998	85.5	5.9	88.7	6.7	70.7	106.7	218.3	86.5	85.5
1999	89.2	4.4	93.2	5.1	76.7	107.3	224.6	82.1	88.1
2000	92.7	3.9	97.0	4.1	82.2	107.8	224.0	83.9	90.6
2001	89.8	−3.1	93.4	−3.7	78.8	104.8	209.5	84.1	90.3
2002	90.1	.3	93.8	.4	79.1	106.0	202.4	80.2	93.0
2003	91.2	1.3	95.1	1.3	81.2	106.2	196.7	80.3	94.5
2004	93.6	2.7	98.0	3.1	85.0	107.8	197.6	80.2	95.9
2005	96.8	3.3	102.0	4.1	90.1	110.6	196.9	79.3	98.0
2006	99.0	2.3	104.6	2.6	94.3	111.2	194.6	81.3	97.7
2007	101.5	2.5	107.5	2.8	99.0	112.5	183.6	81.9	100.7
2008	98.0	−3.5	102.4	−4.8	95.6	105.8	167.5	83.0	100.4
2009	86.8	−11.4	88.3	−13.8	77.8	97.7	140.1	78.7	97.5
2010	91.6	5.5	93.5	5.9	86.2	99.8	129.5	82.4	101.2
2011	94.5	3.2	96.3	2.9	91.5	100.0	123.5	87.7	100.8
2012	97.4	3.0	98.7	2.6	96.6	100.0	116.4	94.7	98.5
2013	99.3	2.0	99.6	.9	98.7	100.0	110.0	100.6	100.7
2014	102.3	3.0	100.7	1.1	101.6	99.3	108.3	111.3	102.0
2015	100.8	−1.4	100.2	−.5	100.5	99.7	103.9	104.6	101.2
2016	98.7	−2.2	99.4	−.8	98.4	100.5	101.0	91.5	100.8
2017	100.0	1.4	100.0	.6	100.0	100.0	100.0	100.0	100.0
2018	103.2	3.2	101.3	1.3	103.1	99.7	96.7	113.3	104.9
2019	102.5	−.7	99.4	−2.0	100.2	98.8	92.6	120.8	104.0
2020	95.3	−7.0	93.1	−6.3	91.5	95.2	85.2	102.7	101.0
2021	100.0	4.9	98.4	5.7	98.7	98.8	85.0	105.9	102.9
2022 [p]	103.8	3.8	101.3	3.0	103.0	100.7	81.3	114.8	106.4
2021: Jan	99.3	−2.0	98.0	−.8	98.4	98.2	86.4	103.1	101.7
Feb	96.2	−5.4	94.6	−4.5	95.5	93.8	88.3	93.8	108.3
Mar	98.9	1.0	97.5	2.9	98.1	97.3	89.7	104.6	99.9
Apr	99.0	16.6	97.3	21.4	97.1	98.3	86.6	105.1	102.1
May	99.8	15.6	98.2	17.3	97.9	99.3	84.0	106.4	101.6
June	100.2	9.2	98.1	9.2	97.8	99.4	82.0	106.9	105.9
July	100.9	5.9	99.2	6.5	99.8	99.6	81.9	107.6	103.6
Aug	100.8	4.9	98.9	4.6	99.3	99.3	84.4	107.6	105.3
Sept	99.8	3.9	98.2	3.7	98.4	98.7	85.0	105.9	103.3
Oct	101.4	4.7	99.8	4.4	100.3	100.2	85.6	109.8	100.4
Nov	102.0	5.0	100.4	4.4	101.0	100.6	84.7	110.2	101.9
Dec	101.8	3.7	100.3	3.9	101.0	100.6	81.7	110.3	100.4
2022: Jan	102.1	2.9	100.0	2.0	101.0	99.9	82.9	109.1	108.4
Feb	102.9	6.9	101.2	7.0	102.3	101.1	84.4	108.5	107.5
Mar	103.6	4.8	102.0	4.6	103.1	101.7	86.7	111.9	103.1
Apr	104.3	5.3	102.4	5.1	104.2	101.5	83.8	112.3	106.7
May	104.2	4.4	101.9	3.8	103.3	101.6	81.6	113.6	107.0
June	103.9	3.7	101.1	3.1	102.7	100.7	80.5	115.4	107.6
July	104.5	3.6	101.5	2.3	103.7	100.5	78.9	116.9	107.7
Aug	104.4	3.5	101.5	2.6	103.6	100.7	78.1	116.9	106.4
Sept [p]	104.6	4.7	101.5	3.4	103.6	100.6	79.5	119.2	104.2
Oct [p]	104.6	3.2	101.9	2.1	104.2	100.8	80.4	119.2	101.5
Nov [p]	104.0	2.0	101.1	.7	102.7	100.6	79.9	117.6	104.3
Dec [p]	102.9	1.1	99.3	−1.0	101.3	98.4	78.0	116.2	109.6

[1] Total industry and total manufacturing series include manufacturing as defined in the North American Industry Classification System (NAICS) plus those industries—logging and newspaper, periodical, book, and directory publishing—that have traditionally been considered to be manufacturing and included in the industrial sector.

[2] Percent changes based on unrounded indexes.

Note: Data based on NAICS; see footnote 1.

Source: Board of Governors of the Federal Reserve System.

TABLE B–35. Capacity utilization rates, 1977–2022

[Percent [1]; monthly data seasonally adjusted]

Year or month	Total industry [2]	Manufacturing				Mining	Utilities	Stage-of-process		
		Total [2]	Durable goods	Nondurable goods	Other (non-NAICS) [2]			Crude	Primary and semi-finished	Finished
1977	83.4	82.5	81.1	84.4	83.2	89.5	86.7	89.1	84.5	79.9
1978	85.1	84.4	83.8	85.3	85.1	89.6	86.9	88.6	86.2	82.3
1979	84.9	84.0	83.9	83.9	85.6	91.1	86.9	89.9	85.8	81.7
1980	80.7	78.7	77.5	79.7	86.7	91.3	85.2	89.3	78.8	79.3
1981	79.5	77.0	75.2	78.8	87.5	90.9	84.1	89.3	77.2	77.5
1982	73.6	70.9	66.4	76.4	87.4	84.1	79.7	82.3	70.4	73.1
1983	74.9	73.5	68.8	79.4	87.9	79.9	79.0	80.0	74.5	73.0
1984	80.5	79.4	77.0	82.1	89.5	86.1	81.6	86.0	81.1	77.2
1985	79.3	78.1	75.8	80.5	90.2	84.7	81.5	84.1	79.8	76.6
1986	78.5	78.5	75.4	81.8	88.7	76.5	80.7	78.5	79.7	77.1
1987	81.2	81.0	77.6	84.8	90.5	80.3	83.3	82.9	82.8	78.7
1988	84.3	84.0	82.0	86.2	88.5	84.0	86.6	86.4	85.9	81.7
1989	83.7	83.3	81.8	85.0	85.5	85.1	86.6	86.8	84.7	81.7
1990	82.4	81.6	79.3	84.2	83.7	87.0	86.3	88.0	82.6	80.6
1991	80.0	78.6	75.6	82.3	80.8	85.4	87.7	85.6	79.9	78.4
1992	80.7	79.7	77.4	82.7	80.2	85.2	86.2	85.9	81.5	78.4
1993	81.6	80.6	78.8	82.7	81.4	85.7	88.0	85.9	83.3	78.5
1994	83.6	82.8	81.7	84.6	81.4	86.7	88.1	87.9	86.3	79.3
1995	83.9	83.1	82.2	84.5	82.2	87.6	89.1	89.0	86.3	79.8
1996	83.3	82.1	81.4	83.1	80.5	90.5	90.5	89.0	85.4	79.3
1997	84.0	83.0	82.2	83.8	85.5	91.8	89.9	90.4	85.8	80.5
1998	82.8	81.6	80.7	82.2	86.8	89.2	92.4	87.0	84.0	80.4
1999	81.8	80.5	80.3	80.0	87.2	86.2	94.0	86.1	84.2	78.1
2000	81.5	79.8	79.7	78.9	87.4	90.5	94.1	88.6	83.8	77.1
2001	76.1	73.8	71.5	75.7	82.9	89.8	90.0	85.5	77.3	72.6
2002	75.0	73.0	70.1	76.0	81.5	85.9	87.5	83.2	77.4	70.6
2003	76.0	74.1	71.2	76.9	81.5	87.7	85.6	85.0	78.2	71.4
2004	78.2	76.5	74.2	78.9	82.4	88.2	84.4	86.6	80.3	73.4
2005	80.2	78.6	76.6	80.5	82.1	88.5	85.0	86.7	81.9	75.8
2006	80.5	78.8	77.7	80.1	79.6	90.1	83.6	88.1	81.4	76.5
2007	80.7	78.9	78.4	79.7	76.8	89.4	85.7	88.7	81.0	77.2
2008	77.7	74.6	74.4	74.4	78.2	90.0	84.1	87.7	76.7	73.9
2009	68.4	65.2	61.2	69.7	67.2	80.8	80.5	78.4	65.4	67.9
2010	73.3	70.3	68.5	73.0	63.1	84.2	82.8	83.6	71.3	70.9
2011	76.0	73.1	72.5	74.7	63.8	86.4	81.3	85.1	74.0	73.4
2012	76.8	74.3	75.1	74.5	62.5	87.8	78.3	85.9	74.4	74.6
2013	77.1	74.5	75.2	74.7	62.3	86.8	79.8	85.8	75.5	73.8
2014	78.7	75.8	77.0	75.3	64.7	89.4	80.7	87.6	77.2	75.0
2015	77.1	76.1	76.4	76.7	65.6	80.6	79.7	79.7	77.1	75.9
2016	75.3	75.4	74.6	76.8	66.9	71.5	78.6	74.2	76.3	74.6
2017	76.5	76.2	75.6	77.5	69.7	77.8	76.9	78.6	77.0	75.1
2018	79.5	78.1	78.1	78.5	70.5	87.3	80.2	86.1	79.8	76.2
2019	78.3	76.9	76.0	78.1	71.2	87.3	78.8	86.0	78.4	75.2
2020	72.6	72.4	69.4	76.1	69.2	71.9	74.8	73.6	72.9	71.9
2021	77.4	77.1	75.1	79.7	73.2	81.4	74.4	81.0	76.6	76.7
2022 p	79.6	79.0	77.5	80.9	74.8	87.3	74.9	85.8	78.3	78.4
2021: Jan	76.4	76.6	74.8	79.0	72.2	76.1	74.3	76.9	75.7	76.8
Feb	74.2	74.0	72.6	75.6	74.1	70.1	79.0	69.2	75.2	74.7
Mar	76.3	76.4	74.6	78.4	75.7	78.9	72.8	77.7	75.5	76.6
Apr	76.6	76.3	73.8	79.3	73.4	80.0	74.2	79.7	76.0	75.9
May	77.3	77.0	74.5	80.2	71.6	81.7	73.7	82.3	76.1	76.4
June	77.7	77.0	74.4	80.3	70.3	82.7	76.6	83.2	76.8	76.3
July	78.2	77.8	75.9	80.4	70.7	83.6	74.8	83.8	77.0	77.3
Aug	78.2	77.7	75.6	80.3	73.2	83.9	75.9	83.3	77.4	77.1
Sept	77.4	77.1	74.8	79.7	74.2	82.7	74.3	81.5	76.9	76.5
Oct	78.6	78.3	76.2	80.9	75.2	85.7	72.1	84.7	77.4	77.3
Nov	79.0	78.7	76.7	81.2	74.8	85.9	73.0	85.0	78.0	77.6
Dec	78.7	78.6	76.6	81.1	72.6	85.8	71.8	84.7	77.5	77.7
2022: Jan	78.9	78.3	76.5	80.6	74.0	84.6	77.3	83.7	78.4	77.7
Feb	79.4	79.2	77.4	81.5	75.9	83.9	76.5	83.4	79.4	78.0
Mar	79.8	79.8	78.0	81.9	78.3	86.1	73.2	85.4	78.8	78.7
Apr	80.2	80.0	78.7	81.7	76.1	86.1	75.6	85.3	79.5	79.1
May	80.0	79.6	77.9	81.7	74.6	86.7	75.7	85.8	79.1	78.8
June	79.7	78.9	77.3	80.9	73.9	87.8	75.9	86.6	78.4	78.2
July	80.0	79.1	78.0	80.7	72.8	88.6	75.9	87.1	78.7	78.4
Aug	79.8	79.0	77.8	80.8	72.5	88.4	74.7	86.7	78.2	78.7
Sept p	79.9	79.0	77.7	80.8	74.2	89.9	73.1	87.6	78.0	78.6
Oct p	79.8	79.2	78.0	80.8	75.5	89.8	71.0	87.4	77.5	79.2
Nov p	79.3	78.5	76.8	80.7	75.4	88.5	72.8	86.3	77.4	78.4
Dec p	78.4	77.1	75.7	78.9	74.0	87.4	76.4	84.9	76.9	77.4

[1] Output as percent of capacity.
[2] See footnote 1 and Note, Table B–34.

Source: Board of Governors of the Federal Reserve System.

TABLE B–36. New private housing units started, authorized, and completed and houses sold, 1977–2022

[Thousands; monthly data at seasonally adjusted annual rates]

Year or month	New housing units started				New housing units authorized [1]				New housing units completed	New houses sold
	Total	Type of structure			Total	Type of structure				
		1 unit	2 to 4 units [2]	5 units or more		1 unit	2 to 4 units	5 units or more		
1977	1,987.1	1,450.9	121.7	414.4	1,690.0	1,126.1	121.3	442.7	1,657.1	819
1978	2,020.3	1,433.3	125.1	462.0	1,800.5	1,182.6	130.6	487.3	1,867.5	817
1979	1,745.1	1,194.1	122.0	429.0	1,551.8	981.5	125.4	444.8	1,870.8	709
1980	1,292.2	852.2	109.5	330.5	1,190.6	710.4	114.5	365.7	1,501.6	545
1981	1,084.2	705.4	91.2	287.7	985.5	564.3	101.8	319.4	1,265.7	436
1982	1,062.2	662.6	80.1	319.6	1,000.5	546.4	88.3	365.8	1,005.5	412
1983	1,703.0	1,067.6	113.5	522.0	1,605.2	901.5	133.7	570.1	1,390.3	623
1984	1,749.5	1,084.2	121.4	543.9	1,681.8	922.4	142.6	616.8	1,652.2	639
1985	1,741.8	1,072.4	93.5	576.0	1,733.3	956.6	120.1	656.6	1,703.3	688
1986	1,805.4	1,179.4	84.0	542.0	1,769.4	1,077.6	108.4	583.5	1,756.4	750
1987	1,620.5	1,146.4	65.1	408.7	1,534.8	1,024.4	89.3	421.1	1,668.8	671
1988	1,488.1	1,081.3	58.7	348.0	1,455.6	993.8	75.7	386.1	1,529.8	676
1989	1,376.1	1,003.3	55.3	317.6	1,338.4	931.7	66.9	339.8	1,422.8	650
1990	1,192.7	894.8	37.6	260.4	1,110.8	793.9	54.3	262.6	1,308.0	534
1991	1,013.9	840.4	35.6	137.9	948.8	753.5	43.1	152.1	1,090.8	509
1992	1,199.7	1,029.9	30.9	139.0	1,094.9	910.7	45.8	138.4	1,157.5	610
1993	1,287.6	1,125.7	29.4	132.6	1,199.1	986.5	52.4	160.2	1,192.7	666
1994	1,457.0	1,198.4	35.2	223.5	1,371.6	1,068.5	62.2	241.0	1,346.9	670
1995	1,354.1	1,076.2	33.8	244.1	1,332.5	997.3	63.8	271.5	1,312.6	667
1996	1,476.8	1,160.9	45.3	270.8	1,425.6	1,069.5	65.8	290.3	1,412.9	757
1997	1,474.0	1,133.7	44.5	295.8	1,441.1	1,062.4	68.4	310.3	1,400.5	804
1998	1,616.9	1,271.4	42.6	302.9	1,612.3	1,187.6	69.2	355.5	1,474.2	886
1999	1,640.9	1,302.4	31.9	306.6	1,663.5	1,246.7	65.8	351.1	1,604.9	880
2000	1,568.7	1,230.9	38.7	299.1	1,592.3	1,198.1	64.9	329.3	1,573.7	877
2001	1,602.7	1,273.3	36.6	292.8	1,636.7	1,235.6	66.0	335.2	1,570.8	908
2002	1,704.9	1,358.6	38.5	307.9	1,747.7	1,332.6	73.7	341.4	1,648.4	973
2003	1,847.7	1,499.0	33.5	315.2	1,889.2	1,460.9	82.5	345.8	1,678.7	1,086
2004	1,955.8	1,610.5	42.3	303.0	2,070.1	1,613.4	90.4	366.2	1,841.9	1,203
2005	2,068.3	1,715.8	41.1	311.4	2,155.3	1,682.0	84.0	389.3	1,931.4	1,283
2006	1,800.9	1,465.4	42.7	292.8	1,838.9	1,378.2	76.6	384.1	1,979.4	1,051
2007	1,355.0	1,046.0	31.7	277.3	1,398.4	979.9	59.6	359.0	1,502.8	776
2008	905.5	622.0	17.5	266.0	905.4	575.6	34.4	295.4	1,119.7	485
2009	554.0	445.1	11.6	97.3	583.0	441.1	20.7	121.1	794.4	375
2010	586.9	471.2	11.4	104.3	604.6	447.3	22.0	135.3	651.7	323
2011	608.8	430.6	10.9	167.3	624.1	418.5	21.6	184.0	584.9	306
2012	780.6	535.3	11.4	233.9	829.7	518.7	25.9	285.1	649.2	368
2013	924.9	617.6	13.6	293.7	990.8	620.8	29.0	341.1	764.4	429
2014	1,003.3	647.9	13.7	341.7	1,052.1	640.3	29.9	382.0	883.8	437
2015	1,111.8	714.5	11.5	385.8	1,182.6	696.0	32.1	454.5	968.2	501
2016	1,173.8	781.5	11.5	380.8	1,206.6	750.8	34.8	421.1	1,059.7	561
2017	1,203.0	848.9	11.4	342.7	1,282.0	820.0	37.2	424.8	1,152.9	613
2018	1,249.9	875.8	13.9	360.3	1,328.8	855.3	39.7	433.8	1,184.9	617
2019	1,290.0	887.7	13.4	388.9	1,386.0	862.1	42.6	481.4	1,255.1	683
2020	1,379.6	990.5	12.3	376.8	1,471.1	979.4	47.2	444.5	1,286.9	822
2021	1,601.0	1,127.2	11.7	462.1	1,737.0	1,115.4	52.9	568.8	1,341.0	771
2022 p	1,554.5	1,004.9	16.4	533.2	1,651.9	972.2	52.7	627.2	1,391.2	641
2021: Jan	1,602	1,117	....	472	1,843	1,217	58	568	1,330	911
Feb	1,430	1,053	....	364	1,743	1,132	50	561	1,332	768
Mar	1,711	1,243	....	446	1,773	1,204	59	510	1,462	881
Apr	1,505	1,061	....	430	1,765	1,152	49	564	1,417	809
May	1,605	1,110	....	485	1,691	1,138	59	494	1,340	740
June	1,664	1,165	....	488	1,661	1,091	49	521	1,305	714
July	1,573	1,124	....	438	1,655	1,051	55	549	1,376	726
Aug	1,576	1,095	....	474	1,772	1,061	43	668	1,302	686
Sept	1,559	1,094	....	455	1,615	1,054	48	513	1,233	732
Oct	1,563	1,079	....	474	1,698	1,077	52	569	1,256	671
Nov	1,706	1,220	....	469	1,729	1,111	48	570	1,406	756
Dec	1,768	1,212	....	553	1,896	1,118	68	710	1,326	839
2022: Jan	1,666	1,157	....	499	1,841	1,197	57	587	1,247	831
Feb	1,777	1,213	....	532	1,857	1,204	54	599	1,380	790
Mar	1,716	1,191	....	511	1,879	1,163	56	660	1,366	707
Apr	1,805	1,173	....	619	1,823	1,109	56	658	1,339	619
May	1,562	1,073	....	459	1,695	1,051	55	589	1,440	636
June	1,575	1,013	....	554	1,696	970	50	676	1,391	571
July	1,377	900	....	462	1,685	932	52	701	1,411	543
Aug	1,508	923	....	565	1,542	900	47	595	1,352	646
Sept	1,465	893	....	555	1,564	870	49	645	1,433	550
Oct	1,426	859	....	553	1,512	841	51	620	1,357	589
Nov p	1,419	807	....	598	1,351	781	52	518	1,539	583
Dec p	1,371	879	....	483	1,337	731	46	560	1,392	625

[1] Authorized by issuance of local building permits in permit-issuing places: 20,100 places beginning with 2014; 19,300 for 2004–2013; 19,000 for 1994–2003; 17,000 for 1984–93; 16,000 for 1978–83; and 14,000 for 1977.

[2] Monthly data do not meet publication standards because tests for identifiable and stable seasonality do not meet reliability standards.

Note: One-unit estimates prior to 1999, for new housing units started and completed and for new houses sold, include an upward adjustment of 3.3 percent to account for structures in permit-issuing areas that did not have permit authorization.

Source: Department of Commerce (Bureau of the Census).

TABLE B–37. Manufacturing and trade sales and inventories, 1980–2022

[Amounts in millions of dollars; monthly data seasonally adjusted]

Year or month	Total manufacturing and trade			Manufacturing			Merchant wholesalers [1]			Retail trade			Retail and food services sales
	Sales [2]	Inventories [3]	Ratio [4]	Sales [2]	Inventories [3]	Ratio [4]	Sales [2]	Inventories [3]	Ratio [4]	Sales [2, 5]	Inventories [3]	Ratio [4]	
SIC: [6]													
1980	327,233	508,924	1.56	154,391	265,215	1.72	93,099	122,631	1.32	79,743	121,078	1.52	....
1981	355,822	545,786	1.53	168,129	283,413	1.69	101,180	129,654	1.28	86,514	132,719	1.53	....
1982	347,625	573,908	1.67	163,351	311,852	1.95	95,211	127,428	1.36	89,062	134,628	1.49	....
1983	369,286	590,287	1.56	172,547	312,379	1.78	99,225	130,075	1.28	97,514	147,833	1.44	....
1984	410,124	649,780	1.53	190,682	339,516	1.73	112,199	142,452	1.23	107,243	167,812	1.49	....
1985	422,583	664,039	1.56	194,538	334,749	1.73	113,459	147,409	1.28	114,586	181,881	1.52	....
1986	430,419	662,738	1.55	194,657	322,654	1.68	114,960	153,574	1.32	120,803	186,510	1.56	....
1987	457,735	709,848	1.50	206,326	338,109	1.59	122,968	163,903	1.29	128,442	207,836	1.55	....
1988	497,157	767,222	1.49	224,619	369,374	1.57	134,521	178,801	1.30	138,017	219,047	1.54	....
1989	527,039	815,455	1.52	236,698	391,212	1.63	143,760	187,009	1.28	146,581	237,234	1.58	....
1990	545,909	840,594	1.52	242,686	405,073	1.65	149,506	195,833	1.29	153,718	239,688	1.56	....
1991	542,815	834,609	1.53	239,847	390,950	1.65	148,306	200,448	1.33	154,661	243,211	1.54	....
1992	567,176	842,809	1.48	250,394	382,510	1.54	154,150	208,302	1.32	162,632	251,997	1.52	....
NAICS: [6]													
1992	540,199	835,800	1.53	242,002	378,609	1.57	147,261	196,914	1.31	150,936	260,277	1.67	167,842
1993	567,195	863,125	1.50	251,708	379,806	1.50	154,018	204,842	1.30	161,469	278,477	1.68	179,425
1994	609,854	926,395	1.46	269,843	399,934	1.44	164,575	221,978	1.29	175,436	304,483	1.66	194,186
1995	654,689	985,385	1.48	289,973	424,802	1.44	179,915	238,392	1.29	184,801	322,191	1.72	204,219
1996	686,923	1,004,646	1.45	299,766	430,366	1.44	190,362	241,058	1.27	196,796	333,222	1.67	216,983
1997	723,443	1,045,495	1.42	319,558	443,227	1.37	198,154	258,454	1.26	205,731	343,814	1.64	227,178
1998	742,391	1,077,183	1.44	324,984	448,373	1.39	202,260	272,297	1.32	215,147	356,513	1.62	237,746
1999	786,178	1,137,260	1.40	335,991	463,004	1.35	216,597	290,182	1.30	233,591	384,074	1.59	257,249
2000	833,868	1,195,894	1.41	350,715	480,748	1.35	234,546	309,191	1.29	248,606	405,955	1.59	273,961
2001	818,160	1,118,552	1.42	330,875	427,353	1.38	232,096	297,536	1.32	255,189	393,663	1.58	281,576
2002	823,234	1,139,523	1.36	326,227	423,028	1.29	236,294	301,310	1.26	260,713	415,185	1.55	288,256
2003	854,700	1,147,795	1.34	334,616	408,302	1.25	248,190	308,274	1.22	271,894	431,219	1.56	301,038
2004	926,002	1,241,744	1.30	359,081	441,222	1.19	277,501	340,128	1.17	289,421	460,394	1.56	320,550
2005	1,005,821	1,314,197	1.27	395,173	474,639	1.17	303,208	367,858	1.17	307,440	471,700	1.51	340,479
2006	1,069,032	1,408,670	1.28	417,963	523,476	1.20	328,438	398,782	1.17	322,631	486,412	1.49	357,863
2007	1,128,176	1,488,229	1.28	443,288	563,043	1.22	351,956	424,608	1.17	332,932	500,578	1.49	369,978
2008	1,160,778	1,465,827	1.31	455,750	543,273	1.26	377,085	445,864	1.20	327,943	476,690	1.52	365,965
2009	988,905	1,331,715	1.38	368,648	505,025	1.39	319,217	398,140	1.29	301,039	428,550	1.47	338,706
2010	1,089,044	1,450,605	1.27	409,273	553,726	1.28	361,600	443,374	1.15	318,171	453,505	1.39	357,081
2011	1,206,873	1,567,464	1.26	457,658	607,035	1.29	407,302	489,035	1.15	341,913	471,394	1.35	383,192
2012	1,267,540	1,658,270	1.28	474,727	625,053	1.30	434,294	525,749	1.18	358,519	507,468	1.38	402,199
2013	1,306,460	1,727,460	1.29	484,511	631,742	1.30	450,346	550,594	1.19	371,603	545,124	1.41	416,895
2014	1,346,595	1,790,353	1.32	490,751	642,655	1.31	469,124	586,084	1.22	386,721	561,614	1.43	434,775
2015	1,303,865	1,823,840	1.39	461,086	638,177	1.40	448,936	597,666	1.33	393,843	587,997	1.46	445,857
2016	1,295,948	1,859,432	1.42	446,966	635,825	1.42	444,974	612,125	1.36	404,008	611,482	1.50	458,830
2017	1,357,498	1,917,746	1.39	462,400	658,986	1.39	475,081	633,371	1.31	420,018	625,389	1.48	477,739
2018	1,437,066	2,001,842	1.36	490,889	677,472	1.37	508,225	671,681	1.28	437,952	652,689	1.46	498,954
2019	1,434,007	2,043,172	1.42	477,871	709,281	1.46	505,946	680,181	1.35	450,189	653,710	1.47	514,585
2020	1,382,229	1,986,925	1.44	435,110	696,711	1.61	482,919	667,974	1.38	464,199	622,240	1.34	518,301
2021	1,622,197	2,203,651	1.28	483,146	759,327	1.51	591,963	793,022	1.22	547,087	651,302	1.13	620,116
2022 [p]	1,821,247	2,481,962	1.31	540,501	807,891	1.47	689,338	933,076	1.28	591,407	740,995	1.21	676,731
2021: Jan	1,524,341	1,998,351	1.31	468,239	698,229	1.49	542,833	676,463	1.25	513,269	623,659	1.22	572,822
Feb	1,502,974	2,012,203	1.34	461,028	705,029	1.53	538,296	682,344	1.27	503,650	624,830	1.24	562,686
Mar	1,586,444	2,012,605	1.27	466,236	707,492	1.52	561,839	688,911	1.23	558,369	616,202	1.10	625,731
Apr	1,594,668	2,011,003	1.26	466,698	710,250	1.52	572,105	695,058	1.21	555,865	605,695	1.09	625,764
May	1,599,215	2,023,512	1.27	473,192	717,919	1.52	575,582	704,470	1.22	550,441	601,123	1.09	622,921
June	1,623,099	2,042,070	1.26	480,651	725,494	1.51	589,404	713,342	1.21	553,044	603,234	1.09	628,881
July	1,634,914	2,056,143	1.26	487,964	729,783	1.50	605,229	720,017	1.19	541,721	606,343	1.12	619,014
Aug	1,636,905	2,074,782	1.27	488,388	735,546	1.51	601,118	729,988	1.21	547,399	609,248	1.11	624,963
Sept	1,657,284	2,092,460	1.26	492,160	743,493	1.51	611,849	740,072	1.21	553,275	608,895	1.10	631,563
Oct	1,689,234	2,118,663	1.25	501,087	749,747	1.50	626,072	757,936	1.21	562,075	610,980	1.09	640,524
Nov	1,711,344	2,152,079	1.26	505,813	756,238	1.50	638,366	771,833	1.21	567,165	624,008	1.10	646,132
Dec	1,710,335	2,203,651	1.29	508,219	759,327	1.49	641,275	793,022	1.24	560,841	651,302	1.16	639,273
2022: Jan	1,759,418	2,231,159	1.27	515,741	765,231	1.48	664,740	802,375	1.21	578,937	663,553	1.15	655,154
Feb	1,776,578	2,263,268	1.27	519,899	770,905	1.48	674,911	821,111	1.22	581,768	671,252	1.15	662,321
Mar	1,805,838	2,317,441	1.28	531,180	781,702	1.47	687,088	843,644	1.23	587,570	692,095	1.18	669,958
Apr	1,817,211	2,348,268	1.29	534,507	787,969	1.47	692,466	862,896	1.25	590,238	697,403	1.18	674,719
May	1,834,718	2,386,601	1.30	545,675	798,203	1.46	697,250	879,642	1.26	591,793	708,756	1.20	677,115
June	1,856,573	2,420,090	1.30	550,206	801,535	1.46	708,222	895,439	1.26	598,145	723,116	1.21	684,084
July	1,838,499	2,433,047	1.32	545,282	801,381	1.47	697,323	900,964	1.29	595,894	730,702	1.23	681,108
Aug	1,844,829	2,455,035	1.33	549,197	800,301	1.46	697,252	913,474	1.31	598,380	741,260	1.24	685,685
Sept	1,845,223	2,461,135	1.33	550,844	801,300	1.45	698,037	918,942	1.32	596,342	740,893	1.24	684,538
Oct	1,852,388	2,466,950	1.33	552,057	804,577	1.46	697,748	924,226	1.32	602,583	738,147	1.22	691,844
Nov	1,830,699	2,475,039	1.35	547,319	804,816	1.47	688,052	932,368	1.36	595,328	737,855	1.24	684,411
Dec [p]	1,819,575	2,481,962	1.36	543,856	807,891	1.49	687,841	933,076	1.36	587,878	740,995	1.26	676,925

[1] Excludes manufacturers' sales branches and offices.
[2] Annual data are averages of monthly not seasonally adjusted figures.
[3] Seasonally adjusted, end of period. Inventories beginning with January 1982 for manufacturing and December 1980 for wholesale and retail trade are not comparable with earlier periods.
[4] Inventory/sales ratio. Monthly inventories are inventories at the end of the month to sales for the month. Annual data beginning with 1982 are the average of monthly ratios for the year. Annual data for 1980–81 are the ratio of December inventories to monthly average sales for the year.
[5] Food services included on Standard Industrial Classification (SIC) basis and excluded on North American Industry Classification System (NAICS) basis. See last column for retail and food services sales.
[6] Effective in 2001, data classified based on NAICS. Data on NAICS basis available beginning with 1992. Earlier data based on SIC. Data on both NAICS and SIC basis include semiconductors.

Source: Department of Commerce (Bureau of the Census).

TABLE B–38. Changes in consumer price indexes, 1980–2022

[For all urban consumers; percent change]

Year or month	All items	All items less food and energy					Food			Energy [4]		C-CPI-U [5]
		Total [1]	Shelter [2]	Medical care [3]	Apparel	New vehicles	Total [1]	At home	Away from home	Total [1, 3]	Gasoline	
	December to December, NSA											
1980	12.5	12.2	15.0	9.9	6.8	7.4	10.2	10.5	9.6	18.0	18.9	....
1981	8.9	9.5	9.9	12.5	3.5	6.8	4.3	2.9	7.1	11.9	9.4	....
1982	3.8	4.5	2.4	11.0	1.6	1.4	3.1	2.3	5.1	1.3	–6.7	....
1983	3.8	4.8	4.7	6.4	2.9	3.3	2.7	1.8	4.1	–.5	–1.6	....
1984	3.9	4.7	5.2	6.1	2.0	2.5	3.8	3.6	4.2	.2	–2.5	....
1985	3.8	4.3	6.0	6.8	2.8	3.6	2.6	2.0	3.8	1.8	3.0	....
1986	1.1	3.8	4.6	7.7	.9	5.6	3.8	3.7	4.3	–19.7	–30.7	....
1987	4.4	4.2	4.8	5.8	4.8	1.8	3.5	3.5	3.7	8.2	18.6	....
1988	4.4	4.7	4.5	6.9	4.7	2.2	5.2	5.6	4.4	.5	–1.8	....
1989	4.6	4.4	4.9	8.5	1.0	2.4	5.6	6.2	4.6	5.1	6.5	....
1990	6.1	5.2	5.2	9.6	5.1	2.0	5.3	5.8	4.5	18.1	36.8	....
1991	3.1	4.4	3.9	7.9	3.4	3.2	1.9	1.3	2.9	–7.4	–16.2	....
1992	2.9	3.3	2.9	6.6	1.4	2.3	1.5	1.5	1.4	2.0	2.0	....
1993	2.7	3.2	3.0	5.4	.9	3.3	2.9	3.5	1.9	–1.4	–5.9	....
1994	2.7	2.6	3.0	4.9	–1.6	3.3	2.9	3.5	1.9	2.2	6.4	....
1995	2.5	3.0	3.5	3.9	.1	1.9	2.1	2.0	2.2	–1.3	–4.2	....
1996	3.3	2.6	2.9	3.0	–.2	1.8	4.3	4.9	3.1	8.6	12.4	....
1997	1.7	2.2	3.4	2.8	1.0	–.9	1.5	1.0	2.6	–3.4	–6.1	....
1998	1.6	2.4	3.3	3.4	–.7	.0	2.3	2.1	2.5	–8.8	–15.4	....
1999	2.7	1.9	2.5	3.7	–.5	–.3	1.9	1.7	2.3	13.4	30.1	....
2000	3.4	2.6	3.4	4.2	–1.8	.0	2.8	2.9	2.4	14.2	13.9	2.6
2001	1.6	2.7	4.2	4.7	–3.2	–.1	2.8	2.6	3.0	–13.0	–24.9	1.3
2002	2.4	1.9	3.1	5.0	–1.8	–2.0	1.5	.8	2.3	10.7	24.8	2.0
2003	1.9	1.1	2.2	3.7	–2.1	–1.8	3.6	4.5	2.3	6.9	6.8	1.7
2004	3.3	2.2	2.7	4.2	–.2	.6	2.7	2.4	3.0	16.6	26.1	3.2
2005	3.4	2.2	2.6	4.3	–1.1	–.4	2.3	1.7	3.2	17.1	16.1	2.9
2006	2.5	2.6	4.2	3.6	.9	–.9	2.1	1.4	3.2	2.9	6.4	2.3
2007	4.1	2.4	3.1	5.2	–.3	–.3	4.9	5.6	4.0	17.4	29.6	3.7
2008	.1	1.8	1.9	2.6	–1.0	–3.2	5.9	6.6	5.0	–21.3	–43.1	.2
2009	2.7	1.8	.3	3.4	1.9	4.9	–.5	–2.4	1.9	18.2	53.5	2.5
2010	1.5	.8	.4	3.3	–1.1	–.2	1.5	1.7	1.3	7.7	13.8	1.3
2011	3.0	2.2	1.9	3.5	4.6	3.2	4.7	6.0	2.9	6.6	9.9	2.9
2012	1.7	1.9	2.2	3.2	1.8	1.6	1.8	1.3	2.5	.5	1.7	1.5
2013	1.5	1.7	2.5	2.0	.6	.4	1.1	.4	2.1	.5	–1.0	1.3
2014	.8	1.6	2.9	3.0	–2.0	.5	3.4	3.7	3.0	–10.6	–21.0	.5
2015	.7	2.1	3.2	2.6	–.9	.2	.8	–.4	2.6	–12.6	–19.7	.4
2016	2.1	2.2	3.6	4.1	–.1	.3	–.2	–2.0	2.3	5.4	9.1	1.8
2017	2.1	1.8	3.2	1.8	–1.6	–.5	1.6	.9	2.5	6.9	10.7	1.7
2018	1.9	2.2	3.2	2.0	–.1	–.3	1.6	.6	2.8	–.3	–2.1	1.5
2019	2.3	2.3	3.2	4.6	–1.2	.1	1.8	.7	3.1	3.4	7.9	1.8
2020	1.4	1.6	1.8	1.8	–3.9	2.0	3.9	3.9	3.9	–7.0	–15.2	1.5
2021	7.0	5.5	4.1	2.2	5.8	11.8	6.3	6.5	6.0	29.3	49.6	6.5
2022	6.5	5.7	7.5	4.0	2.9	5.9	10.4	11.8	8.3	7.3	–1.5	6.6
	Change from year earlier, NSA											
2021: Jan	1.4	1.4	1.6	1.9	–2.5	1.4	3.8	3.7	3.9	–3.6	–8.6	1.6
Feb	1.7	1.3	1.5	2.0	–3.6	1.2	3.6	3.5	3.7	2.4	1.5	1.8
Mar	2.6	1.6	1.7	1.8	–2.5	1.5	3.5	3.3	3.7	13.2	22.5	2.6
Apr	4.2	3.0	2.1	1.5	1.9	2.0	2.4	1.2	3.8	25.1	49.6	4.0
May	5.0	3.8	2.2	.9	5.6	3.3	2.2	.7	4.0	28.5	56.2	4.9
June	5.4	4.5	2.6	.4	4.9	5.3	2.4	.9	4.2	24.5	45.1	5.1
July	5.4	4.3	2.8	.3	4.2	6.4	3.4	2.6	4.6	23.8	41.8	5.0
Aug	5.3	4.0	2.8	.4	4.2	7.6	3.7	3.0	4.7	25.0	42.7	4.8
Sept	5.4	4.0	3.2	.4	3.4	8.7	4.6	4.5	4.7	24.8	42.1	5.0
Oct	6.2	4.6	3.5	1.3	4.3	9.8	5.3	5.4	5.3	30.0	49.6	5.8
Nov	6.8	4.9	3.8	1.7	5.0	11.1	6.1	6.4	5.8	33.3	58.1	6.4
Dec	7.0	5.5	4.1	2.2	5.8	11.8	6.3	6.5	6.0	29.3	49.6	6.5
2022: Jan	7.5	6.0	4.4	2.5	5.3	12.2	7.0	7.4	6.4	27.0	40.0	6.8
Feb	7.9	6.4	4.7	2.4	6.6	12.4	7.9	8.6	6.8	25.6	38.0	7.3
Mar	8.5	6.5	5.0	2.9	6.8	12.5	8.8	10.0	6.9	32.0	48.0	8.1
Apr	8.3	6.2	5.1	3.2	5.4	13.2	9.4	10.8	7.2	30.3	43.6	7.9
May	8.6	6.0	5.5	3.7	5.0	12.6	10.1	11.9	7.4	34.6	48.7	8.1
June	9.1	5.9	5.6	4.5	5.2	11.4	10.4	12.2	7.7	41.6	59.9	8.5
July	8.5	5.9	5.7	4.8	5.1	10.4	10.9	13.1	7.6	32.9	44.0	8.1
Aug	8.3	6.3	6.2	5.4	5.1	10.1	11.4	13.5	8.0	23.8	25.6	8.1
Sept	8.2	6.6	6.6	6.0	5.5	9.4	11.2	13.0	8.5	19.8	18.2	8.1
Oct	7.7	6.3	6.9	5.0	4.1	8.4	10.9	12.4	8.6	17.6	17.5	7.7
Nov	7.1	6.0	7.1	4.2	3.6	7.2	10.6	12.0	8.5	13.1	10.1	7.2
Dec	6.5	5.7	7.5	4.0	2.9	5.9	10.4	11.8	8.3	7.3	–1.5	6.6

[1] Includes other items not shown separately.
[2] Data beginning with 1983 incorporate a rental equivalence measure for homeowners' costs.
[3] Commodities and services.
[4] Household energy--electricity, utility (piped) gas service, fuel oil, etc.--and motor fuel.
[5] Chained consumer price index (C-CPI-U) introduced in 2002. Reflects the effect of substitution that consumers make across item categories in response to changes in relative prices. Data for 2022 are subject to revision.

Source: Department of Labor (Bureau of Labor Statistics).

TABLE B–39. Price indexes for personal consumption expenditures, and percent changes, 1972–2022

[Chain-type price index numbers, 2012=100; monthly data seasonally adjusted]

Year or month	Personal consumption expenditures (PCE)						Percent change from year earlier					
	Total	Goods	Services	Food [1]	Energy goods and services [2]	PCE less food and energy	Total	Goods	Services	Food [1]	Energy goods and services [2]	PCE less food and energy
1972	22.542	33.926	17.441	22.371	10.716	23.856	3.4	2.6	4.2	4.8	2.6	3.2
1973	23.756	35.949	18.284	25.202	11.640	24.764	5.4	6.0	4.8	12.7	8.6	3.8
1974	26.229	40.436	19.833	29.034	15.176	26.726	10.4	12.5	8.5	15.2	30.4	7.9
1975	28.415	43.703	21.533	31.217	16.672	28.958	8.3	8.1	8.6	7.5	9.9	8.4
1976	29.974	45.413	23.027	31.798	17.791	30.718	5.5	3.9	6.9	1.9	6.7	6.1
1977	31.923	47.837	24.770	33.671	19.294	32.694	6.5	5.3	7.6	5.9	8.4	6.4
1978	34.145	50.773	26.674	36.892	20.380	34.861	7.0	6.1	7.7	9.6	5.6	6.6
1979	37.178	55.574	28.911	40.516	25.414	37.403	8.9	9.5	8.4	9.8	24.7	7.3
1980	41.182	61.797	31.918	43.922	33.203	40.840	10.8	11.2	10.4	8.4	30.6	9.2
1981	44.871	66.389	35.187	47.051	37.668	44.419	9.0	7.4	10.2	7.1	13.4	8.8
1982	47.363	68.198	37.949	48.289	38.326	47.306	5.6	2.7	7.8	2.6	1.7	6.5
1983	49.378	69.429	40.280	48.844	38.684	49.727	4.3	1.8	6.1	1.1	.9	5.1
1984	51.243	70.742	42.376	50.312	39.172	51.789	3.8	1.9	5.2	3.0	1.3	4.1
1985	53.031	71.877	44.450	50.859	39.585	53.893	3.5	1.6	4.9	1.1	1.1	4.1
1986	54.184	71.541	46.276	52.056	34.685	55.752	2.2	–.5	4.1	2.4	–12.4	3.4
1987	55.855	73.842	47.660	53.699	35.069	57.548	3.1	3.2	3.0	3.2	1.1	3.2
1988	58.038	75.788	49.939	55.300	35.337	59.994	3.9	2.6	4.8	3.0	.8	4.3
1989	60.572	78.704	52.293	58.216	37.425	62.484	4.4	3.8	4.7	5.3	5.9	4.2
1990	63.231	81.927	54.690	61.060	40.589	65.016	4.4	4.1	4.6	4.9	8.5	4.1
1991	65.345	83.930	56.829	62.977	40.769	67.338	3.3	2.4	3.9	3.1	.4	3.6
1992	67.087	84.943	58.850	63.461	40.959	69.384	2.7	1.2	3.6	.8	.5	3.0
1993	68.758	85.681	60.885	64.348	41.331	71.269	2.5	.9	3.5	1.4	.9	2.7
1994	70.193	86.552	62.540	65.426	41.493	72.864	2.1	1.0	2.7	1.7	.4	2.2
1995	71.671	87.361	64.288	66.844	41.819	74.451	2.1	.9	2.8	2.2	.8	2.2
1996	73.204	88.321	66.051	68.883	43.777	75.863	2.1	1.1	2.7	3.1	4.7	1.9
1997	74.478	88.219	67.914	70.195	44.236	77.201	1.7	–.1	2.8	1.9	1.0	1.8
1998	75.070	86.893	69.351	71.077	40.502	78.183	.8	–1.5	2.1	1.3	–8.4	1.3
1999	76.164	87.349	70.731	72.241	42.143	79.210	1.5	.5	2.0	1.6	4.1	1.3
2000	78.090	89.082	72.740	73.933	49.843	80.625	2.5	2.0	2.8	2.3	18.3	1.8
2001	79.656	89.015	75.063	76.089	51.088	82.153	2.0	–.1	3.2	2.9	2.5	1.9
2002	80.702	88.166	77.004	77.239	48.110	83.526	1.3	–1.0	2.6	1.5	–5.8	1.7
2003	82.398	88.054	79.574	78.701	54.190	84.874	2.1	–.1	3.3	1.9	12.6	1.6
2004	84.443	89.292	82.018	81.157	60.339	86.544	2.5	1.4	3.1	3.1	11.3	2.0
2005	86.876	91.084	84.774	82.575	70.752	88.440	2.9	2.0	3.4	1.7	17.3	2.2
2006	89.322	92.306	87.844	83.963	78.812	90.558	2.8	1.3	3.6	1.7	11.4	2.4
2007	91.614	93.331	90.786	87.239	83.557	92.578	2.6	1.1	3.3	3.9	6.0	2.2
2008	94.325	96.122	93.458	92.552	95.464	94.393	3.0	3.0	2.9	6.1	14.3	2.0
2009	94.062	93.812	94.182	93.651	77.393	95.270	–.3	–2.4	.8	1.2	–18.9	.9
2010	95.747	95.183	96.017	93.931	85.120	96.651	1.8	1.5	1.9	.3	10.0	1.4
2011	98.170	98.773	97.875	97.682	98.601	98.184	2.5	3.8	1.9	4.0	15.8	1.6
2012	100.000	100.000	100.000	100.000	100.000	100.000	1.9	1.2	2.2	2.4	1.4	1.8
2013	101.354	99.407	102.322	100.989	99.109	101.535	1.4	–.6	2.3	1.0	–.9	1.5
2014	102.887	98.920	104.880	102.925	98.279	103.187	1.5	–.5	2.5	1.9	–.8	1.6
2015	103.116	95.896	106.796	104.086	80.641	104.487	.2	–3.1	1.8	1.1	–17.9	1.3
2016	104.148	94.332	109.197	103.009	74.784	106.138	1.0	–1.6	2.2	–1.0	–7.3	1.6
2017	106.054	94.621	111.966	102.866	81.305	107.938	1.8	.3	2.5	–.1	8.7	1.7
2018	108.317	95.334	115.070	103.406	87.828	110.095	2.1	.8	2.8	.5	8.0	2.0
2019	109.933	94.948	117.791	104.434	85.943	111.973	1.5	–.4	2.4	1.0	–2.1	1.7
2020	111.145	94.237	120.133	107.965	78.675	113.464	1.1	–.7	2.0	3.4	–8.5	1.3
2021	115.621	98.824	124.458	111.372	95.002	117.388	4.0	4.9	3.6	3.2	20.8	3.5
2022 p	122.857	107.331	130.733	123.102	119.911	123.280	6.3	8.6	5.0	10.5	26.2	5.0
2021: Jan	112.583	95.315	121.786	108.717	83.466	114.782	1.5	.4	2.0	3.5	–4.5	1.6
Feb	112.961	95.687	122.165	109.011	87.337	114.975	1.7	.8	2.2	3.3	1.8	1.6
Mar	113.632	96.406	122.792	109.259	92.162	115.457	2.5	2.3	2.7	3.0	13.5	2.0
Apr	114.238	97.102	123.324	109.633	90.917	116.186	3.6	4.0	3.5	1.1	24.2	3.1
May	114.819	97.861	123.773	109.985	91.519	116.787	4.0	5.0	3.6	.7	27.5	3.5
June	115.458	98.684	124.277	110.670	93.471	117.349	4.3	5.3	3.7	.9	24.6	3.8
July	115.986	99.159	124.831	111.321	95.004	117.811	4.4	5.4	3.9	2.4	23.9	3.9
Aug	116.444	99.755	125.192	111.783	96.729	118.199	4.5	5.5	4.0	2.8	25.1	3.9
Sept	116.808	100.149	125.531	112.945	97.880	118.446	4.7	6.0	4.0	4.1	25.1	3.9
Oct	117.479	101.224	125.927	113.773	101.735	118.929	5.2	7.3	4.2	4.8	30.3	4.3
Nov	118.200	101.938	126.641	114.502	104.424	119.543	5.9	8.1	4.7	5.6	33.6	4.8
Dec	118.841	102.608	127.253	114.864	105.376	120.193	6.0	8.3	4.8	5.7	29.9	5.0
2022: Jan	119.469	103.540	127.672	115.857	106.527	120.761	6.1	8.6	4.8	6.6	27.6	5.2
Feb	120.178	104.790	128.015	117.517	110.572	121.205	6.4	9.5	4.8	7.8	26.6	5.4
Mar	121.321	106.631	128.690	119.119	123.810	121.651	6.8	10.6	4.8	9.0	34.3	5.4
Apr	121.563	106.443	129.204	120.371	119.991	122.030	6.4	9.6	4.8	9.8	32.0	5.0
May	122.300	107.414	129.780	121.849	124.726	122.488	6.5	9.8	4.9	10.8	36.3	4.9
June	123.512	109.154	130.639	123.053	134.256	123.258	7.0	10.6	5.1	11.2	43.6	5.0
July	123.397	108.682	130.753	124.623	127.651	123.352	6.4	9.6	4.7	11.9	34.4	4.7
Aug	123.728	108.316	131.519	125.588	120.475	124.031	6.3	8.6	5.1	12.3	24.5	4.9
Sept	124.154	108.207	132.275	126.366	117.581	124.607	6.3	8.0	5.4	11.9	20.1	5.2
Oct p	124.666	108.622	132.839	127.043	120.315	124.987	6.1	7.3	5.5	11.7	18.3	5.1
Nov p	124.873	108.363	133.336	127.661	118.645	125.258	5.6	6.3	5.3	11.5	13.6	4.8
Dec p	125.124	107.815	134.078	128.174	114.383	125.727	5.3	5.1	5.4	11.6	8.5	4.6

[1] Food consists of food and beverages purchased for off-premises consumption; food services, which include purchased meals and beverages, are not classified as food.

[2] Consists of gasoline and other energy goods and of electricity and gas services.

Source: Department of Commerce (Bureau of Economic Analysis).

Money Stock, Credit, and Finance

Table B–40. Money stock and debt measures, 1985–2022

[Averages of daily figures, except debt end-of-period basis; billions of dollars, seasonally adjusted]

Year and month	M1	M2	Debt	Percent change		
	Sum of currency, demand deposits, travelers checks, and other checkable deposits; includes savings deposits beginning May 2020 [1]	M1 plus savings deposits, retail MMMF balances, and small time deposits [2]	Debt of domestic nonfinancial sectors [3]	From year or 6 months earlier [4] M1	From year or 6 months earlier [4] M2	From previous period [5] Debt
December:						
1985	619.8	2,492.1	7,341.7	12.4	8.1	16.1
1986	724.7	2,728.0	8,216.7	16.9	9.5	12.0
1987	750.2	2,826.4	8,958.2	3.5	3.6	9.0
1988	786.7	2,988.2	9,777.6	4.9	5.7	9.2
1989	792.9	3,152.5	10,527.9	.8	5.5	7.5
1990	824.7	3,271.8	11,245.9	4.0	3.8	6.6
1991	897.0	3,372.2	11,775.5	8.8	3.1	4.7
1992	1,024.9	3,424.7	12,328.5	14.3	1.6	4.7
1993	1,129.6	3,474.5	13,054.8	10.2	1.5	5.8
1994	1,150.7	3,486.4	13,739.4	1.9	.3	5.2
1995	1,127.5	3,629.5	14,428.1	–2.0	4.1	4.9
1996	1,081.3	3,818.6	15,185.0	–4.1	5.2	5.2
1997	1,072.3	4,032.9	16,029.2	–.8	5.6	5.6
1998	1,095.0	4,375.2	17,110.2	2.1	8.5	6.7
1999	1,122.2	4,638.0	18,288.4	2.5	6.0	6.7
2000	1,088.6	4,925.0	19,172.2	–3.0	6.2	4.8
2001	1,183.2	5,433.8	20,261.2	8.7	10.3	5.8
2002	1,220.2	5,772.0	21,618.2	3.1	6.2	6.7
2003	1,306.2	6,067.3	23,343.4	7.0	5.1	7.8
2004	1,376.0	6,418.3	26,255.1	5.3	5.8	9.1
2005	1,374.3	6,681.9	28,536.4	–.1	4.1	8.7
2006	1,366.6	7,071.6	30,997.4	–.6	5.8	8.6
2007	1,373.4	7,471.6	33,506.8	.5	5.7	8.2
2008	1,601.7	8,192.1	35,292.0	16.6	9.6	5.7
2009	1,692.8	8,496.0	36,260.7	5.7	3.7	3.7
2010	1,836.7	8,801.8	37,678.6	8.5	3.6	4.4
2011	2,165.7	9,660.1	38,891.6	17.9	9.8	3.6
2012	2,460.7	10,459.7	40,549.2	13.6	8.3	4.7
2013	2,664.3	11,028.8	42,147.3	8.3	5.4	4.2
2014	2,940.9	11,681.5	43,699.6	10.4	5.9	3.8
2015	3,095.8	12,344.0	45,423.9	5.3	5.7	4.4
2016	3,340.9	13,209.6	47,362.5	7.9	7.0	4.4
2017	3,610.6	13,852.3	49,469.3	8.1	4.9	4.2
2018	3,763.4	14,358.8	52,128.9	4.2	3.7	4.8
2019	4,007.1	15,319.1	54,553.2	6.5	6.7	4.7
2020	17,828.7	19,118.9	61,340.0		24.8	12.5
2021	20,419.0	21,478.1	65,191.2	14.5	12.3	6.3
2022 *p*	19,734.3	21,236.2		–3.4	–1.1	
2021: Jan	18,101.8	19,367.2		16.0	12.0	
Feb	18,362.8	19,610.6		17.4	13.7	
Mar	18,636.5	19,848.9	62,139.2	17.2	13.8	5.2
Apr	18,921.6	20,104.5		18.0	14.7	
May	19,252.1	20,411.0		18.5	15.3	
June	19,311.3	20,451.7	63,255.6	16.6	13.9	7.2
July	19,481.8	20,605.0		15.2	12.8	
Aug	19,717.7	20,824.2		14.8	12.4	
Sept	19,862.8	20,955.9	63,801.4	13.2	11.2	3.4
Oct	20,053.6	21,133.8		12.0	10.2	
Nov	20,269.0	21,338.4		10.6	9.1	
Dec	20,419.0	21,478.1	65,191.2	11.5	10.0	8.8
2022: Jan	20,576.8	21,640.7		11.2	10.1	
Feb	20,652.4	21,699.2		9.5	8.4	
Mar	20,699.6	21,739.0	66,549.7	8.4	7.5	8.3
Apr	20,618.2	21,643.6		5.6	4.8	
May	20,626.6	21,646.8		3.5	2.9	
June	20,552.3	21,602.0	67,642.9	1.3	1.2	6.5
July	20,527.1	21,635.0		–.5	–.1	
Aug	20,466.2	21,636.8		–1.8	–.6	
Sept	20,279.8	21,516.7	68,463.1	–4.1	–2.0	4.9
Oct	20,107.4	21,432.3		–5.0	–2.0	
Nov	19,987.3	21,400.6		–6.2	–2.3	
Dec *p*	19,734.3	21,236.2		–8.0	–3.4	

[1] Beginning May 2020, M1 includes savings deposits. Prior to May 2020, savings deposits were not included in M1. See the H.6 statistical release for additional details.

[2] Money market mutual fund (MMMF). Savings deposits include money market deposit accounts.

[3] Consists of outstanding debt securities and loans of the U.S. Government, State and local governments, and private nonfinancial sectors. Quarterly data shown in last month of quarter. End-of-year data are for fourth quarter.

[4] Annual changes are from December to December; monthly changes are from six months earlier at an annual rate.

[5] Debt growth of domestic nonfinancial sectors is the seasonally adjusted borrowing flow divided by the seasonally adjusted level of debt outstanding in the previous period. Annual changes are from fourth quarter to fourth quarter; quarterly changes are from previous quarter at an annual rate.

Note: For further information on the composition of M1 and M2, see the H.6 release.

For further information on the debt of domestic nonfinancial sectors and the derivation of debt growth, see the Z.1 release.

Source: Board of Governors of the Federal Reserve System.

TABLE B–41. Consumer credit outstanding, 1972–2022

[Amount outstanding (end of month); millions of dollars, seasonally adjusted]

Year and month	Total consumer credit[1]	Revolving	Nonrevolving[2]
December:			
1972	166,189.10	9,379.24	156,809.86
1973	190,086.31	11,342.22	178,744.09
1974	198,917.84	13,241.26	185,676.58
1975	204,002.00	14,495.27	189,506.73
1976	225,721.59	16,489.05	209,232.54
1977	260,562.70	37,414.82	223,147.88
1978	306,100.39	45,690.95	260,409.43
1979	348,589.11	53,596.43	294,992.67
1980	351,920.05	54,970.05	296,950.00
1981	371,301.44	60,928.00	310,373.44
1982	389,848.74	66,348.30	323,500.44
1983	437,068.86	79,027.25	358,041.61
1984	517,278.98	100,385.63	416,893.35
1985	599,711.23	124,465.80	475,245.43
1986	654,750.24	141,068.15	513,682.08
1987	686,318.77	160,853.91	525,464.86
1988[3]	731,917.76	184,593.12	547,324.64
1989	794,612.18	211,229.83	583,382.34
1990	808,230.57	238,642.62	569,587.95
1991	798,028.97	263,768.55	534,260.42
1992	806,118.69	278,449.67	527,669.02
1993	865,650.58	309,908.02	555,742.56
1994	997,301.74	365,569.56	631,732.19
1995	1,140,744.36	443,920.09	696,824.27
1996	1,253,437.09	507,516.57	745,920.52
1997	1,324,757.33	540,005.56	784,751.77
1998	1,420,996.44	581,414.78	839,581.66
1999	1,531,105.96	610,696.47	920,409.49
2000	1,716,969.72	682,646.37	1,034,323.35
2001	1,867,852.87	714,840.73	1,153,012.14
2002	1,972,112.21	750,947.45	1,221,164.76
2003	2,077,360.69	768,258.31	1,309,102.38
2004	2,192,246.17	799,552.18	1,392,693.99
2005[3]	2,290,928.13	829,518.36	1,461,409.78
2006	2,456,715.70	923,876.78	1,532,838.92
2007	2,609,476.53	1,001,625.30	1,607,851.24
2008	2,643,788.96	1,003,997.04	1,639,791.92
2009	2,555,016.64	916,076.63	1,638,940.01
2010	2,646,811.26	839,102.67	1,807,708.59
2011	2,756,224.86	840,164.23	1,916,060.63
2012	2,912,905.02	839,980.84	2,072,924.18
2013	3,090,467.78	854,138.80	2,236,328.97
2014	3,309,539.85	887,381.64	2,422,158.21
2015	3,400,223.22	898,082.65	2,502,140.57
2016	3,636,435.66	960,095.49	2,676,340.17
2017	3,830,751.67	1,016,806.67	2,813,944.99
2018	4,007,041.89	1,053,847.41	2,953,194.48
2019	4,192,191.40	1,091,988.92	3,100,202.47
2020	4,184,852.51	974,594.43	3,210,258.07
2021	4,430,823.86	1,041,694.48	3,389,129.38
2022 p	4,775,911.96	1,195,986.16	3,579,925.80
2021: Jan	4,195,657.99	971,968.80	3,223,689.19
Feb	4,213,473.58	973,294.93	3,240,178.65
Mar	4,228,549.07	972,935.85	3,255,613.22
Apr	4,247,381.24	975,089.20	3,272,292.04
May	4,274,138.58	980,431.40	3,293,707.19
June	4,297,377.67	989,167.13	3,308,210.54
July	4,313,338.39	994,604.22	3,318,734.17
Aug	4,331,529.22	1,000,679.07	3,330,850.14
Sept	4,355,206.69	1,009,689.11	3,345,517.58
Oct	4,376,025.84	1,018,454.92	3,357,570.92
Nov	4,407,630.94	1,033,573.72	3,374,057.21
Dec	4,430,823.86	1,041,694.48	3,389,129.38
2022: Jan	4,445,531.56	1,050,016.33	3,395,515.24
Feb	4,478,314.10	1,060,126.77	3,418,187.33
Mar	4,523,952.94	1,086,052.39	3,437,900.54
Apr	4,555,230.28	1,102,802.32	3,452,427.96
May	4,582,155.44	1,110,212.36	3,471,943.09
June	4,621,880.16	1,125,824.17	3,496,055.99
July	4,644,406.07	1,136,539.72	3,507,866.35
Aug	4,673,592.58	1,153,224.77	3,520,367.81
Sept	4,698,977.71	1,161,151.68	3,537,826.03
Oct	4,731,239.84	1,173,486.49	3,557,753.36
Nov	4,764,347.02	1,188,785.20	3,575,561.82
Dec p	4,775,911.96	1,195,986.16	3,579,925.80

[1] Covers most short- and intermediate-term credit extended to individuals. Credit secured by real estate is excluded.

[2] Includes automobile loans and all other loans not included in revolving credit, such as loans for mobile homes, education, boats, trailers, or vacations. These loans may be secured or unsecured. Beginning with 1977, includes student loans extended by the Federal Government and by SLM Holding Corporation.

[3] Data newly available in January 1989 result in breaks in these series between the prior period and subsequent months.

Source: Board of Governors of the Federal Reserve System.

TABLE B–42. Bond yields and interest rates, 1952–2022

[Percent per annum]

Year	U.S. Treasury securities					Corporate bonds (Moody's)		High-grade municipal bonds (Standard & Poor's)	Home mortgage yields[4]	Prime rate charged by banks[5]	Discount window (Federal Reserve Bank of New York)[5, 6]		Federal funds rate[7]
	Bills (at auction)[1]		Constant maturities[2]										
	3-month	6-month	3-year	10-year	30-year	Aaa[3]	Baa				Primary credit	Adjustment credit	
1952	1.766	....	....	....	....	2.96	3.52	2.19	....	3.00	....	1.75	....
1953	1.931	....	2.47	2.85	....	3.20	3.74	2.72	....	3.17	....	1.99	....
1954	.953	....	1.63	2.40	....	2.90	3.51	2.37	....	3.05	....	1.60	....
1955	1.753	....	2.47	2.82	....	3.06	3.53	2.53	....	3.16	....	1.89	1.79
1956	2.658	....	3.19	3.18	....	3.36	3.88	2.93	....	3.77	....	2.77	2.73
1957	3.267	....	3.98	3.65	....	3.89	4.71	3.60	....	4.20	....	3.12	3.11
1958	1.839	....	2.84	3.32	....	3.79	4.73	3.56	....	3.83	....	2.15	1.57
1959	3.405	3.832	4.46	4.33	....	4.38	5.05	3.95	....	4.48	....	3.36	3.31
1960	2.93	3.25	3.98	4.12	....	4.41	5.19	3.73	....	4.82	....	3.53	3.21
1961	2.38	2.61	3.54	3.88	....	4.35	5.08	3.46	....	4.50	....	3.00	1.95
1962	2.78	2.91	3.47	3.95	....	4.33	5.02	3.18	....	4.50	....	3.00	2.71
1963	3.16	3.25	3.67	4.00	....	4.26	4.86	3.23	....	4.50	....	3.23	3.18
1964	3.56	3.69	4.03	4.19	....	4.40	4.83	3.22	....	4.50	....	3.55	3.50
1965	3.95	4.05	4.22	4.28	....	4.49	4.87	3.27	....	4.54	....	4.04	4.07
1966	4.88	5.08	5.23	4.93	....	5.13	5.67	3.82	....	5.63	....	4.50	5.11
1967	4.32	4.63	5.03	5.07	....	5.51	6.23	3.98	....	5.63	....	4.19	4.22
1968	5.34	5.47	5.68	5.64	....	6.18	6.94	4.51	....	6.31	....	5.17	5.66
1969	6.68	6.85	7.02	6.67	....	7.03	7.81	5.81	....	7.96	....	5.87	8.21
1970	6.43	6.53	7.29	7.35	....	8.04	9.11	6.51	....	7.91	....	5.95	7.17
1971	4.35	4.51	5.66	6.16	....	7.39	8.56	5.70	7.54	5.73	....	4.88	4.67
1972	4.07	4.47	5.72	6.21	....	7.21	8.16	5.27	7.38	5.25	....	4.50	4.44
1973	7.04	7.18	6.96	6.85	....	7.44	8.24	5.18	8.04	8.03	....	6.45	8.74
1974	7.89	7.93	7.84	7.56	....	8.57	9.50	6.09	9.19	10.81	....	7.83	10.51
1975	5.84	6.12	7.50	7.99	....	8.83	10.61	6.89	9.05	7.86	....	6.25	5.82
1976	4.99	5.27	6.77	7.61	....	8.43	9.75	6.49	8.87	6.84	....	5.50	5.05
1977	5.27	5.52	6.68	7.42	7.75	8.02	8.97	5.56	8.85	6.83	....	5.46	5.54
1978	7.22	7.58	8.29	8.41	8.49	8.73	9.49	5.90	9.64	9.06	....	7.46	7.94
1979	10.05	10.02	9.70	9.43	9.28	9.63	10.69	6.39	11.20	12.67	....	10.29	11.20
1980	11.51	11.37	11.51	11.43	11.27	11.94	13.67	8.51	13.74	15.26	....	11.77	13.35
1981	14.03	13.78	14.46	13.92	13.45	14.17	16.04	11.23	16.63	18.87	....	13.42	16.39
1982	10.69	11.08	12.93	13.01	12.76	13.79	16.11	11.57	16.04	14.85	....	11.01	12.24
1983	8.63	8.75	10.45	11.10	11.18	12.04	13.55	9.47	13.24	10.79	....	8.50	9.09
1984	9.53	9.77	11.92	12.46	12.41	12.71	14.19	10.15	13.88	12.04	....	8.80	10.23
1985	7.47	7.64	9.64	10.62	10.79	11.37	12.72	9.18	12.43	9.93	....	7.69	8.10
1986	5.98	6.03	7.06	7.67	7.78	9.02	10.39	7.38	10.19	8.33	....	6.32	6.80
1987	5.82	6.05	7.68	8.39	8.59	9.38	10.58	7.73	10.21	8.21	....	5.66	6.66
1988	6.69	6.92	8.26	8.85	8.96	9.71	10.83	7.76	10.34	9.32	....	6.20	7.57
1989	8.12	8.04	8.55	8.49	8.45	9.26	10.18	7.24	10.32	10.87	....	6.93	9.21
1990	7.51	7.47	8.26	8.55	8.61	9.32	10.36	7.25	10.13	10.01	....	6.98	8.10
1991	5.42	5.49	6.82	7.86	8.14	8.77	9.80	6.89	9.25	8.46	....	5.45	5.69
1992	3.45	3.57	5.30	7.01	7.67	8.14	8.98	6.41	8.39	6.25	....	3.25	3.52
1993	3.02	3.14	4.44	5.87	6.59	7.22	7.93	5.63	7.31	6.00	....	3.00	3.02
1994	4.29	4.66	6.27	7.09	7.37	7.96	8.62	6.19	8.38	7.15	....	3.60	4.21
1995	5.51	5.59	6.25	6.57	6.88	7.59	8.20	5.95	7.93	8.83	....	5.21	5.83
1996	5.02	5.09	5.99	6.44	6.71	7.37	8.05	5.75	7.81	8.27	....	5.02	5.30
1997	5.07	5.18	6.10	6.35	6.61	7.26	7.86	5.55	7.60	8.44	....	5.00	5.46
1998	4.81	4.85	5.14	5.26	5.58	6.53	7.22	5.12	6.94	8.35	....	4.92	5.35
1999	4.66	4.76	5.49	5.65	5.87	7.04	7.87	5.43	7.44	8.00	....	4.62	4.97
2000	5.85	5.92	6.22	6.03	5.94	7.62	8.36	5.77	8.05	9.23	....	5.73	6.24
2001	3.44	3.39	4.09	5.02	5.49	7.08	7.95	5.19	6.97	6.91	....	3.40	3.88
2002	1.62	1.69	3.10	4.61	5.43	6.49	7.80	5.05	6.54	4.67	....	1.17	1.67
2003	1.01	1.06	2.10	4.01	....	5.67	6.77	4.73	5.83	4.12	2.12	....	1.13
2004	1.38	1.57	2.78	4.27	....	5.63	6.39	4.63	5.84	4.34	2.34	....	1.35
2005	3.16	3.40	3.93	4.29	....	5.24	6.06	4.29	5.87	6.19	4.19	....	3.22
2006	4.73	4.80	4.77	4.80	4.91	5.59	6.48	4.42	6.41	7.96	5.96	....	4.97
2007	4.41	4.48	4.35	4.63	4.84	5.56	6.48	4.42	6.34	8.05	5.86	....	5.02
2008	1.48	1.71	2.24	3.66	4.28	5.63	7.45	4.80	6.03	5.09	2.39	....	1.92
2009	.16	.29	1.43	3.26	4.08	5.31	7.30	4.64	5.04	3.25	.50	....	.16
2010	.14	.20	1.11	3.22	4.25	4.94	6.04	4.16	4.69	3.25	.72	....	.18
2011	.06	.10	.75	2.78	3.91	4.64	5.66	4.29	4.45	3.25	.75	....	.10
2012	.09	.13	.38	1.80	2.92	3.67	4.94	3.14	3.66	3.25	.75	....	.14
2013	.06	.09	.54	2.35	3.45	4.24	5.10	3.96	3.98	3.25	.75	....	.11
2014	.03	.06	.90	2.54	3.34	4.16	4.85	3.78	4.17	3.25	.75	....	.09
2015	.06	.17	1.02	2.14	2.84	3.89	5.00	3.48	3.85	3.26	.76	....	.13
2016	.33	.46	1.00	1.84	2.59	3.67	4.72	3.07	3.65	3.51	1.01	....	.39
2017	.94	1.05	1.58	2.33	2.89	3.74	4.44	3.36	3.99	4.10	1.60	....	1.00
2018	1.94	2.10	2.63	2.91	3.11	3.93	4.80	3.53	4.54	4.91	2.41	....	1.83
2019	2.08	2.07	1.94	2.14	2.58	3.39	4.38	3.38	3.94	5.28	2.78	....	2.16
2020	.38	.39	.42	.89	1.56	2.48	3.60	2.41	3.11	3.54	.64	....	.37
2021	.04	.06	.46	1.45	2.06	2.70	3.39	2.00	2.96	3.25	.25	....	.08
2022	2.04	2.44	3.05	2.95	3.11	4.07	5.07	3.85	5.34	4.86	1.86	....	1.69

[1] High bill rate at auction, issue date within period, bank-discount basis. On or after October 28, 1998, data are stop yields from uniform-price auctions. Before that date, they are weighted average yields from multiple-price auctions.

See next page for continuation of table.

TABLE B–42. Bond yields and interest rates, 1952–2022—*Continued*

[Percent per annum]

Year and month	U.S. Treasury securities: Bills (at auction)[1]: 3-month	U.S. Treasury securities: Bills (at auction)[1]: 6-month	U.S. Treasury securities: Constant maturities[2]: 3-year	U.S. Treasury securities: Constant maturities[2]: 10-year	U.S. Treasury securities: Constant maturities[2]: 30-year	Corporate bonds (Moody's): Aaa[3]	Corporate bonds (Moody's): Baa	High-grade municipal bonds (Standard & Poor's)	Home mortgage yields[4]	Prime rate charged by banks[5]	Discount window (Federal Reserve Bank of New York)[5, 6]: Primary credit	Discount window (Federal Reserve Bank of New York)[5, 6]: Adjustment credit	Federal funds rate[7]
										High-low	High-low	High-low	
2018: Jan	1.43	1.59	2.15	2.58	2.88	3.55	4.26	3.29	4.03	4.50–4.50	2.00–2.00	....	1.41
Feb	1.53	1.72	2.36	2.86	3.13	3.82	4.51	3.54	4.33	4.50–4.50	2.00–2.00	....	1.42
Mar	1.70	1.87	2.42	2.84	3.09	3.87	4.64	3.58	4.44	4.75–4.50	2.25–2.00	....	1.51
Apr	1.76	1.93	2.52	2.87	3.07	3.85	4.67	3.55	4.47	4.75–4.75	2.25–2.25	....	1.69
May	1.87	2.03	2.66	2.98	3.13	4.00	4.83	3.38	4.59	4.75–4.75	2.25–2.25	....	1.70
June	1.91	2.08	2.65	2.91	3.05	3.96	4.83	3.15	4.57	5.00–4.75	2.50–2.25	....	1.82
July	1.96	2.12	2.70	2.89	3.01	3.87	4.79	3.45	4.53	5.00–5.00	2.50–2.50	....	1.91
Aug	2.03	2.18	2.71	2.89	3.04	3.88	4.77	3.58	4.55	5.00–5.00	2.50–2.50	....	1.91
Sept	2.13	2.28	2.84	3.00	3.15	3.98	4.88	3.63	4.63	5.25–5.00	2.75–2.50	....	1.95
Oct	2.24	2.39	2.94	3.15	3.34	4.14	5.07	3.88	4.83	5.25–5.25	2.75–2.75	....	2.19
Nov	2.34	2.46	2.91	3.12	3.36	4.22	5.22	3.64	4.87	5.25–5.25	2.75–2.75	....	2.20
Dec	2.38	2.49	2.67	2.83	3.10	4.02	5.13	3.69	4.64	5.50–5.25	3.00–2.75	....	2.27
2019: Jan	2.41	2.47	2.52	2.71	3.04	3.93	5.12	3.61	4.46	5.50–5.50	3.00–3.00	....	2.40
Feb	2.40	2.45	2.48	2.68	3.02	3.79	4.95	3.57	4.37	5.50–5.50	3.00–3.00	....	2.40
Mar	2.41	2.45	2.37	2.57	2.98	3.77	4.84	3.43	4.27	5.50–5.50	3.00–3.00	....	2.41
Apr	2.38	2.39	2.31	2.53	2.94	3.69	4.70	3.27	4.14	5.50–5.50	3.00–3.00	....	2.42
May	2.35	2.36	2.16	2.40	2.82	3.67	4.63	3.11	4.07	5.50–5.50	3.00–3.00	....	2.39
June	2.20	2.14	1.78	2.07	2.57	3.42	4.46	2.87	3.80	5.50–5.50	3.00–3.00	....	2.38
July	2.13	2.03	1.80	2.06	2.57	3.29	4.28	3.32	3.77	5.50–5.50	3.00–3.00	....	2.40
Aug	1.97	1.91	1.51	1.63	2.12	2.98	3.87	3.61	3.62	5.50–5.25	3.00–2.75	....	2.13
Sept	1.93	1.85	1.59	1.70	2.16	3.03	3.91	3.57	3.61	5.25–5.00	2.75–2.50	....	2.04
Oct	1.68	1.66	1.53	1.71	2.19	3.01	3.93	3.67	3.69	5.00–4.75	2.50–2.25	....	1.83
Nov	1.55	1.55	1.61	1.81	2.28	3.06	3.94	3.26	3.70	4.75–4.75	2.25–2.25	....	1.55
Dec	1.54	1.55	1.63	1.86	2.30	3.01	3.88	3.26	3.72	4.75–4.75	2.25–2.25	....	1.55
2020: Jan	1.53	1.53	1.52	1.76	2.22	2.94	3.77	3.00	3.62	4.75–4.75	2.25–2.25	....	1.55
Feb	1.54	1.50	1.31	1.50	1.97	2.78	3.61	2.66	3.47	4.75–4.75	2.25–2.25	....	1.58
Mar	.46	.45	.50	.87	1.46	3.02	4.29	3.07	3.45	4.75–3.25	2.25–0.25	....	.65
Apr	.15	.17	.28	.66	1.27	2.43	4.13	2.86	3.31	3.25–3.25	0.25–0.25	....	.05
May	.12	.15	.22	.67	1.38	2.49	3.95	2.69	3.23	3.25–3.25	0.25–0.25	....	.05
June	.16	.18	.22	.73	1.49	2.41	3.65	2.69	3.16	3.25–3.25	0.25–0.25	....	.08
July	.13	.15	.17	.62	1.31	2.14	3.31	1.75	3.02	3.25–3.25	0.25–0.25	....	.09
Aug	.10	.12	.16	.65	1.36	2.25	3.27	1.88	2.94	3.25–3.25	0.25–0.25	....	.10
Sept	.11	.12	.16	.68	1.42	2.31	3.36	2.10	2.89	3.25–3.25	0.25–0.25	....	.09
Oct	.10	.11	.19	.79	1.57	2.35	3.44	2.15	2.83	3.25–3.25	0.25–0.25	....	.09
Nov	.09	.10	.22	.87	1.62	2.30	3.30	2.10	2.77	3.25–3.25	0.25–0.25	....	.09
Dec	.09	.09	.19	.93	1.67	2.26	3.16	1.97	2.68	3.25–3.25	0.25–0.25	....	.09
2021: Jan	.09	.09	.20	1.08	1.82	2.45	3.24	1.61	2.74	3.25–3.25	0.25–0.25	....	.09
Feb	.04	.06	.21	1.26	2.04	2.70	3.42	1.13	2.81	3.25–3.25	0.25–0.25	....	.08
Mar	.03	.05	.32	1.61	2.34	3.04	3.74	1.74	3.08	3.25–3.25	0.25–0.25	....	.07
Apr	.02	.04	.35	1.64	2.30	2.90	3.60	1.84	3.06	3.25–3.25	0.25–0.25	....	.07
May	.02	.03	.32	1.62	2.32	2.96	3.62	1.63	2.96	3.25–3.25	0.25–0.25	....	.06
June	.03	.04	.39	1.52	2.16	2.79	3.44	2.16	2.98	3.25–3.25	0.25–0.25	....	.08
July	.05	.05	.40	1.32	1.94	2.57	3.24	2.22	2.87	3.25–3.25	0.25–0.25	....	.10
Aug	.06	.05	.42	1.28	1.92	2.55	3.24	2.38	2.84	3.25–3.25	0.25–0.25	....	.09
Sept	.04	.05	.47	1.37	1.94	2.53	3.23	2.30	2.90	3.25–3.25	0.25–0.25	....	.08
Oct	.05	.06	.67	1.58	2.06	2.68	3.35	2.43	3.07	3.25–3.25	0.25–0.25	....	.08
Nov	.05	.07	.82	1.56	1.94	2.62	3.28	2.30	3.07	3.25–3.25	0.25–0.25	....	.08
Dec	.06	.14	.95	1.47	1.85	2.65	3.30	2.24	3.10	3.25–3.25	0.25–0.25	....	.08
2022: Jan	.14	.31	1.25	1.76	2.10	2.93	3.58	2.47	3.45	3.25–3.25	0.25–0.25	....	.08
Feb	.34	.64	1.65	1.93	2.25	3.25	3.97	2.78	3.76	3.25–3.25	0.25–0.25	....	.08
Mar	.46	.82	2.09	2.13	2.41	3.43	4.29	3.22	4.17	3.50–3.25	0.50–0.25	....	.20
Apr	.80	1.24	2.72	2.75	2.81	3.76	4.66	3.74	4.98	3.50–3.50	0.50–0.50	....	.33
May	.98	1.46	2.79	2.90	3.07	4.13	5.12	4.06	5.23	4.00–3.50	1.00–0.50	....	.77
June	1.48	2.07	3.15	3.14	3.25	4.24	5.27	4.01	5.52	4.75–4.00	1.75–1.00	....	1.21
July	2.24	2.75	3.03	2.90	3.10	4.06	5.21	3.96	5.41	5.50–4.75	2.50–1.75	....	1.68
Aug	2.61	3.01	3.23	2.90	3.13	4.07	5.15	3.99	5.22	5.50–5.50	2.50–2.50	....	2.33
Sept	3.09	3.53	3.88	3.52	3.56	4.59	5.69	4.53	6.11	6.25–5.50	3.25–2.50	....	2.56
Oct	3.67	4.13	4.38	3.98	4.04	5.10	6.26	4.70	6.90	6.25–6.25	3.25–3.25	....	3.08
Nov	4.14	4.47	4.34	3.89	4.00	4.90	6.07	4.52	6.81	7.00–6.25	4.00–3.25	....	3.78
Dec	4.29	4.58	4.05	3.62	3.66	4.43	5.59	4.19	6.36	7.50–7.00	4.50–4.00	....	4.10

[2] Yields on the more actively traded issues adjusted to constant maturities by the Department of the Treasury. The 30-year Treasury constant maturity series was discontinued on February 18, 2002, and reintroduced on February 9, 2006.

[3] Beginning with December 7, 2001, data for corporate Aaa series are industrial bonds only.

[4] Contract interest rate on commitments for 30-year first-lien prime conventional conforming home purchase mortgage with a loan-to-value of 80 percent.

[5] For monthly data, high and low for the period.

[6] Primary credit replaced adjustment credit as the Federal Reserve's principal discount window lending program effective January 9, 2003.

[7] Beginning March 1, 2016, the daily effective federal funds rate is a volume-weighted median of transaction-level data collected from depository institutions in the Report of Selected Money Market Rates (FR 2420). Between July 21, 1975 and February 29, 2016, the daily effective rate was a volume-weighted mean of rates on brokered trades. Prior to that, the daily effective rate was the rate considered most representative of the day's transactions, usually the one at which most transactions occurred.

Sources: Department of the Treasury, Board of Governors of the Federal Reserve System, Federal Home Loan Mortgage Corporation, Moody's Investors Service, Bloomberg, and Standard & Poor's.

TABLE B–43. Mortgage debt outstanding by type of property and of financing, 1962–2022

[Billions of dollars]

End of year or quarter	All properties	Farm properties	Nonfarm properties				Nonfarm properties by type of mortgage					
			Total	1- to 4-family houses	Multi-family properties	Commercial properties	Government underwritten				Conventional [2]	
							Total [1]	1- to 4-family houses			Total	1- to 4-family houses
								Total	FHA-insured	VA-guaranteed		
1962	252.4	15.2	237.2	168.3	26.7	42.2	69.4	62.2	32.3	29.9	167.9	106.1
1963	279.3	16.8	262.4	185.1	30.0	47.3	73.4	65.9	35.0	30.9	189.0	119.2
1964	307.0	18.9	288.1	202.3	34.6	51.2	77.2	69.2	38.3	30.9	210.9	133.1
1965	334.5	21.2	313.3	219.4	38.2	55.7	81.2	73.1	42.0	31.1	232.2	146.3
1966	358.5	23.1	335.5	232.7	41.3	61.5	84.1	76.1	44.8	31.3	251.4	156.7
1967	382.1	25.0	357.0	246.0	44.8	66.2	88.2	79.9	47.4	32.5	268.9	166.0
1968	411.4	27.2	384.2	262.9	48.3	73.0	93.4	84.4	50.6	33.8	290.8	178.5
1969	439.9	29.0	410.9	278.7	53.2	79.1	100.2	90.2	54.5	35.7	310.7	188.5
1970	469.4	30.5	438.9	292.2	60.1	86.5	109.2	97.3	59.9	37.3	329.6	195.0
1971	517.9	32.4	485.5	318.4	70.1	97.0	120.7	105.2	65.7	39.5	364.8	213.2
1972	589.8	35.4	554.4	357.4	82.9	114.2	131.1	113.0	68.2	44.7	423.3	244.4
1973	666.5	39.8	626.7	399.8	93.2	133.7	135.0	116.2	66.2	50.0	491.7	283.6
1974	728.4	44.9	683.5	435.2	100.0	148.3	140.2	121.3	65.1	56.2	543.3	313.9
1975	785.6	49.9	735.7	474.0	100.7	161.0	147.0	127.7	66.1	61.6	588.7	346.3
1976	870.5	55.4	815.1	535.0	105.9	174.2	154.0	133.5	66.5	67.0	661.1	401.5
1977	999.2	63.9	935.3	627.7	114.3	193.3	161.7	141.6	68.0	73.6	773.5	486.1
1978	1,150.7	72.8	1,077.9	738.3	125.2	214.5	176.4	153.4	71.4	82.0	901.5	584.9
1979	1,317.0	86.8	1,230.3	855.8	135.0	239.4	199.0	172.9	81.0	92.0	1,031.3	682.8
1980	1,457.8	97.5	1,360.3	957.9	142.5	259.9	225.1	195.2	93.6	101.6	1,135.3	762.7
1981	1,579.5	107.2	1,472.3	1,030.2	142.4	299.7	238.9	207.6	101.3	106.2	1,233.4	822.6
1982	1,661.3	111.3	1,550.0	1,070.2	146.1	333.7	248.9	217.9	108.0	109.9	1,301.1	852.3
1983	1,850.6	113.7	1,736.9	1,186.3	161.2	389.4	279.8	248.8	127.4	121.4	1,457.1	937.4
1984	2,092.0	112.4	1,979.6	1,321.5	186.1	471.9	294.8	265.9	136.7	129.1	1,684.7	1,055.7
1985	2,368.5	94.1	2,274.5	1,526.9	205.9	541.7	328.3	288.8	153.0	135.8	1,946.1	1,238.1
1986	2,655.6	84.1	2,571.5	1,730.1	239.4	602.0	370.5	328.6	185.5	143.1	2,201.0	1,401.5
1987	2,954.3	75.8	2,878.5	1,928.5	258.4	691.6	431.4	387.9	235.5	152.4	2,447.0	1,540.6
1988	3,271.9	70.8	3,201.1	2,162.8	274.5	763.7	459.7	414.2	258.8	155.4	2,741.4	1,748.6
1989	3,523.6	68.8	3,454.8	2,369.6	287.0	798.2	486.8	440.1	282.8	157.3	2,967.9	1,929.5
1990	3,779.5	67.6	3,711.8	2,606.8	287.4	817.6	517.9	470.9	310.9	160.0	3,193.9	2,135.9
1991	3,930.7	67.5	3,863.2	2,774.7	284.1	804.4	537.2	493.3	330.6	162.7	3,326.0	2,281.4
1992	4,040.8	67.9	3,972.9	2,942.1	270.9	759.9	533.3	489.8	326.0	163.8	3,439.6	2,452.3
1993	4,171.5	68.4	4,103.1	3,101.1	267.8	734.2	513.4	469.5	303.2	166.2	3,589.7	2,631.7
1994	4,336.3	69.9	4,266.3	3,278.6	268.5	719.2	559.3	514.2	336.8	177.3	3,707.0	2,764.4
1995	4,522.1	71.7	4,450.3	3,446.4	274.4	729.5	584.3	537.1	352.3	184.7	3,866.1	2,909.4
1996	4,802.8	74.4	4,728.4	3,682.8	286.7	758.9	620.3	571.2	379.2	192.0	4,108.1	3,111.6
1997	5,115.9	78.5	5,037.4	3,917.6	298.8	821.1	656.7	605.7	405.7	200.0	4,380.8	3,311.8
1998	5,603.2	83.1	5,520.1	4,275.8	334.5	909.8	674.0	623.8	417.9	205.9	4,846.1	3,652.0
1999	6,209.6	87.2	6,122.4	4,701.2	375.2	1,046.0	731.5	678.8	462.3	216.5	5,390.9	4,022.4
2000	6,766.6	84.7	6,681.9	5,125.0	404.5	1,152.5	773.1	719.9	499.9	220.1	5,908.8	4,405.0
2001	7,450.1	88.5	7,361.6	5,678.0	446.1	1,237.4	772.7	718.5	497.4	221.2	6,588.9	4,959.5
2002	8,358.7	95.4	8,263.3	6,434.4	486.3	1,342.6	759.3	704.0	486.2	217.7	7,504.0	5,730.4
2003	9,364.8	83.2	9,281.6	7,260.3	559.7	1,461.6	709.2	653.3	438.7	214.6	8,572.4	6,607.1
2004	10,646.7	95.7	10,551.0	8,292.1	609.3	1,649.6	660.2	604.1	398.1	206.0	9,890.8	7,688.0
2005	12,112.9	104.8	12,008.1	9,448.5	674.3	1,885.3	606.6	550.4	348.4	202.0	11,401.5	8,898.1
2006	13,525.5	108.0	13,417.5	10,530.8	717.5	2,169.2	600.2	543.5	336.9	206.6	12,817.3	9,987.3
2007	14,609.6	112.7	14,497.0	11,252.3	810.5	2,434.1	609.2	552.6	342.6	210.0	13,887.8	10,699.7
2008	14,690.0	134.7	14,555.3	11,150.9	852.9	2,551.5	807.2	750.7	534.0	216.7	13,748.1	10,400.2
2009	14,445.4	146.0	14,299.4	10,961.0	862.9	2,475.5	1,005.0	944.3	752.6	191.7	13,294.4	10,016.7
2010	13,893.0	154.1	13,738.9	10,523.4	863.0	2,352.5	1,227.6	1,156.1	934.4	221.7	12,511.2	9,367.4
2011	13,567.7	167.2	13,400.5	10,281.3	863.3	2,255.9	1,368.6	1,291.3	1,036.0	255.3	12,031.9	8,990.0
2012	13,331.3	173.4	13,157.9	10,047.7	891.2	2,219.0	1,544.8	1,459.7	1,165.4	294.2	11,613.1	8,588.1
2013	13,344.5	185.2	13,159.3	9,959.6	940.9	2,258.8	3,927.2	3,832.6	3,480.8	351.8	9,232.1	6,127.1
2014	13,486.8	196.8	13,290.0	9,936.6	1,009.1	2,344.3	4,130.9	4,028.1	3,615.3	412.8	9,159.1	5,908.5
2015	13,883.3	208.8	13,674.5	10,076.4	1,118.8	2,479.3	4,432.7	4,326.7	3,851.3	475.4	9,241.8	5,749.6
2016	14,333.6	226.0	14,107.6	10,278.8	1,236.3	2,592.4	4,764.8	4,654.9	4,106.9	548.1	9,342.8	5,623.9
2017	14,911.6	236.2	14,675.4	10,595.9	1,363.2	2,716.3	5,079.1	4,958.2	4,344.3	613.9	9,596.4	5,637.8
2018	15,463.8	245.8	15,218.0	10,897.8	1,488.4	2,831.8	5,380.0	5,246.5	4,562.3	684.2	9,838.0	5,651.2
2019	16,033.6	267.9	15,765.7	11,179.2	1,622.1	2,964.4	5,664.1	5,522.9	4,788.6	734.3	10,101.5	5,656.3
2020	16,787.1	288.6	16,498.5	11,648.9	1,754.6	3,095.0	6,053.8	5,908.0	5,108.2	799.7	10,444.7	5,741.0
2021	18,060.2	324.3	17,735.9	12,540.0	1,885.3	3,310.5	6,480.3	6,325.5	5,442.1	883.4	11,255.6	6,214.5
2021: I	16,976.3	297.4	16,678.9	11,780.2	1,782.8	3,115.9	6,160.7	6,012.4	5,193.8	818.6	10,518.1	5,767.9
II	17,291.4	306.3	16,985.1	12,019.2	1,808.4	3,157.5	6,274.4	6,123.7	5,280.7	843.0	10,710.8	5,895.5
III	17,636.1	315.3	17,320.8	12,272.9	1,836.5	3,211.4	6,388.6	6,235.4	5,366.4	869.1	10,932.3	6,037.5
IV	18,060.2	324.3	17,735.9	12,540.0	1,885.3	3,310.5	6,480.3	6,325.5	5,442.1	883.4	11,255.6	6,214.5
2022: I	18,321.0	330.1	17,990.9	12,694.7	1,925.2	3,371.0	6,562.9	6,408.4	5,504.0	904.5	11,428.0	6,286.3
II	18,736.5	336.0	18,400.6	12,970.8	1,967.2	3,462.5	6,640.8	6,485.4	5,562.4	923.0	11,759.7	6,485.4
III [p]	19,058.5	341.9	18,716.6	13,194.5	2,007.3	3,514.8	6,719.7	6,562.8	5,621.9	940.9	11,996.9	6,631.8

[1] Includes Federal Housing Administration (FHA)–insured multi-family properties, not shown separately.

[2] Derived figures. Total includes multi-family and commercial properties with conventional mortgages, not shown separately.

Source: Board of Governors of the Federal Reserve System, based on data from various Government and private organizations.

Table B–44. Mortgage debt outstanding by holder, 1962–2022

[Billions of dollars]

End of year or quarter	Total	Major financial institutions: Total	Depository Institutions [1, 2]	Life insurance companies	Other holders: Federal and related agencies [3]	Mortgage pools or trusts [4]	Individuals and others
1962	252.4	190.5	143.6	46.9	12.2	0.4	49.3
1963	279.3	214.6	164.1	50.5	11.3	.5	52.9
1964	307.0	238.8	183.6	55.2	11.6	.6	56.0
1965	334.5	262.4	202.4	60.0	12.7	.9	58.6
1966	358.5	279.5	214.8	64.6	16.2	1.3	61.5
1967	382.1	296.4	228.9	67.5	18.9	2.0	64.7
1968	411.4	317.3	247.3	70.0	22.6	2.5	69.0
1969	439.9	336.6	264.6	72.0	27.9	3.2	72.2
1970	469.4	352.9	278.5	74.4	33.6	4.8	78.2
1971	517.9	389.2	313.7	75.5	36.8	9.5	82.3
1972	589.8	443.8	366.8	76.9	40.1	14.4	91.5
1973	666.5	500.7	419.4	81.4	46.6	18.0	101.1
1974	728.4	539.3	453.1	86.2	60.7	21.5	106.9
1975	785.6	576.1	486.9	89.2	72.6	28.5	108.4
1976	870.5	640.7	549.1	91.6	76.0	40.7	113.2
1977	999.2	735.3	638.4	96.8	83.7	56.8	123.4
1978	1,150.7	837.5	731.3	106.2	100.2	70.4	142.7
1979	1,317.0	928.6	810.2	118.4	121.2	94.8	172.4
1980	1,457.8	988.0	857.0	131.1	142.9	114.0	213.0
1981	1,579.5	1,034.1	896.4	137.7	160.4	129.0	256.0
1982	1,661.3	1,019.6	877.6	142.0	176.9	178.5	286.3
1983	1,850.6	1,108.4	957.4	151.0	188.5	244.8	309.0
1984	2,092.0	1,248.2	1,091.5	156.7	201.6	300.0	342.2
1985	2,368.5	1,368.7	1,196.9	171.8	213.0	392.4	394.4
1986	2,655.6	1,483.3	1,289.5	193.8	202.1	549.5	420.6
1987	2,954.3	1,631.5	1,419.1	212.4	188.5	700.8	433.4
1988	3,271.9	1,797.8	1,564.9	232.9	192.5	785.7	495.9
1989	3,523.6	1,897.4	1,643.2	254.2	197.8	922.2	506.1
1990	3,779.5	1,918.8	1,651.0	267.9	239.0	1,085.9	535.7
1991	3,930.7	1,846.2	1,586.7	259.5	266.0	1,269.6	549.0
1992	4,040.8	1,770.5	1,528.5	242.0	286.1	1,440.0	544.3
1993	4,171.5	1,770.1	1,546.3	223.9	326.1	1,561.1	514.2
1994	4,336.3	1,824.7	1,608.9	215.8	315.6	1,696.9	499.1
1995	4,522.1	1,900.1	1,687.0	213.1	307.9	1,812.0	502.0
1996	4,802.8	1,982.2	1,773.7	208.5	294.4	1,989.1	537.1
1997	5,115.9	2,084.2	1,877.1	207.0	285.2	2,166.5	580.1
1998	5,603.2	2,194.7	1,981.0	213.8	291.9	2,487.1	629.5
1999	6,209.6	2,394.5	2,163.5	231.0	319.8	2,832.3	663.1
2000	6,766.6	2,619.2	2,383.0	236.2	339.9	3,097.5	710.1
2001	7,450.1	2,791.0	2,547.9	243.1	372.0	3,532.4	754.7
2002	8,358.7	3,089.4	2,839.3	250.1	432.3	3,978.4	858.6
2003	9,364.8	3,387.5	3,126.4	261.2	694.1	4,330.3	952.9
2004	10,646.7	3,926.5	3,653.0	273.5	703.2	4,834.5	1,182.5
2005	12,112.9	4,396.5	4,110.8	285.7	665.4	5,710.0	1,341.1
2006	13,525.5	4,784.0	4,479.8	304.1	687.5	6,629.5	1,424.7
2007	14,609.6	5,065.5	4,738.4	327.1	725.5	7,434.4	1,384.3
2008	14,690.0	5,045.8	4,702.0	343.8	801.1	7,592.7	1,250.4
2009	14,445.4	4,779.4	4,452.0	327.4	816.1	7,649.8	1,200.1
2010	13,893.0	4,585.2	4,266.1	319.2	5,127.5	3,108.4	1,071.8
2011	13,567.7	4,450.3	4,115.7	334.6	5,033.9	3,034.3	1,049.2
2012	13,331.3	4,438.2	4,091.3	346.9	4,935.0	2,947.6	1,010.5
2013	13,344.5	4,412.3	4,046.1	366.3	4,993.2	2,773.5	1,165.5
2014	13,486.8	4,546.7	4,158.5	388.2	4,987.7	2,742.7	1,209.8
2015	13,883.3	4,804.2	4,373.6	430.7	5,036.6	2,793.6	1,248.9
2016	14,333.6	5,096.7	4,631.2	465.5	5,146.9	2,826.6	1,263.4
2017	14,911.6	5,308.0	4,801.3	506.7	5,313.6	2,971.5	1,318.5
2018	15,463.8	5,487.5	4,919.4	568.1	5,457.0	3,143.7	1,375.6
2019	16,033.6	5,709.5	5,090.3	619.2	5,634.5	3,254.3	1,435.3
2020	16,787.1	5,775.7	5,131.0	644.7	6,269.6	3,259.0	1,482.8
2021	18,060.2	5,975.9	5,285.0	690.9	7,057.2	3,382.6	1,644.5
2021: I	16,976.3	5,739.6	5,092.8	646.8	6,480.7	3,256.7	1,499.2
II	17,291.4	5,780.8	5,123.2	657.6	6,689.8	3,286.2	1,534.6
III	17,636.1	5,873.2	5,200.2	673.0	6,868.2	3,316.1	1,578.7
IV	18,060.2	5,975.9	5,285.0	690.9	7,057.2	3,382.6	1,644.5
2022: I	18,321.0	6,062.1	5,354.0	708.1	7,245.1	3,429.2	1,584.6
II	18,736.5	6,262.9	5,540.0	722.9	7,344.2	3,487.9	1,641.6
III p	19,058.5	6,430.2	5,699.4	730.7	7,417.3	3,542.6	1,668.4

[1] Includes savings banks and savings and loan associations. Data reported by Federal Savings and Loan Insurance Corporation–insured institutions include loans in process for 1987 and exclude loans in process beginning with 1988.

[2] Includes loans held by nondeposit trust companies but not loans held by bank trust departments.

[3] Includes Government National Mortgage Association (GNMA or Ginnie Mae), Federal Housing Administration, Veterans Administration, Farmers Home Administration (FmHA), Federal Deposit Insurance Corporation, Resolution Trust Corporation (through 1995), and in earlier years Reconstruction Finance Corporation, Homeowners Loan Corporation, Federal Farm Mortgage Corporation, and Public Housing Administration. Also includes U.S.-sponsored agencies such as Federal National Mortgage Association (FNMA or Fannie Mae), Federal Land Banks, Federal Home Loan Mortgage Corporation (FHLMC or Freddie Mac), Federal Agricultural Mortgage Corporation (Farmer Mac, beginning 1994), Federal Home Loan Banks (beginning 1997), and mortgage pass-through securities issued or guaranteed by GNMA, FHLMC, FNMA, FmHA, or Farmer Mac. Other U.S. agencies (amounts small or current separate data not readily available) included with "individuals and others."

[4] Includes private mortgage pools.

Source: Board of Governors of the Federal Reserve System, based on data from various Government and private organizations.

TABLE B–45. Federal receipts, outlays, surplus or deficit, and debt, fiscal years 1958–2024

[Billions of dollars; fiscal years]

Fiscal year or period	Total			On-budget			Off-budget			Federal debt (end of period)		Addendum: Gross domestic product
	Receipts	Outlays	Surplus or deficit (–)	Receipts	Outlays	Surplus or deficit (–)	Receipts	Outlays	Surplus or deficit (–)	Gross Federal	Held by the public	
1958	79.6	82.4	–2.8	71.6	74.9	–3.3	8.0	7.5	0.5	279.7	226.3	473.5
1959	79.2	92.1	–12.8	71.0	83.1	–12.1	8.3	9.0	–.7	287.5	234.7	504.6
1960	92.5	92.2	.3	81.9	81.3	.5	10.6	10.9	–.2	290.5	236.8	534.3
1961	94.4	97.7	–3.3	82.3	86.0	–3.8	12.1	11.7	.4	292.6	238.4	546.6
1962	99.7	106.8	–7.1	87.4	93.3	–5.9	12.3	13.5	–1.3	302.9	248.0	585.7
1963	106.6	111.3	–4.8	92.4	96.4	–4.0	14.2	15.0	–.8	310.3	254.0	618.2
1964	112.6	118.5	–5.9	96.2	102.8	–6.5	16.4	15.7	.6	316.1	256.8	661.7
1965	116.8	118.2	–1.4	100.1	101.7	–1.6	16.7	16.5	.2	322.3	260.8	709.3
1966	130.8	134.5	–3.7	111.7	114.8	–3.1	19.1	19.7	–.6	328.5	263.7	780.5
1967	148.8	157.5	–8.6	124.4	137.0	–12.6	24.4	20.4	4.0	340.4	266.6	836.5
1968	153.0	178.1	–25.2	128.1	155.8	–27.7	24.9	22.3	2.6	368.7	289.5	897.6
1969	186.9	183.6	3.2	157.9	158.4	–.5	29.0	25.2	3.7	365.8	278.1	980.3
1970	192.8	195.6	–2.8	159.3	168.0	–8.7	33.5	27.6	5.9	380.9	283.2	1,046.7
1971	187.1	210.2	–23.0	151.3	177.3	–26.1	35.8	32.8	3.0	408.2	303.0	1,116.6
1972	207.3	230.7	–23.4	167.4	193.5	–26.1	39.9	37.2	2.7	435.9	322.4	1,216.3
1973	230.8	245.7	–14.9	184.7	200.0	–15.2	46.1	45.7	.3	466.3	340.9	1,352.7
1974	263.2	269.4	–6.1	209.3	216.5	–7.2	53.9	52.9	1.1	483.9	343.7	1,482.9
1975	279.1	332.3	–53.2	216.6	270.8	–54.1	62.5	61.6	.9	541.9	394.7	1,606.9
1976	298.1	371.8	–73.7	231.7	301.1	–69.4	66.4	70.7	–4.3	629.0	477.4	1,786.1
Transition quarter	81.2	96.0	–14.7	63.2	77.3	–14.1	18.0	18.7	–.7	643.6	495.5	471.7
1977	355.6	409.2	–53.7	278.7	328.7	–49.9	76.8	80.5	–3.7	706.4	549.1	2,024.3
1978	399.6	458.7	–59.2	314.2	369.6	–55.4	85.4	89.2	–3.8	776.6	607.1	2,273.5
1979	463.3	504.0	–40.7	365.3	404.9	–39.6	98.0	99.1	–1.1	829.5	640.3	2,565.6
1980	517.1	590.9	–73.8	403.9	477.0	–73.1	113.2	113.9	–.7	909.0	711.9	2,791.9
1981	599.3	678.2	–79.0	469.1	543.0	–73.9	130.2	135.3	–5.1	994.8	789.4	3,133.2
1982	617.8	745.7	–128.0	474.3	594.9	–120.6	143.5	150.9	–7.4	1,137.3	924.6	3,313.4
1983	600.6	808.4	–207.8	453.2	660.9	–207.7	147.3	147.4	–.1	1,371.7	1,137.3	3,536.0
1984	666.4	851.8	–185.4	500.4	685.6	–185.3	166.1	166.2	–.1	1,564.6	1,307.0	3,949.2
1985	734.0	946.3	–212.3	547.9	769.4	–221.5	186.2	176.9	9.2	1,817.4	1,507.3	4,265.1
1986	769.2	990.4	–221.2	568.9	806.8	–237.9	200.2	183.5	16.7	2,120.5	1,740.6	4,526.3
1987	854.3	1,004.0	–149.7	640.9	809.2	–168.4	213.4	194.8	18.6	2,346.0	1,889.8	4,767.7
1988	909.2	1,064.4	–155.2	667.7	860.0	–192.3	241.5	204.4	37.1	2,601.1	2,051.6	5,138.6
1989	991.1	1,143.7	–152.6	727.4	932.8	–205.4	263.7	210.9	52.8	2,867.8	2,190.7	5,554.7
1990	1,032.0	1,253.0	–221.0	750.3	1,027.9	–277.6	281.7	225.1	56.6	3,206.3	2,411.6	5,898.8
1991	1,055.0	1,324.2	–269.2	761.1	1,082.5	–321.4	293.9	241.7	52.2	3,598.2	2,689.0	6,093.2
1992	1,091.2	1,381.5	–290.3	788.8	1,129.2	–340.4	302.4	252.3	50.1	4,001.8	2,999.7	6,416.3
1993	1,154.3	1,409.4	–255.1	842.4	1,142.8	–300.4	311.9	266.6	45.3	4,351.0	3,248.4	6,775.3
1994	1,258.6	1,461.8	–203.2	923.5	1,182.4	–258.8	335.0	279.4	55.7	4,643.3	3,433.1	7,176.9
1995	1,351.8	1,515.7	–164.0	1,000.7	1,227.1	–226.4	351.1	288.7	62.4	4,920.6	3,604.4	7,560.4
1996	1,453.1	1,560.5	–107.4	1,085.6	1,259.6	–174.0	367.5	300.9	66.6	5,181.5	3,734.1	7,951.3
1997	1,579.2	1,601.1	–21.9	1,187.2	1,290.5	–103.2	392.0	310.6	81.4	5,369.2	3,772.3	8,451.0
1998	1,721.7	1,652.5	69.3	1,305.9	1,335.9	–29.9	415.8	316.6	99.2	5,478.2	3,721.1	8,930.8
1999	1,827.5	1,701.8	125.6	1,383.0	1,381.1	1.9	444.5	320.8	123.7	5,605.5	3,632.4	9,479.6
2000	2,025.2	1,789.0	236.2	1,544.6	1,458.2	86.4	480.6	330.8	149.8	5,628.7	3,409.8	10,117.1
2001	1,991.1	1,862.8	128.2	1,483.6	1,516.0	–32.4	507.5	346.8	160.7	5,769.9	3,319.6	10,525.7
2002	1,853.1	2,010.9	–157.8	1,337.8	1,655.2	–317.4	515.3	355.7	159.7	6,198.4	3,540.4	10,828.9
2003	1,782.3	2,159.9	–377.6	1,258.5	1,796.9	–538.4	523.8	363.0	160.8	6,760.0	3,913.4	11,278.8
2004	1,880.1	2,292.8	–412.7	1,345.4	1,913.3	–568.0	534.7	379.5	155.2	7,354.7	4,295.5	12,028.4
2005	2,153.6	2,472.0	–318.3	1,576.1	2,069.7	–493.6	577.5	402.2	175.3	7,905.3	4,592.2	12,840.0
2006	2,406.9	2,655.1	–248.2	1,798.5	2,233.0	–434.5	608.4	422.1	186.3	8,451.4	4,829.0	13,636.8
2007	2,568.0	2,728.7	–160.7	1,932.9	2,275.0	–342.2	635.1	453.6	181.5	8,950.7	5,035.1	14,305.4
2008	2,524.0	2,982.5	–458.6	1,865.9	2,507.8	–641.8	658.0	474.8	183.3	9,986.1	5,803.1	14,796.6
2009	2,105.0	3,517.7	–1,412.7	1,451.0	3,000.7	–1,549.7	654.0	517.0	137.0	11,875.9	7,544.7	14,467.3
2010	2,162.7	3,457.1	–1,294.4	1,531.0	2,902.4	–1,371.4	631.7	554.7	77.0	13,528.8	9,018.9	14,884.4
2011	2,303.5	3,603.1	–1,299.6	1,737.7	3,104.5	–1,366.8	565.8	498.6	67.2	14,764.2	10,128.2	15,466.5
2012	2,450.0	3,526.6	–1,076.6	1,880.5	3,019.0	–1,138.5	569.5	507.6	61.9	16,050.9	11,281.1	16,109.4
2013	2,775.1	3,454.9	–679.8	2,101.8	2,821.1	–719.2	673.3	633.8	39.5	16,719.4	11,982.7	16,665.1
2014	3,021.5	3,506.3	–484.8	2,285.9	2,800.2	–514.3	735.6	706.1	29.5	17,794.5	12,779.9	17,370.8
2015	3,249.9	3,691.9	–442.0	2,479.5	2,948.8	–469.3	770.4	743.1	27.3	18,120.1	13,116.7	18,086.1
2016	3,268.0	3,852.6	–584.7	2,457.8	3,077.9	–620.2	810.2	774.7	35.5	19,539.5	14,167.6	18,536.1
2017	3,316.2	3,981.6	–665.5	2,465.6	3,180.4	–714.9	850.6	801.2	49.4	20,205.7	14,665.4	19,245.7
2018	3,329.9	4,109.0	–779.1	2,475.2	3,260.5	–785.3	854.7	848.6	6.2	21,462.3	15,749.6	20,302.0
2019	3,463.4	4,447.0	–983.6	2,549.1	3,540.3	–991.3	914.3	906.6	7.7	22,669.5	16,800.7	21,159.2
2020	3,421.2	6,553.6	–3,132.5	2,455.7	5,598.0	–3,142.3	965.4	955.6	9.8	26,902.5	21,016.7	21,060.9
2021	4,047.1	6,822.5	–2,775.4	3,094.8	5,818.6	–2,723.8	952.3	1,003.8	–51.5	28,385.6	22,282.8	22,654.0
2022	4,897.4	6,273.3	–1,375.9	3,831.4	5,192.2	–1,360.7	1,066.0	1,081.2	–15.2	30,838.6	24,252.4	25,000.4
2023 (estimates)	4,802.5	6,371.8	–1,569.3	3,604.4	5,159.8	–1,555.4	1,198.1	1,212.1	–14.0	32,692.9	25,909.8	26,335.7
2024 (estimates)	5,036.4	6,882.7	–1,846.4	3,828.2	5,567.2	–1,739.0	1,208.2	1,315.5	–107.4	34,807.7	27,782.7	27,237.5

Note: Fiscal years through 1976 were on a July 1–June 30 basis; beginning with October 1976 (fiscal year 1977), the fiscal year is on an October 1–September 30 basis. The transition quarter is the three-month period from July 1, 1976 through September 30, 1976.

See *Budget of the United States Government, Fiscal Year 2024*, for additional information.

Sources: Department of Commerce (Bureau of Economic Analysis), Department of the Treasury, and Office of Management and Budget.

Table B–46. Federal receipts, outlays, surplus or deficit, and debt, as percent of gross domestic product, fiscal years 1953–2024

[Percent; fiscal years]

Fiscal year or period	Receipts	Outlays		Surplus or deficit (–)	Federal debt (end of period)	
		Total	National defense		Gross Federal	Held by public
1953	18.2	19.9	13.8	–1.7	69.6	57.2
1954	18.0	18.3	12.7	–.3	70.0	58.0
1955	16.1	16.8	10.5	–.7	67.5	55.8
1956	17.0	16.1	9.7	.9	62.2	50.7
1957	17.3	16.5	9.8	.7	58.8	47.3
1958	16.8	17.4	9.9	–.6	59.1	47.8
1959	15.7	18.3	9.7	–2.5	57.0	46.5
1960	17.3	17.3	9.0	.1	54.4	44.3
1961	17.3	17.9	9.1	–.6	53.5	43.6
1962	17.0	18.2	8.9	–1.2	51.7	42.3
1963	17.2	18.0	8.6	–.8	50.2	41.1
1964	17.0	17.9	8.3	–.9	47.8	38.8
1965	16.5	16.7	7.1	–.2	45.4	36.8
1966	16.8	17.2	7.4	–.5	42.1	33.8
1967	17.8	18.8	8.5	–1.0	40.7	31.9
1968	17.0	19.8	9.1	–2.8	41.1	32.3
1969	19.1	18.7	8.4	.3	37.3	28.4
1970	18.4	18.7	7.8	–.3	36.4	27.1
1971	16.8	18.8	7.1	–2.1	36.6	27.1
1972	17.0	19.0	6.5	–1.9	35.8	26.5
1973	17.1	18.2	5.7	–1.1	34.5	25.2
1974	17.8	18.2	5.4	–.4	32.6	23.2
1975	17.4	20.7	5.4	–3.3	33.7	24.6
1976	16.7	20.8	5.0	–4.1	35.2	26.7
Transition quarter	17.2	20.3	4.7	–3.1	34.1	26.3
1977	17.6	20.2	4.8	–2.7	34.9	27.1
1978	17.6	20.2	4.6	–2.6	34.2	26.7
1979	18.1	19.6	4.5	–1.6	32.3	25.0
1980	18.5	21.2	4.8	–2.6	32.6	25.5
1981	19.1	21.6	5.0	–2.5	31.8	25.2
1982	18.6	22.5	5.6	–3.9	34.3	27.9
1983	17.0	22.9	5.9	–5.9	38.8	32.2
1984	16.9	21.6	5.8	–4.7	39.6	33.1
1985	17.2	22.2	5.9	–5.0	42.6	35.3
1986	17.0	21.9	6.0	–4.9	46.8	38.5
1987	17.9	21.1	5.9	–3.1	49.2	39.6
1988	17.7	20.7	5.7	–3.0	50.6	39.9
1989	17.8	20.6	5.5	–2.7	51.6	39.4
1990	17.5	21.2	5.1	–3.7	54.4	40.9
1991	17.3	21.7	4.5	–4.4	59.1	44.1
1992	17.0	21.5	4.6	–4.5	62.4	46.8
1993	17.0	20.8	4.3	–3.8	64.2	47.9
1994	17.5	20.4	3.9	–2.8	64.7	47.8
1995	17.9	20.0	3.6	–2.2	65.1	47.7
1996	18.3	19.6	3.3	–1.4	65.2	47.0
1997	18.7	18.9	3.2	–.3	63.5	44.6
1998	19.3	18.5	3.0	.8	61.3	41.7
1999	19.3	18.0	2.9	1.3	59.1	38.3
2000	20.0	17.7	2.9	2.3	55.6	33.7
2001	18.9	17.7	2.9	1.2	54.8	31.5
2002	17.1	18.6	3.2	–1.5	57.2	32.7
2003	15.8	19.2	3.6	–3.3	59.9	34.7
2004	15.6	19.1	3.8	–3.4	61.1	35.7
2005	16.8	19.3	3.9	–2.5	61.6	35.8
2006	17.6	19.5	3.8	–1.8	62.0	35.4
2007	18.0	19.1	3.9	–1.1	62.6	35.2
2008	17.1	20.2	4.2	–3.1	67.5	39.2
2009	14.5	24.3	4.6	–9.8	82.1	52.2
2010	14.5	23.2	4.7	–8.7	90.9	60.6
2011	14.9	23.3	4.6	–8.4	95.5	65.5
2012	15.2	21.9	4.2	–6.7	99.6	70.0
2013	16.7	20.7	3.8	–4.1	100.3	71.9
2014	17.4	20.2	3.5	–2.8	102.4	73.6
2015	18.0	20.4	3.3	–2.4	100.2	72.5
2016	17.6	20.8	3.2	–3.2	105.4	76.4
2017	17.2	20.7	3.1	–3.5	105.0	76.2
2018	16.4	20.2	3.1	–3.8	105.7	77.6
2019	16.4	21.0	3.2	–4.6	107.1	79.4
2020	16.2	31.1	3.4	–14.9	127.7	99.8
2021	17.9	30.1	3.3	–12.3	125.3	98.4
2022	19.6	25.1	3.1	–5.5	123.4	97.0
2023 (estimates)	18.2	24.2	3.1	–6.0	124.1	98.4
2024 (estimates)	18.5	25.3	3.3	–6.8	127.8	102.0

Note: See Note, Table B–45.

Sources: Department of the Treasury and Office of Management and Budget.

Table B–47. Federal receipts and outlays, by major category, and surplus or deficit, fiscal years 1958–2024

[Billions of dollars; fiscal years]

Fiscal year or period	Receipts (on-budget and off-budget)					Outlays (on-budget and off-budget)										Surplus or deficit (−) (on-budget and off-budget)
	Total	Individual income taxes	Corporation income taxes	Social insurance and retirement receipts	Other	Total	National defense: Total	National defense: Department of Defense, military	International affairs	Health	Medicare	Income security	Social security	Net interest	Other	
1958	79.6	34.7	20.1	11.2	13.6	82.4	46.8	....	3.4	0.5	....	7.5	8.2	5.6	10.3	−2.8
1959	79.2	36.7	17.3	11.7	13.5	92.1	49.0	....	3.1	.7	....	8.2	9.7	5.8	15.5	−12.8
1960	92.5	40.7	21.5	14.7	15.6	92.2	48.1	....	3.0	.8	....	7.4	11.6	6.9	14.4	.3
1961	94.4	41.3	21.0	16.4	15.7	97.7	49.6	....	3.2	.9	....	9.7	12.5	6.7	15.2	−3.3
1962	99.7	45.6	20.5	17.0	16.5	106.8	52.3	50.1	5.6	1.2	....	9.2	14.4	6.9	17.2	−7.1
1963	106.6	47.6	21.6	19.8	17.6	111.3	53.4	51.1	5.3	1.5	....	9.3	15.8	7.7	18.3	−4.8
1964	112.6	48.7	23.5	22.0	18.5	118.5	54.8	52.6	4.9	1.8	....	9.7	16.6	8.2	22.6	−5.9
1965	116.8	48.8	25.5	22.2	20.3	118.2	50.6	48.8	5.3	1.8	....	9.5	17.5	8.6	25.0	−1.4
1966	130.8	55.4	30.1	25.5	19.8	134.5	58.1	56.6	5.6	2.5	0.1	9.7	20.7	9.4	28.5	−3.7
1967	148.8	61.5	34.0	32.6	20.7	157.5	71.4	70.1	5.6	3.4	2.7	10.3	21.7	10.3	32.1	−8.6
1968	153.0	68.7	28.7	33.9	21.7	178.1	81.9	80.4	5.3	4.4	4.6	11.8	23.9	11.1	35.1	−25.2
1969	186.9	87.2	36.7	39.0	23.9	183.6	82.5	80.8	4.6	5.2	5.7	13.1	27.3	12.7	32.6	3.2
1970	192.8	90.4	32.8	44.4	25.2	195.6	81.7	80.1	4.3	5.9	6.2	15.6	30.3	14.4	37.2	−2.8
1971	187.1	86.2	26.8	47.3	26.8	210.2	78.9	77.5	4.2	6.8	6.6	22.9	35.9	14.8	40.0	−23.0
1972	207.3	94.7	32.2	52.6	27.8	230.7	79.2	77.6	4.8	8.7	7.5	27.6	40.2	15.5	47.3	−23.4
1973	230.8	103.2	36.2	63.1	28.3	245.7	76.7	75.0	4.1	9.4	8.1	28.3	49.1	17.3	52.8	−14.9
1974	263.2	119.0	38.6	75.1	30.6	269.4	79.3	77.9	5.7	10.7	9.6	33.7	55.9	21.4	52.9	−6.1
1975	279.1	122.4	40.6	84.5	31.5	332.3	86.5	84.9	7.1	12.9	12.9	50.2	64.7	23.2	74.9	−53.2
1976	298.1	131.6	41.4	90.8	34.3	371.8	89.6	87.9	6.4	15.7	15.8	60.8	73.9	26.7	82.8	−73.7
Transition quarter	81.2	38.8	8.5	25.2	8.8	96.0	22.3	21.8	2.5	3.9	4.3	15.0	19.8	6.9	21.4	−14.7
1977	355.6	157.6	54.9	106.5	36.6	409.2	97.2	95.1	6.4	17.3	19.3	61.0	85.1	29.9	93.0	−53.7
1978	399.6	181.0	60.0	121.0	37.7	458.7	104.5	102.3	7.5	18.5	22.8	61.5	93.9	35.5	114.7	−59.2
1979	463.3	217.8	65.7	138.9	40.8	504.0	116.3	113.6	7.5	20.5	26.5	66.4	104.1	42.6	120.2	−40.7
1980	517.1	244.1	64.6	157.8	50.6	590.9	134.0	130.9	12.7	23.2	32.1	86.5	118.5	52.5	131.3	−73.8
1981	599.3	285.9	61.1	182.7	69.5	678.2	157.5	153.9	13.1	26.9	39.1	100.3	139.6	68.8	133.0	−79.0
1982	617.8	297.7	49.2	201.5	69.3	745.7	185.3	180.7	12.3	27.4	46.6	108.1	156.0	85.0	125.0	−128.0
1983	600.6	288.9	37.0	209.0	65.6	808.4	209.9	204.4	11.8	28.6	52.6	123.0	170.7	89.8	121.8	−207.8
1984	666.4	298.4	56.9	239.4	71.8	851.8	227.4	220.9	15.9	30.4	57.5	113.4	178.2	111.1	117.9	−185.4
1985	734.0	334.5	61.3	265.2	73.0	946.3	252.7	245.1	16.2	33.5	65.8	129.0	188.6	129.5	131.0	−212.3
1986	769.2	349.0	63.1	283.9	73.2	990.4	273.4	265.4	14.1	35.9	70.2	120.7	198.8	136.0	141.3	−221.2
1987	854.3	392.6	83.9	303.3	74.5	1,004.0	282.0	273.9	11.6	40.0	75.1	124.1	207.4	138.6	125.2	−149.7
1988	909.2	401.2	94.5	334.3	79.2	1,064.4	290.4	281.9	10.5	44.5	78.9	130.4	219.3	151.8	138.7	−155.2
1989	991.1	445.7	103.3	359.4	82.7	1,143.7	303.6	294.8	9.6	48.4	85.0	137.6	232.5	169.0	158.2	−152.6
1990	1,032.0	466.9	93.5	380.0	91.5	1,253.0	299.3	289.7	13.8	57.7	98.1	148.8	248.6	184.3	202.4	−221.0
1991	1,055.0	467.8	98.1	396.0	93.1	1,324.2	273.3	262.3	15.8	71.1	104.5	172.6	269.0	194.4	223.4	−269.2
1992	1,091.2	476.0	100.3	413.7	101.3	1,381.5	298.3	286.8	16.1	89.4	119.0	199.7	287.6	199.3	172.1	−290.3
1993	1,154.3	509.7	117.5	428.3	98.8	1,409.4	291.1	278.5	17.2	99.3	130.6	210.1	304.6	198.7	157.8	−255.1
1994	1,258.6	543.1	140.4	461.5	113.7	1,461.8	281.6	268.6	17.1	107.1	144.7	217.2	319.6	202.9	171.5	−203.2
1995	1,351.8	590.2	157.0	484.5	120.1	1,515.7	272.1	259.4	16.4	115.4	159.9	223.8	335.8	232.1	160.3	−164.0
1996	1,453.1	656.4	171.8	509.4	115.4	1,560.5	265.7	253.1	13.5	119.3	174.2	229.7	349.7	241.1	167.3	−107.4
1997	1,579.2	737.5	182.3	539.4	120.1	1,601.1	270.5	258.3	15.2	123.8	190.0	235.0	365.3	244.0	157.4	−21.9
1998	1,721.7	828.6	188.7	571.8	132.6	1,652.5	268.2	255.8	13.1	131.4	192.8	237.7	379.2	241.1	189.0	69.3
1999	1,827.5	879.5	184.7	611.8	151.5	1,701.8	274.8	261.2	15.2	141.0	190.4	242.4	390.0	229.8	218.1	125.6
2000	2,025.2	1,004.5	207.3	652.9	160.6	1,789.0	294.4	281.0	17.2	154.5	197.1	253.7	409.4	222.9	239.7	236.2
2001	1,991.1	994.3	151.1	694.0	151.7	1,862.8	304.7	290.2	16.5	172.2	217.4	269.7	433.0	206.2	243.2	128.2
2002	1,853.1	858.3	148.0	700.8	146.0	2,010.9	348.5	331.8	22.3	196.5	230.9	312.7	456.0	170.9	273.2	−157.8
2003	1,782.3	793.7	131.8	713.0	143.9	2,159.9	404.7	387.1	21.2	219.6	249.4	334.6	474.7	153.1	302.6	−377.6
2004	1,880.1	809.0	189.4	733.4	148.4	2,292.8	455.8	436.4	26.9	240.1	269.4	333.0	495.5	160.2	311.8	−412.7
2005	2,153.6	927.2	278.3	794.1	154.0	2,472.0	495.3	474.1	34.6	250.6	298.6	345.8	523.3	184.0	339.8	−318.3
2006	2,406.9	1,043.9	353.9	837.8	171.2	2,655.1	521.8	499.3	29.5	252.8	329.9	352.4	548.5	226.6	393.5	−248.2
2007	2,568.0	1,163.5	370.2	869.6	164.7	2,728.7	551.3	528.5	28.5	266.4	375.4	365.9	586.2	237.1	317.9	−160.7
2008	2,524.0	1,145.7	304.3	900.2	173.7	2,982.5	616.1	594.6	28.9	280.6	390.8	431.2	617.0	252.8	365.2	−458.6
2009	2,105.0	915.3	138.2	890.9	160.5	3,517.7	661.0	636.7	37.5	334.4	430.1	533.1	683.0	186.9	651.7	−1,412.7
2010	2,162.7	898.5	191.4	864.8	207.9	3,457.1	693.5	666.7	45.2	369.1	451.6	622.1	706.7	196.2	372.6	−1,294.4
2011	2,303.5	1,091.5	181.1	818.8	212.1	3,603.1	705.6	678.1	45.7	372.5	485.7	597.3	730.8	230.0	435.7	−1,299.6
2012	2,450.0	1,132.2	242.3	845.3	230.2	3,526.6	677.9	650.9	36.8	346.8	471.8	541.2	773.3	220.4	458.4	−1,076.6
2013	2,775.1	1,316.4	273.5	947.8	237.4	3,454.9	633.4	607.8	46.5	358.3	497.8	536.4	813.6	220.9	348.0	−679.8
2014	3,021.5	1,394.6	320.7	1,023.5	282.7	3,506.3	603.5	577.9	46.9	409.5	511.7	513.6	850.5	229.0	341.7	−484.8
2015	3,249.9	1,540.8	343.8	1,065.3	300.0	3,691.9	589.7	562.5	52.0	482.3	546.2	508.8	887.8	223.2	402.0	−442.0
2016	3,268.0	1,546.1	299.6	1,115.1	307.3	3,852.6	593.4	565.4	45.3	511.3	594.5	514.1	916.1	240.0	437.9	−584.7
2017	3,316.2	1,587.1	297.0	1,161.9	270.1	3,981.6	598.7	568.9	46.3	533.2	597.3	503.4	944.9	262.6	495.3	−665.5
2018	3,329.9	1,683.5	204.7	1,170.7	270.9	4,109.0	631.1	600.7	49.0	551.2	588.7	495.3	987.8	325.0	480.9	−779.1
2019	3,463.4	1,717.9	230.2	1,243.1	272.1	4,447.0	686.0	654.0	52.7	584.8	651.0	514.8	1,044.4	375.2	538.1	−983.6
2020	3,421.2	1,608.7	211.8	1,310.0	290.7	6,553.6	724.6	690.4	67.7	747.6	776.2	1,263.6	1,095.8	345.5	1,532.6	−3,132.5
2021	4,047.1	2,044.4	371.8	1,314.1	316.8	6,822.5	753.9	717.6	46.9	796.5	696.5	1,647.7	1,134.6	352.3	1,394.1	−2,775.4
2022	4,897.4	2,632.1	424.9	1,483.5	356.9	6,273.3	765.8	726.6	71.7	914.1	755.1	866.1	1,218.7	475.9	1,206.0	−1,375.9
2023 (estimates)	4,802.5	2,327.9	546.0	1,675.2	253.4	6,371.8	814.8	771.3	79.9	891.3	829.9	792.1	1,352.3	660.6	951.0	−1,569.3
2024 (estimates)	5,036.4	2,390.0	666.2	1,742.1	238.1	6,882.7	909.4	863.0	73.7	852.7	850.4	976.4	1,465.8	788.8	965.5	−1,846.4

Note: See Note, Table B–45.

Sources: Department of the Treasury and Office of Management and Budget.

Table B–48. Federal receipts, outlays, surplus or deficit, and debt, fiscal years 2019–2024

[Millions of dollars; fiscal years]

Description	Actual				Estimates	
	2019	2020	2021	2022	2023	2024
RECEIPTS, OUTLAYS, AND SURPLUS OR DEFICIT						
Total:						
Receipts	3,463,364	3,421,164	4,047,111	4,897,399	4,802,483	5,036,384
Outlays	4,446,960	6,553,621	6,822,470	6,273,324	6,371,827	6,882,738
Surplus or deficit (–)	–983,596	–3,132,457	–2,775,359	–1,375,925	–1,569,344	–1,846,354
On-budget:						
Receipts	2,549,061	2,455,736	3,094,788	3,831,424	3,604,388	3,828,230
Outlays	3,540,343	5,598,039	5,818,623	5,192,169	5,159,771	5,567,203
Surplus or deficit (–)	–991,282	–3,142,303	–2,723,835	–1,360,745	–1,555,383	–1,738,973
Off-budget:						
Receipts	914,303	965,428	952,323	1,065,975	1,198,095	1,208,154
Outlays	906,617	955,582	1,003,847	1,081,155	1,212,056	1,315,535
Surplus or deficit (–)	7,686	9,846	–51,524	–15,180	–13,961	–107,381
OUTSTANDING DEBT, END OF PERIOD						
Gross Federal debt	22,669,466	26,902,455	28,385,562	30,838,586	32,692,918	34,807,699
Held by Federal Government accounts	5,868,766	5,885,786	6,102,745	6,586,229	6,783,081	7,025,032
Held by the public	16,800,700	21,016,669	22,282,817	24,252,357	25,909,838	27,782,667
Federal Reserve System	2,113,329	4,445,477	5,433,156	5,634,940	....	....
Other	14,687,371	16,571,192	16,849,661	18,617,417	....	....
RECEIPTS BY SOURCE						
Total: On-budget and off-budget	3,463,364	3,421,164	4,047,111	4,897,399	4,802,483	5,036,384
Individual income taxes	1,717,857	1,608,663	2,044,377	2,632,146	2,327,860	2,390,010
Corporation income taxes	230,245	211,845	371,831	424,865	545,999	666,168
Social insurance and retirement receipts	1,243,113	1,309,955	1,314,088	1,483,527	1,675,236	1,742,081
On-budget	328,810	344,527	361,765	417,552	477,141	533,927
Off-budget	914,303	965,428	952,323	1,065,975	1,198,095	1,208,154
Excise taxes	98,914	86,780	75,274	87,728	91,453	114,089
Estate and gift taxes	16,672	17,624	27,140	32,550	20,899	25,338
Customs duties and fees	70,784	68,551	79,985	99,908	101,656	60,686
Miscellaneous receipts	85,779	117,746	134,416	136,675	39,380	38,012
Deposits of earnings by Federal Reserve System	52,793	81,880	100,054	106,674	....	....
All other	32,986	35,866	34,362	30,001	39,380	38,012
OUTLAYS BY FUNCTION						
Total: On-budget and off-budget	4,446,960	6,553,621	6,822,470	6,273,324	6,371,827	6,882,738
National defense	686,003	724,645	753,901	765,823	814,750	909,377
International affairs	52,739	67,666	46,947	71,699	79,883	73,735
General science, space, and technology	32,414	34,022	35,534	37,404	43,052	44,602
Energy	5,041	7,083	5,977	–9,132	10,655	30,456
Natural resources and environment	37,844	42,450	44,160	41,389	69,400	93,175
Agriculture	38,257	47,298	47,398	33,065	41,414	33,147
Commerce and housing credit	–25,715	572,071	307,847	–19,075	–1,131	21,853
On-budget	–24,612	574,474	310,581	–18,658	–628	24,970
Off-budget	–1,103	–2,403	–2,734	–417	–503	–3,117
Transportation	95,756	145,623	154,291	131,084	136,507	147,140
Community and regional development	26,784	81,878	44,655	69,963	100,474	71,506
Education, training, employment, and social services	136,700	237,754	298,406	677,305	269,046	218,552
Health	584,816	747,582	796,450	914,081	891,297	852,655
Medicare	650,996	776,225	696,458	755,094	829,902	850,446
Income security	514,787	1,263,639	1,647,729	866,097	792,089	976,437
Social security	1,044,409	1,095,816	1,134,586	1,218,663	1,352,268	1,465,820
On-budget	36,130	39,893	34,862	48,524	51,470	57,387
Off-budget	1,008,279	1,055,923	1,099,724	1,170,139	1,300,798	1,408,433
Veterans benefits and services	199,843	218,655	234,282	274,404	304,963	320,970
Administration of justice	65,832	71,997	71,430	71,323	86,259	88,338
General government	23,488	180,109	273,941	133,214	42,505	44,353
Net interest	375,158	345,470	352,338	475,887	660,647	788,772
On-budget	457,662	424,274	425,591	543,625	727,255	855,930
Off-budget	–82,504	–78,804	–73,253	–67,738	–66,608	–67,158
Allowances	....	....	....	....	–17,770	16,430
Undistributed offsetting receipts	–98,192	–106,362	–123,860	–234,964	–134,383	–165,026
On-budget	–80,137	–87,228	–103,970	–214,135	–112,752	–142,403
Off-budget	–18,055	–19,134	–19,890	–20,829	–21,631	–22,623

Note: See Note, Table B–45.

Sources: Department of the Treasury and Office of Management and Budget.

TABLE B–49. Federal and State and local government current receipts and expenditures, national income and product accounts (NIPA) basis, 1972–2022

[Billions of dollars; quarterly data at seasonally adjusted annual rates]

Year or quarter	Total government			Federal Government			State and local government			Addendum: Grants-in-aid to State and local governments
	Current receipts	Current expenditures	Net government saving (NIPA)	Current receipts	Current expenditures	Net Federal Government saving (NIPA)	Current receipts	Current expenditures	Net State and local government saving (NIPA)	
1972	345.6	388.5	–42.9	219.0	268.0	–49.0	157.1	151.0	6.1	30.5
1973	388.8	421.5	–32.7	249.2	287.6	–38.3	173.0	167.4	5.6	33.5
1974	430.2	473.9	–43.7	278.5	319.8	–41.3	186.6	189.0	–2.3	34.9
1975	441.2	549.9	–108.7	276.8	374.8	–97.9	208.0	218.7	–10.7	43.6
1976	505.7	591.0	–85.3	322.6	403.5	–80.9	232.2	236.6	–4.4	49.1
1977	567.4	640.3	–72.9	363.9	437.3	–73.4	258.3	257.8	.5	54.8
1978	646.1	703.3	–57.2	423.8	485.9	–62.0	285.8	280.9	4.9	63.5
1979	729.3	777.9	–48.6	487.0	534.4	–47.4	306.3	307.5	–1.2	64.0
1980	799.9	894.6	–94.7	533.7	622.5	–88.8	335.9	341.8	–5.9	69.7
1981	919.1	1,017.4	–98.2	621.1	709.1	–88.1	367.5	377.6	–10.2	69.4
1982	940.9	1,131.0	–190.1	618.7	786.0	–167.4	388.5	411.3	–22.8	66.3
1983	1,002.1	1,227.7	–225.6	644.8	851.9	–207.2	425.3	443.7	–18.4	67.9
1984	1,115.0	1,311.7	–196.7	711.2	907.7	–196.5	476.1	476.3	–.2	72.3
1985	1,217.0	1,418.7	–201.7	775.7	975.0	–199.2	517.5	519.9	–2.4	76.2
1986	1,292.9	1,512.8	–219.9	817.9	1,033.8	–215.9	557.4	561.3	–4.0	82.4
1987	1,406.6	1,586.7	–180.1	899.5	1,065.2	–165.7	585.5	599.9	–14.4	78.4
1988	1,507.1	1,678.3	–171.3	962.4	1,122.4	–160.0	630.4	641.7	–11.3	85.7
1989	1,632.0	1,810.7	–178.7	1,042.5	1,201.8	–159.4	681.4	700.7	–19.3	91.8
1990	1,713.3	1,952.9	–239.5	1,087.6	1,290.9	–203.3	730.1	766.3	–36.2	104.4
1991	1,763.7	2,072.2	–308.5	1,107.8	1,356.2	–248.4	779.9	840.0	–60.1	124.0
1992	1,848.7	2,254.2	–405.5	1,154.4	1,488.9	–334.5	836.1	907.0	–71.0	141.7
1993	1,953.3	2,339.3	–386.0	1,231.0	1,544.6	–313.5	878.0	950.4	–72.5	155.7
1994	2,097.6	2,417.2	–319.6	1,329.3	1,585.0	–255.6	935.1	999.1	–63.9	166.8
1995	2,223.9	2,536.5	–312.5	1,417.4	1,659.5	–242.1	981.0	1,051.4	–70.4	174.5
1996	2,388.6	2,621.8	–233.2	1,536.3	1,715.7	–179.4	1,033.7	1,087.5	–53.8	181.5
1997	2,565.9	2,699.9	–133.9	1,667.4	1,759.4	–92.0	1,086.7	1,128.7	–42.0	188.1
1998	2,738.6	2,767.4	–28.7	1,789.8	1,788.4	1.4	1,149.6	1,179.7	–30.1	200.8
1999	2,909.7	2,879.5	30.2	1,906.0	1,836.8	69.1	1,222.9	1,261.8	–38.9	219.2
2000	3,139.0	3,019.9	119.0	2,067.8	1,908.1	159.7	1,304.3	1,345.0	–40.6	233.1
2001	3,125.2	3,229.2	–104.0	2,032.4	2,017.3	15.0	1,354.1	1,473.1	–119.0	261.3
2002	2,969.1	3,419.8	–450.7	1,870.9	2,138.7	–267.8	1,386.9	1,569.8	–182.9	288.7
2003	3,045.4	3,624.0	–578.7	1,896.1	2,293.5	–397.4	1,470.9	1,652.2	–181.3	321.7
2004	3,275.0	3,817.4	–542.5	2,028.1	2,421.6	–393.5	1,579.2	1,728.2	–149.0	332.3
2005	3,678.7	4,075.3	–396.6	2,304.7	2,598.5	–293.8	1,717.5	1,820.3	–102.8	343.5
2006	4,013.1	4,320.1	–307.0	2,538.8	2,760.7	–221.9	1,815.3	1,900.4	–85.0	341.0
2007	4,210.6	4,599.6	–389.0	2,668.3	2,928.0	–259.7	1,901.4	2,030.7	–129.3	359.1
2008	4,126.2	4,972.0	–845.8	2,582.1	3,207.0	–624.9	1,915.3	2,136.2	–220.9	371.2
2009	3,699.5	5,284.0	–1,584.5	2,242.1	3,485.2	–1,243.2	1,915.5	2,256.9	–341.3	458.1
2010	3,934.1	5,560.0	–1,625.8	2,446.3	3,764.6	–1,318.4	1,993.1	2,300.6	–307.5	505.2
2011	4,130.3	5,639.5	–1,509.2	2,573.6	3,807.8	–1,234.1	2,029.1	2,304.2	–275.1	472.5
2012	4,311.6	5,667.1	–1,355.5	2,700.8	3,773.5	–1,072.7	2,055.2	2,338.1	–282.8	444.4
2013	4,834.3	5,731.4	–897.1	3,139.6	3,771.3	–631.8	2,144.9	2,410.2	–265.3	450.1
2014	5,054.4	5,889.7	–835.3	3,293.0	3,890.4	–597.4	2,256.4	2,494.4	–237.9	495.0
2015	5,288.5	6,064.5	–776.0	3,449.0	4,009.2	–560.2	2,372.6	2,588.4	–215.8	533.1
2016	5,336.1	6,248.4	–912.3	3,463.8	4,131.4	–667.6	2,429.1	2,673.8	–244.7	556.7
2017	5,467.5	6,429.3	–961.8	3,510.2	4,244.6	–734.4	2,517.7	2,745.2	–227.4	560.4
2018	5,654.1	6,758.8	–1,104.7	3,586.9	4,494.2	–907.3	2,649.8	2,847.2	–197.4	582.6
2019	5,888.9	7,134.5	–1,245.6	3,706.3	4,758.5	–1,052.2	2,791.6	2,985.0	–193.4	609.0
2020	5,950.9	8,894.9	–2,944.1	3,734.1	6,691.5	–2,957.4	3,095.6	3,082.3	13.3	878.9
2021	6,731.8	9,342.3	–2,610.5	4,319.0	7,154.4	–2,835.3	3,525.0	3,300.1	224.9	1,112.1
2022 p	....	8,651.5	....	....	6,020.7	....	....	3,573.5	....	942.8
2019: I	5,794.4	7,021.3	–1,226.8	3,665.7	4,693.9	–1,028.2	2,721.2	2,919.8	–198.7	592.4
II	5,904.5	7,110.3	–1,205.8	3,699.1	4,751.4	–1,052.3	2,820.9	2,974.4	–153.5	615.5
III	5,899.8	7,187.3	–1,287.5	3,699.7	4,787.3	–1,087.6	2,810.5	3,010.5	–199.9	610.4
IV	5,956.8	7,219.1	–1,262.3	3,760.5	4,801.5	–1,041.0	2,813.8	3,035.2	–221.4	617.5
2020: I	5,995.2	7,282.1	–1,286.9	3,785.7	4,875.9	–1,090.2	2,848.0	3,044.7	–196.7	638.6
II	5,619.2	10,566.8	–4,947.6	3,508.0	8,896.4	–5,388.5	3,506.2	3,065.3	440.9	1,395.0
III	5,999.3	9,490.9	–3,491.6	3,743.6	7,116.0	–3,372.5	2,992.8	3,112.0	–119.1	737.1
IV	6,189.8	8,240.0	–2,050.2	3,899.1	5,877.5	–1,978.4	3,035.4	3,107.2	–71.8	744.8
2021: I	6,388.6	10,582.2	–4,193.7	4,058.6	8,179.0	–4,120.3	3,115.0	3,188.4	–73.3	785.1
II	6,692.8	9,282.3	–2,589.4	4,266.9	7,649.6	–3,382.7	4,079.6	3,286.4	793.3	1,653.7
III	6,802.0	8,971.6	–2,169.7	4,394.8	6,709.2	–2,314.4	3,492.2	3,347.5	144.7	1,085.0
IV	7,044.0	8,533.1	–1,489.1	4,555.8	6,079.8	–1,524.0	3,413.0	3,378.1	34.9	924.7
2022: I	7,541.0	8,402.6	–861.6	4,962.6	5,891.6	–929.0	3,518.4	3,451.1	67.4	940.0
II	7,618.1	8,535.8	–917.8	5,055.3	5,935.2	–879.9	3,523.3	3,561.2	–37.9	960.5
III	7,611.6	8,707.3	–1,095.7	5,047.8	6,063.5	–1,015.7	3,517.2	3,597.2	–80.0	953.4
IV p	....	8,960.2	....	....	6,192.7	....	....	3,684.7	....	917.2

Note: Federal grants-in-aid to State and local governments are reflected in Federal current expenditures and State and local current receipts. Total government current receipts and expenditures have been adjusted to eliminate this duplication.

Source: Department of Commerce (Bureau of Economic Analysis).

Table B–50. State and local government revenues and expenditures, fiscal years 1957–2020

[Millions of dollars]

Fiscal year [1]	General revenues by source [2]							General expenditures by function [2]				
	Total	Property taxes	Sales and gross receipts taxes	Individual income taxes	Corporation net income taxes	Revenue from Federal Government	All other [3]	Total [4]	Education	Highways	Public welfare [4]	All other [4, 5]
1957	38,164	12,864	9,467	1,754	984	3,843	9,252	40,375	14,134	7,816	3,485	14,940
1958	41,219	14,047	9,829	1,759	1,018	4,865	9,701	44,851	15,919	8,567	3,818	16,547
1959	45,306	14,983	10,437	1,994	1,001	6,377	10,514	48,887	17,283	9,592	4,136	17,876
1960	50,505	16,405	11,849	2,463	1,180	6,974	11,634	51,876	18,719	9,428	4,404	19,325
1961	54,037	18,002	12,463	2,613	1,266	7,131	12,562	56,201	20,574	9,844	4,720	21,063
1962	58,252	19,054	13,494	3,037	1,308	7,871	13,488	60,206	22,216	10,357	5,084	22,549
1963	62,891	20,089	14,456	3,269	1,505	8,722	14,850	64,815	23,776	11,135	5,481	24,423
1963–64	68,443	21,241	15,762	3,791	1,695	10,002	15,952	69,302	26,286	11,664	5,766	25,586
1964–65	74,000	22,583	17,118	4,090	1,929	11,029	17,251	74,678	28,563	12,221	6,315	27,579
1965–66	83,036	24,670	19,085	4,760	2,038	13,214	19,269	82,843	33,287	12,770	6,757	30,029
1966–67	91,197	26,047	20,530	5,825	2,227	15,370	21,198	93,350	37,919	13,932	8,218	33,281
1967–68	101,264	27,747	22,911	7,308	2,518	17,181	23,599	102,411	41,158	14,481	9,857	36,915
1968–69	114,550	30,673	26,519	8,908	3,180	19,153	26,117	116,728	47,238	15,417	12,110	41,963
1969–70	130,756	34,054	30,322	10,812	3,738	21,857	29,973	131,332	52,718	16,427	14,679	47,508
1970–71	144,927	37,852	33,233	11,900	3,424	26,146	32,372	150,674	59,413	18,095	18,226	54,940
1971–72	167,535	42,877	37,518	15,227	4,416	31,342	36,156	168,549	65,813	19,021	21,117	62,598
1972–73	190,222	45,283	42,047	17,994	5,425	39,264	40,210	181,357	69,713	18,615	23,582	69,447
1973–74	207,670	47,705	46,098	19,491	6,015	41,820	46,542	199,222	75,833	19,946	25,085	78,358
1974–75	228,171	51,491	49,815	21,454	6,642	47,034	51,735	230,722	87,858	22,528	28,156	92,180
1975–76	256,176	57,001	54,547	24,575	7,273	55,589	57,191	256,731	97,216	23,907	32,604	103,004
1976–77	285,157	62,527	60,641	29,246	9,174	62,444	61,125	274,215	102,780	23,058	35,906	112,472
1977–78	315,960	66,422	67,596	33,176	10,738	69,592	68,435	296,984	110,758	24,609	39,140	122,478
1978–79	343,236	64,944	74,247	36,932	12,128	75,164	79,822	327,517	119,448	28,440	41,898	137,731
1979–80	382,322	68,499	79,927	42,080	13,321	83,029	95,467	369,086	133,211	33,311	47,288	155,276
1980–81	423,404	74,969	85,971	46,426	14,143	90,294	111,599	407,449	145,784	34,603	54,105	172,957
1981–82	457,654	82,067	93,613	50,738	15,028	87,282	128,925	436,733	154,282	34,520	57,996	189,935
1982–83	486,753	89,105	100,247	55,129	14,258	90,007	138,008	466,516	163,876	36,655	60,906	205,080
1983–84	542,730	96,457	114,097	64,871	16,798	96,935	153,571	505,008	176,108	39,419	66,414	223,068
1984–85	598,121	103,757	126,376	70,361	19,152	106,158	172,317	553,899	192,686	44,989	71,479	244,745
1985–86	641,486	111,709	135,005	74,365	19,994	113,099	187,314	605,623	210,819	49,368	75,868	269,568
1986–87	686,860	121,203	144,091	83,935	22,425	114,857	200,350	657,134	226,619	52,355	82,650	295,510
1987–88	726,762	132,212	156,452	88,350	23,663	117,602	208,482	704,921	242,683	55,621	89,090	317,527
1988–89	786,129	142,400	166,336	97,806	25,926	125,824	227,838	762,360	263,898	58,105	97,879	342,479
1989–90	849,502	155,613	177,885	105,640	23,566	136,802	249,996	834,818	288,148	61,057	110,518	375,094
1990–91	902,207	167,999	185,570	109,341	22,242	154,099	262,955	908,108	309,302	64,937	130,402	403,467
1991–92	979,137	180,337	197,731	115,638	23,880	179,174	282,376	981,253	324,652	67,351	158,723	430,526
1992–93	1,041,643	189,744	209,649	123,235	26,417	198,663	293,935	1,030,434	342,287	68,370	170,705	449,072
1993–94	1,100,490	197,141	223,628	128,810	28,320	215,492	307,099	1,077,665	353,287	72,067	183,394	468,916
1994–95	1,169,505	203,451	237,268	137,931	31,406	228,771	330,677	1,149,863	378,273	77,109	196,703	497,779
1995–96	1,222,821	209,440	248,993	146,844	32,009	234,891	350,645	1,193,276	398,859	79,092	197,354	517,971
1996–97	1,289,237	218,877	261,418	159,042	33,820	244,847	371,233	1,249,984	418,416	82,062	203,779	545,727
1997–98	1,365,762	230,150	274,883	175,630	34,412	255,048	395,639	1,318,042	450,365	87,214	208,120	572,343
1998–99	1,434,029	239,672	290,993	189,309	33,922	270,628	409,505	1,402,369	483,259	93,018	218,957	607,134
1999–2000	1,541,322	249,178	309,290	211,661	36,059	291,950	443,186	1,506,797	521,612	101,336	237,336	646,512
2000–01	1,647,161	263,689	320,217	226,334	35,296	324,033	477,592	1,626,063	563,572	107,235	261,622	693,634
2001–02	1,684,879	279,191	324,123	202,832	28,152	360,546	490,035	1,736,866	594,694	115,295	285,464	741,413
2002–03	1,763,212	296,683	337,787	199,407	31,369	389,264	508,702	1,821,917	621,335	117,696	310,783	772,102
2003–04	1,887,397	317,941	361,027	215,215	33,716	423,112	536,386	1,908,543	655,182	117,215	340,523	795,622
2004–05	2,026,034	335,779	384,266	242,273	43,256	438,558	581,902	2,012,110	688,314	126,350	365,295	832,151
2005–06	2,197,475	364,559	417,735	268,667	53,081	452,975	640,458	2,123,663	728,917	136,502	373,846	884,398
2006–07	2,330,611	388,905	440,470	290,278	60,955	464,914	685,089	2,264,035	774,170	145,011	389,259	955,595
2007–08	2,421,977	409,540	449,945	304,902	57,231	477,441	722,919	2,406,183	826,061	153,831	408,920	1,017,372
2008–09	2,429,672	434,818	434,128	270,942	46,280	537,949	705,555	2,500,796	851,689	154,338	437,184	1,057,586
2009–10	2,510,846	443,947	435,571	261,510	44,108	623,801	701,909	2,542,231	860,118	155,912	460,230	1,065,971
2010–11	2,618,037	445,771	463,979	285,293	48,422	647,606	726,966	2,583,805	862,271	153,895	494,682	1,072,957
2011–12	2,598,745	445,854	482,172	307,897	48,877	580,604	733,341	2,595,947	870,321	159,498	491,158	1,074,971
2012–13	2,687,495	453,458	503,553	339,666	52,853	583,294	754,672	2,631,945	878,957	160,260	518,035	1,074,693
2013–14	2,768,260	465,100	522,014	343,001	54,558	602,175	781,412	2,723,022	906,016	165,051	547,889	1,104,066
2014–15	2,920,320	484,251	544,359	368,862	57,130	658,012	807,707	2,844,289	934,353	171,084	616,515	1,122,338
2015–16	3,018,372	504,593	559,625	375,310	53,581	693,989	831,274	2,964,238	973,025	177,982	655,532	1,157,699
2016–17	3,119,990	525,233	581,191	384,759	52,806	710,814	865,187	3,077,267	1,014,085	181,262	680,469	1,201,451
2017–18	3,299,409	547,512	617,820	429,849	56,881	740,369	906,978	3,207,278	1,046,754	194,652	710,321	1,255,552
2018–19	3,466,370	577,612	643,722	446,723	67,885	761,438	968,990	3,351,553	1,092,416	202,562	748,867	1,307,708
2019–20	3,624,460	599,990	650,980	424,769	60,620	911,218	976,884	3,497,281	1,131,609	204,258	794,182	1,367,232

[1] Fiscal years not the same for all governments. See Note.

[2] Excludes revenues or expenditures of publicly owned utilities and liquor stores and of insurance-trust activities. Intergovernmental receipts and payments between State and local governments are also excluded.

[3] Includes motor vehicle license taxes, other taxes, and charges and miscellaneous revenues.

[4] Includes intergovernmental payments to the Federal Government.

[5] Includes expenditures for libraries, hospitals, health, employment security administration, veterans' services, air transportation, sea and inland port facilities, parking facilities, police protection, fire protection, correction, protective inspection and regulation, sewerage, natural resources, parks and recreation, housing and community development, solid waste management, financial administration, judicial and legal, general public buildings, other government administration, interest on general debt, and other general expenditures, not elsewhere classified.

Note: Except for States listed, data for fiscal years listed from 1963–64 to 2019–20 are the aggregation of data for government fiscal years that ended in the 12-month period from July 1 to June 30 of those years; Texas used August and Alabama and Michigan used September as end dates. Data for 1963 and earlier years include data for government fiscal years ending during that particular calendar year.

Source: Department of Commerce (Bureau of the Census).

Table B–51. U.S. Treasury securities outstanding by kind of obligation, 1982–2022

[Billions of dollars]

End of fiscal year or month	Total Treasury securities outstanding[1]	Marketable							Nonmarketable				
		Total[2]	Treasury bills	Treasury notes	Treasury bonds	Treasury inflation-protected securities			Total	U.S. savings securities[3]	Foreign series[4]	Government account series	Other[5]
						Total	Notes	Bonds					
1982	1,141.2	824.4	277.9	442.9	103.6	....	....	....	316.8	67.6	14.6	210.5	24.1
1983	1,376.3	1,024.0	340.7	557.5	125.7	....	....	....	352.3	70.6	11.5	234.7	35.6
1984	1,560.4	1,176.6	356.8	661.7	158.1	....	....	....	383.8	73.7	8.8	259.5	41.8
1985	1,822.3	1,360.2	384.2	776.4	199.5	....	....	....	462.1	78.2	6.6	313.9	63.3
1986	2,124.9	1,564.3	410.7	896.9	241.7	....	....	....	560.5	87.8	4.1	365.9	102.8
1987	2,349.4	1,676.0	378.3	1,005.1	277.6	....	....	....	673.4	98.5	4.4	440.7	129.8
1988	2,601.4	1,802.9	398.5	1,089.6	299.9	....	....	....	798.5	107.8	6.3	536.5	148.0
1989	2,837.9	1,892.8	406.6	1,133.2	338.0	....	....	....	945.2	115.7	6.8	663.7	159.0
1990	3,212.7	2,092.8	482.5	1,218.1	377.2	....	....	....	1,119.9	123.9	36.0	779.4	180.6
1991	3,664.5	2,390.7	564.6	1,387.7	423.4	....	....	....	1,273.9	135.4	41.6	908.4	188.5
1992	4,063.8	2,677.5	634.3	1,566.3	461.8	....	....	....	1,386.3	150.3	37.0	1,011.0	188.0
1993	4,410.7	2,904.9	658.4	1,734.2	497.4	....	....	....	1,505.8	169.1	42.5	1,114.3	179.9
1994	4,691.7	3,091.6	697.3	1,867.5	511.8	....	....	....	1,600.1	178.6	42.0	1,211.7	167.8
1995	4,953.0	3,260.4	742.5	1,980.3	522.6	....	....	....	1,692.6	183.5	41.0	1,324.3	143.8
1996	5,220.8	3,418.4	761.2	2,098.7	543.5	....	....	....	1,802.4	184.1	37.5	1,454.7	126.1
1997	5,407.6	3,439.6	701.9	2,122.2	576.2	24.4	24.4	....	1,968.0	182.7	34.9	1,608.5	141.9
1998	5,518.7	3,331.0	637.6	2,009.1	610.4	58.8	41.9	17.0	2,187.6	180.8	35.1	1,777.3	194.4
1999	5,647.3	3,233.0	653.2	1,828.8	643.7	92.4	67.6	24.8	2,414.3	180.0	31.0	2,005.2	198.1
2000	5,622.1	2,992.8	616.2	1,611.3	635.3	115.0	81.6	33.4	2,629.4	177.7	25.4	2,242.9	183.3
2001[1]	5,807.5	2,930.7	734.9	1,433.0	613.0	134.9	95.1	39.7	2,876.7	186.5	18.3	2,492.1	179.9
2002	6,228.2	3,136.7	868.3	1,521.6	593.0	138.9	93.7	45.1	3,091.5	193.3	12.5	2,707.3	178.4
2003	6,783.2	3,460.7	918.2	1,799.5	576.9	166.1	120.0	46.1	3,322.5	201.6	11.0	2,912.2	197.7
2004	7,379.1	3,846.1	961.5	2,109.6	552.0	223.0	164.5	58.5	3,533.0	204.2	5.9	3,130.0	192.9
2005	7,932.7	4,084.9	914.3	2,328.8	520.7	307.1	229.1	78.0	3,847.8	203.6	3.1	3,380.6	260.5
2006	8,507.0	4,303.0	911.5	2,447.2	534.7	395.6	293.9	101.7	4,203.9	203.7	3.0	3,722.7	274.5
2007	9,007.7	4,448.1	958.1	2,458.0	561.1	456.9	335.7	121.2	4,559.5	197.1	3.0	4,026.8	332.6
2008	10,024.7	5,236.0	1,489.8	2,624.8	582.9	524.5	380.2	144.3	4,788.7	194.3	3.0	4,297.7	293.8
2009	11,909.8	7,009.7	1,992.5	3,773.8	679.8	551.7	396.2	155.5	4,900.1	192.5	4.9	4,454.3	248.4
2010	13,561.6	8,498.3	1,788.5	5,255.9	849.9	593.8	421.1	172.7	5,063.3	188.7	4.2	4,645.3	225.1
2011	14,790.3	9,624.5	1,477.5	6,412.5	1,020.4	705.7	509.4	196.3	5,165.8	185.1	3.0	4,793.9	183.8
2012	16,066.2	10,749.7	1,616.0	7,120.7	1,198.2	807.7	584.7	223.0	5,316.5	183.8	3.0	4,939.3	190.4
2013	16,738.2	11,596.2	1,530.0	7,758.0	1,366.2	936.4	685.5	250.8	5,142.0	180.0	3.0	4,803.1	156.0
2014	17,824.1	12,294.2	1,411.0	8,167.8	1,534.1	1,044.7	765.2	279.5	5,529.9	176.7	3.0	5,212.5	137.7
2015	18,150.6	12,853.8	1,358.0	8,372.7	1,688.3	1,135.4	832.1	303.3	5,296.9	172.8	.3	5,013.5	110.3
2016	19,573.4	13,660.6	1,647.0	8,631.0	1,825.5	1,210.0	881.6	328.3	5,912.8	167.5	.3	5,604.1	141.0
2017	20,244.9	14,199.8	1,801.9	8,805.5	1,951.7	1,286.5	933.3	353.2	6,045.1	161.7	.3	5,771.1	112.0
2018	21,516.1	15,278.0	2,239.9	9,154.4	2,127.8	1,376.4	993.4	383.0	6,238.0	156.8	.3	5,977.6	103.4
2019	22,719.4	16,347.3	2,377.0	9,762.8	2,319.1	1,455.7	1,044.9	410.8	6,372.1	152.3	.3	6,133.7	85.8
2020	26,945.4	20,374.9	5,028.9	10,663.8	2,673.5	1,523.2	1,092.7	430.5	6,570.5	148.6	.3	6,196.3	225.3
2021	28,428.9	21,878.7	3,714.1	12,578.9	3,347.6	1,652.7	1,180.2	472.5	6,550.2	143.6	.3	6,243.3	163.0
2022	30,928.9	23,694.1	3,644.6	13,703.8	3,874.4	1,840.5	1,306.8	533.7	7,234.8	166.2	.3	6,929.8	138.5
2021: Jan	27,784.6	21,049.0	4,955.0	11,172.8	2,865.7	1,549.8	1,117.3	432.5	6,735.6	146.6	.3	6,418.2	170.5
Feb	27,902.4	21,158.6	4,859.0	11,312.3	2,919.7	1,560.0	1,118.2	441.9	6,743.8	146.3	.3	6,424.3	173.1
Mar	28,132.6	21,388.1	4,669.0	11,597.2	3,006.3	1,582.0	1,138.3	443.7	6,744.5	145.7	.3	6,420.9	177.6
Apr	28,174.7	21,456.9	4,540.1	11,783.3	3,062.6	1,562.2	1,116.1	446.1	6,717.9	145.2	.3	6,392.6	179.7
May	28,199.4	21,421.7	4,377.1	11,830.4	3,093.8	1,585.7	1,136.6	449.0	6,777.7	144.9	.3	6,451.1	181.4
June	28,529.4	21,739.0	4,275.1	12,106.4	3,179.9	1,618.1	1,165.2	452.9	6,790.4	144.6	.3	6,475.1	170.4
July	28,428.1	21,699.0	4,142.1	12,185.0	3,207.9	1,604.4	1,147.8	456.6	6,729.2	144.3	.3	6,401.5	183.1
Aug	28,427.3	21,932.2	4,038.1	12,411.9	3,294.1	1,628.6	1,158.5	470.2	6,495.1	144.0	.3	6,173.7	177.2
Sept	28,428.9	21,878.7	3,714.1	12,578.9	3,347.6	1,652.7	1,180.2	472.5	6,550.2	143.6	.3	6,243.3	163.0
Oct	28,908.9	22,132.2	3,852.1	12,646.2	3,373.4	1,675.1	1,201.7	473.5	6,776.7	143.5	.3	6,476.6	156.3
Nov	28,908.0	22,351.6	3,786.1	12,854.6	3,433.5	1,695.3	1,220.5	474.8	6,556.4	144.1	.3	6,266.3	145.7
Dec	29,617.2	22,590.1	3,770.1	13,000.5	3,481.5	1,728.6	1,249.9	478.7	7,027.1	146.2	.3	6,739.1	141.6
2022: Jan	30,012.4	22,918.9	3,961.1	13,141.6	3,530.0	1,705.0	1,224.0	481.1	7,093.5	148.8	.3	6,804.3	140.2
Feb	30,290.4	23,196.0	4,055.0	13,227.6	3,589.2	1,720.9	1,227.8	493.1	7,094.4	149.3	.3	6,800.3	144.5
Mar	30,401.0	23,286.1	3,929.0	13,348.5	3,631.5	1,751.9	1,254.8	497.2	7,114.8	149.7	.3	6,814.7	150.2
Apr	30,374.7	23,255.1	3,827.9	13,409.5	3,656.3	1,736.2	1,234.4	501.7	7,119.5	153.1	.3	6,815.3	150.9
May	30,499.6	23,307.2	3,672.9	13,516.3	3,731.4	1,775.8	1,267.5	508.3	7,192.5	157.7	.3	6,891.3	143.3
June	30,568.6	23,311.6	3,523.9	13,583.6	3,766.6	1,806.0	1,294.7	511.3	7,257.0	160.4	.3	6,959.1	137.3
July	30,595.7	23,355.4	3,514.9	13,631.0	3,788.0	1,790.0	1,273.3	516.7	7,240.4	162.5	.3	6,944.6	133.0
Aug	30,936.1	23,675.0	3,725.0	13,672.1	3,844.4	1,824.7	1,291.1	533.5	7,261.1	164.3	.3	6,968.3	128.2
Sept	30,928.9	23,694.1	3,644.6	13,703.8	3,874.4	1,840.5	1,306.8	533.7	7,234.8	166.2	.3	6,929.8	138.5
Oct	31,238.3	23,743.5	3,666.0	13,734.2	3,904.3	1,860.9	1,327.4	533.5	7,494.8	172.5	.3	7,188.2	133.9
Nov	31,413.3	23,953.5	3,811.9	13,717.9	3,941.9	1,881.7	1,347.1	534.6	7,459.8	173.2	.3	7,157.4	129.0
Dec	31,419.9	23,939.5	3,697.4	13,751.9	3,959.9	1,908.3	1,371.6	536.8	7,480.4	173.5	.3	7,179.3	127.3

[1] Data beginning with January 2001 are interest-bearing and non-interest-bearing securities; prior data are interest-bearing securities only.

[2] Data from 1986 to 2002 and 2005 forward include Federal Financing Bank securities, not shown separately. Beginning with data for January 2014, includes Floating Rate Notes, not shown separately.

[3] Through 1996, series is U.S. savings bonds. Beginning 1997, includes U.S. retirement plan bonds, U.S. individual retirement bonds, and U.S. savings notes previously included in "other" nonmarketable securities.

[4] Nonmarketable certificates of indebtedness, notes, bonds, and bills in the Treasury foreign series of dollar-denominated and foreign-currency-denominated issues.

[5] Includes depository bonds; retirement plan bonds through 1996; Rural Electrification Administration bonds; State and local bonds; special issues held only by U.S. Government agencies and trust funds and the Federal home loan banks; for the period July 2003 through February 2004, depositary compensation securities; and for the period August 2008 through April 2016, Hope bonds for the HOPE For Homeowners Program.

Note: The fiscal year is on an October 1–September 30 basis.

Source: Department of the Treasury.

Table B–52. Estimated ownership of U.S. Treasury securities, 2008–2022

[Billions of dollars]

End of month	Total public debt[1]	Federal Reserve and Intra-governmental holdings[2]	Held by private investors: Total privately held	Depository institutions[3]	U.S. savings bonds[4]	Pension funds: Private[5]	Pension funds: State and local governments	Insurance companies	Mutual funds[6]	State and local governments	Foreign and international[7]	Other investors[8]
2008: Mar	9,437.6	4,694.7	4,742.9	125.0	195.4	143.7	135.4	152.1	466.7	646.4	2,506.3	371.9
June	9,492.0	4,685.8	4,806.2	112.7	195.0	145.0	135.5	159.4	440.3	635.1	2,587.4	395.9
Sept	10,024.7	4,692.7	5,332.0	130.0	194.3	147.0	136.7	163.4	631.4	614.0	2,802.4	512.9
Dec	10,699.8	4,806.4	5,893.4	105.0	194.1	147.4	129.9	171.4	758.2	601.4	3,077.2	708.9
2009: Mar	11,126.9	4,785.2	6,341.7	125.7	194.0	155.4	137.0	191.0	721.1	588.2	3,265.7	963.7
June	11,545.3	5,026.8	6,518.5	140.8	193.6	164.1	144.6	200.0	711.8	588.5	3,460.8	914.2
Sept	11,909.8	5,127.1	6,782.7	198.2	192.5	167.2	145.6	210.2	668.5	583.6	3,570.6	1,046.3
Dec	12,311.3	5,276.9	7,034.4	202.5	191.3	175.6	151.4	222.0	668.8	585.6	3,685.1	1,152.1
2010: Mar	12,773.1	5,259.8	7,513.3	269.3	190.2	183.0	153.6	225.7	678.5	585.0	3,877.9	1,350.1
June	13,201.8	5,345.1	7,856.7	266.1	189.6	190.8	150.1	231.8	676.8	584.4	4,070.0	1,497.1
Sept	13,561.6	5,350.5	8,211.1	322.8	188.7	198.2	145.2	240.6	671.0	586.0	4,324.2	1,534.4
Dec	14,025.2	5,656.2	8,368.9	319.3	187.9	206.8	153.7	248.4	721.7	595.7	4,435.6	1,499.9
2011: Mar	14,270.0	5,958.9	8,311.1	321.0	186.7	215.8	157.9	253.5	749.4	585.3	4,481.4	1,360.1
June	14,343.1	6,220.4	8,122.7	279.4	186.0	251.8	158.0	254.8	753.7	572.2	4,690.6	976.1
Sept	14,790.3	6,328.0	8,462.4	293.8	185.1	373.6	155.7	259.6	788.7	557.9	4,912.1	935.8
Dec	15,222.8	6,439.6	8,783.3	279.7	185.2	391.9	160.7	297.3	927.9	562.2	5,006.9	971.4
2012: Mar	15,582.3	6,397.2	9,185.1	317.0	184.8	406.6	169.4	298.1	1,015.4	567.4	5,145.1	1,081.2
June	15,855.5	6,475.8	9,379.7	303.2	184.7	427.4	171.2	293.6	997.8	585.4	5,310.9	1,105.4
Sept	16,066.2	6,446.8	9,619.4	338.2	183.8	453.9	181.7	292.6	1,080.7	596.9	5,476.1	1,015.4
Dec	16,432.7	6,523.7	9,909.1	347.7	182.5	468.0	183.6	292.7	1,031.8	599.6	5,573.8	1,229.4
2013: Mar	16,771.6	6,656.8	10,114.8	338.9	181.7	463.4	193.4	284.3	1,066.7	615.6	5,725.0	1,245.7
June	16,738.2	6,773.3	9,964.9	300.2	180.9	444.5	187.7	281.3	1,000.1	612.6	5,595.0	1,362.6
Sept	16,738.2	6,834.2	9,904.0	293.2	180.0	347.8	187.5	276.6	986.1	624.3	5,652.8	1,355.7
Dec	17,352.0	7,205.3	10,146.6	321.1	179.2	464.9	181.3	274.5	983.3	633.6	5,792.6	1,316.2
2014: Mar	17,601.2	7,301.5	10,299.7	368.4	178.3	474.3	184.3	280.1	1,060.4	632.0	5,948.3	1,173.7
June	17,632.6	7,461.0	10,171.6	409.5	177.6	482.6	198.3	291.0	986.2	638.8	6,018.7	968.8
Sept	17,824.1	7,490.8	10,333.2	471.1	176.7	490.7	198.7	301.4	1,075.8	628.7	6,069.2	920.8
Dec	18,141.4	7,578.9	10,562.6	516.8	175.9	507.1	199.2	310.5	1,121.8	654.5	6,157.7	919.0
2015: Mar	18,152.1	7,521.3	10,630.8	518.1	174.9	447.8	176.7	308.5	1,170.4	663.3	6,172.6	998.4
June	18,152.0	7,536.5	10,615.5	518.5	173.9	373.8	185.7	307.7	1,139.8	652.8	6,163.1	1,100.1
Sept	18,150.6	7,488.7	10,661.9	519.1	172.8	305.3	171.0	310.0	1,195.1	646.0	6,105.9	1,236.8
Dec	18,922.2	7,711.2	11,211.0	547.4	171.6	504.7	174.5	310.1	1,318.3	680.9	6,146.2	1,357.1
2016: Mar	19,264.9	7,801.4	11,463.6	562.9	170.3	524.4	170.4	319.1	1,404.1	694.9	6,284.4	1,333.0
June	19,381.6	7,911.2	11,470.4	580.6	169.0	537.9	185.0	333.7	1,434.2	712.6	6,279.1	1,238.3
Sept	19,573.4	7,863.5	11,709.9	626.8	167.5	545.6	203.8	345.2	1,600.4	710.9	6,155.9	1,353.8
Dec	19,976.9	8,005.6	11,971.3	663.1	165.8	538.0	218.8	334.2	1,705.4	717.3	6,006.3	1,622.4
2017: Mar	19,846.4	7,941.1	11,905.3	657.4	164.2	444.2	239.5	342.6	1,715.2	724.6	6,075.3	1,542.3
June	19,844.6	7,943.4	11,901.1	620.5	162.8	425.9	262.8	352.8	1,645.8	710.1	6,151.9	1,568.5
Sept	20,244.9	8,036.9	12,208.0	610.5	161.7	570.8	266.5	364.3	1,739.6	704.0	6,301.9	1,488.7
Dec	20,492.7	8,132.1	12,360.6	636.7	160.4	432.1	289.4	377.9	1,850.8	735.0	6,211.3	1,667.1
2018: Mar	21,089.9	8,086.6	13,003.3	637.8	159.0	589.7	300.1	366.9	2,048.2	715.8	6,223.4	1,962.5
June	21,195.3	8,106.9	13,088.5	663.1	157.8	605.0	307.3	360.2	1,902.9	726.8	6,225.0	2,140.4
Sept	21,516.1	8,068.1	13,447.9	682.0	156.8	615.3	301.7	361.3	1,957.2	730.7	6,225.9	2,417.0
Dec	21,974.1	8,095.0	13,879.1	769.7	155.7	637.3	367.9	360.5	2,094.9	713.2	6,270.1	2,509.9
2019: Mar	22,028.0	7,999.1	14,028.9	769.5	154.5	443.6	357.6	361.1	2,189.2	752.7	6,474.0	2,526.7
June	22,023.5	7,945.2	14,078.4	808.2	153.4	470.4	382.0	363.6	2,037.0	751.4	6,625.9	2,486.5
Sept	22,719.4	8,023.6	14,695.8	909.4	152.3	691.1	343.5	366.8	2,319.7	766.8	6,923.5	2,222.6
Dec	23,201.4	8,359.9	14,841.5	935.1	151.3	705.3	329.3	368.7	2,412.8	793.1	6,844.2	2,301.7
2020: Mar	23,686.9	9,279.7	14,407.2	947.6	150.0	759.3	325.3	396.8	2,501.7	862.1	6,949.5	1,514.9
June	26,477.4	10,157.7	16,319.6	1,157.9	149.8	767.7	284.7	403.2	3,696.0	1,034.8	7,052.1	1,773.5
Sept	26,945.4	10,371.9	16,573.5	1,241.1	148.6	773.8	309.9	414.3	3,725.3	1,059.7	7,069.2	1,831.6
Dec	27,747.8	10,809.2	16,938.6	1,265.2	147.1	772.2	346.8	398.2	3,784.8	1,111.9	7,070.7	2,041.7
2021: Mar	28,132.6	11,095.5	17,037.1	1,347.9	145.7	750.6	344.8	391.9	3,951.6	1,099.6	7,038.3	1,966.6
June	28,529.4	11,382.9	17,146.5	1,433.1	144.6	769.1	395.9	421.2	3,778.7	1,313.7	7,518.9	1,371.3
Sept	28,428.9	11,579.1	16,849.8	1,540.3	143.6	594.0	406.3	423.8	3,237.3	1,394.2	7,570.9	1,539.3
Dec	29,617.2	12,125.9	17,491.3	1,733.9	146.2	771.7	430.9	419.3	3,410.0	1,440.7	7,740.5	1,398.1
2022: Mar	30,401.0	12,281.3	18,119.7	1,754.1	149.7	775.8	380.0	374.9	3,283.6	1,420.0	7,604.4	2,377.3
June	30,568.6	12,399.7	18,168.9	1,807.6	160.4	767.8	378.7	368.2	2,885.8	1,555.5	7,416.1	2,828.8
Sept	30,928.9	12,264.7	18,664.2	1,740.1	166.2	749.6	366.3	371.6	2,605.8	1,537.4	7,251.5	3,875.7
Dec	31,419.9	12,401.4	19,018.5	....	173.5	....	....	....	....	....	7,314.6	....

[1] Face value.
[2] Federal Reserve holdings exclude Treasury securities held under repurchase agreements.
[3] Includes U.S. chartered depository institutions, foreign banking offices in U.S., banks in U.S. affiliated areas, credit unions, and bank holding companies.
[4] Current accrual value includes myRA.
[5] Includes Treasury securities held by the Federal Employees Retirement System Thrift Savings Plan "G Fund."
[6] Includes money market mutual funds, mutual funds, and closed-end investment companies.
[7] Includes nonmarketable foreign series, Treasury securities, and Treasury deposit funds. Excludes Treasury securities held under repurchase agreements in custody accounts at the Federal Reserve Bank of New York. Estimates reflect benchmarks to this series at differing intervals; for further detail, see *Treasury Bulletin* and http://www.treasury.gov/resource-center/data-chart-center/tic/pages/index.aspx.
[8] Includes individuals, Government-sponsored enterprises, brokers and dealers, bank personal trusts and estates, corporate and noncorporate businesses, and other investors.

Source: Department of the Treasury.

Corporate Profits and Finance

Table B–53. Corporate profits with inventory valuation and capital consumption adjustments, 1972–2022

[Billions of dollars; quarterly data at seasonally adjusted annual rates]

Year or quarter	Corporate profits with inventory valuation and capital consumption adjustments	Taxes on corporate income	Corporate profits after tax with inventory valuation and capital consumption adjustments		
			Total	Net dividends	Undistributed profits with inventory valuation and capital consumption adjustments
1972	117.2	39.1	78.1	30.1	48.0
1973	133.4	45.6	87.8	34.2	53.5
1974	125.7	47.2	78.5	38.8	39.7
1975	138.9	46.3	92.6	38.3	54.3
1976	174.3	59.4	114.9	44.9	70.0
1977	205.8	68.5	137.3	50.7	86.6
1978	238.6	77.9	160.7	57.8	102.9
1979	249.0	80.7	168.2	66.8	101.4
1980	223.6	75.5	148.1	75.8	72.3
1981	247.5	70.3	177.2	87.8	89.4
1982	229.9	51.3	178.6	92.9	85.6
1983	279.8	66.4	213.3	97.7	115.7
1984	337.9	81.5	256.4	106.9	149.5
1985	354.5	81.6	272.9	115.3	157.5
1986	324.4	91.9	232.5	124.0	108.5
1987	366.0	112.7	253.3	130.1	123.2
1988	414.5	124.3	290.2	147.3	142.9
1989	414.3	124.4	289.9	179.6	110.3
1990	417.7	121.8	295.9	192.7	103.2
1991	452.6	117.8	334.8	201.3	133.5
1992	477.2	131.9	345.3	206.3	139.0
1993	524.6	155.0	369.5	221.3	148.2
1994	624.8	172.7	452.1	256.4	195.7
1995	706.2	194.4	511.8	282.3	229.4
1996	789.5	211.4	578.1	323.6	254.5
1997	869.7	224.8	645.0	360.1	284.9
1998	808.5	221.8	586.6	383.6	203.0
1999	834.9	227.4	607.5	373.5	234.0
2000	786.6	233.4	553.1	410.2	142.9
2001	758.7	170.1	588.6	397.9	190.7
2002	911.7	160.7	751.0	424.9	326.2
2003	1,056.3	213.8	842.5	456.0	386.5
2004	1,289.3	278.5	1,010.8	582.2	428.6
2005	1,488.6	379.7	1,108.9	602.0	506.9
2006	1,646.3	430.1	1,216.1	755.1	461.1
2007	1,533.2	391.8	1,141.4	853.5	287.9
2008	1,285.8	255.9	1,029.9	840.3	189.6
2009	1,386.8	203.9	1,182.9	622.1	560.8
2010	1,728.7	272.3	1,456.5	643.2	813.3
2011	1,809.8	280.8	1,529.0	779.1	749.9
2012	1,997.4	334.6	1,662.8	948.7	714.1
2013	2,010.7	362.6	1,648.1	1,009.0	639.1
2014	2,120.2	407.1	1,713.1	1,096.1	617.1
2015	2,060.5	396.3	1,664.2	1,164.9	499.3
2016	2,037.7	376.2	1,661.5	1,189.4	472.1
2017	2,128.6	297.3	1,831.2	1,264.1	567.1
2018	2,311.9	297.7	2,014.3	1,338.4	675.9
2019	2,402.2	297.4	2,104.7	1,531.2	573.5
2020	2,260.1	288.9	1,971.2	1,541.3	429.9
2021	2,771.1	388.2	2,382.8	1,659.3	723.6
2022[p]	....	....	....	1,704.9	....
2019: I	2,341.3	290.3	2,051.0	1,470.9	580.1
II	2,419.3	304.0	2,115.3	1,539.4	575.9
III	2,413.7	283.7	2,130.0	1,553.0	577.0
IV	2,434.3	311.7	2,122.7	1,561.6	561.1
2020: I	2,230.0	264.1	1,965.9	1,566.0	399.9
II	2,001.5	255.5	1,746.1	1,527.2	218.9
III	2,466.3	312.0	2,154.3	1,508.1	646.2
IV	2,342.6	324.2	2,018.5	1,564.0	454.5
2021: I	2,588.2	350.8	2,237.4	1,567.5	669.8
II	2,786.8	385.1	2,401.7	1,645.6	756.0
III	2,843.5	387.1	2,456.4	1,693.8	762.6
IV	2,865.9	430.0	2,435.9	1,730.2	705.7
2022: I	2,869.6	495.1	2,374.6	1,743.6	631.0
II	3,001.3	478.7	2,522.6	1,740.4	782.2
III	3,000.0	457.0	2,543.0	1,683.9	859.0
IV[p]	....	....	....	1,651.7	....

Source: Department of Commerce (Bureau of Economic Analysis).

Table B–54. Corporate profits by industry, 1972–2022

[Billions of dollars; quarterly data at seasonally adjusted annual rates]

Year or quarter	Corporate profits with inventory valuation adjustment and without capital consumption adjustment													
	Total	Domestic industries												Rest of the world
		Total	Financial			Nonfinancial								
			Total	Federal Reserve banks	Other	Total	Manufacturing	Transportation[1]	Utilities	Wholesale trade	Retail trade	Information	Other	
SIC:[2]														
1972	109.3	99.7	19.5	3.3	16.1	80.3	47.6	10.4	....	7.2	7.5	....	7.6	9.5
1973	126.6	111.7	21.1	4.5	16.6	90.6	55.0	10.2	....	8.8	7.0	....	9.6	14.9
1974	123.3	105.8	20.8	5.7	15.1	85.1	51.0	9.1	....	12.2	2.8	....	10.0	17.5
1975	144.2	129.6	20.4	5.6	14.8	109.2	63.0	11.7	....	14.3	8.4	....	11.8	14.6
1976	182.1	165.6	25.6	5.9	19.7	140.0	82.5	17.5	....	13.7	10.9	....	15.3	16.5
1977	212.8	193.7	32.6	6.1	26.5	161.1	91.5	21.2	....	16.4	12.8	....	19.2	19.1
1978	246.7	223.8	40.8	7.6	33.1	183.1	105.8	25.5	....	16.7	13.1	....	22.0	22.9
1979	261.0	226.4	41.8	9.4	32.3	184.6	107.1	21.6	....	20.0	10.7	....	25.2	34.6
1980	240.6	205.2	35.2	11.8	23.5	169.9	97.6	22.2	....	18.5	7.0	....	24.6	35.5
1981	252.0	222.3	30.3	14.4	15.9	192.0	112.5	25.1	....	23.7	10.7	....	20.1	29.7
1982	224.8	192.2	27.2	15.2	12.0	165.0	89.6	28.1	....	20.7	14.3	....	12.3	32.6
1983	256.4	221.4	36.2	14.6	21.6	185.2	97.3	34.3	....	21.9	19.3	....	12.3	35.1
1984	294.3	257.7	34.7	16.4	18.3	223.0	114.2	44.7	....	30.4	21.5	....	12.1	36.6
1985	289.7	251.6	46.5	16.3	30.2	205.1	107.1	39.1	....	24.6	22.8	....	11.4	38.1
1986	273.3	233.8	56.4	15.5	40.8	177.4	75.6	39.3	....	24.4	23.4	....	14.7	39.5
1987	314.6	266.5	60.3	16.2	44.1	206.2	101.8	42.0	....	18.9	23.3	....	20.3	48.0
1988	366.2	309.2	66.9	18.1	48.8	242.3	132.8	46.8	....	20.4	19.8	....	22.5	57.0
1989	373.1	305.9	78.3	20.6	57.6	227.6	122.3	41.9	....	22.0	20.9	....	20.5	67.1
1990	391.2	315.1	89.6	21.8	67.8	225.5	120.9	43.5	....	19.4	20.3	....	21.3	76.1
1991	434.2	357.8	120.4	20.7	99.7	237.3	109.3	54.5	....	22.3	26.9	....	24.3	76.5
1992	459.7	386.6	132.4	18.3	114.1	254.2	109.8	57.7	....	25.3	28.1	....	33.4	73.1
1993	501.9	425.0	119.9	16.7	103.2	305.1	122.9	70.1	....	26.5	39.7	....	45.8	76.9
1994	589.3	511.3	125.9	18.5	107.4	385.4	162.6	83.9	....	31.4	46.3	....	61.2	78.0
1995	667.0	574.0	140.3	22.9	117.3	433.7	199.8	89.0	....	28.0	43.9	....	73.1	92.9
1996	741.8	639.8	147.9	22.5	125.3	492.0	220.4	91.2	....	39.9	52.0	....	88.5	102.0
1997	811.0	703.4	162.2	24.3	137.9	541.2	248.5	81.0	....	48.1	63.4	....	100.3	107.6
1998	743.8	641.1	138.9	25.6	113.3	502.1	220.4	72.6	....	50.6	72.3	....	86.3	102.8
1999	761.9	640.2	154.6	26.7	127.9	485.6	219.4	49.3	....	46.8	72.5	....	97.6	121.7
2000	729.8	584.1	149.7	31.2	118.5	434.4	205.9	33.8	....	50.4	68.9	....	75.4	145.7
NAICS:[2]														
1998	743.8	641.1	138.9	25.6	113.3	502.1	193.5	12.8	33.3	57.3	62.5	33.1	109.7	102.8
1999	761.9	640.2	154.6	26.7	127.9	485.6	184.5	7.2	34.4	55.6	59.5	20.8	123.5	121.7
2000	729.8	584.1	149.7	31.2	118.5	434.4	175.6	9.5	24.3	59.5	51.3	−11.9	126.1	145.7
2001	697.1	528.3	195.0	28.9	166.1	333.3	75.1	−.7	22.5	51.1	71.3	−26.4	140.2	168.8
2002	797.4	640.6	265.3	23.5	241.9	375.3	78.3	−6.5	10.5	53.5	83.3	5.0	151.2	156.8
2003	955.7	796.7	302.8	20.0	282.7	494.0	123.9	4.4	13.2	56.6	87.9	28.1	179.9	158.9
2004	1,217.5	1,022.4	346.0	20.0	326.0	676.3	186.2	12.0	21.1	72.7	94.0	61.6	228.8	195.1
2005	1,629.2	1,403.4	409.5	26.5	383.0	993.9	279.7	28.4	32.4	96.0	123.3	100.7	333.5	225.7
2006	1,812.2	1,572.5	413.1	33.8	379.3	1,159.4	352.9	40.8	55.2	105.0	133.6	115.2	356.8	239.7
2007	1,708.3	1,370.5	300.2	36.0	264.2	1,070.3	321.1	23.3	49.6	102.8	119.4	120.5	333.6	337.8
2008	1,344.5	954.3	94.6	35.1	59.5	859.7	240.0	29.3	30.4	92.7	82.2	98.8	286.3	390.2
2009	1,470.1	1,121.3	362.7	47.3	315.3	758.7	164.7	21.7	23.4	88.9	107.9	87.0	265.1	348.8
2010	1,786.4	1,400.6	405.8	71.6	334.3	994.8	281.8	44.6	30.6	99.3	115.9	102.3	320.4	385.8
2011	1,750.2	1,337.7	378.4	76.0	302.4	959.3	296.0	30.6	10.2	97.2	115.1	95.7	314.5	412.6
2012	2,144.7	1,739.3	482.4	71.7	410.6	1,256.9	403.0	54.4	13.8	137.9	155.7	112.0	380.1	405.4
2013	2,165.9	1,767.1	430.7	79.7	351.1	1,336.3	446.9	45.2	28.3	146.4	153.3	137.6	378.6	398.8
2014	2,266.6	1,861.7	483.1	103.5	379.6	1,378.6	458.7	55.7	32.8	150.6	157.3	126.6	397.0	404.9
2015	2,184.6	1,789.4	447.2	100.7	346.5	1,342.1	427.2	61.0	20.2	152.4	169.3	135.5	376.4	395.2
2016	2,138.8	1,718.9	457.4	92.0	365.4	1,261.5	336.8	64.6	9.4	127.9	175.2	157.8	389.8	419.9
2017	2,148.2	1,649.3	440.4	78.3	362.1	1,208.9	314.8	57.5	11.1	123.3	151.7	142.4	408.0	498.9
2018	2,210.1	1,689.6	453.6	68.0	385.5	1,236.0	345.8	48.0	21.2	114.0	149.9	139.4	417.7	520.6
2019	2,306.2	1,777.5	540.9	63.2	477.6	1,236.7	351.5	37.4	17.6	123.3	155.6	133.2	418.0	528.7
2020	2,373.5	1,943.8	514.6	89.7	424.9	1,429.2	329.5	38.0	25.6	142.2	230.2	138.7	525.1	429.6
2021	2,881.2	2,468.8	585.0	113.1	471.8	1,883.9	447.0	93.8	23.6	159.3	311.3	159.2	689.7	412.4
2020: I	2,285.5	1,791.8	501.2	78.6	422.6	1,290.6	348.0	33.0	17.3	147.5	172.3	136.3	436.2	493.7
II	2,114.1	1,709.7	514.6	86.2	428.4	1,195.1	250.6	26.0	27.3	121.8	220.5	117.9	431.0	404.4
III	2,606.8	2,181.6	515.7	102.6	413.1	1,665.9	361.8	45.6	25.3	146.4	269.4	149.9	667.5	425.2
IV	2,487.4	2,092.2	526.9	91.5	435.3	1,565.3	357.4	47.3	32.4	153.2	258.5	150.9	565.7	395.2
2021: I	2,688.6	2,253.2	530.4	82.1	448.3	1,722.8	387.8	74.6	28.7	136.7	308.9	152.0	634.1	435.4
II	2,883.1	2,503.4	587.5	113.5	474.0	1,915.9	427.6	108.9	17.4	154.1	336.3	166.0	705.5	379.7
III	2,951.8	2,540.1	608.3	128.4	479.9	1,931.8	457.7	94.9	24.6	170.3	301.5	159.2	723.5	411.7
IV	3,001.4	2,578.6	613.6	128.5	485.1	1,965.0	514.9	96.8	23.6	176.0	298.5	159.4	695.8	422.7
2022: I	3,081.6	2,644.7	593.4	142.7	450.7	2,051.3	548.1	89.4	26.2	190.3	297.3	161.7	738.3	436.9
II	3,252.7	2,790.4	552.4	130.7	421.8	2,237.9	616.9	124.4	27.9	184.9	307.4	151.8	824.6	462.3
III	3,288.0	2,841.2	555.8	42.5	513.3	2,285.3	635.7	121.6	36.0	229.8	312.0	152.4	797.8	446.8

[1] Data on Standard Industrial Classification (SIC) basis include transportation and public utilities. Those on North American Industry Classification System (NAICS) basis include transporation and warehousing. Utilities classified separately in NAICS (as shown beginning 1998).

[2] SIC-based industry data use the 1987 SIC for data beginning in 1987 and the 1972 SIC for prior data. NAICS-based data use 2002 NAICS.

Note: Industry data on SIC basis and NAICS basis are not necessarily the same and are not strictly comparable.

Source: Department of Commerce (Bureau of Economic Analysis).

TABLE B–55. Historical stock prices and yields, 1949–2003

End of year	Common stock prices (end of period)[1]									Common stock yields (Standard & Poor's) (percent)[5]	
	New York Stock Exchange (NYSE) indexes[2]						Dow Jones industrial average[2]	Standard & Poor's composite index (1941–43=10)[2]	Nasdaq composite index (Feb. 5, 1971=100)[2]	Dividend-price ratio[6]	Earnings-price ratio[7]
	Composite (Dec. 31, 2002=5,000)[3]	December 31, 1965=50									
		Composite	Industrial	Transportation	Utility[4]	Finance					
1949							200.52	16.76		6.59	15.48
1950							235.42	20.41		6.57	13.99
1951							269.23	23.77		6.13	11.82
1952							291.90	26.57		5.80	9.47
1953		13.60					280.90	24.81		5.80	10.26
1954		19.40					404.39	35.98		4.95	8.57
1955		23.71					488.40	45.48		4.08	7.95
1956		24.35					499.47	46.67		4.09	7.55
1957		21.11					435.69	39.99		4.35	7.89
1958		28.85					583.65	55.21		3.97	6.23
1959		32.15					679.36	59.89		3.23	5.78
1960		30.94					615.89	58.11		3.47	5.90
1961		38.93					731.14	71.55		2.98	4.62
1962		33.81					652.10	63.10		3.37	5.82
1963		39.92					762.95	75.02		3.17	5.50
1964		45.65					874.13	84.75		3.01	5.32
1965	528.69	50.00	50.00	50.00	50.00	50.00	969.26	92.43		3.00	5.59
1966	462.28	43.72	43.13	47.56	90.38	44.91	785.69	80.33		3.40	6.63
1967	569.18	53.83	56.59	49.66	86.76	53.80	905.11	96.47		3.20	5.73
1968	622.79	58.90	61.69	56.27	91.64	76.48	943.75	103.86		3.07	5.67
1969	544.86	51.53	54.74	37.85	77.54	67.87	800.36	92.06		3.24	6.08
1970	531.12	50.23	52.91	35.70	81.64	64.34	838.92	92.15		3.83	6.45
1971	596.68	56.43	60.53	49.56	78.78	73.83	890.20	102.09	114.12	3.14	5.41
1972	681.79	64.48	70.33	47.69	84.34	83.34	1,020.02	118.05	133.73	2.84	5.50
1973	547.93	51.82	56.60	37.53	68.66	64.51	850.86	97.55	92.19	3.06	7.12
1974	382.03	36.13	39.15	26.36	53.30	39.84	616.24	68.56	59.82	4.47	11.59
1975	503.73	47.64	52.73	32.98	66.94	45.20	852.41	90.19	77.62	4.31	9.15
1976	612.01	57.88	63.36	42.57	82.54	59.23	1,004.65	107.46	97.88	3.77	8.90
1977	555.12	52.50	56.43	40.50	81.08	53.85	831.17	95.10	105.05	4.62	10.79
1978	566.96	53.62	58.87	41.58	75.38	55.01	805.01	96.11	117.98	5.28	12.03
1979	655.04	61.95	70.24	50.64	73.80	63.45	838.74	107.94	151.14	5.47	13.46
1980	823.27	77.86	91.52	76.19	76.90	70.83	963.99	135.76	202.34	5.26	12.66
1981	751.90	71.11	80.89	66.85	80.10	73.68	875.00	122.55	195.84	5.20	11.96
1982	856.79	81.03	93.02	73.63	86.94	85.00	1,046.54	140.64	232.41	5.81	11.60
1983	1,006.41	95.18	111.35	98.09	92.48	94.32	1,258.64	164.93	278.60	4.40	8.03
1984	1,013.91	96.38	110.58	90.61	103.14	97.63	1,211.57	167.24	247.35	4.64	10.02
1985	1,285.66	121.59	139.27	113.97	126.38	131.29	1,546.67	211.28	324.93	4.25	8.12
1986	1,465.31	138.59	160.11	117.65	147.54	140.05	1,895.95	242.17	348.83	3.49	6.09
1987	1,461.61	138.23	167.04	118.57	134.62	114.57	1,938.83	247.08	330.47	3.08	5.48
1988	1,652.25	156.26	189.42	146.60	149.38	128.19	2,168.57	277.72	381.38	3.64	8.01
1989	2,062.30	195.04	232.76	178.33	204.00	156.15	2,753.20	353.40	454.82	3.45	7.42
1990	1,908.45	180.49	223.60	141.49	182.60	122.06	2,633.66	330.22	373.84	3.61	6.47
1991	2,426.04	229.44	285.82	201.87	204.26	172.68	3,168.83	417.09	586.34	3.24	4.79
1992	2,539.92	240.21	294.39	214.72	209.66	200.83	3,301.11	435.71	676.95	2.99	4.22
1993	2,739.44	259.08	315.26	270.48	229.92	216.82	3,754.09	466.45	776.80	2.78	4.46
1994	2,653.37	250.94	318.10	222.46	198.41	195.80	3,834.44	459.27	751.96	2.82	5.83
1995	3,484.15	329.51	413.29	301.96	252.90	274.25	5,117.12	615.93	1,052.13	2.56	6.09
1996	4,148.07	392.30	494.38	352.30	259.91	351.17	6,448.27	740.74	1,291.03	2.19	5.24
1997	5,405.19	511.19	630.38	466.25	335.19	495.96	7,908.25	970.43	1,570.35	1.77	4.57
1998	6,299.94	595.81	743.65	482.38	445.94	521.42	9,181.43	1,229.23	2,192.69	1.49	3.46
1999	6,876.10	650.30	828.21	466.70	511.15	516.61	11,497.12	1,469.25	4,069.31	1.25	3.17
2000	6,945.57	656.87	803.29	462.76	440.54	646.95	10,786.85	1,320.28	2,470.52	1.15	3.63
2001	6,236.39	589.80	735.71	438.81	329.84	593.69	10,021.50	1,148.08	1,950.40	1.32	2.95
2002	5,000.00	472.87	583.95	395.81	233.08	510.46	8,341.63	879.82	1,335.51	1.61	2.92
2003[3]	6,440.30	572.56	735.50	519.58	265.58	655.12	10,453.92	1,111.92	2,003.37	1.77	3.84

[1] End of period.

[2] Includes stocks as follows: for NYSE, all stocks listed; for Dow Jones industrial average, 30 stocks; for Standard & Poor's (S&P) composite index, 500 stocks; and for Nasdaq composite index, over 5,000.

[3] The NYSE relaunched the composite index on January 9, 2003, incorporating new definitions, methodology, and base value. (The composite index based on December 31, 1965=50 was discontinued.) Subset indexes on financial, energy, and health care were released by the NYSE on January 8, 2004 (see Table B–56). NYSE indexes shown in this table for industrials, utilities, transportation, and finance were discontinued.

[4] Effective April 1993, the NYSE doubled the value of the utility index to facilitate trading of options and futures on the index. Indexes prior to 1993 reflect the doubling.

[5] Based on 500 stocks in the S&P composite index.

[6] Aggregate cash dividends (based on latest known annual rate) divided by aggregate market value based on Wednesday closing prices. Monthly data are averages of weekly figures; annual data are averages of monthly figures.

[7] Quarterly data are ratio of earnings (after taxes) for four quarters ending with particular quarter-to-price index for last day of that quarter. Annual data are averages of quarterly ratios.

Sources: New York Stock Exchange, Dow Jones & Co., Inc., Standard & Poor's, and Nasdaq Stock Market.

Table B–56. Common stock prices and yields, 2000–2022

End of year or month	Common stock prices (end of period)[1]							Common stock yields (Standard & Poor's) (percent)[4]	
	New York Stock Exchange (NYSE) indexes (December 31, 2002=5,000)[2, 3]				Dow Jones industrial average[2]	Standard & Poor's composite index (1941–43=10)[2]	Nasdaq composite index (Feb. 5, 1971=100)[2]	Dividend-price ratio[5]	Earnings-price ratio[6]
	Composite	Financial	Energy	Health care					
2000	6,945.57	....	....	....	10,786.85	1,320.28	2,470.52	1.15	3.63
2001	6,236.39	....	....	....	10,021.50	1,148.08	1,950.40	1.32	2.95
2002	5,000.00	5,000.00	5,000.00	5,000.00	8,341.63	879.82	1,335.51	1.61	2.92
2003	6,440.30	6,676.42	6,321.05	5,925.97	10,453.92	1,111.92	2,003.37	1.77	3.84
2004	7,250.06	7,493.92	7,934.49	6,119.07	10,783.01	1,211.92	2,175.44	1.72	4.89
2005	7,753.95	7,996.94	10,109.61	6,458.20	10,717.50	1,248.29	2,205.32	1.83	5.36
2006	9,139.02	9,552.22	11,967.88	6,958.64	12,463.15	1,418.30	2,415.29	1.87	5.78
2007	9,740.32	8,300.68	15,283.81	7,170.42	13,264.82	1,468.36	2,652.28	1.86	5.29
2008	5,757.05	3,848.42	9,434.01	5,340.73	8,776.39	903.25	1,577.03	2.37	3.54
2009	7,184.96	4,721.02	11,415.03	6,427.27	10,428.05	1,115.10	2,269.15	2.40	1.86
2010	7,964.02	4,958.62	12,520.29	6,501.53	11,577.51	1,257.64	2,652.87	1.98	6.04
2011	7,477.03	4,062.88	12,409.61	7,045.61	12,217.56	1,257.60	2,605.15	2.05	6.77
2012	8,443.51	5,114.54	12,606.06	7,904.06	13,104.14	1,426.19	3,019.51	2.24	6.20
2013	10,400.33	6,353.68	14,557.54	10,245.31	16,576.66	1,848.36	4,176.59	2.14	5.57
2014	10,839.24	6,707.16	12,533.54	11,967.04	17,823.07	2,058.90	4,736.05	2.04	5.25
2015	10,143.42	6,305.68	9,343.81	12,385.19	17,425.03	2,043.94	5,007.41	2.10	4.59
2016	11,056.89	6,961.56	11,503.76	11,907.20	19,762.60	2,238.83	5,383.12	2.19	4.17
2017	12,808.84	8,235.89	11,470.58	14,220.58	24,719.22	2,673.61	6,903.39	1.97	4.22
2018	11,374.39	6,969.48	9,341.44	15,158.38	23,327.46	2,506.85	6,635.28	1.90	4.66
2019	13,913.03	8,700.11	10,037.30	18,070.10	28,538.44	3,230.78	8,972.60	1.93	4.53
2020	14,524.80	8,292.85	6,502.78	20,045.67	30,606.48	3,756.07	12,888.28	1.89	3.28
2021	17,164.13	10,175.36	9,146.18	24,345.65	36,338.30	4,766.18	15,644.97	1.38	3.79
2022	15,184.31	8,668.77	13,051.89	23,439.84	33,147.25	3,839.50	10,466.48	1.57	....
2020: Jan	13,614.10	8,535.85	9,007.57	17,753.73	28,256.03	3,225.52	9,150.94	1.80	....
Feb	12,380.97	7,701.35	7,770.44	16,364.87	25,409.36	2,954.22	8,567.37	1.84	....
Mar	10,301.87	5,972.42	5,319.36	15,554.24	21,917.16	2,584.59	7,700.10	2.30	4.50
Apr	11,372.34	6,467.31	6,190.56	17,500.36	24,345.72	2,912.43	8,889.55	2.20	....
May	11,802.95	6,612.69	6,262.28	18,041.17	25,383.11	3,044.31	9,489.87	2.08	....
June	11,893.78	6,709.21	6,242.11	17,505.30	25,812.88	3,100.29	10,058.77	1.95	3.20
July	12,465.05	6,849.26	6,024.80	18,380.12	26,428.32	3,271.12	10,745.27	1.89	....
Aug	13,045.60	7,181.16	6,014.26	18,853.66	28,430.05	3,500.31	11,775.46	1.78	....
Sept	12,701.88	6,860.62	5,161.75	18,559.43	27,781.70	3,363.00	11,167.51	1.79	2.92
Oct	12,429.28	6,761.94	4,912.48	17,847.94	26,501.60	3,269.96	10,911.59	1.76	....
Nov	14,006.46	7,887.93	6,232.84	19,390.40	29,638.64	3,621.63	12,198.74	1.69	....
Dec	14,524.80	8,292.85	6,502.78	20,045.67	30,606.48	3,756.07	12,888.28	1.62	2.51
2021: Jan	14,397.20	8,072.62	6,733.84	20,208.09	29,982.62	3,714.24	13,070.69	1.55	....
Feb	15,010.47	8,853.18	7,774.59	19,760.30	30,932.37	3,811.15	13,192.35	1.49	....
Mar	15,601.74	9,240.02	7,995.97	20,388.89	32,981.55	3,972.89	13,246.87	1.48	3.23
Apr	16,219.33	9,773.10	8,005.80	21,141.32	33,874.85	4,181.17	13,962.68	1.39	....
May	16,555.66	10,112.15	8,440.17	21,494.66	34,529.45	4,204.11	13,748.74	1.38	....
June	16,555.35	9,889.35	8,787.30	21,796.88	34,502.51	4,297.50	14,503.95	1.37	3.69
July	16,602.29	9,923.19	8,163.13	22,679.73	34,935.47	4,395.26	14,672.68	1.34	....
Aug	16,806.44	10,162.18	8,052.76	23,180.04	35,360.73	4,522.68	15,259.24	1.32	....
Sept	16,144.92	9,934.02	8,784.79	21,846.16	33,843.92	4,307.54	14,448.58	1.33	4.07
Oct	17,016.41	10,455.70	9,460.44	23,131.46	35,819.56	4,605.38	15,498.39	1.33	....
Nov	16,318.97	9,756.72	8,829.04	22,267.26	34,483.72	4,567.00	15,537.69	1.29	....
Dec	17,164.13	10,175.36	9,146.18	24,345.65	36,338.30	4,766.18	15,644.97	1.29	4.15
2022: Jan	16,659.78	10,200.96	10,648.50	22,894.30	35,131.86	4,515.55	14,239.88	1.33	....
Feb	16,313.89	9,875.64	11,142.11	22,757.28	33,892.60	4,373.94	13,751.40	1.38	....
Mar	16,670.91	9,971.24	12,065.19	23,828.90	34,678.35	4,530.41	14,220.52	1.41	4.37
Apr	15,615.25	9,139.65	11,791.27	22,944.86	32,977.21	4,131.93	12,334.64	1.42	....
May	15,827.05	9,297.74	13,336.34	23,217.06	32,990.12	4,132.15	12,081.39	1.55	....
June	14,487.64	8,313.35	11,252.27	22,640.69	30,775.43	3,785.38	11,028.74	1.64	5.08
July	15,327.71	8,901.55	12,171.38	23,258.76	32,845.13	4,130.29	12,390.69	1.64	....
Aug	14,801.25	8,563.40	12,304.08	21,713.32	31,510.43	3,955.00	11,816.20	1.56	....
Sept	13,472.18	7,747.27	11,004.62	20,936.54	28,725.51	3,585.62	10,575.62	1.71	5.22
Oct	14,747.03	8,481.92	13,240.72	22,560.24	32,732.95	3,871.98	10,988.15	1.78	....
Nov	15,780.02	9,083.61	13,551.07	23,695.65	34,589.77	4,080.11	11,468.00	1.70	....
Dec	15,184.31	8,668.77	13,051.89	23,439.84	33,147.25	3,839.50	10,466.48	1.72	....

[1] End of year or month.
[2] Includes stocks as follows: for NYSE, all stocks listed (in 2022, over 3,000); for Dow Jones industrial average, 30 stocks; for Standard & Poor's (S&P) composite index, 500 stocks; and for Nasdaq composite index, in 2022, over 3,600.
[3] The NYSE relaunched the composite index on January 9, 2003, incorporating new definitions, methodology, and base value. Subset indexes on financial, energy, and health care were released by the NYSE on January 8, 2004.
[4] Based on 500 stocks in the S&P composite index.
[5] Aggregate cash dividends (based on latest known annual rate) divided by aggregate market value based on Wednesday closing prices. Monthly data are averages of weekly figures, annual data are averages of monthly figures.
[6] Quarterly data are ratio of earnings (after taxes) for four quarters ending with particular quarter-to-price index for last day of that quarter. Annual data are averages of quarterly ratios.

Sources: New York Stock Exchange, Dow Jones & Co., Inc., Standard & Poor's, and Nasdaq Stock Market.

Table B–57. U.S. international transactions, 1972–2022

[Millions of dollars; quarterly data seasonally adjusted]

Year or quarter	Current Account [1]												Current account balance as a percentage of GDP
	Goods [2]			Services			Balance on goods and services	Primary income receipts and payments			Balance on secondary Income [3]	Balance on current account	
	Exports	Imports	Balance on goods	Exports	Imports	Balance on services		Receipts	Payments	Balance on primary income			
1972	49,381	55,797	–6,416	17,842	16,867	973	–5,443	14,764	6,572	8,192	–8,544	–5,796	–0.5
1973	71,410	70,499	911	19,832	18,843	989	1,900	21,809	9,656	12,153	–6,914	7,140	.5
1974	98,306	103,811	–5,505	22,591	21,378	1,212	–4,293	27,587	12,084	15,503	–9,248	1,961	.1
1975	107,088	98,185	8,903	25,497	21,996	3,500	12,403	25,351	12,565	12,786	–7,076	18,117	1.1
1976	114,745	124,228	–9,483	27,971	24,570	3,402	–6,082	29,374	13,312	16,062	–5,686	4,296	.2
1977	120,816	151,907	–31,091	31,486	27,640	3,845	–27,247	32,355	14,218	18,137	–5,227	–14,336	–.7
1978	142,075	176,002	–33,927	36,353	32,189	4,164	–29,763	42,087	21,680	20,407	–5,788	–15,143	–.6
1979	184,439	212,007	–27,568	39,693	36,689	3,003	–24,566	63,835	32,961	30,874	–6,593	–285	.0
1980	224,250	249,750	–25,500	47,585	41,492	6,093	–19,407	72,605	42,533	30,072	–8,349	2,318	.1
1981	237,044	265,067	–28,023	57,355	45,503	11,851	–16,172	86,529	53,626	32,903	–11,702	5,029	.2
1982	211,157	247,642	–36,485	64,078	51,750	12,330	–24,156	96,522	61,359	35,163	–16,545	–5,537	–.2
1983	201,799	268,901	–67,102	64,307	54,973	9,335	–57,767	96,031	59,643	36,388	–17,311	–38,691	–1.1
1984	219,926	332,418	–112,492	71,168	67,748	3,418	–109,074	115,639	80,574	35,065	–20,334	–94,344	–2.3
1985	215,915	338,088	–122,173	73,156	72,863	294	–121,879	105,046	79,324	25,722	–21,999	–118,155	–2.7
1986	223,344	368,425	–145,081	86,690	80,147	6,543	–138,539	102,798	87,304	15,494	–24,131	–147,176	–3.2
1987	250,208	409,765	–159,557	98,661	90,788	7,874	–151,683	113,603	99,309	14,294	–23,265	–160,655	–3.3
1988	320,230	447,189	–126,959	110,920	98,525	12,394	–114,566	141,666	122,981	18,685	–25,274	–121,153	–2.3
1989	359,916	477,665	–117,749	127,087	102,480	24,607	–93,142	166,384	146,560	19,824	–26,169	–99,487	–1.8
1990	387,401	498,438	–111,037	147,833	117,660	30,173	–80,865	176,894	148,345	28,549	–26,654	–78,969	–1.3
1991	414,083	491,020	–76,937	164,260	118,459	45,802	–31,136	155,327	131,198	24,129	9,904	2,897	.0
1992	439,631	536,528	–96,897	177,251	119,566	57,685	–39,212	139,082	114,845	24,237	–36,635	–51,613	–.8
1993	456,943	589,394	–132,451	185,920	123,780	62,141	–70,311	141,606	116,287	25,319	–39,811	–84,805	–1.2
1994	502,859	668,690	–165,831	200,395	133,057	67,338	–98,493	169,447	152,302	17,145	–40,265	–121,612	–1.7
1995	575,204	749,374	–174,170	219,183	141,397	77,786	–96,384	213,661	192,771	20,890	–38,074	–113,567	–1.5
1996	612,113	803,113	–191,000	239,489	152,554	86,935	–104,065	229,530	207,212	22,318	–43,017	–124,764	–1.5
1997	678,366	876,794	–198,428	256,087	165,932	90,155	–108,273	261,357	248,750	12,607	–45,062	–140,726	–1.6
1998	670,416	918,637	–248,221	262,758	180,677	82,081	–166,140	266,244	261,978	4,266	–53,187	–215,062	–2.4
1999	698,524	1,035,592	–337,068	278,001	196,742	81,258	–255,809	302,540	292,566	9,974	–40,777	–286,612	–3.0
2000	784,940	1,231,722	–446,783	298,023	220,927	77,096	–369,686	365,612	350,980	14,632	–46,863	–401,918	–3.9
2001	731,331	1,153,701	–422,370	284,035	222,039	61,997	–360,373	311,364	288,120	23,244	–56,953	–394,082	–3.7
2002	698,036	1,173,281	–475,245	288,059	233,480	54,579	–420,666	306,391	288,886	17,506	–52,949	–456,110	–4.2
2003	730,446	1,272,089	–541,643	297,740	252,340	45,401	–496,243	346,931	317,677	29,254	–55,300	–522,289	–4.6
2004	823,584	1,488,349	–664,766	344,536	290,609	53,927	–610,838	432,839	386,256	46,583	–71,634	–635,890	–5.2
2005	913,016	1,695,820	–782,804	378,487	312,225	66,262	–716,542	536,294	492,108	44,186	–76,876	–749,232	–5.7
2006	1,040,905	1,878,194	–837,289	423,086	349,329	73,756	–763,533	669,919	653,945	15,974	–69,088	–816,646	–5.9
2007	1,165,151	1,986,347	–821,196	495,664	385,464	110,199	–710,997	816,938	752,582	64,356	–89,910	–736,550	–5.1
2008	1,308,795	2,141,287	–832,492	540,791	420,650	120,142	–712,350	820,244	708,225	112,019	–96,192	–696,523	–4.7
2009	1,070,331	1,580,025	–509,694	522,461	407,538	114,923	–394,771	653,222	537,684	115,539	–100,496	–379,729	–2.6
2010	1,290,279	1,938,950	–648,671	582,041	436,456	145,584	–503,087	723,223	553,311	169,911	–98,834	–432,009	–2.9
2011	1,498,887	2,239,886	–740,999	644,665	458,188	186,477	–554,522	791,469	589,038	202,431	–103,211	–455,302	–2.9
2012	1,562,630	2,303,749	–741,119	684,823	469,610	215,213	–525,906	791,613	593,754	197,859	–90,134	–418,181	–2.6
2013	1,593,708	2,294,247	–700,539	719,413	465,736	253,678	–446,861	811,501	616,041	195,460	–88,115	–339,516	–2.0
2014	1,635,563	2,385,480	–749,917	757,051	491,086	265,965	–483,952	845,858	645,623	200,235	–86,339	–370,056	–2.1
2015	1,511,381	2,273,249	–761,868	769,397	498,305	271,092	–490,776	824,929	639,724	185,205	–102,882	–408,453	–2.2
2016	1,457,393	2,207,195	–749,801	783,431	513,088	270,343	–479,458	857,240	660,798	196,442	–113,199	–396,216	–2.1
2017	1,557,003	2,356,345	–799,343	837,474	548,475	288,999	–510,344	995,442	737,501	257,942	–108,618	–361,021	–1.9
2018	1,676,913	2,555,662	–878,749	865,549	565,395	300,155	–578,594	1,102,964	847,689	255,275	–116,530	–439,850	–2.1
2019	1,655,098	2,512,358	–857,260	891,177	593,594	297,584	–559,676	1,136,799	893,244	243,555	–129,836	–445,957	–2.1
2020	1,432,218	2,346,103	–913,885	726,433	466,537	259,896	–653,989	936,236	773,146	163,090	–128,799	–619,698	–2.9
2021	1,761,364	2,851,660	–1,090,296	795,273	550,025	245,248	–845,047	1,052,080	912,587	139,493	–140,800	–846,354	–3.6
2019: I	419,131	635,292	–216,161	218,205	147,252	70,953	–145,208	284,627	221,798	62,829	–34,931	–117,311	–2.2
II	413,503	637,510	–224,007	225,170	149,587	75,583	–148,424	290,862	227,027	63,835	–32,606	–117,195	–2.2
III	412,182	628,942	–216,760	223,618	148,400	75,218	–141,542	284,951	223,263	61,688	–29,798	–109,652	–2.0
IV	410,282	610,614	–200,331	224,184	148,354	75,830	–124,501	276,359	221,157	55,202	–32,501	–101,800	–1.9
2020: I	400,424	597,750	–197,327	203,550	135,929	67,621	–129,705	255,495	200,009	55,486	–33,200	–107,420	–2.0
II	288,969	511,718	–222,749	168,227	101,064	67,163	–155,586	209,064	175,235	33,829	–30,527	–152,283	–3.1
III	357,652	600,719	–243,067	172,092	108,063	64,030	–179,037	234,068	192,517	41,551	–33,806	–171,293	–3.2
IV	385,173	635,915	–250,743	182,564	121,482	61,082	–189,661	237,610	205,386	32,224	–31,266	–188,702	–3.5
2021: I	410,395	675,663	–265,268	187,935	119,858	68,077	–197,191	255,625	214,719	40,906	–32,455	–188,740	–3.4
II	435,556	702,985	–267,429	194,691	130,977	63,714	–203,715	256,960	228,932	28,027	–30,714	–206,402	–3.6
III	441,893	714,472	–272,579	199,688	146,251	53,437	–219,142	267,976	234,408	33,568	–40,800	–226,375	–3.8
IV	473,521	758,540	–285,019	212,959	152,939	60,020	–225,000	271,520	234,527	36,993	–36,831	–224,837	–3.7
2022: I	487,899	829,575	–341,676	216,829	157,904	58,925	–282,751	278,059	239,239	38,819	–38,608	–282,540	–4.6
II	539,793	850,668	–310,875	229,176	171,904	57,272	–253,603	298,761	241,547	57,214	–42,338	–238,727	–3.8
III p	547,019	818,159	–271,139	234,043	173,502	60,542	–210,598	313,971	268,350	45,621	–52,129	–217,106	–3.4

[1] Current and capital account statistics in the international transactions accounts differ slightly from statistics in the National Income and Product Accounts (NIPAs) because of adjustments made to convert the international statistics to national accounting concepts. A reconciliation can be found in NIPA table 4.3B.

[2] Adjusted from Census data to align with concepts and definitions used to prepare the international and national economic accounts. The adjustments are necessary to supplement coverage of Census data, to eliminate duplication of transactions recorded elsewhere in the international accounts, to value transactions according to a standard definition, and for earlier years, to record transactions in the appropriate period.

See next page for continuation of table.

TABLE B–57. U.S. international transactions, 1972–2022—*Continued*

[Millions of dollars; quarterly data seasonally adjusted]

Year or quarter	Balance on capital account [1]	Financial account											Statistical discrepancy
		Net U.S. acquisition of financial assets excluding financial derivatives [net increase in assets / financial outflow (+)]					Net U.S. incurrence of liabilities excluding financial derivatives [net increase in liabilities / financial inflow (+)]				Financial derivatives other than reserves, net transactions	Net lending (+) or net borrowing (–) from financial account transactions [5]	
		Total	Direct investment assets	Portfolio investment assets	Other investment assets	Reserve assets [4]	Total	Direct investment liabilities	Portfolio investment liabilities	Other investment liabilities			
1972	....	14,497	7,747	619	6,127	4	22,171	948	13,123	8,100	....	–7,674	–1,879
1973	....	22,874	11,353	672	11,007	–158	18,388	2,800	4,790	10,798	....	4,486	–2,654
1974	....	34,745	9,052	1,853	22,373	1,467	35,228	4,761	5,500	24,967	....	–483	–2,444
1975	....	39,703	14,244	6,247	18,363	849	16,870	2,603	12,761	1,506	....	22,833	4,717
1976	....	51,269	11,949	8,885	27,877	2,558	37,840	4,347	16,165	17,328	....	13,429	9,134
1977	....	34,785	11,891	5,459	17,060	375	52,770	3,728	37,615	11,427	....	–17,985	–3,651
1978	....	61,130	16,057	3,626	42,179	–732	66,275	7,896	30,083	28,296	....	–5,145	9,997
1979	....	66,053	25,223	12,430	27,267	1,133	40,693	11,876	–13,502	42,319	....	25,360	25,647
1980	....	86,968	19,222	6,042	53,550	8,154	62,036	16,918	23,825	21,293	....	24,932	22,614
1981	....	114,147	9,624	15,650	83,697	5,176	85,684	25,196	17,509	42,979	....	28,463	23,433
1982	....	142,722	19,397	12,395	105,965	4,965	109,897	27,475	19,695	62,727	....	32,825	38,362
1983	....	74,690	20,844	2,063	50,588	1,195	95,715	18,688	18,382	58,645	....	–21,025	17,666
1984	....	50,740	26,770	3,498	17,340	3,132	126,413	34,832	38,695	52,886	....	–75,673	18,673
1985	....	47,064	21,241	3,008	18,957	3,858	146,544	22,057	68,004	56,483	....	–99,480	18,677
1986	....	107,252	19,524	8,984	79,057	–313	223,854	30,946	104,497	88,411	....	–116,602	30,570
1987	....	84,058	39,795	7,903	45,508	–9,148	251,863	63,232	79,631	109,000	....	–167,805	–7,149
1988	....	105,747	21,701	4,589	75,544	3,913	244,008	56,910	86,786	100,312	....	–138,261	–17,108
1989	–207	182,908	50,973	31,166	75,476	25,293	230,302	75,801	74,852	79,649	....	–47,394	52,299
1990	–7,221	103,985	59,934	30,557	11,336	2,158	162,109	71,247	25,767	65,095	....	–58,124	28,066
1991	–5,129	75,753	49,253	32,053	210	–5,763	119,586	34,535	72,562	12,489	....	–43,833	–41,601
1992	1,449	84,899	58,755	50,684	–20,639	–3,901	178,842	30,315	92,199	56,328	....	–93,943	–43,776
1993	–714	199,399	82,799	137,917	–22,696	1,379	278,607	50,211	174,387	54,009	....	–79,208	6,313
1994	–1,112	188,758	89,988	54,088	50,028	–5,346	312,995	55,942	131,849	125,204	....	–124,237	–1,514
1995	–221	363,555	110,041	143,506	100,266	9,742	446,393	69,067	254,431	122,895	....	–82,838	30,951
1996	–8	424,548	103,024	160,179	168,013	–6,668	559,027	97,644	392,107	69,276	....	–134,479	–9,706
1997	–256	502,024	121,352	121,036	258,626	1,010	720,999	122,150	311,105	287,744	....	–218,975	–77,995
1998	–7	385,936	174,751	132,186	72,216	6,783	452,901	211,152	225,878	15,871	....	–66,965	148,106
1999	–6,428	526,612	247,484	141,007	146,868	–8,747	765,215	312,449	278,697	174,069	....	–238,603	54,437
2000	–4,217	587,682	186,371	159,713	241,308	290	1,066,074	349,124	441,966	274,984	....	–478,392	–72,257
2001	12,170	386,313	146,041	106,919	128,442	4,911	788,345	172,496	431,492	184,357	....	–402,032	–20,120
2002	–3,825	319,175	178,984	79,532	56,978	3,681	821,844	111,056	504,155	206,634	....	–502,668	–42,734
2003	–8,499	371,104	195,218	133,059	44,351	–1,524	911,660	117,107	550,163	244,390	....	–540,556	–9,768
2004	–4,344	1,058,661	374,006	191,956	495,505	–2,806	1,600,881	213,642	867,340	519,899	....	–542,220	98,014
2005	950	562,996	52,591	267,290	257,210	–14,094	1,277,056	142,345	832,037	302,673	....	–714,059	34,223
2006	–7,439	1,324,623	283,800	493,366	549,830	–2,373	2,120,480	298,464	1,126,735	695,280	–29,710	–825,567	–1,482
2007	–6,057	1,563,467	523,889	380,807	658,649	122	2,190,087	346,615	1,156,612	686,860	–6,222	–632,841	109,765
2008	–172	–317,592	343,584	–284,269	–381,754	4,848	462,408	341,091	523,683	–402,367	32,947	–747,053	–50,358
2009	–5,877	131,082	312,597	375,883	–609,654	52,256	325,644	161,082	357,352	–192,789	–44,816	–239,379	146,227
2010	–6,891	958,737	349,829	199,620	407,454	1,835	1,391,042	264,039	820,434	306,569	–14,076	–446,381	–7,481
2011	–9,020	492,556	436,615	85,365	–45,301	15,877	983,522	263,499	311,626	408,397	–35,006	–525,972	–61,650
2012	931	171,359	377,239	243,182	–453,522	4,460	632,034	250,343	747,017	–365,327	7,064	–453,611	–36,361
2013	–6,559	626,189	392,796	457,734	–221,242	–3,099	1,052,068	288,131	511,987	251,949	2,222	–423,657	–77,582
2014	–6,535	865,694	387,528	581,668	–99,920	–3,583	1,109,443	251,857	697,607	159,979	–54,335	–298,084	78,506
2015	–7,940	144,104	302,072	107,154	–258,831	–6,292	503,468	511,434	213,910	–221,876	–27,035	–386,400	29,993
2016	–6,606	336,438	299,814	37,489	–2,955	2,090	706,693	474,388	231,265	1,040	7,827	–362,427	40,394
2017	12,394	1,161,984	409,413	540,728	213,533	–1,690	1,559,219	380,823	790,810	387,586	23,998	–373,237	–24,610
2018	–4,261	429,710	–130,720	381,863	173,578	4,989	712,178	214,716	303,075	194,387	–20,404	–302,872	141,238
2019	–6,456	307,192	105,677	–11,453	208,310	4,659	831,045	314,743	233,469	282,834	–41,670	–565,524	–113,111
2020	–5,532	943,091	271,798	406,364	255,956	8,974	1,634,965	148,914	946,560	539,490	–5,107	–696,980	–71,751
2021	–2,474	1,278,599	421,749	719,095	23,763	113,993	1,977,294	448,325	676,112	852,857	–41,902	–740,597	108,231
2019: I	–2,733	80,054	–11,162	–54,228	145,236	208	149,861	92,635	–16,702	73,928	–21,383	–91,189	28,855
II	–866	54,250	64,857	18,343	–31,309	2,359	294,098	101,976	145,860	46,262	–9,642	–249,490	–131,430
III	–899	148,842	–1,682	28,859	119,783	1,882	283,012	73,541	123,979	85,492	–6,382	–140,552	–30,001
IV	–1,957	24,045	53,664	–4,427	–25,401	210	104,075	46,591	–19,669	77,152	–4,263	–84,293	19,465
2020: I	–2,878	860,256	35,047	104,831	720,622	–245	984,920	37,217	29,069	918,633	–25,136	–149,799	–39,502
II	–957	–222,493	59,130	35,817	–322,400	4,960	–147,569	–58,227	324,300	–413,642	–11,702	–86,626	66,614
III	–561	55,475	133,765	137,090	–217,200	1,820	255,526	109,797	170,786	–25,057	28,425	–171,626	228
IV	–1,136	249,853	43,855	128,627	74,933	2,438	542,088	60,127	422,405	59,556	3,306	–288,929	–99,091
2021: I	–2,740	466,636	88,583	346,286	33,867	–2,100	642,074	72,763	390,072	179,240	–2,216	–177,654	13,826
II	–881	296,073	180,545	173,874	–58,823	477	428,362	116,823	146,867	164,672	–8,611	–140,900	66,382
III	2,990	466,485	87,710	305,649	–39,476	112,603	676,601	161,484	200,804	314,312	–7,980	–218,096	5,289
IV	–1,844	49,404	64,912	–106,715	88,194	3,013	230,257	97,255	–61,631	194,633	–23,095	–203,948	22,734
2022: I	–1,888	414,584	134,008	227,966	51,678	932	656,055	125,653	246,077	284,325	5,762	–235,710	48,718
II	–3,815	409,870	99,641	276,714	32,334	1,181	516,175	70,929	443,379	1,867	–45,911	–152,216	90,326
III p	5,198	410,967	56,720	368,923	–15,474	797	671,186	101,387	463,168	106,631	–33,940	–294,159	–82,251

[3] Includes U.S. government and private transfers, such as U.S. government grants and pensions, fines and penalties, withholding taxes, personal transfers, insurance-related transfers, and other current transfers.

[4] Consists of monetary gold, special drawing rights (SDRs), the U.S. reserve position in the International Monetary Fund (IMF), and other reserve assets, including foreign currencies.

[5] Net lending means that U.S. residents are net suppliers of funds to foreign residents, and net borrowing means the opposite.

Source: Department of Commerce (Bureau of Economic Analysis).

TABLE B–58. U.S. international trade in goods on balance of payments (BOP) and Census basis, and trade in services on BOP basis, 1993–2022

[Billions of dollars; monthly data seasonally adjusted]

Year or month	Goods: Exports (f.a.s. value)[1, 2]							Goods: Imports (customs value)[6]							Services (BOP basis)	
	Total, BOP basis[3, 4]	Census basis (by end-use category)						Total, BOP basis[4]	Census basis (by end-use category)							
		Total, Census basis[3, 5]	Foods, feeds, and beverages	Industrial supplies and materials	Capital goods except automotive	Automotive vehicles, parts, and engines	Consumer goods (nonfood) except automotive		Total, Census basis[5]	Foods, feeds, and beverages	Industrial supplies and materials	Capital goods except automotive	Automotive vehicles, parts, and engines	Consumer goods (nonfood) except automotive	Exports[4]	Imports[4]
1993	456.9	465.1	40.6	111.8	181.7	52.4	54.7	589.4	580.7	27.9	145.6	152.4	102.4	134.0	185.9	123.8
1994	502.9	512.6	42.0	121.4	205.0	57.8	60.0	668.7	663.3	31.0	162.1	184.4	118.3	146.3	200.4	133.1
1995	575.2	584.7	50.5	146.2	233.0	61.8	64.4	749.4	743.5	33.2	181.8	221.4	123.8	159.9	219.2	141.4
1996	612.1	625.1	55.5	147.7	253.0	65.0	70.1	803.1	795.3	35.7	204.5	228.1	128.9	172.0	239.5	152.6
1997	678.4	689.2	51.5	158.2	294.5	74.0	77.4	876.8	869.7	39.7	213.8	253.3	139.8	193.8	256.1	165.9
1998	670.4	682.1	46.4	148.3	299.4	72.4	80.3	918.6	911.9	41.2	200.1	269.5	148.7	217.0	262.8	180.7
1999	698.5	695.8	46.0	147.5	310.8	75.3	80.9	1,035.6	1,024.6	43.6	221.4	295.7	179.0	241.9	278.0	196.7
2000	784.9	781.9	47.9	172.6	356.9	80.4	89.4	1,231.7	1,218.0	46.0	299.0	347.0	195.9	281.8	298.0	220.9
2001	731.3	729.1	49.4	160.1	321.7	75.4	88.3	1,153.7	1,141.0	46.6	273.9	298.0	189.8	284.3	284.0	222.0
2002	698.0	693.1	49.6	156.8	290.4	78.9	84.4	1,173.3	1,161.4	49.7	267.7	283.3	203.7	307.8	288.1	233.5
2003	730.4	724.8	55.0	173.0	293.7	80.6	89.9	1,272.1	1,257.1	55.8	313.8	295.9	210.1	333.9	297.7	252.3
2004	823.6	814.9	56.6	203.9	327.5	89.2	103.2	1,488.3	1,469.7	62.1	412.8	343.6	228.2	372.9	344.5	290.6
2005	913.0	901.1	59.0	233.0	358.4	98.4	115.3	1,695.8	1,673.5	68.1	523.8	379.3	239.4	407.2	378.5	312.2
2006	1,040.9	1,026.0	66.0	276.0	404.0	107.3	129.1	1,878.2	1,853.9	74.9	602.0	418.3	256.6	442.6	423.1	349.3
2007	1,165.2	1,148.2	84.3	316.4	433.0	121.3	146.0	1,986.3	1,957.0	81.7	634.7	444.5	256.7	474.6	495.7	385.5
2008	1,308.8	1,287.4	108.3	388.0	457.7	121.5	161.3	2,141.3	2,103.6	89.0	779.5	453.7	231.2	481.6	540.8	420.7
2009	1,070.3	1,056.0	93.9	296.5	391.2	81.7	149.5	1,580.0	1,559.6	81.6	462.4	370.5	157.7	427.3	522.5	407.5
2010	1,290.3	1,278.5	107.7	391.7	447.5	112.0	165.2	1,939.0	1,913.9	91.7	603.1	449.4	225.1	483.2	582.0	436.5
2011	1,498.9	1,482.5	126.2	501.1	494.0	133.0	175.3	2,239.9	2,208.0	107.5	755.8	510.8	254.6	514.1	644.7	458.2
2012	1,562.6	1,545.8	133.0	501.2	527.2	146.2	181.7	2,303.7	2,276.3	110.3	730.6	548.7	297.8	516.9	684.8	469.6
2013	1,593.7	1,578.5	136.2	508.2	534.4	152.7	188.8	2,294.2	2,268.0	115.1	681.5	555.7	308.8	531.7	719.4	465.7
2014	1,635.6	1,621.9	143.7	505.8	551.5	159.8	199.0	2,385.5	2,356.4	125.9	667.0	594.1	328.6	557.1	757.1	491.1
2015	1,511.4	1,503.3	127.7	427.0	539.5	151.9	197.7	2,273.2	2,248.8	127.8	486.0	602.5	349.2	594.2	769.4	498.3
2016	1,457.4	1,451.5	130.5	397.3	519.7	150.4	193.7	2,207.2	2,186.8	130.0	443.3	589.7	349.9	583.1	783.4	513.1
2017	1,557.0	1,547.2	132.8	465.2	533.4	157.9	197.7	2,356.3	2,339.6	137.8	507.0	639.8	358.2	601.4	837.5	548.5
2018	1,676.9	1,665.8	133.1	541.2	563.2	158.8	206.0	2,555.7	2,536.1	147.3	574.6	690.9	371.1	645.4	865.5	565.4
2019	1,655.1	1,645.9	131.0	529.5	550.5	163.1	205.6	2,512.4	2,491.7	150.5	520.6	674.8	374.5	653.0	891.2	593.6
2020	1,432.2	1,428.5	139.3	466.2	462.7	128.8	174.8	2,346.1	2,330.8	154.3	478.8	643.5	309.2	638.8	726.4	466.5
2021	1,761.4	1,754.3	164.7	636.9	520.6	144.1	222.2	2,851.7	2,831.1	182.1	649.8	761.1	347.1	766.3	795.3	550.0
2022 p	2,085.6	2,064.8	180.0	827.8	571.6	158.4	246.4	3,277.3	3,246.7	208.3	810.7	864.7	399.1	842.6	924.2	680.5
2021: Jan	135.2	134.9	14.0	45.3	41.6	12.6	16.1	221.6	220.3	13.8	43.0	59.8	32.0	62.9	62.3	39.8
Feb	131.2	130.8	13.7	45.6	39.3	12.0	15.3	219.5	218.0	13.4	46.6	59.9	28.2	60.5	62.2	39.2
Mar	144.0	143.6	13.7	52.0	42.5	12.8	16.9	234.6	233.0	14.2	50.3	62.6	30.2	65.6	63.3	40.8
Apr	143.9	143.4	13.7	51.4	44.4	11.9	16.7	231.4	229.7	14.7	49.7	63.4	29.1	63.3	63.7	42.0
May	145.3	144.8	13.9	52.4	43.7	11.5	17.8	233.4	231.6	15.2	51.9	62.3	29.1	63.3	64.9	43.5
June	146.3	145.7	13.2	53.5	43.6	11.7	18.2	238.2	236.3	15.8	56.3	63.2	28.7	62.2	66.0	45.5
July	147.9	147.3	13.3	53.1	44.4	12.1	18.8	235.6	234.0	15.7	54.8	63.0	29.4	60.7	66.2	47.9
Aug	149.5	148.9	12.6	57.1	43.7	11.3	18.9	238.2	236.2	15.6	56.4	63.2	28.1	62.9	66.4	49.1
Sept	144.5	143.9	12.6	52.3	42.7	11.0	20.1	240.6	239.0	15.6	57.9	65.3	26.1	62.8	67.1	49.3
Oct	157.6	156.9	14.8	57.6	45.1	12.3	20.8	243.9	242.2	15.9	58.1	65.0	27.4	64.1	68.3	50.2
Nov	156.5	155.7	15.0	57.6	44.4	12.1	20.7	254.8	252.8	16.4	63.7	65.9	28.5	66.3	71.6	51.3
Dec	159.4	158.6	14.3	58.9	45.2	12.7	21.9	259.9	258.1	15.8	61.1	67.4	30.3	71.7	73.1	51.4
2022: Jan	156.5	155.6	14.0	58.3	46.3	12.4	19.0	264.4	262.4	17.0	62.3	68.9	32.5	71.7	70.8	50.5
Feb	160.1	159.1	14.7	59.8	46.0	12.2	20.4	266.5	264.4	16.8	65.3	70.2	29.7	71.8	72.2	53.1
Mar	170.0	168.1	15.2	67.1	46.2	12.9	20.3	295.8	293.3	17.8	76.0	74.1	32.3	82.0	73.8	54.4
Apr	176.3	174.0	17.4	69.4	47.4	13.0	20.7	283.0	280.3	18.2	70.7	71.6	33.7	75.6	75.6	55.6
May	179.3	177.2	15.8	73.3	47.2	13.3	21.3	283.1	280.2	18.1	72.5	71.3	34.1	74.1	76.4	57.7
June	182.8	180.4	16.7	77.5	46.0	12.8	21.0	281.7	279.0	17.9	73.1	72.2	31.4	74.6	77.2	58.5
July	182.9	181.2	15.4	76.6	48.1	13.7	20.3	273.7	270.9	16.9	71.4	72.7	33.3	67.2	77.5	56.9
Aug	183.6	181.3	15.6	75.0	48.4	12.7	21.6	269.3	266.6	17.4	66.7	71.5	34.3	67.3	77.7	57.2
Sept	179.2	177.3	13.5	72.1	49.6	13.3	21.5	272.2	269.4	17.1	64.8	74.9	34.9	68.4	78.8	59.4
Oct	175.7	173.9	14.0	69.7	49.6	13.7	19.5	274.6	272.0	17.6	65.8	74.4	35.5	67.8	80.8	59.3
Nov	171.1	169.7	13.5	66.0	48.3	13.9	21.0	254.3	251.8	16.7	62.4	71.5	32.3	59.0	81.3	59.1
Dec p	168.1	166.9	14.1	62.9	48.5	14.5	19.9	258.8	256.6	16.7	59.6	71.5	35.2	63.1	82.0	58.8

[1] Department of Defense shipments of grant-aid military supplies and equipment under the Military Assistance Program are excluded from total exports through 1985 and included beginning 1986.

[2] F.a.s. (free alongside ship) value basis at U.S. port of exportation for exports.

[3] Beginning with data for 1989, exports have been adjusted for undocumented exports to Canada and are included in the appropriate end-use categories. For prior years, only total exports include this adjustment.

[4] Beginning with data for 1999, exports of goods under the U.S. Foreign Military Sales program and fuel purchases by foreign air and ocean carriers in U.S. ports are included in goods exports (BOP basis) and excluded from services exports. Beginning with data for 1999, imports of petroleum abroad by U.S. military agencies and fuel purchases by U.S. air and ocean carriers in foreign ports are included in goods imports (BOP basis) and excluded from services imports.

[5] Total includes "other" exports or imports, not shown separately.

[6] Total arrivals of imported goods other than in-transit shipments.

[7] Total includes revisions not reflected in detail.

[8] Total exports are on a revised statistical month basis; end-use categories are on a statistical month basis.

Note: Goods on a Census basis are adjusted to a BOP basis by the Bureau of Economic Analysis, in line with concepts and definitions used to prepare international and national accounts. The adjustments are necessary to supplement coverage of Census data, to eliminate duplication of transactions recorded elsewhere in international accounts, to value transactions according to a standard definition, and for earlier years, to record transactions in the appropriate period.

Data include international trade of the U.S. Virgin Islands, Puerto Rico, and U.S. Foreign Trade Zones.

Source: Department of Commerce (Bureau of the Census and Bureau of Economic Analysis).

TABLE B–59. U.S. international trade in goods and services by area and country, 2000–2021

[Millions of dollars]

Item	2000	2005	2010	2015	2017	2018	2019	2020	2021
EXPORTS									
Total, all countries	1,082,963	1,291,503	1,872,320	2,280,778	2,394,477	2,542,462	2,546,275	2,158,651	2,556,637
Europe	298,654	366,823	510,935	608,049	655,211	705,063	735,529	632,898	719,097
Euro area [1]	174,591	214,207	292,815	350,142	377,617	403,640	433,677	377,427	428,506
France	30,821	35,241	45,279	50,074	53,913	58,237	60,012	42,908	47,134
Germany	45,379	55,246	75,023	81,185	88,604	93,262	96,758	87,688	97,402
Italy	16,666	18,557	22,787	24,628	27,249	32,506	33,279	25,770	28,096
United Kingdom	73,995	83,456	104,891	126,762	131,514	145,472	147,130	120,186	129,279
Canada	204,237	246,292	307,571	341,366	348,666	368,992	362,297	309,695	364,501
Latin America and Other Western Hemisphere	228,633	259,832	416,623	551,388	556,797	594,182	584,967	475,341	609,662
Brazil	22,112	21,574	53,766	58,667	63,854	65,834	66,966	49,397	62,071
Mexico	127,581	141,856	187,487	267,794	275,645	299,176	289,849	235,019	307,112
Venezuela	9,476	9,396	15,918	14,212	7,477	9,160	3,623	2,272	3,103
Asia and Pacific	301,451	342,228	523,350	633,923	697,440	731,554	716,471	628,184	738,247
China	21,862	50,685	113,577	163,329	187,875	180,596	167,474	166,274	192,038
India	6,730	13,294	29,243	38,838	47,936	55,831	58,012	43,354	58,407
Japan	101,554	93,383	104,991	106,619	114,299	122,537	124,627	102,387	112,092
Korea, Republic of	35,106	37,866	56,700	66,254	73,680	80,779	80,967	69,242	86,086
Singapore	24,557	26,657	39,743	43,050	50,515	57,044	54,105	52,320	65,124
Taiwan	30,604	29,103	36,896	39,017	37,236	41,921	42,910	39,792	47,258
Middle East	28,616	48,702	70,477	102,159	97,237	98,238	102,183	76,070	82,390
Africa	17,203	22,890	40,278	41,229	36,511	41,533	41,748	33,075	38,926
IMPORTS									
Total, all countries	1,452,649	2,008,045	2,375,406	2,771,554	2,904,820	3,121,057	3,105,952	2,812,640	3,401,685
Europe	359,220	493,562	566,372	704,961	743,880	808,185	854,847	775,870	902,046
Euro area [1]	216,802	304,574	341,235	444,164	464,993	506,179	537,764	465,673	550,047
France	41,344	47,725	56,563	66,202	68,609	72,413	78,327	57,136	68,951
Germany	75,709	110,076	114,861	158,863	153,738	160,095	163,932	146,710	170,617
Italy	31,593	39,768	37,779	53,781	60,542	66,247	69,466	53,967	66,998
United Kingdom	70,963	84,200	96,034	115,152	114,404	124,396	128,547	104,983	117,887
Canada	253,313	319,543	310,340	334,249	341,332	362,898	363,420	306,163	398,270
Latin America and Other Western Hemisphere	255,760	362,652	468,191	528,383	545,442	588,303	597,624	509,922	627,353
Brazil	15,340	26,401	30,095	35,155	35,730	36,619	37,469	27,932	36,482
Mexico	148,493	188,384	248,695	327,768	345,898	378,266	393,624	346,162	418,633
Venezuela	19,192	34,662	33,394	16,215	12,689	13,474	2,144	317	443
Asia and Pacific	507,527	682,521	841,359	1,091,820	1,152,332	1,226,094	1,180,459	1,142,075	1,358,918
China	103,340	251,791	377,619	499,696	524,042	558,324	469,541	448,880	526,807
India	12,480	23,426	44,940	69,771	76,888	83,990	87,526	77,408	102,111
Japan	164,972	162,613	147,993	164,738	172,505	178,615	181,060	152,801	167,010
Korea, Republic of	45,726	51,175	59,292	82,529	80,172	85,328	89,206	86,452	108,443
Singapore	21,837	19,242	23,668	25,232	27,722	35,798	37,216	41,715	40,857
Taiwan	44,272	40,690	41,740	47,629	49,647	53,221	61,678	66,722	86,908
Middle East	44,500	81,361	95,039	79,353	79,637	88,661	70,170	49,422	68,758
Africa	31,075	69,516	93,001	32,713	42,120	45,381	39,346	29,130	44,865
BALANCE (excess of exports +)									
Total, all countries	–369,687	–716,542	–503,087	–490,776	–510,344	–578,594	–559,676	–653,989	–845,048
Europe	–60,566	–126,739	–55,436	–96,912	–88,668	–103,121	–119,318	–142,972	–182,949
Euro area [1]	–42,211	–90,367	–48,420	–94,021	–87,376	–102,538	–104,087	–88,247	–121,542
France	–10,523	–12,484	–11,284	–16,129	–14,696	–14,175	–18,315	–14,228	–21,815
Germany	–30,331	–54,830	–39,838	–77,679	–65,134	–66,832	–67,174	–59,021	–73,216
Italy	–14,928	–21,211	–14,991	–29,154	–33,293	–33,742	–36,187	–28,198	–38,902
United Kingdom	3,033	–744	8,856	11,611	17,110	21,077	18,584	15,204	11,392
Canada	–49,076	–73,252	–2,770	7,116	7,334	6,094	–1,124	3,532	–33,769
Latin America and Other Western Hemisphere	–27,127	–102,820	–51,567	23,006	11,355	5,879	–12,657	–34,581	–17,691
Brazil	6,772	–4,826	23,672	23,512	28,125	29,215	29,496	21,465	25,589
Mexico	–20,912	–46,528	–61,208	–59,974	–70,254	–79,090	–103,775	–111,144	–111,521
Venezuela	–9,716	–25,266	–17,476	–2,003	–5,211	–4,315	1,479	1,955	2,660
Asia and Pacific	–206,077	–340,293	–318,009	–457,897	–454,892	–494,541	–463,988	–513,891	–620,672
China	–81,478	–201,106	–264,042	–336,368	–336,167	–377,729	–302,066	–282,606	–334,769
India	–5,749	–10,132	–15,698	–30,934	–28,953	–28,160	–29,514	–34,054	–43,703
Japan	–63,419	–69,230	–43,002	–58,118	–58,206	–56,077	–56,433	–50,414	–54,918
Korea, Republic of	–10,620	–13,308	–2,593	–16,275	–6,492	–4,549	–8,240	–17,210	–22,357
Singapore	2,719	7,415	16,076	17,818	22,793	21,245	16,890	10,605	24,267
Taiwan	–13,668	–11,587	–4,843	–8,612	–12,411	–11,300	–18,768	–26,930	–39,650
Middle East	–15,883	–32,659	–24,561	22,806	17,600	9,577	32,013	26,648	13,632
Africa	–13,872	–46,625	–52,723	8,516	–5,610	–3,848	2,402	3,946	–5,940

[1] Euro area consists of Austria, Belgium, Finland, France, Germany, Ireland, Italy, Luxembourg, Netherlands, Portugal, Spain and Greece (beginning in 2001), Slovenia (2007), Cyprus and Malta (2008), Slovakia (2009), Estonia (2011), Latvia (2014), and Lithuania (2015).

Note: Data are on a balance of payments basis. For further details, and additional data by country, see *Survey of Current Business*, October 2022.

Source: Department of Commerce (Bureau of Economic Analysis).

Table B–60. Foreign exchange rates, 2002–2022

[Foreign currency units per U.S. dollar, except as noted; certified noon buying rates in New York]

Period	Australia (dollar)[1]	Brazil (real)	Canada (dollar)	China, P.R. (yuan)	EMU Members (euro)[1,2]	India (rupee)	Japan (yen)	Mexico (peso)	South Korea (won)	Sweden (krona)	Switzer-land (franc)	United Kingdom (pound)[1]
March 1973	1.4129	....	0.9967	2.2401	....	7.55	261.90	0.013	398.85	4.4294	3.2171	2.4724
2002	.5437	2.9213	1.5704	8.2771	0.9454	48.63	125.22	9.663	1,250.31	9.7233	1.5567	1.5025
2003	.6524	3.0750	1.4008	8.2772	1.1321	46.59	115.94	10.793	1,192.08	8.0787	1.3450	1.6347
2004	.7365	2.9262	1.3017	8.2768	1.2438	45.26	108.15	11.290	1,145.24	7.3480	1.2428	1.8330
2005	.7627	2.4352	1.2115	8.1936	1.2449	44.00	110.11	10.894	1,023.75	7.4710	1.2459	1.8204
2006	.7535	2.1738	1.1340	7.9723	1.2563	45.19	116.31	10.906	954.32	7.3718	1.2532	1.8434
2007	.8391	1.9461	1.0734	7.6058	1.3711	41.18	117.76	10.928	928.97	6.7550	1.1999	2.0020
2008	.8537	1.8326	1.0660	6.9477	1.4726	43.39	103.39	11.143	1,098.71	6.5846	1.0816	1.8545
2009	.7927	1.9976	1.1412	6.8307	1.3935	48.33	93.68	13.498	1,274.63	7.6539	1.0860	1.5661
2010	.9200	1.7600	1.0298	6.7696	1.3261	45.65	87.78	12.624	1,155.74	7.2053	1.0432	1.5452
2011	1.0332	1.6723	.9887	6.4630	1.3931	46.58	79.70	12.427	1,106.94	6.4878	.8862	1.6043
2012	1.0359	1.9535	.9995	6.3093	1.2859	53.37	79.82	13.154	1,126.16	6.7721	.9377	1.5853
2013	.9683	2.1570	1.0300	6.1478	1.3281	58.51	97.60	12.758	1,094.67	6.5124	.9269	1.5642
2014	.9034	2.3512	1.1043	6.1620	1.3297	61.00	105.74	13.302	1,052.29	6.8576	.9147	1.6484
2015	.7522	3.3360	1.2791	6.2827	1.1096	64.11	121.05	15.874	1,130.96	8.4350	.9628	1.5284
2016	.7445	3.4839	1.3243	6.6400	1.1072	67.16	108.66	18.667	1,159.34	8.5541	.9848	1.3555
2017	.7671	3.1910	1.2984	6.7569	1.1301	65.07	112.10	18.884	1,129.04	8.5430	.9842	1.2890
2018	.7481	3.6513	1.2957	6.6090	1.1817	68.37	110.40	19.218	1,099.29	8.6945	.9784	1.3363
2019	.6952	3.9440	1.3269	6.9081	1.1194	70.38	109.02	19.247	1,165.80	9.4604	.9937	1.2768
2020	.6899	5.1587	1.3422	6.9042	1.1410	74.14	106.78	21.546	1,180.56	9.2167	.9389	1.2829
2021	.7515	5.3958	1.2533	6.4508	1.1830	73.94	109.84	20.284	1,144.89	8.5812	.9144	1.3764
2022	.6951	5.1605	1.3014	6.7290	1.0534	78.58	131.46	20.121	1,291.78	10.1177	.9550	1.2371
2021: I	.7729	5.4845	1.2656	6.4817	1.2045	72.90	106.17	20.374	1,114.81	8.4031	.9067	1.3798
II	.7701	5.2944	1.2285	6.4594	1.2050	73.79	109.43	20.013	1,121.30	8.4177	.9110	1.3981
III	.7344	5.2299	1.2600	6.4699	1.1784	74.10	110.07	20.030	1,160.08	8.6499	.9182	1.3779
IV	.7289	5.5889	1.2604	6.3914	1.1437	74.94	113.64	20.748	1,183.29	8.8557	.9216	1.3486
2022: I	.7249	5.2230	1.2664	6.3478	1.1216	75.24	116.36	20.506	1,206.18	9.3467	.9241	1.3407
II	.7144	4.9213	1.2764	6.6084	1.0646	77.19	129.73	20.053	1,260.46	9.8436	.9652	1.2564
III	.6833	5.2455	1.3062	6.8520	1.0066	79.78	138.35	20.234	1,341.11	10.5552	.9666	1.1767
IV	.6574	5.2550	1.3577	7.1120	1.0218	82.15	141.36	19.681	1,359.38	10.7252	.9636	1.1754

Trade-weighted value of the U.S. dollar

Period	Nominal			Real[6]		
	Broad index (January 2006=100)[3]	Advanced foreign economies index (January 2006=100)[4]	Emerging market economies index (January 2006=100)[5]	Broad index (January 2006=100)[3]	Advanced foreign economies index (January 2006=100)[4]	Emerging market economies index (January 2006=100)[5]
2002	....	....	....	....	....	....
2003	....	....	....	....	....	....
2004	....	....	....	....	....	....
2005	....	....	....	....	....	....
2006	98.6005	97.6833	99.8103	98.9357	98.3159	99.7520
2007	93.8100	92.0715	96.1170	94.2696	93.6198	95.1227
2008	90.8801	88.4517	94.1271	90.9839	90.8430	91.2092
2009	96.7509	92.8232	101.9953	95.3414	94.7210	96.1195
2010	93.0541	90.1336	97.1416	90.8045	92.0390	89.6167
2011	88.7767	84.8522	93.9916	86.3069	87.3412	85.3008
2012	91.6361	88.0233	96.5231	88.5167	90.8658	86.1946
2013	92.7611	90.6492	96.0312	88.7296	93.8601	83.8221
2014	95.5876	93.4349	98.9391	90.7229	97.0261	84.7836
2015	108.1696	108.1483	109.5239	101.1916	111.8303	91.5859
2016	113.0665	109.3636	118.1858	105.4110	114.0195	97.3978
2017	112.8113	108.9531	118.0912	104.8598	114.1634	96.2894
2018	112.0066	106.4922	119.0091	104.0918	112.2341	96.4658
2019	115.7368	110.2693	122.7198	107.1994	116.7233	98.3771
2020	117.7778	109.0592	128.3883	108.7699	116.4064	101.4855
2021	113.1139	104.5232	123.5478	106.2938	114.1803	98.8358
2022	120.6657	115.1260	128.0614	115.1378	127.0414	104.5105
2021: I	112.3724	103.4286	123.1729	104.2806	111.3393	97.4936
II	111.8371	102.8353	122.6943	104.8256	112.1988	97.7850
III	113.3104	104.9378	123.5115	106.8490	115.1189	99.0834
IV	114.9769	106.9356	124.8499	109.2201	118.0642	100.9810
2022: I	115.5273	108.3922	124.4619	110.3796	119.8988	101.6071
II	118.9357	113.5264	126.1623	113.6835	125.7374	102.9598
III	123.4386	118.7803	129.9911	117.7361	131.1673	105.9360
IV	124.7657	119.7883	131.6568	118.7520	131.3621	107.5393

[1] U.S. dollars per foreign currency unit.

[2] European Economic and Monetary Union (EMU) members consists of Austria, Belgium, Finland, France, Germany, Ireland, Italy, Luxembourg, Netherlands, Portugal, Spain and Greece (beginning in 2001), Slovenia (2007), Cyprus and Malta (2008), Slovakia (2009), Estonia (2011), Latvia (2014), and Lithuania (2015).

[3] Weighted average of the foreign exchange value of the U.S. dollar against the currencies of a broad group of major U.S. trading partners.

[4] Subset of the broad index. Consists of currencies of the Euro area, Australia, Canada, Japan, Sweden, Switzerland, and the United Kingdom.

[5] Subset of the broad index currencies that are emerging market economies. For details, see *Revisions to the Federal Reserve Dollar Indexes*, January 2019.

[6] Adjusted for changes in consumer price indexes for the United States and other countries.

Source: Board of Governors of the Federal Reserve System.

TABLE B–61. Growth rates in real gross domestic product by area and country, 2004–2023

[Percent change]

Area and country	2004–2013 annual average	2014	2015	2016	2017	2018	2019	2020	2021	2022[1]	2023[1]
World	4.1	3.5	3.4	3.3	3.8	3.6	2.8	−3.0	6.2	3.4	2.9
Advanced economies	1.6	2.0	2.3	1.8	2.5	2.3	1.7	−4.4	5.4	2.7	1.2
Of which:											
United States	1.8	2.3	2.7	1.7	2.3	2.9	2.3	−3.4	5.9	2.0	1.4
Euro area[2]	0.9	1.4	2.0	1.9	2.6	1.8	1.6	−6.1	5.3	3.5	.7
Germany	1.3	2.2	1.5	2.2	2.7	1.0	1.1	−3.7	2.6	1.9	.1
France	1.2	1.0	1.1	1.0	2.4	1.8	1.9	−7.9	6.8	2.6	.7
Italy	−0.3	.0	.8	1.3	1.7	.9	.5	−9.0	6.7	3.9	.6
Spain	0.7	1.4	3.8	3.0	3.0	2.3	2.1	−10.8	5.5	5.2	1.1
Japan	0.7	.3	1.6	.8	1.7	.6	−.4	−4.6	2.1	1.4	1.8
United Kingdom	1.2	3.0	2.6	2.3	2.1	1.7	1.7	−9.3	7.6	4.1	−.6
Canada	1.9	2.9	.7	1.0	3.0	2.8	1.9	−5.2	5.0	3.5	1.5
Other advanced economies	3.5	3.0	2.3	2.6	3.1	2.8	2.0	−1.7	5.3	2.8	2.0
Emerging market and developing economies	6.4	4.7	4.3	4.4	4.8	4.6	3.6	−1.9	6.7	3.9	4.0
Regional groups:											
Emerging and Developing Asia	8.5	6.9	6.8	6.8	6.6	6.4	5.2	−.6	7.4	4.3	5.3
China	10.3	7.4	7.0	6.9	6.9	6.8	6.0	2.2	8.4	3.0	5.2
India[3]	7.7	7.4	8.0	8.3	6.8	6.5	3.7	−6.6	8.7	6.8	6.1
ASEAN-5[4]	5.4	4.7	5.0	5.1	5.5	5.4	4.9	−3.4	3.8	5.2	4.3
Emerging and Developing Europe	4.4	1.8	1.0	1.9	4.1	3.4	2.5	−1.7	6.9	.7	1.5
Russia	4.3	.7	−2.0	.2	1.8	2.8	2.2	−2.7	4.7	−2.2	.3
Latin America and the Caribbean	4.0	1.3	.4	−.6	1.4	1.2	.2	−7.0	7.0	3.9	1.8
Brazil	4.0	.5	−3.5	−3.3	1.3	1.8	1.2	−3.9	5.0	3.1	1.2
Mexico	2.3	2.9	3.3	2.6	2.1	2.2	−.2	−8.1	4.7	3.1	1.7
Middle East and Central Asia	5.0	3.4	3.0	4.2	2.6	2.6	1.7	−2.7	4.5	5.3	3.2
Saudi Arabia	4.6	3.7	4.1	1.7	−.7	2.5	.3	−4.1	3.2	8.7	2.6
Sub-Saharan Africa	5.6	5.0	3.2	1.5	3.0	3.3	3.2	−1.6	4.7	3.8	3.8
Nigeria	7.3	6.3	2.7	−1.6	.8	1.9	2.2	−1.8	3.6	3.0	3.2
South Africa	3.4	1.4	1.3	.7	1.2	1.5	.3	−6.3	4.9	2.6	1.2

[1] All figures are forecasts as published by the International Monetary Fund. For the United States, the second estimate by the Department of Commerce shows that real GDP rose 2.1 percent in 2022.

[2] Euro area consists of Austria, Belgium, Finland, France, Germany, Ireland, Italy, Luxembourg, Netherlands, Portugal, Spain and Greece (beginning in 2001), Slovenia (2007), Cyprus and Malta (2008), Slovakia (2009), Estonia (2011), Latvia (2014), and Lithuania (2015).

[3] Data and forecasts are presented on a fiscal year basis and output growth is based on GDP at market prices.

[4] Consists of Indonesia, Malaysia, Philippines, Thailand, and Vietnam.

Note: For details on data shown in this table, see *World Economic Outlook*, October 2022, and *World Economic Outlook Update*, January 2023, published by the International Monetary Fund.

Sources: International Monetary Fund and Department of Commerce (Bureau of Economic Analysis).

www.ingramcontent.com/pod-product-compliance
Lightning Source LLC
LaVergne TN
LVHW061217100826
845148LV00004B/782

9781839315107